The Development of the Church

The Mercersburg Theology Study Series
Volume 3

The Mercersburg Theology Study Series presents attractive, readable, scholarly modern editions of the key writings of the nineteenth-century theological movement led by Philip Schaff and John Nevin. It aims to introduce the academic community and the broader public more fully to Mercersburg's unique blend of American and European, Reformed and Catholic theology.

Published Volumes

1. *The Mystical Presence and the Doctrine of the Reformed Church on the Lord's Supper*
Edited by Linden J. DeBie
2. *Coena Mystica: Debating Reformed Eucharistic Theology*
Edited by Linden J. DeBie
4. *The Incarnate Word: Selected Writings on Christology*
Edited by William B. Evans
6. *Born of Water and the Spirit: Essays on the Sacraments and Christian Formation*
Edited by David W. Layman

Volumes in Progress

5. *"One, Holy, Catholic, and Apostolic": Nevin's Writings on Ecclesiology*
Edited by Sam Hamstra
7. *Selected Writings of Emanuel V. Gerhart*
Edited by Annette Aubert
8. *The Early Creeds*
Edited by Charles Yrigoyen
10. *The Heidelberg Catechism*
Edited by Lee Barrett

Volumes Planned
(Details Subject to Change)

9. *Essays in Church History*
Edited by Nick Needham
11. *The Mercersburg Liturgy*
Edited by Michael Farley
12. *Schaff's America and Related Writings*
Edited by Stephen Graham
13. *Philosophy and the Contemporary World*
Edited by Adam S. Borneman
14. *Mercersburg and Its Critics*
Edited by Darryl G. Hart

The Development of the Church

"The Principle of Protestantism" and other Historical Writings of Philip Schaff

By
PHILIP SCHAFF

Translated by
JOHN WILLIAMSON NEVIN

Edited by
David R. Bains and Theodore Louis Trost

General Editors
W. Bradford Littlejohn,
Lee C. Barrett, and David W. Layman

Foreword by
Leigh Eric Schmidt

WIPF & STOCK · Eugene, Oregon

THE DEVELOPMENT OF THE CHURCH
"The Principle of Protestantism" and other Historical Writings of Philip Schaff

The Mercersburg Theology Study Series 3

Wipf & Stock
An Imprint of Wipf and Stock Publishers
199 W. 8th Ave., Suite 3
Eugene, OR 97401

www.wipfandstock.com

PAPERBACK ISBN: 978-1-62564-523-4
HARDCOVER ISBN: 978-1-4982-8789-0
EBOOK ISBN: 978-1-5326-1020-2

Manufactured in the U.S.A. JANUARY 3, 2017

Contents

Contributors

David R. Bains, S. Louis and Ann W. Armstrong Professor of Religion at Samford University. He is the author of "Conduits of Faith: Reinhold Niebuhr's Liturgical Thought" and has contributed essays to many publications including *The Wiley-Blackwell Companion to World Christianity* and *Understanding Religions of the World.*

Lee C. Barrett, Henry and Mary Stager Professor of Theology at Lancaster Theological Seminary. A former president of the Kierkegaard Society, he has published extensively on the thought of Kierkegaard and other nineteenth-century theologians. He is the author of *Makers of Modern Theology: Kierkegaard* and *Eros and Self-Emptying: Intersections of Augustine and Kierkegaard.*

Charles Hodge (1797–1878), professor at Princeton Theological Seminary, was the leading Old School Presbyterian theologian of his generation. He was the editor of the journal *Biblical Repertory and Princeton Review.*

David W. Layman earned his Ph. D. in Religion from Temple University in 1994. Since then, he has been a lecturer in religious studies and philosophy at schools in south-central Pennsylvania. He is editor for volume 6 of the Mercersburg Theological Study Series, *Born of Water and the Spirit: Essays on the Sacraments and Christian Formation.*

W. Bradford Littlejohn, Director of the Davenant Trust, a nonprofit organization sponsoring historical research at the intersection of the church and academy. He is author of *The Mercersburg Theology and the Quest for Reformed Catholicity* and *Richard Hooker: A Companion to His Life and Work.*

John Williamson Nevin (1803–86), professor successively at Western Theological Seminary, the Theological Seminary of the German Reformed Church at Mercersburg, and Franklin and Marshall College. He was a leading nineteenth-century theologian and founding editor of *Mercersburg Review.*

Philip Schaff (1819–93), a professor at the Theological Seminary of the German Reformed Church at Mercersburg (1844–63), and Union Theological Seminary in New York (1870–93). He founded the American Society of Church History and was nineteenth-century America's leading church historian and proponent of Christian unity.

Leigh Eric Schmidt, Edward C. Mallinckrodt Distinguished University Professor in the Humanities at Washington University in St. Louis. Among his many books are *Holy Fairs: Scottish Communions and American Revivals in the Early Modern Period* and *Restless Souls: The Making of American Spirituality.*

Theodore Louis Trost, Professor in Religious Studies and New College at the University of Alabama. Among other writings, he is the author of *Douglas Horton and the Ecumenical Impulse in American Religion.*

Foreword
by Leigh Eric Schmidt

In introducing his translation of Philip Schaff's *The Principle of Protestantism*, John Williamson Nevin defended his new colleague's tome from the charge of sounding "too German." Schaff, only recently arrived in the United States, was "entitled to indulgence" for having not yet become "fully American." Why, Nevin asked, should Schaff "denationalize himself" in order to communicate with his new American audience? The pieces collected in this volume of the Mercersburg Theology Study Series show how little danger there was of Schaff forgetting Berlin upon landing in Reading, Pennsylvania. If anything, his expatriate status made him, at least in the near term, more resolutely German—a scholarly émigré in a country not well matched to his professorial attainments. In each of his three works that appear here—*The Principle of Protestantism*, *What Is Church History?*, and "German Theology and the Church Question"—Schaff presumed that Germany was "the proper home of Protestant theology" and that American Christians very much needed to soak up that higher knowledge—the sooner, the better. Schaff's corrective observations about sectarianism, theological education, and church history all depended upon the sharp juxtaposition of Germany and America in which his new home was found conspicuously wanting. Schaff would eventually become a more sympathetic commentator on the American religious scene, but he very much began with a missionary's assertive stance.

From Roger Williams to Ralph Waldo Emerson, the American Protestant mythos seemed designed to produce churches of one member. With the right of private judgment exalted, if not fetishized, the spiritual hankerings of the lone individual overtook the collective authority of the church time and again. As Schaff saw it, an atomistic sectarianism had found its most fertile ground in the United States, an unfortunate consequence of the nation's Puritan and Congregational ancestry. In America he discovered "a variegated sampler of all conceivable religious chimeras and dreams;" here was a land in which "the arbitrary fancies and baseless opinions of an individual" repeatedly superseded the church as a historical body and living communion. Schaff necessarily turned to German theological learning to provide antidotes to these sectarian poisons, a dose of Lutheran rationalism along with a deep engagement with the full scope of church history. To move his adopted country forward and, more importantly, to move the church forward, the American infatuation with "evangelical liberty" would itself need to be reformed.

To chasten American Protestantism's sectarian impulses required convincing his new compatriots that they had much to gain from engaging the theological life of Germany. Some, of course, hardly needed convincing. That included Princeton's Charles Hodge whose broad-ranging review of *The Principle of Protestantism* is also included in this volume. For Hodge, who had spent time in Halle and Berlin, Schaff was a welcome interlocutor, another bridge for the transatlantic exchange of theological ideas. But, Schaff hardly counted on such a hospitable reception from most Americans, many of whom seemed only contemptuous of German philosophical thinking, seeing little practical benefit in it. "Has it ever manufactured a steamboat, or so much even as a pin?" Schaff imagined an uncultured American asking. Here again Schaff was a missionary—for Germany as the leader in all departments of higher learning from philology to history. The remedy for American anti-intellectualism was procurable through the studious embrace of Germany's scientific consciousness.

Specifically, Schaff offered his new American comrades a more encompassing understanding of church history—one that he hoped would free evangelical Protestantism of both its riotous anti-Catholicism and its naïve biblical primitivism. Again, when it came to historical awareness, Schaff found most Americans sadly lacking; they were consumed so much with the present that they cared little about the past. Attending to the long development of Christianity, especially bringing the venerable treasures of the medieval church into a continuous relationship with Protestantism, would transmute American evangelicalism's "low esteem for history." The bigoted, wholesale dismissal of the Church of Rome would give way to a far more irenic appreciation of the sacramental texture, theological sophistication, and artistic splendor of the Middle Ages. Protestants would come to see themselves as organically related to the entire flow of church history, not in ruptured opposition to all things Catholic. Schaff's vision of evolving union, discerned especially through a more comprehensive knowledge of church history, flew in the face of American Protestantism's fiery war on popery and earned him the notoriety of a heresy charge. He was vindicated, but the allegation highlighted the stakes involved in Schaff's historical enterprise.

As with previous volumes in the Mercersburg Theology Study Series, this one is marked by its extensive editorial apparatus and erudition. Thoroughly introducing each of the pieces, as well as offering a general introduction to the whole, the editors have made these texts freshly accessible to a twenty-first-century audience. The editors have also provided careful translations of the Latin, German, French, and Greek texts that Schaff employed as well as a large "Glossary of Names" to help the reader enter more fully into the wide circle of expositors in which Schaff moved and studied. This is the sort of painstaking critical edition that facilitates scholarship for the long term. For those interested in nineteenth-century American religion, Christian ecumenism, and the theological consequence of church history, this volume is a welcome and valuable addition.

Leigh Eric Schmidt
Edward C. Mallinckrodt Distinguished University Professor
John C. Danforth Center on Religion and Politics
Washington University in St. Louis

Editorial Approach and Acknowledgments

The purpose of this series is to reprint the key writings of the Mercersburg theologians in a way that is both fully faithful to the original and yet easily accessible to non-specialist modern readers. These twin goals, often in conflict, have determined our editorial approach throughout. We have sought to do justice to both by being very hesitant to make any alterations to the original, but being very free with additions to the original in the form of annotations.

We have taken a few liberties in altering punctuation (essentially just comma usage) and some abbreviations for clarity, consistency, and ease of reading. We have also divided some particularly long paragraphs. In keeping with modern conventions, we have italicized book titles and non-English words. We have, however, aimed to leave spelling, capitalization, and emphasis exactly as in the original. There are two exceptions to this. First, clear typographical errors have been silently corrected. Second, following Schaff's style in *The Principle of Protestantism* we have represented his emphasis of the names of people by small capitals in *What is Church History?* and "German Theology and the Church Question," rather than the italics originally used. This eliminates any confusion introduced by our italicization of adjoining book titles.

The entirety of the text has been re-typeset and re-formatted to render it as clear and accessible as possible; pagination, of course, has accordingly been changed. Original section headings have been retained and additional section headings added in brackets for the reader's convenience. Almost all of these in *The Principle of Protestantism* are based on the book's detailed table of contents and employ Schaff's language and capitalization.

Readers should be aware that various spellings of individual names appear in these pieces. This is particularly true of German names containing a vowel with an umlaut. Sometimes they were typeset with the umlaut (e.g., Möhler, Müller), sometimes they were typeset following the alternative convention of adding an "e" after the umlauted vowel (Moehler, Mueller). In every case the original spelling has been retained.

Original footnotes are retained, though for ease of typesetting, they have been subsumed within the series of numbered footnotes that includes the annotations we have added to this edition. Our own annotations and additions are wholly enclosed in square brackets, whether that be within a footnote that was original, or around an entire footnote when it is one that we have added. In the very few cases where square brackets were used in the original publication, one of two approaches has been followed. In bracketed footnotes inserted by Nevin as translator, his name appears at the beginning of the note. In short insertions into a quoted passage, the original brackets have been silently converted to parentheses since they appear to have been more commonly used for editorial insertions in these pieces.

Source citations in the original have been retained in their original form, but where necessary, we have provided expanded citation information in brackets or footnotes, and directed the reader toward modern editions of these works, where they exist. Where citations are lacking in the original, we have tried as much as possible to provide them in our footnotes. Given the historiographic character of Schaff's pieces, many works are mentioned in passing. In each case we have provided a citation of the work referenced. These provide the full name of the author, usually the short title, and the original publication date.

All three pieces by Schaff were composed and first disseminated in German. Most of the works he cites are also German. In the main text, however, the original translator often rendered their titles in English. This does not indicate that the works were available in English to Schaff's initial readers. When English translations did appear, they often had slightly different titles. If the work has now been translated into English, the translation appears in the entry for the work in the bibliography. If the work is particularly important or if it had been translated prior to the publication of Schaff's work, the citation for the English translation is provided in the footnote. Where no English title is given and where it cannot be discerned from obvious cognates, a translation has been provided. In many places the translator did not translate the German terms for volume, edition, and page, but left them or their abbreviations in German. While we have translated these in brackets on first reference, we have left them untranslated on later reference so as not to encumber the page with multiple bracketed insertions. *Band* (Bd.) designates volume, *Theil* (Th.) designates part, *Abtheil* (Abth.) designates section, *Seite* (S. or s.) designates page.

In the annotations we have added (almost entirely in the footnotes, though occasionally in the form of brackets in the body text), we have attempted to be comprehensive without becoming cumbersome. In addition to offering citations for works referenced in the original, these additions fall under four further headings:

1. Translation
2. Unfamiliar terms and historical figures
3. Additional source material
4. Commentary

Given the large number of persons named in these pieces, and the fact that they reappear in the different writings in this volume, we placed the biographical information for most people in a glossary of names. Each individual's entry is listed under the first spelling of the name as it appears in Schaff's writings in this volume (e.g., whether Möhler or Moehler). The alternative spellings and forms of these and other names are also included in the glossary. Occasionally due to the usage of the time, or the idiosyncrasies of his translator, Schaff's reference to an individual appears under a form that is unusual today (e.g. Vincens of Paula, rather than Vincent de Paul). In each case Schaff's form is the form used first in the glossary, with other more common forms noted. Following standard usage, both we and Schaff shorten German names containing the participle "von" to the name itself when only the last name is used. If an individual only appears once in this volume, we have often provided the pertinent information in a footnote and not in the glossary.

We have attempted to be comprehensive in providing translations of any untranslated quotations in these works, and have wherever possible made use of translations in standard modern editions.

Additional annotations serve to elucidate unfamiliar words, concepts, or (especially) persons to which our authors refer, and where applicable, to provide references to sources where the reader may pursue further information (for these additional sources, only abbreviated citations are provided in the footnotes; for full bibliographical information, see the bibliography). Interestingly, one of our chief aids in compiling this information was the *New Schaff-Herzog Encyclopedia of Religious Knowledge* (Grand Rapids, MI: Baker, 1949–50), the descendant of Schaff's original celebrated reference work. Other reference works used include T*he Oxford Dictionary of the Christian Church*, edited by F. L. Cross and Elizabeth A. Livingstone, Third Edition (New York: Oxford University Press, 1997); *The Oxford Encyclopedia of the Reformation*, edited by Hans J. Hillerbrand (New York: Oxford University Press, 1996); and *American National Biography*, edited by Mark C. Carnes and John A. Garraty (New York: Oxford University Press, 1999).

We have also sought to shed light on the issues under discussion. Although most commentary on the texts has been reserved for the general introduction and the editors' introductions to each work, further brief commentary on specific points of importance has been provided occasionally in footnotes to facilitate understanding of the significance of the matter under discussion. We hope that our practice throughout will help bring these remarkable texts to life again for a new century, while also allowing the authors to be heard in their own authentic voices.

Acknowledgements

Volume Editors

David Bains would like to thank the Department of Religion in the Howard College of Arts and Sciences at Samford University for a sabbatical leave in spring 2014. Some of the work on this text was completed then. A number of the department's undergraduates assisted early in the process. Codi Norred rendered great help in transcription. Casey Bell, Hannah Holland, Zachery Pittman, and Chelsea Rolo aided in proofreading scanned texts. Joy Berkhouse assisted in helping find the translations of some Latin texts. The assistance of Gail Barton and others in Samford's interlibrary loan office was vital to completing annotations.

Theodore Louis Trost would like to thank the Religious Studies Department, New College, and the College of Arts and Sciences at the University of Alabama for a sabbatical leave during the academic year 2013–14. Some of the work on this text was completed during that period as a Visiting Fellow in the School of Philosophy, Religion, and the History of Science at the University of Leeds, England. Virginia Langley, as an office assistant in the Religious Studies Department, carefully transcribed the entire text of *The Principle of Protestantism*. Thanks are also extended to the Mercersburg Society, for the invitation to deliver an address on Schaff's ecumenical perspective at the annual convocation in June 2015.[1]

Both editors extend thanks to the Reformed Theology and History Group and the Nineteenth-Century Theology Group of the American Academy of Religion for sponsoring a session on the Mercersburg Theology at the 2013 annual meeting. We are also grateful to *Theology Today* for the opportunity to publish a revised form of our conference paper.[2] We are particularly grateful for the ongoing support of W. Bradford Littlejohn, the inaugurator of the Mercersburg Theology Studies Series. In addition to careful editorial work he assisted greatly with Latin translations and provided some annotations. We are also very grateful to Lee C. Barrett. He rendered invaluable assistance at a propitious moment during the production of this volume.

General Editors

Brad Littlejohn would like to thank David Bains and Ted Trost for their persistence, dedication, and attention to extraordinary detail in a volume that posed numerous unforeseen editorial challenges that might have deterred many fainter hearts. I am also extremely grateful to David Layman and Lee Barrett for assuming the responsibilities of general editorship this past year and seeing this volume to completion when it became impossible for me to continuing giving the project the attention it deserved

1. Trost, "The Ecumenical Trajectory of the Mercersburg Movement."
2. Bains and Trost, "Philip Schaff."

Lee Barrett and David Layman thank Bradford Littlejohn for exercising the imagination and initiative to inaugurate this series that aspires to make a significant but under-appreciated theological tradition available and intelligible to new generations of scholars and general readers. For this particular volume, David Bains and Theodore Trost deserve lasting gratitude for their meticulous labors in producing critical editions of some of the most crucial texts by Philip Schaff and John Nevin, and for illuminating the rather alien world of those authors with their helpful introductions and commentary.

Abbreviations

ANF	*Ante-Nicene Fathers*. Edited by Philip Schaff and Henry Wace. New York: Christian Literature, 1885–96.
C&C	Pelikan, Jaroslav, and Valerie R. Hotchkiss, eds. *Creeds & Confessions of Faith in the Christian Tradition*. 4 vols. New Haven, CT: Yale University Press, 2003.
DEC	Tanner, Norman P., ed. *Decrees of the Ecumenical Councils*. 2 vols. Washington, DC: Georgetown University Press, 1990.
LW	*Luther's Works*. Saint Louis: Concordia, 1955–.
MTSS	Mercersburg Theology Study Series. Edited by W. Bradford Littlejohn. Eugene, OR: Wipf and Stock, 2012–.
NPNF	*Nicene and Post-Nicene Fathers*. Edited by Philip Schaff and Henry Wace. New York: Christian Literature, 1890.

General Introduction
by Theodore Louis Trost, Lee C. Barrett, and David Bains

Philip Schaff's Life and Work

Early Education

Philip Schaff—"the founder of the discipline of church history in America"[1]—began his journey inauspiciously and far away, in the Swiss village of Chur. In 1818, Anna Louis Schindler had ventured to this irenic locale shortly after abandoning her husband in a near-by village.[2] She met and courted (or was courted by) a local carpenter of limited means named Philipp Schaf, whom she took to court prior to the birth of their mutually conceived progeny, thereby successfully forcing the carpenter into acknowledging his paternal responsibility. Their son, "Philipp Schaf," was born on January 1, 1819.

Chur is located near the source of the Rhine River, some fifty miles southeast of Zürich. It became the capital of the Graubünden canton, or district, when the region joined the Swiss Republic in 1803. In the early 1800s, the village was made up of both Protestants and Catholics. While the majority of the citizenry spoke a dialect of German, a significant number of Italian-speaking people also resided there. These various folk lived side-by-side and in relative harmony with one another.

Despite the pacific environment, the troubles facing Philip's family continued after his birth. Soon after his baptism in the Reformed church, his mother was expelled from the village as a consequence of bearing Philip out of wedlock and in breach of her prior marriage contract. Within a year, his father died and the orphaned infant was eventually placed in foster care as a ward of the state. He only came to know his mother in later life and he never knew his father at all.

Perhaps on account of this lack, the spelling of his name remained unsettled into his adult life—his given name spelled interchangeably with one or two p's and his family name sometimes spelled "Schaaf," and at other times "Schaf," or "Schaff."

1. Graham, *Cosmos in the Chaos*, xvii.

2. This account of the circumstances surrounding Schaff's birth and early childhood is derived from Gäbler, "Philipp Schaff in Chur."

He eventually subtracted a "p" from his first name and, several years after his emigration to the United States, definitively added an "f" to the end of his last name.[3] In his autobiographical reminiscences, Philip Schaff does not elaborate on the particulars of his humble origins—indeed, of some of the particulars he may never have been aware. He does, however, credit his upbringing in "poverty and obscurity" as key to the development of his character. He writes:

> But poverty has its redeeming features: it stimulates energy, breeds industry, and develops the spirit of self-reliance and manly independence. It proves to be a better capital to start with than wealth and the prestige of pedigree. I have nothing to complain of. What my parents lacked was not their fault. And God has overruled any disadvantages of my early childhood for my own good.[4]

Schaff's intellectual abilities were recognized early on by his parish pastor, Paul Kind, who served as mentor to the boy from the beginning of his studies in primary school. With his matriculation into secondary school, Schaff's boarding expenses as well as the tuition for his education were paid for by the *Armenkommission*, the "Commission for the Poor" in Chur. This arrangement arose in response to the lad's consistent level of achievement at or near the top of his class.[5] However, as a result of his involvement in an incident of perceived indecency at the age of fifteen, Schaff ran afoul of the school administration. Along with four of his schoolmates, he was suspended from the *Kantonsschule* for committing the "secret sin" of Onan, or masturbation. As recorded in the school's official records, the secret sin "had been a group practice, with young Philip standing out as one of the leaders."[6] The same kind of devotion to upright behavior that eventuated in his mother's expulsion from Chur might have brought Philip's academic career to an end were it not for the intervention of Paul Kind (whose family name in German means "child," but when given the long vowel sound in English evokes kindness). Pastor Kind by this time had been elevated to the position of "*Antistes*" or presiding minister in the synod of Chur; he was, therefore, an influential figure and a convincing advocate on Philip Schaff's behalf. In consultation with the Commission for the Poor, whose members remained impressed by Schaff's academic accomplishments, Kind arranged for the teenager to enter the Kornthal academy for boys in the Württemberg region of Germany.

As a pastor and theology instructor, Antistes Kind belonged to a network of religionists who advanced the virtues of Pietism in the church and the community.

3. Philip Schaff's lifelong friend, William Julius Mann (1819–92), speculated that the additional "f" suggested the musical notation "ff," *fortissimo* (just as, perhaps, the absence of a second "p" exchanged *pianissimo* for *piano*). Meanwhile, Mann elaborated, the word *Schaff* was derived from the verb *schaffen*, "to create," as distinct from the less powerful *Schaf*, that is to say: "sheep" (or even, colloquially *Dummkopf* or, in British English, "twit"). See Mann, *Erinnerungsblätter*, 45.

4. David S. Schaff, *Life of Philip Schaff*, 2.

5. Gäbler, "Philipp Schaff in Chur," 157.

6. Penzel, *German Education*, 12.

German Pietism arose at the end of the seventeenth century as a critique of orthodox Lutheranism, with its emphasis on doctrinal formulation and theological disputation. The movement was led by Jacob Spener, who had studied theology among the Lutherans at Strasbourg before venturing, like Calvin before him, to Geneva, the capital of Reformed Protestantism. Eschewing strict adherence to one or another confessional tradition, Spener, instead, "stressed the necessity of biblical devotion, heartfelt decision for Christ and a morally perfected life."[7] As heir to Spener's legacy, August Hermann Francke helped to institutionalize the pietistic impulse in German Protestantism through his position as chair of Greek and oriental languages at the newly-established university in the Saxony town of Halle, where he also founded a world-renown orphanage.[8] Elsewhere in Saxony in 1722, Count Ludwig von Zinzendorf welcomed the Moravian Brethren to his estate where they established the Herrnhut community. The Moravians held goods in common, developed schools to advance pietistic principles, and inaugurated missionary activities.

Under the leadership of Johann Bengel and Friedrich Ötinger, Pietism exerted significant influence in the region of Württemberg in the eighteenth century. Some Pietists, following the millennial inclinations of Bengel, tended toward separation from the established Lutheran church; others with a more irenic disposition asserted their pietistic principles from within the church. By the nineteenth century a second awakening movement (parallel to the Second Great Awakening in England and North America) was underway in Württemberg. This time around, Pietists inclined toward a commitment to the established church with a particular concern to combat the rationalist tendencies that had developed within the church as a consequence of the Enlightenment.

The academy at Kornthal to which Anistes Kind had conveyed Philip Schaff was established by a community of German Pietists in 1819 as an independent, self-supporting institution. It was modeled after the schools associated with the Moravian Brethren and privileged rigorous academic training alongside personal piety and a commitment to the general welfare.[9] Although he was only at the academy for eight months, Schaff attributed great significance to the transformation that occurred as a result of his retreat there. Upon his arrival from Chur, Schaff had been plagued by an overwhelming sense of what he termed "homesickness"—a psychological reaction, perhaps, to the unfortunate circumstances that resulted in his exodus out of Switzerland.[10] But then, "one day, at three o'clock in the morning," he found himself in a forest

7. Penzel, *German Education*, 19.

8. Francke's work for social reform was well-known beyond the provinces of Germany as suggested by the efforts of Puritan minister, Cotton Mather, to correspond with him. See, for example, Splitter, "The Fact and the Fiction of Cotton Mather's Correspondence with August Herman Francke."

9. Appel, "Life of Dr. Philip Schaff," 90. See also, Penzel, *German Education*, 20–21. Orphanages and training schools for Christian missionaries were among the earliest institutions established by the Pietists.

10. See Penzel, *German Education*, 31.

at prayer, crying in intense agony; suddenly he experienced a "new birth" and began to understand that peace with God was made possible "through the atoning blood of Christ which washes away all sin." It is not clear if Schaff's reference to "sin" was the judgment he himself passed on his prior activities across the border. What is clear, however, is that after essentially actualizing the paradigmatic pietistic "conversion," he dedicated himself thenceforth to the "service of God."[11]

Philip Schaff had been baptized in the Reformed Church at Chur on Epiphany Sunday; he was confirmed in the Lutheran Church at Kornthal on Easter during his sixteenth year. His movement from Switzerland to German lands and from Reformed to Lutheran suggested an unbound spirit—an irenic nature that affirmed similarities and a pietistic tendency to overlook, or overcome, confessional differences.[12] His brief stay at the academy was followed by a much longer period of study at the *Gymnasium* in nearby Stuttgart, the Württemberg capital. There Philip boarded for a time in the home of prominent merchant, Johann Georg Mann, who hosted many "awakened" pastors and leaders of the Pietist movement. Philip shared lodging with the merchant's son, William Julius Mann, and the two roommates became life-long friends. In assessing the importance of the Württemberg period on Schaff's development as a theologian, his son and biographer concluded:

> The social and religious influences of these days in Stuttgart left a deep impression on the boy's mind and heart, and had much to do in keeping him during his university career from being drawn into rationalistic teaching. He always retained much of the fervor of Württemberg pietism.[13]

University Education

The discipline of theology in German universities was enjoying a golden age during Schaff's student years, which began at the age of eighteen after his graduation from the *Gymnasium* at Stuttgart.[14] Prior to this period, the reputations of many German universities, particularly the theology faculties, had declined as the champions of the Enlightenment ridiculed them for being antiquated, obscurantist, and narrow-minded. Even worse, many of them had been closed during the Napoleonic era as French armies imposed the anti-clerical values of the French Revolution on much of Europe.

11. David Schaff, *Life of Philip Schaff*, 12–13.

12. Conser, *Church and Confession*, 32.

13. David Schaff, *Life of Philip Schaff*, 16. Philip Schaff maintained a life-long affiliation with Stuttgart and its environs. His friend, W. J. Mann emigrated from there to Pennsylvania and served for a time as a pastor in the German Reformed Church before settling among the Lutherans in Philadelphia. Schaff's son, David, studied at the Kornthal academy prior to entering college at Yale—where he helped found Yale's first football team. Philip Schaff returned to Stuttgart many times, notably in 1865 when he established Germany's first Sunday school there.

14. See Howard, *Protestant Theology*.

This was particularly true of Prussia after its crushing defeat by Napoleon at Jena in 1806. However, with the collapse of Napoleon's regime and the restoration of the various traditional monarchies, principalities, and empires in 1815, many universities were reestablished or reformed according to "modern" principles. Under the control of the progressively more centralized national governments, the universities were reconceived as research institutions in the service of the bureaucratized state. The expanded administrative aspirations of the state required that it educate its people to be responsible citizens and to practice the critical thinking that technological progress demanded. The schools were expected to encourage systematic investigative methods and the habit of free inquiry so that students could discover the inner workings of all phenomena and then use that knowledge for humane purposes (as defined by the state).

This state-sponsored rejuvenation of academic life affected theology in major ways. In order to justify its existence, theology had to demonstrate that it too was "scientific" (*wissenschaftlich*). This meant that academic theology became less confessional and ecclesial, and more reliant upon the current standards of intellectual rigor. Schaff inherited the concern for finding an appropriate method, particularly in regard to the historical investigation of the development of Christianity.

With the new nationalism sweeping post-Napoleonic Europe, not only the universities but also the churches were subjected to increasing governmental supervision and regulation.[15] The various German states all sought to encourage a religious and moral consensus in their territories in order to foster ideological cohesion. Therefore, most German principalities promoted an inclusive, or "ecumenical,"[16] view of Christianity that downplayed confessional differences. Some states even ordered the union of the Lutheran and Reformed churches, most famously Prussia during the tercentenary celebration of the Reformation in 1817. The non- or post-partisan nature of the united church was affirmed in its adoption of the name *Evangelische Kirche in den Königlich-Preußischen Landen* (The Evangelical Church in the Royal Prussian Lands). The word "Evangelical" suggested a united Protestantism unconstrained by an exclusive Lutheran or Reformed confessional position. In addition, religious minorities were often granted more rights, and efforts were made to accommodate

15. See Conser, *Church and Confession.*

16. The word "ecumenical" is something of an anachronism when applied to cooperative or ecclesiological ventures in the nineteenth century. At the time, the word functioned as an adjective, but most commonly in relation to confessions on the one hand and ecclesiastical councils on the other. Thus the ecumenical creeds, according to the Lutheran *Book of Concord*, included the Apostles', the Nicene, and the Athanasian; more precisely, the Nicene Creed was ecumenical inasmuch as it was accepted universally by the churches of the East and the West. Similarly, the first seven councils of the church beginning with the Council of Nicaea in 325 constitute the seven ecumenical councils since they were recognized by both Eastern Orthodox and Roman Catholics. Roman Catholics extended the title to later councils as well, including the Vatican Council of 1870. Non-Catholics usually referred to the Vatican council as ecumenical with a hint of derision owing to the exclusion of Protestant and Orthodox Christians from it.

Catholics or even give them parity with Protestants. Consequently, theologians were promoted who encouraged a generous latitudinarianism. Often this involved favoring theologians with Pietist leanings, for Pietists had always minimized the significance of doctrinal differences. Schaff's rescue from ignominy in Switzerland, and his subsequent nurturing among the Pietists in Württemberg, offered significant exposure to an embracive orthodoxy, an ecumenical spirit that would profoundly and indelibly shape his theological sensibilities.

During the early nineteenth century two theological trends epitomized the "scientific" approach, one was known as speculative idealism and was represented in different ways by G. W. F. Hegel and Friedrich Schelling, and the other was based in the religious experience of the individual and championed by Friedrich Schleiermacher. Hegel discerned a divine spirit surreptitiously operating in the history of the human spirit, impelling it forward to more fulfilling forms of cultural, ethical, and political life.[17] The dialectical dynamic of history revealed the progressive reconciliation of seemingly opposed partial perspectives into higher unities that preserved the best of both poles. This evolving spirit expressed itself implicitly in the history of art and religion, and had become most fully and explicitly aware of itself in contemporary philosophy. Because the difference between the divine spirit and the spirit of humanity was not clear in Hegel's writings, many Christian thinkers denounced Hegel, or at least his left-wing followers, as pantheistic, a suspicion that Schaff shared.[18] In spite of fears that Hegel's system had no room for a transcendent, personal God, Schaff embraced his analysis of historical progress whereby inadequate worldviews were overtaken or cast off by more satisfying ones.

Schelling's idealism differed somewhat from that of Hegel. Schelling's thought had gone through several periods, and each of them left a continuing legacy in European intellectual life. In his early career Schelling had stressed the underlying identity of subject and object, and of the infinite and the finite, thereby suggesting a sort of monistic mysticism in which the self and the divine were merged. By the time Schaff encountered his work in Berlin in the early 1840s, Schelling was developing a more "positive philosophy" that posited God's freedom and will as the basis of all reality and all reasoning.[19] Only a free act, he argued, could account for the existence of anything, for nothing exists by virtue of logical necessity. Contrary to Hegel, Schelling insisted that reality was prior to reason, and that God is the utterly free act of the origin of everything. Schelling concluded that we cannot know anything about God unless it is revealed by God. The objectivity and epistemic priority of the revelation of God in Jesus became a foundational theme for Schaff.

The other major new trend in theology, diverging sharply from speculative idealism, was inspired by the theologian Friedrich Schleiermacher. Schleiermacher, who

17. Hegel, *G. W. F. Hegel.*

18. Schaff, *Germany*, 159.

19. Schelling, *Philosophie der Offenbarung.*

was himself indebted to Pietism, based theological reflection on the inner experience of the Christian believer.[20] Faith was not primarily a matter of cognitive assent to doctrinal propositions, nor was it primarily a matter of correct moral behavior. Rather, faith was an immediate feeling of being absolutely dependent upon God. Accordingly, Schleiermacher redefined theology as the articulation of Christian self-consciousness, and thereby capitalized on Romanticism's prioritization of emotion over reason. For Schleiermacher, this self-consciousness revolved around the experience of having been redeemed through Christ from the sense of alienation from God. Redemption was the communication of Christ's perfectly resilient God-consciousness to the faithful. In this soterio-centric view, Christ is the Second Adam in whom new life is made available to humanity. The task of theology, then, was to express this experience in a way that would be comprehensible and plausible to a given cultural situation.

The reflections of Hegel, Schelling, and Schleiermacher were communicated to Schaff in numerous ways.[21] Many of the professors under whom Schaff studied were known as "mediating theologians," because they sought to integrate Protestant doctrines and the claims of philosophy and science, tradition and culture, rationalism and supernaturalism, and revelation and reason. The Protestant tradition, they were convinced, must be interpreted in the light of modern culture and its reigning concepts. They also sought to mediate between subjectivity and objectivity, claiming that theology must integrate faith experience with objective revelation. The Spirit, they were convinced, illumined the theologian and gave insight into textual and historical objectivities. The interpreter needed the proper subjectivity to discern the meaning of Scripture, although biblical exposition also required the careful work of historical analysis and reconstruction.

Schaff was exposed to these intellectual trends through his studies with mediating theologians at three different universities.[22] In 1837 Schaff attended Tübingen University in the kingdom of Württemberg. While Württemburg was predominantly Lutheran, it had absorbed many Reformed influences from neighboring Switzerland and was predisposed to minimizing confessional differences, owing to its strong tradition of Pietism. Following the example of Prussia, the Lutheran and Reformed churches had united into one Evangelical church in 1827. Attempts were also made to accommodate the Catholic population, and after the Napoleonic wars, the university added a Catholic faculty to its Protestant one. This created a very dynamic theological situation. The Catholic professors, following Johann Adam Möhler, tended to regard the church as an evolving organism, and therefore devoted much attention to the history of the church's dynamic tradition. Doctrine, they maintained, was progressive, not static.

20. Schleiermacher, *Christian Faith*.

21. See Penzel, *German Education*.

22. Schaff, *Germany*, 62–101.

The Protestants were divided among confessionalist Lutherans who wanted to recover a doctrinally pristine past, liberals who critiqued many inherited beliefs as relics of the mythological world-view of early Christianity, and the mediators who sought to combine the virtues of modern learning with traditional convictions. One recently dismissed liberal faculty member, David Friedrich Strauss, had just caused a sensation through the publication of his *The Life of Jesus Critically Examined* in 1835, which epitomized a type of "higher criticism" influenced by Hegel. The higher criticism sought to approach the Bible without dogmatic presuppositions such as, for example, the belief in miracles. It challenged the historicity of some biblical accounts and endeavored to uncover the original contexts in which the New Testament writings were composed. F. C. Baur exhibited this trend in a less threatening way, but he too cast doubt on the apostolic authorship and dating of the canonical writings. Although Schaff regarded Strauss as a heretic and denounced "Straussian infidelity," Schaff did come to appreciate the theme of historical development from Baur. Schaff was particularly influenced by Baur's distinction of the ecclesial visions of Peter, James, Paul and John, a theme reinforced by the more conservative professor Friedrich Schmid.

At Tübingen, Schaff gravitated to Isaak August Dorner, a mediating theologian who employed some of the strategies of both Hegel and Schleiermacher to clarify the truths of supernatural revelation. According to Dorner, first the theologian must possess the immediate certainty of faith, and then the theologian could pursue the scientific explication and verification of what faith believes. Dorner believed that the success of this method, in which the natural capacities of human reason complete faith's immediate experience of the divine, demonstrates that humanity was created for union with God. He argued that there was a religious impulse latent in the self and, therefore, an original affinity between God and the self. Tragically, this potential of created human life for spiritual communion with God was frustrated by the fall. However, this impulse has been restored and brought to fruition in Jesus, in whom human nature was perfected. Given his focus on the centrality of union with God, Dorner concluded that God's primary attribute was love. He also insisted that faith was primarily a communal experience; the faith of the church shaped the religious experience of the individual. All of these themes would be taken up Schaff and elaborated throughout his career.

After Tübingen, Schaff travelled to the University of Halle. Its tradition of Pietism, established at the time of Francke, had weathered a number of challenges, notably the rationalistic spirit that came to prominence during the second half of the eighteenth century under the influence of Johann Salomo Semler. Because Halle was part of a Saxon province that belonged to Prussia, it became part of the Church of the Prussian Union after 1817. The Awakening movement inspired numerous followers in the region and in 1826 Friedrich August Gustav Tholuck, a leading theologian in Pietist circles in Berlin, was appointed professor of theology at Halle, where he steered the institution back toward its Pietist roots. During his time at Halle, Philip Schaff lived in the home of Tholuck (whose wife was the niece of Hegel's wife); there he dined regularly with the Tholuck household that often included many colleagues from Berlin and elsewhere, and served as the professor's secretary. Like Schleiermacher, Tholuck based his theology on an analysis of Christian subjectivity. He identified the dreadfulness of sin as the motivating factor in the evolution of Christian faith, elaborating the severity of despair as one discovers the emptiness of the inner self. Tholuck's colleague Julius Müller also stressed sin as a free act and insisted upon the difference of God from all finite and fallen reality. The triumph of Pietism at Halle reinforced Schaff's sensitivity to the importance of subjectivity in Christianity, a theme to which he had been drawn at least since his days at the Kornthal academy.

Schaff then moved on to the University of Berlin, which had been founded in 1810, and was intended to be the premier research university of Europe. In Berlin, Schaff met another mediating theologian, church historian August Neander, whom he came to regard as his most significant mentor. Neander, like all those who had been influenced by the Awakening and by Romanticism, rooted theology in the heart, in the individual's interiority. Neander was intensely Christocentric and interpreted all theological themes in the light of the incarnation and the believer's living union with Christ. He related all events to the incarnation as the center point of history, and therefore focused more on intellectual and spiritual history than on institutional developments. Neander's theological convictions about the nature of the church and his approach to writing about the church ultimately inspired Schaff to pursue church history as a theological discipline.

Also during this period, Schaff learned much from Ernst Hengstenberg, later a leader of the confessional Lutheran party, but a strong advocate of the "evangelical" position associated with the Church of the Prussian Union during the period when Schaff was under his influence. Hengstenberg was professor of Old Testament and the editor of the newspaper *Evangelische Kirchenzeitung*, to which Schaff contributed some of his earliest writings.[23] In the circle of Hengstenberg and the nobleman Ernst Ludwig von Gerlach (whose father had been the mayor of Berlin just after the Napoleonic occupation of the city), Schaff came to appreciate the historic church as the body of Christ, and to value the visible church and its teaching authority in a way that Pietists like Neander and Tholuck typically did not. From his more confessional friends like Gerlach, Schaff also began to discern a deep continuity between Catholicism and Protestantism.

While Schaff was at Berlin, Schelling was articulating the historical dialectic of Petrine authority, evident in Catholicism, and Pauline freedom, manifested in Protestantism. This considerably simplified the more complex schema that Schaff had learned from Baur and Schmidt. According to Schelling, these one-sided emphases were to be synthesized in the Johannine theme of love. Schaff did not personally hear

23. David Schaff, *Life of Philip Schaff*, 511.

Schelling's lectures[24] for he was travelling in Italy at the time they were delivered, but the subsequent excitement about Schelling's vision of the *telos* of Christian history left a permanent mark upon his own conception of the development of the faith as demonstrated in all three of Schaff's texts included in this volume.

Schaff completed his doctoral dissertation, "The Sin against the Holy Spirit," in the spring of 1841. A somewhat speculative work, it included a review of existing scholarship that sought to clarify the precise nature of this "unforgiveable sin" as it appears in the context of Matthew 12:31–33. Schaff concluded that it was impossible to determine with infallible certainty when the sin against the Holy Spirit had been committed.[25] The writing later proved a source of controversy for Schaff because in it he speculated about the possibility of an intermediate state, after death, for those who had rejected or had not known Jesus Christ during their lifetimes. The dissertation was passed *non sine laude* ("not without praise"), a moderate commendation, by his examiners, including Hengstenberg and Neander. While the work was not particularly original, it exhibited familiarity with a wide range of primary sources. Schaff was granted the degree of licentiate of theology from the University of Berlin.

Travels and the Call to Mercersburg

At the recommendation of Hengstenberg, Schaff had served as tutor to the son of noblewoman Frau von Kröcher shortly after his arrival in Berlin. With his studies completed, he embarked upon a fourteen-month sojourn with mother and son through Switzerland and Italy beginning the summer of 1841.[26] They came eventually to Rome, where Schaff preached the Palm Sunday sermon in the Holy City's Protestant chapel before the Prussian princes Friedrich and Wilhelm. After Easter, his visit culminated in an audience with the Pope Gregory XVI. Schaff was twenty-two years old. His uneasiness with the formality of kissing the pontiff's red slippers was noted in his diary. Schaff further observed that "the nostrils of [the pope's] capacious nose were soiled with snuff." This observation revealed a kind of literal proximity to the pope that later detractors would attribute figuratively to Schaff. After their exodus from Rome, the von Kröcher party reposed for a time among the Waldensians at Turin.[27]

When Schaff returned to Berlin, he assumed the role of *Privatdozent* or "independent lecturer," at the university and taught, among other things, the theology of Schleiermacher. His close associations with Hengstenberg and his inner circle led, eventually, to a meeting with Benjamin Schneck and Theodore Hoffeditz, two emissaries from the German Reformed Church in Pennsylvania. The delegation had traveled

24. Although in later life Schaff recalled Schelling's lectures as if he had been there, his actual whereabouts during the time of their delivery are noted in Penzel, "The Reformation Goes West," 225.

25. Theodore L. Trost, Jr., "Philip Schaff's Concept of the Church," 40–41.

26. Appel, "Life of Dr. Philip Schaff," 90–91.

27. David Schaff, *Life of Philip Schaff*, 53–58.

to Prussia in the effort to convince world-famous preacher Friedrich Krummacher to become a professor at their denomination's seminary in Mercersburg. Krummacher, whose newspaper *Palmblätter* ("palm leaves") was widely read in the United States, declined the invitation and recommended Philip Schaff in his stead.[28] Conversations begun during this visit led, eventually, to the unanimous election of Schaff to the chair of Church History and Biblical Literature in the Theological Seminary at Mercersburg, Pennsylvania. A call was formally extended to Schaff on October 19, 1843, by the Synod of the German Reformed Church, which was meeting in Winchester, Virginia. The president of the synod, the Reverend Joseph Berg, signed the document announcing Schaff's election. In less than a year this same Pastor Berg would become Schaff s chief antagonist in the German Reformed Church.

On April 12, 1844, Philip Schaff's ordination service took place at Elberfeld in the Wuppertal region (near Barmen) under the auspices of the Pastor's Aid Society, a missionary society that was organized to assist emigrants to America. So Schaff, who had been baptized in the Swiss Reformed Church and confirmed in the Lutheran Church, was ordained into the Evangelical Church of the Prussian Union.[29] It might be said that Schaff's religious career reflected a process of growth, a dialectic progress, that was central to his thinking about the nature of church history. The ordination service was conducted by Dr. Krummacher, who also delivered the charge to the new minister. Krummacher drew upon the text of Jeremiah 1:17: "But you, gird up your loins; arise and say to them everything that I command you. Do not be dismayed by them, lest I dismay you before them." From Krummacher's point of view, Schaff was called to rescue the original dignity of the German character, a dignity that had been lost in the uncivilized west. Schaff was to venture forth as "the bearer of a pure German national spirit, to assist in restoring to new life a German population whose national character is already half destroyed by the admixture of foreign elements."[30] Schaff's was a call to arms:

> The many-headed monster of pantheism and atheism, issuing from the sphere of German speculation, as it has there [in America] become flesh and broken forth into actual life, in concrete form, spreading desolation and terror, you are called to meet in the armor of the shepherd boy of Bethlehem and to smite with incurable wounds.[31]

28. Krummacher would later serve as court preacher to the King at Potsdam. Schaff stayed at his residence for over a week in advance of his ordination. He returned to the Krummacher residence in 1854 while writing the lectures that would be incorporated into his book *America*. See Theodore Louis Trost, "Exposing, Experiencing, and Explaining America," 4. Portions of this section first appeared in that article.

29. Shriver contends that the Lutheran rite was followed. Shriver, "Phillip Schaff: Heresy at Mercersburg," 20. However, the "Rhine Rite" (a Reformed liturgy) is reported in "Dr. Schaff's Sermon at Elberfeld," 1866.

30. "Krummacher's Address," 1866.

31. Ibid. Also cited in Miller, editor's introduction, xvii-xviii.

Like young Jeremiah, Schaff was being sent forth to admonish a people gone astray. Like young David, his mission was to do battle against the gigantic enemies of God's people.

Schaff did not hesitate to draw his sling. The text for his ordination sermon was the call of the Macedonian man from the shores of Europe to the apostle Paul across the Aegean Sea in Asia Minor: "Come over and help us!" (Acts 16:8). Schaff interpreted this as the call of the German-American community from another distant shore, a call that was intended for him. Like Krummacher, Schaff assumed that the situation in America was desperate. It was a place where "men thirty and forty years of age, descendants of German ancestors, have not been so much as baptized!"[32] Even Puritans and Quakers were more religious than German immigrants! Not only that, the country was overrun by sects: "every enthusiast in whose brain has engendered overnight a new theological concept, builds the next day a chapel and baptizes it with his own name as a legacy for future generations."[33]

But Schaff believed his mission into the wilderness on behalf of the church would be successful. Armed with German scholarship and a certain sense of responsibility, Schaff ventured forth with confidence. His sermon concluded with an eschatological vision of a united Christendom gathered into one triumphant throng and the suggestion that it was toward the actualization of such a universal church that he would labor in America. His journey was not merely to America, then, but toward another destination

> far beyond sea and land, mountain and valley. . . space and time. . . sin and death, into the land of true liberty endlessly manifold and yet one, where there shall be no Europe, no America, no Catholicism and no Protestantism, but an undivided Kingdom of God: No Old World, and no New World, but one glorious Church of the redeemed.[34]

On his journey to America, Schaff stopped for a few weeks in Oxford, England, and met with Edward Pusey. Pusey had studied theology in Göttingen. He also traveled to Berlin and Bonn during the late 1820s, where he made the acquaintance of numerous scholars including Schleiermacher, Tholuck, Neander, and Hengstenberg.[35] These names were all quite familiar to Schaff, of course. Pusey's name, meanwhile, had become associated with the Oxford Movement, a movement within the Church of England that sought to reassert the faith and practice of the church fathers. It regarded the English church, along with the Roman Catholic and Eastern Orthodox churches, as legitimate branches of the one true church which had retained apostolic succession through bishops. Schaff took an interest in this conservative development within

32. "Dr. Schaff's Sermon at Elberfeld," 1869.

33. Ibid.

34. Ibid., 1869–70.

35. Conser, *Church and Confession*, 183–84.

Anglicanism and it would figure centrally in the argument he was developing for his inaugural address. He also visited with various other religious groups in England even though his English ability was quite limited at the time.[36] This habit of meeting people face-to-face, even people with whom he had strong disagreements, was characteristic of Schaff's traveling practice for the rest of his life.

The American Scene

Schaff's background in German mediating theology was dramatically different from the theological education of his American peers, and would lead to many hostile reactions to his work. His use of organic and dialectical concepts to understand the history of the church made him an anomaly in his new intellectual context. Schaff's training in philosophy, particularly in the various forms of German idealism, was dramatically at odds with the preferred philosophical orientation of most American Protestant theologians in the early nineteenth century.[37] American theologians were enamored of the "Scottish Common Sense" philosophers, particularly Thomas Reid and Dugald Stewart.[38] In the eighteenth century Scotland had enjoyed a rare flowering of innovative intellectual activity in response to the challenge of the European Enlightenment.[39] During this period of ferment Reid and his colleagues had reacted negatively to the thorough-going empiricism of David Hume, the notorious epistemologist who had argued that we humans are only conscious of discrete bits of experience. Hume's unsettling radicalism was rooted in his rejection of John Locke's celebrated distinction of an object's primary qualities (like extension in space), which were taken to be objective properties, and secondary qualities (like color and taste), which were taken to be the products of the observer's perceptual apparatus. According to Hume, all we can ever know about anything are our own fleeting sensations, for perceiving something like extension is just as much a sensory phenomenon as is experiencing a taste. Reid and his colleagues feared that Hume's epistemology reduced all propositions about external states of affairs to statements about mental events, and implied a drastic skepticism about the "objective" world. In opposition to this, Reid claimed that the mind directly apprehends external objects (and not merely subjective impressions of the alleged objects), and that veridical knowledge of reality can be extrapolated from

36. Richards, "Life and Work of Philip Schaff," 161–62.

37. By the time of Schaff's arrival, German idealism's principal influence in America had been on New England Transcendentalism through Samuel Taylor Coleridge, *Aids to Reflection*. This was first published in the U. S. by the Calvinist James Marsh in 1829. Holifield, *Theology in America*, 414–51. Only gradually would it appeal to others who became dissatisfied with the Scottish Common Sense. Kuklick, *Churchmen and Philosophers*, 117–229; Noll, *America's God*, 247–50; Aubert, *German Roots of Nineteenth-Century American Theology*, 23–35.

38. See Reid, *An Inquiry into the Human Mind*; Stewart, *Elements of the Philosophy of the Human Mind*.

39. See Broadie, *Scottish Enlightenment*.

these acts of cognition. According to Reid, there is an experiential difference between having a sensation (like being cold) and perceiving an object (like seeing an ice cube).

Although the Scottish Common Sense philosophers did in certain ways anticipate Immanuel Kant's contention that the mind provides some indubitable assumptions governing the processing of information, unlike Kant they did not believe that the mind's own contribution to the construction of knowledge in any way jeopardized knowledge of things as they really are. Rather, for them the mind was more like a mirror of nature, accurately recording data. This epistemology led Reid and his fellow travelers to champion inductive reasoning in all areas of life and to regard all general statements about the cosmos as summations of empirical data. As a result, they favored the collection, analysis, collation, and classification of particular observations of phenomena as articulated by Francis Bacon, and lauded the empirical method as the basis for any valid science. They also continued to insist upon a strict differentiation of the perceiving subject and the perceived object, matter and spirit, and the finite and the infinite. Moreover, Reid argued for the existence of an innate, universal faculty of moral knowledge that grounded all imperatives concerning right and wrong behavior. For him, this moral sense and the self-evident ethical intuitions which it generated undergirded objective judgments about the ethical domain and established human responsibility.

All of these implications attracted American theologians who wanted to emphasize the historic Reformed differentiation of Creator and creature, and of spirit and matter.[40] The Scottish Common Sense philosophy provided a conceptuality that resisted the reduction of ethics to utilitarian calculations of pleasure and pain or to the arbitrary customs of a particular culture. Most attractively, it suggested that objective knowledge, including objective knowledge of divine things, is possible. Theology is not merely the expression of subjective experiences, nor is it a futile attempt to describe the ineffable. Theology can be a science like any other science, the only difference being that its data is supplied by revelation rather than by the observation of nature. Moreover, the inductive method encouraged a hermeneutic strategy that regarded traditional doctrinal truths as valid generalizations based on the collation of discrete biblical passages, a style of biblical interpretation that would evolve into various forms of Fundamentalism.

Scottish Common Sense philosophy was introduced to America by John Witherspoon, a Scottish émigré who in 1768 became president of the College of New Jersey, later known as Princeton University. From Princeton it spread rapidly to such diverse theological institutions as Andover, Harvard, and Yale.[41] Almost every denomination, from Unitarian to Methodist, felt its impact. Its popularity had enormous consequences for the teaching of church history in American seminaries and divinity schools. Church history was presented mainly as a series of discrete events illustrating

40. See Noll, *Princeton and the Republic.*

41. Noll, *America's God*, 93–113. 127–30; Holifield, *Theology in America*, 173–80.

the perpetual struggle between the eternal verities of Protestant orthodoxy and the perennial temptations of heresy, or as the gradual articulation of general theological truths that had always been implicit in the original biblical data.

At Princeton Seminary Samuel Miller, a church historian who was profoundly influenced by the Scottish Common Sense philosophy, continued to use the work of the mildly rationalistic J. L. Mosheim as his basic text. As John Nevin recalled, the result was a view of church history as a fall from original orthodoxy into a period of superstition and prelatical despotism, followed by an advance into an era of Protestant recovery of the pristine truths.[42] During the great apostasy of the Middle Ages, the true faith had endured only in isolated enclaves, like the Waldensians. The particularistic empiricism of the Scottish Common Sense philosophy reinforced the tendency in Protestant America to regard history as a chronicle of disparate facts, with little sense of organic development and little interest in teleology. For historians like Miller, it certainly was not the case that foundational doctrines like the Trinity could undergo any significant evolution. The history of Christianity was a confusing tale of the periodic oscillations in the church's recognition of static theological truths.

The insistence of American theologians influenced by the Scottish Common Sense philosophy upon the possibility of grasping the objective meaning of biblical revelation, apart from the church's subjective appropriation it, did not sit well with Schaff's appreciation of the importance of ecclesial experience. Moreover, their static view of history was at odds with Schaff's more developmental and organic understanding. A clash was inevitable.

The Mercersburg Theology

On October 25, 1844, Philip Schaff delivered his "Inaugural Address" in German on the "principle of Protestantism" to the Synod of the German Reformed Church assembled in Reading, Pennsylvania. His topic was not intended to be controversial; rather, he offered "a sort of scientific religious confession that may serve to explain distinctly the ground on which I intend to stand in your midst."[43] Still, almost every point of Schaff's lecture was a potential point of controversy in an American church whose self-understanding was quite different from that of her sister churches across the sea. While the structure and the content of *The Principle of Protestantism* are discussed in greater detail in the next chapter, it is necessary here to introduce some of the key elements of the address in order to account for the reaction it induced within the German Reformed Church as it welcomed Schaff to America and into its company.

Schaff began his discussion of Protestantism with a retrospective look at the Reformation, what he called "the legitimate offspring, the greatest act of the Catholic

42. Nevin, *My Life*, 40–42.

43. Schaff, *The Principle of Protestantism* in this volume, 61..

Church."[44] Schaff insisted upon maintaining the connection between Roman Catholicism and Protestantism because, despite numerous aberrant practices, Catholicism had brought Christianity forward in time to the point where reformation was both necessary and possible. Protestantism, from this point of view, did not represent an effort to overthrow the cardinal doctrines of the church (e.g., the two natures of Christ; the doctrine of the Trinity); rather, it carried these doctrines forward into the light of new insight. Nor was Protestantism mainly an effort to subvert hierarchy and the papacy. The whole point of Protestantism was to "eradicate popedom from the heart."[45] In short, it was *not* in *protest* against Roman Catholicism that Protestants found their true identity.

Schaff's assessment of Roman Catholicism, certainly, had been nurtured in the various benign environments he traversed on his way to America: the religious diversity of his hometown in Switzerland; the contested *and* congenial atmosphere of the university at Tübingen; the cooperative ethos of the Prussian unionists in Berlin. But he also posed a series of theological reasons for insisting upon the relationship between Protestantism and Catholicism. First, he pointed to Christ's promise in the gospel: "Lo, I am with you always even to the end of the world" (Matt 28:20). If Christ were actually absent from the church for centuries and then suddenly appeared on the scene during the Reformation what would become of Christ's reliability as one who promises? Here Schaff placed himself in opposition to those Anabaptists and spiritualists of the Reformation era and their nineteenth-century counterparts who would leap over the entire history of the Roman Catholic Church in an effort to recapture a pristine New Testament Christianity untainted by Roman distortions. For Schaff, New Testament Christianity was indeed determinative but only in the sense that seed and tree are related.

A second point arose for Schaff in this context. The Christian religion was not an escape from history, it was a movement through history, through time, toward that great day when Christ would it be all in all. Christianity was involved in a process of organic development. Schaff used available biblical metaphors to convey this sense. Like the mustard seed, Christianity grew invisibly for long periods of time before it would become the tallest of all trees (Matt 13:31–32). It was the unseen leaven that eventually leavens the entire loaf (Gal 5:9). Like the roots and branches of the tree, Protestantism and Roman Catholicism were, therefore, intimately connected; they needed each other. The role of Protestantism was to move the whole Christian church forward. "Truth can be said to advance only as error is surmounted and thrown to the rear," wrote Schaff's approving Mercersburg colleague, John Nevin, in his introduction to the English publication of *The Principle of Protestantism*.[46] The church was no mere bystander in the advance of the kingdom of God. Human history, from Schaff's

44. Ibid., 75.
45. Ibid., 78.
46. Ibid., 51.

point of view, was the stage upon which the great drama of the kingdom is played, and only through the actions of Christians, as they engaged each other and the world around them, could that play grow toward its final conclusion.

If Schaff's notion of organic development suggested the influence of German Romanticism, a third factor that contributed to his understanding of the relationship between Protestantism and Catholicism was derived from Hegel. For Schaff, history advanced toward the consummation of time dialectically. In the case of Christianity, then, opposing forces both inside and outside of the church competed to direct the church's course. To every thesis there was an antithesis. Extremes on both sides diverted the course of the church and might even carry it backwards for a while. But forward progress was maintained in the mainstream, in the waters that ran deep and to which the shallow waters that languished along opposing shores would ultimately return. Schaff located the reforming principle which gave birth to Protestantism in this mainstream:

> To be true to its own idea a reformation must hold its course midway, or through the deep rather than between the two extremes. In opposition on the one side to revolution, or the radical and violent overthrow of an existing system, it must attach itself organically to what is already at hand, and grow forth from the trunk of history in regular living union with its previous development. In opposition to simple restoration or a mere repetition of the old, it must produce from the womb of this the birth of something new.[47]

In Schaff's over-arching conception of church history, the dialectic process was at work everywhere. Schaff saw Christianity moving toward a balance of the principles of freedom and order and toward the church of John, which, as his mentors from Baur to Schelling had imagined it, would be ruled by love. Accordingly, the extreme forms of both Protestantism and Roman Catholicism would co-mingle and flow back into mainstream.

If Protestantism was retrospectively a legitimate development of Roman Catholicism, in its prospective aspect it represented a move beyond Catholicism. As already noted, Protestantism was for Schaff not primarily a *protest* against Rome; rather, Protestantism was a positive force in history. This force had to do with the primacy of scripture. But the Protestant principle of scripture alone led to particular problems in America. Schaff suggested that the greatest threat to Christianity in America came from the proliferation of sects. In the "sect system" no allegiance to any historic faith community was necessary or required. Anyone could presumably pick up the Bible and understand immediately what it had to say, since its truths were obvious to anyone endowed with common sense. Thus it was not the "single pope of the city of seven hills" who endangered the well-being of Christianity in America; rather the true foes were "the numberless popes—German, French, English, and American—who would

47. Ibid., 62.

fain enslave Protestants once more to human authority . . . in the form of mere private judgment and private will."[48]

In the end, Schaff blamed the problem of sectarianism on what he called Puritanism—the guiding force behind most of American Protestantism, as he understood it from his European perspective. Ultimately Puritanism would lead to full atomism. It resisted development. It ran counter to the whole stream of history by asserting isolation against union; it mistook a part for the whole; and it denied organic connection to the living stream of the Church in that it maintained no historical connection to the community of saints (or other contemporary Christian communities) through confession or creed. Schaff went so far as to insist that Puritanism was not biblical. John 17, according to Schaff's exegesis, "Inflicts the death blow on the whole sectarian and denominational system."[49]

In the aftermath of his recent visit to Oxford, Schaff turned his attention to the Anglo-Catholic movement. In "Puseyism" he saw an effort to cure the sectarianism disease. He considered the high-church movement among American Episcopalians and their English counterparts as "an entirely legitimate reaction against rationalism and sectarian pseudo-Protestantism as well as the religious subjectivity of the low church party."[50] But it was a misdirected reaction. It tried to put tradition on a par with scripture, finding its legitimating authority in an apostolic succession instead of a priesthood of all believers. It was a retreat rather than an advance. Schaff respected the movement for what it was trying to accomplish but in the end it sacrificed too much. It surrendered the scriptures to the institutional church; it subscribed anxiously to the "dogma of Trent."[51] It moved inevitably back to Rome in its search for certainty and thereby utterly misapprehended "the significance of the Reformation with its consequent development—that is the entire Protestant period the Church."[52]

In concluding his address, Schaff anticipated a Protestantism in America that would be historically grounded—one that would absorb the various sects as they served out their corrective purposes and flowed back into the mainstream of Protestantism. For all of church history was coming together: "The future belongs to union," Schaff proclaimed, perhaps in affirmation of his experience in the Evangelical Church of the Prussian Union. And he foresaw this union within the church first of all as a sign to the world of the coming kingdom: "for the end or scope of all history is this, that the world may resolve itself into the kingdom of God." From this point of view, Protestantism could not be consummated without Catholicism; the "truth of both tendencies must be actualized as the power of one and the same life in the full

48. Ibid., 140.

49. Ibid., 138.

50. Ibid., 142.

51. Ibid., 147.

52. Ibid., 144.

revelation of the kingdom of God."[53] And so, Schaff's address ended on a hopeful note. He looked forward to an emerging "Evangelical Catholicism" on the soil of the New World: a magnificent union that would complete in the nineteenth century the Reformation that was begun in the sixteenth century.

It would be an exaggeration to say that Schaff shocked the entire German Reformed community with his address. Most of the assembly applauded and appreciated the young scholar's insights. Indeed, only a couple of months earlier, John Nevin had preached a sermon on "Catholic Unity" to open the Triennial Convention of the Dutch Reformed and German Reformed Churches at Harrisburg. Schaff concluded that Nevin's sermon was fully sympathetic with the catholic ethos of his own address and had the sermon published as an appendix to *The Principle of Protestantism* when it appeared in English.[54] In Nevin himself Schaff found a very likeminded colleague who championed his insights. Nevin had long admired the histories of Neander, crediting them with awakening him from his "dogmatic slumber."[55] He had also long been concerned with the role of the church in the work of grace and the development of the Christian faith. His initial Mercersburg colleague Friederich Rauch had become the first person to introduce Hegel's ideas to America through his *Psychology* (1840) before his untimely death in 1841. Through Rauch, Nevin had encountered more fully contemporary German views of the "organic" process of faith and history.[56]

The prevailing conditions in America, however, disposed many to reject Schaff's views. In 1837, the Presbyterians of the Old School had opened up the missionary field to Latin America claiming that the Roman Catholic baptism was not a Christian baptism at all.[57] Following this religious reasoning, Roman Catholics fell into the same category for many American Protestants as the Muslim or the "heathen." Politically considered, Roman Catholics were even less appreciated. In the early 1830s they had begun to push for public funding of parochial schools, hoping to avoid altogether the Protestant influences in the public schools. Then again many Protestants perceived the papal system to be antithetical to the principles of freedom and equality so dear to all Americans. The Catholic Church was indeed openly hostile in its proclamations to the democratic system and preferred a close relationship between church and state to the separation of church and state that existed in America.

The opposition to Schaff's address was led by Joseph Berg, pastor of the Race Street Church in Philadelphia. Berg considered the Roman Catholic Church to be no church at all or the church of the Antichrist. In this regard he was fairly typical of

53. Ibid., 189.

54. Ibid., 25–192. In a note to Henry Harbaugh written some time after 1860, Nevin listed "Catholic Unity" as the second of his own contributions to what became the "Mercersburg Theology" (the first was his book *The Anxious Bench*). See Nevin, "Mercersburg Theology," v-vi.

55. DeBie, "Biographical Essay," xvii.

56. Layman, general introduction, 12–18; Aubert, *German Roots*, 25–27.

57. Schaff refers to this decision of the Old School Presbyterian General Assembly in His "Lectures on Church History." Cited in Shriver, "Phillip Schaff: Heresy at Mercersburg," 52–53.

many Protestant divines in the mid-nineteenth century. Indeed only a few months before Schaff arrived in Pennsylvania, Berg's own neighborhood in Philadelphia experienced extensive anti-Catholic rioting. Ironically, just one week before Schaff's inaugural address, Berg himself had given a speech to the Synod's opening assembly. In his address, Berg argued that the undefiled doctrines of the German Reformed Church had been maintained in their purity and strength from of the original apostolic church through various Christian communities after the second century in the south of France and adjacent areas. These *protesting* churches were entirely uncontaminated by Roman influence. Their witness culminated in the fourteenth century in the Waldensian community: the true parent of the German Reformed Church in the United States, according to Berg. Berg insisted that there was indeed a viable apostolic succession that animated the German Reformed tradition. It consisted in a succession of protesting communities that had no dealings whatsoever with the pope. Berg summarized his argument accordingly:

> If others can claim apostolic relation and succession, so can we; if others establish the right to trace their descent from Waldensian witness, much more we . . .; if others may animate their churches with zeal to emulate the piety and devotion of their fathers, all these resources are abundantly ours. Let us use them.[58]

The whole point of Joseph Berg's history was to elevate the concept of a static Protestant orthodoxy that had been handed down in pristine glory to the contemporary church, thereby avoiding any connection whatsoever with the Roman Catholic Church, the "Church of the Antichrist." As Berg contended in a later writing: "If we admit that the Church of Rome has ever been the Church of Christ you concede the whole ground."[59] A starker contrast with Schaff, who spoke before the same assembly a week later, is hardly imaginable. For Berg, Schaff's position could only be an alien alchemy. Organic historical development was worse than useless in his conception; indeed, it was nothing less than a heretical concept. So Berg convened a committee of the Philadelphia Classis in September 1845 to pursue charges of heresy against Schaff. The examination itself was anticlimactic: the Berg faction was completely dismissed. *The Principle of Protestantism*, if fairly understood, was declared to "promote the true interests of religion." Both Schaff and Nevin—who defended Schaff's work tirelessly in articles in the denomination's newspaper—were praised for their efforts to "build up and honor the welfare of the church."[60]

58. Cited in Thompson and Bricker, editors' preface, 13.

59. Berg, *Old Paths*, viii.

60. "Acts and Proceedings of the Synod, York, Pennsylvania, 1845"; 80. Cited in George H. Shriver, "Philip Schaff: Heresy at Mercersburg," 39. This and a subsequent heresy trial are the subjects of Shriver's chapter. See also Shriver, "Philip Schaff (1819–1893)."

Schaff was exonerated, or more precisely: his book was. And so he decided to commit himself to life in America. Recalling his transition, his progress, to America forty-seven years later, Schaff remarked:

> the Synod acquitted of me. . . with an overwhelming majority. With such a record I thought I ought to venture upon the honorable state of matrimony and married a Mary from Maryland, but this is a private matter.[61]

A private matter too, it would appear, was Dr. Berg's relentless opposition to Professor Schaff. Within a year after Schaff's vindication, Berg brought new charges forward. This time they focused upon Schaff's dissertation, "The Sin against the Holy Spirit." In this admittedly speculative work Schaff wrote about an intermediary state after death, a second chance for those who had known Christ in this life. The work had been translated into English and appeared in the Dutch Reformed paper *The Christian Intelligencer* on July 16, 1846. Its translator, a Reverend Gulden, charged Schaff of advancing a "doctrine akin to purgatory." Dr. Berg drafted a resolution against the doctrine of the middle state but the board that reviewed Berg's complaint "refused to censure one of our professors simply because his view on a single doctrine did not correspond with the view of the majority."[62]

As it happens, theological speculation at Mercersburg was not curtailed because of Berg's actions. Classroom notes from Schaff's students show that he continued to wonder about the possibility of a middle state until his departure from Pennsylvania in 1863.[63] Meanwhile the possibility of a middle state caused Schaff's colleague, John Nevin, to rethink the whole Calvinistic doctrine of predestination and influenced all of Nevin's later writings. Indeed, Nevin preached a sermon at the funeral service of President James Buchanan in which an intermediate state akin to the one Schaff had described was suggested.[64] Thus the proximity of the kingdom of God to all human beings—even beyond the grave—was introduced by Schaff into American theological discussion.[65] As for Joseph Berg, he abandoned the German Reformed Church in 1852 and aligned himself with the Dutch Reformed Church.

61. "Dr. Schaff's Farewell Address to the Synod of the German Reformed Church" in Schaff, *Reformed and Catholic,* 13.

62. Cited in Shriver, "Heresy at Mercersburg," 45.

63. Ibid., 55.

64. This theme is explored in Theodore L. Trost, Jr., "Philip Schaff's Concept of the Church," 114–15.

65. Forty years later, this idea—which originated with Dorner—would be reintroduced into American theological discourse by Charles Briggs and Newman Smyth. See William R. Hutchison, *Modernist Impulse*, 84.

Schaff's Life Work: The Reunion of Christendom

After an uneasy beginning at Mercersburg, Schaff settled down to the work that would comprise the major headings of the twentieth-century ecumenical movement, as James Hastings Nichols had put it.[66] He labored in the German Reformed Church until 1863, when the Civil War's proximity to Mercersburg led to an extended sabbatical. Schaff moved to middle Manhattan where he initially worked on behalf of the Sabbath Society. He also lectured at Andover and Hartford seminaries. In 1870 he became a professor at Union Theological Seminary and remained there for another twenty-two years. Schaff continued to be guided by his vision of an evangelical catholicism, which he pursued in a variety of venues and in numerous activities after his arrival in America.

First, Schaff continued his defense of historical development in his writings, notably *What is Church History?* (1846) and "German Theology and the Church Question" (1852) which are included in this volume. He considered writing church history key to the idea of the church itself and to the church's development. His famous seven-volume *History of the Christian Church* (1882–92) and his scholarly collection of *Nicene and Post Nicene Fathers* (1886–90) are two fruits of this conviction.

Second, he pursued his effort to draw German and American churches into dialogue. He published the journal *Der Deutsche Kirchenfreund* (1848–53), which strived to place the greatest scholarship from Germany before United, Lutheran, Moravian and Reformed churches of German descent in America. The watchwords for this publication were those of Meledinius: "In essentials unity, in non-essentials liberty, in all things charity."[67] When Schaff resigned from his editorial duties, his friend, William Julius Mann, took over responsibilities as editor. He also lectured abroad about the state of religious affairs in America, resulting, for example, in the publication of his book *America: A Sketch of the Political, Social, and Religious Character of the United States of North America* (1855). And he wrote about events and people in Germany for an American audience, as in his book *Germany: its Universities, Theology and Religion* (1857).

Third, Schaff was active in liturgics and other aspects of church life. He helped develop the German Reformed Church's provisional liturgy of 1857 that reflected his Christocentric understanding of the church and affirmed its historical nature by including forms and phrases that extended back to before the Reformation.[68] He

66. "The agenda of the twentieth-century ecumenical movement . . . (at least on its faith and order side) reads like the heads of the Mercersburg controversy." See Nichols, *Romanticism in American Theology*, 310–11. Portions of this section appeared in Theodore Louis Trost, "The Ecumenical Trajectory."

67. The maxim was initially attributed to Augustine in the *Kirchenfreund*. In a 1999 article, H. J. M. Nellen argued that the maxim originated in a tract written by the archbishop of Split, Marco Antonio de Dominis, in 1617. See Nellen, "De zinspreuk 'In necessariis unitas,'" 99–106.

68. See Michael Farley, ed. *The Mercersburg Liturgy*, MTSS, vol. 11 (forthcoming). Maxwell, *Worship and Reformed Theology*.

produced a German hymnbook (1859) for use in the churches of various denominations and also a *Catechism for Sunday Schools and Families* (1862). Schaff also placed contemporary churches into communication with their forbears through the publication of the *Creeds of Christendom* (1877).

Fourth, he served as an ambassador for the church universal. In this capacity he fostered face to face encounters across denominational lines, as in the Evangelical Alliance, and within confessional communities, as in the Alliance of Reformed Churches.[69] He also established a number of societies and fostered conversations and generated scholarly collaborations, such as the American Society of Church History and the Society of Biblical Literature. And remarkably, for a non-native English speaker, he traveled between Great Britain and the United States as chair of the translation committee to revise the King James Version and make a more accessible and scholarly sound Bible available to the English-speaking world.

Schaff delivered his final address—it could be called his last will and testament—in Chicago at the World's Parliament of Religions in 1893. Entitled "The Reunion of Christendom," the speech surveyed the religious landscape of the entire world, celebrated the progress of Christianity throughout the world, and envisioned in this development signs of the coming kingdom, to be achieved, or granted, perhaps, in the coming century. Notable in the address is Schaff's delineation of types of unified action that would lead to the reunion of Christendom: voluntary associations of individuals such as the Evangelical Alliance; federal union in which groups retain separate identities but cooperate together for a common purpose such as mission (the Alliance of Reformed Churches was one example); and organic union, in which a common governing principle unites all parties as in the Prussian Union Church. His attitude toward denominationalism had moderated greatly. As reunions among Protestant groups advanced, Schaff anticipated the greater work of uniting with the Roman Catholic and Orthodox churches.[70]

In remarkable contrast to *The Principle of Protestantism* and along lines he first developed in his book *America*, Schaff now distinguished between sectarianism and denominationalism. He affirmed that each denomination offered a particular theological gift for the larger church. This may be the philosophy behind the fourteen-volume American Church History Series that Schaff proposed but did not live to see. For this series, Schaff had contracted authors such as Williston Walker, Leonard Bacon, and Joseph Dubbs to write histories of their particular denominations. This attitude of a positive embrace of denominations is reflected in "The Reunion of Christendom" in a series of benedictions in which Schaff calls many (but not all) denominations

69. For Schaff's key role in the Alliance of Reformed Churches, see Jordan, "Cooperation without Incorporation," 13–35. For Schaff's role in the history of the Evangelical Alliance, see Jordan, *Evangelical Alliance.*

70. For a skillful elaboration of these matters see John Payne, "Philip Schaff: Christian Scholar and Prophet of Ecumenism."

"glorious." So, for example whereas at the beginning of his career, he criticized Congregationalists for their sectarianism, at the end of it he says:

> The Congregational Church is a glorious church: for she has taught the principle and proved the capacity of congregational independence and self-government based upon a living faith in Christ, without diminishing the effect of voluntary cooperation in the Master's service.

The Principle of Protestantism placed emphasis on what Schaff and his contemporaries called "the church question" and ended, in its final thesis, with the fulfillment of the eschatological trajectory initiated by Jesus' prayer for his followers in John 17. At the end of his career, "The Reunion of Christendom" advanced this same vision:

> Before the reunion of Christendom can be accomplished, we must expect providential events, new Pentecosts, new reformations—great as the ones that have gone before. The twentieth century has marvelous surprises in store for the world, which may surpass even those of the nineteenth. History now moves with telegraphic speed, and may accomplish the work of years in a single day. The modern inventions of the steamboat, the telegraph, the power of electricity, the progress of science and of international law (which regulates commerce by land and by sea, and will in due time make an end of war), link all the civilized nations into one vast brotherhood.[71]

This developmental and providential vision of the church's progress toward union and the kingdom of God animated Schaff's career and grounded the theological movement he and John Nevin led. He provided his most direct and expansive description of it in these early writings from Mercersburg.

71. Schaff, "The Reunion of Christendom," *Historian and Ambassador* 334.

DOCUMENT 1

The Principle of Protestantism as Related to the Present State of the Church
by Philip Schaff (1845)

Editors' Introduction

On Friday, October 25, 1844, the synod of the German Reformed Church assembled in Reading, Pennsylvania. As part of the proceedings, Philip Schaff was installed as professor of biblical literature and ecclesiastical history in the denomination's seminary at Mercersburg. Speaking in his native German, Schaff introduced himself to his new coreligionists in a protracted lecture entitled "*Das Princip des Protestantismus*." An expansion of the address was completed in December and published soon thereafter.[1] By June, John W. Nevin, completed an English translation entitled *The Principle of Protestantism*. As bookends to Schaff's monograph, Nevin included his own apologetic introduction and a concluding sermon on "Catholic Unity," in which Nevin developed his understanding of the true church with particular reference to its visible nature.[2]

In his introduction, Nevin addresses the key points of controversy that resulted both from Schaff's ordination sermon in Elberfeld in Germany prior to his departure for America and his later inaugural address in Reading. As a collaboration, *The Principle of Protestantism* constituted the first concerted expression of the Mercersburg theology—with Nevin defending Schaff's scholarship and Schaff offering appreciation for Nevin's collegiality and their common convictions concerning catholicity.

Schaff interpreted his call to America as an invitation to become a "missionary of science"; his purpose was to bring German scholarship in its fullness into active participation in the life of the American church. *The Principle of Protestantism* offers a comprehensive summary of Schaff's university studies in ecclesiology. It includes a well-organized, carefully argued discussion of Protestantism's two-fold principle: the primacy of scripture and salvation by grace through faith. It surveys the development

1. Schaff, *Das Princip des Protestantismus*.

2. This volume of the MTSS contains all of the writings from the 1845 edition of *The Principle of Protestantism* except the sermon "Catholic Unity," which appears in *"One Holy, Catholic, and Apostolic": John Nevin's Writings on Ecclesiology*, ed. Sam Hastra, Jr. MTSS, vol. 5 (forthcoming). The sermon was included in the original volume at Schaff's request. As Schaff explains in the text of *The Principle of Protestantism* and, as Nevin elaborates in a footnote to Schaff's text (see p. 185. footnote 86), there was a fortuitous agreement between the two professors on the matter of the future unity of the church and the need for a real and visible manifestation of that "catholic" unity.

of Christianity in Germany and its contributions to German intellectual life. It also includes a lengthy discussion of the organic development of the church through time, both into the future, and in relation to its medieval Catholic past. Finally in several places, particularly in the footnotes, Nevin and Schaff engage in detail with the controversies of their day. Some of these, like the allure of the Anglo-Catholic position, may be familiar to twenty-first century readers. More particular affairs revolving around George Bush, Johannes Ronge, and Benjamin Onderdonk grounded the discussion for the original reader. Today's reader may rely on the editors' footnotes or the glossary of names for clarifications about these less well-known personages.

The book itself is a display of Germanic erudition. Schaff intended his work to build bridges between German churches in America and churches in Germany for the thoughtful conveyance of a living and vigorous Anglo-German theology. Klaus Penzel describes the most important ingredients in *The Principle of Protestantism* as:

> . . .the high-church notion of the church as the Body of Christ, the *Christus-prolongatus*; the romantic-idealistic philosophy of history with its novel principle of historical development; the Neander-Schmid distinction of the three apostolic types of Peter, Paul, and John as key to understanding the nature and history of the New Testament church; and the romantic vision of an "Evangelical Catholicism."[3]

The motivating issue behind the book is "the Church Question," as he and his German contemporaries called it: What is the nature of the true church? How should it be ordered and related to other aspects of society, including the state, the arts, and culture? The church question had been central to Schaff's education and continued to preoccupy his early career.[4] Schaff's ecclesiology, his theological understanding of church history as developed in relation to his incarnational Christology, is first articulated in *The Principle of Protestantism* and is subsequently elaborated upon in *What is Church History?* and "German Theology and the Church Question." These expositions constitute Schaff's foundational theological contribution to the Mercersburg Theology.

In accordance with other proponents of a "high church" theology, Schaff insisted that the church must be seen not simply as a gathering of like-minded Christians, but as a divinely constituted, historical, and visible institution.[5] But in contrast to the other major American movements concerned with the nature of the church, Schaff saw it neither as strictly bound to one institution, such as the Church of Rome, nor to a static orthodoxy such as the Calvinism articulated in the Westminster Confession of Faith (1646) or the twenty eight articles of the Lutheran Augsburg Confession

3. Penzel, editorial introduction, *Philip Schaff*, xli.

4. Penzel, *German Education*, 87–124. Portions of the following discussion are derived from Bains and Trost, "Philip Schaff," 418–23.

5. Holifield, *Theology in America*, 245–51, 276–78, 298–301, 331–40, 408–14, 415–33.

(1530). Instead, using the imagery of the Romantic era that had infused the works of Beethoven and Goethe with such passion, Schaff argued that the church was a flowing stream or a living organism; its development had been nurtured by Rome, by Augsburg, and by Westminster, of course, and by some dissenting sects and irreligious movements as well. He believed that through it all, and despite misadventure, the kingdom of God was growing toward fruition.

Overview of the Work

Schaff organized his writing into two parts. The first considers Protestantism in relation to the Roman Catholic Church. The longer second part discusses the nature of Protestantism in relationship to its development since the Reformation. In the first part, he names two principles, the "material principle" of the doctrine of justification by grace through faith and the "formal principle" of the normative authority of the scriptures.[6] While Schaff's insistence that justification by faith is the foundational and primary principle offers a critique of Protestantism as rooted primarily in biblicism, there is little in his discussion of these two principles themselves that would have given the book notoriety or made it especially memorable.

In relationship, however, they are foundational to the idea of organic historical development that Schaff's critics rejected. The formal principle of the Bible is the root of the objective forms that Schaff believes must exist and be respected in the church, while the material principle of faith is the root of the subjective experience that makes the church not an ossified institution or a collection of denominations only spiritually united, but a stream of tradition flowing onward to the kingdom of God. As Schaff says in the second part, "Protestantism is the principle of movement, of progress in the history of the Church" (176). Because of its foundational principles, Protestantism's essential contribution to the church is not restoration or revolution, but continual reformation, change, movement, and progress. As such it accomplishes "an *ever-deepening appropriation* of Christianity as the power of a divine life, which is destined to make *all* things new" (176–77).

Schaff introduces this theme at the very beginning of the first part where it cannot escape the reader's attention. He distinguishes the Protestant Reformation from a revolution that rejects the past and from a restoration that looks to restore a lost condition. In contrast to those kinds of movements, the Reformation is the product of what came before it and thus "the legitimate offspring, the greatest act of the Catholic church" (75). Protestantism is not grounded in the rejection of Catholicism any more than Christianity rejects Judaism. Rather, like the relationship of Christianity to Judaism, Protestantism is the fulfillment of Catholicism, the next stage in the

6. Klaus Penzel traces the origin of these categories to K. G. Bretschneider *Handbuch der Dogmatik der evangelisch-lutherischen Kirche* (1814; 4th edition 1838). See Penzel, "Toward a New Reformation," 76, n3.

historical development of the church (73). In this survey of the medieval history of Christianity, Schaff not only praises so-called "reformers before the reformers" such as the Waldensians, John Wycliffe, and Jan Hus, but also the Renaissance, and Italian leaders of the Catholic Reformation such as Gasparo Contarini. Yet it is not only the leading figures of the new movements of the late Middle Ages that Schaff praises as playing an essential role in preparing for the Reformation but even the Roman Catholic Church's system of law and authority which controlled the nations until they were ready for appropriation of "the evangelical principle and the use of an independent manly freedom" (74).

Schaff's discussion of the material and formal principles of the Reformation is easily the most systematic and well-documented part of his work. His notes provide extensive citations of Roman Catholic, Lutheran, and Reformed authorities. While he gives careful and respectful attention to the Catholic view, on the issues of justification and the primacy of scripture he is forthright in charging them with "serious defects" and in defending the Protestant position from the attacks of its Roman Catholic and rationalist critics. Schaff cautioned Protestants that the two principles are "inseparably joined as contents and form, will and knowledge, and strictly taken constitute but two sides of the same maxim: Christ in all" (115). They must be held together or distortions would emerge. Justification without a searching of the scripture tends toward narrow orthodoxy. Scripture alone, without justification, leads to individualized interpretations. Creeds he regarded as particularly important, not because they were an independent source of revelation from scripture, as Roman Catholics might argue, but because with scripture they were "the one fountain of the written word, only rolling itself forward in the stream of church consciousness" (110).[7] While such an insistence on creeds would be controversial among many American Protestants, it was mainly Schaff's emphasis on the stream of the church as developed in other parts of the work that awakened his contemporaries' hostile response.

Schaff begins the second part with a paean of praise to Protestantism and its development, particularly its German theology and missionary expansion. The remainder of the book is divided into three distinct sections. The first presents the two major "diseases" afflicting Protestantism; the second acknowledges a prominent but insufficient solution; the third presents a wide-ranging discussion of what Schaff sees as the ultimate solution, "Protestant Catholicism."

The two diseases of rationalism and "sectarianism" are both rooted in "one-sided subjectivism" that is a distortion of a Protestant strength, rationalism in a theoretic subjectivism, sectarianism in a practical one. Schaff's discussion of rationalism was controversial because he claimed it was a greater evil than Catholicism. "Romanism," he estimated as "only *half*-pelagian and half-rationalistic." Rationalism, on the other hand, "dreams of being able to do *all* by its own strength, and to know *all* by reason simply"

7. Under Schaff's editorial direction, the texts of the seven ecumenical councils (325–787) were published as volume 14 in the second series of *NPNF*.

(125). For a man of pious convictions, nurtured by the thought and example of scholars like Neander and Tholuck, it was the greater evil. He also jabbed at his new countrymen who regarded rationalism and infidelity as a German disease incubated through too much thinking. "Where a man does not think, it requires no great skill to be orthodox," he allowed. But such an approach left the church undefended against the rising intellectual life of rationalism present, he noted, in many of the German-American newspapers that had attacked him based on reports of his ordination sermon (126).

Sectarianism, however, was the more dangerous of the two diseases because it was "dressed in the imposing garb of piety: Satan transformed into an angel of light" (129). While the German scientific inclination nurtured the disease of rationalism, the "practical" tendency of the English and America made sects their special plague (130). Schaff develops this stereotypical view of the different national characters at length, and it would be an important theme that he would return to in *America* and other works of his later career—usually with an increasing appreciation for the practical orientation of the American people and an appreciation of denominations rather than a condemnation of sects.

Schaff traces the history of sectarianism in America back to the Church of England and the Puritan protest against the "bad forms" and rigidity under archbishop William Laud (132). Puritanism's "deep moral earnestness" was a gift to the church, but its rejection of all forms and complete disregard for history broke the unity of the church and created in America not one Pope, as in the Catholic church, but numberless popes who advanced not divine truth, but "private judgment and private will" (140). Schaff prized historical development and unity. He concluded that Puritanism led to "full atomism" (135). Against the flow of history toward union, the sect system asserted isolation; sects mistook a part for the whole; sects denied organic connection to the living stream of the church by maintaining no historical connection to the communion of saints—or other contemporary Christian communities—through confession or creed. Schaff was deeply impressed by the vision of unity he experienced in the Union Church in Germany and assumed he should find the same in America. Sectarianism flourished particularly in America with its "free institutions and the separation of church from the state" (129). While he knew that many Americans regarded their various denominations as a natural product of evangelical liberty and saw them all as one, he was unable to find biblical evidence to support this position and condemned "Puritanism" as unbiblical: "John 17 inflicts the death blow on the *whole* sectarian and denominational system," he proclaimed (138).[8] Furthermore, only through unity could Protestantism contend with Romanism to bring about "the One Church of God" (140).

8. Given the nature of this preliminary assessment, at least, it is ironic that Schaff's denomination would subsequently merge with the Puritan's decedants in the Congregational Christian Churches one hundred or so years later to form the United Church of Christ (1957). Or perhaps Schaff would see this union as an inevitable consequence of historical development.

After outlining these two diseases, Schaff takes up a controversial contemporary movement related to them both, "Puseyism" or the Oxford Movement as it would be better known. In this movement, led by Edward B. Pusey, John H. Newman, and others, Schaff saw an effort to cure the disease. It represented "an entirely legitimate reaction against rationalistic and sectarian pseudo-Protestantism" (142). But it was a misdirected reaction. It tried to find its legitimating authority in a legalistic, apostolic succession of bishops. "This is the old leaven of the Pharisees!" Schaff declared (144). He respected the movement for what it was trying to accomplish, but it sacrificed too much. It abandoned both the formal and material principles of Protestantism, adding tradition to the Bible and celebrating works-righteousness rather than faith. It also countered the principle of historical progress in its quest for a restoration of the church of the church fathers. Mere restoration along this line completely denied "the significance of the Reformation [and] the entire Protestant period of the church." Contrary to its claims, it fatally lacked "the true idea of development altogether" (144).[9] Thus while Puseyism lacked the individualism of the sects, it was equally motivated by an ahistorical primitivism that did not acknowledge the progress of the church to the present and from the present to the future.

Schaff's final section commends what he calls "Protestant Catholicism" or historical progress. The tenor of this section is evoked in the first paragraph, where he likens the life of the church to the pilgrimage of the people of Israel through the wilderness to the promised land. In this journey, God guides and sustains Christians, but they must follow his historical will and guard against any premature attempt to make their permanent home at a place or through a form of the church other than that which God ordains. This is the error of the Anglo-Catholics, the Old Lutherans, and the American champions of "New Measures" revivals: they build homes in the wilderness and refuse to follow the flow of history as it advances (albeit slowly) onward.

His discussion of Protestant Catholicism is divided into four parts. In the first, Schaff reveals his firmly dialectical developmental view of *all* of modern culture and shows that rationalism and sectarianism have a necessary role to play in the development of the church. They are not "the work of Satan *only*;" God is using rationalism to bring out the "natural side of Christianity," such as the expression of sacred truth through the individuality of the biblical authors (132, 152). Likewise, the sects urge the church "to new life and a more conscientious discharge of her duties" (153).

The second part of this section might be said, in modern terms, to be an appraisal of the process of secularization. He considers its merits and the typical Catholic and Protestant responses to it. His thesis about the work of the church is that it must cooperate with Christ in making "all things new" allowing Christ to be "all in all." In this respect he praises the medieval church for its sense of comprehension of all of

9. Like Schaff's *Principle of Protestantism*, John Henry Newman's *Essay on the Development of Christian Doctrine* was published in 1845. For Schaff's initial response to it see *What is Church History?*, 233 in this volume.

human life. Here Schaff cites the Latin statement of Terence "nothing that is human is alien to me" that Schaff would later adapt to be the motto of the American Society of Church History ("nothing Christian is alien to me"). Schaff also celebrates the accomplishments of the Middle Ages and scoffs at those who would write them off as "Dark Ages" (157). He, however, faults the Roman Catholic Church for retreating from this comprehensiveness and failing to respect the world's own rights, particularly the rights of the state. On this count, given his formation in the state-created Church of the Prussian Union, it is worth noting that Schaff supports the independence of the church stating that making Caesar pope "is no whit better than making the pope to be Caesar" (160).

Schaff praises modern advances in philosophy and art even as he notes that advancement of the latter has generally been without explicit religious focus. Yet these advancements of modern life in philosophy, art, and technology are not something that the church should separate itself from. It should neither regard them as part of the secular life of Christians, as many Protestants would, nor scorn them as evil. Rather, since they are rooted in the European Christian civilization from which they developed, they should be "reconciled" or "subdued" by the church and thereby folded into the kingdom of God. For Schaff the fulfillment of the natural development of secular philosophy, art, society, and government is for them to acknowledge their rootedness in God and to lay their fruits at the church's altar. He valued all major developments of human culture and looked for them to find an explicitly Christian consummation.

In the third part of his discussion of Protestant Catholicism, Schaff explores signs of a new era in theology, first in Germany and then in America. Germany comes out decidedly better. Its theology seems poised on the cusp of a great advance. It is particularly invigorated by the developmental and incarnational philosophy of Schelling and Hegel. Schaff insists that the usefulness of their philosophy should not be judged by the rationalistic inclination of left-wing Hegelians. In an extended footnote he thoroughly disputes the Andover-trained theologian Calvin Stowe's recent review of German metaphysics in the *Biblical Repository*. In a more general fashion, Schaff praises recent German historiography and philology for their role in the advancement of Christian knowledge. He closes with praise for the creation of the Union of the Lutheran and Reformed churches in Germany, though given the indifferentism toward theology of many supporters of the union, he also has kind words for the Old Lutherans who oppose it. Schaff is convinced, however, that "the future belongs to the 'Union'" and that it is only the first step in a trajectory that will necessarily involve significant progress, particularly in the development of new theological confessions (171).

When his outline requires him to turn to America, he has difficulty doing so. While this is understandable for a new arrival, it can throw a reader familiar with his carefully balanced discussion of the two principles of Protestantism off guard. Rather than discussing American theology, Schaff notes that Americans have little interest in theology and enters into a lengthy exhortation on the importance of theology and of theology from Germany, "the proper home of Protestant theology," in particular (177). This discussion did little to endear him to German Reformed leaders in America and less to other American readers.

Turning in his discussion of America from theoretical life to the practical, Schaff continued his complaint by identifying the need for "an antidote to the sect plague" (183). Here he offered no solutions, just more exhortation, and an attack on the dominant solutions to the problem: Anglo-Catholicism and Roman Catholicism. These attacks, at least, enabled him to build common ground with other American Protestants.

In his peroration, Schaff returns to his major theme. The future of Protestantism rests not in the abolition of Catholicism, but as a "reconciliation with it finally in a higher position, in which all past errors shall be left behind whether Protestant or Catholic" (189). Following Friedrich Schelling, Schaff uses Trinitarian apostolic types to designate types and stages of Christianity. Peter, "the apostle of the Father," is linked to Moses and represents law and authority and thus Roman Catholicism. Paul, "the apostle of the Son," is linked to Elijah and represents "the principle of movement" and justifying faith and thus Protestantism. John the Evangelist, "the apostle of the Holy Ghost," represents love in which "law and freedom shall both be perfect in one" and thus represents the reconciliation of the divergent principles of the church in a higher more glorious state. Schaff closes with the hope that the New World would be the place where this would occur "bringing all the scattered members of Christ's body into true catholic union" (191).

The Principle of Protestantism introduces central themes of the Mercersburg Theology and of Philip Schaff's career. This includes the importance of the church, church unity, trans-Atlantic cooperation, the valuing of creedal and liturgical forms, and most importantly an organic understanding of the development of church history. His affirmation that Roman Catholicism, with all its errors, was part of the church of Christ and grim view of American denominationalism caused many hearers and readers to take offense at his words. As explained in the general introduction, Joseph Berg quickly organized a heresy trial against him. Also, George Cheever, the influential editor of the *New York Evangelist*, took considerable issue with Schaff's view of the relationship of Protestantism and Catholicism and Schaff responded to him directly in *What is Church History?* The most substantial review of *Principle of Protestantism*, however, came from Charles Hodge. Further discussion of the book's reception will be found in the editors' introduction to Hodge's review.

TITLE PAGE OF 1845

THE

PRINCIPLE OF PROTESTANTISM

as related to the

PRESENT STATE OF THE CHURCH

By
PHILIP SCHAF, Ph. D.
Professor of Church History and Biblical Literature
in the Theological Seminary of the Ger. Ref. Church.

TRANSLATED FROM THE GERMAN
with an
INTRODUCTION
By JOHN W. NEVIN, D.D.

Chambersburg, Pa.
"PUBLICATION OFFICE" OF THE GERMAN REFORMED CHURCH.
1845

Translator's Introduction
[by John W. Nevin]

The work of which a translation is here presented to the English public has grown out of the author's INAUGURAL ADDRESS, delivered at Reading on the 25th of October, 1844, and still retains to some extent its original form. Only a part of the Address, however, as previously prepared, was spoken at that time; and it has been since considerably changed and enlarged in the way of preparation for the press. It is now accordingly more like a book than a pamphlet. If this may be supposed to require any apology, it is found in the difficulty and importance of the subject, and in the anxiety of the writer to have his views with regard to it fully understood, from the first, by the Church which has called him into her service. Both the difficulties and perils of the subject indeed were felt to be greater in the progress of the work than had been anticipated at the start; and hence it became necessary that the investigation, only to do justice to itself, should be extended in the same proportion.

It is trusted that the circumstances which have led to the publication will exonerate the author, in the view of all reasonable persons, from the charge of any improper presumption in venturing so soon before the American public with the discussion of so momentous a theme. He has himself felt sensibly the delicacy of his position in this respect; and would have been glad in the end to have kept back the work entirely, if circumstances had permitted, until he might have become more fully acquainted with the relations of the Church in this country, so that no room might have been left for the semblance of impropriety even in his making them the subject of public remark. But the case has been one which he had no power, properly speaking, to control. His inauguration made it necessary that he should deliver an address; and he felt it to be due to the solemnity of the occasion that he should select a theme of central interest, belonging to the life of the age, and suited to reveal his own general position with regard to the Church. The theme, as already mentioned, has controlled the character of the discussion. The publication of the whole in its present form has been in obedience simply to the law by which, in the nature of the case, every such address is required to appear also in print. The work besides has been prepared primarily and immediately for the use of the German Reformed Church in this country and with an eye mainly upon the German community in general. As now translated, moreover, it is still a work intended directly of course for the German Church so far as this has become English; though it is expected, of course, that it will command in this form a still wider interest. In any view, however, the responsibility of the translation belongs not to the author.

[German Theological Scholarship]

In the circumstances described, it is not strange certainly that the work should be pervaded with a true transatlantic German tone from beginning to end. I have endeavored indeed to make the translation run smooth and free in English, so far as the mere language is concerned. But the method, argument, and thought will be found to a great extent invincibly German still. How could it in fact be otherwise? The writer's entire nature and constitution are German. His whole *Entwicklung*[1] besides has proceeded from the first in the element of German thought and feeling—under the active power of a thoroughly German education—up to the moment when, without all previous expectation on his own part, he found himself as by a divine voice constrained to quit Berlin for Mercersburg. In such a case, who would expect him to appear here in any different character? He is entitled to indulgence, at least, as not yet having had time to become fully American. But we may go farther and say that no such renunciation of the German order of thinking, if it were even possible in such a case, would be either desirable or proper. He had no reason certainly to anticipate that, in coming to this country, he would be required to divest himself of his old life and become absolutely reconstructed as a preliminary condition to all right activity in his new sphere. And the Church never intended certainly to insist on any such conditions. Why call a professor from Germany, if all that is German in the man is to be left behind, or as soon as possible forgotten? Is he to receive all from those to whom he comes, and bring to them nothing of his own? Must he denationalize himself, lay aside his own nationality as barbarous and false; or not rather seek to make it available, as far as it may have value, for the improvement of the new life which has received him into its bosom? These questions it might seem hardly necessary to ask. And yet it is possible that some may be disposed after all to find fault with the present work as too German; just as if in the circumstances it either could have been, or should have been, in the fullest sense "Native American."[2]

1. [*Entwicklung* is the German word for "development," "progress," "growth," or "evolution." In this context, Nevin is referring to the German environment in which Schaff's education, spiritual discernment, and intellectual faculties were nurtured.]

2. The case of Professor Schaf has been somewhat singular. No man could well be more thoroughly German in his whole constitution and character. Perhaps no one has ever come into the country with more zeal for the consecration and advancement of all properly German interests as such. And yet, strange to tell, no foreigner has ever before encountered among us, within the same time, such a tide of reproach from his own countrymen, on the charge of being untrue to the honor of his nation. Within

Some indeed seem to have the idea that whatever is characteristically German

---

three months from the time of his arrival upon our shores, a perfect whirlwind of excitement may be said to have been raised against him among the foreign German population, from one end of the land to the other; which has only of late begun to subside, in the way of sheer self-exhaustion; for even whirlwinds, if they are let alone, must in the end blow themselves to rest.

The occasion of the uproar was a sermon preached by Professor Schaf in connection with his ordination at Elberfeld, in Prussia, just before he came to America; with reference particularly to the moral desolations of the field in which he was called to labor. In the nature of the case, the dark side of the subject was brought into view, especially as constituted by the character to some extent of the emigration itself from Germany to America, including, as it was known to do, in connection with much good, a large portion also of very different material. Various classes in particular were described who might be said to have left their country for their country's good, carrying with them to the new world dispositions and tendencies unfriendly to all right order in the State and all true religion in the Church. The sermon was afterwards translated and published in this country.

In this form, it fell under the eye of some who immediately set themselves at work to turn it to mischief. A single paragraph was retranslated into German and sent thus to circulate through the political German prints of the land, without the least regard to its original connections, with such inflammatory comments as malignant passion was pleased to invent. Various communications appeared at different points, intended to rouse, if possible, general indignation. The author of the sermon, it was said, had slandered and vilified the whole German emigration; betrayed his country; sold himself to the service of the Native American party; and deserved properly to be tarred and feathered, or drummed out of the land, as not worthy to enjoy its free air.

The German mind is vastly excitable and not particularly noted for its moderation when under excitement. It was soon thrown accordingly into a perfect tempest of commotion, through the whole length and breadth of the United States. The name of Dr. Schaf was at once made famous, in every direction. Within the course of a few weeks, as many perhaps as thirty different papers were poured in upon him, to let him know how heartily he was hated and cursed. Indignation meetings were held at a number of places at which valorous speeches, and still more valorous resolutions, were exploded in vindication of the German honor. All this on the part of a vast body of people, not one of whom probably had ever seen the original sermon of Professor Schaf as published in Krummacher's *Palmbletter* [*Palmblätter* 1 (May/June, 1844) 49], not one in a thousand of whom probably had ever seen the translation of it, as published in the *Weekly Messenger* ["Ordination of Professor Schaf," *Weekly Messenger* 9 (Sept. 4, 1844) 1869–70]; and of whose whole number, not one of a hundred perhaps could say when, where, or how the offense had occurred with which they were called to be so terribly displeased.

In fact, however, the movement is to be referred to a much deeper ground. The whole occasion has served, beyond any previous development, to reveal the true character of the foreign German population in our country. This is reckoned to be now more than a million, perhaps a million and a half strong, and is rapidly increasing every year. Beyond all doubt, it includes a large amount of virtuous and excellent character. At the same time, it has been equally certain all along that elements of an infidel, disorganizing order, have been comprehended in it to a serious extent. But no demonstration has before occurred so well suited as the one now in view, to set the matter in its true light, and to awaken apprehension in the direction here noticed. Because it has been abundantly evident to all who have been in a situation to understand the case that the uproar which it has been contrived to create against Professor Schaf is attributable properly not to an honest zeal for the credit of the German name as such, but to a secret hostility to the religious views and principles of which he is considered a distinguished representative.

At the bottom of the whole movement is to be traced distinctly the spirit of political libertinism and intolerant rationalistic fanaticism; answering too truly to a part of the sketch presented in the Elberfeld sermon and lending it light and confirmation beyond all that could have been anticipated in the same form previously. The active part taken in the business by certain rationalist ministers serves only of course to establish this charge. The papers which have been making a noise in the case reveal their irreligious character in general with very little disguise; and the same thing may be said of the proceedings of the indignation meetings. In some instances, the displays of rationalism have been

must be theologically bad. Especially the philosophy of Germany is regarded as almost universally either infidel or absurd and incapable altogether of being turned to any serviceable account in connection with religion. Now I would be sorry to appear as the apologist of either the German philosophy or the German theology as a whole. Few probably have been exercised with more solemn fears than myself in this very direction. One thing however is most certain. The zeal affected by a large class of persons in this country against German thinking is not according to knowledge. A judgment which is based, in any such case, on the assumption that there is nothing defective or one-sided in the system of thought and life out of which it has itself sprung, especially if it proceed from such as show palpably that they have never been able to transcend that system in its traditional form at a single point, and who may be possibly altogether ignorant besides even of the language which includes the foreign mind they presume to charge with folly: such a judgment so circumstanced, I say, can never be entitled to much respect. It is an immense mistake to assume that the Anglo-American order of religious life is all right and the German life in the same respect all wrong.[3] Both forms of existence include qualities of the highest value with corresponding defects and false tendencies. What is needed is a judicious union of both, in which the true and good on either side shall find its proper supplement in the true and good of the other, and one-sided extremes stand mutually corrected and reciprocally restrained. Realism and Idealism, practice and theory, are both—separately taken—unsound and untrue. Their truth holds—can hold only—in their union. We are a practical people pre-eminently and are entitled to great credit on this account. But it is in vain to expect that in this character simply we shall be able to do our duty to the world or to the Church of Christ. All great epochs in the world's development,

---

carried to the point of downright blasphemy. One sheet in New York has shown itself particularly vile and abominable in this way. Altogether the movement has been carried forward in the most low and ribald style.

It has however served one important purpose in the case of Professor Schaf, besides revealing more than had been revealed before of the spirit of this section of our foreign population. It has shown clearly in how little sympathy he stands with the Rationalism and Radicalism with which we are so unfortunately invaded from abroad. From no quarter has he been so immediately and violently repelled, as with an instinctive consciousness of irreconcilable opposition. This in the circumstances must be counted a high advantage; one of the greatest recommendations in fact, under which a learned German divine could make his appearance in our country.

3. [In these opening paragraphs, and in the lengthy footnote above, Nevin depicts Schaff's arrival in America as fraught with conflict. On the one hand, Schaff's description of the religious condition of the Germans in America as outlined in his ordination sermon in Elberfeld was quoted out of context in the German American press. These Germans felt that Schaff was playing into the hands of the "Native American party," anti-immigrationists who were suspicion of foreigners, especially German and Irish laborers who provided relatively cheap labor and who were often Roman Catholic. While the German American press accused Schaff of being insufficiently "German," he was also criticized for being "too German" by others, including those in his own denomination, like Joseph Berg, who felt that Schaff's historical appreciation of Roman Catholicism and his embrace of philosophy, among other things, made him an enemy of American Protestantism. Some of these sentiments are articulated in Charles Hodge's review of *The Principle of Protestantism* (see 209–222 in this volume).]

after all, owe their presence primarily to theory and speculation. Our religious life and practice can be sound and strong only in connection with a living, vigorous theology. But to be thus living and vigorous, our theology must be more than traditional. It must keep pace with the onward course of human thought, subduing it always with renewed victory to its own power. Not by ignoring the power of error, or fulminating upon it blind ecclesiastical anathemas, can theology be saved from death; but only by meeting and overcoming it in the strength of the Lord. Now this requires, in our day, a legitimate regard in this form to the errors of Germany in particular. For it is preposterous to suppose that in the most speculative portion of the whole Christian world these errors stand in no connection with the general movement of the world's mind, or that they do not *need* to be surmounted by a fresh advance on the part of truth, as being only the dead repetition of previously vanquished falsehood. In immediate contact with the evil, the friends of religion in Germany itself know the case to be different. There it is felt that theology *must* advance so as fairly to conquer or die. *We* may not feel the pressure of the same necessity. But this is no evidence that we stand on higher or surer ground. In the end, our theology, to be worth anything as a science, must be carried over this limitation. It may not devolve on us possibly to achieve the work for ourselves. We may trust, rather, that this precisely is the special commission of the Church in Germany itself, the land of Luther and the glorious Reformation. Certainly at this very time, the struggle with error may be regarded as most auspicious and full of promise. And if there be one country in the whole compass of the Church where at this moment orthodox theology is not dead, but full of life and spirit and power, that country is Germany. We may hope then it will be found sufficient for its own work. This however when accomplished, must be viewed as a work properly for the whole Christian world; and we owe it to ourselves, at least, to be willing to take advantage of it in its progress and to employ it for the improvement of our own position, if it can be so used.

This much I have thought it proper to say on this point, merely to counteract, if possible, the poor prejudice that some may feel towards the present work, simply because of its German source and German complexion; as if all must needs be either rationalistic or transcendental that breathes a thought in common with Hegel, or owns a feeling in sympathy with the gifted, noble Schleiermacher.

[The Church Question]

But after all, the work stands in no special need of apology in this direction. It is more likely to be met with distrust, in certain quarters, under a different view. It may seem to occupy suspicious ground with regard to the Church question. With the argument for Protestantism, in the first part, in its positive, separate character, even the most rigid in their zeal for this interest, can hardly fail to be generally satisfied. But some may not like the relations in which it is made to stand, nor the consequences it is made to involve. And then they are still less likely of course to be pleased with the formal development of these consequences in the part that follows. They may think that too much is surrendered in the controversy with Oxford and Rome. They may not be willing to endure that the nakedness of Protestantism, in its modern position, should be so freely exposed. It is always difficult, in the case of earnest, violent controversy, to have an eye for anything less than extremes. All must be right in one direction and all must be wrong in the other; although in fact, no great controversy in the Church is ever precisely of this character. So at this time, the excitement which prevails on the subject of Popery and Puseyism, and for which undoubtedly there is good reason, must naturally render it hard for many to exercise any moderate judgment upon questions that lie in this direction. In such circumstances then particularly, there is some danger that the present publication may not escape censure in the view already mentioned.[4]

This much, however, is certain at the same time. The work will not be regarded by Puseyites and Papists as a plea in their favor. Rather, if I am not much mistaken, it will be felt by them, so far as it may come under their observation, to be one of the most weighty and effective arguments they have yet been called to encounter, in this country, in opposition to their cause. For it is not to be disguised that a great deal of the war which is now carried on in this direction is as little adapted to make any impression on the enemy as a battery of popguns in continual fire. Instead of being alarmed or troubled on its account, the enemy is no doubt pleased with it at heart. Nothing can be more vain than to imagine that a blind and indiscriminate warfare here can lead to any true and lasting advantage. Not with circumstances and accidents simply must the controversy grapple, but with principles in their inmost life to reach any result. The present argument, accordingly, in throwing itself back upon the true principle of Protestantism with a full acknowledgment of the difficulties that surround it, while proper pains are taken to put them out of the way, may be said to occupy the only ground on which any effectual stand can be made against the claims of Rome.

To contend successfully with any error, it is all important that we should understand properly and acknowledge fairly the truth in which it finds its life. The polemic who assails such a system as Popery or Puseyism with the assumption that its pretensions are built upon sheer wind, shows himself utterly unfit for his work and must necessarily betray more or less the cause he has undertaken to defend. All error of this sort involves truth, apprehended in a one-sided and extreme way, with

4. [Throughout this Introduction, Nevin has clearly in mind the reaction to Schaff's critique of religion in America as announced in his sermon at Elberfeld and as outlined in the work to which Nevin's Introduction is attached. In particular, Schaff's insistence that Protestantism is historically dependent up Roman Catholicism and that the Anglican Oxford Movement (or Puseyism) represents an important, though flawed, corrective to the concept of church within Protestantism are key arguments to which Nevin expects strong opposition. This matter endures as a key Mercersburg concern and is the primary focus of the article "German Theology and the Church Question," 322–341 in this volume.]

the sacrifice of truth in the opposite direction. Hence a purely negative opposition to it, bent simply on the destruction of the system as a whole, must itself also become inevitably one-sided and false, and can only serve so far to justify and sustain what it labors to overthrow. Romanism includes generally some vast truth in every one of its vast errors; and no one is prepared to make war upon the error who has not felt, in his inmost soul, the authority of its imprisoned truth, and who is not concerned to rescue and save this while the prison itself is torn to the ground. In this view, no respect is due to an infidel or godless zeal when it may happen to be turned in this direction; and that must be counted always a spurious religious zeal, which can suffer itself to be drawn into communion with such an irreligious element simply because for the moment it has become excited against Rome. It is greatly to be feared that the spirit into which some are betrayed in this way is unhallowed and profane, even where they take to themselves the credit of the most active zeal for the glory of God. So with regard to Puseyism, nothing can well be more shallow than the convenient imagination that the system is simply a religious monstrosity, engrafted on the body of the Church from without, and calling only for a wholesale amputation to effect a cure. Such a supposition is contradicted, to every intelligent mind, by the history of the system itself. No new phase of religion could so spread and prevail as this has done, within so short a period of time, if it did not embody in itself, along with all its errors, the moving force of some mighty truth whose rights needed to be asserted and the want of which had come to be felt in the living consciousness of the Church, vastly farther than it was clearly understood. If the evils against which the system protests were purely imaginary, it could never have acquired so solid a character itself, as it has done in fact. Most assuredly the case is one that calls for something more than a merely negative and destructive opposition. Only by acknowledging and honoring that which is true and good in the movement is it possible to come to any right issue with it so far as it is false. The truth which it includes must be reconciled with the truth it rejects, in a position more advanced than its own, before it can be said to be fairly overcome. In this view, it is not saying too much to affirm that a large part of the controversy directed against it thus far has been of very little force. It has been too blind and undiscriminating, as one-sidedly false in its own direction at times as the error it has opposed in the other. Our newspapers, and reviews, and pamphlets, and books show too often that the question is only half understood by those who undertake to settle its merits. While they valiantly defend the citadel of Protestantism at one point, they leave it miserably exposed to the attacks of its enemies at another. With many it might seem to be the easiest thing in the world to demolish the pretensions of this High Church system. Its theory of the Church is taken to be a sheer figment; its idea of the sacraments, a baseless absurdity; its reverence for forms, a senseless superstition. The possibility of going wrong in the opposite direction is not apprehended at all. Such a posture, however, with regard to the subject, is itself *prima facie* evidence that those who occupy it are not competent to do justice to the case.

Some have told us that the controversy comes simply to this: whether we shall have a religion of forms or a religion of the spirit. They claim accordingly to be the friends of inward, living, practical piety, and charge upon the opposite tendency a secret disaffection to this great interest as exalting the letter above the life and substituting for the fact its mere sign. But the issue in this form is false. Religion is the union of soul and body, spirit and matter. To resolve it into naked forms is indeed to part with the substance for mere show; but it is just as vain to think of holding the substance where forms are treated with contempt. The man who takes the issue in the way now stated shows himself to be disqualified for the controversy. Because it is not a question with him then simply as to the quality or quantity of forms—whence they shall come and how far they shall reach—but a question as to whether the right forms have to be included in the idea of religion at all; in the case of which he shows clearly that his own conception of the true nature of religion is one-sided and false. He will be a spiritualist only, and not a formalist. Why not then become at once a Quaker? In its own nature, the issue is false. No such alternative, as it supposes, has any place in the idea of religion. It separates what God has joined together. Not soul *or* body, but soul *and* body, is the formula that represents humanity as truly after its union with Christ as before. The issue is false, monstrously false; and the champion who takes ground upon it is not fit to be entrusted with the interests of truth—in opposition to Oxford or in any other direction.

Again we are told the controversy has for its object the question, whether salvation be an individual concern or something that comes wholly by the Church; the fruit of a private, separate transaction of the subject with God's word and Spirit, or the product of a more comprehensive, inexplicable force residing in the mystical body of Christ and showing itself particularly in and through the sacraments. But here again the issue is false and those who plant themselves upon it only betray their own incompetency for intermeddling with the subject. Ecclesiasticism, as held by Rome and also by Oxford, is indeed a terrible error; but it does not follow that the mere negation of ecclesiasticism is the truth. The error itself includes a truth—a vast great precious, glorious truth; and if our negation annihilate this along with the error, it has become itself an error as false as the other. The position that religion is an individual interest, a strictly personal concern, a question between a man singly and his maker, is one which it would be treason to the gospel to reject. He that believeth shall be saved; he that believeth not shall be damned [Mark 16:16]. Every tree that bareth not good fruit is hewn down and cast into the fire [Matt 7:19]. Here is a vast, vital truth. But if it be so held as to exclude the dependence of the individual spiritual life on the general life of the Church, it becomes necessarily one-sided and false. Individualism without the Church is as little to be trusted as ecclesiasticism without individual experience. Both separately taken are false, or the truth only in a one-sided way; and the falsehood, sooner or later, must make itself practically felt. The full truth is the union of the two. Every issue, then, which puts them apart must be counted an untrue issue; and as before said, the very fact that any man should make it, in contending with Popery or Puseyism, proves him unfit for the task he has been pleased to assume.

So again, when the controversy is made to lie between the liberty of private judgment and the authority of the Church, the issue is equally false. And the matter is not mended at all, but only made worse, when the alternative is exhibited as holding between the Bible and the Church. It is indeed an abominable usurpation when the Church claims to be the source of truth for the single Christian separately from the Bible, or the absolutely infallible interpreter of the sense of the Bible itself, and so requires him to yield his judgment blindly to her authority and tradition. But it is a presumption equally abominable for a single individual to cast off all respect for Church authority and Church life and pretend to draw his faith immediately from the Bible only and wholly through the narrow pipe-stem of his own private judgment. No one does so in fact. Our most bald, abstract sects, even, show themselves here as much under authority almost as Papists themselves. Where shall we find a greater traditionist than the Scotch Seceder?[5] Who less free ordinarily in the exercise of what he calls his private judgment, upon the sense of scripture? His ecclesiastico-theological system, as handed down by his Church, or fraction of a Church, sways his interpretation at every point. Such a thing as an absolutely abstract private judgment we meet with in no denomination, party, or sect. But if we had it, what would it be worth? Or so far as we find anything like an approximation to it, to what honor or confidence is it entitled? For at the last, what sort of comparison can there be between the naked judgment of a single individual and the general voice of the Church? The argument from prescription here is one which no spiritually sane mind can despise. We employ it with overwhelming force against the Anti-trinitarian, the Anti-pedobaptist, the Anti-sacramental Quaker, and the whole host of fanatical upstarts who modestly undertake to make the world believe that the City of God has been buried for eighteen centuries like Herculaneum and Pompeii and is now to be dug out of the scriptures for the first time by such as themselves. Even the theories of a learned man are deservedly borne down by the weight of this authority; clothed in such a form, for instance, as it carries in opposition to the fancy of Prof. Bush when he tries to persuade us that the resurrection of believers takes place at their death.[6] The private judgment of a Grotius, *as such*, is a small thing as compared with the judgment of the Church. But we are

5. [The Scottish Seceders withdrew from the Church of Scotland in 1733 because they felt that the authority of the church was compromised by its establishment status. They particularly objected to the right of wealthy lay patrons to appoint clergy. Whitley, *Great Grievance*.]

6. [At the time that Nevin wrote, New York University's professor of Hebrew, George Bush, had caused a considerable stir among his fellow Princeton alumni and American Christians generally with his book, *Anastasis: or the Doctrine of the Resurrection of the Body, Rationally and Scripturally Considered* (New York: Putnam, 1845). In it he argued that the doctrine of the bodily resurrection of the dead agreed neither with science nor with the teachings of scripture. Instead the dead entered into a new sphere of existence in their spiritual bodies at the time of death. His conclusions agreed with those followers of Emanuel Swedenborg who had founded the Church of the New Jerusalem, which Bush soon joined.]

told, the issue is properly, not between a Grotius or a George Fox and the Church, but between the Bible and the Church, evangelism and ecclesiasticism. As if the Bible could interpret itself, without the intervention of a human judgment, either public or private! There is gross sophistry in the alternative as thus presented. In any true statement of the case, neither the judgment of the Church nor that of the individual is to be exhibited as a professedly separate *source* of truth. Romanism and Rationalism, in this view, fall here in opposite directions under the same condemnation. The only fair alternative lies between the Bible as apprehended by the Church and the same Bible as apprehended by an individual, or by some party or sect to which he may happen to belong. Shall the Church interpret the Bible for the single believer, or shall he interpret it for himself? The question comes at last to this. But the issue in such form is false. Neither side of the alternative separately taken is true; and yet neither is absolutely untrue. The Church may err; and every man is bound to exercise his own reason in things pertaining to his salvation. But still the Church is the pillar and ground of the truth. The Bible lives and has power as God's word only in and by the Church, the body of Christ. It is most certain then that private judgment extrinsical to all felt communion with the life of the Church, as a continuation through all centuries of the life of Jesus Christ, is entitled to no confidence whatever. Private judgment, or if any one please, the use of the Bible in this form, is a sacred right, to be parted with for no price by those whom the truth has made free; but it can hold only in the element of true Church authority. In proportion precisely as the sense of that general life which has constituted the unity of the Church from the beginning is found to be wanting in any individual; in proportion precisely as it is possible for him to abjure all respect for the organic whole, in virtue of which only he can have any life as a part; in proportion precisely as he is ruled by the feeling that the Bible is to be interpreted as a revelation just fallen from heaven without any regard to the development of its contents, the stream of its living waters as carried forward in the faith of Christendom from the beginning down to the present time; in the same proportion, I say, precisely, must such an individual (be his qualifications and resources in other respects what they may) be counted an unsafe expounder of God's word, either for himself or for others. The Bible mirrored from his mere private judgment, as thus sundered from all proper Church consciousness, is likely to reveal but little of the mind of the Spirit. The issue then as made between the Bible and the Church is false and sophistical; and the polemic who takes ground upon it as though it were of any real force only shows himself again unequal to the wants of this great controversy.

The case requires a reconciliation of these unhappily divided interests in such form that the truth which each includes may be saved in the union of both. This, of course, is not to be reached by yielding to Rome. The very nature of the papacy is that it sacrifices the rights of the individual wholly to the authority of the Church, which so far at the same time becomes itself false and dead. Puseyism is but a return towards the same error. We need not this. But as little may we feel ourselves abidingly satisfied with the mere contrary. What is to be reached after, as the true normal form of the Christian life, is such an inward marriage of the two general tendencies as shall be sufficient to make them one. There is no reason at all why zeal for experimental godliness and zeal for the idea of the Church should not go hand in hand together. The single case of Paul, to say nothing of Augustine, and Anselm, and Luther, and many others that might be named, may furnish full proof to the contrary. Who more zealous for all that is comprehended in the personal piety and personal freedom of the single believer? And yet who more carried away and ruled continually by the idea of the Church as the body of Christ and the organic whole in which and by which alone all individual Christian vitality must be upheld and carried forward to its proper perfection? This is the only form in which religion can deserve to be considered complete. This is to be regarded as the true consummation of the Church, in which the life of the whole body and the life of all its parts may be expected to proceed harmoniously and vigorously together. Towards the full and final accomplishment of this glorious result should be directed the prayers and efforts of all who love the prosperity of Zion or seek the salvation of the world.

Or will it be seriously pretended by any, competent to discern the signs of the time, that the state of the Church at present involves no necessity for looking or reaching after any such new position? Is all that is wanted for the great ends of the gospel—that is, for the actualization in full of the idea of the Kingdom of God in the world—the simple annihilation of all the elements and tendencies embraced in the objective Church system as such, and the undisputed supremacy of the opposite subjective interest in the form in which it now prevails in the Protestant world? Can we say of Protestantism that, as it now stands, it forms the true, complete, symmetrical, and ultimate state of Christianity; or that this requires at most, only that its existing tendencies should be carried out still farther in the same direction? They must be dull of vision truly, who can impose upon themselves so far as this. Vast evils and tendencies that must, if carried out, inevitably defeat the whole movement are palpably incorporated at this time with its very constitution. These must be acknowledged and put away before it can be expected to prevail. Taking the present state of Protestantism as ultimate and complete, we must despair of its being able to stand against its enemies. Our faith in its divine mission can be intelligent only as we confidently trust that it will yet in due time surmount its own present position, and stand forth redeemed and disenthralled from the evils that now oppress it, to complete the Reformation so auspiciously begun in the sixteenth century. The necessity of some such new order of things is coming to be more and more sensibly felt; and may we not trust that the way for it is fast being prepared—though to our narrow view, chaotically still and without light—in the ever deepening and extending agitation with which men's minds are beginning to be moved, as it might seem all the world over, in this direction. The feeling that we are on the eve of some vast religious revolution, by which a new epoch shall be constituted in the development of the history of the Church as a whole, has taken strong possession of many of the first minds in Europe. And it is quite evident that in this country too, a sentiment of the same general sort is steadily gaining ground. Men feel that they have no right to be satisfied with the actual state of the Church and they are not satisfied with it in fact.

That there is reason in these circumstances for looking with apprehension towards Popery, particularly in these United States, is not to be doubted. Both the author and translator of the present work participate in this apprehension to a greater extent probably than most of those who may be ready to exclaim against it as treasonable to the Protestant interest. The danger, however, is of a much deeper kind than is often imagined. It lies principally in the fact that we have come to such a crisis in the history of religion as has just been mentioned: involving for the moment at least a reaction in the direction of Rome, and making it necessary for the Protestant interest to advance to a new position, in order to save itself; while at the same time, those who stand forth in its defense show themselves too generally ignorant of the true posture of the case and not infrequently by their blind misguided zeal only help on in fact the cause they oppose. Meantime Romanism, with an instinctive sense of the importance and critical opportunity of the time, is putting forth vast policy and immense effort for the purpose of securing the land. The system is growing rapidly. It is beginning to assume a bold and confident tone. All its works are on a large scale and all its enterprises are crowned with success. No religious body is advancing at the same rate. Then it is a united, well-organized phalanx from one end of the land to the other. Protestantism, alas, is a divided interest. Most assuredly the danger that threatens us on the side of Popery is real and great. But for this very reason it is not to be turned aside by superficial declamation, hard names, or blind opprobrious epithets; especially if with all this no corresponding zeal be shown to build up and clothe with strength the positive life of Protestantism itself. Still we will hope that the end of all these things is destined to be different from what might seem to be their tendency at this time. It belongs to the crisis of the age that, along with this new impulse imparted to Popery in the way of life, the same system is itself made to tremble at other points with infirmities and disorders that threaten its very existence. All this is included in the chaotic struggle by which the way is to be opened for that new epoch which seems to be at hand and which, it may be with good assurance expected, will be not a retrogression of the Church to papal bondage, but an advance by the grace of God to the true standpoint of Protestant Catholicism.[7]

7. [While the Roman Catholic presence in the thirteen colonies was limited primarily to Maryland during the colonial era, immigration into the United States increased significantly during the nineteenth century so that, by 1850, Catholics made up 4 percent of the U.S. population. Methodists, by contrast, accounted for roughly 38 percent of the population while the German Reformed denomination constituted less than 1 percent of the population. During the famine, the Irish population rose to 25 percent or more in some major American cities including Boston, Baltimore, and Philadelphia. It is worth noting that "the most bloody religious riots in American history" between Protestants and Catholics took place in Philadelphia beginning on May 6, 1844. Two months later (just a few months

[The Organic Progress of Christianity]

The present state of Protestantism is only interimistic. It can save itself only by passing beyond itself. In this country particularly, our sect system is an evil that may be said to prey upon the very vitals of the Church. The evil itself however is but the index of a false element, incorporated with the life of Protestantism itself. The case then is not to be remedied by any merely external change. We are not called to a crusade against sects as they stand, as though by storming them to the ground, we could do for Christianity all that is needed in this direction. Only as the sect principle can be reached and cured in the inward habit of the Church may any such revolution (in connection with the openings and orderings of God's providence) be expected to take place, as the existing crisis demands. Not by might, nor by power, but by my Spirit, saith the Lord [Zech 4:6]. We are not to run before God, nor to take his work rashly and violently into our own hands. All true redemption and salvation, in the case of the Church, must come in the way of historical development, self-mediated under God, and in a certain sense self-produced. Still it may not be said that on this account we are at liberty to sit absolutely still, inwardly as well as outwardly, passively content with the present, in the midst of the onward flow of the counsels of the Almighty. If our present position be unsound, it is right that we should feel it and lay it solemnly to heart; that we may not cling to the old superstitiously like the Papists in the age of the Reformation, when the fullness of time is come for the new. Though we may not be able to see at once how our sect leprosy is to be healed, it must be a great evil still to justify it as something compatible with good health, or to acquiesce in it patiently as merely a necessary inconvenience. What is first of all and most of all needed, in the circumstances, as a preliminary to the coming of a more glorious Church epoch, is that the Protestant Christian mind generally should be brought to see more and more the actual wants of the time, and thus be engaged to sigh and reach after the deliverance, which in that case might be supposed to be at hand.

Some, I know, have no faith in this idea of Church progress. Rather, they regard it as derogatory to the perfect character of the gospel and false to the true unity of the Christian life. The subject is one of great importance and very liable to be misapprehended; and as the light particularly in which it has lately been exhibited by Professor Bush in his *Anastasis* or theory of the resurrection, cannot be regarded perhaps as exactly the most fortunate, it seems proper to bestow upon it here some additional consideration.[8]

---

prior to Phillip Schaff's arrival in Reading on October 25), several churches had been burned, thirteen people had been killed, and over fifty people were injured. Graham, *Cosmos in the Chaos*, 48. Irwin, "Chaos in the Streets." It is perhaps pertinent to note that these riots occurred to the north and the south of First Reformed Church where Joseph Berg served as pastor.]

8. [George Bush began his book with an essay claiming that the knowledge of revelation was progressive. By this he meant that human knowledge of God's revelation in nature and scripture improves over time through research into both the natural world (including human physiology) and the

The knowledge of revelation, Mr. Bush tells us, is progressive. But the progress he seems to have in his mind may be said to be more of an outward than inward sort. The knowledge of the truth is expected to grow only by accretion, accumulating new material in an external, mechanical way. A certain number of truths are taken to be at hand for all, clear and complete from the beginning. But along with these are many dark things in the Bible, which come to be understood gradually, by dint of study and helps of science, improved hermeneutical apparatus, and new external facilities and opportunities generally. The discoveries thus made are to be added from age to age to the knowledge previously collected, so that the quantity of it may be continually increased; and this is what we are to understand by the law of progress and gradual development in the sphere of religion. Now it is certainly true that the case does include the conception of such enlargement simply from without; although it is clear that the form in which this conception is presented by Professor Bush is perilous as Rationalism itself. For if all foreign science as such have a right to require that its discoveries, so far as they may seem to be related to religion, shall be allowed to assist in shaping its structure and making out the sum of its contents in a merely external, mechanical way, the independent life of Christianity may be considered gone at the same time. But in opposition to this we say, with Schleiermacher, that Christianity is a new living creation in itself that can be enlarged properly speaking only from within, and not at all from without. Not by mechanical accumulation or accretion can it be said to grow, but only in the way of organic development. These conceptions are entirely different and it is of the first importance that the difference should be understood and felt in the present case. The outward gain that may be secured for the interpretation of the Bible, or that may be found in the actual results of such interpretation, can become important only as it is taken up by the inward life of Christianity itself, and is made subservient to its progress in this view.

Christianity we say is organic. This implies, in the nature of the case, development, evolution, progress. The law of its life moreover in this form includes its whole life. It is not as though the knowledge of some truths had been absolutely complete, and so stationary from the beginning, while the knowledge of other truths has been numerically added to it from time to time. But the whole, in all its parts, is comprehended more or less in the same law; since no truth can be absolutely complete separately from the rest, though the general process may require that some should be developed to a certain point at least, as it might seem, in advance of others. In this view Christianity has an inward history vastly more important than that which is simply outward; and all its leading doctrines have a history too; and cannot be understood, it may be added, apart from their history. The idea of such a development does

meaning of the Bible in its original language and context. Bush argued that while reason must accept what God has taught, it "must still act *in determining the true sense of what He has taught*." Bush, *Anastasis*, x. In the following paragraph, Nevin offers a fair summary of Bush's view of progress before offering his own quite different view.]

not imply of course any change in the nature of Christianity itself. It implies just the contrary. It assumes that the system is complete in its own nature from the beginning, and that the whole of it too is comprehended in the life of the Church, at all points of its history. But the contents of this life need to be unfolded, theoretically and practically, in the consciousness of the Church. What it includes potentially and in principle or idea, requires to be actualized or made real in Humanity as a new creation in Christ Jesus. All this is something very different from such a *Fortbildung des Christenthums* ["development of Christianity"] as has been commended to us by the rationalist Ammon.[9] Christianity can never transcend itself. It can never become absolutely more than it has been from the beginning, in the person of Christ and in the truth of the gospel. It belongs to its very nature however, that it should not remain in the person of Christ or the letter of the gospel, but pass over into the life of the Church. This implies development. In its very constitution, the Church involves a process which will be complete only when the "new heavens" shall reflect in full image the "new earth wherein dwelleth righteousness" [2 Pet 3:13]. And still all this will be nothing more than the full evolution of the life that was in Christ from the beginning; and the full power of which has been always present in the Church, struggling through all ages towards this last glorious "manifestation of the sons of God" [Rom 8:19].

I am not able to see how any intelligent person, with a distinct understanding of what is meant in the case and any tolerable knowledge of history, can refuse to admit this view at least to some extent. Can any such person seriously imagine that the consciousness of the Church at the beginning of the second century, in the days of Ignatius and Polycarp, included all that properly belonged to it in the century following, or all that it reveals in the sixteenth century through the persons of Luther, Melanchthon, Calvin, and the Reformers in general? Was the new spiritual creation in Christ Jesus exhibited from the start as a finished system, clearly bounded and defined at every point; or was it not rather the power of a divine life that was expected to subdue the surrounding elements to its own law, and organize itself continuously from within? No one surely can read the masterly Church history of Neander without being compelled to yield his mind in some measure to the force of this idea; and for one who has at all entered into the spirit of the work, the impression is never likely to be erased.[10] Without this idea indeed, Church history may be said to be shorn of all its interest and meaning. It is no longer entitled to the name of history; and for all practical ends must be counted the most barren and useless of all studies; while in fact in its true form, it is a river of instruction, deep, broad and full, conveying life to every other department of theology and religion. No man who rejects this idea entirely can

9. [Christoph Friedrich von Ammon. *Die Fortbildung des Christenthums zur Weltreligion* (The development of Christianity into a world religion) 4 vols. (1833–40).]

10. [Only partially complete in both German and English translation when Nevin wrote, this complete work was published in English as August Neander, *General History of the Christian Religion and Church* (1872).]

penetrate the spirit of any of the early centuries or do justice to the character of a single Church father.

But has not the Church in fact gone backwards at times, instead of forwards? Have not doctrines been obscured? Has not Christianity been vastly corrupted? And what shall we say of the law of progress, in view of such facts? Does the great Roman apostasy constitute part of the development of Christ's body? Is the tenth century to be held in advance of the third?

To one who has any right sense of history, questions like these will not be particularly confounding. Assuredly those who hold the idea of historical progress with any proper knowledge do not conceive of it as a continuous movement, under the same form, in the same direction. They mean by it only a movement whose general, ultimate tendency is forwards and not backwards; and which, though it may seem at times to be differently turned, is still found in the end steadily recovering and pursuing its original course—as a stream of water carried aside, or pressed back upon itself by some obstruction, does but force for itself a more circuitous way, or only gather strength to burst or overflow the barrier, that so it may roll onward as before. Truth can be said to advance only as error is surmounted and thrown into its rear. But this requires that the error should always, in the first place, make itself known and felt. A position in which the elements of a still latent error are included is of course less advanced than a position which has been gained by overcoming the same error after it has come to light; and as this can be reached only through the manifestation of the error, we may say that the intermediate stage itself in which such manifestation takes place, though it may seem to be a falling away as compared with the period before, is nevertheless also an onward movement in fact. In certain circumstances it may be absolutely necessary that false tendencies should work themselves out through a long, vast experiment of disastrous consequences before they can be so brought home to the consciousness of the Church in their root and principle as to admit a radical cure. Whole centuries even may be comprehended in the circuit of such a process. With this explanation then, we need not shrink from saying that the course of the Church has always been onward in periods of apostasy as well as at other times; onward in such sense, that the position gained in surmounting such apostasy has never been just the same ground that was occupied before, but an actual advance upon it that could not have been made in any other way. The proposition of course holds good only of the proper central stream in which the one life of the Church is organically comprehended and carried forward without regard to separate, particular movements, that may refuse to go along with this in its general course. In this view, the Middle Ages form properly speaking no retrogression for Christianity. They are to be regarded rather as the womb in which was formed the life of the Reformation itself. For it is perfectly unhistorical to imagine that this might have connected itself directly with the life of the fourth century, or third, or second, in the way of simple continuation in the same direction and under the same form. Palpably the tendencies which at last produced the papal system as a whole were all in operation as early as the end of the second century. The Middle Ages then as the resolution of the latent mystery of iniquity, in connection with the life of the Church, stood nearer the redemption that followed, not only in time, but also in constitution, than the period that went before. The tenth century, with all its darkness, must be considered in advance of the third.

And so too, according to the view presented in the present work, it is our privilege to believe that the course of Protestantism (comprehending since the Reformation the main, central stream of the history of the Church) involves in the same way a true onward movement of Christianity; although manifestly it has included from the start certain false tendencies which are working themselves out interimistically in great and sore evils. If it should prove inadequate in the end to rise superior to these, it must stand convicted of falsehood. Our faith is, however, that it will in due time surmount them, and thus throw into the rear the epoch of the sixteenth century itself, by taking a position in which the elements of such aberration shall no longer be found; which in such case must be regarded of course as the end towards which, through all seeming retrogression in the way of heresy and division, the Church of the Reformation has been steadily tending from the beginning.

Such a view of Church progress is certainly much more full of encouragement than any theory in which the idea is rejected. What a depressing imagination, if only it were properly laid to heart, is that by which the papacy is taken to have been for eight long centuries the grave of all true Christianity; and the honor of the Reformation is supposed to require that the whole life of the Middle Ages should be relinquished to Rome, as part and parcel of the great apostasy, instead of being claimed as the catholic heritage of the Reformation itself. If Protestantism be not derived by true and legitimate succession from the Church life of the Middle Ages, it will be found perfectly vain to think of connecting it genealogically with the life of the Church at any earlier point. For if it might even be imagined possible to effect a junction, say, with the fifth century, or the fourth, or the third, by means of the small sect of the Waldenses and other such "witnesses of the truth" (than which no dream can well be more visionary), still, who that has the least true knowledge of history can feel that the Reformation was in fact the continuation simply of the life of the Church as it stood in either of these centuries, secretly carried forward to the age of Luther in any such way?[11] The life of the Church in the fifth, fourth, and third centuries looks indeed towards the

11. [The Waldensians were a movement within Roman Catholicism that originated in Lyon during the eleventh century. They claimed allegiance to the Bible as the legitimate authority in religious matters and were declared heretics in 1215. They survived, however, as a small group into the modern era; as noted in the general introduction, Philip Schaff visited their community during his sojourn through Italy in 1842. Although their origin is usually traced to Peter Waldo (1140–1218), who had helped translate the Bible into the vernacular Provençal, Joseph Berg devised a more elaborate genealogy for the sect, tracing their origin all the way back to the apostolic church. In *The Old Paths*, Berg referred to the Waldensians as "God's remnant in the dark ages" (169) and argued that they were the true progenitors of the German Reformed Church.]

age of Luther; but not immediately nor directly. It looks towards it only *through* the Middle Period that was to come between, the entire constitution of which it may be said to have carried in its womb. If the Reformation had indeed sprung directly from the life of the third century, it must have been something widely different from what we find it to have been in fact; a birth that could only have repeated, in its subsequent development, the general course of the Roman apostasy itself—as we may see exemplified, to some extent, in the tendencies of Puseyism as borrowed from this distant antiquity. That Protestantism in its true character has been something immeasurably better is owing altogether to the fact that it did not spring in the way of direct historical continuation from the fourth century, or the third, or the second; but strictly and fully from the more advanced life of the Middle Ages, by means of which only the way was prepared for it to surmount, as it has done, the gigantic errors that have been left in its rear.

As it regards to the present state of the Church, there can be no comparison again between the two theories: that which admits and that which rejects the idea of progress in the same general view. Only as we can believe that Protestantism is itself a process which three hundred years have not yet conducted to its issue, and that its very diseases, monstrous as they may seem, are only helping it onward to a triumphant resolution of its appointed problem, does it appear possible to be intelligently satisfied with the present posture of the great experiment.

Thus much it has been thought proper to say on this subject of the progressive development of Christianity—as it is one which is very liable, in certain quarters, to be misunderstood and misrepresented. The difficulty which is made with regard to it comes partly from this: that no proper distinction is made between Christianity itself in its ideal character, and the same Christianity as actually apprehended and realized in the life of the Church; and partly also from the fact, that so far as some notion of such a distinction may prevail, the relation between the two is still contemplated as outward and mechanical, rather than inward and organic. In any true view of the case, however, Christianity must be regarded as the only proper idea of humanity itself. It is not to be joined with its other modes of existence externally to make them complete; but it is to penetrate all modes of existence alike with its own life and take them up organically into its own constitution. Till this be done, humanity must remain imperfect and the idea of Christianity cannot be said to be fully evolved in the world. And yet who will dare to say that the history of the Church has not this evolution for its object; which, however is only to say, in other words, that it is such a process as has now been represented. In the case of the individual believer, something of the kind is generally admitted. His religion is expected to pervade his entire nature, not at once, but gradually and progressively, like leaven, till in the end the whole man, soul and body, shall appear transfused and transfigured with the power of it at every point. Here is a process, beginning at regeneration and ending in the resurrection; and yet at the last it cannot be said properly to include more than it has included from the first; only that which existed at first in principle merely, or potentially, in a state of involution, is fully actualized or evolved in the end in the perfect life of its subject. But such a process in the case of single Christians, separately considered, can never fully represent the relation of Christianity to our nature. The life of man, in any view, is not something single and separate. To a great extent, it holds in the order and constitution of his nature as a whole. Humanity is not an aggregation merely of men, but an organic unity, rather, in which all men are one. And so Christianity also as the perfect conception of humanity must take possession of it not by separate individuals simply, separately taken, but genetically. It must penetrate and transform into its own image the life, the whole life of the race, as such; and not till this shall have been done can it be said to have fulfilled its mission, or actualized its idea, or accomplished its full development in the consciousness of the world. Thus we have in the Church as a whole necessarily the same progressive, leaven-like action of the Christian life, which we have just seen to hold in the history of the single believer. The kingdom of heaven here also is like leaven, not simply as diffusing itself extensively through the world, but in a still more important sense as transfusing itself intensively into the life of humanity itself, as an organic whole. Now we see not yet the life of humanity in this view thus transfigured, just as little as we see the single saint made perfect in holiness and glory. Science, and art, and government, and social life, are by no means yet taken up organically into the living constitution of the Church. How then can it be imagined, that the life of the Church involves in its totality no process? And does it not lie clearly in the nature of the case that this process must actualize or evolve from the idea of Christianity, age after age, what was not apprehended in the consciousness of the Church before, till it shall become complete finally in the new heavens and the new earth? Only indeed as it is comprehended in this general process can the particular process by which the salvation of the single Christian is accomplished, from the new birth to the morning of the resurrection, be carried successfully forward. He is saved in the Church, the mystical body of Christ; and can become complete, only as the whole is made complete of which he is a part. His resurrection accordingly, the last result of the organic power of his new nature, will be reached only in connection with the consummation of the life of the Church as a whole, when in the fullest and most glorious sense, old things shall have passed away and all things become new.

[Conclusion]

The great question of the age undoubtedly is that concerning the Church. It is evidently drawing to itself all minds of the more earnest order, more and more, in all parts of the world. Where it comes to be apprehended in its true character, it can hardly fail to be of absorbing interest; nor is it possible perhaps for one who has become thus interested in it to dismiss it again from his thoughts. Its connections are found to reach in the end, through the entire range of the Christian life. Its issues are of the most momentous nature, and solemn as eternity itself. No question can be less of merely curious or speculative interest. It is in some respects just now of all practical questions decidedly the most practical. In these circumstances, it calls for attention, earnest, and prayerful, and profound. At the same time, the subject is clearly one of great difficulty and hazard; as we may see from the strange confusion and contradiction in which the controversy with regard to it has come already to be involved. A subject manifestly that is not to be disposed of in any way satisfactorily in such flippant wholesale style as with some might seem to be considered sufficient for the purpose. Both the solemnity and difficulty of it have been deeply felt in the preparation of the present work. It is the fruit of painfully severe thought, baptized it is trusted in the element of prayer. Not without true spiritual conflict does it make its appearance in the world. And not without prayerful anxiety is its course followed, now that it is launched from the press, as the first fruit of the author's labors in this form, in the new hemisphere. Should the views it offers be disapproved in any direction, it is desired only that it may be in the same spirit of earnestness in which they are presented. If anyone can show them to be wrong, not by declamation or positive assertion, but with deeper and more thorough exposition of the question itself, it will be not only respectfully but thankfully received. For the theme is one that calls for light; and if the publication should only indirectly serve this end by leading to the exhibition of some higher and better view in which its own position shall be fairly and truly surmounted, it will be felt that it has not appeared in vain. The author however *does* deprecate all hasty and superficial judgment in which ignorance and presumption may prevail more than a heartfelt reverence for truth. Especially he protests solemnly beforehand against all false or partial statement of his views: an evil, to which from the nature of the subject and the posture of the times with regard to it, he cannot help feeling that he is particularly exposed.

J. W. N.
Mercersburg,
March 4, 1845.

Original Table of Contents
(from 1845 edition)

Preliminary remarks. The idea of progress in the history of the Church. False views of the principle of Protestantism.

1. The *material* principle of Protestantism (*principium essendi*), or the *doctrine of justification by grace alone through faith*; in opposition to all pelagian and semi-pelagian error, or the overvaluation of the natural will.

A. The Roman Catholic doctrine of justification, with its presupposed conditions and necessary consequences.

B. The Protestant doctrine.

C. The principal papistical and rationalistic objections answered.

2. The *formal* principle of Protestantism (*principium cognoscendi*), or the *doctrine of the normative authority of the sacred scriptures*; in opposition to the dogma of tradition, or the overvaluation of human reason, whether that of the Church in Romanism or that of the individual in Rationalism.

A. The Roman Catholic doctrine of scripture and tradition.

B. The Protestant doctrine.

C. Principal objections answered.

3. The *mutual relation* of the two principles. Supplementary sides only of one and the same principle. Their living interpenetration the criterion of genuine, orthodox Protestantism.

PART SECOND.

The Principle of Protestantism in its Relation to the later development of the Protestant Church and its state at the present time.

General survey of the historical course of Protestantism.

I. *Diseases* or *Caricatures* of Protestantism; unchurchly subjectivism in theory and practice.

1. *Rationalism* or onesided *theoretic* subjectivism; developed especially in Germany and in the bosom of the Lutheran Church.

A. History and character of Rationalism.

B. Its relation to orthodox Protestantism.

C. The altered posture thus of the time.

2. *Sectarism* or one-sided *practical* subjectivism; developed especially in England and America, in the bosom of the Reformed Church.

A. *History and character of Sectarism.*

B. *Its relation to the bible and to orthodox Protestantism.*

C. *The altered posture thus of the time.*

II. *Puseyism*, a well meant, but insufficient attempt to remedy these diseases.

1. Its historical justification and weight in opposition to unchurchly subjectivism.

2. Its unprotestant character, involving a tendency backwards instead of forwards.

III. The standpoint of *regular historical progress* or *Protestant Catholicism.*

1. Rationalism and Sectarism viewed as a relatively necessary transition stage to a higher development of theology and the Church.

2. The separation of the secular spheres of life from the Church since the Reformation, viewed as an advance in the naturalization process of Christianity.

3. Signs of a new era in the history of theology and the Church.

A. *In Germany.*

B. *In America.*

4. Ultimate prospect.

SUMMARY. One hundred and twelve theses for the time.

APPENDIX. Sermon on *Catholic Unity.*[12]

12. [For John Nevin's "Sermon on Catholic Unity," see Nevin, *"One Holy, Catholic, and Apostolic": John Nevin's Writings on Ecclesiology*, ed. Sam Hamstra, MTSS, vol. 5 (forthcoming).]

Introduction

Brethren Beloved and honored in the Lord,

Guarded and led by the almighty hand which rules the winds and the waves, I find myself standing at length in your midst, on the threshold of my new sphere of labor. But little more than a year ago, I had not the most distant idea of ever visiting the new world; while to you all my very existence was unknown. You had sent two worthy representatives of your Church to the mother country, to secure for your Theological Seminary a man whose name simply, carrying with it such a charm as it does for the friends of the gospel on both sides of the Atlantic, was sufficient to clothe the institution with new importance and credit; for whose sake alone, you were led to embark in so bold and weighty a movement.[1] In the hands of Him who so often frustrates the prayers and plans of his people in one form to establish them contrary to their short-sighted wisdom in another, this distinguished servant of God became the medium by which you were conducted to myself. In no turn of my life have I ever held myself more passive than in this removal to America; in none, at the same time, have I endeavored more conscientiously and steadily to surrender myself entirely to the guidance of the Lord.

Strong indeed was the temptation, I confess, to remain in the world-renowned metropolis of German science, where my academic career had just begun to open under favorable auspices in the society of so many cultivated, profound, and noble minds, well fitted to enlarge and invigorate my inexperienced powers, and under the fostering care of a pious and highly gifted monarch, who has rendered his name immortal also in the annals of your Church by the magnanimous interest he has shown in its welfare; there, along with the German Evangelical Church and Theology, though only as one of the least in her service, to fall or conquer in the deadly war that now

1. [Schaff refers here to the vagaries of his call to become professor at Mercersburg. As discussed in the volume introduction, initially two representatives of the German Reformed Church approached Frederick W. Krummacher, pastor of the largest Reformed congregation in Germany, concerning the position. Krummacher eventually declined. Later they visited Schaff in Berlin and recommended him for the position. An official invitation to become chair of Church History and Biblical Literature was extended to Schaff on October 19, 1843. Shriver, *Philip Schaff*, 12–15; Trost, "Exposing, Experiencing, and Explaining America," 4.]

rages with fire and sword in the spiritual life of the old world. But the voice of nature became dumb when the most competent judges in Germany, honored instructors and beloved friends, men long conspicuous in the religious history of the age, with strange unanimity joined in recommending me as one specially qualified for the vacant post at Mercersburg; and when your Synod subsequently, after the most earnest and mature deliberation, saluted me, as from the mouth of a single man, with the solemn call, *Come over and help us!* [Acts 16:9].[2]

And thus I stand here today with the consoling consciousness by which all darkness is made light, that in forsaking literary connections, country, kindred and friends as a missionary of science, I have not pursued a road cast up by my own hands. How could I do otherwise than I have done? Israel's pillar of cloud and fire has gone before me, in clear unbroken vision, from the palaces of Berlin to the foot of the Blue Mountains; so that I almost tremble in view of the vast perspective that is made to open upon me through such foretokening, and under an unfeigned sense of my own weakness am ready to ask misgivingly, with one greater than myself, *Who am I, Lord, that thou shouldst send me!*[3] Yes, I speak it plainly in your presence, when I consider the vast expectations that rest upon me, and the unmerited marks of honor which attended my reception on the 12th of August,[4] before all service on my own part, I should be cast down utterly, were it not for the stay I find in God's encouraging word: *I will be with thy mouth and will teach thee what thou shalt do. Fear thou not; for I am with thee; be not dismayed, for I am thy God. I will strengthen thee; yea, I will help thee, I will uphold thee with the right hand of my righteousness. Behold, I give power to the faint, and increase strength to them that have no might. Even the youths shall faint, and he weary, and the young men shall utterly fall; but they that wait upon the Lord shall renew their strength; they shall mount up with wings as eagles; they shall run and not be weary, and they shall walk and not faint* [Exod 4:12; Isa 41:10; 29–31].

Whether now I shall close my earthly career in the western world, or find myself called to the temporary service simply of scattering some germs that may be watered afterwards and brought to perfection by more competent hands, then to return to my original home, enriched with such observation and experience touching the Church as are to be gathered from a land, mirroring like this her youthful infirmities and the fresh practical zeal of her first love, in one picture; this, I say, is a question, which it is not for me, nor for any one else, at this time, to decide. God's thoughts are not our

2. [Schaff makes reference here to the plea from a man of Macedonia directed to the apostle Paul at Troas during a night vision. Schaff had used these words as the text for his ordination sermon at Elberfeld on April 12, 1844. Schaff, "Ordination of Philip Schaf," 1869; Graham, *Cosmos in the Chaos*, 3–4; Penzel, *German Education*, 131–32; Pranger, *Philip Schaff*, 60–63.]

3. [Cf. Moses's response to God's call, "Who am I, that I should go unto Pharaoh?" (KJV, Exod 3:11b).]

4. [Schaff arrived in the village of Mercersburg on the evening of August 12, 1844. He was greeted by students of the seminary and welcomed with a torchlight procession and speeches in German and English. See Penzel, *German Education*, 139.]

thoughts, neither are his ways our ways; and the man is to be counted happy, who by humble renunciation of his own counsels and passive surrendry [sic] of his course to the conduct of his heavenly Father, provides against painful disappointments; planting his feet on the firm ground of the actual present and devoting his entire strength to its claims, free of all useless cares or empty dreams for the future. Now at least I am *here* to serve your Church, and in and through this the Church *universal* of Jesus Christ. At present, no field is before me save that to which I have been called in America, and I have no ear for any call besides, cheerfully resigned to any issue that may follow. "Whether we live, we live unto the Lord," it matters not where, in the old world or in the new; "and whether we die, we die unto the Lord. Whether we live therefore or die, we are the Lord's" [Rom 14:8].

In such a frame of mind, I proceed, according to ancient, venerable custom before entering formally on my appointed work, to lay down in your presence, as representing here the German Reformed Church in this country, a sort of scientific religious confession that may serve to explain distinctly the ground on which I expect to stand in your midst. I find myself at no loss, in these circumstances, in choosing my theme. On the practical relations of the service to which I am called, I have already spoken in my ordination sermon, at another place. Here we have to do with its theoretic side; in such method, however, as to hold in full view at the same time the connection of this with the other interest, and the end towards which it should continually reach in the life of the Church. I may say then comprehensively, that the foundation on which I stand, since by the grace of God I have come to any clear consciousness of religion and theology, is no other than the orthodox Protestant, or what in my view is the same, the Reformed Catholic faith; as it was preached loudly and powerfully by the reformers of the sixteenth century, or rather by the Spirit of God in their persons, at once purifying the Church from the springs of its primitive life and raising it besides into a new and higher form. Upon this ancient, venerable rock accordingly, against whose front so many hostile waves have already been broken, I propose to build, with divine help, in my present vocation; making due account at the same time of the past history of our Church as a medium of instruction, and having constant respect also to the special wants of our own country and our own age.

Allow me then to speak of THE PRINCIPLE OF PROTESTANTISM AND ITS RELATION TO THE PRESENT POSTURE OF THE CHURCH, PARTICULARLY IN THE UNITED STATES.

PART FIRST

The Principle of Protestantism in its original relation to the Roman Catholic Church

[Preliminary Remarks. Reformation, as distinguished from Revolution and Restoration]

To be true to its own idea, a Reformation must hold its course midway, or through the deep rather, between two extremes. In opposition on the one side to Revolution, or the radical and violent overthrow of an existing system, it must attach itself organically to what is already at hand, and grow forth thus from the trunk of history, in regular living union with its previous development. In opposition to simple Restoration, on the other side, or a mere repetition of the old, it must produce from the womb of this the birth of something new. Christianity was such a Reformation, not simply of Judaism, but of Humanity as a whole. With what gentle and loving accommodation the Savior and his Apostles applied themselves to meet the general wants of the human heart, and those particularly of their own time? Towards the institutions of the old dispensation, disfigured though they were with arbitrary human additions, and towards its official ministers also, however poorly for the most part their personal character comported with their Office, they exhibited all becoming respect. No iconoclastic zeal distinguished their steps; no revolutionary whirlwind gave token of their presence. Christ must *fulflil all righteousness* [Matt 3:15] himself, and charged his hearers to observe and do what was commanded by those *who sat in Moses's seat* [Matt 23:2]. Paul, as he informs us himself, became to the Jew a Jew, to the Gentile a Gentile, and in one word *all things to all men*, that he might if possible gain all to Christ [1 Cor 9:19–21]. John was ready to allow the gift of prophecy to Caiaphas in his character of high priest [John 11:49]; and found no difficulty in admitting, that the everlasting light of the *divine Logos had shined in darkness* through all ages, gradually preparing the way for its personal manifestation [John 1:5]. And yet the watchword both of himself and his fellow apostles, openly and broadly proclaimed upon their common banner, was the

Lord's declaration, *Behold I make all things* NEW [Rev 21:5]! And what was the result of their mission? In the end, these humble, unlettered fishermen of Galilee caused both the Jewish and Pagan systems to fall to the ground together, and turned the history of the world into a different channel altogether.

The same two-fold character belongs to the vast ecclesiastico-religious movement of the sixteenth century. This too carries upon its standard the sacred field motto, "*I am not come to destroy, but to fulfil!*" [Matt 5:17]. And thus neither the unhistorical radical on the one hand, nor the motionless slave of the past on the other, can find in the true representatives of the Reformation either precedent or pattern.

The case requires to be surveyed under both aspects, in order that the principle of our Church may be fully comprehended, and its position turned to right account for the purposes of God's kingdom.

I. The Retrospective Aspect of the Reformation; or its catholic union with the previous history of the Church.

In the first place, we contemplate the Reformation in its strictly *historical conditions*, its CATHOLIC UNION WITH THE PAST. This is a vastly important point which thousands in our day appear to overlook entirely. They see in the 31st of October, 1517, it is true, the birth day of the Evangelical Church, and find her certificate of baptism in the ninety-five theses of LUTHER; but at the same time cast a deep stain upon the legitimacy of this birth itself, by separating it from all right relation to the time that went before. In this way all interest is renounced in the spiritual wealth of the Middle Ages which, however, belongs to us of right as fully at least as it does to the Church of Rome. And what is worse still, the lie is given practically to the Lord's promise itself: "Lo, I am with you always, even unto the end of the world" [Matt 28:20]!

No work so vast as the Reformation could be the product of a single man or a single day. When LUTHER uttered the bold word which called it into being, the sound was at once echoed back again, as in obedience to an enchanter's wand, not only from every quarter of Germany, but from England also, and France and Italy, and Spain. He gave utterance to what was already darkly present to the general consciousness of his age and brought out into full view that which thousands before him, and in his own time, had already been struggling in various ways to reach. Genuine Protestantism is no such sudden growth, springing up like a mushroom of the night, as the papist, and certain narrow-minded ultra-protestants, would fain have us believe. Its roots reach back to the day of Pentecost. In all periods of the Church, in connection with the gradual progress of Romish corruption, it has had its witnesses, though not always fully conscious of their own vocation. And it was only when it had become fully prepared in all parts of the Christian world, both negatively and positively, to stand forth in full separate, objective manifestation, that the Lord of the Church in the end, from an obscure corner of Germany, called into life the herald whose word was to solve the oppressive riddle with which all Christendom had been so long burdened—the spiritual Columbus that should open the way into the territory, still unknown though long at hand, of evangelical freedom.[1]

As the several departments of human life are bound together by an inward organic union, like the members of the same body; while religion in particular, which takes hold upon the entire man in the inmost ground of his personality, must exert a modifying influence in every other direction; the case requires that we should take account of the tendencies which led the way to the Reformation in the spheres of *Politics* and *Science*, as well as in that of the *Church* strictly taken.

[1. Preparation in the sphere of Politics and Popular Literature.]

As it regards the first, it is clear that both Romanism and Protestantism rest constitutionally upon a *national basis*. Christianity, in its eternal and everlasting character, is raised indeed above every distinction of nation or race. It is a religion for the whole world. Still, on its first publication, it found on all sides a given historical development, a settled system of society, already at hand. This, of course, it did not seek to demolish and reconstruct, but simply to transfuse with the power of its own divine life. In this way, it became possible for the old order of existence to break into view again, with all its characteristic faults and virtues in the bosom of the Church itself, reflecting the Christian religion under its own peculiar image. Where previously the eagle of the war god spread forth his powerful talons and the earnest, manly spirit of pagan Rome was enabled to organize and hold together by the force of one gigantic and yet minutely specific system of law, the entire world lying submissive at her feet; there, now, a new empire appeared, Rome restored in the Church; built up in part by the same agencies as before, invigorated only by the presence of a higher principle; subduing the most barbarous nations under the banner of the cross and binding the most distant to a common center; but at the same time repeating the lightnings of the Capitol in the thunders of the Vatican, directed against every motion of freedom, and in its conflict with the world gradually taking up all the elements of the world's corruption into its own constitution.

In both cases we meet essentially the same features of character: immovable resolution, iron constancy, a restless grasping after universal dominion, and confidence of perpetual stability; but in connection with all this, an artful cunning policy, disguised

1. ["Evangelical" translates Schaff's *evangelisch*, and should not be confused with Anglo-American revivalistic Protestantism, with its emphasis upon the "born again" experience. "Evangelical" asserts the centrality of the "*evangelium*"—that is to say, the gospel story of Jesus' life, death, and resurrection—as the source of Christian authority; therefore, it is intimately related to what Schaff calls the formal principle of Protestantism, "Scripture alone." In Schaff's immediate German context, the word *evangelisch* was used to suggest a version of Protestantism that transcends, or at least includes, confessional differences between the Lutheran and Reformed as advanced in the Prussian Union church. See the general introduction, 64.]

beneath a show of urbanity, the Jesuitic maxim of the end sanctifying the means, and a heartless disregard to both national and individual rights in the midst of vast pretensions to liberality and broad-hearted pliant toleration. *The papacy is a Christian universal monarchy erected on the popular spirit of ancient Rome.* And as it is necessary that authority should go before independence, the general before the particular and single—which implies that barbarous tribes require the force of a heavy disciplinary institute, in the first instance, to bring them to a full free knowledge of themselves—no unprejudiced historian will dispute the merits of the Romish system as eminently fitted for this service. Nay, in view of such countries as Italy, Spain, and Ireland, which have not yet outgrown their political minority, must we not allow a relative necessity for it, even in our own day?

Protestantism springs, as all know, from the *German* life, which may be considered constitutionally its proper womb and cradle; as we find prophetically indicated by many voices of the Middle Period[2] even, like that of Mechtildis, with her *remansurum pauperem et afflictum coetum in Germania, qui pie ac pure Deum colat.*[3] It was not a matter of mere chance therefore, or something indifferent in its nature, that the father of the Reformation, surpassing all his followers both at home and abroad, should have borne upon him the impress of this particular nationality in its purest, most original, and most perfect form; and that his German translation of the bible became the recruiting call to so many thousands, to rally round the standard of the new, or rather, renovated faith. In LUTHER, all the essential traits of the German nationality are found collected as it were into a single focus: indomitable energy, earnest childlike integrity and simplicity, unaffected humility, and a predominant tendency towards the world of thought and feeling; to which must be added, it is true, a blunt carriage, running not infrequently into downright rudeness, and a certain undervaluation of the outward costume of life, not to be approved in any case. Such a nationality is fitted constitutionally for a deep, inward apprehension of the Christian system; while the Roman and Romanist spirit, as naturally, was led to embrace it prevailingly in a more outward way, as a body of mere rules and statutes. Those forms of character, which have distinguished the German nature from the beginning, its love and truth, its geniality and depth, should be regarded as a prophetical preparation for Christianity. They were so more emphatically even than the penitential discipline of the Hindus, or

2. [That is, the middle ages.]

3. [Trans. "They who devoutly and purely worship God in Germany are sure to remain a poor and afflicted company." The likely source for Schaff's quotation of this line is the *Catalogus Testium Veritatis* of Matthias Flacius Illyricus (Argentinae, 1562), 529. Mechtildis (also Matilda and Mechtild) of Magdeburg (c. 1212–80) was a Beguine and mystic who described her visions of God in *The Flowing Light of the Godhead.*] "Only the inwardness of the German nation," says HEGEL ([*Vorlesungen über die*] *Philosophie der Geschichte.* Works, 1st ed. vol. 9 [(Berlin: Duncker und Humblot, 1837),] p. 417), "was the soil of the Reformation; only from such simple, straight-forward character, could the great work proceed. While other nations were wholly taken up with worldly dominion, conquests, and discoveries, a plain monk toiled after perfection in his spirit and brought it to pass."

the earnest idealistic longings of the Platonic philosophy; the latter, as it is well known, served the purpose of a bridge to conduct so many of the early fathers to Christ.

These two opposite orders of life, which might have seemed to be forever disjoined by inward ineradicable mutual hatred, no less than by the heaven climbing mountains of snow that separated them outwardly, found the middle wall of partition between them broken down, notwithstanding, by the power of Christianity, as the religion of the world. But now in proportion as the German tribes, under the motherly supervision of Rome, began to wake to self-consciousness, the old struggle of Arminius also, which may be said to have foreshadowed the disruption of the papal yoke by Christian Germany, was gradually renewed. The entire Middle Period is full of the conflicts of the imperial power in Germany with the papal authority at Rome. German blood was poured out like water on the battlegrounds of Italy. As far back as the time of the Hohenstaufen, a sect in Swabia declared the pope a heretic; and it was long a popular tradition in Germany that Frederick the Second would one day return, or an eagle spring from his blood, to overthrow the Romish Church. The conflict grew always more violent and fierce in proportion as the papacy surrendered itself, more and more, to the Machiavellian policy of employing mere worldly influences for the accomplishment of its ends and laid itself out, under cover of the Church, to advance the private interests simply of the popes and their courtiers, directing the sword of St. Peter against every liberal movement that came in their way. Such foul prostitution of things sacred and divine to mere secular ends, carried to the most shameless climax at last in the traffic in indulgences as conducted by Tetzel, together with such hierarchal despotism intolerant of all right and all freedom, could not fail to shock the moral earnestness of the German spirit in the most serious manner. How could it be otherwise in the case of a people, which in its purest representatives has ever subordinated national, political, simply egoistic interests to the world-embracing claims of the spirit, as embodied in the Church; and that in the 16th century, in particular—when almost every other nation either remained altogether in communion with Rome, or stood forth simply on general protestant ground—chose to be torn in pieces of its own children, and to see its fields laid waste and its fair territory divided, rather than to give up eternal truth for a political advantage, the momentous issue which divided the two Confessions, to save the unity of the nation.

The long cherished opposition just mentioned, passed over, towards the close of the Middle Ages, into the most distinguished popular productions of the German national literature, particularly in its epic, dramatic, and satiristic forms. It is sufficient to remind those who are acquainted with the subject, of the *Eulenspiegel,* the German version of *Reineke Fuchs*, and the *Fastnachtspiele* of Hans Rosenblut.[4] All these compositions served to bring continually nearer to the consciousness of the people the

4. ["Til Eulenspiegel" and "Reineke the Fox" were prankster heroes of popular medieval German folk tales. These characters, and those featured in Hans Rosenplüt's (or Rosenblut's) carnivalesque stories, exposed the folly and hypocrisy of medieval society.]

faults of the time, and especially the corruption of the clergy and the pernicious consequences of transalpine influence. In the end the tendency of the popular national literature found its most eloquent expounders, simultaneously with the appearance of Luther, in the persons of ULRICH VON HUTTEN and the celebrated HANS SACHS.

But with all the importance of this political and literary opposition to Italy, it is by no means sufficient of itself to explain the Reformation. To suppose this would be superficial in the extreme; as is shown at once by the fact that a large part of Germany still continues, though in a more inward and free way than other nations, to do homage to the see of Rome. It would have been a calamity, rather, if the political tendency had drawn the direction of the Reformation into its own hands. Luther found no pleasure in the later enterprises of *Hutten* and *Sickingen*; taking the ground against them that the Church was not to be revived by means of outward, carnal weapons, but only by means of the divine word from which it had its life in the beginning. The war of the Peasants, which rose like a dark column of smoke in connection with the pure flame of the Reformation, was repudiated by him as a miserable caricature of his work; and just as little respect did he show for the Anabaptists and their wild dreams of liberty and equality.[5]

[2. Preparation in the sphere of Polite Learning and Profane Science.]

The way of the Reformation was prepared, in like manner, in the smaller circle of the learned, by the *revival of the sciences*; and it is a circumstance accordingly not to be overlooked that the representatives of the movement, in particular MELANCHTHON, CALVIN and BEZA, surpassed in thorough humanistic culture almost all their contemporaries. The emigration of learned Greeks to the West, which took place after the destruction of Constantinople, and the fruitful labors of PETRARCH had contributed to extend still more and more the study of the ancient languages; the darkness of ignorance and superstition was coming gradually to disperse; the spiritual horizon of the nations had begun to grow clear. In Italy, the ancient life, through living contemplation of the monuments of classic art, stood forth in fresh reproductions, revolutionizing on a large scale the entire literature, and indeed the whole order of thinking. Almost

5. [The direction of Schaff's thought moves from an early resistance to papal authority during the period of the Hohenstaufen rulers (1158–1252; see Glossary); to a critique of medieval German society in literature; to political resistance against Roman Catholic Church domination as expressed in the actions of knights such as Hutten, Sachs, and Franz von Sickingen; to a revolutionary extreme as exemplified in the later activities of Hutten and Sickingen during the so-called "Knights' Revolt" (1522); to the Peasants' War, and the revolutionary actions of the Anabaptists. Encouraged by notions of freedom advanced in Reformation rhetoric, especially by the Reformer Thomas Müntzer, the *Bauernkrieg* or Peasants' War (1524–26) resulted in up to 100,000 deaths. Luther wrote *Against the Robbing and Murdering Hordes of Peasants* in *LW* 46: 45–65, in opposition to the revolt and in support of the princes. The Anabaptists advanced a radical critique of emerging Protestant practice, including the nature of sacraments and the use of images. Luther's many writings in opposition to them include *Against the Heavenly Prophets in the Matter of Images and Sacraments* (1525) in *LW* 40: 63–223.]

all the philosophical systems of Greece and Rome were honored again with living adherents and advocates. Platonism once more, as in the first ages of the Church, excited a longing for something higher and better than all that was offered by the present. We see this particularly in Marsiglio Ficino, who may be taken as the representative of a widely extended feeling, and who especially in his latter years—a sort of Christian Plutarch—endeavored to reconcile the culture of the age with Christianity. The knowledge of the Hebrew and Greek languages, promoted with untiring zeal by Reuchlin and Erasmus, furnished the key to the understanding of the Old and New Testaments, and enabled the Reformers (indispensable for the purpose) to translate them into the vernacular tongues, and so to open the way for them into the life of the people. It deserves notice particularly, that the two first editions of the *Greek New Testament*, that of Erasmus in the year 1516 and that of the *Complutensian Polyglot* in the year 1520, appeared simultaneously with the commencement of the Reformation; and under protection too of the papal authority, which dreamed not yet of the powerful assault that was to be made upon it soon from this book. The edition of Erasmus was repeated in a short time, over and over again, and thus by means of the art of printing—not long before discovered—found its way into thousands of hands.

It shows strikingly how very general the feeling of opposition to the superstition and immorality of the clergy had become, that this same small, cowardly and cautious Erasmus was enabled to occupy so successfully as he did the apparently bold and perilous position in which he stood. No one attacked the vices of the clergy so sharply, with the same cutting wit and inexhaustible humor. His hatred for the monks seemed to be constitutional. He made it his great business to draw theological study off from the reigning scholastic method and back to the fathers of the Church and the New Testament; and to this last, not as exhibited in the Vulgate, which he was bold enough to convict of an immense mass of errors, but as found in the original text. And still this man stood in the most honorable correspondence with the leading men of his time. Presents and marks of respect were showered upon him from all sides. Wreaths of fame adorned his person. His presence was courted, with special invitation, in all parts of the world. And his *Encomium Moriae*, the most severe of all his works against the clergy, passed during his lifetime through twenty-seven editions, and made its appearance in every cultivated language of the age.[6]

But still these scientific and humanistic tendencies again are not sufficient to account for the Reformation. Many, by the study of the ancient languages and philosophy, were led, in Italy particularly, into the most decided infidelity, which is worse of course than superstition itself. Erasmus himself, it is known, drew back in his latter years always more and more from the work of the Reformation. We cannot pronounce him void of all regard for evangelical truth; but altogether his influence was mainly of the negative sort and was just as likely, but for the intervention of the Reformation

6. [Erasmus's *Encomium Moriae* (*The Praise of Folly*) was a satirical work published in 1511 exposing many of the corruptions in the Catholic Church.]

in its true form, to have called forth a false and perilous action in the free thinking, liberalistic style, as it was to serve the cause in question. "He knew well," as Luther tells us, who saw through him completely, "how to expose errors, but not how to teach the truth." Indeed if science and art could have produced the Reformation, Leo X, in whom they found so zealous a patron, must have been one of the best reformers. The learning and cultivation of the age were primarily of the nature of a mere instrument, which, as it came to be associated either with piety or with the spirit of the world, might be made subservient to exactly opposite ends.

[3. Preparation in the sphere of Theology and the Church]

Leaving behind now the outer court of politics, popular literature, and profane science as thus far surveyed, we approach nearer to the proper sanctuary of the Reformation and fix our attention on the movements by which its way was prepared in the sphere of *Theology* and the *Church*. Here however we must distinguish carefully between simply negative action, so directed against error as to make war upon the truth more or less at the same time, and that of a positive character springing from the life of the Church itself.

[In a negative respect]

The first we find exemplified, in general, by the sects of the *Albigenses*, the *Beghards* and *Beguines*, the *Bogomiles*, and *Catharists*;[7] and by such men moreover as ARNOLD *of Brescia*, AMALRICH *of Bena*, DAVID *of Dinanto*, and others,[8] who, without any proper Church-feeling and under the influence of hyper-spiritualistic and not unfrequently Manichean and pantheistic views, set themselves in opposition to truth and error promiscuously. The Catholic Church regarded all these properly as heretics but employed carnal weapons, instead of the sword of the Spirit, to put them down, and in this way rendered them only so much the more dangerous.

7. [The Albigenses thrived in southern France during the twelfth and thirteenth centuries; the Beghards (males) and Beguines (females) were lay communities in the Low Countries starting in the twelfth century. The Bogomiles arose in the region of contemporary Macedonia and thrived between the tenth and the fifteenth centuries. The Catharists, influenced by the Bogomiles, were located in northern Italy and southern France during the twelfth and fourteenth centuries. The Albigenses, Bogomiles, and Catharists maintained a dualistic (Manichaean in Schaff's terms, or gnostic) view of the world. All the groups were critical of the practices of Catholic clergy.]

8. [These three men were heretics of the twelfth or early thirteenth centuries. Arnold of Brescia (c.1090–1155) was an Italian priest who called on the Church to renounce property ownership and the accumulation of money. He was executed in Rome. Amalrich of Bena (d. 1204) was a Paris theologian forced by Pope Innocent III to recant for his pantheistic tendencies. Ten of his followers were burnt before the gates of Paris in 1209. David of Dinanto (c. 1160–c. 1217) was also a French theologian, and possibly a follower of Amalrich, his "*Quaternuli*" (Little notebooks) were condemned by a provincial council in 1210, forcing him to flee Paris.]

[In a postive respect]

[By religious bodies]

Of much greater account, of course, is the positive tendency of the Theology and Church of the Middle Ages towards the Reformation. Here we meet whole *communities* and also *single* voices. Among the first, a principal place belongs to the *Waldenses* who accompany us, in spite of the fierce persecutions of the papacy, like a lamp in the night, from the middle of the twelfth century down to the time of Luther; and whose life of simplicity and strict virtue is still perpetuated indeed, even in our own time, amidst surrounding Romish superstition, in the valleys of Piedmont, near to Turin. They based their opposition to the reigning Church upon the holy scriptures, which many of their members knew almost entirely by heart; so that, in some instances, they were called in even by the Romish ecclesiastics themselves to assist them in their disputations with heretics.

Wickliffe in Oxford, and Huss in Prague, though apparently overwhelmed by the ruling hierarchy, had not labored in vain in contending against abuses and false doctrine, and in calling men's minds away from externals to inward godliness, and from human traditions to the word of God as the only fountain of true theology. We find a large number of *Wickliffites* in England; and from the *Hussites* arose by degrees the *Bohemian* and *Moravian Brethren*, who made it their object to restore the simplicity, spirituality, and strict discipline of the apostolic age.[9] They had already as many as two hundred churches and houses for prayer in the beginning of the sixteenth century.

The Society of the *Fratres communis vitae* ["Brothers of the Common Life"] also, instituted by Gerhard Groot, towards the close of the 14th Century, must not be forgotten. It proposed to preserve what was true and good in the conventual system of the age without its excrescences. Thus for instance it allowed no monastic vows, but only free resolutions in dependence on God's grace. From this association proceeded many distinguished men, with Thomas à Kempis at their head; who preached the word of God in the vernacular tongue; devoted themselves earnestly to the instruction of the young; insisted in a style very different from the Pharisaic formality of the times on deep, inward, practical piety; and in opposition to the prevalent dry learning of the schools, acknowledged no wisdom but such as carried with it at the same time a sanctifying power.[10]

9. [The Moravian Brethren, also known as the Moravian Church or *Unitas Fratrum* ("Unity of the Brethren") stemmed from the Hussite movement in Bohemia and Moravia. In 1722, a group of these Christians settled on the estate of the Lutheran nobleman Nikolaus Ludwig Graf von Zinzendorf in Germany. Recognizing them as the remnant of a church that predated the Reformation, he supported their formation as a modern Pietist, Protestant community. Active in missionary work and practicing communal living, their American settlements included Bethlehem in Pennsylvania and Salem in North Carolina. Atwood, *Theology of the Czech Brethren*; Atwood, *Community of the Cross*. For Wyclif and the English Lollard movement see Rex, *The Lollards*.]

10. [With their emphasis on education and the inner life the Brothers of the Common Life were

Attention is due further to an association that rose in Italy, and formed an interesting analogy of the German Protestantism, though for reasons easily understood it fell far short of it in its development. An *Oratory of Divine Love* was established in the church of St. Sylvester and Dorothea, across the Tiber at Rome, where in the time of Leo X as many as fifty or sixty distinguished men, including such names as CONTARINI, SADOLET, GIBERTO, CARAFFA, and LIPPOMANO, were accustomed to meet statedly for mutual religious edification.[11] These men, some of whom afterwards struck into a very different path when they came to be adorned with the cardinal's cap, had come to the very threshold of the evangelical doctrine of justification! CONTARINI composed a treatise on the subject, which led Pole to say, in writing to him, "You have brought into the light a precious jewel, which was before half concealed in the keeping of the Church."[12] Another member of this association, M. A. FLAMINIO, writes in his epistle to Theodorina Sauli:

> The gospel is nothing else than the glad tidings, that the only begotten Son of God, clothed in our flesh, has rendered satisfaction to the righteousness of the eternal Father on our account. *He who believes this* enters into the kingdom of God, finds universal forgiveness, is changed from a carnal to a spiritual nature, from a child of wrath to a child of grace and leads a life of sweet peace in his conscience.[13]

But among all the movements and connections in which a reformatory element may be discovered to have been at work before the time of Luther, none is more worthy of being noticed than the interest of mysticism. Its influence was felt indeed by several of the associations to which we have already referred, particularly by the Brethren of

at the center of the movement for spiritual revival known as the *Devotio Moderna*. Van Engen, *Sisters and Brothers of the Common Life*.]

11. [Many locally organized institutions inspired by the life and charitable work of St. Catherine of Genoa (1447–1510) were known as the Oratory of Divine Love. The one to which Schaff refers was established by members of Pope Leo X's court sometime between 1514 and 1517. Like the others, it focused on the spiritual renewal of its members through the observance of religious exercises, common prayer, fasting, confession, frequent communion, and works of charity, While this oratory disbanded after the sack of Rome in 1527 by troops of Emperor Charles V, it inspired Thomas de Vio Cajetan and Giovani Pietro Carafa to found the Theatine order, which gave more structured expression to many of the oratory's ideals. Biographical notes on the members to whom Schaff refers are in the Glossary. Black, *Italian Confraternities*; Jorgensen, "The Oratories of Divine Love and the Theatines."]

12. [Gasparo Contarini, Reginald Pole, and Marcantonio Flaminio were all representatives of the spirituali, a small group of Italian Catholics who affirmed the importance of the doctrine of justification by faith. Contarini's major work on justification was Epistola de iustificatione (1541) written as an apology for the article on justification he drafted which was approved by Lutherans and Catholics at the Regensburg Colloquy in 1541. Gleason, *Gasparo Contarini*, 190–201, 229–35.]

13. For more on the subject of this interesting tendency, the influence of which extended even to the gay, pleasure-seeking Naples, the reader is referred to LEOP. RANKE'S *Die Römischen Päpste im 16ten und 17ten Jahrhundert* (2nd ed. [Berlin: Duncker und Humblot, 1839]), Vol. I, p. 134. [This work has been translated as *The Ecclesiastical and Political History of the Popes of Rome during the 16th and 17th Centuries* (1841).]

the Common Life. But we find it besides running in various forms, with more full development, through the entire Middle Age; and the influence of it, in this view, on Luther himself, is not to be mistaken. He was the affectionate disciple of John von Staupitz, in whom a profound, Augustinian, mystical tendency strongly prevailed; and he was the publisher and eulogist of the old treatise entitled, "*The German Theology*," which may be regarded as the flower of the ascetico-speculative spirit in this form.[14] The reformatory bearing of the mystical system appeared in this, that it drew attention away from mere externals, in which the idea of religion and the Church had become well nigh lost, to the exercises of the heart; and breaking through the barriers that had been interposed between man and his Maker by the hierarchical framework of the papacy, and in defiance at the same time of the dialectics of the schools, threw itself directly into the stream of the divine life itself. In its view, religion was to be apprehended not as a system of forms, but as the inmost life of its subject. It thirsted after direct communion with God. Mysticism however had no power, of itself, to produce a reformation. It is deficient in practical energy. Predominantly subjective in its nature and resting too exclusively in mere feeling, it has no capacity to overcome the world. Its life proceeds accordingly, in lonely retirement, without action, like the mysterious flower that unfolds its petals in the stillness of the night, but gathers them in again with shrinking sensitiveness as soon as they are touched by a hand.

[By single persons]

Not less significant, however, than these collective tendencies, are the *separate* strivings towards the Reformation to be considered, which show themselves in particular individuals with growing frequency in the course of the 15th century and with the opening of that which followed. These sprang partly from a practical religious interest and partly from an interest in theology as a science, and in both forms wrought powerfully, in the way of controversy and in the way of quiet positive teaching, to prepare the way for the new era that was at hand.

The celebrated councils of Constance and Basel, which had insisted on a reformation of the Church in its head and members, though with their self-contradictory constitution they could not accomplish the work; and the deep toned lamentations, of a Nicolas of Clamenge (de Clemangis), Pierre d'Ailly, John von Gerson, and others, over the reigning corruption, had served to disseminate a longing desire for a better state of religion through all sections of Europe.[15] This feeling found its organs

14. [This mystical text from the late fourteenth century is also commonly known by its Latin (*Theologica germanica*) and German (*Eine deutsche Theologie*) names. Luther published a partial edition in 1516 and a more complete edition in 1518. For Luther's introduction to the latter edition see *LW* 31: 73–76; for a complete translation of Luther's edition, *The Theologia Germanica of Martin Luther*, trans. Bengt Hoffman (New York: Paulist Press, 1980).]

15. [The Council of Constance (1414–18) and the Council of Basel (1431–49) were the height of the conciliar movement. During the Great Western Schism (1378–1417), the allegiance of Catholic

in such men as the Dominican SAVONAROLA *of San Marco* in Florence, who preached with prophetic indignation, in the boldest style, not without a hurtful mixture indeed of political zeal, against the licentiousness that had come to abound in the Church, and sealed his testimony with his blood in the year 1498. Such also were JOHN VON WESEL (*de Wesalia*), Professor of Theology at Erfurth (d. 1482), JOHN VON GOCH, a native of Cleves (d. 1475), and the Frieslander, JOHN WESSEL (d. 1489). These all insisted more or less clearly on the Augustinian doctrine of grace in opposition to the prevailing Jewish idea of righteousness by works and bondage to the law, and appealed to the sacred scriptures as the only sure ground and source of Christian doctrine. This was carried so far indeed in the case of *John Wessel*, who went beyond all others before the Reformation in his apprehension of the Protestant doctrine of justification, that LUTHER, undervaluing it is true his own merits, did not hesitate to say: "If I had read Wessel previously, my adversaries might have supposed that Luther had borrowed all from Wessel, so well do our views agree." In none of these men however was there found such a union of all the powers that are needed for a reformation, as was possessed by LUTHER and CALVIN, for whom it was reserved accordingly to accomplish so great a work.

[Preparation in the sphere of Practical Religion]

Enough has been said already to vindicate an absolute historical necessity to the Reformation and to expose in its utter emptiness and nakedness the reproach, cast upon it by its enemies, as an uncalled for innovation. We go farther, however, and affirm that *the entire Catholic Church as such, so far as it might be considered the legitimate bearer of the Christian faith and life*, pressed with inward necessary impulse towards Protestantism, just as Judaism—not in its character of Pharisaism and Sadduceeism indeed, but as a divinely appointed preparatory institute, and viewed in its true historical import—rolled with steady powerful stream, in its interior legal, symbolical and prophetical principle, directly towards Christianity as the fulfillment of the law, the prototype of all its symbols, and the accomplishment of all its prophecies. The Councils of Constance and Basel alone furnish proof that the call for a reformation had its ground, not simply in the sects, and in single individuals more or less estranged from the objective life of the Church, but in the heart of the Church itself, and in the persons of those who were most fully penetrated with its life. This affirmation, as well as the appeal to the case of Judaism, may require some additional illustration.

Europe was divided among two, and then three popes. In response, conciliarists sought to establish the supremacy of councils over the pope and to enact other reforms, particularly to combat corruption among the clergy. Pope Eugenius broke with the Council of Basel in 1438 when he convoked the Council of Ferrara-Florence (1438–45) to replace it. This was the beginning of the end of the conciliarist movement. Some members of the Council of Basel refused to accept the new council and did not close theirs until 1449.]

The Catholic Church of the Middle Ages, as already intimated, was a Church of law and authority; well fitted, by means of its vast disciplinary system, turning on a single living center and perfectly complete in all its parts, to exercise a wardship over the nations, still in their childhood, till such time as they might be ripe for a fuller appropriation of the evangelical principle and the use of an independent manly freedom. In saying this, we do not question the presence of the gospel in the communion of the Roman Catholic Church, any more than we doubt the comfort of the promise that went hand in hand with the development of the Old Testament law. Still, the *predominant* spirit, in both cases, was legal; as might easily be proved, in minute detail, if this were the proper place.[16] Now it belongs always to the nature of the law to excite in man a feeling that reaches beyond itself and refuses to be satisfied by its means; a feeling that craves reconciliation with the lawgiver, and the full possession of that righteousness which he requires. More definitely expressed, the law is a schoolmaster to bring men to Christ, who has fulfilled its requisitions in their largest extent, and makes over to us the benefit of this obedience as a free unmerited gift, by the power of his Spirit. Thus the Jewish dispensation looked always towards the gospel; and in like manner the discipline of the Roman Church involved an inward struggle that became satisfied at last only in the evangelical emancipation of Protestantism.

It is only from this point of view we come to understand fully the personal life of Luther, in which the genesis of our Church itself is reflected with the most clear and graphic representation. It was no political, national, scientific, or theological interest, even, that impelled him to his work. The immediate, original ground of it is to be sought in the very center of the religious life of the Catholic Church itself, as it stood at the time. This Church he was proud at one time to call his mother and his separation from her visible head cost him a struggle, a self-immolation, of which, now that the great rupture is past, it is hard for us to form any clear conception. The most faithful and conscientious of monks, he subjected himself intellectually to the logical discipline of the schools, and bore practically the prescribed penances and other legal burdens of the Catholic Church, as those of Judaism had been borne by Paul. To become righteous before God, to appear as a saint in his presence, was the object for which he wrestled without intermission. But the longer he continued in this hard school, he became sensible the more of his own weakness, and of his immeasurable distance from the ideal he was laboring to reach, and in the same proportion was

16. This legal character of the Middle Ages was clearly perceived by many of the forerunners of the Reformation themselves. Specially worthy of notice in this respect is an uncommonly striking description of *Cornelius Graphaeus* of Flanders (born 1482), which is to be found in the classic work of my much esteemed friend Ullmann, entitled, *Reformatoren vor der Reformation*, Vol. 1. [Hamburg, 1841] p. 153 ff. All who wish to become acquainted with the forerunners of the Reformation in Germany and the Netherlands, may find all they need for the purpose in this thoroughly learned, and well-written work, presented in the most entertaining form. May the learned author soon add to the two volumes which have already appeared, a further continuation on what still remains of his general subject, at least so far as the philological and humanistic precursors of the Reformation are concerned. [Carl Ullmann, *Reformers before the Reformation*, 2 vols. (Edinburgh: T. & T. Clark, 1841).]

brought to long after a redeemer from the body of such death and the terrible conflict between the law in his members and the law of the Spirit; till in the end, like his great apostolical pattern, he beheld the Crucified in his spiritual glory, and by faith in him received at once, in all its fullness, as a free gift, all that he had been vainly endeavoring to secure by his own strength before. Of a truth, we may say, the pains endured in the mortification of the flesh and in legal wrestlings after righteousness with God by the noblest spirits of the Middle Ages, the Mystics in particular, with the anxiously religious Augustinian monk at their head, are to be regarded as the true birth-pangs of our Protestant Church.[17]

As the result then of this whole representation, we reach the following—for the vindication of Protestantism vastly important, and even indispensable—proposition: *The Reformation is the legitimate offspring, the greatest act of the Catholic Church; and on this account of true catholic nature itself, in its genuine conception: whereas the Church of Rome, instead of following the divine conduct of history, has continued to stick in the old law of commandments, the garb of childhood, like the Jewish hierarchy in the time of Christ, and thus by its fixation as Romanism has parted with the character of catholicity in exchange for that of particularity.*[18]

II. The Prospective Aspect of the Reformation; or the Protestant Principle in its positive force.

[Preliminary remarks]

With this proposition we have already touched upon the second essential constituent of the Reformation, according to which it is to be viewed as a *historical advance* on the part of the Church; and in the closest connection with the pressure of previous long accumulating want, a new birth from the womb of its life in the old form. The subject however in this aspect calls now for closer elucidation in a direct way.

17. We may observe in *Calvin* also, and to a greater extent indeed than in Luther, the traces in every direction of the severe legal discipline, intellectual and practical, which the Catholic Church, in spite of all her corruptions, still continued to exercise at least over minds of the more serious order. It would be wholly beyond the capacity of our own age to produce such an amount of resolute, vigorous, large proportioned character, as is presented to us in the Reformers. We have lost almost entirely the consciousness of the power of the law as it is felt always in the earlier stages of life. Along with our scientific seminaries, we stand in great want of institutions expressly for the cultivation of character; and in this particular, we might, and should, learn much from the Romish Church, the schools especially of the Jesuits.

18. Compare, on the difference between Catholicism and Romanism, my articles in the *Literar. Zeitung* of Berlin, 1843, No. 87 and No. 100. [Schaff, "Katholizismus und Romanismus," *Literarische Zeitung* (Berlin) 20, no. 87 (Oct. 31, 1843): 1385–90, no. 100 (Dec. 16, 1843): 1597–603.]

[The idea of progress in the history of the Church]

It must be remarked in the first place, that when we speak of advance or progress here, we do so with reference only to the previous *apprehension* of Christianity in the Church, and not to Christianity itself as exhibited in its original and for all times absolutely normal character in the writings of the New Testament. Our comparison of the relation of the Evangelical Church to the Roman Catholic, with the relation of Christianity to Judaism, must be taken therefore with a material limitation. Christianity stands related to Judaism, not simply as fulfillment to presentiment, enlargement to compression, substance to shadow; but is at the same time specifically a new creation. No expansion simply of the idea of the Old Testament, as such, was sufficient for its production. This could take place only by the creative act of God, in his incarnation, his life, sufferings, death and resurrection, as God and man in one person, and in the real and full communication of the Holy Ghost, which had irradiated the human consciousness before only in a transient and sporadic way.

Beyond Christianity itself however, as thus introduced into the world, there can be no similar advance. Our faith must be subverted in its very ground, if now that Christ has appeared, "the fullness of the Godhead bodily" [Col 2:9], and given his Spirit to the apostles to "lead them into all truth" [John 16:13], we should allow ourselves to expect, like the Jews, a still higher revelation. In its own nature, as a new order of life, Christianity has been complete from the beginning; and there is no room to conceive that any more perfect order can ever take its place, or that it may be so improved as in the end to outgrow entirely its own original sphere. But notwithstanding this, we are authorized to speak of advance or progress in the case of the Church itself, and on the part of the Christianized world; and of this not merely as extensive, in the spread of the gospel among pagans, Mohammedans and Jews; but as intensive also in the continually growing cultivation and improvement of those four great interests of the Church: doctrine, life, constitution, and worship.

The Church, not less than every one of its members, has its periods of infancy, youth, manhood, and old age. This involves no contradiction to the absolute character of Christianity; for the progress of the Church, outward or inward, is never in the strict sense creative, but in the way only of reception, organic assimilation, and expansion. In other words, all historical development in the Church, theoretical and practical, consists in *an apprehension always more and more profound of the life and doctrine of Christ and his apostles, an appropriation more full and transforming always of their distinctive spirit, both as to its contents and its form.* Only so far as a doctrine or ordinance of the Church bears this character, may it be allowed to have normative and enduring force. If it could be clearly shown for instance, that the doctrines of the Trinity and the two natures in Christ, as dogmatically developed and symbolically established in opposition to heretical errors in the fourth and fifth centuries, are not contained so far as substance is concerned in the New Testament, but contradict it rather, their authority must fall before the culture of the age to make room for a different view in consonance with the scriptures.

In this sense then, the Reformation is an advance, not of Christianity itself, but of its tenure at least upon the consciousness of the Christian world. We may bring forward indeed many passages from the writings of AUGUSTINE, ANSELM, BERNARD OF CLAIRVAUX, and other men occupying a position near to the Reformers, which seem to teach the cardinal doctrine of justification by grace; and it may be affirmed with truth, that all real Christians, from the beginning, had lived upon this doctrine at bottom, unconsciously to themselves. But still their piety, in its general character, must be admitted to carry with it more or less of a legal complexion. Only in single, exalted moments of their existence at best, were they enabled to lay hold of the freedom, the assurance of salvation, and full triumphant faith, to which we have been raised by the Reformation. This merit at least belongs to the Reformers, that they have brought into clear consciousness what existed only darkly before in the soul, and have made that to be common property in the Church which had belonged previously only to single and highly gifted individuals. On the other hand, when we bring the soteriological ground principle of the Reformation into the light of the New Testament, particularly the epistles of Paul, we find it ratified here with such clear and distinct enunciation that we are ready to wonder why the Church should not have come to the knowledge of it a great while sooner. But to penetrate from the surface into the depth, from the shell to the kernel, is something far more difficult than it seems; a work belonging to God's chosen instruments, the architects of the world's history, the wakers of slumbering centuries.

[False views of the principle of Protestantism]

The new vital principle of the Reformation, as compared with the form in which Christianity had been held previously, is not to be sought in the sphere of the objective, more theoretic doctrines, such for instance as the Trinity, the incarnation, or the relation of the divine and human natures in the person of Christ. These it incorporated into itself rather, as they had been previously perfected by the great oecumenical councils, asserting and maintaining thus its catholic interest in the true spiritual acquisitions of the ancient Church.

On the contrary, the sixteenth century was the classic period for the full exposition of the Christian soteriology as standing in the subjective appropriation of the work of redemption. The re-appearance of Unitarian and Arian errors at the time must be considered a mere accidental excrescence, such as we find attending every great historical occasion.[19] The essential, fundamental doctrines of the Reformation then fall within a sphere which had not previously been occupied by the decision

19. [For the anti-trinitarian movements of the sixteenth-century see Williams, *The Radical Reformation*, 943–1049, 1079–176.]

of any general council, as in the case of the Trinity and the constitution of Christ's person, and where accordingly it was possible to advance new scriptural statements, without contradicting the true Catholic Church. The movement in this view was not an effort to overthrow and reconstruct the work of this Church in the case of its great cardinal doctrines as already positively defined by the general councils; but to carry forward and complete that work rather, by going on to define and settle what had not yet been made the subject of action, in the same positive style.

As little may we say that the Reformation stood essentially in an effort to subvert the papacy and hierarchy, although this is often affirmed. Those who regard it in this light, do not consider that Luther had already uttered his positive life principle before he thought of a breach with the pope; and that much later even Melanchthon, in subscribing the Articles of Smalcald, professed himself willing to accept the pope as *de jure humano* ["by human law"] head of the Church. Such a principle besides would give no distinction between the Protestant Church and the Greek, or common sects even, which all agree in rejecting the primacy of Rome to the same extent. The great point was to eradicate popedom from the heart itself, which is too prone away from all connection with Rome to make an idol of mere human authority, in forms that may appear more plausible perhaps, but are often more intolerably tyrannic on this very account.

Still more prevalent is the view by which the essence of the Reformation is placed in the emancipation of the human mind subjectively considered, that is, in the triumphant assertion of the liberty of faith and conscience, as well as of unlimited scientific inquiry. Rightly understood, this to be sure has its truth; but as commonly represented, it is a sheer caricature of history. It is made to mean very often, for instance, a full liberation of the subject from every sort of restraint, the overthrow of all authority as such. But of such escape from discipline and rule the Reformers had no thought. Their object was rather to bind man to the grace of God and to lead his conscience captive to God's word. In every view, the act of protesting is not the first and main constituent in the Reformation, but the result only of a positive affirmation going before. This last accordingly is the great point, from which alone its true importance springs. Only in connection with such an original positive life principle, and as flowing from it, can deliverance from the papacy and the restitution of private judgment to its rights, find any right sense, any religious value. Apart from this connection, they fall over to the province of infidelity, with which the Reformation has nothing to do.

Such a positive religious principle now is the doctrine of the exclusive authority of the sacred scriptures as a rule of faith; and it is a very current idea, particularly in the *Reformed* Church, that this doctrine forms the proper center and root of Protestantism. But this also we cannot admit, although the Christian life of the Reformers was shaped from the beginning by the scriptures. For this principle is formal only, and so secondary, presupposing the presence of a definite substance which it must include. In order that the scriptures may be taken as the exclusive source and measure of Christian truth, it is necessary that the faith in Christ of which they testify should be already at hand, that their contents should have been made to live in the heart by the power of the Holy Ghost accompanying the word and the Church. And so all turns upon the particular constitution of this faith. The Socinians, Swedenborgeans, later Unitarians, and other sects, made the same strenuous appeal to the scriptures as their only authority; but they stood quite off from the true living ground of the Reformation notwithstanding, and gave accordingly a wholly different sense to the bible, in the most weighty points.[20]

[1. The material principle.]

That we may come to the furthest source then, we must inquire after the material or life principle (*principium essendi*) of the Reformation. This, according to history, is no other than the great doctrine which is presented by Paul especially as the entire sum of the gospel: the doctrine of the *justification of the sinner before God by the merit of Christ alone through faith*. This doctrine was the fruit of LUTHER's earnest spiritual conflicts already noticed; and it formed the proper soul, the polar star and center of his life, from the commencement of his reformatory career on to his last breath.[21] The

20. [Socinians refers to followers of an antitrinitarian theology that emerged from the theology of Lelio Francesco Maria Sozini (1525–62) and his nephew Fausto Paolo Sozzini (1539–1604). It took root in sixteenth-century Poland. See Williams, *Radical Reformation*, 876–85, 965–89, 1169–75. Swedenborgians followed the teachings of Emanuel Swedenborg (1688–1772), a Swedish scientist who reported receiving a divine call in the 1740s to interpret the Bible and found a new church. His mystical and antitrinitarian teachings emphasized the doctrine of correspondence between the physical and mystical worlds. For Swedenborg's broad influence in America see Albanese, *Republic of Mind and Spirit*.]

21. Hence he says himself in the Articles of Smalcald, p. 305 (*Edition of the Symb. Books* by HASE): *De hoc articulo cedere aut aliquid contra illum largiri aut permittere nemo piorum potest, etiamsi coelum et terra et omnia corruant. Non enim est aliud nomen hominibus datum, per quod salvari possimus (inquit Petrus,* Act. 4:12) *et per vulnera ejus sanati sumus* (Esaj. 53:5). *Et* in hoc articulo sita sunt et consistunt *omnia, quae contra Papam, Diabolum, et universum mundum, in vita nostra docemus, testamur et agimur. Quare oportet nos de hac doctrina esse certos et minime dubitare,* alioquin actum est prorsus, *et Papa et diabolus et omnia adversa jus et victoriam contra nos obtinent.* [Schaff cites from Karl von Hase, *Libri Symbolici Ecclesiae Evangelicae, sive Concordia*, 1st ed. (Leipzig: Johannes Suehring, 1827). Trans. "Nothing in this article can be given up or compromised, even if heaven and earth and things temporal should be destroyed. For as St. Peter says, 'There is no other name under heaven given among men by which we must be saved,' Acts 4, 'And with his stripes we are healed,' Isaiah 53. *On this article rests all* that we teach and practice against the pope, the devil, and the world. Therefore we must be quite certain and have no doubts about it. *Otherwise all is lost*, and the pope, the devil, and all our adversaries will gain the victory." *C&C*, 2:126.] Comp. *Formula of Concord* p. 683 [*C&C*, 2:176] and Melanchthon, *Locus de gratia et justification*, where he says of the doctrine of justification: *Hic locus continet summam evangelii* [Trans. "This doctrine contains the whole sum of the gospel." This was the first sentence of the chapter (or *locus*) *de gratia et justificatione* beginning with the second edition of Melanchthon's *Loci Communes Theologici* (1535).]. When the younger BENGEL (*Archiv für die Theol.*, Bd. 1., St. 2., S. 469 [vol. 1, issue 2, p. 469]), and the celebrated historian PLANCK (*Worte des Friedens an die kath. Kirche*, [Göttingen: Vandenhöck und Ruprecht] 1809, p. 47 f.) represent the whole controversy between the Protestants and Romanists on the doctrine of justification as of no

Romish Church may be said to urge precisely her most earnest and pious members always towards this point; as we see in the case of the *Jansenists*, condemned indeed by the pope, and in our own day in such men as Sailer, Veith, Gossner, Boos, and others. For all earnest legal wrestling after righteousness and holiness leads naturally, at last, to the abandonment of every fleshly confidence and a reliance on God's grace alone. It was this doctrine which first made the scriptures for the Reformers what they claimed to be; and Luther, it is known, employed it as a measure for the sacred canon itself, not allowing it to include as God's normative word anything that might carry an opposite sense. His harsh censures on certain portions of the established Church canon, the Epistle of James, the Epistle to the Hebrews, and the Revelation of St. John, we do not of course defend, but reject them rather as one-sided and rash. They form an interesting fact however, in illustration of the point immediately in hand, the posture of the doctrine of justification relatively to the great reformatory movement as its true life principle. Pressed as he was by his Romish adversaries, with whom James especially was always a favorite authority, Luther's unfavorable judgment of the books just named arose altogether from his not being able to find in them his cardinal truth, justification by faith only.[22]

[The Roman Catholic doctrine of justification]

It devolves upon us now to go into a somewhat closer examination of this material principle of the Reformation; and for this purpose it is necessary to direct our view

vital account, a mere logomachy in fact, the thing finds its explanation in the dogmatic indifferentism of the age to which these men belonged. But it is incomprehensible how at the present time, when the difference of the Confessions has come to be more clearly felt again in a recurrence to its foundations, the latest Protestant expositor of the Catholic system, Koellner (in his otherwise very accurate and learned *Symbolik der heil. apost. kath. römischen Kirche*, Preface, p. XIX) [W. H. D. E. Köllner, *Symbolik aller christlichen Confessionen*, vol. 2, *Symbolik der heiligen apostolischen katholischen römischen Kirche* (Hamburg: F. Perthes, 1844)], should affirm the same thing, and find on the contrary the main difference in the outward relations, constitution, and worship of the two churches.

22. From this it appears with how much wrong the modem negative criticism makes its appeal to Luther's example. He, standing in the element of God's unwritten word and animated by the one all regulating principle of justification, uttered his judgment against certain parts of the canon handed down by the Church, because they seemed to him to be in conflict with that word, as the essence of the gospel itself. Luther's criticism in one word was the action of faith in the free grace of God in Christ, against all human distortion of the truth. The modern criticism of a Strauss or Bruno Bauer on the other hand, in full reverse, starts from unbelief in this grace, and is aimed destructively against the positive ground of the gospel itself (Comp. my articles on "True and False Criticism" in the *Literar. Zeitung* of Berlin, 1843, No. 40 and No. 61). [Schaff, "Ein Wort über die theologische Kritik: I Wahre und falsche Kritik," (A word about theological criticism: true and false criticism), *Literarische Zeitung* 20, no. 40 (May 20, 1843): 633–37; "Ein Wort über die theologische Kritik: II Der Selbstvernichtungsprocess der neueren Evangelienkritik," (The self-destructive process of the newer criticism of the gospels) *Literarische Zeitung* 20, no. 61 (Aug. 2, 1843): 969–75.] Let any one read Luther's judgment upon the Epistle of James continuously in *Walch*, Vol. 14, p. 148 f. [Martin Luther, *Sämtliche Schriften*, ed by Johann Georg Walch (Halle: J. J. Gebauer, 1740–53); also *LW* 35:395–97] and he will be fully satisfied of the truth of our representation.

first, in brief, to the opposite tenet of the Romish Church. The Christian salvation rests upon the primary truth that Jesus Christ, the absolute God-man, is the only Redeemer and Mediator between man as a sinner and his offended Maker. It is long, however, before man is brought to take up this doctrine in its full import into his consciousness and to part radically with the Judaism that is in him from his birth. So we find it in the experience of the individual child of God at all times; and so it has been with the life of the Church as a whole, from the beginning. In the Church of Rome, we find the doctrine, according to the Council of Trent, acknowledged objectively and *in thesi* ["as a matter of general opinion"], but always laid under restriction as soon it comes to a particular explanation of the way in which the atonement is carried over into the life of its subject and made available for his salvation. In opposition, not only to Pelagianism, but to Semi-pelagianism also (which may be charged indeed upon the papal bull, *Unigenitus*, A. D. 1711, and the whole practice of the Church, but not on the Council of Trent), she teaches, it is true, that the grace of God, as *gratia praeveniens* ["prevenient grace"] commences the work of conversion in man by calling him to the salvation which is in Christ.[23] In her view however, the natural condition of man is not as with us, a state of positive corruption, but holds simply in the absence of supernatural endowments, as *defectus justitiae originalis* ["want of original righteousness"] on the one hand, and a mere debilitation of the natural powers of reason and freedom on the other;[24] and so the natural man is made to take part also in the work

23. *Conc. Trid.*, S. VI. decr. I. c. 5–6. [Council of Trent, Session VI, canons 5–6. "Unigenitus" was a papal bull promulgated in 1713 (not 1711) by Pope Clement XI against the Jansenists. Pelagianism describes the teaching that humans by their good works can merit salvation apart from divine grace. Semi-pelagianism describes the teaching that while grace is necessary for salvation, it requires the cooperation of the human will, actively receiving this grace, before it can become operative.]

24. S. VI, Decr. I, c. 1, and can. 4. 5. 7. BELLARMINE consequently (*Disputt. etc. de gratia primi hominis* I. 1) states the doctrine of his Church correctly, when he says: *Docent enim (catholici Doctores), per Adae peccatum totum hominem vere deteriorem esse factum, et tamen* nec liberum arbitrium neque alia naturalia dona, *sed solum supernaturalia perdidisse.* And what he remarks, *de gratia primi hom.* c. 5, agrees with this fully: *Quare non magis differt status hominis post lapsum Adae a statu ejusdem in puris naturalibus, quam differat* spoliatus a nudo; *neque deterior est humana natura, si culpam originalem detrahas, neque magis ignorantia et infirmitate lahorat, quam esset et laboraret in puris naturalibus condita. Proinde corruptio naturae non ex alicujus doni naturalis carentia, neque ex alicujus malae qualitatis accessu, sed ex sola doni supernaturalis ob Adae peccatum amissione profluxit.* [Robert Bellarmine, *In disputationes de controversiis christianae fidei adversus hujus temporis haereticos.* Schaff likely uses the Rome edition of 1832. The authoritative edition is contained in the *Opera omnia* (Paris: Vives, 1870–74), and citations will be given for this edition. No English translation of this work has been made to date. Trans. "For they (the catholic Doctors) teach, that through the sin of Adam the whole man was indeed made worse, and yet has lost *neither free will nor any other natural gifts*, but only the supernatural ones." *In disp. de contr.*, XIII (*De gratia generi humano*).1.1 (Vives, 5:169b).—"Therefore the state of man after the fall of Adam differs no more from his state of pure nature than *a 'stripped man' differs from 'a naked man.'* Nor is human nature worse, if you take away original sin, when it comes to purely natural matters, than in the condition in which it started, nor does it toil under more ignorance and infirmity. Thus the corruption of nature proceeds not from the lack of any natural gift, nor from the addition of any bad quality, but only from the loss of the supernatural gift on account of the sin of Adam." *In disp. de contr.*, XIII (*De gratia generi humano*).1.5 (Vives, 5:179a).]

of his own conversion and justification. When the power towards good, which is still in him though debilitated by original sin, is again set free and invigorated in his gracious calling, he disposes himself, we are told, to the acquisition of justification; so that God's grace (*gratia operans*) and the human will (*voluntas humana cooperans*) work now in conjunction, the first in the way of illumination, and the other freely consenting and moving towards God.[25] As the result of this twofold action justification in due time takes place—not suddenly however, but gradually, partly by faith, and partly by works of love. For justification here, agreeably to the etymology of the word indeed, but against both classical and Biblical use, is taken to mean making righteous in the proper sense; whence it is made the same substantially with sanctification, and regarded as a property residing in the man personally, *justitia inhaerens or infusa* ["inherent or infused righteousness"].[26] The objective ground of justification, according to the Council of Trent, is in every view the propitiatory death of Christ; but the apprehension of it is not by faith alone. This has justifying power only so far as it is the beginning of salvation, the root of justification, *humanae salutis initium, fundamentum et radix omnis justificationis.*[27] Full justification however it cannot effect, if it were only for the reason that in the Romish view of it, differing from the evangelical, it is exhibited prevailingly as simple historical assent.[28] The grace becomes complete

25. *Conc. Trid.*, S. VI, can. 4: *Si quis dixerit, liberum hominis arbitrium a Deo motum excitatum nihil* cooperari *assentiendo Deo excitanti, atque vocanti quo* ad obtinendam justificationis gratiam se disponat ac praeparet, *neque posse dissentire, si velit, sed veluti inanime quoddam nihil omnino agere, mereque passive se habere; anathema sit.* In the 5th and 6th cap. of the same session, this is made the subject of further positive explication. [Trans. "If anyone says that a person's free will when moved and roused by God, gives no *co-operation* by responding to God's summons and invitation *to dispose and prepare itself to obtain the grace of justification*; and that it cannot, if it so wishes, dissent but, like something inanimate, can do nothing at all and remains merely passive: let him be anathema." *DEC*, 2:679.]

26. S. VI, cap. 7: *Hanc dispositionem seu praeparationem justificatio ipsa consequitur, quae non est sola peccatorum remissio, sed* et sanctificatio et renovatio *interioris hominis per voluntariam susceptionem gratiae et donorum, unde homo* ex injusto fit justus *et ex inimico amicus, ut sit haeres secundum spem vitae aeternae.* Comp. can. 16. [Trans. "This disposition and preparation precede the actual justification, which consists not only in the forgiveness of sins but *also in the sanctification and renewal* of the inward being by a willing acceptance of the grace and gifts whereby *someone from being unjust becomes just,* from being an enemy becomes a friend, so that he is an heir in hope of eternal life." *DEC*, 2:673.]

27. [Trans. "the beginning of human salvation; the foundation and the root of justification."] S. VI, cap. 8. Comp. can. 9, 11, and 12. In the 9th can. it is said: *Si quis dixerit, sola fide impium justificari, ita ut intelligat nihil aliud requiri, quod* ad justificationis gratiam consequendam cooperetur *et nulla ex parte necesse esse eum suae voluntatis motu praeparari atque disponi; anathema sit.* [Trans. "If anyone says that the sinner is justified by faith alone, meaning thereby *that no other co-operation is required for him to obtain the grace of justification*, and that in no sense is it necessary for him to make preparation and be disposed by a movement of his own will: let him be anathema" *DEC*, 2:679.]

28. S. VI, cap. 6: *credentes vera esse, quae divinitus revelata et promissa sunt.* [Trans. "[they] believe to be true what has been divinely revealed and promised." *DEC*, 2:672.] Comp. *Cat. Rom.* I. 1, 1 : *Nos de ea fide loquimur, cujus vi omnino assentimur iis, quae tradita sunt divinitus.* [Trans. "We speak of that faith, by force of which we yield our entire assent to whatever has been divinely delivered." *The Catechism of the Council of Trent*, trans. Theodore Alois Buckley (London: Routledge, 1852), 19.] Bellarmine, *de justific.*, I, 4: *Catholici fidem in* intellectus *sedem habere docent.* [Trans. "Catholics teach

only by means of good works flowing from faith; and has different degrees accordingly answerable to the character and number of these works.[29] In this way a proper merit is held to belong to such works; a *meritum de congruo* ["congruent merit"] as they speak, to those which precede justification, and a *meritum de condigno* ["condign or deserved merit"] to those which follow.[30]

Practically however this co-ordination simply of faith and works, as producing justification, cannot be preserved; but the chief weight must be given to the last, since they can be multiplied indefinitely, coming thus under the category of number and quantity, whilst faith is one act properly flowing over into a continuous state. The Romish Church accordingly has carried her estimate of human virtue so far that she not only holds a perfect fulfillment of the law to be possible[31] but in broad opposition to that scripture, *When ye have done all, say, We are unprofitable servants* [Luke 17:10], has to tell even of a surplus meritoriousness of good works, her so called *opera supererogationis* ["works of supererogation"], in which a man may do more than his duty and raise himself to the character of a saint. Such super-meritorious works are deposited in the treasury or fund of the Church, which has the right to dispose of the trust at pleasure and may employ it to cover the sins of less advanced Christians, or of souls even that have already passed into purgatory.[32] Hence sprang the traffic in

that faith has its seat in the *understanding*." *In disp. de contr.*, XIV.ii (*De iustificatione impii*).1.4 (Vives, 6:154a).]

29. S. VI, cap. 10: *Sic ergo justificati et amici Dei ac domestici facti, euntes de virtute in virtutem, renovantur, ut Apostolus inquit, de die in diem; h. e., mortificando membra carnis suae et exhibendo ea arma justitiae in sanctificationem, per observationem mandatorum Dei et ecclesiae, in ipsa justitia per Christi gratiam accepta, cooperante fide, bonis operibus crescunt atque* magis justificantur. [Trans. "So those justified in this way and made friends and members of the household of God, going from strength to strength, are (as the Apostle says) renewed from day to day by putting to death what is earthly in themselves and yielding themselves as instruments of righteousness for sanctification by observance of the commandments of God and of the church. They *grow and increase in that very justness* they have received through the grace of Christ, by faith united to good works." *DEC*, 2:675.] Comp. can. 13, 14, and 24. In the last it is said: *Si quis dixerit, justitiam acceptam non conservari atque etiam non* augeri *coram Deo* per bona opera, *sed opera ipsa fructus solummodo et signa esse justificationis adeptae, non autem* ipsius augendae *causam; anathema sit.* [Trans. "If anyone says that justice once received is neither preserved nor *increased* in the sight of God *by good works*, but that the works themselves are no more than the effects and signs of the justification obtained, and not also a cause of *its increase*: let him be anathema." *DEC*, 2:680.]

30. Comp. the way in which this doctrine was carried out by the scholastics with the notices furnished in Koellner's *Symbolik der heil. apost. kath. römischen Kirche* (Hamburg, 1844), pp. 325 ff.

31. *Conc. Trid.*, S. VI, cap. 16.

32. The *Conc. Trid.* indeed does not utter itself clearly on this point (comp., however, S. VI, cap. 11, can. 18 and 32; S. XXI, de reform, c. 9); and it is remarkable that the *Cat. Rom.* has not a word on the subject. But the doctrine had already become complete with the scholastics, particularly Thomas Aquinas; and the Council informs us, S. XXV, *decr. de indulg.*, that it was to be held agreeably to the authorities, and only the practical abuses of it to be put away. The Roman Catholic divines accordingly bring it forward without reserve. Comp. Bellarmine, *de indulg.*, I. 1: *Exstat in Ecclesia thesaurus satisfactionum ex Christi passionibus infinitus, qui nunquam exhauriri poterit.*—Ad hunc thesarum superfluentium satisfactionum pertinent etiam passiones b. Mariae virginis et omnium aliorum sanctorum, qui plus passi sunt, quam eorum peccata requirerent.— Cap. 14. *Res autem certissima est et apud*

indulgences, the abomination that gave the first shock to the moral sensibilities of Luther. In this scandalous trade, that which forms the inmost sanctuary of man's life, the pardon of sin and holiness, was put to sale for the most paltry and outward of all interests, money. The profits thus made were applied to the building of St. Peter's church to gratify the ambition of the popes. But the completion of this dome, whose Sistine chapel Michelangelo had decorated with the scene of the Last Judgment, might be said to have brought with it at the same time the *last judgment* for the Romish Church itself, thus fallen into the arms of the world.

Where full justification is thus made to depend on the fluctuating subjective ground of human works and merit, it is impossible, on the other side, for a Christian, however honest and humble, to attain to any certainty of his salvation; and all such assurance is expressly condemned accordingly by the Council of Trent, unless as it may be the product of a special revelation.[33] Thus it happens very generally, that the piety of precisely the most excellent and earnest members of this Church carries with it a legal, fettered, anxious character, that never allows them to come to the full joy of faith, the glorious liberty of the children of God. The farther the man advances, the more he sees and feels what is still wanting; while such as can be satisfied with themselves, only show the absence of all right judgment and feeling by this fact. Such self-righteousness no doubt is much more common in the Roman Catholic Church than rigid self-probation or self-knowledge.

The Tridentine view then of this most momentous dogma, in which all subjective Christianity is comprehended, is fairly chargeable with the following serious defects: (1) a very superficial knowledge of human sinfulness, in affirming a *dispositio, praeparatio* and *cooperatio* on the part of man as necessarily preceding and making way for justification; (2) a confounding of *justificatio* with *sanctificatio* in the conception of the central idea itself; (3) a most insufficient representation of the nature of faith; (4) an over-valuation of good works after conversion, investing the whole Christian life with a Pelagianistic complexion; and (5) lastly, an entire want of evangelical freedom and assurance.

catholicos indubitata, indulgentiis juvari posse animas, quae in purgatorio poenas luunt. [Trans. "There exists in the church a treasury of satisfactions from the infinite sufferings of Christ, which can never be exhausted." Robert Bellarmine, *Tractatus de indulgentiis* I.2 (Schaff's reference to ch. 1 is in error) (Vives, 7:20a). "*To this treasury of extra satisfactions belong also the sufferings of the blessed Virgin Mary and all the other saints, who suffered more than their sins required.*" *Tract. de indulg.* I.2 (Vives, 7:20b). "Moreover, it is a thing most certain and undoubted among catholics that with indulgences souls are able to helped, which pay the penalties in purgatory." *Tract. de indulg.* I.14 (Vives, 7:51a).] Theologians of more evangelical views in the Romish Church, such as Hirscher, regard indulgences, to be sure, as the regular continuation simply of the early penitential discipline, a remnant of the old church punishments. But the whole practice of the Church serves to confirm the other view.

33. Sess. VI, cap. 9 and 12, and can. 13–16.

[The Protestant doctrine of justification]

Now in all these points, which are inseparably connected with the doctrine of justification itself, the Protestant system, both as Lutheran and orthodox Reformed, exhibits a greater depth of Christian consciousness, and an advance consequently upon the soteriology of the Middle Ages. The doctrine as it stands in this system presupposes necessarily a much more thorough knowledge of sin, the guilt of which is to be taken away by justification. The natural state of man, or his original depravity, is viewed not simply as a debilitation of the moral powers, *egestas naturalis, justitiae debitae nuditas* ["a natural lack, a want of the righteousness due"], as Thomas Aquinas expresses it; but as a real corruption of these powers, of such sort, that before the introduction of a new life-giving principle into his person, so far as a *justitia spiritualis* ["spiritual righteousness"] is concerned on which all turns in the case, he is unable to produce from himself anything that is good. After the will has once made choice of evil, it is no longer free, no longer an undecided *liberum arbitrium* ["free will"]; but on the contrary, it is filled with the contents of evil, sold under its power, and thus an object of divine wrath.[34] The only disposition then which Protestantism can require, and in fact does require,[35] as a prerequisite to justification, is the consciousness of guilt awakened by the judicial function of the law, that "schoolmaster to Christ," and grounded on this the felt need of redemption, which is still included in our nature in spite of its corruption, and without which indeed redemption could have no place. This repentance and desire however are so little operative and meritorious as it regards justification that they form rather the sense of complete unworthiness, the feeling of absolute emptiness and want, resembling bodily hunger, which craves food, but has no power to satisfy its own call.

The renovation of the sinner can proceed only from the creative grace of God. If the divine goodness in the first creation formed for itself its own object, this is necessary much more in redemption, where its object is in the first place its opposite

34. That the tract may not be unduly extended, we must limit ourselves mostly to mere references, leaving the reader to consult the proof passages for himself, as every Protestant divine at any rate should have them within reach. We cite the Lutheran symbols from the edition of Hase (*Libri Symbolici*, 1837); the Reformed, as published by Niemeyer (*Collectio Confessionum in Ecclesiis Reformatis publicatarum*, [Leipzig: Klinkhardt,] 1840). On original sin, and the whole state of the unregenerate, see *Confessio Augustana* [Augsburg Confession, 1530], Art. 2, pp. 9 ff; *Apologia Confessionis* [*Apology of the Augsburg Confession*, by Philipp Melanchthon, 1530], Art. 1, *de peccato origine*, pp. 50 ff; *Articuli Smalcaldici* [Articles of Smalcald, 1537], III, 1, pp. 317 ff. On the Reformed side, *Confessio Helvetica* II [Second Helvetic Confession, 1566], c. 8–9, pp. 477 ff.; *Catechismus Heidelbergensis* [Heidelberg Catechism, 1563], quaest. 7–8, p. 431; *Articuli Anglicani* [Thirty-Nine Articles of Religion of the Church of England, 1563], Art. 9, p. 603; *Confessio Fidei Gallicana* [Gallican, or French Confession, 1559], Art. 10–11, p. 332; *Confessio Belgica* [Belgic Confession, 1561] Art. 15, p. 370; *Confessio Scoticana* I, Art 3, p. 342; *Canones Synodi Dordrechtanae* [Canons of the Synod of Dordt, 1618], cap. 3, Art. 1–3, p. 708 ff.; and *Confessio Fidei Westmonasterienses sive Puritanae* [Westminster Confession of Faith, 1647], c. 6, § 1–6; c. 9, § 1–5.

35. Comp., for example, *Formula Concordiae* [Formula of Concord, 1577] V. de lege et evangelio ["Of Law and Gospel"], p. 711.

also and enemy (Rom. 5:10). Not the love we bear to God, but the love with which he has loved us in Christ, is the ground of our salvation (1 John 4:10). This love accordingly has prevented [preceded] us; it has borne all sin and expiated all guilt in our stead, but fulfilled at the same time all righteousness, as required by the law, that is the published will of God. This all-sufficient satisfaction of Christ takes hold upon the individual subjectively in justification. This is a judicial, declarative act on the part of God, by which he first pronounces the sin-crushed, contrite sinner free from guilt as it regards the past, for the sake of his Only Begotten Son, and then ("freely": Rom 3:24; "without the deeds of the law": v. 28; "by grace, through faith, and not of himself ": Eph 2:8) makes over to him, in boundless mercy, the full righteousness of the same, to be counted and to be in fact his own. It is in this way (1) negatively *remissio peccatorum* ["a remission of sins"] (Ps 32:12; Rom 3:25; 4:7; Luke 11:4; 2 Cor 5:19) and (2) positively *imputatio justitiae* ["an imputation of righteousness"] and *adoptio in filios Dei* ["an adoption as sons of God"] (Rom 4:5; 5.9; 2 Cor 5:21; Gal 3:6; Phil 3:9). Man by justification steps into the place of Christ, as Christ had previously stepped into the place of man. What he did altogether, he did not for himself, but out of free self-sacrificing love towards the human race, of which he is the head.[36]

36. *Conf. Aug.*, Art. 4, p. 10; *Apol. Conf.*, Art. 2, p. 71 ff; *Form. Conc.*, Art. 3, pp. 683ff.: *Unanimi consensu credimus, docemus et confitemur, . . . quod homo peccator coram Deo justificetur, h. e. absolvatur ab omnibus suis peccatis et a judicio justissimae condemnationis, et adoptetur in numerum filiorum Dei, atque haeres aeternae vitae scribatur, sine ullis nostris meritis aut dignitate, et absque ullis praecedentibus aut sequentibus nostris operibus, ex mera gratia tantummodo, propter unicum meritum perfectissimamque obedientiam, passionem acerbissimam, mortem et resurrectionem Dom. nostri J. Chr., cujus obedientia nobis ad justitiam imputatur.* [Trans. "We unanimously believe, teach, and confess, . . . that poor sinful people are justified before God, that is, absolved—pronounced free of all sins, and of the judgment of damnation that they deserved and accepted as children and heirs of enternal life ——without the least bit of our own 'merit or worthiness,' apart from all preceding, present, or subsequent works. We are justified on the basis of sheer grace, because of the sole merit, entire obedience, and bittersuffering, death, and resurrection of our Lord Christ, whose obedience alone is reckoned to us as righteousness." *Formula of Concord*, part II, article III, in Robert Kolb and Timothy J. Wengert, ed., *Book of Concord: The Confessions of the Evangelical Lutheran Church* (Minneapolis: Fortress, 2000), 563.] Reformed symbols: *Conf. Helv.*, c. 15, pp. 494 ff: *Justificare significat-Apostolo in disputatione de justificatione, peccata remittere, a culpa et poene absolvere, in gratiam recipere et justum pronunciare etc.* [Trans. "What is justification? According to the apostle in his treatment of justification, to justify means to remit sins, to absolve from guilt and punishment, to receive into favor, and to pronounce a man just." *C&C*, 2:486.]; *Cat. Heidelb.*, quaest. 60, p. 443: *Ut . . . sine ullo meo merito* (Rom. 3:24) *ex mera Dei misericordia* (Tit. 3:5; Eph. 2:8, 9) *mihi perfecta satisfictio* (1 John 2:2), *justitia et sanctitas Christi* (1 John 2:1) *imputetur ac donetur* (Rom. 4:4,5; 2 Cor. 5:19*), perinde ac si nec ullum ipse peccatum admisissem, nec ulla mihi labes inhaereret, imo vere quasi eam obedientiam, quam pro me Christus praestitit, ipse perfecte praestitissem* (2 Cor. 5:21)—a most clear, complete and valuable definition. [Trans. "That. . .without any merit of my own, out of pure grace, [God] grants me the benefits of the perfect expiation of Christ, imputing to me his righteousness and holiness as if I had never committed a single sin or had ever been sinful, having fulfilled myself all the obedience which Christ has carried out for me." *C&C*, 2:440.] *Art. Anglic.*, Art. 11, 12, pp. 603 ff.; *Conf. Gallic.*, Art. 18, p. 334; *Conf. Belg.*, Art. 22, p. 374; *Conf. Scot.*, Art. 12, p. 346; *Declar. Thorum.*, de gratia, p. 673 [Declaration of Thorn, 1645, "On Grace"]; *Can. Syn. Dordr.*, III, c. 10, p. 710; *Conf. Westmonast.*, cap. 11, de justif. § 1–6, and c. 12.

In this way, all Pelagian and Semi-Pelagian self-righteousness is torn up by the roots; humility is exhibited as the ground of piety; and all rightful honor is secured to Jesus Christ as the only and all sufficient Mediator between God and man.

While the merit of Christ is thus viewed as the only ground, the efficient cause (*causa efficiens* and *emeritoria*) of this righteousness, the only means of its appropriation (*causa instrumentalis, instrumentum, organon lepticon*) ["the cause instrumental, the instrument, the receiving organism"] is presented to us in faith. This is not a natural product of man, although it finds a basis in the possibility and want of redemption belonging to his fallen nature; but the free gift of God, which is offered and imparted to him through the word and sacraments.[37] Nor is it moreover, as regarded in the Romish system (and this is a very essential point) a mere historical assent, and so a theoretic process simply; but along with this, and principally, a cordial unconditional *trust* in the atoning efficacy of Christ's merit, a *personal appropriation* of it to the entire spiritual life of the subject.[38] It holds, back of the psychological distinction of understanding and will, in the inmost depth of man's personality, and so works

37. *Conf. Aug.*, V, p. 11: *Nam per verbum et sacrementa, tamquam per instrumenta, donatur Spiritus Sanctus, qui fidem efficit, ubi et quando visum est Deo, in iis, qui audiunt evangelium, etc.* [Trans. "For through the word and the sacraments, as through instruments, the Holy Spirit is given, and the Holy Spirit produces faith, where and when it pleases God, in those who hear the gospel." *C&C*, 2:61.] *Conf. Helv.*, Art. 16, p. 496: *Haec autem fides merum est Dei donum, quod solus Deus ex gratia sua electis suis, secundum mensuram, et quando, cui et quantum ipse vult, donat, et quidem per spiritum sanctum, mediante praedicatione evangelii et oratione fideli.* [Trans. "But this faith is a pure gift of God which God alone of his graces gives to his elect according to his measure when, to whom, and to the degree he wills. And he does this by the Holy Spirit by means of the preaching of the gospel and steadfast prayer." *C&C*, 2:488.]

38. Besides the passages already cited, comp. *Conf. Aug.*, Art. 20, p. 18. More fully in his *Loci theologici*, p. 226 (1562 ed.) [Melanchthon, *Loci communes theologici* (Basel: Ioannem Oporinum, 1562), 226], MELANCHTHON describes the nature of faith, first as an *assentiri universo verbo divino* [Trans. "assenting to the entire word of God"], and further as a *fiducia misericordiae Dei* [Trans. "trust in the mercy of God"], and then proceeds: *Fiducia est* motus in voluntate, *necessario respondens assensioni, seu quo voluntas* in Christo acquiescit. [Trans. "For trust is *an action of the will* which of necessity responds to the assent, or an action by which the will *meets Christ*." Philipp Melanchthon, *Loci Communes 1543*, trans. J. A. O. Preus (St. Louis: Concordia, 1992), 89–90.] Comp. CALVIN's *Instit. Chr. Rel.*, III, 2, 8; *Conf. Helv.*, Art 16, p. 496: *Fides Christiana non est opinio et humana persuasio, sed* firmissima fiducia *et* evidens ac constans animi assensus, *denique* certissima comprehensio veritatis Dei, *propositae in scripturis et symbolo apostolico, atque adeo* Dei ipsius, *summi boni, et praecipue promissionis divinae et Christi, qui omnium promissionum est colophon.* [Trans. "Christian faith is not an opinion or human conviction, but *a most firm trust and a clear and steadfast assent of the mind*, and then *a most certain apprehension of truth of God* presented in the Scriptures and in the Apostles' Creed, and thus also *of God himself*, the greatest good, and especially of God's promise and of Christ who is the fulfillment of all promises." *C&C*, 2:488.] Most masterly also, and drawn from the deepest experience, is the definition of faith by the *Heidelberg Catechism* in its answer to the 21st question. No such deep views of the constitution of faith had been taken since the time of the apostles. SARPI [Paolo Sarpi the *History of the Council of Trent*, trans. Nathanael Brent, (London, 1676). It was first published in Italian in 1619.] relates that the bishops of the Council of Trent were not able to conceive of it as anything more than assent simply to historical truth; and that they were brought into the greatest embarrassment with the subject, since they could find no satisfactory light, either from the fathers or the schoolmen, on what had not before come under thorough discussion.

with like influences upon both. The later Protestant theologians tried accordingly to exhaust the conception of faith, as much as might be, under three characters. The first is *notitia*, the knowledge of its object, Jesus Christ namely and his all sufficient merit; the second, *assensus*, free inward consent to all the scriptures teach of the mercy of God in Christ; the third, which is most essential and full of comfort, *fiducia*, or the act of the will moving towards Christ and resting in him for redemption, the confidence that this grace is not only of general objective force, but personally proper also to the believing subject himself.

In what relation now does this justification stand to *holiness*, faith as thus described to *works*? Decided as Protestantism is in limiting all justifying efficacy to the apprehension of Christ's merit by means of faith, it is just as far from denying, however remotely, the necessary connection between this grace and a godly life. This even the most shrewd, clear-sighted and profound of modern opposers of the system, has been constrained to admit when he says: "It would be *in the highest degree unfair* however, not to add that according to the Lutheran theory, the apprehension of this free remission of sins must always draw after it the renewal of the sinner, and a transformation of his life to holiness."[39]

Genuine Protestantism has ever in its eye the faith of Paul that works by love—or to speak with the Helvetic Confession, the *fides, nulla operum fiducia* is at the same time *operum fæcundissima.*[40] Its very being consists in the appropriation of Christ, the holy and the just. How then should it *not* produce good works as necessarily as a good tree must yield good fruit? It is the parent of all virtues. As soon as we have known and believed the love which God has towards us (1 John 4:16), we cannot but love him in return (v. 19).[41] This relation between faith and love is of such inward force

39. [This is probably a translation of a sentence from Möhler, *Symbolik*.]

40. [Trans. the "faith that has no confidence in works" is at the same time "of works the most fruitful." *First Helvetic Confession,* article 14, in Schaff, *Creeds of Christendom*, 2:219.]

41. *Conf. Aug.*, Art. 6, p. 11; Art. 20, pp. 15, 16; *Apol. Conf.*, Art. 3, pp. 83, 85. In the latter, pp. 133 ff., it is said: *Ideo justificamur, ut justi bene operari et obedire Legi Dei incipiamus. Ideo regeneramur et Spiritum Sanctum acoipimus, ut nova vita habeat nova opera, novos affectus, timorem, dilectionem Dei, odium concupiscentiae, etc.* ["We are justified for this very purpose, that, being righteous, we might begin to do good works and obey god's law. For this purpose we are reborn and receive the Holy Spirit, that this new life might have new works and new impulses, the fear and love of God, hatred of lust, etc." *Apology of the Augsburg Confession,* Tappert, *Book of Concord,* 160. (The more recent Kolb and Wengert, *Book of Concord* uses a different edition of the *Apology* than Schaff cites.)] *Form. Conc.* epit. Art. 3, p. 586; Art. 4, p. 589; sol. decl. Art. 3, p. 688. The noble passage of Luther in his *Preface to the Epistle to the Romans*, is known: "Oh, it is a living, busy, active, mighty thing with faith, that it cannot possibly cease from working good. It does not ask either if good works are to be done, but before the question is put it has done them already and is doing them still. . . .; so that it is impossible to sunder works from faith, as much so verily, as that burning and shining should be sundered from fire." [*Preface to the Epistle of St. Paul to the Romans* (1546) in *LW* 35:370.] The Reformed symbols, without exception, press this point in terms equally strong, and in actual life indeed this Church has shown herself more zealous for good works even than her sister. I refer only to *Conf. Helv.* II, Art. 16, pp. 496 ff.; and *Cat. Heidelb.*, Q 64, p. 444: *neque enim fieri potest, quin ii, qui Christo per fidem insiti sunt, fructus proferant gratitudinis.* [Trans. "For it is impossible for those who are engrafted into Christ

that this last also can have no place without the first, as little as one may gather grapes from thorns. Faith is always necessarily presupposed in love; for what does not spring from faith is sin, and so not love—the essence of which is a forsaking of self, while self-seeking forms the inmost nature of evil.

> Good religious works make never a good religious man, but a good religious man maketh good religious works. So that always the person must first be religious and good before all good works, and good religious works follow and go forth from the religious good person. As the tree must be before the fruit, so must the man be first good or bad in his person, before he doeth good or bad works. The like we see in all handiwork. A good or bad house maketh not a good or bad carpenter, but a good or bad carpenter maketh a good or bad house. No work maketh a master, such as is the work; but as the master is, his work also is such. . . . Works, as they make not believing, so they make not pious either. But faith, as it maketh pious, so doth it make good works also.[42]

Protestantism in this way only places faith and love in their natural relation to each other without detracting in the least from the dignity of the last. Rather, with the apostle Paul, it puts this highest, for the very reason that it comes last; as the beginning is always the less perfect that points to a more complete form of existence. The Evangelical morality, as the product of free love and gratitude, is also much more sound, pure, deep, than the Roman Catholic, which even in its highest exhibitions must be allowed to include a sinful mixture of spiritual pride or mechanical formality.

Good works then, in the Protestant system, are held to be acceptable to God; and it is taught even that God rewards them graciously.[43] But no room is left for the

---

by true faith not to bring forth the fruit of gratitude." *C&C*, 2:441.]

42. LUTHER's sermon on the Liberty of a Christian Man; one of his most profound productions (edition by Gerlach, vol. V, pp. 37 ff.) [*The Freedom of a Christian* in *LW* 31: 327–77]. The two theses of LUTHER, "*If faith be not without all work, it maketh not righteous*" and "*It is impossible that justifying faith should be without constantly many good works*," have been tiresomely paraded by the papists as an irreconcilable contradiction. To this however SARTORIUS has rightly answered that both agree admirably, and the more the truth of the one is seen, the more true must the other show itself to be at the same time (*Evangel. Kirchenzeitung*, 1835. p. 826). In proportion as the man, renouncing himself, ascribes his salvation only and altogether to God's preventing love, the more deep and inward will be the devotion of his love in return, and his grateful zeal in all good works; which flow the more richly from faith, as its fruit, the less they are made to go before it, or take rank with it, in the way of principle or ground. As for the dictum finally of the same great reformer, so ignorantly misconstrued, *Si in fide fieri posset adulterium, peccatum non esset* [Trans. "if adultery could be committed in faith it would not be a sin"]: we must bear in mind the bold, reckless, wholesale, sweeping style in which he was accustomed to speak; and then reflect further, that with him no such sin could be committed in faith, that he argues simply *ex impossibili*.

43. *Apol. Conf.*, Art. 3, pp. 96, 135; *Form. Conc.*, Art. 4, pp. 70 ff.; *Conf. Helv.* II. c. 16, p. 498: *Placent vero approbanturque a Deo opera, quae a nobis fiunt per fidem. —Etenim docemus Deum bona operantibus amplam dare mercedem. —Referimus tamen mercedem hanc, quam Dominus dat, non ad meritum hominis accipientis, sed ad bonitatem, vel liberalitatem et veritatem Dei promittentis atque dantis, qui cum nihil debeat cuiquam, promisit tamen, etc.* [Trans. "Now the works which we do by faith are pleasing to God and are approved by him.—For we teach that God gives a rich reward to those

imagination that we can earn salvation by their means, much less to think of any surplus merit. The entire Christian life is made to appear as a *debt of gratitude* for the boundless, eternally to be praised, love and mercy of God manifested towards us in Jesus Christ.[44] When we have done all accordingly, we have at best done only what was our duty (Luke 17:10). Sanctification however is in its nature a continually progressive work that becomes complete only when the whole body of the Church, of which the individual Christian is a member, has reached its state of perfection. Yea, strictly considered, even the best works of the believer, so long as he sojourns in the body, by reason of the continued presence of sin in his person, are not good absolutely, but only so much and so far as they are wrought in him and through him by the Spirit of God.[45] If he might say even with the apostle, "I know nothing by myself," that is am conscious of no wrong, he must with, him, also, still add, "yet am I not hereby *justified*" [1 Cor 4:4]. His confidence of salvation consequently can never rest upon his works of love, but only upon the objective rock of Christ's merit, whose he feels himself to be in faith. Even Paul himself, the apostle, at the end of his career—a career such as no saint of the Romish Church certainly can exhibit—declares it to be the highest object of his desire that he might not have his own righteousness, which was of the law, but a foreign righteousness, which was of faith in Christ, the righteousness namely that is of God by faith (Phil 3:9).

The last point of difference in the case before us regards the *assurance* of justification. Being justified by grace through faith, we have peace, the apostle tells us, with God (Rom 5:1–5). This peace is a state of mind, which necessarily attends the exercise

who do good works.—However, we do not ascribe this reward, which the Lord gives, to the merit of the man who receives it, but to the goodness, generosity, and truthfulness of God who promises and gives it, and who, although he owes nothing to anyone, nevertheless promises." *C&C*, 2:490–91.] *Conf. Belg.*, Art. 24, p. 378: *Interea non negamus, Deum bona opera in suis remunerari; sed id mera sua gratia fieri dicimus, ut qui dona sua in nobis coronet.* [Trans. "Yet we do not wish to deny that God rewards good works—but it is by his grace that he crowns his gifts." *C&C*, 2:417.]

44. With admirable judgment accordingly, the Heidelberg Catechism has comprehended all Christian practice under the article of Gratitude. The *Conf. Helv.* II, Art. 16, p. 497, agreeing with this says: *(Bona opera) fieri debent, non ut his promereamur vitam aeternam, Donum Dei enim est, ut apostolus ait, vita aeterna; neque ad ostentationem, quam rejecit Dominus Matth. 6; neque ad quaestum, quem et ipsum rejecit Matth. 23; sed ad gloriam Dei, ad, ornandam vocationem nostram gratitudinemque Deo praestandam, et utilitatem proximi.* [Trans. "These same works ought not to be done in order that we may earn eternal life by them, for, as the apostle says, eternal life is the gift of God. Nor are they to be done for ostentation which the Lord rejects in Mathew 6, nor for gain which he also rejects in Matthew 23, but for the glory of God, to adorn our calling, to show gratitude to God, and for the profit of the neighbor." *C&C*, 2:489.] *Artic. Ang.*, Art. 14.

45. *Conf. Helv.* II, c. 16, p. 499: *Sunt multa praeterea indigna Deo, et imperfecta plurima inveniuntur in operibus etiam sanctorum.* [Trans. "Moreover, in the works even of the saints there is much that is unworthy of God and very much that is imperfect." *C&C*, 2:491.] Luther's word is known: *Justus in omni bono opere peccat.* [Trans. "The just man sins in every good work." The form of this statement quoted here by Schaff is that attributed to Luther by Leo X in the bull *Exsurge Domine.* It is listed as #31 in the catalog of Luther's errors, which appears to be a paraphrase of statements made by Luther in *Against Latomus.* See *LW* 32:159 ff., 253–54; cf. also *LW* 31:323.]

of faith. For God is the fullness of all blessedness; and faith is the possession of God; consequently in itself of beatifying nature, in itself the assurance of salvation. To be united to God in Christ is to be saved. But faith is the consciousness of this communion. As nothing makes a man living but life, nothing makes him joyful or loving but joy or love, so he can be made blessed only by faith, which is the same thing with blessedness itself.[46] At the same time to be sure, since faith is at one time large and strong, as Luther says, at another small and weak, this assurance of justification must naturally rise and fall in the same way.[47]

[Principal objections answered]

Before passing over to the formal principle, it may be well, in view of the immense importance of the Protestant doctrine of justification, to notice the most acute and weighty objections that have been urged against it on the part of Roman Catholic and pseudo-Protestant, or rationalistic opposers.

1. One of the most common reproaches is that "the Protestant theory of justification encourages a thoughtless reliance on grace and neglect of good works." Here however the curse turns into a blessing. For the same reproach was brought against the doctrine of the apostle Paul;[48] and it serves to show consequently that we agree

46. This assurance of salvation, as secured to us by faith, is proclaimed in the loftiest style by the old Church psalmody, and by LUTHER himself in a thousand places; as for instance in his sermon on the gosp. D. 20. p. trin. [Luther, *Church Postil*, Gospel for the 20th Sunday after Trinity] where among other things he says: "If death make onset, so have I Christ; he is my life. If sin make onset, so have I Christ; he is my righteousness. If hell and damnation make onset, so have I Christ: he is my salvation. Set in upon me thus what may, still I have Christ; him I can hold forward as my shield, so that nothing can do me harm." CALVIN's Instit. III, 2, 16—*In summa: vere fidelis non est, nisi qui solida persuasione Deum sibi propitium benevolumque patrem esse persuasus, de ejus benignitate omnia sibi pollicetur; nisi que divinae erga se benevolentiae promissionibus fretus, indubitatam salutis expectationem praesumit.* [Trans. "Briefly, he alone is truly a believer who, convinced by a firm conviction that God is a kindly and well-disposed Father toward him, promises himself all things on the basis of his generosity; who relying upon the promises of divine benevolence toward him, lays hold on an undoubted expectation of salvation." John Calvin, *Institutes of the Christian Religion*, ed. John T. McNeill, trans. Ford Lewis Battles (Philadelphia: Westminster Press, 1960) 1:562.]

47. CALVIN's *Instit.* III, 2, 17: *Nos certe dum fidem docemus esse debere certam et securam, non certitudinem aliquam imaginamur, quae nulla tangatur dubitatione, nec securitatem, quae nulla sollicitudine impetatur; quin potius dicimus, perpetuum esse fidelibus certamen cum sua ipsorum diffidentia. Tantum abest ut eorum conscientias in placida aliqua quiete collocemus, quae nullis omnino turbis interpelletur.* [Trans. "Surely, while we teach that faith ought to be certain and assured, we cannot imagine any certainty that is not tinged with doubt, or any assurance that is not assailed by some anxiety. On the other hand, we say that believers are in perpetual conflict with their own unbelief. Far, indeed, are we from putting their consciences in any peaceful repose, undisturbed by any tumult at all." Calvin, *Institutes*, 1:562.]

48. Rom. 3:8: "We be slanderously reported, and some affirm that we say, Let us do evil that good may come." Rom. 5:10 compared with 6:1; Gal. 5.13. When Peter says, in his 2nd epistle, 3:16, that "there are some things in the epistles of Paul hard to understand, which they that are unlearned and unstable wrest to their own destruction," he has the doctrine of justification mainly in his eye.

with him. As he could triumphantly point such calumniators to the moral exhortations contained in all his epistles and also to his own life, so do we with like confidence hold up to our opponents our symbolical books, and the lives of the Reformers themselves, whose moral earnestness and untiring practical activity were such as to cast all their cotemporaries into the shade.

2. "It is not possible that God, who is truth itself, can declare a man to be righteous, and treat him as such, when he is not such in fact." The mere *treatment* involves no difficulty. Even in the sphere of the natural life, God treats us better than we deserve, causing the sun to shine and giving rain for the benefit of the ungodly as well as of the good and pious. The nature of grace, which falls it is true beyond the range of abstract justice, consists always in this, that the offender is released from merited punishment and put into the positive enjoyment of freedom, that being thus subdued and humbled, he may be led to pursue a better life. Love also in general, of which grace is only a particular modification, shows in its highest utterances the very same character, without which it could never be exercised towards an enemy. When some unfortunate has fallen into the water, the philanthropist stops not to inquire, even if it be his own enemy, whether he is worthy of being rescued, but plunges at once into the stream, and by his noble, self-forgetting conduct wins the heart of him whose life he saves.

The whole difficulty then in the case before us must turn, not upon God's treatment of the believer, but upon the idea of his *declaring* a man to be what he is not in fact. If however practice and judgment are to be saved from irreconcilable contradiction with each other, the first must involve here the supposition again of the second. When God is represented by the apostle as having loved men while they were yet sinners, it does not mean that he loved them as sinners, which would be to have loved sin itself in them, whereas this is always his abomination; but he loved them as creatures, who were capable of redemption, and in this view worthy of being loved. He loved the divine nature which was in them potentially, having reality indeed only in his own purpose, but destined, through the manifestation of his grace and love, to actualize itself and become real subjectively also in man himself.

Men are declared righteous then by God, not so far as they are sinners, but so far only as they are in Christ, and have thus in this objective way the principle of righteousness in fact; and this justifying act becomes itself the occasion by which the principle is actualized in its subject, having creative force, quickening the dead, and calling into existence that which had no existence before. The justifying grace of God does not stand over against the convicted sinner in an abstract form, but passes over to him through the medium of faith, sets him in its own element, and thus lodges in his person a life germ altogether new, in which is comprehended from the start the entire growth of holiness. So Abraham was called a father of many nations, before he was so actually.[49] Ideally however, in the divine plan he was such in the fullest sense.

49. [Gen 17:5.]

God, before whom the dimensions of time all give way in the same vast eternity, looks upon men in their inmost nature as rooted in Christ, with whom they are brought into living union by faith. For the relation of Christ to humanity is not outward, but inward and essential. He is the second Adam, the spiritual head of the race, the true center of all its individual personalities, in which only the idea of the whole is fully realized and made complete. This whole objection then proceeds upon a perfectly abstract conception of the doctrine of justification, which admits the thought of a judgment in the divine mind that is not at the same time creative; and only against such a conception of the case can it be allowed to have any force. Many of the Lutheran theologians did indeed lean towards this extreme, in their anti-Pelagian zeal; but it was not so with the Reformed. They always acknowledged the true element here in the catholic doctrine, without sanctioning its Pelagianistic trait.[50] For there still remains always this great distinction, that the principle of righteousness in man as answering to the justifying act of God never flows even in part from his own subjective constitution, but only and altogether from his believing union with the objective Christ, and that the actualization of this principle in his person is itself conditioned by the declaratory act, creative at the same time, going before.

3. "It is unreasonable to ascribe all justifying and saving power to faith and to deny such virtue to love, when the apostle Paul nevertheless, who is in such great authority with Protestants, places love above faith, 1 Cor 13:13."[51] We too proclaim love to be the highest, the always abiding; but precisely for this reason it is not to be found in guilty man, immersed in selfishness and sin, but only in God himself,

50. Comp. particularly the whole 11th chapter of the third book of Calvin's *Institutes*; for example, § 6, where this agreement and difference are both very clearly stated: *Sicut non potest decerpi Christus in partes, ita inseparabilia esse haec duo, quae simul et conjunctim in ipso percipimus, justitiam et sanctificationem. Quoscunque ergo in gratiam recipit Deus, simul spiritu adoptionis donat, cujus virtute eos reformat ad suam imaginem. Verum, si solis claritas non potest a calore separari, an ideo dicemus luce calefieri terram, calore vero illustrari? Hac similitudine nihil ad rem praesentem magis aceomodum: sol calore suo terram vegetat ac fecundat, radiis suis illustrat et illuminat: hic mutua est ac individua connexio, transferre tamen quod unius peculiare est, ad alterum, ratio ipsa prohibet.* [Trans. "As Christ cannot be torn into parts, so these two which we perceive in him together and conjointly are inseparable—namely, righteousness and sanctification. Whomever, therefore, God receives into grace, on them he at the same time bestows the spirit of adoption by whose power he remakes them to his own image. But if the brightness of the sun cannot be separated from its heat, shall we therefore say that the earth is warmed by its light, or lighted by its heat? Is there anything more applicable to the present matter than this comparison? The sun, by its heat, quickens and fructifies the earth, by its beams brightens and illumines it. Here is a mutual and indivisible connection. Yet reason itself forbids us to transfer the peculiar qualities of the one to the other." Calvin, *Institutes*, 1:732.]

51. In similar style the argument was pressed by an opponent upon Melanchthon: *dilectio est maxima virtus; ergo dilectio justificat.* [Trans. "Love is the greatest virtue: therefore, love justifies."] Melanchthon, however, draws from the proposition just the opposite conclusion: *dilectio est maxima virtus, atqui nos eam* minime *praestamus; ergo per dilectionem* minime *justi sumus.* [Trans. "Love is the greatest virtue, but in fact we perform it *the least*. Therefore by love we are justified *the least*." Melanchthon responds to this argument from opponents, but without this exact response, in *The Chief Theological Topics: Loci praecipui theologici 1559*. trans. J. A. O. Preus (St. Louis: Concordia, 2011), 205–7.]

the fountain of all love. So the only way of coming to God and becoming assured of his love in Christ, through the knowledge and apprehension of which we are made first capable of love in return, is no other than faith itself; which is simply what our doctrine asserts. The fruit is better than the root; and yet this last carries the tree, and not the first. In this objection moreover, it is forgotten that all justifying and saving power, causatively considered, is lodged according to our view neither in human faith, to which we attribute only instrumental efficacy, nor in human love, but exclusively in God's grace, that the glory of this may remain complete.

4. Adroitly constructed is the objection: "Faith in the protestant view is justifying, not as a dead historical assent, but in the character of inward humility and trust, as a longing after the Redeemer, as love consequently though in its infancy; and thus the theory, to preserve itself, falls back again unwittingly to the Roman Catholic dogma." Now we may well allow that there *is* an ultimate point where faith may be regarded as a constituent in the development of love, taken in its broadest sense. But unless all ideas are to lose themselves in one another promiscuously, we must distinguish and separate on the one hand, as closely as we seek connecting relations on the other. Only in the use of such reflective separation is any scientific knowledge possible. We say then, that fallen man, sold under the power of selfishness, which is the very opposite of love, in order that he may come to the exercise of this grace—in its true Christian, self-renouncing, self-sacrificing form—must first become conscious of the divine love in its relation to himself personally, must *yield* himself to *Christ's love*; and this is itself the exercise of faith. The receptive element must go before the spontaneous; humble apprehension before self-subsisting action. We are always brought back accordingly to the Protestant thesis that man is justified and saved, not by the love which he exercises himself, but by the love he receives from abroad, that is by faith.

[2. The formal principle]

So much for the *material* principle of Protestantism, by which direct and full access has been made good for man to the grace of God in Christ. This doctrine was brought to the consciousness of the Reformers, in their inward spiritual conflicts, by means of the written word of God. While tradition as it then stood contradicted it entirely, directing men for salvation not to faith, but to mechanical outward observances and forms, the almost forgotten bible was felt to preach the glorious truth, distinctly and loudly, from beginning to end.[52] Thus as Christ became to them all in all, his word

52. This experience is described in a lovely way by Luther himself: "Then (after coming to a clear sense of justification by faith) at once I felt that I was new born, and had now found a wide, open door to enter into paradise itself; *saw now moreover the precious scriptures in a very different light, from all they seemed before; ran accordingly soon through the whole bible, and gathered in other passages also according to this rule all its expositions of what is meant by God's work, God's righteousness, and God's faith*. And as before I hated this little word right heartily—God's righteousness!—so I began now to hold the same high and dear as the sweetest and most comforting to me of all words, and this same

also was taken for the separate and sufficient fountain of their religious knowledge. To the material or life principle of the Reformation accordingly, is joined as its necessary complement the *formal* or *knowledge principle*; which consists in this, that the *word of God*, as it has been handed down to us in the canonical books of the Old and New Testaments, *is the pure and proper source as well as the only certain measure of all saving truth.*

We find here now a similar relation to that which we have already met in the case of the material principle, and a correspondence between the terms on both sides. The word of God answers to faith, and tradition to love. As the doctrine of justification refers back to the doctrine of sin as its necessary presupposition, so does the doctrine of the authority of the scriptures also to a corresponding view of the relation of the natural reason to revelation. The more favorable the view that is taken of the will of man in its natural state, the less will be the account made of the blindness of the understanding as going hand in hand with sin, and the higher the consequence attached to the word of man, as well as to his works, in the business of salvation; and so the reverse will hold also in every point. Hence Romanism, as it makes faith and works to be parallel sources of justification and lays the main stress in fact practically upon the last, is only consistent with itself when it invests, here also in the sphere of the formal principle, the word of God and human tradition with equal authority as sources of religious knowledge, and gives the second in reality the preference above the first. Protestantism, on the contrary, places both powers in each case in their natural relation to each other, in the relation namely of ground and consequence, cause and effect, origin and process. Faith alone justifies, but produces at the same time good works as its necessary fruit; the word of God is the only fountain and norm of knowledge, but it flows forward in the Church, and comes there continually to clearer and deeper consciousness. As moreover, according to this view, the value of works is estimated by the measure of the faith that forms their ground, so the worth of tradition also is determined by its organic connection and agreement with the word of God.

Inasmuch however as history is ever developed by means of more or less one-sided antagonisms, it was natural that with the Reformation, in opposition to the reigning overvaluation of *man's works and man's word*, the principal emphasis should be placed upon *God's* grace and *God's* word; not with the repudiation indeed, but with some neglect at least of the other side. This was the case particularly with regard to tradition.[53] The neglect here is the more to be excused, since the Church of Rome

passage in St. Paul became to me of a truth the very gate of paradise." [Preface to the Wittenberg edition of *Luthers Werke* (1545); *Weimarer Ausgabe* LIV, 185 ff. *LW* 34:337.]

53. We may notice here incidentally, in passing, a very important fundamental peculiarity of the Lutheran Church as distinguished from the Reformed. This communion, in its genuine form and life, has more respect for tradition than the Reformed, and its development accordingly has been more historical and gradual, and more largely conservative of what was old; whilst the Reformed, in Puritanism particularly, proceeded more violently, and by its contempt for history furnished occasion, in part at least, for the multiplication of sects. On the other hand, the Reformed Church is

under the credit of apostolical tradition, had smuggled into her communion the most shocking errors and brought the word of God almost entirely into oblivion, had repeatedly prohibited it to the laity indeed in express terms. Tradition was in fact, as Chemnitz says in his *Examen. Conc. Trid.*, the box of Pandora, *cujus operculo omne genus corruptelarum, abusuum et superstitionum in ecclesiam invectum fuit.*[54]

As both principles are thus inwardly connected, being only two different sides indeed of one and the same principle, our exposition of the formal, which is now before us, will be materially assisted by the acquaintance we have formed with the other.

[A. The Roman Catholic doctrine of scripture and tradition]

The Council of Trent receives, according to the first decree of the fourth session, two sources for the knowledge of divine revelation, the word written or the sacred scriptures, and the word unwritten or tradition; and these she makes co-ordinate, in the first instance, as the product of the same Holy Ghost (*pari pietatis affectu ac reverentia suscipit et veneratur*[55]). Such a co-ordination serves itself to depreciate the written word.[56] But this is done still more effectually through the further definitions and restrictions to which it is subjected. In actual practice, the scriptures fall behind tradition, as in the case of the material principle faith falls behind works. For under the written word of God, the Church of Rome understands not merely, as we do, the canonical books of the Old and New Testaments, but in open contradiction to the oldest and purest tradition of an Origen, Athanasius, Eusebius, Hilary, and even her otherwise so much respected Jerome, incorporates into it also the Apocrypha; mere human productions, whatever may be their worth.[57] The distinction between the divine and human is thus unsettled. This pantheistic feature runs through the whole system, culminating in the respect shown towards the pope, as lawfully holding and exercising the threefold office of Christ himself. Too much again is allowed to human agency in the formation of the sacred scriptures by limiting the inspiration of the

more strenuous than the Lutheran in its view of the necessity of good works, and has always displayed accordingly uncommon practical activity in the Christian life; whilst the sister body, reveling in free justification, presses hard on the confines of antinomianism; having been carried in the person of one of her principal champions quite over to the maxim, "Good works hinder salvation!" An exaggeration, which of course the Church soon disowned.

54. [Trans. "under whose cover every kind of corruption, abuse, and superstition has been brought into the church." Chemnitz, *Examination of the Council of Trent*, trans. Fred Kraemer (St. Louis: Concordia, 1971), 1:219.]

55. [Schaff quotes from the Council of Trent, Session IV, *Decretum de canonicis scripturis.* Trans. "accepts and venerates with a like feeling of piety and reverence." *DEC*, 2:663.]

56. For it involves the assumption that there is much wanting in the scriptures that is necessary to salvation, and that they are consequently incomplete; as Bellarmine, *de verbo Dei*, IV, 3, expressly asserts.

57. *Conc. Trid.*, Sess. IV, *decr. de can. script.*, where at the same time the Protestants, for rejecting the Apocrypha, are laid under an anathema.

Holy Ghost to mere assistance and guidance (*assistentia et directio*).[58] Still further, the Latin translation of JEROME, a work of course proceeding from a particular Church position and reflecting its image, is not only placed on a par with the original text, but in actual use preferred to it altogether.[59] In the fourth place, the charge of darkness and ambiguity is brought against the scriptures;[60] whence tradition is held to be necessary for their interpretation; and it is counseled that the laity should not read them, except in cases of special qualification, of which the bishop is to be the judge.[61] In short, the

58. BELLARMINE, *de verbo div.*, I, 15. *Aliter Deus adfuit prophetis, aliter historicis. Illis revelavit futura et simul adstitit, ne aliquid falsi admiscerent in seribendo; his non semper revelavit ea, quae scripturi erant, sed excitavit duntaxat, ut scriberent ea, quae vel viderant, vel audierant, quorum recordabantur, et simul adstitit, ne quid falsi scriberent, quae assistentia non excludebat laborem.* [Trans. "God was active in one way in the prophets, and in another way in the historical writings. To the former he revealed future things and at the same time assisted them, so that nothing false would be mixed with their writing; to the latter he did not always reveal the things which were written, but He merely stirred them up that they might write those things which they had either seen or heard, of which they recalled, and at the same time he assisted so that they might not write anything false, which assistance would not exclude their labor." *In disp. de contr.*, I (*De verbo dei*).1.1 (Vives, 1:100). The Vives text differs considerably from the text of Schaff's quotation here, though without altering the meaning substantially.] The Jesuits proceeded further and admitted without reserve the possibility of error, and even of falsehood outright in the Gospels; as, for example, ALB[ertus] PIGHUIS [1490–1542], *Hierarch. eccles.* 1, 2: *Matthaeus et Ioannes evangelistae potuerunt et* labi memoria *et* mentiri, *etc.* [Trans. "Lapses of memory and false statements may be attributed to the Evangelists Matthew and John." Albrecht Pigghe, *Heirarchiae ecclesiasticae absertio* (Cologne: Neuss, 1544). Translation from Francis Ernest Gigot, *General Introduction to the Holy Scriptures* (New York: Benziger, 1904), 264.]

59. *Conc. Trid.*, Sess. IV, *decr. de edit. et usa s. libr.*, [*Decretum de editione et usu sacrorum librorum*] where the Vulgate is pronounced *authentica*, and the rejection of it, that is all departure from it in interpretation, is prohibited. Comp. BELLARMINE (*de verbo Dei*, II, 10), who with proper consequence maintains that the Vulgate is free from all material error in translation.

60. Comp. KLEE's *katholische Dogmatik*, vol. 1, p. 277, 2nd ed. [Mainz: Schott und Thielmann, 1839]. LINDANUS (*de opt. script. interpret.*) [William Damasus Lindanus, *De optimo scripturas interpretandi genere* (Cologne: M. Cholinus, 1558)] is not ashamed to say even that the scriptures without the aid of tradition have no more value than Aesop's Fables: *Sacram scripturam, si auctoritas ecclesiae disideratur, non plus per se valere quam Aesopi fabulas.* [Trans. "Holy Scripture, if the authority of the Church is lacking, is worth no more in itself than the stories of Aesop."] Comp. also the *Instruction pastorale* I, of BOSSUET, cap. 43. [Jacques Bénigne Bossuet, *Ordonnance et instruction pastorale . . . sur les états d'oraison* (Paris: Jean Anisson, 1695), chapter 43.]

61. The symbols, it is true, are silent on the point, and in all times there have been Catholics who have earnestly recommended the study of the bible (comp. *Extracts on the necessity and use of bible reading, from the fathers and other catholic writings*, by LEANDER V. ESS, 2nd ed., Sulzbach, 1816). But in strict Roman Catholic lands, such as Italy and Spain, the people are fearfully ignorant of the bible, and the priests oppose every effort of the protestants to circulate it, frequently indeed have committed large numbers of bibles to the flames. It is a fact further, that the reading of the scriptures has been prohibited to the laity by several popes, from Gregory VII down to our own time, and also by several provincial councils; as the *C. Tolosanum*, 1229 (*can.* 14. *Prohibemus etiam, ne libros Vet. T. aut N., laici permittantur habere: nisi forte Psalterium, vel Breviarium pro divinis officiis aut horas B. Mariae aliquis ex devotione habere velit. Sed ne praemissos libros habeant in vulgari translatos, arctissime inhibemus*) [Trans. "We prohibit also that the laity should be permitted to have the books of the Old or New Testament; unless anyone from motive of devotion should wish to have the Psalter or the Breviary for divine offices or the hours of the blessed Virgin; but we most strictly forbid their having any translation of these books" Council of Toulouse in Edward Peters, ed. *Heresy and Authority in*

whole tendency of the Roman Catholic Church has for its object to subordinate the bible to tradition, and then to make itself the infallible judge of both; with power to determine at pleasure what is God's word and the doctrine of the Church, and to anathematize every thing that may go beyond its past decisions, even though, as in the case of the Reformation and Jansenism, it should be an actual deepening of the Christian consciousness itself.

As already remarked, tradition in the Romish sense is the unwritten portion of divine revelation; by which is meant simply, that it was not committed to writing in the beginning by its author, however it may have been reduced to this form since in the symbolical books and other productions of the Church. Its contents are partly expository and partly supplementary to the bible; it springs in part from Christ himself, and in part from the apostles under the guidance of the Holy Ghost; it is thus of like origin and like dignity with the written word; and has transmitted itself through the Church all along, pure and true, under the constant care of God's Spirit.[62] Articles of tradition are, for example, infant baptism, the worship of the saints, the doctrine of purgatory, the sacrifice of the mass, the forty days fast before Easter. Its compass is determined of course by the Church, that is by the Roman Catholic Church, which is taken to be the Church universal, and so the rightful bearer of this trust. What she has declared to be apostolical tradition, through her organs, the popes and councils, must be received in this character. She decides in the case however according to a fixed rule,

---

Medieval Europe: Documents in Translation (Philadelphia: University of Pennsylvania Press, 195] so the *C. Tarraconense*, 1234 [Council Tarragona]. In any case, according to the whole system of the Church, the reading of the scriptures is not regarded as necessary, and the people are referred to the priests as a nearer and surer fountain of instruction.

62. The Council of Trent speaks on this difficult subject in its 4th Session, but for reasons easily understood goes not into it minutely. Even to have raised a question here, must have been to put at stake a number of her most important doctrines and usages. Bellarmine, *de verba Dei*, IV, 2, divides traditions into: 1st *traditiones divinae*, communicated by Christ to the apostles; 2nd *traditiones apostolicae*, proceeding from the apostles, though not in their writings; and 3rd *traditiones ecclesiasticae*, ancient Church usages and customs. The first stand parallel in value with the Gospels; the second, with the writings of the apostles; and the third, with the written decrees and constitutions of the Church. Moehler's view of tradition, on the contrary, is by no means strictly orthodox, but ideal, showing a Protestant tinge. Here, as in his celebrated book also on the unity of the Church, the theology of Schleiermacher was evidently felt. Thus he distinguishes in his *Symbolik* (pp. 362 ff. of the 5th ed., 1838) between a tradition in the subjective, and a tradition in the objective sense. The first is nothing more than "the Christian sense belonging to the Church, and handing itself down by means of Church training, the word continuously living in the hearts of the faithful"; the same thing thus with what Schleiermacher styles the Christian consciousness. Tradition in the objective sense is made to be "the aggregate faith of the Church through all ages as exhibited in external historical testimonies." But this is to say nothing characteristic of it as distinguished from the sacred Scriptures, which also belong to the aggregate faith of the Church in this form. It is easy enough, in such fashion, to escape the difficulties of the case, which begin precisely where it comes to the question of the concrete contents of tradition as differing from the bible. [Quotations from Johann Adam Möhler are Nevin's own translation of Schaff's German. For the English edition see Johann Adam Möhler, *Symbolism: Exposition of the Doctrinal Differences between Catholics and Protestants as Evidenced by their Symbolical Writings*, trans. James Burton Robertson (1843, New York: Crossroad, 1997).]

the criterion of catholicity namely presented by VINCENTIUS LIRINENSIS: *quod ubique, quod semper, quod ab omnibus creditum est.*[63] All valid traditions, consequently, must have been universally acknowledged by the Christian Church from the beginning.

But just here comes the knot that the Church of Rome is not able to unloose, but only to cut in a violent way. The universality in time and space which is called for by the criterion now mentioned cannot be shown in favor of a single one of all her traditions as different from the bible. This point has been largely handled by CHEMNITZ with great learning. Very many dogmas and usages rose clearly in the Middle Age, or at least after the time of Augustine; and in the best cases, the alleged universality reduces itself to a relative majority of voices merely, which was often very small, and not unfrequently besides the result of outward influences entirely. In the discussion on tradition itself, in the fourth session of the Council of Trent, nothing like absolute unanimity was to be found. The bishop of Chiozza maintained that the gospels contain all that man needs for salvation; and another prelate declared decidedly, that God's word consisted not of two parts, that it was a reproach to divine providence to assume that a portion of its revelation had not been committed to writing, and that we must rather follow therefore the example of those fathers who confined themselves always to the bible alone. In the discussion on the doctrine of justification a still more considerable want of unity appeared. The archbishop of Sienna, the bishop della Cava, Giulio Contarini bishop of Belluno, and with them five theologians, joined in declaring faith to be the only ground of justification; love and hope its attendants; and works its evidence or proof; while the general of the Augustinians, Seripaudo, brought forward the view of Gaspar Contarini, which took a middle course between the two systems.

But the voice of history, with its thousand tongues, is overwhelmed, not answered, by the Church of Rome, with the declaration that she is absolutely infallible, the unerring organ of the Holy Ghost, to which all private judgment, all historical inquiry, must yield implicit submission.[64] To this point in the end the whole controversy of

63. [The so-called "Vincentian canon" coined by Vincent of Lérins: "that which is believed everywhere, always, and by all."]

64. The Council of Trent of course takes this position everywhere for granted and utters all its decisions accordingly. In the nature of the case, at the same time, it could not be subjected to particular investigation and proof. This would have been nothing less than a *petitio principii*; since to be able to show its divine authority, the Synod must have assumed the fact as already given. The *Cat. Rom.*, I, 10, 18, ascribes to the Roman Church, and to this exclusively, freedom from all error in *fidei ac morum disciplina tradenda* [Trans. "delivering the discipline of faith or morals" *Catechism of the Council of Trent*, 104. The passage occurs at I. 10. 16 in this edition.]; and so likewise, BELLARMINE, *eccl. milit.* c. 14. *Nostra igitur sententia est* ecclesiam absolute non posse errare, *nec in rebus absolute necessariis, nec in aliis, quae credenda vel facienda nobis proponit, sive habeantur expresse in scripturis, sive non: et quum dicimus, ecclesiam non posse errare, id intelligimus tam de universitate fidelium quam de universitate episcoporum.* [Trans. "Therefore our opinion is that the Church is *absolutely not able to err*, neither in absolutely necessary matters, nor in other matters which it determines we must believe or do, whether they are expressly contained in Scripture or not: and when we say that the Church is not able to err, we understand it so concerning the whole body of the faithful and the whole body of the bishops." *In disp. de contr.*, IV (*De ecclesia militante*) 3.14 (Vives, 2:349–350).]

right comes; with it the entire Roman Catholic system stands or falls. But this highest principle precisely of the infallibility of the papal hierarchy, like the highest principle of most philosophical systems, is merely asserted, *never proved.* It forms the *proton pseudos*, the grand falsehood, on which the whole system rests; and at the same time its central sin, creature deification, making itself identical with the universal Church, yea, with the absolute kingdom of God, out of which all are heretics only and children of perdition.

[The Protestant doctrine of scripture and tradition]

Protestantism has shaken this foundation from its place. It plants itself on the principle that infallibility belongs to Christ and his word alone, and to all else so far only as it may be joined to him in living union. This union however, in the present world, is progressive, and so always incomplete. In the case of the single Christian, this is as clear as day. As in the best works of the regenerate, sin still continues to work with more or less power, so that they can never become the ground of justification; so also error still cleaves to his knowledge as long as he tabernacles in the body, and on this account the truth which is unto salvation can never be built on human tradition. For error and sin are ever inseparably related, like the understanding and the will. Sin is practical error, and error is theoretic sin. If this hold in the case of the individual, it is hard to see why the same should not be true of the Church also, since this is nothing else than the organic complex of individual Christians. A bishop does not become another man in appearing as the member of a Synod, made free as by a magic wand from error and sin. As little is this the case with the whole body. Many sinners make no saint, many blind no one with the gift of sight, as little as a quantity of wood can yield iron, or a quantity of stones bread. Error and truth differ not gradually, but specifically.

If the Church militant then be not free from sin, which no one in the face of history will maintain, so neither is she free from error. True, she has the unerring word of God, and is styled by Paul "the pillar and ground of the truth" [1 Tim 3:15]. The truth accordingly can never disappear from her communion; and this is the right and sound side of the Roman Catholic dogma. But this by no means involves the idea of a positive infallibility. Rather, the Church has error along with the truth, by which this may be corrupted and obscured, though never absolutely lost. She bears the golden treasure in earthen vessels; along with her ideal, divine nature, she possesses also a real, human existence, which is subject to the conditions of the finite, and thus also to the laws of process and growth. In the Church herself, as well as in her members singly taken, we must distinguish different periods of life. She is not made perfect at once, but is engaged in a gradual process of development, which holds just in this: that she is ever extricating herself more and more from the Judaism and Paganism, sin and error, that still cleave to her by nature; by entering always more deeply into the word of God, in her hands but not for this reason fully understood from the beginning; and by incorporating it more fully always with her thinking, feeling and acting; till in the end she shall appear the full grown body of Christ, without spot or wrinkle, infirmity or disease, thus ceasing at the same time to be a militant Church, and passing over into the kingdom of God triumphant.

For every unprejudiced person, history confirms this by incontrovertible facts. Even the most celebrated councils have been sufficiently characterized by contention and strife, contradictory feelings and views; and human passions and errors have come into play in their proceedings as fully as in other places. Add to this that popes and councils have not unfrequently appeared in direct contradiction—a circumstance fatal at once to the claim of infallibility. Thus, in the Arian controversy, several synods, just as large and constitutional as those afterwards acknowledged to be orthodox, declared in favor of this heresy; and while the Council of Constantinople, in 754, by imperial will the Seventh Oecumenical, composed of 300 bishops, fanatically damned all religious images, the next universal synod, held at Nicaea in 787, proclaimed the whole proceeding to be wind.[65] More frequent still have been the cases of contradiction on the part of the popes among themselves, and especially to the Church as represented by the great reformatory synods of Constance and Basel; so that with regard to this point, the Roman theologians themselves have not been able to agree.

The Protestant Church however can appeal, in favor of her view, not simply to the history of councils and popes, but also to the express testimony of the most ancient Church fathers; as ATHANASIUS and AUGUSTINE, for example, without qualification *allow the possibility of error even in the highest administration of the Church.*[66] The

65. [The Council of Constantinople (754) was held at the insistence of the Emperor Constantine Copronymous. All 330 delegates were Eastern bishops. This undermined its claim to be "oecumenical." The subsequent Second Council of Nicaea (787) is accepted by both Roman Catholic and Eastern Orthodox churches as the "Seventh Oecumenical Council." Schaff, *History of the Christian Church* 4 (New York: Scribner's, 1891), 454–64.]

66. Thus [Augustine, in] *de baptismo contra Donatist*, II, 3, says: *Quis autem nesciat S. Scripturam. . . omnibus episcoporum litteris ita praeponi, ut de ilia omnino dubitari et disceptari non possit. . . episcoporum autem literas. . . per sermonem forte sapientiorem cujuslibet in ea re peritioris, et per aliorum episcoporum graviorem auctoritatem doctioremque prudentiam et per concilia licere reprehendi, si quid in eis forte a veritate deviatum est: et ipsa concilia, quae per singulas. . . provincias. fiunt*, plenariorum conciliorum *auctoritati quae fiunt ex* universo orbe christiano, *sine ullis ambagibus cedere*, ipsaque plenaria saepe priora a posterioribus emendari, *quum aliquo experimento rerum aperitur quod clausum erat et cognoscitur quod latebat.* If the general councils themselves admit and require thus improvement and correction from those that follow, they cannot be infallible. [Trans. "But who can fail to be aware that the sacred canon of Scripture, . . . stands so absolutely in a superior position to all later letters of the bishops, that about it we can hold no manner of doubt or disputation . . .; but that all the letters of bishops are liable to be refuted if there be anything contained in them which strays from the truth, either by the discourse of some one who happens to be wiser in the matter than themselves, or by the weightier authority and more learned experience of other bishops, by the authority of Councils; and further, that the Councils themselves, which are held in the several districts and provinces, must yield, beyond all possibility of doubt, to the authority of *plenary Councils* which are formed for the *whole Christian world*; and that *even of the plenary Councils, the earlier are often corrected by those which follow them*, when, by some actual experiment, things are brought to light which were before

idea of a positive infallibility, excluding all and every error, and clothing the decisions of councils with the character of divine oracles, was first uttered by the Council of Chalcedon, A. D. 451, with reference to that of Nicaea—whose decrees, it was directly affirmed, were given not by the fathers of the synod themselves, but by the Holy Ghost speaking through their persons.

[Protestant teaching on scripture]

If there be then any unerring fountain of truth needed to satisfy religious want, it can be found only in the *word of God*, who is himself the truth; and this becomes thus consequently the *highest norm* and *rule* by which to measure all human truth, all ecclesiastical tradition, and all synodical decrees.[67] Having in this way no rival at their side, the sacred scriptures must take a far higher place in the Protestant system than they are allowed to hold in that of Rome, similarly to the view taken of faith also in the two churches. Our older theologians cannot be charged certainly with any want of respect for the bible; rather fault is to be found with the inspiration theory of the 17th century, that it did not sufficiently recognize the individuality of the sacred writers, which without the least prejudice to the divinity of the matter, mirrors it nevertheless in every case under a peculiar form. These bible fathers, as I may style them with Daub, have resolved the excellence predicated of the scriptures into the following properties.

1. The character of *fontal* and *normal authority* immediately in view.

2. *Perfection* as to compass and contents (*perfectio s. sufficientia*) ["perfection or sufficiency"]; not of course in the absolute sense, as containing all that can possibly be known of God and divine things; but relatively, reaching to all that is necessary to salvation, as distinctly expressed in the symbolical books (*continet omnia, quae ad salutem consequendam sunt necessaria* ["contains all things which are necessary to be followed for salvation"]. All traditions accordingly, unless they be mere consequences

concealed, and that is known which previously lay hid. Augustine, *On Baptism against the Donatists*, book 2, chapter 3, *NPNF* 1st ser. 4:427.]

67. *Artic. Smalc.*, I, 2, 15, p. 308: *Ex patrum enim verbis et factis non sunt extruendi articuli fidei. . . . Regulam autem aliam habemus, ut videlicet verbum Dei condat articulos fidei, et praeterea nemo, ne Angelus quidem.* [Trans. "It will not do to make articles of faith out of the holy fathers' words or works. . .we have another rule, namely, that the word of God shall establish articles of faith and no one else, not even an angel." *C&C*, 2:128.] Luther, as early as the conference at Augsburg, would be "confuted only from the scriptures"; and at Worms, as is known, he put forward the *testimonia scripturarum* and declared his conscience bound by God's word. *Form. Conf. praef.*, p. 570, where the bible is styled *unica regula et norma* ["sole rule and standard"] of all doctrines; also *sol. decl.*, p. 632 ["The Solid Declaration of the Formula of Concord." The pagination here, as in the other citations of Protestant creeds, continues to be from Hase, *Libri symbolici*]. The Reformed Church proclaims this formal principle throughout with still more distinctness and decision so that it is almost superfluous to refer to proof passages: *Conf. Helv.*, II, Art. 1–2, pp. 467 ff.; *Artic. Anglic.*, Art. 6.; *Conf. Belg.*, Art. 3–5, pp. 361 ff.; *Conf. Gallic.*, Art. 2–5 pp. 329 ff.; *Conf. Westmonast.*, c. 1, § 1–10.

drawn from the bible, are either positively false, or contain only subordinate and unessential truth.[68] It might be presumed indeed beforehand, that the divine wisdom and goodness, in the case of the new covenant as well as in that of the old, would provide for a true and full record of the truth as needed for salvation, in a written form; since a merely oral tradition, in the nature of the case, must be subject to change and distortion, making it impossible at last to distinguish truth from falsehood. In such passages as Acts 20:27; 26:22; 2 Tim. 3:14–17; Gal. 1:8; Rev. 22:18, the scriptures ascribe this character to themselves quite directly; and the claim is made good continually in practical life. The more any one enters into the contents of the bible, the more he learns to say with Luther that it resembles an herb that by every rubbing becomes only the more odoriferous; a tree that by every shaking throws down only a richer supply of golden apples. Every valuable exegetical work discloses to us new treasures; and our Church, after having lived upon it already three hundred years, must still with Paul exclaim in amazement, "O the depth of the riches both of the wisdom and knowledge of God!" [Rom 11:33].

3. As it regards form, the bible has the quality of *Perspicuity* (*perspicuitas*); not absolutely again, as excluding every mystery; but so as that all things indispensably necessary to salvation may be known by every member of the Church from the scriptures, without the aid of tradition or councils, if only the proper conditions are at hand for the purpose. These include not simply the general command of intellect and knowledge that are requisite for the understanding of every human book, by which the loose spiritualism of the Quakers is disowned, but a living sense also of spiritual need, and a proper affinity with the Spirit from which the scriptures proceed. And here the Protestant Church appears in full opposition to Rationalism, in the case of which the natural understanding, that cannot discern the things of the Spirit according to Paul (1 Cor. 2:14; 12:3; 2 Cor. 3:5), is made the principle of interpretation. That it is properly the Holy Ghost only which can interpret the scriptures, is admitted by the Romish Church also; and so all controversy here turns upon the question:

68. SCHLEIERMACHER, *Der christl. Glaube*, 3rd ed. [Berlin: Reimer, 1835], Vol. 2, § 103, pp. 120 ff., says with much truth: "This original revelation of God in Christ is moreover so sufficient, and at the same time so inexhaustible, that so far as this first point is concerned Christ stands forth at once as the crown and consummation of all prophecy. For it is not possible, either for any representation of our relation to God to take place, out of the sphere in which Christ is already known, that shall not fall behind this revelation; or for any such advance ever to be made within the Christian Church, as may show anything imperfect in the doctrine of Christ itself, for which something better might be substituted, or to conceive for the understanding of man, as it regards his relation to God, anything more spiritual, deep and complete, than has been done by Christ. With the idea of such a perfectibility of the Christian doctrine, as might allow us to go beyond Christ himself, the idea of his peculiar excellence must fall to the ground. On the contrary, all later excellence here can never be anything else than the right development of what is either comprehended in his declarations as handed down to us, or in such relation to them as to have been necessarily present to his mind." That SCHLEIERMACHER has in his mind the contents of the bible here, as the measure which none can transcend, must be clear to all who are acquainted with his system.

Where is this Holy Ghost?[69] The Church of Rome of course arrogates its presence, and with this the right interpretation of the bible, entirely to herself, her bishops and her popes; and thus in fact exalts herself above the bible, as its infallible judge.[70] The Protestant, on the other hand, binds the Spirit that "bloweth where it listeth" [John 3:8], not to a particular form and section of the Church, but to the word alone (comp. John 8:31–32). Where the word is read and preached, there the Spirit lives and moves and creates light; that is, in other words, the scriptures interpret themselves.[71] When, notwithstanding, controversies arise, as they unavoidably must, and opposite parties contend for different senses of the word in their own favor, the Protestant requires, it is true, a subjection of the individual to some general authority; whether it be a small body of theologians, as that which framed the Formula of Concord, or a regular synod, as of Dort, Westminster, etc., which establishes a standard of faith for all within its jurisdiction. On this ground, it is known, the Reformers were earnestly urgent for a general council in which the controversies of the time might be decided. But here still this important difference prevails between the Protestant and Romish systems: that in the view of the first no such ecclesiastical authority is permitted to draw its decisions from tradition, but always again from the bible itself only; and thus the principle of its self-interpretation in the Holy Ghost remains unimpaired.[72]

69. Bellarmine, *de verb. Dei*, III, 3: *Convenit etiam inter nos et adversarios scripturas intelligi debere eo spiritu, quo factae sunt, i. e., spiritu sancto. . . . Toto igitur quaestio in eo posita est, ubi sit iste spiritus.* [Trans. "It is agreed between us and our opponents that the Scriptures must be understood by that spirit by whom they were made, i.e. the Holy Spirit. . . .Therefore the whole question concerns where that Spirit may be." *In disp. de contr.*, I (*De verbo dei*).3.3 (Vives, 1:175–76).]

70. Bellarmine, 1, c. 3, 9, [Schaff would appear to here be citing *In disp. de contr.*, I (*De verbo dei*).3.3, I.3.9] has poorly sustained his usual logical acumen at this point. He maintains, that as the bible is the subject of controversy, we must not appeal to it as judge in the case, but only to something external to it, that is the Church. But the Church is also a party; and so not qualified to act as judge, unless in the most partial, and in the worst sense, extra-biblical style.

71. *Scriptura sacra est sui ipsius legitimus interpres.* ["The Holy Scripture is its own legitimate interpreter."] Comp. especially the Reformed symbols; for example, *Conf. Helv.*, II. c. 2, p. 469: *illam duntaxat scripturarum intepretationem pro orthodoxa et genuina agnoscimus, quae ex ipsis est petita scripturis. . . cum regula fidei et caritatis congruit et ad gloriam Dei hominumque salutem eximie facit.* [Trans. "We hold that interpretation of the Scriptures to be orthodox which is gleaned from the Scriptures themselves. . . and which agrees with the rule of faith and love, and contributes much to the glory of God and man's salvation." *C&C*, 2:462.]

72. The Lutheran divines distinguish accordingly thus: (l) *Judex* principalis *est spiritus s.*; (2) *judex* instrumentalis *est s. scriptura*; (3) *jud.* ministerialis (also inferior) *est ministerium ecclesiasticum*. This last however may not "*pro suo arbitrio sententiam pronunciare, sed juxta normam a supremo judice praescriptam, videl. juxta scripturam s., quam propterea vocem judicis supremi et normam judicis inferioris et judicem directivum appellamus*." [Trans.: (1) "the *principle* judge is the Holy Spirit; (2) the *instrumental* judge is Holy Scripture; (3) the *ministerial*, or *inferior* judge is the ministry of the church." This last however may not "by its own will pronounce an opinion, except in accord with the rule prescribed by the supreme judge, that is, in accord with Holy Scripture, to which for this reason we appeal as the voice of a supreme judge and thus both the rule and directing judge for lesser judges."] Calvin treats of the point I*nstit*. IV, c. 9. § 13, where the remarkable passage occurs: "*Nos certe libenter concedimus, si quo de dogmate incidat disceptatio, nullum esse nec melius nec certius remedium, quam si verorum episcoporum Synodus conveniat, ubi controversum dogma excutiatur. Multo enim plus ponderis habebit*

4. The last character of the scriptures is the power (*efficacia*) with which they operate through the Holy Spirit on the soul of man, in the way of illumination and renewal. This however is of no essential consequence to our present investigation.

When all this is taken together, we may say, leaving out of view a number of the fathers and mediaeval divines, very prominent men it is true, that the holy scriptures were first instated in their proper rights, in a general way, by the Reformers. It is felt accordingly to be a sacred duty with Protestantism, which in this view also forms a decided advance in the history of the Church, to circulate them as widely as possible in the languages accessible to the people; whilst it lies in the interest of popery universally, to restrain their circulation, and to anathematize all bible societies; under the convenient plea of course, that the editions are heretical and the translation corrupt.

[Tradition in Protestant theology]

We are now to investigate the relation of the Protestant bible principle to tradition, or the place assigned to *tradition* in the Protestant system. To do justice however to this difficult point, we must first reduce the idea to its constituent parts; since the word is used in very different senses, and by the Council of Trent in particular is made so general as to embrace the whole mass of what has been handed down in the Church. We may take up the whole compass of its meaning under the distinction of *ritual*, *historical*, and *dogmatic* tradition. To all these forms, the general relation of Protestantism is such that it *affirms their historical necessity, whilst at the same time it places them neither parallel with the scriptures, nor over them, but under them only, and measures their value by the extent of their agreement with this standard.*

1. The first class corresponds in the main, with what Bellarmine styles ecclesiastical traditions. It comprises the ancient customs and usages, pertaining to order and worship, which have gradually acquired the character of catholicity; for example, the distinctions of the clergy, the Church festivals, the arrangement of divine service, the specifications of Church discipline, and the whole range of Church symbolism, as the custom of praying with the face towards the East, the consecration of the baptismal

ejusmodi definitio, in quam communiter ecclesiarum pastores, invocato Christi spiritu, consenserint, quam si quisque seorsum domi conceptam populo traderet, vel pauci homines privatim eam conficerent." [Trans. "We indeed willingly concede, if any discussion arises over doctrine, that the best and surest remedy is for a synod of true bishops to be convened, where the doctrine at issue may be examined. Such a definition, upon which the pastors of the church in common, invoking Christ's Spirit, agree, will have much more weight than if each one, having conceived it separately at home, should teach it to the people, or if a few private individuals should compose it." Calvin, *Institutes*, 2:1176.] He then goes on to establish this view, in part exegetically (from 1 Cor. 14:29), in part historically; adding in the end however that the Holy Ghost may forsake an entire synod, so that the decisions of such a body are not necessarily free from error, as history shows. *Hoc autem perpetuum esse nego, ut vera sit et certa scripturae interpretatio, quae concilii suffragiis fuerit recepta.* [Trans. "But I deny it to be always the case that an interpretation of Scripture adopted by vote of a council is true and certain." Calvin, *Institutes*, 2:1177.]

water, making the sign of the cross, etc. That these points in general were established *after* the age of the apostles needs, in the present posture of historical inquiry, no further argument. It entered not into the design of Christ and the apostles, to lay down more than the most essential ground regulations for the order and worship of the Church. They wished not to burden the new organization with forms and ceremonies. This would have been wholly contrary also to the free genius of the gospel, which was expected rather to create its own body according to time and circumstances, as its wants might require (comp. Rom. 14; Gal. 4:9–10; 5:4; Coloss. 2:16–18). To insist on *one* constitution and *one* worship, as alone true and valid, in the case at least of the militant Church, is to fall back again into fleshly Judaism. So in the Church of Rome itself, many primitive customs have gone into disuse, and others again have been introduced much later, which now form an essential part of the system; as the papacy in its present form, the pomp connected with the mass, the splendid clerical attire, the festivals of Mary and the saints, the details with regard to fasts and penances, praying by the rosary, and the like.

Now in all these secondary things, Protestantism recognizes throughout no normative force, as is done by the Church of Rome, but claims the right to exercise a free evangelical criticism in the case; rejecting absolutely all that conflicts with the true life of the Church, and serves merely to promote a dead mechanical religion; whilst it retains only what is found to embody with suitable form and expression the Christian spirit.[73] As however at the time of the Reformation, the Church had well nigh petrified in these outward forms with the loss in a great measure of all inward life, as it was with Judaism at the time of Christ; whilst the apostolic age, as far as we can gather from the New Testament, was characterized by the greatest simplicity and

73. *Conf. Aug.*, Art. 15, pp. 13 ff.: *De ritibus ecclesiasticis docent, quod ritus illi servandi sint, qui sine peccato servari possunt et prosunt ad tranquillitatem et bonum ordinem in Eccleeia, sicut certae feriae, festa et similia. De talibus rebus tamen admonentur homines, ne conscientiae onerentur, tamquam talis cultus ad salutem necessarius sit. Admonentur etiam, quod traditiones humanae institutae ad placandum Deum, et promerendam gratiam et satisfaciendum pro peccatis, adversentur evangelio et doctrinae fidei. Quare vota et traditiones de cibis et diebus etc., institutae ad promerendam gratiam et satisfaciendum pro peccatis inutiles sintet contra evangelium.* [Trans. "Our churches teach that those rites should be observed which can be observed without sin and which contribute to peace and good order in the church. Such are certain holy days, festivals, and the like. Nevertheless, men are admonished not to burden consciences with such things, as if observances of this kind were necessary for salvation. They are also admonished that human traditions which are instituted to propitiate God, merit grace, and make satisfaction for sins are opposed to the gospel and the teaching about faith. Wherefore vows and traditions about foods and days, etc., instituted to merit grace and make satisfaction for sins, are useless and contrary to the gospel." *C&C*, 2:66.] Comp. Art. 22, p. 20 (*falsa enim calumnia*, etc.), and the whole admirable 8th section in the *Apol. Conf. de traditionibus humanis in eccles.*, pp. 205–23. Chemnitz, in his *Exam.*, lays down in relation to ritual traditions the following very sound rule: *Ceremoniae in ecclesia sint genere indifferentes, numero paucae, sint piae et utiles ad aedificationem, ordinem et decoram; haeant extra casum scandali liberas observationes.* [Trans. "ceremonies may be according to their nature adiaphora, few in number, good and profitable for edification, order, and decorum, and that this whole kind, except in the case of offense, should be observed in freedom." *Examination of the Council of Trent*, trans. Kramer 1:269.] Cf. *Conf. Helv.* II, Art. 27, pp. 530 ff.

spirituality; it was quite natural that the Reformers should have been carried too far at times in opposition to the existing system. At the same time, this was not the case so much with the Lutheran and *German* Reformed Church, as it was with the Reformed Church in Scotland and France. For the Romanic nations, and the English also, are much more disposed to attach an undue value to form than the inward minded, idealistic Germans; and for this very reason, it was natural for them, when the spirit was roused to the consciousness and assertion of its superior rights, to fall over unduly to the opposite side, on the principle that one extreme begets another. Puritanism in particular, I am constrained here openly to acknowledge, through a false spiritualistic tendency and an utter misapprehension of the significance of the corporeal and outward, showed itself in this case rash in its zeal, and has sacrificed many beautiful customs by which religious ideas were sweetly interwoven with common life, and outward opportunities continually supplied for the favorable application of truth to the heart. All this, it is much more difficult to recover, than to cast away. It is always more easy to destroy, than it is to build. The culminating point of this abstract spiritualism has been reached in the system of the Quaker, which rejects even the ministry and the sacraments as mere forms; but strangely enough, against its own will, swings clear over at the same time to the very opposite extreme. For of all others, the Quakers are the greatest slaves of form, and the most barren and unmeaning besides in their profession; a palpable satire upon all such naked inwardism, an involuntary argument for the necessity of externalization.[74]

2. To the *historical* tradition must be referred, as of first account, the testimonies of Christian antiquity on the genuineness and integrity of the sacred books, the time and place of their composition, and the settlement of the canon. This tradition the Lutheran and Reformed Church hold to be of great account, and they have retained, as is known, the canon of the Catholic Church. But still faith in the scriptures is made to rest, in the end, not on these testimonies of the fathers, but on the inward testimony of the Holy Spirit, and is not allowed to have any true worth while it continues a simple blind trust in authority. Then again, these traditions are for Protestantism by no means infallible and binding, but simple historical testimonies only, whose worth is to be estimated, partly according to the general credibility of the writer concerned, and partly also, and mainly, according to the measure of their connection with the apostolic age. It is sufficient to show them not infallible, that previously to the Council of Hippo in the year 393, they are known not to agree with one another, in relation to several books of the New Testament, the so called *antilegomena* of Eusebius. The Church of Rome has so much the less room for casting reproach upon us here, since in open contradiction to the oldest and best accredited tradition, which we have once

74. [In this discussion of Quakers, the Religious Society of Friends founded by George Fox, Schaff alludes to highly regulated Quaker practices of plain dress and plain speech. An equally biting, but more nuanced discussion may be found in Möhler, *Symbolism*, 401–7. For description of Quaker practices see Hamm, *The Quakers in America*, 101–2. For the use of Quakers in American cultural discourse see Ryan, *Imaginary Friends*.]

more restored to its rights, she has rejected the distinction of canonical and apocryphal books, and so invested with traditional authority this false co-ordination itself.

Under the same head, in a wider sense, may be reckoned *exegetical* tradition. The Council of Trent understands by this the pretended consent of the fathers; and it was ordained, in the fourth session, that this should govern the interpretation of the scriptures.[75] This tradition also Protestantism prizes, without overvaluation. It is well pleased to find a Church father in harmony with the true explanation of a passage; as may be sufficiently seen for instance, from CHEMNITZ's *Examinis Concilii Tridentini*, and GERHARD's celebrated system of theology.[76] The religious life rests on the deepest feeling of communion. It may be safely affirmed moreover, that for every peculiar exposition of the Reformers, at least an analogy may be found in the ancient Church, particularly with AUGUSTINE. But still the Reformers by no means allow a normative authority to the fathers. Respect for them is not suffered to shackle the further progress of exegesis, as in the Church of Rome.[77] The fathers, in their interpretation, proceeded in part on wholly unsound principles, as those of Alexandria for instance with their extravagant allegory; and of a full agreement, except only in the most essential particulars, it is idle to speak.[78] The scripture expositions of the Reformers show not only far more agreement, but also sounder sense and tact, and saving the single case of AUGUSTINE, who however like all philosophical thinkers is a better theologian than interpreter, are characterised by much greater acuteness and depth.

3. The *dogmatico-moral* traditions finally, on which most hangs, may be taken first in the *material* view; comprehending thus, in the Romish system, all doctrines

75. *Ut nemo. . . contra unanimem consensum Patrum ipsam scripturam sacram interpretari audeat.* [Trans. "That no one . . . shall dare to interpret the sacred scriptures contrary to the unanimous consent of the fathers." *DEC*, 2:664.]

76. [Martin Chemnitz, *Examination of the Council of Trent*, trans. Fred Kramer 4 vols. (Saint Louis: Concordia, 1971) (First published in 1563–73); Johann Gerhard, *Loci Theologica*, 9 vols. (Jena, 1610–25).]

77. *Conf. Helv*. II, Art. 2, p. 469: *Proinde non aspernamur sanctorum patrum Graecorum Latinorumque interpretationes neque reprobamus eorundem disputationes ac tractationes rerum sacrarum cum scripturis consentientes; a quibus tamen recedimus modeste, quando aliena a scripturis aut his contraria adferre deprehenduntur. Nec putamus illis ullam a nobis hac re injuriam irrogari, cum omnes uno ore nolint sua scripta aequari canonicis. . . Eodem in ordine collocantur etiam conciliorum definitiones vel canones.* With this agrees the whole practice of the orthodox Protestant interpreters and theologians. [Trans. "Wherefore we do not despise the interpretations of the holy Greek and Latin fathers, nor reject their disputations and treatises concerning sacred matters as far as they agree with the Scriptures; but we modestly dissent from them when they are found to set down things differing from, or altogether contrary to, the Scriptures. Neither do we think that we do them any wrong in this matter; seeing that they all with one consent, will have their writtings equated with the canonical Scriptures. . . In the same order also we place the decrees and canons of councils." *C&C* 2:462.]

78. This MOEHLER himself is constrained to allow, *Symbolik* (5th ed.), p. 390: "With the exception of the interpretation of a very few classic passages, a general agreement here is to be found only in this, that all educe from the holy scriptures the same doctrinal and moral views" (even this however holds only in the case of the veriest essentials); "everyone, at the same time, in his own peculiar way; so that some as expositors are distinguished models for all times, others rise not above mediocrity, and others still are entitled to respect only for their good intention and their love to the Savior."

that are referred to Christ or the apostles without being found in the scriptures. These we might look for most naturally in the apostolical fathers and the ecclesiastical writers of the second and third centuries. But we find here no utterances of Christ and the apostles that are not more clearly and fully presented to us in the New Testament. At times besides, something wholly unsuitable and absurd is attributed to them; as *Papias* for instance, in Irenaeus, puts an allegorical saying into the mouth of Christ, which he could never have uttered.[79] It becomes necessary accordingly to proceed here with the utmost critical caution, and there remains no rule by which to discriminate the true from the false but the scriptures. Our Romish opponents however set more store by the dogmatic traditions of the *Middle Ages*; which are referred at once to a divine origin on the grievously arbitrary principle of Peter à Soto: *quorum observationum initium, auctor et origo ignoratur vel inveniri non potest, illas extra omnem dubitationem ab apostolis traditas esse.*[80] All these doctrines, however, which not only have no foundation in the bible, but for the most part contradict it outright, such as the worship of the virgin Mary and the saints, the scholastic theory of justification, purgatory, satisfactions, indulgences, etc., are with full right rejected by Protestantism under the authority of the apostle's word: "Though an angel from heaven should preach unto you any other gospel than that which we have preached unto you, let him be accursed" [Gal 1:8]. For how can the Spirit of Christ contradict itself? And where do we find it written that the Church has the power at pleasure to create or sanction new doctrines? These then are no apostolical, but in their later Romish form at least, altogether human, arbitrary traditions; like the self-made Jewish ordinances of the Pharisees and Sadducees, and the false doctrines against which we are expressly warned by Christ and his apostles (Matth. 15:2; Mark 7:3; 5.13; Gal. 1:14; Col. 2:8).

Quite different however, in the second place, is the case of the *formal* dogmatic tradition. This is such as has not for its contents something different from what is contained in the bible, but forms the channel by which these contents are conducted forward in history; the onward development thus of Church doctrine and Church life, as comprehended first dogmatically in the so called rules of faith, above all in the Apostles' creed; and then in the oecumenical creeds, that of Nice [Nicaea] and the Athanasian; and still further as orally carried forward, apart from all written statement, through the entire course of Church history, so that every one, before he wakes even to self-consciousness, is made involuntarily to feel its power. Tradition in this sense is absolutely indispensable. By its means we come first to the contents of the bible; and from it these draw their life for us, perpetually fresh and new, in such way that Christ and his apostles are made present, and speak to us directly, in the Spirit which breathes in the bible, and flows through the Church as her life's blood. *This tradition therefore is not a part of the divine word separately from that which is written,*

79. [Irenaeus, *Against Heresies*, V, xxxiii, 4. *ANF*, 1:563.]

80. [Trans. "As for those observances of which the beginning, author, and origin is unknown or cannot be found, those beyond all doubt have been handed down from the apostles."]

but the contents of scripture itself as apprehended and settled by the Church against heresies past and always new appearing; not an independent source of revelation, but the one fountain of the written word, only rolling itself forward in the stream of Church consciousness. Much to the same purpose, Martin Chemnitz says: "*Haec est vera et vetus apostolorum traditio, quae nihil tradit extra et praeter scripturam, sed complectitur summam totius scripturae.*"[81]

This tradition Protestantism can and must allow without a surrender of its principle. For the Reformers in their great controversy had always in their eye, not this conception, but the material tradition only, as a fountain of knowledge independent of the scriptures, and having different contents. Many Protestants are to be found, to be sure, in our own time particularly, who entirely overlook the importance of this point; which makes it so much the more necessary to give it emphasis. But we can appeal boldly to history for its support.

In the first place, an argument for holding fast to tradition in this form is found in the whole historical connection of the Reformation itself with the period going before, as this has been already brought into view. Then we have it expressly declared by the leaders of this vast movement that men can be saved only in connection with the true Christian Church as it has stood from the beginning, against which the gates of hell cannot prevail; and that all reformation therefore, and further development of doctrine and life, must maintain essential unity with the collective consciousness of the Christian Church.[82] Lastly, our affirmation is confirmed by the practice of the

81. *Examen Conc. Trident.*, Part I. p. 120, ed. Francof. [Trans. "This is the true and ancient tradition of the apostles which does not hand down anything outside of and beyond the Scripture but embraces the summary of the whole Scripture" *Examination of the Council of Trent*, trans. Kramer, 1:244.]

82. Particularly worthy of note in this view, is a passage found in a letter of Luther to the Duke Albert of Prussia in the year 1532. He is speaking of the real presence of the Lord in the eucharist—a doctrine denied it is true by Zwingli, but firmly held by Calvin, as he expressly declares particularly in his *defensio ad Westphalum*, and also in his *Instit.* "This article moreover," the letter proceeds, "has been clearly believed and held from the beginning of the Christian Church to this hour; *which testimony of the entire holy Christian Church, if we had nothing besides, should be sufficient for us. For it is dangerous and terrible, to hear or believe anything against the united testimony, faith and doctrine, of the entire holy Christian Church*, as this hath been held now 1500 years, from the beginning, unanimously in all the world. Whoso now doubted thereon, it is even the same as though he believed in no Christian Church, and he condemneth thus not only the entire holy Christian Church as a damnable heresy, but also Christ himself and all the apostles and prophets, who have established and powerfully attested this article, where we say 'I *believe in a holy Christian Church*'; Christ namely, Matth. 28:20: 'Lo I am with you always, even unto the end of the world'; and Paul, 1 Tim. 3:15: 'The Church of God, which is the pillar and ground of the truth.'" *Conf. Helv.* II, c. 17, p. 503: Communionem vero cum ecclesia Christi vera tanti facimus, ut negemus eos coram Deo vivere posse, qui cum vera Dei ecclesia non communicant, sed ab ea se separant. *Nam ut extra arcam Noe non erat ulla salus, pereunte mundo in diluvio, ita credimus extra Christum, qui se electis in ecclesia fruendum praebet, nullam esse salutem certam: et proinde docemus, vivere volentes non oportere separari a vera Christi ecclesia.* [Trans. "*But we esteem fellowship with the true Church of Christ so highly that we deny that those can live before God who do not stand in fellowship with the true church of God, but separate themselves from it.* For as there was no salvation outside Noah's ark when the world perished in the flood; so we believe that there is no certain salvation outside Christ, who offers himself to be enjoyed by the elect in the church; and

Reformed and Lutheran Churches. For these have appropriated to themselves unhesitatingly the oecumenical symbols as true expressions of this Church consciousness, that is: as agreeing with the scriptures to which they refer still as the unerring fountain and norm of religious knowledge.[83] Then again, they formed in their own bosom a peculiar Reformed and Lutheran tradition, carrying forward thus the stream of Church consciousness in themselves, and giving it representation in their symbolical books. This too is in no respect contrary to their bible principle. For the Protestant symbols are likewise formal dogmatic traditions that contain nothing different from the scriptures, but simply express the faith of Protestantism in the scriptures themselves, and its apprehension of their contents. *They are the evangelical answer to the interrogation of the divine Word;*[84] which founded the Church at first, and by which it must be con-

hence we teach that those who wish to live ought not to be separated from the true church of Christ." *C&C*, 2:495.] The idea of the Church is developed in a masterly style by CALVIN, *Instit. Chr. Rel.* IV, c. 1. § 1 ff: "He who has God for his Father, he tells us, has the Church also for his mother; and this not simply under the law, but after the coming of Christ likewise, who will have us to be children of the new and heavenly Jerusalem" (Gal. 4:16). He then goes on to say, §4: *Verum quia nunc de visibili ecclesia disserere propositum est, discamus vel uno* Matris *elogio, quam utilis sit nobis ejus cognitio, imo necessaria: quando non alius est in vitam ingressus, nisi nos ipsa concipiat in utero, nisi pariat, nisi nos alat suis uberibus, denique sub custodia et gubernatione sua nos tueatur, donec exuti carne mortali similes erimus angelis. Neque enim patitur nostra infirmitas a schola nos dimitti, donec toto vitae cursu discipuli fuerimus. Adde quod extra ejus gremium nulla est speranda peccatorum remissio, nec ulla salus, teste Iesaja* (37:32) *et Joele* (2:32). [Trans. "But because it is now our intention to discuss the visible church, let us learn even from the simple title 'mother' how useful, indeed how necessary, it is that we should know her. For there is no other way to enter into life unless this mother conceive us in her womb, give us birth, nourish us at her breast, and lastly, unless she keep us under her care and guidance until, putting off mortal flesh, we become like the angels. Our weakness does not allow us to be dismissed from her school until we have been pupils all our lives. Furthermore, away from her bosom one cannot home for any forgiveness of sins or any salvation as Isaiah (37:32) and Joel (2:32) testify." Calvin, *Institutes*, 2:1028.] With the greatest severity he then reproves all those, who without imperious necessity of conscience separate themselves from the reigning Church. This whole section in fact sounds so strongly catholic, that MOEHLER (*Symbolik*, pp. 443 ff.) accuses CALVIN of being in perfect contradiction here with himself in leaving the Catholic Church. But this reproach is fully answered by the second chapter of the same book, where CALVIN, with that overwhelming moral earnestness which is peculiar to him, exhibits the papacy as a false Church because by its ordinances it directly contradicted the word of God. He estimates thus the worth of a Church by its agreement with this unerring standard, the charter of the covenant, and the depository of all truth. Till the papists can show what has not yet been done, that their Church agrees with the word of God, CALVIN stands fully justified. For the sake of his connection with the true Catholic Church, he was compelled to separate from a communion which in its spiritual insolence claims to be the only true Church, without being able to bring anything more than its own assertion in proof of the pretension. The true Church, before the Reformation, existed no doubt in the dominion of the pope; but the papacy must by no means be identified for this reason with the true Church; as little as Christianity in the beginning was to be considered one with Judaism because Christ and his apostles stood in this system, visited the temple, and took part in its service.

83. *Conf. Gallic.*, Art. 5, p. 330: *Quamobrem tria ilia symbola, nempe Apostolicum, Nicaenum et Athanasianum, idcirco approbamus, quod sint illi verbo Dei scripto consentanea.* [Trans. "And therefore we confess the three creeds, to wit: the Apostles', the Nicene, and the Athanasian, because they are in accordance with the word of God." *C&C*, 2:376.]

84. Hence the known expression *symbola non imprimunt credenda, sed exprimunt credita.* They

tinually set free from remaining alloy, and carried forward from one degree of light and power to another, till at last the word itself shall be fully corporealized in its life, and the written letter thus will be no more needed in the plenitude of the spirit.

With this view firmly secured in our minds, we escape the insuperable difficulties that do in fact encumber the protestant position as held by many, particularly in our own time, who invest the bible with the most abstract, isolated character, interposing a lifeless void of eighteen centuries between its completion and the present time; while yet, in spite of their own theory, they do themselves in fact hold it only through the medium of tradition, and see and understand it too only as mirrored in the present consciousness of the particular Church to which they belong. A gross inconsequence truly, and glaring contradiction, of which the Romish theologians are well pleased to take advantage.

[Principal objections answered]

Before closing this part of our discussion, and passing over to the consideration of the *present* posture of Protestantism, we have still to notice the principal Roman Catholic objections to the scripture principle, and then to make clear, in a comprehensive view, its relation to the *material* principle.

1. One of the most frequent objections is: "The Church is older than the holy scriptures, these proceed from her; this relation between them ought not then to be reversed, as it is with Protestantism." True, the Church was in being, before any book of the New Testament existed; but not before the unwritten word of Christ and the apostles, which rather was the foundation of the Church, and in substance is the same with the written.[85] Now however this originally oral communication is fixed and secured against corruption by the scriptures. Why then should we have recourse besides to unwritten tradition, as though these were not sufficient? As long as the apostles lived, the inspired bearers of the divine word, such tradition was sufficiently safe. In case of corruption or perversion, the apostles might apply the necessary correction. But the case must be wholly different after the death of these unerring witnesses. If the gospel was to be perpetuated in its purity, it became indispensable that it should

---

are not *norma fidei*, but *norma doctrinae*, according to which the scriptures are to be taught. [Trans. "creeds do not impress what must be believed, but they express what is believed." They are not "norms of faith" but "norms of teaching."]

85. Quenstedt replies to the objection in hand: *Quando Pontificii argumentantur in hunc modum: Ecclesia est antiquior scriptura, ergo majorem habet auctoritatem etc., respondeo: Distinguendum inter verbum Dei in scripturis propositum et ipsum scribendi actum, sive inter scripturae* substantiam, *quae est verbum Dei, et hujus accidens, quod est scriptio. Syst. Theolog.*, 1702, p. 93. [Trans. "When Papists argue in the following way: The church is more ancient than scripture, therefore it has greater authority, etc. I respond: One must distinguish between the Word of God declared in scripture and the actual act of writing, or between the substance of the scriptures, which is the Word of God, and the accident, which is the writing of them." Johann Andreas Quenstedt, *Theologia didactico-polemica, sive, System theologicum* (Leipzig: Thomam Fritsch, 1702), 93.]

be committed to writing; since all merely oral tradition, in proportion as it becomes removed from its source, is found to grow more and more turbid through the accession of foreign matter, till in the end it is no longer possible, without the intervention of a new revelation, to make any sure distinction between the truth and the error. Against such disaster God has provided under the new dispensation, as before under the old, by causing his word to be committed to writing, and wonderfully preserving it in this form from age to age. Allowing then, as all reasonable protestants will be ready to do, that the written word was not necessary for the rise of the Church, it must still be considered indispensable for its continuance, as the perpetual, pure fountain, and only certain measure of saving truth.[86]

2. "It is through tradition only we have the scriptures themselves, and are assured of their authenticity, integrity, and divine character. So likewise we are referred to the Church for the determination of the sacred canon, which fixes the limits of the written word. Now it is inconsistent, when protestants accept the canon thus handed down to them by the Church, and yet in theory reject tradition." With regard to this, it has been already observed that these testimonies of the Church on the genuineness, integrity, and number of the sacred writings, have no claim to infallible authority; but

86. We can appeal here even to the testimony of the most important Roman Catholic theologian of the present age. MOEHLER, in his spirited work, Über die Einheit der Kirche (Tübingen, 1825), p. 60, says: "*Without the holy scriptures*, in which the gospel was first embodied, *the Christian doctrine would not have been preserved in its purity and simplicity; and it is certainly a great want of right feeling towards God, to speak of them as accidental*" (which however is just what many Romish theologians, in opposing protestants, have done, and are doing still), "*because they may seem to have sprung from merely accidental occasions. What a conception of the regency of the Holy Spirit in the Church!* Without the scriptures moreover, the first link of the Church would be wanting, leaving it thus without any proper beginning, and for this reason unmeaning, confused and chaotic. Without a continuous tradition, on the other hand, all higher sense for the scriptures would fail us too, since without intermediate links we could be conscious of no connection. Without the scriptures, we could form no complete image of the Redeemer, as trustworthy material would be wanting, and all must be made uncertain through fables; without a continuous tradition the spirit and interest would be wanting to form for ourselves any such image, and the material again likewise, for without tradition we should have no scripture. Without the scriptures the peculiar form of the discourses of Jesus would be withheld from us, we should not know how the God-man spake, etc." [This translation is by Nevin from Schaff's German manuscript, for a complete English translation see *Unity in the Church or the Principle of Catholicism: Presented in the Spirit of the Church Fathers of the First Three Centuries*, trans. Peter C. Erb (Washington, DC: Catholic University of America Press, 1996).] What is here said, with as much beauty as truth, of tradition, impairs not at all the force of the passage in favor of Protestantism. For tradition is not taken here in the true Roman Catholic sense, as we have before noticed in the case of MOEHLER, but as the regenerated reason, the Christian consciousness of the Church; which stands not beside the scriptures as an independent fountain, hut is simply the stream of their contents reaching to us through the life of the Church, embracing always only what is contained in the scriptures themselves; the same view accordingly that we freely and cheerfully admit on Protestant ground itself. The distinguished champion of popery says indeed explicitly, that without the scriptures we should be left without trustworthy matter, *all being involved in fables*; and this, of course applies with fair consequence also to tradition in the Romish sense, so far as it is made to hold contents of its own, not derived from the scriptures. Comp. also BAUR, *Der Gegensatz des Katholicismus und Protestantismus* ([Tubingen: L.F. Fues], 1834), pp. 348 ff.

are primarily of mere historical character, subject fairly to critical trial external and internal, and become fully valid to the individual Christian at last, only through the self-evidencing power of the scriptures themselves to his spirit by the Holy Ghost. Properly too, they utter nothing new, give no contents, are no voice beyond the scriptures, but only *upon* the scriptures. "The Church," as Nitzsch says,[87] "has not made the scriptures genuine by acknowledging them, but the scriptures have demonstrated themselves to her, and now make the Church genuine." And in the same way, apart also from these patristic testimonies, they still demonstrate themselves as genuine and divine, to every earnest reader, by the Spirit of God speaking through them to his heart.

3. "By rejecting tradition, which imposes definite rules and limits on the interpretation of scripture, we throw open the door to lawless subjectivity. This is shown by the actual state of the protestant world, as rent into various conflicting parties, which without exception appeal to the scriptures in support of the most opposite doctrines and principles." Here indeed a disadvantageous side of Protestantism is brought to view, which we are constrained to acknowledge with deep sorrow, as will appear hereafter. Still however, while we readily allow that the curse of sects is to be ascribed, in large part, to the contempt of Church authority and the abuses of protestant liberty, we must decidedly reject the allegation that tradition alone, and that in the Romish sense as an infallible judge of scripture, forms a sufficient remedy for the cure of this disease. The prescription at best leaves us where we were before, if it bring us not into a plight still worse. For tradition itself is capable also of various interpretations, and to a greater extent indeed than the bible, in proportion as the writings in which it is to be found are of greater compass. It is prodigious injustice to ascribe all clearness to man's word, and all darkness to the word of God. The history of the Church besides informs us plainly that different sects have stayed themselves on tradition as well as upon the holy scriptures. This was done, for instance, by the Gnostics, and again by the Arians at the Council of Antioch;[88] also by the Artemonites, who, according to Eusebius,[89] affirmed that their error with regard to the person of Christ had been held by the apostles and the whole Church down to the time of the Roman bishop Victor, and was first exchanged for a different view under his successor Zephyrinus. It is known too that different views still prevail in the Church of Rome, without loss of orthodoxy, on several by no means unimportant articles of the Tridentine system; and it is owing only to the outward force she employs to restrain all tendencies of the more free sort, as in the case of Jansenism and Hermesianism, that these differences come

87. *System der christlichen Lehre*, 4th ed. [Bonn: Marcus, 1839], p. 93.

88. Socrates, *Hist. Eccles.*, II, 10. [Socrates of Constantinople, *Ecclesiastical History*, *NPNF*, 2nd ser., vol. 2, 39–40.]

89. *Hist. Eccles.*, V, 28. [Eusebius, *Ecclesiastical History*, *NPNF*, 2nd ser., vol. 1, 246–48. The Artemonites were folloers of Artemon or Artemas (c. 235–80), a proponent of monarchism, or anti-trinitarianism and leader of the small group in Rome. He taught that Christ was a mere man filled with divine power.]

not to more open contradiction and collision.[90] In this way however, the disease is not cured, but only covered over: to break forth the more dangerously again, in its own time. Such tyranny over the conscience and against free inquiry is contrary in the view of our Church to the free nature and spiritual constitution of the gospel. As little as the present, so sadly divided condition of the Evangelical Church may be considered her proper normal and perfect state, it still forms an advance as compared with the posture of the Church of Rome, to which the crisis is still future. What vital energy must not Protestantism possess to endure so long and renew its youth continually, in spite of such distraction!

In directing our view now to the relation of the two principles to each other mutually, it may be observed that they are inseparably joined as contents and form, will and knowledge, and strictly taken constitute but two sides of one and the same principle, which resolves itself into the maxim: *Christ all in all.* All sects accordingly that either deny justification by faith alone, as the Socinians, Unitarians, and Swedenborgians, or reject the written word, as the Schwenckfeldians and Quakers, are to be excluded from the territory of orthodox Protestantism, however they may claim to belong to it and seem to stand in its connection.[91] Wherever either element comes to be held in a one-sided way, a deviation has already taken place from the original character of the Reformation. Christ, or in an immediate view his Spirit, is ever in the word and with the word; never without or beyond the word, written or preached; yea, he is himself the living, personal word. The word again can be understood only by faith, in union with the spirit of Christ speaking to us through the letter. By the word, the objective Spirit bears witness to the subjective spirit, that it is born of God.[92] The material element without the objective basis of the formal, becomes swarming inwardism, and in the end sheer subjectivity. The formal element without the material, on the other hand, conducts to stiff, lifeless and soulless externalism, the idolatry of the let-

90. [See in glossary Hermes, Georg.]

91. [The followers of Caspar Schwenckfeld (1490–1561) held that the "outer word," which included the scriptures, only pointed to the "inner word," the glorified Christ who worked directly on the soul. By the nineteenth-century their principal community was in Pennsylvania. Erb, *Schwenkfelders in America.*]

92. The relation is happily exhibited by CALVIN, *Instit.*, III, c. 2, § 6. *Principio admonendi sumus, perpetuam esse fidei relationem cum verbo, nec magis ab eo posse divelli, quam radios a sole, unde oriuntur. —Quare si ab hoc scopo, quem collimare debet, vel minimum deflectit fides, naturam suam non retinet, sed incerta est credulitas et vagus mentis error. Idem verbum basis est, qua fulcitur et sustinetur, unde si declinat, corruit. Tolle igitur verbum, et nulla jam restabit fides. —Unde et fidem definit Paulus obedientiam, quae praestatur, evangelio* (Rom. 1:5). [Trans. "First, we must be reminded that there is a permanent relationship between faith and the Word. He could not separate the rays from the sun from which they come. . . . Therefore if faith turns away even in the slightest degree from this goal toward which it should aim, it does not keep its own nature, but becomes uncertain credulity and vague error of mind. The same Word is the basis whereby faith is supported and sustained; if it turns away from the Word, it falls. Therefore, take away the Word and no faith will then remain. . . . And for this reason, Paul defines faith as that obedience which is given to the gospel (Rom1.5)." Calvin, *Institutes*, 1:548–49.]

ter; and comes besides to no right understanding of the scriptures, to which the key is found only in justifying faith as produced by the Spirit of God. We have a like result in Philosophy, where Idealism and Realism come not to a living interpenetration. The first sundered from the second becomes a barren, merely formal thought-thinking; the second without the first sinks into rough empiricism and materialism.

In thus breaking through the interposed obstruction of hierarchical authority, vindicating to Christ his exclusive and all sufficient mediatorial rights, bringing man back from dead works to God's grace, from vain traditions to God's word, and thus by means of both obtaining for him direct access to his Savior and through him to his heavenly Father, Protestantism at the same time gave no countenance to loose and unrestrained willfulness in thought or practice. On the contrary, the freedom it has introduced is such as has solid contents, not excluding but including allegiance to law and order. *It has bound the religious spirit indissolubly to God's grace and God's word, and by so doing set it free from all human ordinances running counter to the same.* The positive element is accordingly the first. Our Church is primarily Evangelical. Protestation is its second character, and has respect only to that which invades destructively the objective ground of the gospel. Positively evangelical, it becomes at the same time negatively Protestant towards all opposing error. In short, its freedom is the blessed liberty of the children of God, which stands in unconditional obedience to the Lord and to his word, and is identical thus with moral necessity.[93]

93. Excellent instruction on this point is to be found in the truly masterly sermon of Luther, "On the Liberty of a Christian Man"; where he handles the seemingly contradictory propositions: "A Christian Man is a free lord over all things," and "A Christian Man is a bound servant of all things, and subject to every man in Christ." [Luther, *The Freedom of a Christian* in *LW* 31:327–77.]

Part Second

The Principle of Protestantism in its Relation to the Later Development and Present State of the Protestant Church

The new religious views comprehended in Protestantism accomplished a re-modification of the entire world, in government, science, art, and social life. Modern history is an inexplicable riddle without the Reformation. We are not called however to quit the strictly theological sphere. Rather, having now completed the historico-doctrinal part of our subject, we must pass on to consider THE RELATION OF THE PROTESTANT PRINCIPLE TO THE POSTURE AND WANTS OF THE CHURCH IN OUR OWN AGE.

[General Survey of the Historical Course of Protestantism]

It must be acknowledged something remarkable always, that the last days of LUTHER and MELANCHTHON, who had attained to such a full measure of evangelical liberty and joy, should have been characterized nevertheless by a deep melancholy. Only ill will can attribute this to their personal character, and only the most superficial reflection reckon it to the discredit of their work.[1]

1. The distinguished critic and historian THOMAS CARLYLE, who has well apprehended and described the character of LUTHER, at least in its human greatness and historical significance, observes of his melancholy very beautifully (*Heroes and Hero Worship*, p. 164) [*On Heroes, Hero-Worship & the Heroic in History* (New York: Appleton, 1841)]: "The basis of his life was sadness, earnestness. In his latter days, after all triumphs and victories, he expresses himself heartily weary of living; he considers that God alone can and will regulate the course things are taking and that perhaps the day of judgment is not far. As for him, he longs for one thing: that God would release him from his labor and let him depart and be at rest. They understand little of the man who cite this in discredit of him! I will call this Luther a true great man; great in intellect, in courage, affection and integrity; one of our most loveable and precious men. Great, not as a hewn obelisk; but as an alpine mountain—so simple, honest, spontaneous, not setting-up to be great at all; there for quite another purpose than being great! Ah, yes, unsubduable granite, piercing far and wide into the heavens; yet in the clefts of it, fountains, green beautiful valleys with flowers! A right spiritual hero and prophet; once more a true son of nature and fact, for whom these centuries, and many that are to come yet, will be thankful to heaven."

They were sad, not on their own account, but on account of the Church, which lay immeasurably more near to their hearts than all personal prosperity. And the men were not imposed upon by their own imagination; their sad forebodings, in view of the perils outward and inward to which Protestantism stood exposed, after its glorious pentecostal period, had in fact a prophetical character. The great rent, from which Christendom still continues to bleed, had now taken place; the Church hitherto one was divided; individuals and whole nations were set loose from the bonds of hierarchical discipline. The Reformers had not sought the separation; it was however unavoidable. They must themselves set their seal to it, after the pope had uttered his damnatory sentence, if they would obey God and their own conscience rather than men, and honor Christ's crown of thorns above the triple crown of gold with its arbitrary decrees.

It was simply the objective course of history itself, and with this, one would think, they might have set their hearts at rest. But history, since the presence of sin, unfolds itself only through extremes in the way of action and reaction. A religious principle, once uttered, becomes the property of the whole world, communicates itself like fire to all other departments of life, rushes onward restless and one-sided to its extreme consequences; and then, by inherent dialectic process, strikes over into its opposite. Dislodge a heavy rock from its place on the summit of a mountain and it rests not till it finds the bottom of the valley below, and there breaks into a thousand pieces. All flesh is as grass; only the word of God abideth forever [1 Pet 1:24–25]. This was well understood by the great men of whom we speak. Already indeed they had been compelled to witness with their own eyes much fleshly misunderstanding of their pure work; false consequences drawn from it; confusion and division by its means, though not by its fault. In all this, they saw now the slender beginnings of greater distraction to come, and were made sorrowful by the prospect. Time has since verified their fears. What they thus despondingly anticipated lies painfully disclosed before our eyes.

Protestantism has now a history of three hundred years in its rear—a short, but most stirring and active life. True, it has built no Gothic domes, painted no Raphaelian madonnas, founded no monastic orders; in such spheres, its laurels are not found. But it possesses a scholasticism, less philosophically deep perhaps, but quite as acute, as that of the Middle Ages, and at the same time much more biblically sound and solid. It carries in its bosom a mysticism, not less inward and full of feeling, speculative and practical, than that which preceded it in the Roman Church. Its hymns and chorales, in Germany at least, may stand comparison with the richest creations of Church art in earlier times. From the snows of Greenland to the islands of the South Sea, from the sundered walls of the mammoth Asiatic State to the western shores of America, its missionaries are scattered among the heathen, vying in devoted and untiring zeal with those of the ancient Church. It calls a literature its own, which is truly a literature for the *world*, and the power of which continues to be felt with boundless influence upon the civilization of the human race. To it belongs, at all events again in Germany, a theology, to which, in point of mobility, learning, spirit, penetration, freedom from prejudice, and skilful delineation, nothing equal is to be found in the earlier history of the Church. From it also has sprung the modern philosophy, with its succession of systems, which in their kind are something no less bold and grand than the papacy itself and its dogmatic image, the metaphysics of the schools. It has organized states and given them immunities that our age for no price would commute again with the servitude of the ancient hierarchy. Compare Prussia with Italy, England with Spain, the Free States of North America with Brazil, and the truth of this declaration will be at once felt.

To Romanism itself, though serving on the one hand to fix it in its own principle, it imparted on the other a new impulse: calling into life the Jesuits, for its defense; purifying like a storm its moral atmosphere, so that it could venture no more to nominate such a pope as Sixtus IV, Alexander VI, or Julius II. It stands indeed continually over against its powerful adversary still, as a corrector and waker from sleep. And who will not admit that the greatest modern defenders of popery, a MOEHLER, a GOERRES, for instance, are so formidable as they are, simply because they have sharpened their weapons on the whetstone of Protestant science? In short, without this influence the vast communion of Rome, like the Greek Church (at least in great part), must have passed over into a state of putrefaction so as to present at best only the spectacle of a praying corpse.

Traverse the lands in which Protestantism has fixed its seat, from the northern boundary of Sweden to the Sandwich Islands, from the southern declivities of the Himalayan to the banks of the Mississippi; almost everywhere you may find theologians victoriously contending against infidelity and superstition; preachers, who like Paul are not ashamed of the gospel of Christ crucified [Rom 1:16], but hold all the glory of the world in contempt for its sake; a strict moral order; a blooming domestic life; an acquaintance with the bible; a freedom and joy of faith in the inward man; such as you may seek in vain in the central seat itself of the Church of Rome. There is still sufficient salt in the system, with all its diseases, to save it from corruption; full as much certainly as belonged to the Catholic Church toward the close of the Middle Ages; material enough therefore for a new Reformation. High and low, learned and unlearned, die happily within its bosom every day, with nothing but the bible in their hands and faith in the free unmerited grace of God in their hearts. Only blindness itself can deny that Protestantism still continues the great moving force of the time, holding the helm of the world's political and spiritual history; while every other form of action comes to have deep significance, only as standing with it in hostile or friendly relation.

I. The Diseases of Protestantism.

We may not however, and will not, for this reason, close our eyes to the shadow that falls from this gigantic system, on the other side. In its inmost center there is lodged, as in the heart of the Catholic Church at the time of the Reformation, a dangerous disease; and, woe to us, if we look not round betimes for a remedy. This must be sought, not beyond the system itself, but only again within its own bosom, in that same apostolic circle into which the Judas has crept, as was the case also, according to our previous showing, with the Reformation itself. Along with the bright aspects just noticed, Protestantism has also its *Revolutions*, its *Rationalism*, its *Sects*—which are all the more dangerous as foes, inasmuch as they all claim to be its most true and legitimate offspring.

With the first, the spirit of political revolution, we have here no concern. It falls not within the theological territory. To the other two however our attention must now be directed; then to the reaction of Puseyism; and finally to the true remedy for these diseases, in its most essential points.

1. Rationalism; or one-sided theoretic subjectivism.

[A. History and character of Rationalism,]

Rationalism has developed itself mainly in the Lutheran Church upon what may be styled its classic soil. Germany is the proper home, not only of the Reformation, but of all the deeper spiritual movements which have been called forth by this during the last three hundred years. Thither then we must first direct our view. To the creative period of the Lutheran Church, which came to a close with the Formula of Concord, succeeded immediately that of logical comprehension; as in the Catholic Church the patristic, dogma-producing time was followed by the scholastic. This protestant school learning was accompanied indeed, like that which preceded it in the Church of Rome, with mystical tendencies of various sorts; but still it gave tone to the age. Its great effort accordingly was to reduce to system the theological acquisitions of the period of the Reformation, with a demonstration, in part dialectic and in part biblical, extending to the smallest separate particulars. Our business here, is not to bring into view the many merits of this period, in which such men as John Gerhard, Hutter, Quenstedt, Calovius, rise before our vision, but only to show in what respect it tended necessarily to call forth opposition. Shutting itself up from the start within the narrow circle of the Formula of Concord, it stood in a perfectly exclusive relation, not only toward the Reformed system of doctrine, but also toward the diverging peculiarities of the Melanchthonian school; and thus gradually degenerated, like the scholastic theology of the Middle Ages, into dry dogmatism and stiffened orthodoxy, in which religion was made to consist in sound knowledge, and its practical nature thrust wholly out of sight. Justification was separated abstractly from holiness; while as it regarded the formal principle, the theory of inspiration, contrary to the more free view of the Reformers, became so overstrained, that the scriptures were made to assume a magical character, in which their human, natural side was not allowed at all to appear. All this opened the way for an opposite movement.

The reaction showed itself first in the sphere of the material principle under the form of *Spenerian Pietism*, which in opposition to such forms of outward intellect successfully asserted the vast importance of holiness and the verification of faith in practice. This mission it fulfilled with great earnestness; but not without a certain one-sidedness, particularly in its later character, which gave its orthodox adversaries, with their superior science, the advantage of right in many points. Pietism contributed much—along with its kindred spirit among the UNITED BRETHREN,[2] by whom all confessional distinctions were undervalued—to disseminate a religion of sickly sentiment and sighs, aversion to clear definite conceptions, and to a regularly digested system of theology; and since the confession of the truth is the ground of the Church, along with all this a want of true Church feeling.

This was the first step, we may say, towards Rationalism; the nature of which holds in this, that it allows the idea of religion to resolve itself into simple morality, or in the end into mere good citizenship, a result full as one-sided as the error of identifying it with theoretic orthodoxy. Men who could acknowledge the truth belonging to Pietism, while they still continued to stand firm on the solid ground of the old Church faith—such as the great J. A. BENGEL, who stands out to view as the religious ornament of the eighteenth century and of his native Württemberg in particular—were not common; and their number grew always more small as the century advanced towards its close. The chord once struck found every day a clearer response. The undervaluation of the Church and her symbols led gradually to the undervaluation of the apostles and their writings, and terminated finally in a denial of the divinity of Christ himself. The transition of the pietistic tendency over into the rationalistic is strikingly exhibited in the case of the celebrated professor of Halle, SEMLER, who was brought up in the pietistic school and continued to adhere to it all his life also, in the way of what he called "private piety"; but became nevertheless, through his special dislike to doctrine, and his bold critical and historical investigations, the proper father of the German neology, and contributed beyond all others to unsettle the received views with regard to the canon and the subject of inspiration. Other elements, in part foreign—the English deism, the French infidelity—whose leaders found unfortunately so powerful a protector in Frederick the Great [1712–86], and lastly the immeasurably flat philosophy of Wolff, making all in heaven and on earth clear by making all shallow, came in to support this fatal tendency; so that towards the close of the revolutionary century it had almost universal possession of the pulpit and professor's chair, and was fairly and fully at home with the visible rulers of the Church, the general superintendents and counselors of consistory.

2. [Schaff is referring here to the *Brüdergemeinde*: Moravians who came under the protection of Count Zinzendorf in Germany, some of whom later repaired to Pennsylvania. He is not referring to the United Brethren in Christ, a group that was formed under the direction of Philip Otterbein, a German Reformed pastor in York, Pennsylvania. This latter group broke away from the German Reformed Church.]

Rationalism again, however, has its own historical development. In its first stage, it appeared as a shallow, popular *Aufklärung* ["enlightenment"], by which religion and the Church were both cleared of all deeper meaning. Afterwards, by means of the philosophy of Kant, which had in the meantime taken hold on the consciousness of the age, it assumed a more scientific form. The familiar, everyday style of thinking, was made to give place to intellectual, philosophically cultivated reflection. Finally, it culminated in the destructive speculative theology, or *untheology* rather, which within a short period past has burst, like a wild monster, with terrific desolation, from the camp of the negative criticism and Hegelian logic. Compared with this, the old common Rationalism is only a harmless child. The critical and doctrinal writings of Strauss, Feuerbach, Bruno Bauer, and their associates, may be regarded as a complete concentration, full of spirit and keen penetration, of all assaults heretofore made upon Christianity; so that if they should be fully overcome, apologetic divinity might hold a true triumph, and allow her armor to hang long without use. Rationalism, it is true, even in its first stage, had exchanged the Protestant doctrine of justification for pelagianism, and put the holy scriptures into the same class with mere human books. It still left standing however some fundamental religious truth, as the being of God, his providence, the freedom and immortality of man, and paid great respect particularly to the morality of Christianity. It is not to be denied, that Kant's *Critique of the Practical Reason* is animated with great moral earnestness, and may have served as a schoolmaster to bring some to Christ. Being separated however in itself from the personal ideal of morality, Jesus Christ, the absolute God-man, it was pervaded with the poison of stoic self-righteousness, and could make no stand therefore against the ever-growing stream of the negative movement.

The speculative Rationalism has now fully demolished the brittle structure, and thus realized in the world of thought what the French Revolution under Robespierre accomplished in actual life. The entire sacred history of our Savior is resolved into a collection of myths, unconsciously produced by the imagination of the infant Church, and forming a tissue of inward and outward contradictions. One Church dogma after another is given to the winds, as an imperfect conception, self-annihilated gradually by the onward course of scientific criticism. Yea, the whole supernatural world is drawn over into the present life as a mere product of the religious fancy without all objective reality, and the infinite Godhead itself must shrink into the finite spirit of man. This is Pantheism in the most scientifically complete and perilous form the world has ever yet seen, exalting the general idea of humanity to the throne of the universe, and proclaiming it the creator, preserver, and redeemer of all things. No further progress seems possible in this direction, unless it be to reduce the theory to practice by building temples for the worship of genius, as has been already proposed, and in some parts of the New World actually carried into effect; and by composing liturgical forms, in which the human spirit may offer prayers and sing speculative hallelujahs, in measured logico-dialectic process, to the honor and glory of itself.[3]

[B. Its relation to orthodox Protestantism.]

It would be an error however to suppose that the representatives of this tendency are agreed among themselves. They stand to one another, in part at least, in the most contradictory relation; so that the negative theological literature of Germany, at the present time, appears a tumultuating chaos of systems and theories, whose affinity often is such as holds between fire and water. In the nature of the case, when the human understanding is raised to the highest tribunal, full scope is given to the willfulness of private judgment at the same time.

This extreme climax of unbelief proclaims itself to be the ultimate necessary result of Protestantism. To this we answer however in the words of the apostle John, concerning the anti-Christian errorists of his own day: "*They went out from us* (in the way of outward, historical derivation), *but they were not of us.* For if they had been of us, they would no doubt have continued with us" (1 John 2:19). It belongs to the very nature of the Reformation, as we have seen, that it makes the clearest distinction between sinful man and a holy God, prostrates utterly the imagination that the human will may redeem itself, or the natural understanding know the truth by its own power, and requires an unconditional submission on the part of the sinner to God's grace and God's word. Here, on the contrary, the divine grace is taken to be a mere objective reflex of the power belonging to man himself, and the subjective reason, or understanding rather,[4] is made the fountain and norm of knowledge. If there was ever a radical confusion of things totally heterogeneous, we have it in the pretension just mentioned. The tendency in question deserves to be regarded only as a Christianly refined paganism, whose very character stands in a deification of the universe, and the worship of the forces, either physical or spiritual, in which it has its constitution. It might be shown that all the heathen mythologies find their image in this modern infidel cultivation.

3. [Schaff may be referring to non-theistic religious humanist societies formed by German-American freethinkers in the United States, or to other religious humanist communities and practices emerging out of Unitarianism and Transcendentalism.]

4. Rationalism arrogates to itself the title of rationality or reason as specially its own. In truth however, it moves not at all in the sphere of reason, but only in that of the abstract understanding, the region of mere finite thinking, entangled in contradictions and external appearances, the standpoint of reflection. Reason, on the contrary is the power of perceiving the supernatural, the infinite, the harmonious unity, the essence of things, the primal idea of the absolute. It is the longing of the spirit after its true country, its home-drawing towards God and the revelation he has made of himself in Christ; just as conscience is the point of contact between the human will and the ground of all will in God. Reason then, in its inmost nature, is a receptive faculty, that must go beyond itself for its contents.

[C. The altered posture thus of the time.]

From this it may now be seen clearly that the standpoint of our time is wholly different from that of the Reformers. The most dangerous enemy with which we are threatened on theoretic ground is not the catholicism of Rome, but the foe within our own borders; not the hierarchic papacy of the vatican, but the worldly papacy of the subjective understanding, and protestant infidelity; not the *Concilium Tridentinum*, but the theology of unbelief, as proclaimed by a Roehr, a Wegscheider, a Strauss, a Feuerbach, and others of the same stamp. Must not all serious believing Protestants feel themselves more closely related in spirit to a Bellarmine or a Moehler, who agree with them in acknowledging the trinity, the deity of Christ, atonement by his blood, and the divine inspiration and infallibility of the scriptures, than they are to Strauss and Bruno Bauer, by whom all these articles are rejected? I will by no means deny indeed, that a certain affinity also may be traced, in another view, between protestant Rationalism and the Catholicism of Rome; in the fact that the tradition principle of the one corresponds with the reason principle of the other, while both rest upon a pelagian basis in which all right apprehension of the deep corruption of sin is wanting.[5] Even the pantheistic character of the latest Rationalism is not without its analogies, in the absolute infallibility and supremacy in Church and State claimed by the papacy, and in the doctrine of transubstantiation, according to which the priest by his consecrating act produces the body of the Lord, the creature the Creator, and sensible elements are taken to be the immediate contents of the Savior's flesh and blood.

5. This is allowed by the more discerning and honorable Roman theologians. Thus the powerful Moehler, in the preface to the first edition of his *Symbolik*, from which all the recent apologists of popery who are of any account, draw their material (p. xi): "*The Catholic has this advantage moreover, that his system includes as well what the Rationalists honor one-sidedly or exclusively in Christianity*, as what is made prominent in the same Christianity just as one-sidedly or exclusively by the orthodox protestantism. *These two extremes are in fact, in his faith, balanced and fully reconciled. It holds as much affinity with the one as with the other*; and the catholic accordingly can comprehend both, since his system is the unity of both. The naturalistic protestants are indebted to Luther directly only for this, that he has procured for them the freedom of daring to profess what is directly opposite to him and to the religious communion which he established; and the orthodox protestants are bound with them by nothing, but the oppressive feeling that Luther has founded a Church whose conception constrains them to tolerate patiently such opposers in their midst, as a case admitting no help. The catholic on the contrary has an inward affinity on the ground of his faith with both, and thus stands higher than both and overlooks both. He has what belongs to both, only without their one-sided defects." [Moehler, *Symbolik* 1st ed. (Mainz: F. Kupferberg, 1832).] Compare the description which Melanchthon gives of the rationalistic and pelagianistic theology of his time in the *Apol. Conf.* and his *Loc. Theol.* [See *Apology of the Augsburg Confession*, Article IV, 9–21 in Kolb and Wengert, *Book of Concord*, 121–24.] We may refer also to the fact that the more free investigations which gradually led to Rationalism had their origin in part in the Catholic Church, as we may see in the case of Petavius in dogmatic history, and Richard Simon in the criticism and history of the bible. The Jesuits first proclaimed the principle of the sovereignty of the people, which produced the French Revolution, and by their casuistry opened the way for the formal overthrow of all morality, with which all religious faith also must necessarily fall at the same time.

But a great difference holds notwithstanding between the two systems, of which we must not lose sight, if we would be equal to the questions of the time.

For Romanism, in the first place, is in this respect at most only *half*-pelagian and half-rationalistic, that it makes the grace of God and the sacred scriptures co-ordinate with works and tradition, and equally necessary as the ground and fountain of salvation; whilst Rationalism, in true stoic style, dreams of being able to do *all* by its own strength, and to know *all* by reason simply, separated from its proper divine contents and contradicting thus its own design; on which account the idea of a supernatural revelation is rejected, and Christ himself is degraded to a natural hero of virtue, a second Socrates, a mere man accordingly however ideally apprehended. A further difference consists in this, that Romanism in making works necessary to justification and salvation looks to the deeds of the *whole Church*, and by tradition, as a fountain of knowledge and rule of faith supplementary to the bible, intends properly the reason of *all Christian history*, showing itself thus in the character of *objective, churchly semi-pelagianism and semi-rationalism*; while protestant Rationalism holds the *isolated* will and reason of the *individual* sufficient for the purposes of salvation, and in this way is altogether *subjective and unchurchly* in its nature. This then, as already said, stands in vastly more direct opposition to the essence of Christianity and orthodox protestantism than the enemy that the Reformers were called to combat. LUTHER and CALVIN, if they should make their appearance now, would act very differently, in the altered state of things, from what they did three hundred years ago. Their main zeal would be directed no doubt against such purely negative pseudo-protestantism as something altogether worse than popery itself.

We need to bear this in mind in our activity for religion and the Church at the present time; that we may not lose sight of our true character and calling as protestants, in view of the false pretensions with which we are surrounded on the part of the unbelieving and ungodly, who profess to stand upon the same ground and to glory in the same name; and who show themselves loudest possibly in their cry against popery and jesuitism, only to cover their hostility to all faith and righteousness. Such have a nominal title only, but none that is historical, to appear in the protestant character. That caution is needed here in a high degree, in our present circumstances, is not to be doubted. By making common cause with such destructive protestants in their opposition to Catholicism, whether the immediate object be political or religious, we must render the most efficient support and aid to this interest itself; which has already indeed, with serpent wisdom, contrived to draw immense advantage from such anti-protestant connections between Christ and Belial.[6] The attack intended to overwhelm the enemy recoils in this case necessarily, in the way of self-annihilation, upon its source. Rather let us never forget the much that we hold in common with the Roman Church, the bond of union by which she is joined with us in opposition to absolute

6. ["And what concord hath Christ with Belial? Or what part hath he that believeth with an infidel?" (2 Cor 6:15).]

unbelief; whose wild ravages are displayed also in her own bosom, particularly in France. Let us first with united strength expel the devil from our own temple, into which he has stolen under the passport of our excessive toleration, before we proceed to exorcise and cleanse the dome of St. Peter. At least, let this be our main business.

It may be said however perhaps that Rationalism, at least in the philosophical form now described, has for our own country no danger. But it should be remembered that the evil does not hold simply in the form. The main thing is the principle from which it grows; the general standpoint of a cold, abstract intellection, to which all that is mystical or supernatural in Christianity is found displeasing. In this view, we may discover affinities with the German Rationalism, not only in the Unitarian and Universalist heresies of this country, but in much also that passes for orthodoxy. That unbelief has not yet acquired here the same giant force is not owing so much to the greater prevalence of personal piety, or to the moral earnestness of the English character, as to the one-sided practical tendency and want of scientific spirit generally predominant. Where a man does not think, it requires no great skill to be orthodox. But the orthodoxy that includes no thought is not worth a farthing.[7] In countries where scientific feeling has prevailed, though with less force, as Holland and France, results have appeared quite analogous with the course of things in Germany. In Holland particularly the old established orthodoxy, having degenerated in great part into dry and lifeless forms, found itself assailed by Arminianism, which itself again ran out finally into formal Pelagianism and Rationalism.[8]

In the case before us, it may be expected that the disposition to explore a given principle, and carry it out to its proper consequences, will continually gain ground; and with this change, if no scientific counterpoise be provided in season, Rationalism must assume among us a more dangerous form. Why should it not find its way into England and America, even as the Deism of the first country, from which it is descended, wandered formerly over into Germany, to complete there its university training? Time and space are continually becoming more compressed; the intercourse of the nations more active and free. Emigration from the Old World is on the increase. Acquaintance with German literature is extending daily; and it would not be difficult to show that many respectable divines of this country, who employ themselves with it only under its abstract intellectual form, have without their own knowledge or will

7. [These pointed indictments of the shallowness of American orthodox Protestantism reveal the considerable potential for animosity between Schaff and his new American colleagues and co-religionists.]

8. [Jacob Arminius (1560–1609) was a Dutch Reformed theologian at the University of Leiden who came to oppose orthodox scholastic Calvinism and its doctrine of predestination. After his death his supporters authored the *Remonstrance* (1610) which articulated their objections to Calvinism in five points. These were subsequently condemned by the Synod of Dort (1618–19). Nevertheless a small Remonstrant community continued, achieving state recognition in 1795 and becoming an enduring liberal Protestant church, while the original Arminian objections to Calvinist orthodoxy gained progressively widespread acceptance among American Protestant churches from the late eighteenth through early twentieth centuries.]

admitted the rationalistic principle, which needs only to be cultivated, as a germ in the earth, by those who may come after them without their piety, to grow upwards in a short time into a mighty tree. Shall I say that even in the liturgies and hymn books of the German American churches rationalistic elements are by no means rare, without being perceived by those who use them? In many cases, clergymen who were educated at the German universities in the palmy day of Rationalism, have been here improved indeed in their hearts under the salutary influence of practical piety, but have at the same time retained the poison, for which no scientific antidote was at hand, in their heads and communicated it also involuntarily to others.

I will simply notice the fact besides, as of a kind to justify anxiety, that so many of the German periodicals of the country, particularly in the West, are lending themselves as organs more or less expert, to the service of infidelity, with the worst influence on the more common class especially of our emigrant population. True, these sheets, so far as they are known to me, are mostly both in matter and style beyond description miserable; such as dare not show themselves in Germany at all, unless in the lowest ale-houses. The great body of their readers however, of course, are not aware that all this style of pretended light and liberality has been fairly exterminated by German science in its most recent form, or we may say even by the Romantic school itself; and then, practically, it comes to much the same, whether infidelity goes about in the antiquated coat and cue style of a Bahrdt and Edelmann, or in the modern philosophical cloak of a Strauss or Feuerbach. We have good reason therefore to stand upon our guard in this quarter also, and to prepare ourselves before hand for the crisis that may come.[9]

9. As many of my readers probably never see the publications referred to, while at the same time it is important that they should know something of the infernal spirit which is at work to undermine the faith of the German population in America, I will submit here to the by no means pleasant task of furnishing a sample of its character; selecting for the purpose a few striking passages only from the collection of various papers I have received, on account of attacks they have contained against me for my ordination sermon, as mentioned in the Introduction. I might bring forward quite a body of political sheets published only by immigrant Germans; but it may be better to limit myself to two of religious, or much better anti-religious pretension, which appear in wholly opposite sections of the union.

The "Licht-Freund," published by C. Muehl and Strehly in Hermann, Missouri, contains in No. 6 of its 5th year, along with other products of the most superficial, spiritless and jejune form of rationalism, an essay on *baptism* in which it is represented as an old usage of pagan and Jewish origin which "Rabbi Jesus" was pleased to retain in his system, but that has now become wholly unmeaning, or rather "irrational" and "grossly superstitious."—"Of a trine immersion or sprinkling with water," we are told, "nothing was known in the beginning; but this was introduced only after the introduction, at a later period, of the nonsensical doctrine of *one God consisting of three persons* of which, as we have shown on a different occasion, no trace is to be found in connection with early Christianity."—"Have children sins then," sneeringly inquires this apostle of infidelity, this jack-o'-lantern philosopher, "that call for forgiveness? On the topic of original sin, as discussed by us in our preceding year, we have handled this point at large and exposed the *ridiculousness of the Church doctrine*."—"It is said of baptism further" (the reference is to Luther's Catechism), "that it redeems us from death and the Devil. But this is still more false; since baptized and unbaptized alike die; and as for the Devil, it is well understood that *this is an invention simply of diseased imagination that carries us back to the times of the*

2. Sectarism; or onesided practical subjectivism.

most gross superstition and rudeness. The devil who plays specter in the doctrine of the Church, is long since killed dead, and no longer creates fear; though it cannot be denied that there is still devil enough in the world, and particularly in America." This last remark has certainly much truth, of which the writer himself may be taken as good practical proof.—In the same number we read: "This bugbear" (of the *orthodox* Lutheran and Reformed Church) "is the old theology which has long since outlived itself. For who in our time can still believe in three Gods, a propitiation of God by blood, a descent into hell, and other devil's play, as expounded here to a hair in the largest style. . . . Let no one say however that people do not play with puppets when they grow large and old. The history of religion, ancient and modern, teaches us that men continue to be children, however old they may be." The religious history of Hermann in Missouri appears however to form a special exception; and the most learned Messrs. Muehl, Strehly, and company, are to be regarded, we presume, as the only truly rational men the world has yet seen. What a pity no one should think of making them professors of theology and philosophy! It is enough to drive one mad, such a perverse world, with its childish religious history.—In No. 10 of the same year a characteristic article is found abusing the Pennsylvania synods, which however is too long to be presented here; also a report on the rationalist associations in Hermann and Augusta, exhibiting in the case of the first, among others, the following spirited resolution: "That we hold all and every title, assumed by the clerical tribe, such as Reverend, Ehrwürdig, Hochwürdig, etc. for a ridiculous, aristocratic pretension, repugnant to free, republican feeling, which every free man should reject with scorn." That these honest heroes of liberty should abolish such titles among themselves must be approved as altogether rational and natural; though we should think it hardly necessary; for none surely who care for decency or truth are likely to burden them with any titles of the sort.

[Edward Muehl (Mühl) and his brother-in-law Carl Procopius Strehly published the *Licht-Freund* in Hermann, Missouri. (Schaff's reference to C. Muehl, appears to be an error.) Mühl first published the *Licht-Freund* in Cincinnati, Ohio, but relocated to Hermann, a German colony, in 1843. Mühl and Stehly were freethinkers who emphasized the supremacy of reason. Mühl, the major literary voice of the paper, acquired a widespread reputation. Most controversially, the *Licht-Freund* advocated the abolition of slavery. The paper discontinued upon his death. Bek, *The German Settlement Society of Philadelphia*, 164–70. *Missouri*, 394.]

The *Licht-Freund* however sheds but the pale glimmer of a glowworm, as compared with the full blazing brightness of another periodical, which makes its appearance at New York, edited by Samuel Ludvigh, under the blinding title *Die Fackel* ["The Torch"]; with the motto, "Out of the ruins of Judaism and Christianity, rationalism will raise its head; out of the rubbish of temples and churches will rise halls of science." Here we read, in No. 4 of the 2nd year (14. Dec. 1844), among other things, such blasphemies as we find it almost too much to copy: "*Dass nach der Lehre des Herrn V. die Asteroiden Bruechstuecke eines grossen Planeten seien, ist in meinen Augen ebenso richtig, als der heilige Geist eines Gottessohn machen koenne. Wenn Planeten Junge machen koennen, so bleibe man doch ja fein im Glauben des alten Gottes, und lasse ihn durch seinen heiligen Geist hier auf Erden noch andere goettliche Jungfern-Kinder erzeugen. Wie aber seine keuschen Marien in jenen Planeten aussehen muessen, das begreift mein Hirnkasten nicht!*" [Trans. "The notion that the Holy Ghost could make a son of God is just as legitimate, from my point of view, as Herr V's teaching that asteroids are supposed to be the broken bits of a great planet. If planets could make boys then one might well remain secure believing in the old God, leaving it to him to produce other divine virgin children through his Holy Ghost here on earth. But what his chaste Marys are supposed to look like on all those planets – that boggles my mind!" Note, while Schaff deemed this "*almost* too much to copy," Nevin decided it was too much to translate!]

The same writer presents his confession of faith, or no faith rather, which is pronounced by Herr Ludvigh: "the quintessence of the highest human spirit." It is to be found with him, inscribed on glass, and all "whose means allow them to honor such a pearl" can be furnished with it there for five dollars. It is of such sort as to throw Feuerbach himself into the shade, whose *Wesen des Christenthums* [*Essence of Christianity*] is diligently turned to account by the *Fackel*. "I believe" (thus speaks this "very distinguished scholar" of Boston) "in an inexplicable, exalted eternal existence, whose name no tongue has ever yet uttered, which was, is, and shall be, past, present and future, in all three eternally

We turn now to the other grand disease which has fastened itself upon the heart of Protestantism, and which must be considered only the more dangerous because it appears ordinarily in the imposing garb of piety, Satan transformed into an angel of light. This is the sect system, which reigns especially in our own land, favored by its free institutions and the separation of the Church from the State, and is entitled accordingly to our particular attention. While Rationalism has been nurtured mainly in the bosom of the Lutheran Church, the poisonous plant of sectarianism has flourished most on Reformed ground, and with the practical nations, England, and her now full grown, emancipated daughter America.

This difference has its ground in the national character of the Germans and the English, who stand in a relation to each other similar to that of the ancient Greeks

---

without change; which was, is, and shall be, one and the same in endless union with itself and the majestical whole; whose power comprehends itself and all, from eternity—that I also have sprung from its bosom, and as a shoot of its eternal endure forever—that my eternal deposited in my mother as seed, impregnated into a germ and brought into the world, formed my present—that I have here heaven and hell, joy and sorrow alike—that when my present shall here dissolve, its elements will be reduced again to the mass out of which I was taken by my birth—that no miracle can occur in the course of the whole—that man and spirit are but spokes in the eternal wheel, no one of more account than another to its movement—that no dead shall or can come ever again—that the judgment of the living must have place here as the consequence of their actions, and that for the dead none is needed—that the most glorious temple is nature under the vault of heaven, and that a God among the stars, crowned with suns, must blind us to the pomp and splendor of churches, and is too high for human worship—that what the priests teach is only falsehood and delusion, and the hope of a life to come a mere contrivance for gain—that the consciousness of praiseworthy actions is a true paradise and a state of divine peace—that an affectionate faithful wife, and loving children, are the true heavenly angels, and in the opposite case also they are the hateful devils—that man needs a wise teacher, for his own welfare and that of others—that I must respect myself, before I can deserve to be respected by others—that I must do right, before I exact right—that the noble man is a god of the earth, but a rough, unprincipled one the most hateful of all venomous monsters—that when I have lived as a man, and loved my fellow men, I can peacefully resign my ashes to corruption in the urn of oblivion, and finally—that something from my eternal thus laid down shall be my resurrection." What this residuum shall consist in, we are informed by the great dogmatist himself. Moscowy leather for boot soles! And this nauseous filth of a demented brain is offered for five dollars! Utilitarianism, in such a case, may well be indulged with its *Cui bono*? The Bostonian philosopher seems himself to have but small hope of replenishing his hungry purse from the profits of his system. He confesses to his friend Ludvigh: "A real dog's life among men, who are like asses and tigers! I have had much, and still have much to bear; my old skin is tanned to moscowy leather. Whoever shall work it into boot soles hereafter, he will have soles that may be expected to last."

[Samuel Ludvigh immigrated from the Austrian empire in 1837, becoming editor of the *Alte und neue Welt* (Old and new world), a German language paper in Philadelphia. In 1843 he moved to New York City and established *Die Fackel. Literaturblatt zur Förderung geistiger Freiheit* (The Torch: literary journal for the promotion of intellectual freedom) which he published until his death. He traveled widely, lecturing in German-American communities and publishing many books. The Boston scholar who wrote the passages Schaff quotes is a Transcendentalist. Since his words were published in German by Ludvigh and then translated back into English by Nevin, he cannot be easily identified. Since Ralph Waldo Emerson had delivered his Divinity School Address in 1838 and Parker published his *Transient and Permanent* in 1841, the rebellion of Transcendentalism within New England Unitarianism was well established by the time Schaff wrote. That he deems it necessary to quote the Boston scholar at length says as much about Schaff as about Ludvigh.]

and Romans. For the better understanding then of this part of our subject, a short ethnographic digression may not be out of place.

The German, when true to his better nature, is distinguished by inwardness, heartiness, and a tendency to contemplation and deep thought. His favorite home is the ideal region of truth and beauty. He possesses at the same time inexhaustible energy and endurance. He can devote his whole life to the development of a philosophical thought or some learned investigation, and feel himself happy while so doing under the most unfavorable circumstances, even sitting on a shoemaker's bench, like Jacob Boehm, or suffering hunger with Kepler. He reckons among his countrymen, the greatest philosophers and artists. An idealist by profession, he has but little tact for practical life. Readily and easily he adapts himself to all outward relations, foreign countries and new tongues, not setting himself to remold them to his own taste, if only he may be left free to follow his inward theoretic bent. He seeks his highest crown in the *Gemütlichkeit*[10] that forms especially the ornament of the German woman, and in science, the pride and joy of the man. Hence accordingly almost all movements in the German Church have turned upon doctrine. She produced all the leading ideas of the Reformation, but left to other nations the business of outward organization. She presents at this time in particular a mixed mass of systems and schools, a pattern chart of all possible views and tendencies. But they all continue notwithstanding in one Church connection, only in rare instances run into separation, schism, sectdom. In Germany, one may often meet with disputations among the younger class, where different persons contend, amid clouds of tobacco smoke, with the greatest keenness and most thorough learning, bringing out the inmost principles of their subject, making them stand forth like day and night, and not resting till they are pushed to their most extreme consequences. But at last, their strength exhausted, they join in the friendly glass and song, and exchange a general kiss, as though nothing had occurred. When however it does come to separation, a case exemplified too often among Germans in this country, we find this usually in an eccentric style. For the German cannot well observe moderation. He has a decided tendency to extremes, both in politics and religion. As he can rise very high, so he can fall very low.

Quite different is the Englishman, and the American resting on the same basis. True, he shares with his kindred Germanic race the same ethical force, which no storms can overcome. But since the time of William the Conqueror, a strong Romanic element has been found associated with his nature. The energy of his will accordingly takes a different direction, one which is outward, namely into practical life. A born realist, he possesses the greatest talent for organization; shrinks from no difficulty, where the call is for order and form; his character is marked and strong. For philosophy and art in their higher forms he cares but little; single praiseworthy examples excepted, as among later writers particularly Coleridge and Carlyle. Such studies are for him not sufficiently

10. [A quality of hospitality or a general disposition, Schaff describes *Gemütlichkeit* below as consisting in the "expression of full, warm, heartfelt tenderness."]

practical, useful, tangible. He laughs at the speculations of the modern German philosophers as unfruitful, baseless, fantastic visions, and still continues to cherish a truly superstitious veneration for the empiricism of LOCKE. The German *Gemütlichkeit*, with its expression of full, warm, heartfelt tenderness, he regards with distrust as effeminate weakness, or sickly sentimentality. So far is he from making himself at home with passive self-renunciation, in foreign relations, he seeks rather everywhere to bend and cut them to his own nature. Go where he may, he remains always an Englishman. Even when he travels into other lands, he expects more accommodation to his national peculiarities on the part of the people than he is prepared to yield to theirs. So in this country, his will, language, manners and customs are made the measure to which Spaniards, Swedes, Hollanders, and French must adjust themselves as they best can; and it is quite possible that the German nationality also, as it now holds among us under a distinct form, both in language and life, may gradually be swallowed up at last in the same Anglican ocean. A result however that must be considered calamitous, and which all Germans should endeavor with all their might to avert. In conformity with this character, the controversies belonging to the history of the English and North American Churches turn not so much on doctrine as on the constitution and forms of the Church. In place of schools and systems we have parties and sects, which in many cases appear in full inexorable opposition, even while occupying the platform, of the very same confession. The mere question of patronage has produced in Scotland, during the last century and in our own time, very important secessions; though the freedom of the Established Church in that country is of a high order, as compared with the condition of the German Church; which nevertheless has no thought of a separation from the State on this account; content if she may be internally free, in the midst of the deductions of philosophy and the creations of art.[11]

[A. History and character of Sectarism.]

Sects, it is true, do not owe their origin to the Reformation. They have root in the general nature of man, its sinful ambition and pride. The apostles were called to oppose the evil, in the very infancy of the Church, as we may learn from 1 Cor. 1:10 ff.,

11. [There were three significant secessions from the Church of Scotland in this period. All were rooted in protests against the right of wealthy landowners, instead of church members and leaders, to appoint ministers. The first, in 1733, created the Associate Synod. In 1761, the second created the Relief Church. The third, known as the Disruption, occurred in May 1843. Approximately a third of the clergy and perhaps half the members withdrew to form the Free Church of Scotland. Not only polity, but theology and piety were involved in each schism, particularly the last when the evangelicals who withdrew were discontent with the moderates' controling the church. Schaff's lack of appreciation of these movements for the autonomy of the church is striking given his embrace in *What is Church History?* of the positive revaluations being offered by Protestant historians of the similarly motivated reforms led by Cluny and Pope Gregory VII in the tenth and eleventh centuries. This disjuncture is best understood by the contrast between the Prussian and Scottish churches that he mentions. Whitley, *A Great Grievance*; Roxburgh, *Thomas Gillespie*; Brown and Fry, *Scotland in the Age of the Disruption*.]

as well as from other passages. The first centuries exhibit a vast number of sects, and they extend through the whole Middle Age. The Catholic Church however has gradually overwhelmed them, partly by spiritual superiority and partly by outward force. Through the emancipation of a large portion of Christendom from the Roman yoke in the 16th century, much more ample scope was secured for the action of subjective freedom, so that it became possible for such separations to acquire independent strength and clothe themselves with a regular constitution. Still they were held back, at the beginning, by the thunder of Luther's voice, and the colossal weight of his person. Calvin too had such a religious horror of heresies and sects that he hewed to pieces without mercy the unprincipled Libertines of Geneva with the sword of his spirit, and even suffered the distinguished Spanish physician, Michael Servetus, to be burned, for denying the doctrine of the trinity.[12]

In England, the energetic government of Elizabeth was enabled to unite the conflicting tendencies of protestantism, though not indeed without violence towards the most stubborn opposers, under a common head, in the form of a complete state-church organization. But under her successors, this degenerated continually more and more into mere external formalism. The consequence was the *Puritan* revolution, by means of which under Cromwell the more free protestant element gained the ascendancy, though only for a short time. Laud atoned for the hierarchical Charles I and for the political sins of the new protestant popedom, each with the sacrifice of his own life. The deep moral earnestness, the stern self-discipline, the unbending force of character exhibited in Puritanism, must fill the unprejudiced historian with high admiration. There was reason in its war against the tyranny of false forms. When it is beheld with inexorable zeal for the first and second commandments, storming the altars and turning St. Paul's cathedral into a stall for horses, it strikes us as a divine judgment, the scorn of the Most High himself, directed against the proud creations of men; and one is reminded of the conduct of Moses, when with indignation at the calf worship of the Israelites, he dashed the tables of the law to pieces [Exod 32:19].[13]

But here precisely lies the weakness also of this tendency. Puritanism has a zeal for God, but not according to knowledge.[14] Inflamed against the despotism of bad

12. [The Libertines were Geneva citizens, who tended toward pantheistic beliefs and who were accused of sexual promiscuity. Calvin famously prevented them from partaking of the Lord's supper. His treatise "Against the Fantastic and Furious Sect of the Libertines who Call Themselves 'Spirituals'" was composed in view of their activities and against their doctrine of the flesh.]

13. [The development of the Church of England was shaped by those who embraced the policies of Queen Elizabeth I, including the Book of Common Prayer, the retention of some medieval ceremonies, and governance by bishops, and those who desired a more complete reform, often in the direction of Calvin's Geneva. William Laud became archbishop of Canterbury in 1633 and enforced a stronger high church policy, requiring the reintroduction of certain pre-Reformation practices and liturgical conformity. This was among the factors precipitating the beginning of the English Civil War in 1642 between the largely puritan Parliamentarians and the Anglican Royalists. As a result of it Oliver Cromwell became England's principal ruler, Laud was executed in 1645, Charles I in 1649.]

14. [An allusion to Paul's indictment of Jews who seek to justify themselves by works in Rom 10:2.]

forms, and the abuse of such as are good, it makes war upon form in every shape, and insists on stripping the spirit of all covering whatever, as though the body were a work of the Devil. If the choice were simply between a bodiless spirit and a spiritless body, the first of course must be at once preferred. But there is still a third condition, that of a sound spirit in a sound body; and this is the best of all, alone answering to the will and order of God. For the body is the divinely formed, natural habitation of the spirit, without which it wanders about ghostlike, exposed to all inclement powers, and must in the end perish with cold. It is worthy of notice that a large part of the puritan or presbyterian congregations in England, and also a considerable section of the congregational interest in North America, in the beginning of the last century, fell over to Unitarianism. The failure of life was a failure of orthodoxy at the same time. Whereas in the case of organizations better secured by forms, the orthodoxy in the same circumstances has still maintained itself at least with statute force, so that when life has returned again, after a period of collapse (against which no constitution as such can make the Church secure), it has found at once its established Church channels, by which to flow forth among the people.

With this rugged, abstract spiritualism stands closely connected the unhistorical, revolutionary tendency of Puritanism. It has no respect whatever for history. It would restore pure, primitive Christianity, with entire disregard to the many centuries of development that lie between, as though all had been labor in vain, and the Lord had not kept his own promise to be with the Church always to the end of the world. It is not surprising, on this account, that CROMWELL, who overturned in such stormful style the ecclesiastical creations of an older time and even stained himself with the blood of a king and an archbishop, should hardly be named without horror in the bosom of the Episcopal Church, and that the great and lofty qualities which undoubtedly belonged to his character should be so generally overlooked, or regarded without respect.[15] He that tramples father and mother underfoot, has no reason to find fault with his children, when they treat him in the same way, and prove the instruments of a divine Nemesis to bring him to a sense of his own wrong committed against history.

With vastly more wisdom, prudence, and moderation, did the founders of Methodism commence and carry forward their work of reformation. WHITEFIELD and the two WESLEYS never laid aside their respect for the mother Church, but notwithstanding its degeneracy labored in its communion and died within its bosom. The Wesleyan movement, it is true, included a secessional element from the beginning, which the force of circumstances soon rendered too strong to be restrained; and the result was the establishment of a separate Church. The divorce however was unnatural and wrong; and the form into which Methodism has since run, in this country particularly (the fair evolution of its original one-sided subjectivity), is not suited certainly

15. An attempt indeed to do him justice has been made recently by THOMAS CARLYLE in his book *Heroes and Hero Worship*, Sect. VI: "The Hero as a King." Carlyle however is constitutionally no Episcopalian, but a Scotch Presbyterian. [Thomas Carlyle, *On Heroes*, 233–287.]

to unsettle this judgment.[16] In the nature of the case, the contemporaneous Secession from the Church of Scotland, notwithstanding the eminent piety of the principal actors in it, must fall under the same condemnation. The results of it as transplanted again to American soil, furnish a painfully ridiculous commentary on the false tendency involved in it from the start.[17]

Puritan protestantism forms properly the main basis of our North American Church. Viewed as a whole, she owes her general characteristic features, her distinctive image, neither to the German or Continental Reformed, nor to the German Lutheran, nor to the English Episcopal communion, but to that band of Independents, who for the sake of their faith and a good conscience forsook their native land before the time of Cromwell, sought refuge first in Holland, and finally landed with prayers and tears on the shores of Massachusetts Bay. To this New England influence must be added indeed the no less important weight of Presbyterianism, as derived subsequently from Scotland and Ireland. But this may be regarded as in all essential respects the same life. The reigning theology of this country is neither that of the Heidelberg Catechism, nor that of the Augsburg Confession, nor that of the Thirty Nine Articles. It is the theology of the Westminster Confession.

We may never ungratefully forget that it was this generation of godly pilgrims which once for all stamped upon our country that character of deep moral earnestness, that spirit of strong intrepid determination, that peculiar zeal for the sabbath and the bible, which have raised it to so high a place in the history of the Christian Church, and enable it now to compare so favorably with the countries of the Old World. For our German emigration in particular it must be counted a high privilege that it is here brought into contact with the practical piety of the English community,[18] and by degrees also imbued more or less with its power; though with the loss, to be regretted on the other side, of many German peculiarities. Thousands of souls that might have died in vanity and unbelief in their native land have been thus rescued, we may trust, from eternal perdition.

But while we thankfully and joyfully acknowledge this, we have no right still to overlook the fact that along with the same tendency an unhistorical and unchurchly character has inserted itself also into the inmost joints of our religious life. The scriptures are the only source and norm of saving truth, but tradition is the channel by which it is carried forward in history.[19] The letter of revelation transforms itself con-

16. [For Methodism's global expansion see Hempton, *Methodism*. On the early development of American Methodism see Wigger, *Taking Heaven by Storm*.]

17. [Schaff refers to the formation of the Associate Presbytery (1753), later the Associate Reformed Synod (1782), as a separate body from the main Presbyterian denomination in the U.S. See Smylie, *A Brief History*, 62, 82–83.]

18. [Here and elsewhere, Schaff employs the vernacular of German Americans. By "English," he means "English-speaking." He by no means intends to exclude the Scots or other British-American ethnicities.]

19. When we speak here, and afterwards occasionally in favor of tradition, the reader is requested

tinuously into life and action, and this not simply in the individual believer as such, but in the Christian Church as a whole, to which as his mother the individual must hold himself subordinate as indeed it is only through her he receives the scriptures themselves. The plan of redemption, moreover, calls for more than the rescue simply of individual souls. God's will is that the body of the redeemed should exhibit an organic communion that may be the image of the union that holds between himself and the Only Begotten Son. This conception of the communion of the Church, however, as the body of Christ, few here seem to have reached in its depth and glory.

The principle of Congregationalism, which has exercised such vast influence upon the entire conformation of our religious views and relations, leads legitimately to full Atomism. The bible principle, in its abstract separation from tradition, or Church development, furnishes no security against sects. They make their appeal collectively to the sacred volume; the Devil himself does so, when it suits his purpose. Strongly also as Puritanism and Congregationalism, in their theocratic, state Church period, endeavored to secure a religious and civil union of their members, a subordination of the individual to the general, the system is clearly impotent in this direction. It includes no limitation for the principle of sects. In its own nature it is unhistorical and one-sidedly spiritualistic, and has no reason on this account to require or expect that its children should be bound by its authority, more than it has itself been bound by the authority of its own spiritual ancestry. The theocratic period accordingly soon ran its course. With the Revolution, the separation of Church and State became general and fixed. As there was now no hierarchic bond on the one hand, as in the Church of Rome, so neither was there any civil supremacy on the other, as in Germany, the Episcopal Church of England, and the Greek Church of Russia, by which the single elements might be held together.[20] The emigration from the Old World increased meanwhile with every year, transporting with it the germs of sectarian distinction and material for new religious formations. Tendencies, which had found no political room to unfold themselves in other lands, wrought here without restraint. All the circumstances of the country, in one word, have contributed to precipitate the Church into those evils, precisely, with which she was least qualified in her original character successfully to contend.

Thus we have come gradually to have a host of sects, which it is no longer easy to number, and that still continues to swell from year to year.[21] Where the process of

---

to bear always in mind what we have already said of the different kinds of tradition. We plead for it, not of course in the Romish sense, which makes it a source of knowledge independent of the bible, and co-ordinate with it in rank, but as exhibiting the consciousness the Church has of the contents of the bible, the Christian reason in the form of history, the *living word* of God in the Church as it flows forth from the word written.

20. [The disestablishment in 1833 of the Congregational churches in Massachusetts was the last act of church-state separation in the United States following the Revolutionary War.]

21. The latest work on the American Church, *An Original History of the Religious Denominations at Present Existing in the United States, Etc.*, by I. D. Rupp (Philadelphia[: J.Y. Humphreys], 1844), gives

separation is destined to end, no human calculation can foretell. Any one who has, or fancies that he has, some inward experience and a ready tongue, may persuade himself that he is called to be a reformer; and so proceed at once, in his spiritual vanity and pride, to a revolutionary rupture with the historical life of the Church, to which he holds himself immeasurably superior. He builds himself of a night accordingly a new chapel in which now, for the first time since the age of the apostles, a pure congregation is to be formed; baptizes his followers with his own name, to which he thus secures an immortality, unenviable it is true, but such as is always flattering to the natural heart; rails and screams with full throat against all that refuse to do homage to his standard; and with all this though utterly unprepared to understand a single book, is not ashamed to appeal continually to the scriptures, as having been sealed entirely, or in large part, to the understanding of eighteen centuries, and even to the view of our Reformers themselves, till now at last God has been pleased to kindle the true light in an obscure corner of the New World! Thus the deceived multitude, having no power to discern spirits, is converted not to Christ and his truth, but to the arbitrary fancies and baseless opinions of an individual, who is only of yesterday. Such *con*version is of a truth only *per*version; such *theo*logy, *neo*logy; such exposition of the bible, wretched imposition. What is built is no Church, but a chapel, to whose erection Satan himself has made the most liberal contribution.

Such is the aspect of our land. A variegated sampler of all conceivable religious chimeras and dreams, in connection with more sober systems of sectarian faith! Every theological vagabond and peddler may drive here his bungling trade, without passport or license, and sell his false ware at pleasure. What is to come of such confusion is not now to be seen.[22]

[B. Its relation to the bible and to orthodox Protestantism.]

Nor is it enough that all these poisonous weeds shoot up thus wild and luxuriant, in our protestant garden. Even those divisions of the Church that are essentially rooted in the same evangelical soil, and that cannot well be included in the category of sects, stand for the most part in such hostile relation to one another, and show so little inclination or impulse towards an inward and outward union in the Lord, that one might weep to think of it. There are indeed single cases of honorable exception, which I know how to value. Without them, we might well nigh despair. In a broad general view of the case however, particularly as it is exhibited in the periodical organs of the

---

an account of not less than forty-one protestant sects, but is notwithstanding by no means complete.

22. [From another point of view, this process might be perceived as the process of "democratization" in American religion as witnessed by Tocqueville and described by Nathan Hatch, *The Democratization of American Christianity*. Schaff's attitude toward the proliferation of denominations softens during his first decade of American residency; he explains the situation quite differently in his lectures on religion in America delivered in Berlin and subsequently published as *America* (1855). See Schaff, *Schaff's "America" and Related Writings*, ed. Stephen R. Graham, MTSS vol. 11 (forthcoming).]

different denominations, the evidences of a wrong spirit are sufficiently clear. Jealousy and contention, and malicious disposition in various forms, are painfully common. We see but little of that charity, which suffereth long and is kind, envieth not, vaunteth not itself, is not puffed up, doth not behave itself unseemly, seeketh not her own, is not easily provoked, and thinketh no evil; that rejoiceth not in iniquity, but rejoiceth in the truth, wherever it may be found, that beareth all things, believeth all things, hopeth all things, endureth all things [1 Cor 13:4–7]. No, alas; with shame and humiliation be it confessed, the different sections of our orthodox Protestantism also are severally bent on securing absolute dominion, take satisfaction too often in each other's damage, undervalue and disparage each other's merits, regard more their separate private interest than the general interest of the kingdom of God, and show themselves stiff-willed and obstinately selfish wherever it comes to the relinquishment, or postponement even, of subordinate differences for the sake of a great common object.

To the man who has any right idea of the Church as the communion of saints, this state of things must be a source of deep distress. The loss of all his earthly possessions, the death of his dearest friend, however severely felt, would be as nothing to him, compared with the grief he feels for such division and distraction of the Church of God, the body of Jesus Christ. Not for the price of the whole world, with all its treasures, could he be induced to appear as the founder of a new sect. A sorrowful distinction that in any view; and one besides that calls for small spiritual capital indeed in these United States.

I am well aware that many respectable Christians satisfy their minds on the subject of sectism, by looking at it as the natural fruit of evangelical liberty. In the main matter, the leading orthodox Protestant parties, they tell us—Episcopalian, Presbyterian, Methodist, Lutheran and Reformed—are all one; their differences have respect almost altogether to government and worship only, that is to the outward conformation of the Church, in the case of which the Lord has allowed large freedom; and so far as they may have a doctrinal character, they may be said to regard not so much the substance of the truth itself, as the theological form simply under which it is apprehended. The separation of these Churches, in the mean time, is attended, we are told, with this great advantage, that it serves to stimulate their zeal and activity, and to extend in this way the interest of religion. This last point we shall not pretend here to dispute; but the advantage, so far as it may exist, is to be ascribed, not to the divisions in question as such, but only to God, who in his wisdom can bring good out of all evil. In the balance of the last judgment moreover, good works that proceed from ambition and emulation only will be found to carry but little if any weight.

From those however who undertake to justify the sect system as a whole, the apologists of religious fanaticism and faction, I would fain require some biblical ground in favor of what is thus upheld. Not a solitary passage of the bible is on their side. Its whole spirit is against them. The Lord is come to make of twain one; to gather the dispersed children of God, throughout the whole world, into one fold, under one

Shepherd [John 10:16]. His last command to his disciples was that they should love one another, and serve one another, as he had loved and served them [John 13:34–35; 15:12, 17]. His last prayer, before his bitter passion, was that all his followers might be made perfect in one, as he was in the Father and the Father in him [John 17:21–23]. Of the first Christians we read, in the Acts of the Apostles, that they were of one heart and one mind, and continued steadfast in the apostles' doctrine and fellowship, and in the breaking of bread and prayer [Acts 2:32, 42]. Paul exhorts the Corinthians in the name of Jesus Christ, that they should all speak the same thing and that there should be no divisions among them; but that they should be perfectly joined together in the same mind and in the same judgment. They must not call themselves after Paul, or Apollos, or Cephas, or Christ in the way of party or sect. For Christ was not divided; and Paul had not been crucified for them; and no one had been baptized into the name of Paul, but all into the name of Christ [1 Cor 1:10–15].[23] The entire view taken by this apostle of the nature of the Church, as the one body of Christ, whose members all partake of the same life blood and are set for mutual assistance; having one hope of their calling, one Lord, one faith, one baptism, one God and Father of all; endeavoring to keep the unity of the one body and one spirit in the bond of peace [Eph 4:3–6]; this view, I say, inflicts a death blow, with one stroke, on the whole sectarian and denominational system. Peter describes the Church as a single spiritual temple, built up with living stones on the same living foundation, Jesus Christ [1 Pet 2:5–8]. John places one great mark of Christianity in love to the brethren; and when in his old age he was carried to the church, having no strength more for any long address, he would still repeat that one exhortation, as comprehending all besides, *Children, love one another* [John 13:34].[24]

Perhaps however the sect system must still be regarded as at all events the last necessary consequence and unavoidable fruit of Protestantism. So many protestants even, and of course all papists, affirm. If such were the fact, the Reformation must stand in direct contradiction to the holy scriptures, and be adjudged by its own umpire to condemnation as a sinful work of man. But, God be praised, the case is not thus bad. The reproach is of the same order with that other, which as we have already seen would shove us into the arms of Rationalism and Pantheism, as our only legitimate resting place.

As in that case, so in this, we repel the alliance as unnatural and false. The sect system, like Rationalism, is a prostitution and caricature of true Protestantism and

23. [Schaff's gloss on 1 Cor 1:12, that no one should call themselves "Christ in the way of party or sect" related especially to the nineteenth century, where various restoration movements, such as the churches of Christ, the Disciples of Christ, the Christadelphians, the Church of Jesus Christ of Latter-day Saints, made Christ central to their name. While these movements all sought Christian unity, they ended up being sects or denominations. Casey and Foster, *Stone-Campbell Movement*.]

24. [Mutual love is a key theme of the first two letters of John, as well as the Gospel of John, all of which Schaff followed tradition in ascribing to John, son of Zebedee. The tradition about his repeated exhortation may be found in Jerome's commentary on Galatians 4:10. *St. Jerome's Commentaries*, trans. Scheck, 266.]

nothing else. We have shown, in the first part of this tract, that the Reformation was no arbitrary novelty, but the fruit of all the better tendencies of the Catholic Church itself; that the Reformers aimed at no separation from the reigning Church, but that this was wholly the work of the pope. Had they been permitted to preach the pure word of God with freedom, and to administer the sacraments according to Christ's appointment, they would have remained in their original communion. But in what orthodox protestant party of our day is this forbidden? No man is in danger with us of being burned or deposed for preaching the gospel. Both in the Reformed Church and in the Lutheran, thank God, the word may be proclaimed in its purity; in both the conversion of souls may go forward without hindrance. In this view therefore our position is wholly different; so that modern sectaries have no good reason whatever for breaking communion with the Church. True, there are defects and faults enough in each of these Churches. But these may and should be reproved *within* the communion itself, that so if possible the whole body may be healed. When moreover the Reformers, for conscience sake, and because they would obey God and his word rather than men and their ordinances [Acts 5:29], proceeded to form a communion of their own, nothing could be further from their intention in doing so, than to throw open the door for the system of sects. Their object was not to upset the Church and break the regular course of its historical life; but only to restore to it once more the clear light and sure rule of God's word; not to emancipate the individual to uncontrolled freedom, but to bind him to the definite objective authority of God's truth and grace. LUTHER exhibited the doctrine of justification as precisely the true ground of Christian union, and fought with all the strength of his gigantic spirit against the fanatical and factious tendencies of his time. His last wish, as that of MELANCHTHON also, wrestled for the unity of the Church. His most depressing fear was still: "After our death, there will rise many harsh and terrible sects. God help us!" CALVIN utters himself against sectaries with his own peculiar cutting severity,[25] and repulses the reproach that Protestantism itself was a sect, in the strongest terms.[26]

25. *Instit.* IV, c. 1.

26. Ibid. IV, c. 2, §. 5. *Jam vero quod reos schismatis et haereseos nos agunt (Romanenses), quia et dissimilem praedicemus doctrinam, et suis legibus non pareamus, et seorsum conventus ad preces, ad baptismum, ad coenae administratonem aliasque sacras actiones habeamus:* gravissima quidem est accusatio, *sed quae nequaquam longa aut laboriosa defensione opus habet. Haeretici et schismatici vocantur, qui dissidio facto ecclesiae communionem dirimunt.* [Trans. "Now they treat us as persons guilty of schism and heresy because we preach a doctrine unlike theirs, do not obey their laws, and hold our separate assemblies for prayers, baptism and the celebration of the Supper, and other holy activities. This is indeed a *very grave accusation* but one that needs no long and labored defense. Those who, by making dissension, break the communion of the church are called heretics and schismatics." Calvin, *Institutes*, 2:1046.] This communion however with the true Church and her only head Christ, he goes on to say, the Protestants have maintained, and for this reason have been thrust out from the false Church, as the apostles formerly, who had the true spirit of the Old Testament, were expelled from the Jewish synagogues. *Eant nunc (§ 6) et clamitent haereticos nos esse, qui ab ipsorum ecclesia recesserimus,* quum nulla alienationis causa fuerit, nisi haec una, quod puram veritatis professionem nulla modo ferre possunt. *Taceo autem, quod anathematibus et diris nos expulerunt. Quod tamen ipsum satis*

[C. The altered posture thus of the time]

From all this it appears that in this practical respect also, as well as in its theoretic relations as before considered, the posture of the Protestant principle is different now from what it was at the time of the Reformation. The most dangerous foe with which we are called to contend is, again, not the Church of Rome but the sect plague in our own midst; not the single pope of the city of seven hills, but the numberless popes, German, English, and American, who would fain enslave Protestants once more to human authority, not as embodied in the Church indeed, but as holding in the form of mere private judgment and private will. What we need to oppose to these is not our formal principle; for they all appeal themselves to the bible, though without right; but the power of history, and the idea of the Church, as the pillar and ground of the truth, the mother of all believers, with due subordination always to the written word. In this controversy we may be said rather to have the Roman Church, in a certain sense, on our side; though we may never employ against sects the same carnal weapons, and propose not for ourselves *such* unity as is offered to us from her hand. For this in the end is an outward sameness only, in which the divinely ordained prerogatives of the individual subject are disregarded and trampled under foot, and all opposition as it rises from time to time, is either covered with a hypocritical mask, or kept down by the strong hand of power. Hence accordingly when it comes to full strength, and can no longer be repressed, its violence proves vastly more destructive than it would be in connection with Protestantism; as we see strikingly illustrated in the case of the French Revolution. We ought never to forget however, that Romanism has already drawn, and continues to draw still, its principal advantage from the pseudo-protestant sect system, as well as from Rationalism. Its recent show of new life and power finds here precisely its proper explanation. Continually its laugh of malicious triumph is going up, in view of our cancerous affection. If then we would contend successfully with Romanism, we must first labor to put away from ourselves the occasions that now lay us open so broadly to its attacks. Away with human denominations, down with religious sects! Let our watchword be: One spirit and one body! One Shepherd and one flock! All conventicles and chapels must perish, that from their ashes may rise the One Church of God, phoenix-like and resplendent with glory, as a bride adorned for her bridegroom.[27]

---

superque nos absolvit, nisi apostolos quoque schismatis damnare velint, quibuscum similem habemus causam. [Trans. "Now let them go and shout that we who have withdrawn from their church are heretics, *since the sole cause of our separation is that they could in no way bear the pure profession of truth.* I forbear to mention that they have expelled us with the anathemas and curses—more than sufficient reason to absolve us, unless they wish to condemn the apostles also as schismatics, *whose case was like our own.*" Calvin, *Institutes*, 2:1047–48.]

27. [The piety Schaff favored in his youth (or with which he was favored in his youth) disdained separation. Following Schleiermacher, Schaff accepted the union of Reformed and Lutheran in the Prussian Church as a necessary development in the history of the Church. From this perspective, then, the anti-historical nature of American Protestantism posed the greatest threat to the Church

Rationalism and Sectarism then are the most dangerous enemies of our Church at the present time. They are both but different sides of one and the same principle, a one-sided, false subjectivity, sundered from the authority of the objective. Rationalism is theoretic Sectarism; Sectarism is practical Rationalism.

II. Puseyism, the reaction of these diseases, but not their remedy.

Who now will guide the vessel of orthodox Protestantism safely between these rocks? In such peril, the helmsman looks anxiously around for help, come whence it may. Possibly the reefs draw still closer together, so that the ship proceeding in the same course must at last inevitably founder. Were it not best then, that it should tack about, and seek again the old haven from which it started?

So think the Puseyites, so named from their leader, or the Tractarians, as they are styled from their principal organ, the *Tracts for the Times*, or the Anglo-Catholics, as they choose to be called themselves.[28] Let us see whether they have found the true remedy for the complaints of the Protestant Church.

It is scarcely more than ten years since the tendency in question appeared in the ancient metropolis of English theology, in the midst of the venerable remains of Church antiquity, and upon the same seats of instruction where once along with schoolmen and papists the voice of Wickliffe sounded, and where the *Institutes* of Calvin were afterwards for a long time honored as the highest dogmatic authority. Within this short period, it has spread throughout the Old and New Worlds. Sympathies long prepared for its reception have been met by it in every direction; particularly in the old anti-"Union" Lutheranism of Germany, which has been transplanted also to this side of the Atlantic.[29] It has brought into clear consciousness, on all sides, spiritual tendencies and wants which were not previously understood. Already thus it appears clothed with a world-historical importance. I have myself hardly ever before

and underscored the urgency of "the Church Question" as Schaff commenced his missionary labors in the New Land.]

28. [This Catholic revival within the Church of England, began in 1833 among professors and students at Oxford University, hence it is most commonly known as the Oxford Movement. The essential argument of this wide-ranging movement was that the Church of England was Catholic, rather than Protestant. The movement's self-understanding was that it was reasserting the faith and practice of the church fathers. It regarded the English church, along with the Roman and Eastern Orthodox churches, as legitimate branches of the one true church which had retained apostolic succession through bishops. The ideas of the movement were developed and spread through a series of pamphlets published under the title *Tracts for the Times* (1833–41), edited by John Henry Newman. Among its other prominent leaders was Edward B. Pusey, from whom the movement took one of its names. Nevin reviewed the movement in "The Anglican Crisis," *Mercersburg Review* 3 (1851): 359–98.]

29. [The Old Lutherans were opposed to the union of Lutheran and Reformed churches under the banner of the Prussian Church. Beginning in the late 1830s, various groups of them immigrated to the United States in part for greater religious freedom. The Lutheran Church-Missouri Synod descends from the Old Lutherans.]

had such an impression of the objective power of the "idea," as during the course of my late travel, through Germany, Switzerland, Belgium, England, and North America; encountering as I did everywhere, in the persons of distinguished ministers and laymen, if not precisely Puseyism itself, at least aspirations and endeavors of a more or less kindred spirit. Of what avail against such a life question, the true burden of the age itself, can be the hue and cry of "Popery!" "Romanism!" nonsensically kept up by our intelligence and anti-intelligence prints?[30] Grapple with the subject in earnest. Bring the fire engines. Extinguish the flame. If ye do but idly stare at it, or stand before it lamenting and railing with folded hands, assuredly it will soon burst triumphantly through the roof, and leave you at last houseless and bare. Nothing can well be more shallow and miserable, and full of senseless pretension withal, than the style in which the controversy with Popery and Puseyism is to a great extent conducted in our religious periodicals.[31] It may be said to be for the most part ammunition expended in vain, time and labor lost for writer and reader alike. If the tendencies in question encounter nothing more solid than such ephemeral opposition, their victory may be counted sure.

[1. Its historical justification and weight in opposition to unchurchly subjectivism.]

I look upon Puseyism as *an entirely legitimate and necessary reaction against rationalistic and sectaristic, pseudo-Protestantism, as well as the religious subjectivism of the so called Low Church Party*, with which the significance of the Church has been forgotten, or at least practically undervalued, in favor of personal individual piety, the sacraments in favor of faith, sanctification in favor of justification, and tradition in its right sense in favor of the holy scriptures. I make indeed no question, but that with many who belong to this neo-catholic school a feeling of poetical romance is more prevalent than true religious conviction; that others again, among the clergy especially, are swayed more or less by hierarchic interest; and that still a third class, largest of all perhaps, are carried along with the alluring movement by the current of mere fashion. But with all these allowances, when we take the movement in its whole compass as exhibited in its authors and leaders in England, we must admit that it rests upon decidedly religious and true Church ground, and springs from grief on the one hand over the disjointed, discinctured character of the age, and an endeavor after Christian catholicity and unity on the other.[32] Hence we find it characterized by deep moral earnestness, reverential solemnity, and a certain spiritual dignity of tone and manner even in controversy itself. It has a proper feeling of respect for history; looks reverently after the remains of the religious life of other days; cherishes a filial homage

30. [Schaff is parodying the common title of many nineteenth-century newspapers, "Intelligencer."]

31. [See Billington, *Protestant Crusade*; Franchot, *Roads to Rome*; Shea, *Lion and Lamb*.]

32. ["Discintured" is from cincture, a girdle or belt. Here it means "ungirded" or "disheveled."]

towards the Christian Past. It exalts the authority of the general over all that is simply single, and makes the reason of the Church to be more than that of the individual; counteracting thus the rage for independence that rules the time. It holds fast to the importance of the sacraments, as objective institutions of the Lord that hang not on the precarious state of the subject, but include an actual living presence of Christ for the purposes they are intended to secure, as real as that by which he stood among his disciples in the days of his flesh. It restores the week services, the Church festivals, and frequent communions after the example of the first ages; lays stress on religious discipline for the whole man outward as well as inward; seeks to revive the sense of sacrificial consecration to God; has an open eye for Church art, and takes pleasure in beautifying sanctuaries and altars on the principle that what is best should belong to the Lord, and that such decoration is only the natural expression of childlike love, as it might be expected to show itself even towards a human friend, being well suited at the same time to assist devotion in the way of support and elevation through the senses. With all this it designs not at all to fall back to Romanism, but only to revive once more the fair usages, lost and forgotten, of the undivided, universal primitive Church, as nearest to the age of the apostles and so to the fountain of Christianity; and thus also to hold within the Protestant communion such as feel themselves urged to forsake it, through dissatisfaction with the usual nakedness and barrenness of its worship.[33]

In all this, considered by itself, I find nothing that is absolutely wrong. Rather it is my firm conviction that we must ourselves appropriate fully some of the more general views lying at the ground of Puseyism, to be secure against its advances, and to prevent its errors from spreading continually more and more along with its truth. We too must take a wider range, and our faith in the one universal Christian Church must show itself to be not merely a confession of the mouth, but power and truth, life and act. We too may not seek the perfection of our own communion, apart from the perfection of the entire Christian Church. We too must be like the good householder who gathers up even the fragments, appropriating to ourselves from the stores of early Christian history in particular, what has sprung from God and proved a blessing to thousands and millions. We too must bear in mind that the single can hold with advantage only in due subordination to the general, and that there can be no true freedom save in the form of subjection to the authority of God.

33. [The movement to revive Catholic art, architecture, and ritual within the Anglican Communion was centered at Cambridge and in many respects distinct from the Oxford Movement. This development of "ritualism" and "ecclesiology" (the "laws" of church building) was only emerging as Schaff wrote. White, *Cambridge Movement*. Yates, *Buildings, Faith, and Worship*.]

[2. Its unprotestant character, involving a tendency backwards instead of forwards.]

So far we go with the young Oxford hand in hand, at the hazard even of being called reformed Catholic, or catholic Protestant. So soon however as it comes to the choice of the means by which the object in view is to be reached, we are constrained to part with it as unsound and unsafe. Its "tracts for the times" are not just "tracts for eternity." Its grand defect, forming an impassable gulf between it and our position, is *its utter misapprehension of the divine significance of the Reformation, with its consequent development, that is of the entire Protestant period of the Church.* As to Romanism, so to Puseyism also, there is wanting the true idea of *development* altogether. It regards the Church as a system handed down under a given and complete form that must remain perpetually the same. It confounds with Christianity itself, which we may never and can never transcend, and which is always equally perfect, the measure of its *apprehension* on the part of mankind, or its *appropriation* into the consciousness of the Church, which like the life of the spirit universally, from first to last, has the character of a genesis or process, and passes through different stages of growth. With all their historical feeling, the Puseyites show themselves with regard to the Reformation absolutely unhistorical. They wish to shut out of view the progress of the last three centuries entirely; to treat the whole as a negation, if possible; and by one vast leap to carry the Church back to the point where it stood before the separation of the Oriental and Western communions, when however the tendencies were already at work which led with historical necessity afterwards to the popish system in its worst form. Turn and twist as they may, with their external, mechanical conception of the Church and episcopacy, the Reformation can be to them properly an *apostasy only* from the true Church, and they must unchurch entirely all those Protestant bodies that have parted with the episcopal constitution.

Their doctrine of episcopal succession, with its denial of the universal priesthood of all believers, the episcopal and apostolical character of every inwardly and outwardly called minister of Christ, involving the papistical idea of a clerical mediatorship between God and man—this is the old leaven of the Pharisees, which has never been thoroughly purged out of the Anglican Church, and that may be said now to offend Protestant feeling in the writings of the Oxford school in particular, from beginning to end. If this succession were taken as one simply of doctrine and ministry, *successio Spiritus Dei, doctrinae evangelii*, and *ministerii divini*,[34] it would carry a perfectly rational meaning, necessarily included in the conception of the Church as the abiding and indissoluble communion of believers in Christ; and in this view it might be confidently claimed by the whole orthodox Protestant interest, with which both word and sacrament, ministry and ordination, are continued, and the founders of which derived their own ordination regularly from the Catholic Church. But instead

34. [Trans. "A succession of the Spirit of God, of gospel teaching, and of the divine ministry."]

of this, the idea is limited to the order of the bishops, unscripturally sundered from the laity and lower clergy, as though they were specifically different in their nature, and were alone competent to transmit ministerial power. All ends in a personal, outward, mechanical succession. The Spirit of God, whose very nature it is to be free, is thus bound to a particular ecclesiastical structure for which no sure authority can be found in the New Testament; and the apostolical legitimacy of a Church is made to turn upon a question of history, in the case of which besides by reason of the darkness that hangs over certain periods, during the earlier part especially of the Middle Ages *no satisfactory result* is possible. Altogether a most crazy foundation on which to build so momentous an interest. According to this theory, Paul was illegitimate fully, because he had his ordination neither from the Lord nor from an apostle, but from a simple presbyter in Damascus. His judaizing adversaries, who had already in substance the Puseyite view, were right then in divesting him at once of all apostolical credit. How monstrous again is the position, necessarily involved in the same theory, that the dead Armenian and Greek denominations, because they have bishops, belong regularly to the Holy Church Catholic, while the German Reformed, Lutheran, and Presbyterian bodies, with all their religious life, are flatly denied any such character, and even their most godly and successful ministers are branded as ecclesiastical bastards, or mere hirelings privily smuggled into the sanctuary. God be praised, for that word of the Lord, "By their *fruits* ye shall know them" [Matt 7:16] and that *love* is made, in another place, the criterion of discipleship [John 13:35].

Let it be allowed that the Tractarians are right, and all unbishoped churches are left without hope, till their clergy submit to have their character made valid by the hands of his Grace of Canterbury, or some diocesan ONDERDONK on this side the Atlantic;[35] unless indeed they should prefer to have recourse at once to the holy father at Rome, or the patriarch no less holy of Constantinople. Preposterous imagination! Can the Church be renovated by putting on a new coat? I have all respect for the episcopal system. It possesses in fact many undeniable advantages, and by its antiquity besides must command the veneration of all who have any right historical feeling. But the thought must be utterly rejected that it carries in its constitution as such the proper and only remedy for the existing wounds of Protestantism. Does it offer any sure guaranty for union? The contests with which the English Episcopal Church has been torn, especially for the last ten years (to say nothing of the posture of our American Episcopacy at this moment), sufficiently show the contrary. Or does it furnish more efficient means for the promotion of true inward piety? Let the state of the Greek Church, always true to the episcopal succession, be taken in reply; or the Roman Church as it stood towards the close of the Middle Age, and as it stands still in

35. [Henry Ustick Onderdonk (1789–1858) was the Episcopal bishop of Pennsylvania. Benjamin Treadwell Onderdonk (1791–1861) was Episcopal bishop of New York. Both were High Churchmen who became the center of controversies over the Oxford Movement. As discussed on p. 185 in this volume, their active ministries ended in 1844 because they were convicted of moral charges.]

entire countries; or the Church of England itself, as it appeared under the last Stuarts and during the eighteenth century. No, we need something higher and better than anointed lords and consecrated gentlemen. Such aristocratic hierarchs and proud bearers of the apostolical succession precisely, like the Pharisees and high priests of Judaism, have themselves again and again secularized the Church, rocking it into the sleep of lifeless formalism or religious indifference. *Timeo Danaos et dona ferentes.*[36] Little children, keep yourselves from idols [1 John 5:21], be afraid of false gods even under episcopal attire! It is the Spirit that maketh alive; the letter killeth [2 Cor 3:6].

As the Puseyites, in this question of government and order, which they invest with undue religious importance both doctrinal and practical, stand upon essentially Roman Catholic ground,[37] it is quite natural that they should surrender in its behalf also what has been gained in point of doctrine by the Reformation. The points in which they still declare their system to be different from popery are comparatively subordinate and unimportant. Of the true Protestant principle they have no conception, or else seek to cover it over, as Newman in tract No. 90 on the Thirty Nine Articles, with Jesuitical interpretation.[38] The *sola fide* on which the Reformers lived and died, they

36. [Virgil, *Aeneid* II, 49: "I fear the Greeks, even those bearing gifts."]

37. The papists at the time of the Reformation appealed in just the same style to the *perpetua episcoporum successio* [trans. "unbroken succession of bishops"]. Calvin (*Instit.* IV, c. 2, § 2) answers well: *Primum ab illis quaero, cur non Africam citent et Aegyptum et totam Asiam. Nempe quia in omnibus illis regionibus desiit sacra haec episcoporum successio, cujus beneficio se ecclesias retinuisse gloriantur. Eo igitur recidunt, se ideo veram habere ecclesiam, quia ex quo esse coepit, non fuerit episcopis destituta, perpetua enim serie alios aliis successisse. Sed quid si Graeciam illis regeram? Quaero igitur iterum ab ipsis, cur apud Graecos periisse ecclesiam dicant, apud quos numquam interrupta fuit illa episcoporum successio, unica, eorum opinione, ecclesiae custos et conservatrix. Graecos faciunt schismaticos. Quo jure? quia a sede apostolica desciscendo privilegium perdiderunt.* Quid? annon multo magis perdere merentur qui a Christo ipso deficiunt? *Sequitur ergo evanidum esse praetextum successionis, nisi Christi veritatem quam a patribus per manum acceperint, salvam et incorruptam posteri retineant ac in ea permaneant.* [Trans. "First, I ask them why they do not mention Africa, Egypt, and all Asia. The reason is that in all these districts this sacred succession of bishops, by virtue of which they boast that the churches have been maintained, has ceased to be. They therefore revert to the point that they have the true church because from its beginning it has not been destitute of bishops, for one has followed another in unbroken succession. But what if I confront them with Greece? I therefore ask them once more why they say that the church perished among the Greeks, among whom the succession of bishops (in their opinion the sole custodian and preserver of the church) has never been interrupted. They make the Greeks schismatics; with what right? Because in withdrawing from the apostolic see, they lost their privilege. *What? Would not they who fall away from Christ deserve to lose it much more?* It therefore follows that this pretense of succession is vain unless their descendants conserve safe and uncorrupted the truth of Christ which they have received at their fathers' hands, and abide in it." *Institutes*, 2:1043.] Comp. § 3 where he refers to the relation of the prophets to the bearers of the Jewish hierarchy, who in the same way laid claim to temple, ceremonies, and succession as all their own, and bitterly persecuted these divine messengers, the bearers of the Holy Ghost, and so the true succession.

38. [In his *Remarks on Certain Passages in the Thirty-Nine Articles* (1841), better known as *Tract 90*, John Henry Newman argued that the *Articles* were written not to establish a Protestant position over against Catholicism, but rather to address distortions in medieval Catholic doctrine as a corrective measure. Furthermore, since the *Articles* were written prior to the Council of Trent, they could not be assumed to condemn its teachings. Thus, they could be subscribed to by Anglican clergymen who held to such Roman Catholic doctrines as transubstantiation, purgatory, the invocation of saints,

have never had experience of probably in themselves, and accordingly they let it go for a small price. The sanctity on which they insist appears thus on closer examination to carry rather the character of an outward legalism, an unfree, anxious piety, reminding us of monkhood, with undue stress laid upon the observance of particular Church forms, fasts and self-imposed discipline. In the *Lives of the Saints*, as brought forward under the direction of MR. NEWMAN, the old Jewish work-righteousness presents itself again in its full arrogant parade.[39]

With the scripture principle it fares no better in the hands of these gentlemen. It has been abandoned, almost from the start, for the Roman dogma of tradition. They wish to bind upon our necks all that has come down to us from the fathers, without any critical sifting by means of science or God's word, even the extravagant and utterly unsound, though often ingenious allegoristic interpretations of the Alexandrian school. Quite a compliment to us certainly, not simply as protestants in general, but as the friends also of a sound grammatico-historical Scripture exegesis!

So, very recently, the organ of Puseyism in this country, the *New York Churchman*, has gone so far as to defend in many respects the last bull of his Holiness of Rome against Bible Societies.[40] The case of Mr. Carey, too is well known, who was ordained by bishop ONDERDONK, though he had distinctly declared that he could subscribe to the decrees of the Council of Trent.[41]

Altogether Puseyism shows itself, in this way, to be no safe guide in the present great need of the Church. Its mission must be regarded as preparatory only to that more full and perfect dispensation, by which in the end the captivity of Jacob is to be restored. It has done much, and may do still more, to bring the great problem of the age home to the consciousness of the Protestant world. But for the solution of the problem itself, it is found to be utterly incompetent. It were to be wished now indeed,

and the authority of ecumenical councils. Newman accomplished this by insisting on ignoring the intent of the authors of the *Articles*, taking the writings of Anglican divines out of context, and creating strained definitions of words. This manner of interpretation, as well as the position Newman defended, was condemned by Schaff and others as "Jesuitical." Ker, *John Henry Newman*, 216–27; Turner, *John Henry Newman*, 358–82.]

39. [Newman, ed., *Lives of the English Saints*, 14 vols. (London: James Toovey, 1844–45).]

40. [Gregory XVI, *Inter praecipuas*, May 8, 1844. The editor of the *New York Churchman* was Samuel Seabury. When the American Bible Society was founded in 1816, Seabury's mentor, Bishop Henry Hobart, refused to support this non-denominational organization. Because of his high church convictions, Hobart held that Episcopalians should not participate in such non-denominational organizations, but support their own Bible societies. Controversy over this decision continued for several years. Mullin, *Episcopal Vision/American Reality*, 50–59.]

41. According to the representation of DRS. SMITH and ANTHON, in their [*The True Issue for the True Churchman:*] *Statement of Facts in Relation to the Recent Ordination in St. Stephen's Church*, New York[: Harper and Brothers], 1843. [Arthur Carey was a graduate of the General Theological Seminary. His rector, Hugh Smith, refused to support his ordination because he doubted Carey's orthodoxy. Appointed to an eight-person committee by New York bishop Benjamin Onderdonk to examine Carey, Smith was joined by Henry Anton in the minority of a six-to-two vote against Carey's ordination. As discussed below (185–186), the controversy over this ordination helped end Onderdonk's active ministry. Mullin, *Episcopal Vision/American Reality*, 161–62.]

that the whole question might he wrested out of such unskillful hands, since the truth which lies at the ground of the movement is in danger of being brought into general discredit, at least for a time, by the false style in which it is here presented.

III. The true Standpoint: Protestant Catholicism or Historical Progress.

Puseyism then looks backward; we look forward. It tends towards Rome and is there in spirit already, even though it should never outwardly complete the transition. We move towards Jerusalem, the new, the heavenly, the eternal. Its way is turned towards the fleshpots of Egypt, the old ignominious servitude of the house of bondage. Ours is onward to the land of promise that flows with milk and honey. Possibly when it shall have reached the last consequences of its principle, and stands confronted with the tyrannic scepter beyond the Red Sea, the better part of it at least may penitently smite upon its breast and turn back again upon its own way; even at the hazard of being doomed to wander yet forty years in the Protestant wilderness. There are still to be found in this [wilderness] refreshing encampments, shady groves of palm and fruitful oases, heavenly manna and quails in abundance. Before us still moves the fiery cloudy pillar of Israel; at our side, fresh water flows from the rock, at the bidding of God; and full in view is the lifted brazen serpent, the symbol of the promised Messiah, to which every sin wounded soul may look and be healed. Patience only, under the weight of our weary way! Canaan must be reached at last. No premature catholicity and unity factitiously produced that must prove after all only a transient mask! The Lord himself will help his people and complete the work of the Reformation, in due time, by a new and more glorious creation; or conduct it rather to its own true and triumphant result. The less we presume to take the matter willfully into our own hands, the more we wait humbly on the leadings of the divine will, following step by step along the quiet, true historical way, the nearer and more sure is the hour when he shall appear, to gather the *disjecta membra ecclesiae* ["scattered fragments of the church"] once more together, and form them into a more glorious body than the world has ever yet beheld.[42]

Let us never forget that fidelity to her inherited patrimony, on the part of the Church, is indispensable to her further prosperity. We must declare against Puseyism on the historical or catholic principle itself. For genuine catholicism holds in organic union with the pure history of the Church, and through this with the apostles, through them with Christ, and through him finally with the eternal Father himself, whose thoughts of love and peace are unfolded in more large and glorious measure always with the flow of time. We are faithless apostates if we allow ourselves with

42. [Schaff here grounds the notion of historical progress in the protracted biblical narrative of the Exodus. He alludes to the extended sojourn undertaken by Moses and his community that constitutes portions of Exodus, Leviticus, Numbers, and Deuteronomy before the arrival in the Promised Land with the crossing over to the western bank of the Jordan River in the Book of Joshua.]

overweening presumption to trample under foot the work of the Reformers. Puseyism occupies extreme ground here, on two sides. Towards the Church fathers it is *slavishly* true, taking upon itself the yoke of human bondage; towards the Reformers it is even to the point of perfidy ungrateful. LUTHER and MELANCHTHON, CALVIN and BEZA, were indeed sinful and fallible men, like ourselves. Of this they had the most full consciousness themselves, and have declared us free accordingly from all bondage to men. We will not then fall into the error that they have themselves most sharply reproved. We readily allow that in their zeal for the purification of the Church they threw away more than was necessary or wholesome. But we cannot consent to give up anything material of their *positive* conquest particularly in the form of doctrine. Assuredly they need not shun a comparison here with the deepest, most intellectual, and most pious among the Church fathers and schoolmen. They sought not their own, but the honor of God. No human doctrine, but God's word only, would they exalt to absolute supremacy. This they preached with unshaken boldness and the most noble disinterestedness; and so when their hard day's work was done died happily in the faith of Jesus Christ Crucified, as their righteousness and salvation. The Lord has spoken his *yea* and *amen* upon their work; and the Church which sprang from it still stands fast in its strength, in spite of the numberless storms that have passed over it from without, in spite of the deadly foes to which it is still exposed within its own bosom.

But we must go still further. As the Puseyites *in contradiction to the Reformation* affect to be catholic (in the Roman sense, catholic in show, particularistic in fact),[43] so as a matter of course they are unprepared altogether to understand or appreciate the subsequent development of the Protestant principle. In the history of the Protestant Church they can see *only* progressive *falling away*; in rationalism and sectarism, a work *purely of the devil*. This is a second point on which we differ from them; and where we come into collision also with the stiff confessionists, the hyper-orthodox Lutherans of the old stamp, the sons of ABRAHAM CALOVIUS and ERNEST VALENTINE LOESCHER. These indeed acknowledge the divine character of the Reformation, at least in its Lutheran form, and in this respect we stand on common ground with them against English and American Puseyism. But they will not allow the development of the Church to extend beyond this point. Whatever progress may have had place before, all must be considered complete with the orthodoxy of the sixteenth century; circumscribed and made fast in the narrow bounds of the *Formula of Concord*. With blind mis-estimation of the rights and prerogatives of the Reformed Church, and of the special wants precisely of our time, they make Lutheranism to be the same thing with the ideal or absolute Church itself, and fall thus into an error as bad as that of Rome, to whose view all that lies beyond its own borders is but damnable heresy and schism. This form of thinking bears, it is true, the name of LUTHER; but with his

43. [Here Schaff appeals to the root meaning of catholic: universal. His inclusive evangelical catholicism, he avers, is more truly catholic than that of Roman or Anglo Catholics, committed as they are to particular boundaries.]

boundlessly free spirit it stands in no affinity whatever; just as little, we may say, as another section of the same *nominal* interest in this country, which has long since sacrificed the original spirit of the Lutheran Church, along with the German language itself, to the totally different genius of Methodism. It is the presentiment and earnest hope of the greatest German theologians that we stand at this time on the eve of a more comprehensive Reformation than that which is past, which is to crown and complete the work of our fathers, bind together again what has been separated, and actualize the last absorbing wish of Luther and Melanchthon, of which notice has already been taken. Of course, the *Formula of Concord*, worthy as it is in itself of all respect, can never bring us to any such result as this. As little at the same time however can we be helped towards it, by methodistical "New Measures," the anxious bench and other such like quack appliances and medicaments, that work upon the nerves far more than the soul. The old measures employed by Christ and the apostles, which have stood the test of historical experiment from the beginning, are vastly more to be relied upon. Eighteen centuries of use have not worn away their edge or force; rather it is their invaluable quality that they become always more keen and effective the more frequently they are applied. With such methods moreover we reach results that are solid and radical, instead of deceptive appearances only that soon pass away, and leave the case worse too often than it was before.[44]

We condemn, without qualification, both Rationalism and Sectarism. Still our historical sense itself will not allow us to look upon them as the work of Satan *only*. God, who brings good out of evil, has been wisely active also in the immense system of destruction that has been going forward in the Christian world in these forms, since the beginning of the last century. "God writes on a crooked line," says an old Portuguese proverb. Through the heathenish larva of rationalist, pantheist, sectarian, and factious irreligion with which the age is marred, we discern the regenerated psyche; in the process of corruption, the still living germ that may be expected to burst its decaying shell, and leave the earth behind, and grow upwards into a tree beneath whose shadow the world may rest. Like the development of the papacy during the Middle Ages, the Rationalism and Sectarism of the modern Protestant Church also has its conditional historical necessity, and along with this a certain justification, an element of truth, that needs to be incorporated into the process with which theology and the Church are to be still further developed. Let us illustrate this, in the way of hint at least, by two or three general observations; though of a kind, it is true, to be fully intelligible only to such as are thoroughly acquainted with Church history. The details of the subject and its application to particulars may then be carried out by the intelligent for themselves.

44. [Schaff here echoes his new colleague Nevin's critique of revival techniques as enumerated in *The Anxious Bench* (1843). Especially in the second edition of the book (1844), Nevin opposed the "system of the catechism" to the "system of the bench." See John Nevin, *The Anxious Bench*, in *"One Holy, Catholic, and Apostolic": John Nevin's Writings on Ecclesiology*, ed. Sam Hamstra, MTSS, vol. 5 (forthcoming).]

As Catholicism towards the close of the Middle Ages settled into a character of hard, *stiff objectivity*, incompatible with the proper freedom of the individual subject, now ripening into spiritual manhood, so Protestantism has been carried aside, in later times, into the opposite error of a *loose subjectivity*, which threatens to subvert all regard for Church authority. These extremes as such are both equally false. Both however involve a principle that is true and divine; the falsehood results from the one-sided way in which this is held in each case. Necessity and freedom, dependence and independence, generality and singularity, are the two poles around which human existence and all history revolve. The perfection of both is the union of both. The highest freedom stands in the service of God. The divine law is at the same time the true expression of particular will, the only form of free inward power. Genuine obedience towards the Church coincides with the highest degree of personal piety. The life of the single member in the body and for the body as a whole constitutes also its own most healthy and vigorous state. Separated from the body, it is given over at once to a process of dissolution.

[1. Rationalism and Sectarism as a transition stage to a higher development of theology and the Church]

Rationalism and Sectarism then are false and hateful, not simply as they are subjective and appertain to the sphere of the individual, but as they are *one-sidedly* subjective, *in opposition* to the general, and *with contempt* of the principle of authority, as embodied in the Church. So far accordingly as the just claims of the subjective reach, both may be said to have their vindication as necessary and important in Church history. In what this right, this element of truth, consists is now to be shown.

Rationalism shows its bright and dark sides in this, that it fixes its view one-sidedly on the human in Christ, in Christianity and in the Church, the earthly body only of their incarnate divinity, and is so carried away towards what is natural and visible merely, as to have no sense or perception of the supernatural, eternal and divine. Its principle is the abstract understanding, which walks the treadmill of mere finite categories and contradictions, without coming ever to the last ground and inmost unity of its subject. So far however as Christianity and the Church fall within the finite, earthly sphere of man's existence, Rationalism also must be considered in place, and not without its merits. It has served to overthrow many false prejudices, and has made many contributions of permanent worth to history and criticism. But besides this, its influence has been salutary, in a certain sense, on the whole tone and spirit of the later evangelical German theology. Only ignorance or prejudice can deny that the older orthodoxy, including its first protestant form also, made too little account of the conditions under which only the revelation of our religion in the way of history could take place. Hence, for instance, its resort to unsound and extravagant allegory, and its fairly magical conception of inspiration, overlooking entirely the human individuality of the sacred writers, which notwithstanding stares us in the face in every single book.

In this respect, the scientific Rationalism of Germany, by bringing in a severe criticism and grammatico-historical exegesis, which form the natural ground and necessary condition of all theological knowledge of the bible, has wrought clearly with purifying power in the Church, the traces of which are not to be mistaken in the most orthodox works of the modern evangelical school. The old faith has sustained in this way no loss. It remains essentially the same. It has come forth from this critical fire, improved only in its form and argument, and cleared of all sorts of dross. It has lost nothing in living power, inwardness and depth, while it has gained in freedom and solid scientific strength. We must not refer Rationalism to sheer ungodliness as its source, but are bound to acknowledge in it also a scientific conscience that the old orthodoxy, though with the best intention, too often wounded in the most sensible manner. The latest speculative Rationalism has this merit besides, that it has helped to destroy the common Rationalism with which it was preceded; as Strauss, for instance, in his *Life of Jesus*,[45] has exposed with great acuteness the unnaturalness of the so-called natural explanation of miracles, as conducted by Paulus of Heidelberg; and the former style of attack also against the doctrine of the Trinity and the divine incarnation has been long since shorn of its force by the Hegelian speculation. It must be admitted however, that the most recent productions of this speculative Rationalism fall back again rather to the old trivial and popular, scientifically surmounted standpoint, so that the system is involved thus in self-condemnation.

But readily as we allow that we are indebted to this transition phase of theology generally considered, for an understanding in part of history and the natural side of Christianity, we must still maintain that this understanding can become true and complete only where, with the good side of the tendency in question, there is found united the determined faith of the old orthodoxy. For the body is the product of the soul, which it [the soul] forms as an organ for its own use. It is the eternal Word that has become flesh in the person of Jesus of Nazareth, in the sacred scriptures, and in the Church. He then who has the flesh only without the word, the body without the spirit, has in the end no more than a corpse.

As it regards Sectarism, in the second place, it must also be allowed that it almost always has its ground in certain practical defects of the Church, as that of Rationalism holds in the flaws and infirmities of the orthodox theology, and in this direction is not without right. Thus Quakerism appeared in opposition to the outward mechanism and dead formality that had taken possession of the Church of England in the beginning of the seventeenth century. Anabaptism finds its apology in the melancholy fact that many baptized persons in the Church live like heathen, the consequence in a great measure of the want of proper Christian education. Modern Methodism, in its various

45. [David Friedrich Strauss, *The Life of Jesus, Critical Examined*, ed. Peter C. Hodgson, trans. George Eliot (Philadelphia: Fortress Press, 1973). The first German edition was published in 1835–36.]

forms, has its well-grounded complaints to present against a dead Church orthodoxy, which is found too often along with unsound life, rejecting all life; along with protracted prayer meetings, all serious prayer; and along with wild fanatical awakenings, conversion in every form, making thus no distinction in its zeal. In almost every sect we may find some particular side of the Christian life clearly and strongly marked; where, as in a mirror, the Church should see her own defects, the wrinkles or spots that mar her visage, so as to do penance for her unfaithfulness, by which so many of her best members have been led to forsake her communion. The divine significance of sects then, their value in the history of the Church, consists in this: that they are a disciplinary scourge, a voice of awakening and admonition by which the Church is urged to new life and a more conscientious discharge of her duties. The system has a favorable operation further, as it tends to spread religious interest and stimulate Christian zeal. In this country perhaps, if there were no sects, we should not have half as many congregations and houses of worship as we have now, and many sections in the West particularly would be destitute of the blessings of the gospel altogether.

But while this is thankfully admitted, two things still need to be kept in view. A sect, in the first place, loses its right to exist, in the same degree in which the body from which it is a secession has corrected the faults that led to it. If it persist in its separation notwithstanding, it is either carried into full unbelief, or sinks into a slavish observance of particular lifeless forms, preparing in this way its own grave, as is strikingly illustrated by many cases in Church history. Then again, a sect as such, can never, in its subjective isolation, provide successfully even for the particular interest to which it is pedantically devoted; since every single religious truth belongs to a great organically constituted whole, and can become complete accordingly only in connection with this as the source of all its life. Christianity is an indivisible unity; its truths are links only of an indissoluble chain returning into itself. Here exactly we may see the spiritual pride and narrow-mindedness of sectarism, that it fancies it can prosper and reach perfection, standing on its own frail feet, in abstract separation from the general life of the Church.[46] Break a branch from the vine, and it must soon wither. Separate a ray from the sun, and it is extinguished. Remove a child from the care of parents and guardians, and it will grow wild. Cut a hand from the body, and it will fall into decay. *If sects then would be true to themselves, they must as soon as they have*

46. [Schaff here operates with the two categories, church and sect that were developed subsequently as "types" by Ernst Troeltsch in *The Social Teachings of the Christian Churches* (1912). American theologian H. Richard Niebuhr, in *The Social Sources of Denominationalism* (1929), introduced a third category of analysis, namely, the denomination. For Niebuhr, the denomination had become a preserve that maintained race and class commonalities. After ten years in America, Schaff would develop an appreciation for the denomination in his book *America* (1854) as a middle course, as it were, between church and sect. See See Schaff, *Schaff's "America" and Related Writings*, ed. Stephen R. Graham, MTSS, vol. 11 (forthcoming). In current scholarly parlance a denomination is "*a* voluntary church" that concedes, often selectively, the authority of other denominations even as it claims its own. Thus, like a sect it is a voluntary group, but like a church seeks to include all and to exercise a custodial role over the culture. Richey, "Denominations and Denominationalism," 76.]

fulfilled their commission unite themselves again with the general life of the Church, that they may thus as organic members of the body acquire new vital energy; and the Church, on her side, should make special efforts to gather once more under her motherly protection and care, the children that have forsaken her and are now estranged from her bosom. To this duty the Reformed Church is specially called, as the largest part of these modern separatistic movements have sprung from her communion.

[2. The separation of the secular spheres of life from the Church as an advance in the naturalization process of Christianity.]

We must now quit for a moment the field of theology and the Church, in the narrower sense, and cast a glance on the development of Protestantism in its relation as a vast whole to the general course of the world's history; that we may discover how far there is included in it in this view also, the promise of a new, glorious future. We shall then be prepared to bring all together in a general image.

To the Lord and his kingdom belongs the whole world, with all that lives and moves in it [Acts 17:28]. *All* is yours, says the apostle [1 Cor 3:21]. Religion is not a single, separate sphere of human life, but the divine principle by which the entire man is to be pervaded, refined and made complete. It takes hold of him in his undivided totality, in the center of his personal being; to carry light into his understanding, holiness into his will, and heaven into his heart; and to shed thus the sacred consecration of the new birth, and of the glorious liberty of the children of God, over his whole inward and outward life. No form of existence can withstand the renovating power of God's Spirit. There is no rational element that may not be sanctified; no sphere of natural life that may not be glorified. The creature, in the widest extent of the word, is earnestly waiting for the manifestation of the sons of God, and sighing after the same glorious deliverance. The whole creation aims towards redemption; and Christ is the second Adam, the new universal man, not simply in a religious but also in an absolute sense. The view entertained by Romish monasticism and Protestant pietism, by which Christianity is made to consist in an abstract opposition to the natural life, or in *flight from the world*, is quite contrary to the spirit and power of the gospel, as well as false to its design. Christianity is the redemption and renovation of the WORLD. It must make *all things* new [Rev 21:5].

Such morbid views are powerfully counteracted in this country by the sound practical feeling which so generally prevails. A different mistake however, nearly as false, is widely established according to which science, art and politics, are placed in a relation, not of absolute hostility indeed, but of entire *indifference* to religion, that is properly in no relation to it at all. The idea seems to be that a man's piety is deposited in one corner of his spirit, his politics in another, and his learning in a third. All good and necessary in their place, but having nothing whatever to do with one another! According to this view, it might seem to be expected further that religion should never come into any closer union with the common secular departments of life. It must be counted pernicious, if the Church should be drawn into nearer contact with the State, or art be made more extensively subservient to divine worship, if Christian morality should seek to occupy all social relations, or Christian theology presume to incorporate with itself the results of worldly science, philosophy in particular.

It were a vast object gained for the interests of American Protestantism, if this radically false and miserably narrow prejudice, opposed as it is to all true and proper progress on the part of the Church, could be effectually subverted. The theme is indeed one of the very highest consequence. It enters into the inmost life of the time, and includes in itself the most momentous questions with which the time is concerned. The following historical hints, which we are not permitted here further to pursue, may serve possibly, in some measure at least, to direct attention to the subject.

We set out then with the assumption that Christianity stands in an absolutely negative, hostile relation only to sin and death, while all that is properly human, the world with its several spheres—government, science, art, and social life—is regarded by it as of divine institution and force; which religion is required accordingly neither to annihilate nor yet to overlook as foreign to its nature, but on the contrary to occupy and fill with its own heavenly spirit. This itself serves to show the universal character of the gospel, and the catholicity of the Church. It follows of course, that no one of these spheres of natural life can reach its highest stage, its true perfection, until it has come to be thoroughly transfused with the leaven of Christianity. In the absolute view of the case therefore, there can be no perfect scholar or philosopher, no perfect ideal artist, whether architect, or sculptor, or painter, or musician, or poet, no perfect statesman, and finally no truly moral man, who is not at the same time animated throughout with the living power of faith. It follows again with equal necessity from the same view, that the Church cannot be said to have completed its career till the whole world shall appear transfigured with its divine spirit, and states, and sciences, and arts, with all their glory, shall fall down before the altar of the Most High in full, free worship.

Let us now apply this standard to history for the purpose of determining according to it the relation between Catholicism and Protestantism, in the direction here noticed, and also the proper wants of our own time so far as the same view is concerned.

Catholicism, particularly in its mediaeval Romano-Germanic period, carried with it, if we put out of view its monastic institutions, a very distinct sense of the *nihil humani a me alienum puto*[47] as just described. It is this precisely which renders the Middle Ages so grand and venerable, that religion in this period appears the all moving, all ruling force, the center around which all moral struggles and triumphs, all thought, poetry and action, are found to revolve. All sciences, and philosophy itself, the science of the sciences, were handmaids to theology, which based itself on the principle of Augustine, *Fides praecedit intellectum* ["faith precedes understanding"]. Before the pope, as the head and representative of Christendom, all states bowed them-

47. [Trans. "nothing that is human is alien to me," Terence (d. c. 159).]

selves with reverent homage; and even the German emperor himself could not feel secure in his place, save as formally acknowledged by the chief bishop of the Church. Princes and people arose at his bidding, forsook country and friends, submitted to the most severe privations, to kneel at the Savior's tomb and water it with thankful tears. According to the reigning idea, the State stood related to the Church like the moon to the sun, from which it borrows all its light. All forms of life, all national manners, were suffused with magic interest from the unseen world. The holy sacraments ran like threads of gold through the whole texture of life, in all its relations, from infancy to old age. The different arts vied with each other in the service of the Church. The most magnificent and beautiful buildings of the period are the cathedrals: those giant stone flowers, with their countless turrets, storming the heavens and bearing the soul on high; and their mysterious devotional gloom, visited never by the light of the natural day, but only by mystic irradiations poured through stained glass; domes, the authors of which stood so completely in the general life of the Church, and were so occupied only with the honor of God in their work, that with a divine carelessness they have left even their own names to perish in oblivion. The maxim was, Let the best house belong to the Lord. The richest paintings were madonnas and images of the saints as produced by a Fra Beato Angelico da Fiesole; a Fra Bartolomeo; a Leonardo Da Vinci; a Perugino; a Raphael; and a Michael Angelo. It was felt that the fairest among the sons of men, and the connections in which he stood, must furnish the most worthy material for the pencil. The most lofty and impressive music, according to Old Testament example, resounded in the public worship of God. Poetry sang her deepest and most tender strains to the Lord and his bride; and the greatest poet of the Middle Ages, Dante, has left behind him in his *Divine Comedy* an image simply of the religious spirit and theological wisdom of the age, as occupied with eternity itself and all its dread realities. Truly a great time, and for one who is prepared to understand it, fraught with the richest spiritual interest. He that has no heart for the excellencies of this period, the beauty that belongs to the Middle Ages, must be wanting in genuine culture, or at least in all right historical feeling.

The true Church historian leaves to every age its own peculiar advantages, without concern. He presumes not with narrow prejudice to reduce all to one measure, but recognizes with joyful satisfaction, under the most different forms, wherever found, the footsteps of the Lord, the presence of his Spirit, as secured to the Church by his own promise through all ages. He does not *construct* history, after the measure of some poor conceptions of his own; he does not *correct* it by the standard of the time in which he himself lives; but he takes it up and *reproduces* it, as God has allowed it to occur, in the progressive explication of his plan of redemption, which apparent obstructions even, yea the rage of diabolic passion itself, must only help forward in the end. However firmly settled he may be for himself in a particular standpoint, he thinks not of circumscribing the boundless fullness of the divine life by the narrow horizon of his own view. With all his respect for the Reformation as a true work of

God, he is not rendered insensible by it to what was excellent and beautiful in earlier times, in which also men of immortal name lived and worked and suffered, and when also God made his presence gloriously felt, and kept watch over the Church continually with the eye of his love.

That must be regarded certainly as a most unwise policy, by which Protestants for a long time allowed themselves to renounce all interest in this period, and resign its treasures wholly to the Church of Rome, as though nothing but darkness and barbarism belonged to its history. The error indeed is still widely prevalent in this country—for the most part however, a sin of profound ignorance—so that the stereotype title for that period is simply, *The Dark Ages*! O, thou light of the nineteenth century! How hast thou tarried with thy rising, hiding thyself for a thousand years behind the clouds, in cowardly fear of those dying men, the popes! Come now, ye poor unfortunate children of darkness—ye LEOS and GREGORYS, ye EMPERORS of the house of SAXONY and the HOHENSTAUFEN, ANSELM, and THOMAS AQUINAS, BONAVENTURA, and BERNARD OF CLAIRVAUX, DANTE ALIGHIERI and PETRARCH, ERWIN OF STEINBACH and BRAMANTE, LEONARDO DA VINCI and RAPHAEL, FRANCIS OF ASSISI and THOMAS À KEMPIS—come forth from your graves and be illuminated by the light that *now* reigns; learn how to govern Church and State, from our synods, consistories, and advocates; study philosophy and theology at Andover and New Haven; practice poetry, Church building, and painting, amid the encouragement that is given to the arts in practical, money loving America; and take lessons of piety from the "camp meetings" of the Albright Brethren, and sects of the same spirit.[48] But they have no desire to come back, the mighty dead! With a compassionate smile, they point our dwarfish race to their own imperishable giant works, and exclaim: "Be humble, and learn that nothing beseems you so well."

In Germany this foolish prejudice, God be praised, has been happily surmounted, since through HERDER and WIELAND, and still more by the Romantic school, particularly TIECK, NOVALIS, and the two SCHLEGELS, the poetic wealth of the Middle Ages has been brought to view; their significance in the general history of the world, by MOSER, JOHN VON MUELLER, and LEO; their universal human interest, by GOETHE in his *Faust* and *Goetz von Berlichingen*; and finally their ecclesiastical magnificence and theological depth, as well scholastic as mystical, by the later works on Church history and the development of doctrines, and in particular also by various monographs on

48. [Schaff here assembles great luminaries of the High Middle Ages of all sorts: popes and German emperors, scholastic theologians (Anselm, Aquinas, and Bonaventura), monastic leaders and mystics (Bernard of Clairvaux, Francis of Assisi, and Thomas à Kempis), poets (Dante and Petrarch), architects (Erwin of Steinbach and Bramante), and painters (Da Vinci and Raphael). He sarcastically contrasts their achievements—relegated by the reigning historiography, to the so-called "Dark Ages"—to the works of the present "enlightened" age, suggesting a qualitative difference between the contributions of the two ages, historically speaking.

Led by Jacob Albright, the Albright Brethren broke away from the German Reformed Church in 1800 under the influence of Methodism. They officially named themselves the Evangelical Association in 1816.]

INNOCENT III, HUGO OF ST. VICTOR, ANSELM OF CANTERBURY, BERNARD OF CLAIRVAUX, HENRY SUSO, TAULER, SAVONAROLA, JOHN WESSEL, and others.[49] It should be borne in mind, that the Middle Ages after all are the cradle of the Reformation. They exhibit to us, not simply the Roman, but the Romano-Germanic Catholicism, in whose arms the Reformation is borne like the infant Christ by the madonnas of Raphael. True, the madonna appears in the foreground, after the Romish style. But still the highest beauty of the virgin mother, surrounding her with the loveliness of heaven itself, flows mainly from the adoring, blissful gaze with which she is absorbed in the divine child, that smiles and plays upon her bosom, and yet bears the world upon its hand. So too the Middle Ages have their richest charm in the longing and earnest expectation with which they look forward to the Reformation, as the ripe fruit of the previous struggles of the Church, the strong and joyous child of her deep birth-pangs endured for long centuries before.

Even now the Roman Catholic Church, which since the sixteenth century lives almost entirely on her past greatness, retains much of the character under consideration, though no longer the mistress of the world. She embraces all spheres of human life, attends it through all its stations from the cradle to the grave, pervades all conditions with her spirit, anoints all occupations with her consecrating oil, and in this way exercises a much greater power than Protestantism over the consciences and spirits of those who stand in her communion. In the midst of the visible world, remembrancers of the world unseen meet us on all sides, in crosses, churches, images of saints, relics, and expressive symbols of every kind. True we encounter in the same quarter also, all sorts of superstition, error and abuse. These it is an easy thing to assault with rude hand, and anathematize incontinently as the work of the devil. Instead of this however it might be well if more pains were taken to fathom and bring home to ourselves (as could be done with great profit and no great difficulty, where proper knowledge and feeling were combined in the inquiry) the original truth, and the deep religious want, that lie at the ground of almost every abuse and error, and impart to it its tough life. "Prove all things, and hold fast that which is good" [1 Thess 5:21].

Notwithstanding all now said however, one radical fault characterizes the relation of the Roman Church to the world. She does not sufficiently respect the world in its own divine rights, and seeks to subject it to herself in a violent, unnatural, premature way, without regard to the measure of her own development. Instead of waiting humbly, and following the course of tribulation prescribed by Christ, she would anticipate in a fleshly way the ideal state, when "the kingdom and dominion, and the greatness of the kingdom under the whole heaven, shall be given to the people of the saints of the Most High, whose kingdom is an everlasting kingdom" (Daniel 7:27), and when it shall be said, that "salvation, and strength, and the kingdom of our God, and the power of his Christ is come" (Rev. 12:10). Thus the heathen mythologies also

49. [For Schaff's discussion of German historiography on these figures see *What is Church History?*, section I (239–252 in this volume).]

were a fleshly prolepsis of the mystery of the incarnation.[50] The papacy in the Middle Ages conducted itself tyrannically towards the State, and trampled on the rights of the nations; it permitted not science and inquiry to take their own course in a free way; it surrounded the arts with arbitrary bounds; in a word, it affected to swallow up the world at once in a wholesale way. The world however, thus overwhelmed but not assimilated to the true life of the Church, has re-asserted its rights in the bosom of the Church itself, and taken revenge upon it by impressing this with its own character, especially at the papal court. Romanism forms accordingly a secular state, at the expense of the free, quietly advancing, inward character of Christianity. Its worship has an outwardly pompous complexion; filling the senses; half heathenish. Even in doctrine, this remarkable dialectic process may be seen, particularly in the dogma of transubstantiation, according to which, on the one hand, the divine is revealed only through the annihilation of the natural substances, bread and wine, here representing the world, and this in virtue of the consecration of the priest, of course the act of a mere creature; while however, on the other hand, these transmuted elements, retaining still in fact their natural character, are made the object of divine worship, by which means a paganizing creature deification comes to prevail. Thus we find explained the seemingly inexplicable contradiction of the system, its contempt for the world in one direction and its undue regard for it in another. Monkish austerity and pelagian secularity dwell harmoniously together in the same cell.

The powers of the world under the legal discipline of the Middle Ages became gradually mature. The Church however, refusing to distinguish between different periods of life, and unwilling to put away the rod at the proper time, paid no respect to the change. The world then avenged itself on a large scale, by breaking away from the Church entirely, and entering upon a new course of development for itself. This took place with the Reformation. It is accordingly in this respect also a process of emancipation; but as such here too not yet complete; requiring still a closing act, to unite once more what has been disjoined.

The world since the sixteenth century has reached a measure of cultivation such as it never possessed before. The Protestant States are incomparably superior to those which have been or are now under the staff of the Roman bishop; showing altogether more order, obedience, and contentment; whereas the pope has often enough preached insurrection against the temporal powers, released subjects from their oath

50. A similar thought is uttered also by J. P. Lang (*Vermischte Schriften*, Vol. IV [Mörs: Rheinischen Schulbuchhandlung 1841], p. 84), when he says in his striking way: "The characteristic fault of the papacy is the show it makes of a perfect Christianity. In popery, the Christian world-renovation is exhibited in a premature, hypocritical, violent way—exhibited *à tout prix*. All that is human is sacrificed, all truth, all reality, development itself, to secure this dazzling show of Christian perfection. Popery is thus the impatience of shallow, unsound Christian feeling, that cannot wait quietly for the end of the world, and so will have it before its time; through impatience settled, and by its settled character again impatient. All is forced; that which is a process must appear throughout an issue (*das Werden ein Gewordenes*) though the truth itself even should be lost, yea openly resisted, to secure the point."

of allegiance, and favored and sanctioned state conspiracy and the murder of kings. In place however of the former slavish dependence on the Church, the opposite extreme has come to prevail. The Protestant States have either separated themselves entirely from the Church (at least this is the case with our own), or in contradiction to the principles of the Reformation have subjected it more or less to their dominion, as in Germany, England, and Switzerland, so that out of Church states have arisen state Churches. For in these countries, the governments have taken the supreme administration of the Church into their own hands, and thus in practice at least make Caesar to be pope, which is no whit better than making the pope to be Caesar. It is true indeed, that in a number of States the freedom of the Romish Church too is restrained by the secular authority, as in Austria, and still more latterly in Russia, Spain, and Portugal. With inflexible consistency however, she steadily protests against every such invasion, and always contrives in the end to make good again her pretensions; as is strikingly shown by the noted affair of Cologne, and recent events in Spain, as well as by the controversy on the subject of Church instruction in France.[51]

Protestant science, philosophy in particular, is so far from being the mere handmaid of theology and the Church that it appears just as often at least arrayed against them. Above all in Germany, philosophy is regarded commonly as the all-comprehending, absolute science of reason itself, of which theology is only a single branch. We cannot hesitate a moment to bestow the title *Christian* on the scholastic philosophers of the Middle Ages, an Anselm, a Peter Lombard, or a Thomas Aquinas; but there is no room for this, in the strict sense, in the case of Locke, Hume, Wolf, Kant, Fichte, etc., if for no other reason, for this alone that they show themselves destitute of humility and penitence, which are the ground of all piety. On the other hand however, considered in the way of pure science only, the modern systems, internally united like the links of a chain from Leibnitz down (a view to be sure but dimly apparent in this country, where the empiricism of Locke still sways its despotic scepter over the most republican spirits) exhibit a vastness, depth and comprehensive variety, that find no parallel in the Church of Rome, whose only approved philosophy, indeed may be said to be the scholastic Aristotelian. The advantage of all this to the Protestant theology is at least so much that it has become more scientific.

A like aspect of things is presented to us in the sphere of the Arts and Polite Literature. These too, since the Reformation, have emancipated themselves more or less from the Church. If we except our sacred hymns and chorales—in the case of which certainly a wonderful productivity has appeared in the German Church, the Lutheran especially during the sixteenth and seventeenth centuries—we possess almost no works of Church art that are fairly entitled to the name. All artistic ornament has been banished from the churches on principle; and our modern structures bear more resemblance often to a theatre, or a Grecian temple, than to the true idea of a

51. [When construction of the Catholic cathedral in Cologne resumed in 1842, the Protestant rulers of Prussia agreed to help fund it.]

Christian house of worship. THORWALDSEN has indeed formed statues also of Christ and the apostles; but they are by no means equal to his mythological representations.[52] The painters since the Reformation until very recently—the DÜSSELDORF school, OVERBECK, CORNELIUS, KAULBACH (in his *Destruction of Jerusalem*), and other masters, partly catholic and partly protestant began to bring in a change again—have had recourse to the kingdom of nature and to profane history for their subjects, rather than to the bible and the Church.[53] So the Dutch painters in particular. The greatest modern composers, even such as are catholic, as MOZART, BEETHOVEN, and the Italian school, are not certainly to be counted Church artists in the strict sense. The prayers and priest choirs of the *Magic Flute* and the Nemesis in *Don Juan*, as well as the *Requiem*, show only that the modern world is impregnated with Christian ideas and feelings, without surrendering still its natural character; and of BEETHOVEN's incomparable symphonies it has been strikingly observed by one fully at home in the subject, that they are so many monologues of the absolute "ME" of the present age, that with desperate struggle to stand upon itself, sinks into immeasurable grief and braves it again with saucy humor, bringing as it were all its resources together to sustain itself in the arduous task. Our poets of the first rank, (among whom we cannot reckon the pious but tedious singers MILTON and KLOPSTOCK) take them altogether, are forms that spring from nature only. SHAKESPEARE belongs rather of right to the Middle Period, whose traditions have supplied him with almost all his poetic material. He is in a certain sense the completion of DANTE, in whom is mirrored the religious glory of that time. GOETHE has his bright and dark side both in this, that he is all *nature*, in the largest and most comprehensive sense of the word. Where he introduces Christianity, it is exhibited (except perhaps in *Faust*, which however moves rather in the mediaeval elements), not at all as the universal life-power by which the whole world is to be pervaded and renewed, but as being itself simply a remarkable object in nature, *one* only among the countless phenomena in which the universal genius is required to feel the same interest. Characteristic in this view is the episode style, in which the confessions of a virtuous soul are presented in the midst of gay actresses and amiable coquettes. SCHILLER's ideal is abstract, moral nature; the gigantically struggling, Stoic will. The religious element with him, where it appears in objective dramatic form, is Catholic, as in the *Maid of Orleans*, in *Maria Stuart*, and in *Wallenstein*; and where it proceeds from his own breast, a mere home-sickness, an unsatisfied longing, as it flows upon us for instance, in sorrowful wise, in the poem "Ach aus dieses Thales Gruenden." BYRON shows himself a stranger in full to the peace whispering accents of the gospel,

52. [The most famous of Bertel Thorvaldsen's (1770–1844) religious statues is his rendering of the resurrected Christ, *Christus* (1838). It is widely reproduced, especially by the Church of Jesus Christ of Latter-day Saints.]

53. [The painters of religious subjects mentioned here are Johann Friedrich Overbeck (1789–1869), Peter von Cornelius (1784–1867), and Wilhelm von Kaulbach (1805–74). The Düsseldorf school was led by Friedrich Wilhelm Schadow (1789–1862).]

and to all true humility. His home is the howling storm of all wild passions. He is the demoniacally inspired poet of despair.

Still who may refuse his admiration to the vast poetical powers and resources, the natural greatness simply of these extraordinary men; who persuade himself that God has introduced such colossal figures into our modern world without purpose, and allowed them to exert so measureless an influence on the culture of millions for no end whatever? No! Such a mass of thought and beauty cannot possibly be lost for the kingdom of God. Rather it challenges the Church to the high and solemn task of subduing this gigantic life to the power of her own spirit, that so she may rise above it, and attain thus to a higher position than any to which she has yet come.[54]

As it regards finally the order of common social life, we may say that Christianity wears no longer a distinguishing priestly dress, but the ordinary citizen's coat. The almost universal banishment of the gown from the pulpit itself, in this country, is characteristic in this view; a novelty at the same time which is by no means to be approved, as savoring of an unhistorical spiritualism and a want of proper respect for what is sacred. The abstract, extramundane character of religion has been laid aside, and the claims of the present life are more fully appreciated. Marriage is no longer depressed beside celibacy as a higher grade of sanctity; but the minister is expected to let the light of his example shine before his congregation, as a husband and a father. Monkery is abolished, and men are directed to exercise their virtue in the natural employments of life; and while standing and working in the world, to keep themselves unspotted from it. True at the same time, purely material interests, traffic and trade, industry and steam, and along with all this utilitarianism and selfism, have acquired an importance to which they are not entitled. For the spirit *ought* to reign over matter. But still, in the hand of God, even steamships and railroads must serve to extend more rapidly his kingdom.

This whole posture of the world towards the Church carries now both a discouraging and a cheering aspect, as has already been intimated in the notice of particulars. It is an unsound condition; since all divinely constituted forms and spheres of life should stand, and must in the end stand, in perfect harmony with one another. It serves to show the weakness of the Church, that she has allowed these natural interests thus to overtop her in her growth, instead of mastering them, and so directing them continually to the glorification of their Creator. It is crying ingratitude besides on the part of the world, that luxuriating now in her own prosperity, she affects to be independent of Christianity, yea even presumes to oppose it broadly; while yet she is indebted to it for the best she has, and without an inward reconciliation to the Church, a full return to the element of religion, can never fulfill at all her own highest destiny. For the end or scope of all history is this: that the world may resolve itself into the

54. [Schaff argues here along the lines of Schleiermacher in his *On Religion: Speeches to its Cultured Despisers* (1799) that where the culture attains its highest artistic achievements, there, too, is religion. See below for an elaboration of this point.]

kingdom of God; reason into revelation; morality into religion; and earth into heaven. All sciences must be raised and refined into theosophy, all government into theocracy, all art into divine worship, and the whole of life into a joyful proclamation of the glory of God.[55]

Since however this ultimate identification of the world with Christianity may be apprehended also as an absolute molding of the Church into all the forms of the world, the full identification of Christianity with nature, we must recognize again on the other side an encouraging advance towards this end, in the present relation of the two systems. The Christian principle by means of it has become more naturalized, more at home in the world. It stands no longer in mere abstract opposition to the natural life; has the world no longer under itself as a foreign element; but is forming it into itself, much as this may be denied by the world in its present stage. The modern culture is not that of heathenism, but is carried throughout on the shoulders of christianity, draws from this constantly its most substantial life, and must on this very account, however unwillingly, come into subjection to it in the end. In this respect also then, Protestantism is only an apparent regression; in truth it has carried the Church materially forward. Roman Catholicism here has remained behind the time; and has either refused altogether, with willful bigotry, to admit the advance of modern cultivation; or has yielded to the force of it to a certain extent, only for the most part where it has stood in near contact with Protestantism, and always in consequence at least of its influence either direct or indirect. The more recent Catholic theology, for instance, springs from Germany, and is conditioned in its best productions by Protestant elements. Let any one think only of Hug, Moehler, von Drey, Gehring, Hirscher, Staudenmaier, Papst, and Guenther.[56] The principal seats of Romanism—Italy, Spain, and Portugal—have done little or nothing in this sphere, within the last centuries, and as regards the education of the people, are incredibly far back.

Thus in this case also our contemplations point us, not backward, but forward to a rich future for Protestantism that will leave all the glory of the Catholic Church far in the rear. The better tendency of the time is indeed toward *objectivity*; not towards that of the Middle Ages however, that could be upheld only by violently crushing, or willfully restraining, the rights of the individual subject; but it seeks the objective rather in a higher form, *in which it shall be enriched and spiritualized by all that has been gained on the part of the subjective, the good fruits of the development of Protestantism through a period of three hundred years*. The day must come when all the forms of life which God has constituted in the world shall feel that they need a union with religion and

55. [The words "theosophy" and "theocracy" should be understood according to their Greek roots, "God's wisdom" and "God's rule." Schaff is not advocating esotericism or clerical control of civil government.]

56. [These Catholic theologians are Johann Leonhard Hug (1765–1846) of Freiburg, Johann Sebastian von Drey (1777–1853) of Tübingen, Franz Anton Staudenmaier (1800–56) of Frieburg, and Anton Guenther (1783–1863) of Vienna. For Moehler and Hirscher see the glossary. Gehring and Papst cannot be identified.]

the Church, to realize in full their own idea, and when they shall voluntarily return to the Lord, and lay their richest products upon his altar. That memorable word of Bacon, *Philosophia obiter libata abducit a Deo, penitus hausta reducit ad eundem,*[57] may be applied with just as much force to Art, Politics, and Social Order, and must be fulfilled sooner or later in all.

[3. Signs of a new era in the history of theology and the Church]

That our hope of a new life for Protestantism, to be secured through its full reconciliation with the objective idea of the Church is no empty dream, many appearances of the present time, in part still incomplete indeed and solitary, serve to show. These now demand our attention, which will be directed again first to Germany, and then to America.

[A. In Germany.]

Germany is still far from having completed her part in the world's history. Such as are acquainted with the present state of the country, as it regards science, morals and religion, and viewed in comparison with what it was during the last century and the beginning of this, will understand the force of this remark. What a melancholy time was that, when English deism, French frivolity, and superficial German popular philosophy, were joined in common conspiracy against the Church. Pietism indeed had still its representatives; for the most part however spiritual cripples, who placed the substance of Christianity in a few poor forms, and turned the fresh air of life into an uncomfortable, gloomy chamber of death. The Moravian Brethren, it is true, were not without influence; but it was exerted, apart from theology, in the stillness only of retired practical life. True again, supranaturalism, technically so called, the last scientific stand on the part of orthodoxy, mustered, in men like Reinhard and Storr, learned and venerable theologians in opposition to the Rationalists;[58] but its position was one-sided, in the way particularly of a too abstract conception of the formal principle of

57. [Trans. "Philosophy sipped in passing leads away from God; but drunk deeply leads back to him." The quote appears to be from Francis Bacon's *Two Bookes of the proficience and advancement of learning, divine and human* (London: 1605) where the thought is given in English as "a little or superficiall knowledge of philosophie may incline the minde of man to atheisme, but a further proceeding therein doth bring the mind backe again to religion" (p. 6); Schaff appears to be quoting from Bacon's own 1623 expanded Latin edition of this work, *De Dignitate et Augmentis.*]

58. [Gottlob Christian Storr (1746–1805) was founder of "the older" Tübingen school of Protestant theology that emphasized "biblical supernaturalism." Moving away from Lutheran scholasticism, he sought to establish the integrity and authenticity of the Bible from historical evidence, and thereby the sole authority of Christ. His exegesis of scripture, later faulted for not taking into consideration the historical and literary context of the Bible's various parts. Franz Volkmar Reinhard (1753–1812) was a Lutheran theologian and popular preacher who also offered rationalistic arguments for the authority of the Bible.]

Protestantism, and it treated with the enemy so far, that in the end it fairly fell over to his side, as we see in the case of SCHOTT, AMMON and BRETSCHNEIDER. Its whole standpoint was outward and empirical; of the Holy Ghost in the Church it had no sense whatever, and could not possibly therefore keep its ground. So dry and waste had the German Church then become, that minds of the deeper, more earnest order, such as STOLBERG, NOVALIS, and FRIEDRICH SCHLEGEL, were fain to take refuge in the bosom of Catholicism. And the revolutionary epoch was so shorn of all religious life and consciousness that SCHLEIERMACHER, in his masterly *Discourses on Religion*, of the year 1799, found it necessary to start from the beginning; taking his stand as it were in the Court of the Gentiles, to teach his Wolffian, Kantian, and Philanthropistic contemporaries, the nature of religion first in general, that he might gain footing again for an intelligible representation of the Christian system.[59]

And how does it now stand with the German theology? I am well aware indeed of the fearful episode that has broken in from the left side of the Hegelian philosophy upon the quiet, regular course of its development, already ripening towards the best results—an episode like the storm of the July Revolution, which may be said to have brought up the rear of the political convulsions, through which France was carried with the close of the last century. Taking however a broad, general view, and looking especially to the most recent movements, we may say with full confidence that the theology which now has the floor of the age is not rationalism, but orthodoxy resuscitated with a higher life from its ruins. With the decision, power, and fervor of the old Church faith, it unites at the same time that scientific freedom, disentanglement from prejudice, and full roundness of method, which have become possible only through the modern development of rationalism and philosophy. Look now where we may either in the widely extended school of SCHLEIERMACHER, with its numerous derivations, the most independent of which are presented to us in NEANDER, NITZSCH and J. MUELLER; or among those who are more or less ruled by the conservative elements of the *Hegelian* philosophy, in the writings especially of a GOESCHEL, ROTHE, DORNER, MARTENSEN, HOFFMANN, HASSE; either to the productions of the orthodox *Unionist* tendency of a HENGSTENBERG and his spiritual colleagues, or the *New Lutheran* theology of a HARLESS and others; everywhere, it is true, we find much mixed disputation and hard conflict, the result however in part of mere misapprehension; but still everywhere also the spring-breath of a newly-wakened faith, and the bursting germs of a new, bright and fruitful era in theology. This must be rich and full, in proportion as the boundless range of history has been brought more fully and clearly into view, by the untiring, most learned and profound researches, *monumenta aere perenniora*[60] of German scholarship and German diligence combined. What is most animating

59. [For an English translation of the original 1799 text see Friederich Schleiermacher, *On Religion: Speeches to Its Cultured Despisers*, trans. Richard Crouter (Cambridge: Cambridge University Press, 1988).]

60. [Trans. "monuments more lasting than bronze," Horace (65 BCE–25 CE).]

however is the genial union of free scientific interest and true Church feeling that is showing itself in some of the theologians who have been named, and in many more especially who are now coming forward. This Church feeling shows itself moreover in the formation continually more and more of ministerial associations for conference on reigning defects and mutual encouragement in efforts after improvement; and particularly also in the concern now so general, which is felt to have the Church service renewed and enriched, by thrusting aside all watery, rationalistic pretended improvements, and falling back in a proper way to the incomparable treasures of the old Church songs and liturgies. Here again however the new which is at hand will be not a mere repetition, but an enlargement and rectification of the old; inasmuch as by means of the vast researches of science, in which Rationalism itself has fulfilled an important part, the wealth of all centuries, as already intimated, is now rendered accessible to such an extent as never before. In short, the German Church and Theology, in spite of all difficulties and dangers, may be said to have a fair wind, and it were disgraceful cowardice just now to draw in the sails, and stand despairingly inactive with hands folded upon the bosom. It is the period emphatically for hope and action.

And from what quarter has this favorable change proceeded? Not wholly from theology and the Church themselves, but in large part, and indeed mainly, from the side of the secular life, involving thus to some extent already a verification of the idea that all natural relations are to be pervaded in a new way by the spirit of religion. This precisely is striking and peculiar in Germany, that the same foe, the same science in particular, which inflicted such deep wounds upon its orthodoxy, has again turned round of its own accord and furnished the means for their cure.[61] For this very reason however, the cure must prove vastly more thorough than such soundness as may be maintained in other lands, where all the attacks of philosophy and secular culture against Christianity are repelled only with the rusty armor of the old apologetic methods, or simple proofless appeals to pious feeling. It is justly remarked by Tholuck, in his learned and spirited work against the *Leben Jesu* of Strauss, that the shallow race of rationalistic illuminatists, at whose head Nicolai of dull and tedious memory once stood, received its death blow first among the laity, by the powerful wing-stroke of the Romantic writers, Tieck, Schlegel and Novalis; after which it was consumed to the bone by the lixivium of ingenious satire, and so remanded back again to its original nothing.[62] The Romantic school indeed fixed its view not so much upon the holiness of religion as its beauty, making it an object of aesthetic enjoyment, which the ironic "me" saw *under* itself; but it helped mightily nevertheless to put an end to the reign of

61. [This is a fine example of how Schaff goes to the middle: not afraid of secular or rational methods and convinced that "progress" animates and annihilates (or *aufheben*) oppositions.]

62. [August Tholuck, *Die Glaubwürdigkeit der evangelischen Geschichte: zugleich eine Kritik des* Lebens Jesu *von Strauss: für theologische und nicht theologische Leser* (Hamburg: F. Perthes, 1837). Partial English translation by J. R. Beard as *The credibility of the evangelical history illustrated* in *Voices of the Church, in Reply to Dr. D.F. Strauss . . . Comprising Essays in Defence of Christianity* (London: Simpkin, Marshall, 1845), 117–60.]

the mere bald understanding. The abstract separation of Christianity and art has since that time disappeared more and more from the consciousness of the cultivated in Germany. Art itself, in many of its most important representatives has again become religious, in particular painting, and music, and poetry. True, the poetry of despair and of sentimental world grief is still to be met with on all sides; but it has of late pronounced its own doom by plunging into politics and all sorts of projects for the world's amelioration, which contradict entirely the very idea of art.

A second powerful agent in the production of the change that has been mentioned, is presented to us in the modern philosophy since the rise of SCHELLING. He freed German science and with it theology also, from the bonds of KANT's standpoint of reflection, and Fichte's subjective idealism, and led forth the spirit again into the objective world both of nature and history. Speak as men may against German transcendentalism, as the word passes here in a wholesale way, this at least no one acquainted with the subject can deny: that at the very time when the most celebrated theologians cast away the cardinal evangelical doctrines of the incarnation and atonement as antiquated superstitions, SCHELLING and HEGEL stood forth in their defense, and claimed for them the character of the highest reason; and that while the reigning view saw in history only an aggregate of arbitrary opinions, a chaos of selfish passions, they taught the world to recognize in it the ever-opening sense of eternal thoughts, an always advancing rational development of the idea of humanity and its relations to God. Such a view must gradually overthrow the abrupt revolutionary and negative spirit which characterized the last century, restoring respect for the Church and its history, and making room for the genuine power of the positive.[63] It is true indeed,

63. Just after I had written this, the article of Professor STOWE, in the *Bib. Repos.*, Jan. 1845 entitled "Teutonic Metaphysics or Modern Transcendentalism," [*Biblical Repository and Classical Review*, 3rd ser., 1, no. 1 (January 1845): 64–97] came to my sight; and as it has been already welcomed in several papers as highly important and seasonable, I do not feel at liberty to pass it over in silence. I am truly sorry to find myself disappointed in Dr. STOWE. In view only of his relations to my honored instructor and friend Dr. DORNER, now counselor of consistory and professor of theology at Königsberg, I held him capable of understanding and appreciating the German philosophy and theology, much beyond what he has shown in this unfortunate article. It is not in my mind at all to undertake a wholesale defense of any system of German philosophy as such; for I prize too much the liberty of thought to be bound by any philosophical school, and yield my reason to be led only by the bible. But men like KANT, FICHTE, SCHELLING and HEGEL, who have devoted their whole life to the most laborious and profound inquiries, and who beyond all question belong to the greatest names in the history of the world, should be treated in different style by such a man as STOWE, in justice only to his own character. Instead of saying a word to us on the contents of the later positive system of SCHELLING, he informs us of his controversy with Dr. PAULUS of Heidelberg, which has nothing in the world to do with the matter in hand; and even takes the part of this wretched rationalist, who closed his career as a writer with a literary theft, against the great philosopher—not dreaming at all, as it would seem, that it is precisely the acknowledged merit of this last, to have overcome the standpoint of the abstract understanding, from which the old common Rationalism made war upon all the deeper truths of Christianity. For this "common sense," entitled as it is to all respect in its own sphere, the region of the simply finite will always hold the doctrines of the Trinity and incarnation for nonsense; since according to its shallow, empty way of reasoning, three cannot be one nor one three, God cannot be man nor man God. If then no higher principle be allowed to prevail in theology, it must be shorn of all its deeper import. Such

that one section of the Hegelian school (the so-called *left side*) has produced the latest and most dangerous form of Rationalism, in which the doctrine of myths and pantheistic hero-worship are made to play so large a part. But this tendency is diametrically opposed to the historical, objective element that clearly rules the spirit if not always the letter of the great philosopher's writings, and cannot be regarded therefore at all events as a complete application of his system to theology. And then again it must be considered that the movement in question is rendered so dangerous, just because it has received into itself, pantheistically caricatured to be sure, so many truths of Christianity, for which the old Rationalism had no organ whatever, and because it is conducted also with so much more spirit and depth; which itself again is to be referred to a general advance, that may be easily remarked also in the form of the later theology as more scientific than before. The very latest speculation besides, in the person of the still living founder of the Identity System, Schelling himself has taken a direction decidedly towards positive revelation; and it may be said now with good certainty at least, that the bloom period of the pantheistic logic and purely negative anti-theology

a higher principle is the *reason* by which we apprehend the super-sensuous, the infinite, the divine. But it is Schelling precisely who has successfully asserted the supremacy of this principle in science. To be convinced of this, let Dr. Stowe read Schelling's *Lectures on the Method of Academic Study* [*Vorlesungen über die Methode des academischen Studium* (Tübingen: T.G. Cotta, 1803)], particularly the fifth and sixth. He will find there a most masterly and powerful argument against the presumption of the mere understanding, in thrusting itself with its poor surface-skimming nature into the region of the higher sciences, which have to do with everlasting ideas—making all flat by trying to make all clear. Hegel's works Prof. Stowe tells us he has "waded through"—so long since however, or in such cursory style, that he can no longer recollect of how many volumes they consist, missing the mark entirely in his general guess (p. 86). No wonder that his memory should be found still more at fault, as it regards the actual contents of this exceedingly difficult system. In fact he does not pretend to draw from the fountain itself, but only from the *Conversations-Lexicon* [*der neuesten Zeit und Literatur* (Encyclopedia of recent times and literature)] of Brockhaus [4 vols. (Leipzig: Brockhaus, 1832–34)]: an ass's bridge notoriously for superficial and lazy thinkers, used by shopkeepers' clerks, but by no true German scholar, at least in so weighty a case. After giving us in this way a most lean skeleton, translated as he himself says not *ad sensum*, but only *ad verbum*, he informs us with all honesty that he cannot understand the philosopher at all. He cannot find out indeed "what the man means by anything he says in all his writings," so far as examined. Yet he adds, "Let no one say I have caricatured the system"—as if a translation of isolated fragments *ad verbum* only, could possibly in such a case be anything else than caricature! What a man by his own confession does not comprehend, it might be as well perhaps that he should not undertake to explain. Especially so, where as in the present instance the explanation is expected to carry with it a sort of "official authority" for the general public. Hegel has errors and sins enough to answer for, no doubt. But this is no reason why he should be loaded with misrepresentation, and made to appear little better than a fool at the bar of the common understanding. It is always however sheer, gross misrepresentation, when his words or thoughts are violently sundered from their true historical life, and forced to stand by abstract translation in new connections and relations entirely, in which inevitably all their original sense is transmuted, for the popular mind especially, into bare nonsense.

[The controversy between H. G. E. Paulus and Friedrich Schelling to which Calvin Stowe referred concerned Paulus's hiring of a student to attend and transcribe Schelling's Berlin lectures of 1841–42 and then publishing them with his own biting notes without Schelling's permission. Schelling sued for damages and lost. Stowe, who had personally met the elderly Paulus, sided with him in finding Schelling's philosophy lacking in substance. Stowe, "Teutonic Metaphysics," 89–91.]

is already over. STRAUSS and his colleagues, by reason of the much greater weight of religious and Church feeling they have been called to encounter, have outlived themselves much sooner than their predecessors PAULUS, WEGSCHEIDER, etc.; and BRUNO BAUER, the object now of almost universal aversion, has been formally deprived of his office, a thing of whose like no body scarcely would have dreamed twenty years ago. Such as are acquainted with the state of things in this quarter must allow that the latest critical and philosophical opposers of Christianity have in a great measure, by their own contradictions and extravagance, destroyed themselves; so that, as before remarked, the leaders of the orthodox theology, after a brief interregnum, are again at the helm of the vessel under the most encouraging auspices.

In Germany, philosophy, as the spirit of the age exalted to scientific consciousness, exerts a controlling influence, over all departments of higher knowledge. From the school of SCHELLING accordingly, in such men as ESCHENMEYER, STEFFENS, SCHUBERT, a decidedly religious tone has been imparted to investigations in the sphere of nature, by which this department has been effectually rescued from the hands of atheism and abstract deism. STEFFENS in particular has made it the great object of his life, in his scientific and poetic representations, to reconcile nature with religion, the cultivated world consciousness with the consciousness of Christianity. So also the greatest later historians, as LEO, RANKE, HAUG, show a special interest in religion and the Church as forming the central force and life pulse properly of the world's history; and bring them continually into the view of their readers, unfettered by the old spiritless pragmatism, with living reproduction, and that freedom from prejudice and love of justice, peculiar to the German mind, by which every age is allowed to enjoy its own proper greatness unimpaired.

Philology itself, both oriental and classical, has come by its inward development to stand in a new relation to the holy scriptures. The earlier Rationalism imposed its own arbitrary hypotheses and neological dreams on the Old and New Testaments by a fearful grammatical recklessness and truly wheel-breaking exegesis; and even the Supra-naturalism of the same period, as exhibited by STORR and others, lies open to censure in the same view. But before the bar of the later philology, this is no longer possible. Professor WINER, of Leipzig, whose grammatical authority as free from all theological bias is universally acknowledged, says unreservedly, "Our exegetical controversies have led back usually to that sense as correct, which the Protestant Church held in the beginning."[64] Such a man as K. FR. AUG. FRITZSCHE, who stands in no inward affinity with the spirit of the bible, but who as it regards philological learning and accuracy (at times even pushed to excess) is fairly rivaled among recent interpreters only by HARLESS and BLEEK, finds himself constrained, from the grammatico-

64. *Leipziger Literatur Zeitung* (1833), N. 44. Comp. the Preface to the third edition of his *Grammar of N. T. Idioms*, p. iv ff., [George Benedikt Winer, *Grammatik des neutestamentlichen Sprachidioms als sichere Grundlage der neutestamentlichen Exegese*, 3rd ed. (Leipzig: F.C.W. Vogel, 1830)] as well as the whole admirable work itself. A similar regeneration has been effected by EWALD and HITZIG in the department of the Old Testament.

historical standpoint alone, to prefer in the most important cases the interpretations of a Chrysostom, Augustine, Luther, Calvin, Beza, Bengel, to those of the Rationalistic school. And Strauss himself has rendered good service to the cause of truth, in his *Leben Jesu*, by the overwhelming force with which he has employed the *reductio ad absurdum* upon the violent exegetical processes made use of by the older Rationalism, in carrying out its so called natural explanation of miracles. Unbelief is thus forced to look in future for help in some different direction; it can no longer cover its nakedness with a philological mantle. The scientific study of language itself, by its own inward development and without any regard to Christianity, has led to the immensely important result that the Church, orthodox Protestantism in particular, has understood the bible in substance correctly, and must be allowed therefore to have all right against Rationalism at the bar of science, if only the assumption of the divine inspiration of the scriptures be securely established.

Finally, the political circumstances of Germany have also contributed much to the new impulse which has been given to religion. In the war for freedom particularly against the French Usurper, both princes and people were overpowered with an ever-memorable, sacred enthusiasm, when the Lord of hosts, after long-continued, well-deserved oppression, interposed so powerfully by the thunder of battle, and revealed himself so clearly in the direction of events. Since that time too, the State has begun to change its posture materially towards the Church. Formerly this was treated too generally as the mere creature of Caesar, being regarded simply as *one* among the several institutions by which the State was expected to serve its own purposes. Now however it is coming to be understood and felt, that the Church has a life of its own, and that the State consults its own welfare best, when this life is respected as an independent interest, and suffered to develop itself freely from its own nature. If any one will compare the administration of the present kings of Prussia and Württemberg with that of their predecessors, particularly Frederick the Great, he will at once admit the great change that has taken place in this respect.

From the State moreover, under Frederick William III, proceeded in the first instance that *Union* of the Lutheran and Reformed Churches, which has since become almost universal in Germany, and must be regarded now as a great step gained towards the catholicity and unity necessarily involved in the idea of the Church itself. It is not good either, that Christ's bride should bear the name of a mere man, as *Lutheran*, and the like.[65] The title *Evangelical* is much more catholic and appropriate; though not in

65. The designations *Presbyterian, Congregational, Protestant Episcopal* are also unsatisfactory, as referring only to government; which however is clearly but a secondary element of the Church, belonging not to its spirit but to its outward form. Our title, *Reformed*, coupled only if need be with the national distinction, is plainly the best. For it implies no dependence whatever on any particular man, and includes the view besides that we are no new body, but the old Catholic Church itself, only regenerated and purified from human additions. As however this term has acquired in Germany a definite historical sense, in opposition to the idea of Lutheranism, it was altogether proper that the title *Evangelical* should be preferred. Names in so weighty a case are not mere smoke, but the

the sense to be sure which it is frequently made to carry in our western States, when used as a mere cloak for rationalism and indifferentism. The stiff, absolute Old Lutheranism of Prussia and Bavaria may be considered indeed a salutary reaction against the indifference of many of the friends of the Union to doctrines; and in this view, we are glad to find its representatives in this country also. But apart from this particular advantage, it is certainly a crying, stubborn misapprehension of the wants of our time, which reach far beyond its narrow horizon. It is truly ridiculous indeed, thus to fancy the Formula of Concord the absolute perfection of theology, and to require virtually that not only the Greek and Roman Churches, but the Reformed also with its German, Low Dutch, French, English, Scotch and American branches, should make it their great business to subscribe it and submit themselves to Lutheran baptism. The future belongs certainly to the "Union," and within its range precisely the most religious life is to be found at the present time.[66] The most important and pious theologians of Germany, such as NEANDER, HENGSTENBERG, TWESTEN, MARHEINEKE, SARTORIUS, THOLUCK, MÜLLER, HUPFELD, NITZSCH, SACK, BLEEK, KLING, HASSE, HAHN, LANGE, HOFFMANN, LÜCKE, LIEBNER, ULLMANN, ROTHE, UMBREIT, SCHMIDT, DORNER, LANDERER go with it fully; though for themselves a number of them prefer, in a doctrinal respect at least, the Lutheran standpoint.[67] To be sure the Union, in its present form, is to be viewed merely as a beginning; and the closer adjustment of it, especially in the symbolical direction, creates just at this time no small difficulty.[68] Nor can it be denied that the measures of the government to promote Church improvement in Prussia labor under the defect of more or less irresolution. Good will is present, but there is a lack of fixed principles and talent for practical organization; for which at all events, the German, whose spiritual universalism is always multiplying possibilities and doubts before him, has never been particularly distinguished. The case however is in its own nature immensely difficult, and becomes still more so by the manifold spiritual tendencies, and peculiarly diversified forms of culture that enter into the constitution of the Prussian State; enough to confound the most thorough practical skill that is not

impression of the idea; and it is known that LUTHER most decidedly disapproved the designation of his followers after his own name.

66. [Schaff here reveals his loyalty to the Church of the Prussian Union as well as his sense that the prevailing arrangement in that communion between church and state advances the Christological principle informing his idea of history: "Christ all in all." From this point of view, the separation between church and state as it exists in America has not yet sufficiently developed and, indeed, the proliferation of sects would seem to disrupt progress.]

67. [Most of these theologians may be found in the glossary. The others are Hermann Hupfeld (1796–1866) of Marburg and later Halle, Karl Heinrich Sack (1789–1875) of Bonn, Christian Friedrich Kling (1800–82) of Marburg and later Bonn, August Hahn (1792–63) of Leipzig, Karl Theodor Albert Liebner (1806–71) of Kiel, Charles Guillaume Adolphe Schmidt (1812–95) of Strasburg, and Maximilian Albert von Landerer (1810–78) of Tübingen. Significantly, Schaff uses the adjective "pious" to suggest the "evangelical" quality of these theologians—including those who are confessionally inclined toward Lutheranism.]

68. [By the "symbolical direction," Schaff refers to the development of new theological confessions that will reconcile the Lutheran and Reformed heritages.]

prepared to violate all the rights of history. And then it must not be forgotten that the whole Evangelical Church is at present in an interimistic state, involved in a process of fermentation and transition, which brings along with it necessarily a measure of uncertainty and experiment. In any case, this is something better however than to repose lazily on pillows worn out by use, or to dream with unbounded self-complacency and pretension of being in a condition already complete.

[B. In America.]

Let us leave however the king of Prussia, with his spiritual and secular counselors, to work out as they best may, under the favor of heaven, the problem they are called to solve, and turn our attention once more upon our own land. What prospect is there here, in the way of encouragement for the Church? May we hope to see our Protestant Zion conducted safely out of the Babylonish captivity of sectarism and faction, without being carried to old Rome or young Oxford?

We have no such deep scientific conflicts among us, as those we have just had in our view. The philosophical life questions of Germany, the relation of the Church to the arts and to the State, with which the greatest minds there are exercised in the severest way, bring no trouble whatever to the American. "*Cui bono*?" ["to whose benefit?"] he is ready to exclaim, in view of every speculation of the sort; dubbing it perhaps with the convenient title *transcendentalism* or *mysticism*, to justify his contempt. What has it accomplished for the souls of men or their bodies? Can it fill an empty pocket, or an empty stomach? Has it ever manufactured a steamboat, or so much even as a pin? Such is the style, in substance if not in form, in which the interest of philosophical thinking is too often undervalued in this country, in favor of what is practical and useful. With such a spirit, of course, I can feel no sympathy. It is greatly to be lamented that the German Churches of America in particular should be so sadly defective in theological and philosophical culture, and without a single literary institution after the pattern of the German *Gymnasia* or universities. The result of this must be in the end that our congregations will lose themselves in the English denominations, with the sacrifice of their own proper character entirely, unless they can be brought betimes into spiritual communication with the mother Church in Germany. On the other hand, if they might be led thus to participate with proper life in the later movements of German theology, they would take a position peculiar to themselves, and must exercise gradually an important influence also on their English sister churches.[69] For these too need a vastly more thorough and vigorous theology to carry them prosperously forward, and make them superior to the foes that now threaten them from every side. Theology is no less necessary for the regeneration of Protestantism now than it was for the accomplishment of the Reformation in the sixteenth century. To prevent

69. [This idea that one group is able to share its influence on others was already in Schaff's day a common justification for denominationalism. It is one he would champion in later writings.]

misunderstanding, it may be well to be a little more particular on the importance of theology in its relation to practical Church life.

Some take ground on principle against all theological training as injurious to the interests of living, practical piety. Such are welcome to the illiterate declaimers in whom they choose to take delight, with all their rant and noise and animal excitement; men who trample under foot the apostolic caution with regard to this point (James 3:1)[70] and in their wretched spiritual pride deal forth the stale conceits and fantastic soap bubbles of their own poor brain, for the inspirations of the Holy Ghost. Alas for the congregations whose want of discernment leads them to accept such husks for bread. Show us then, ye opposers of knowledge, which the apostle makes the element of eternal life, where are the men whom a miraculous illumination of the Spirit has constituted theologians with a single stroke; and no one will be more ready to show them respect than ourselves. But ye substitute your own fanatical feeling for the Holy Ghost. Pentecosts are not common days in history; and according to the general rule and order of God, which we are bound humbly to observe, even our spiritual bread is to be earned by the sweat of our brow. Our intellectual and moral faculties are given us, not to be buried or left to rust, but to be put to use and made productive. We are directed to search the scriptures continually, and to grow in all wisdom and knowledge. If the apostles themselves, after an intercourse of three years with the Master of all masters, needed still an extraordinary furniture of divine gifts for their work, it must certainly be considered no small presumption, when a little religious experience merely, and this often in the most superficial form, together with some tolerable fluency of speech, is held, as with many in this country at the present time, a sufficient preparation for the most important and difficult of all offices. Let us hope, that the age of such presumption may soon come to an end. For nothing is more adapted to bring the ministry into disrespect, to strip the pulpit of its true sacred dignity, and to make the Church itself in the end an object of general indifference and derision.

Others pronounce theology *useful* at least; and regard this as quite a fine compliment paid to the science. These are your utilitarians and materialists, who measure the value of all things in heaven and upon earth by the interest they bring. While seeming to praise it, they sink the first of all sciences into the same category with a bushel of potatoes; and indeed lower, since these last may lay claim to a much more general and palpable utility. Theology is neither useful nor harmful; it is raised immeasurably above the poor category of serviceableness; it is no means, with which to procure something beyond itself, as we employ money or a mechanical instrument; but an end in itself, and for anyone who will hold a prominent place in the Church just as indispensable as the knowledge of law for a statesman or the knowledge of nature for a physician. It is absolutely *necessary*; so that no well ordered condition of the Church is to be thought of where theology does not flourish.

70. ["Let not many of you become teachers, my brothers, for you know that we who teach shall be judged with greater strickness" RSV.]

The necessity for it does not spring from mere outward occasions, but from the inmost nature of the Christian faith itself. Our religion is not simply for feeling or for the will separately taken, but full as much for the faculty of knowledge also, the understanding and reason; it seeks to penetrate and pervade harmoniously all the powers of man's nature, and thus to refine and perfect him in the undivided totality of his person. It belongs to the inmost nature of faith, that it should raise itself continually to clearer consciousness, attain always to a more distinct and full knowledge of its object, that is, of God as revealed in Christ. *Pistis* ["faith"] is in itself the fruitful germ of a true *gnosis* ["knowledge"], and rests not till it becomes at last the vision of God face to face, which is at the same time also the conception of the full blessedness of heaven itself. If faith be true, it must allow this to be shown, so far as this may be possible in the present world. Christianity is not against reason, but only above reason.[71] Only superficial knowledge is irreligious; true, thorough knowledge stands in covenant with faith, and is not possible without it. But faith should be ever struggling to become knowledge; Christianity should enter always more and more into the comprehension of reason. "*Negligentiae mihi videtur, si postquam confirmati sumus in fide, non studemus quod credimus intelligere.*" Thus speaks the greatest theologian of the Middle Ages, one of the most eminently pious men at the same time belonging to the history of the Church.[72] So Augustine, whose name is above all praise, and before whose powerful spirit both the Catholic and Protestant Churches bow with almost equal reverence, represents growth in theological knowledge to be a growth of God in the soul itself.

> "*Crescat ergo Deus, qui semper perfectus est, crescat in te. Quanto enim magis intelligis Deum et quanto magis capis, videtur in te crescere Deus. . . . Intelligebas heri modicum, intelligis hodie amplius, intelliges cras multo amplius: lumen ipsum Dei crescit in te. . . . Sic est et interior homo: Proficit quidem in Deo, et Deus in illo videtur crescere; ipse tamen minuitur, ut a gloria sua decidat, et in gloriam Dei surgat.*"[73]

71. Or, to speak with Pascal: "*La foi dit bien ce que les sens ne disent pas, mais jamais le contraire. Elle est* au dessus, *non* pas contre." [Trans. "Faith addresses matters that the senses do not, but never contrary to the senses. Faith is *above, not against* reason."]

72. [Trans. "It seems to me negligence if, after we have been confirmed in the faith, we do not make an effort to understand what we believe."] Anselm of Canterbury, in the beginning of his work, *Cur Deus homo*? [book 1, chapter 1 *The Major Works*, ed. Brian Davies and G. R Evans (New York: Oxford University Press, 1998), 266].

73. In *Evang. Joann.*, c. 3, Tract. 14. [Trans. "So let God, who is always perfect, increase; let him increase in you. The more you know God, after all, and the more you understand, the more God seems to frown in you. . . . Yesterday, you were understanding a little, today, you are understanding more, you will understand much more tomorrow; the very light of God is growing in you. . . . It is like that too with your inner self; you make progress in God, and God seems to grow in you; yet in fact you are diminishing, so that you may fall away from your own glory and rise up to the glory of God." Augustine, *Homilies on the Gospel of John 1–40*, part 3, vol 12 of *The Works of Saint Augustine: A Translation for the 21st Century*, (Hyde Park, NY: New City Press, 2009), 264–65.]

Theology appears thus an indispensable organ in the life of the Church; its head, its consciousness, and so its ornament and joy; theology of course in the sense of our protestant ancestors, in whose production are joined *oratio, meditatio*, and *tentatio*, the *theologia regenitorum*, ["prayer, meditation, and trial, the theology of the regenerate"] besides which indeed there is none that is entitled to the name.

Happy is he who has attained to this exalted view! A generation that crawls in the dust may style him, in pity or derision, an idealist, perchance even a fantasist. But all this he counts an honor. For he knows that it is not gold nor steam, but *ideas* that rule the world, and constitute the soul, the heart's blood of history, producing in it all that is either true or abiding. For no price would he separate himself from the *regina scientiarum* ["queen of the sciences"]; all the glory of the world, all the praise of men, are to him as nothing, in comparison with the excellency of the knowledge of God in Christ.

It follows then with logical necessity that the progress of the Church moves hand in hand with the progress of theology. Where ignorance rules an age, where the diligent study of the scriptures is neglected, there at the same time the whole Christian life grows sickly, and one form of error after another creeps into the sanctuary. On the contrary, where genuine piety flourishes, where the whole Church is made to feel the life giving presence of God's Spirit, there knowledge shows itself clear and fresh to the same extent. What is it we admire so much in the age of the apostles? The striking union of the deepest insight into the character and works of God with the most vigorous activity; the full-toned harmony of all the powers of the soul, filled and governed by one and the same principle. Paul, who labored more than all the rest of the apostles, is also a master in the way of knowledge, to whom we are indebted for the fullest development of doctrine, a wonderfully profound exhibition of Christian truth, and most powerful confutation of error at the same time. By his scriptural arguments, and his keen logical combinations and conclusions, he so handled his adversaries, both heathen and Jewish, as to leave them ever after without excuse for their unbelief. John, the apostle of love, has been styled not without reason by the Church, the "Theologian" *per eminentiam*. For by the eagle flight of his believing speculation into the depths of God and his Word, made flesh for our salvation, as existing before the world, he may be said to have led the way to Christian theology in its bold and glorious course.[74] His love is only the strong will-force of knowledge; his knowledge

74. Hence the ancient hymn sings of him:

Volat avis sine meta,
Quo nec vates nec propheta
Evolavit altimus.
Tam implenda, quam impleta
Numquam vidit tot secreta
Purus homo purius.

[Trans. "He flies like a bird without limit, / in that neither seer nor prophet / ever flew higher. / As much what would be fulfilled as what has been, / never were so many secrets seen / so purely by a pure

but the keen vision of love. The whole history of the Church furnishes proof that the men who have exerted the greatest and most happy influence, the wakers of a new life, the pillars in the temple of God, have always been distinguished also above their cotemporaries by a thorough scientific cultivation. It is sufficient to call up the names simply of such men as Irenaeus, Origen, Cyprian, Athanasius, the Cappadocian Gregory, Basil the Great, Augustine, Anselm, Thomas Aquinas, Luther, Melanchthon, Calvin, Beza, Johann Gerhard, Spener, Bengel, Wesley, Edwards. Where a new religious movement is not rooted at the same time in a solid doctrinal ground (the case of our later awakenings too generally), it is found also to have no enduring force, or at all events cannot carry the Church forward as a whole.

Shall now the general rule as established by the history of the Church have no application to the time in which we ourselves live? There is an opinion indeed that the Reformers and theologians of the seventeenth century have accomplished in theology all that is to be done, so that we need now only to hold fast this Protestant tradition, and hand it on mechanically to the next generation. This principle of stagnation is openly advocated by one at least of the most influential theological journals of the country, whose authority with a large portion of the American Church is counted well nigh infallible.[75] With all our respect however for the piety and standing of its conductors, we must protest decidedly against every such view. How inconsistent, to admit a perfectibility and actual progress, both of the individual and of the race, in all departments of mind, in the natural sciences, in jurisprudence, in the knowledge of history, in political development, in all material or outward interests, in morality and piety, only *not* in philosophy and theology. Is then the bible alone a book so clear and plain that all its depths are already exhausted? Are then the powers of the human mind so abstractly separate from one another that one may become absolutely complete without the rest? Have our Protestant ancestors perhaps declared themselves to be infallible, requiring us to receive their decisions as oracles; or have they not rather set us free from all bondage to men? Did their work too, in its theoretic character only, spring forth at once complete like Minerva from the head of Jupiter; or was it not rather a gradual process, in which they were themselves led from one view and one measure of clearness still onward to another? If Protestantism be indeed the blind faith of authority, an unthinking rehearsal of what has been handed down, let us then confess at least that we have no reason to reproach popery on this score. But the case stands not thus. Protestantism is the principle of movement, of progress in the history of the Church; progress, not such as may go beyond the bible and Christianity, but such as consists in an *ever-extending knowledge* of the bible itself, and an *ever-*

man." Jeffrey F. Hamburger, *St. John the Divine: The Deified Evangelist in Medieval Art and Theology* (Berkeley: University of California Press, 2002), 209.]

75. [Schaff refers to the *Biblical Repertory and Princeton Review* edited by Charles Hodge. In a speech marking his fiftieth anniversary at Princeton Seminary in 1872, Hodge famously boasted that "a new idea never originated in this Seminary." In the biography of his father, his son made a similar claim about the journal. A. A. Hodge, *Life*, 521, 257.]

deepening appropriation of Christianity as the power of a divine life, which is destined to make *all* things new. Our Church should be always prepared to give an account of her faith with joy, and to contend manfully against all human distortions of the truth, against every false and injurious representation of the gospel. She dare not, unless she would renounce herself, stiffen into lifeless stability, and suffer herself to be left in the rear by her adversaries in the way of scientific movement. Rather she must explore still further and further the inexhaustible mines of God's word, and seek a more full and free representation continually of her own principle; remembering always that there is still beyond measure much to be learned, and that she can never become complete in herself, except as her knowledge also may be carried to the highest point.

But the proper home of Protestant theology is Germany, and hence we may say that those who refuse to make account of the German theology set themselves in fact against the progress of Protestantism. The land which gave birth to the Reformation stands pledged by that movement itself, not to rest till the great work shall have been made complete; when the revelation of God in Christ shall be apprehended in full, and the contents of faith shall be reduced to such form as to carry with them also the clearest evidence and most incontrovertible certainty in the way of knowledge. We wish not to depreciate in the least the merits acquired in former times, by the Dutch and the English in particular, in the way of biblical study, critical, exegetical and antiquarian. The German is always disposed rather to put an undue value on what is foreign, and has long since appropriated the results of these investigations, and worked them into the process of his own cultivation. But what is all this, beside the gigantic creations of the German theology! All its heresies cannot destroy my respect for it. In England and America one learns first to prize it according to its true worth. It must not be forgotten, that even the German Rationalism, worthy of all reprobation as it is, gives evidence, at least in its better forms, of an extraordinary scientific energy and a deep interest in the investigation of truth, from which we are authorized to draw a favorable conclusion on the opposite side. For only an archangel can become a devil. As England and America would not have been able at all to produce so fearful an enemy of Christianity as David Friedrich Strauss, so must they have been much less able to meet him with a proper refutation; and I shudder at times, to think of the desolation his writings must occasion, if they should come to be much read—which may God prevent—in this country.[76] It must be borne in mind also on the other side that there is a species of orthodoxy, by no means rare, which rests upon the foundation of mere convenience or intellectual indolence, or the lowest motive possibly of self-interest, and is consequently no whit better, yea by reason of such hypocrisy in its constitution is even much worse, than open and honest unbelief.

76. I was informed by a friend, one of the Fellows of Baliol College in Oxford, that two prominent young clergymen of the English Church had fallen upon the *Life of Jesus* by Strauss, and were so overpowered by it as absolutely to despair of all scientific help in opposition to it, with the resources or from the standpoint of the English theology as it has stood thus far.

If we look into Church history, we shall be still less disturbed in our estimate of the German theology by the heretical elements that belong to it, since they must appear to us only as negative conditions of a new doctrinal conquest. Thus the full determination and clear, close definition of the doctrines of the Trinity and of the relation of the two natures in Christ, as exhibited to us in the oecumenical councils, were conditioned throughout by a succession of heresies in the direction of these articles. The Pelagian error must serve, in the hand of God, to unfold and establish more profoundly, through Augustine, the doctrine of divine grace and human liberty. At the Reformation also, heretical tendencies, Socinianism, Anabaptism, antinomianism, etc., come into view; as in a period of such vast excitement was to be expected. They wrought with salutary force on the development of orthodox Protestantism, making it necessary for it to understand more clearly its own commission, to discriminate more closely its proper sphere, and to fortify itself against unauthorized consequences and various misapprehensions of its true character. So we may say that the later heresies of Germany are but the negative side of the process by which the theology of that country has been advancing towards higher and more solid ground than it occupied before. In this view, nothing can well be more unfair than to confound them with the idea of German theology itself. Those who do so, only show their own ignorance of the actual posture of things in the German Church at the present time.

It is to be lamented indeed, that the representations usually exhibited of German theology in this country, by those who pass for its friends as well as others, have been, and to a great extent still continue to be, borrowed from a period which has been fairly surmounted and left behind in Germany itself: the period of the older Rationalism, in which the truth might be said to have become for a time so entangled in the folds of error, as hardly to be distinguished from it, even in the writings of its most orthodox defenders. There is reason to believe that this rationalistic orthodoxy, as represented for instance by such men as Ernesti and Morus, has indeed been made the vehicle by which more or less of a truly pernicious neological spirit has been introduced into the American Church, in the name of German theology. Undoubtedly at least, rationalistic elements and tendencies are extensively involved in the religious thinking of the country, even under what are regarded often as its most orthodox forms—elements and tendencies that need only to be carried out consistently to their proper consequences to show themselves in their true light. Elements and tendencies, it may be added, which the orthodox German theology of the present day, all slandered as it is, would reject as heretical and false, no less decidedly than it rejects the entire standpoint of a Bretschneider himself. Nothing, I repeat it, can well be more unfair than to confound the true, positive theology of Germany, now so successfully asserting its spiritual independence, with the negative heretical entanglements of a former time, from which it has extricated itself in large part already, and is in the way of extricating itself still more triumphantly, we may hope, in time to come.

It is not to be desired of course that the mighty struggles of the German philosophy and theology should repeat themselves, in their whole compass, in this country. Rather it may be trusted that the victory achieved by believing science in Germany, over both the popular and speculative forms of Rationalism, will redound to the general benefit of the entire Protestant Church. But what we wish is this: that the spirit of the German theology in its better form, as now predominant, might be transplanted into our midst, and with proper modification of course and adjustment to our circumstances made to enter organically into our religious life.[77] Here all must be more practical; science must go hand in hand with the proper activities of the Christian life. As we will have no order of priests specifically different from the laity, so we want no separate order of theologians, restricting to itself all sacred wisdom. Such a union of the German scientific and English practical tendencies would furnish a better form of existence than either of these separately taken; which it might seem to be the vocation of America in particular to realize, where German elements, in the Middle and Western States especially, are entering so largely, and with such vast increase every year, into the social mass. I regret not in the least the modification, which the science of Germany, and its theology in particular, must thus undergo, to be turned here to any good account. Rather I rejoice in it, with all my heart. For decided foe as I am to the mere utilitarian principle, I am well aware that German science is but too prone to run to an extreme in the other direction, and thus to lose itself in unprofitable speculations and subtleties that come in the end to nothing.[78] Nor should it be forgotten that a large proportion of the German emigration has been, and still is, of such a character, that we must wish to see it brought under the force of the English nationality for its own sake, and have reason to bless God for the favorable change it has been made to undergo by this means in part already.[79] But this is not enough. May we not trust that the time is at hand, when the American Germany shall again rise from the ruins of its own nationality and language, purified and enriched with the advantages belonging to the English character, and so enter upon a new career of its own, that shall be fraught with lasting benefit to the whole country.

77. [This mission to transport German theology to American shores is the charge Schaff received at his ordination in Elberfeld.]

78. To which the well known verse in Goethe's *Faust* [Part V, lines 1830–3] may be applied in all its force:

> *. . . . Ein Kerl, der speculirt,*
> *Ist wie ein Thier, auf duerrer Heide*
> *Von einem boesen Geist im Kreis herumgefuehrt,*
> *Und rings umher liegt schoener gruene Weide.*

[Trans. "A chap who speculates / is like an animal in a scorched meadow / driven around in circles by an evil spirit / while all about lies a beautiful green field.]

79. [Here Schaff echoes the concern he expressed in his ordination sermon that a fair portion of German immigrants were undisciplined "adventurers and vagabonds." Schaff, "Ordination of Professor Schaf."]

Altogether there seems to be reason to believe that the way is opening at least towards such an order of things as the wants of the time are found to demand. There are indications certainly which imply that our Church relations are destined, before a great while, to assume in one way or another a new form. The system of thinking which has hitherto prevailed is coming to lose its authority, at different points. Difficulties are causing themselves to be felt, where formerly they were not imagined to exist. Ideas of deep and far reaching import are steadily working their way, where only a few years since perhaps hardly a trace of their presence was to be found.

The absolute despotism of the metaphysics of Locke is in a measure broken. In spite of the earnest warnings of certain influential literary organs, the general unconditional confidence with which the system was formerly held, has been seriously shaken; particularly, it would seem, in New England. Let us hear on this point Professor Stowe, of Lane Seminary, who will not at least be suspected of any improper leaning towards German transcendentalism. "The metaphysics of Locke," he tells us,

> under various modifications, have prevailed over English and French mind, the most effective mind in the civilized world, for more than a century; a long period certainly in an active and thinking age, for any one system of mental science to maintain its dominion. This style of philosophizing did not long retain its ascendency among the Germanic nations, but was there entirely overthrown more than sixty years ago; and for about twenty-five years past, there has been a gradual but certain undermining of its influence, in France, England, and the United States. *Almost all the ardent, youthful, investigating mind in these countries, now feels that the system of Locke, in all its modifications, is meager, unspiritual and unsatisfying, and is anxiously looking for something better.*[80]

This change has been produced mainly, by the writings, on the one hand, of the French eclectic Cousin, who is known to have borrowed largely from the later German philosophy, and by the works of Coleridge and Thomas Carlyle on the other, both of them thoroughly steeped in the element of German thought. Coleridge, a noble, fertile, half poetic, half philosophic spirit, proceeded from the school of Schelling, which is characterized by a tendency towards the objective and historical; whence it is not strange that his numerous disciples in England sympathize to a certain extent with the Puseyite movement, though not so as to yield themselves to it in a slavish way. One of the most able and interesting productions called forth in this connection is *The Kingdom of Christ* by Fr. Dan. Maurice of London.[81] Carlyle's mind is more of the

80. [Stowe, "Teutonic Metaphysics or Modern Transcendentalism,"] *The Biblical Repository and Classical Review* [3rd ser., 1, no.1] (New York, January 1845), p. 65. [As the reader is aware from p. 167, fn. 63 above in this volume, Stowe offered an extensive critique of "German transcendentalism" in this article.]

81. [Frederick Denison Maurice, *The Kingdom of Christ*, 2 vols. (1838; Cambridge: Lutterworth, 2002).]

negative, critical order with a strong leaning to pantheism; as is seen particularly, in his hero worship, which reaches even to MOHAMMED, and towards GOETHE rises into extravagance itself. By the uncommon richness of his intellect however, and his keen portraits, he exerts a kindling influence on youthful, excitable spirits, and at all events enlarges the field of their vision and opens before them new regions of thought. He sees the defects of our time indeed, and of our present Protestantism, only too well; but has no power to direct us to any positive remedy. Hence a certain character of gloomy dissatisfaction, not to say cynical despair, runs through all his writings. Still the knowledge of the disease must always precede its cure; and in this view the widely extended influence of this energetic writer is to be considered favorable, as leading beyond itself to something that may be better.

In theology itself, directly or indirectly, Germany is coming to be more and more widely felt. An almost absolute authority having been exercised for nearly a hundred years in Church history by the learned chancellor of Göttingen, MOSHEIM, long since thrown into the background in his own country by those who have come after him, the works of NEANDER and GIESELER have at length made their appearance here also in an English dress. These it is known are distinguished for the most conscientious study of original sources; to which must be added in the case of the first the genial presence of a deep religious spirit that lovingly welcomes the manifestations of the divine life under all forms, and causes them to live again upon the historic page with magic reproduction. We could wish only it were pervaded with deeper *Church* feeling. *The History of the Reformation*, also, by MERLE D'AUBIGNÉ, which has had such an immense circulation in this country, is properly speaking, in its main parts, a skilful working up of German material, particularly the *Geschichte der Reformation* by MARHEINECKE,[82] which still remains superior to it in the estimation of all competent judges.[83]

82. [Jean Henri Merle d'Aubigné, *History of the Reformation of the Sixteenth Century*, trans. Henry White, 4 vols. (New York: American Tract Society, 1835–45) was the first American edition of this popular work. Philipp Marheinecke, *Geschichte der deutschen Reformation*, 2 vols. (Berlin: Nicolais, 1816).]

83. The recent production of the celebrated Genevan Doctor [Merle d'Aubigné], translated for *The Biblical Repository* (Jan 1845) under the title, "Lutheranism and the Reform: their Diversity Essential to their Unity," [*The Biblical Repository and Classical Review*, 3rd ser., 1, no. 1 (January 1845): 130–68], can make still less pretension to originality. We hold this essay important on account of its catholic spirit and tendency, and for the acknowledgment it contains that the question concerning the Church has now become the first question, "the greatest, the all engrossing subject." We have been really surprised however, to see how Dr. MERLE allows himself to plunder German authors. One idea is taken from the first volume of [August] TWESTEN's [*Vorlesungen über die*] *Dogmatik* [*der evangelisch-lutherischen Kirche* (Lectures on the dogmatics of the Evangelical Lutheran Church)], 2 vols. (Hamburg: Perth, 1837–38)]; three ideas are borrowed from LANGE's academical inaugural address at Zurich; all the rest are found in the well-known book of [Max] GOEBEL on the "Union" [*Die religiöse Eigenthümlichkeit der lutherischen und der reformirten Kirche* (The religious characteristic of the Lutheran and Reformed Church) (Bonn: Adolph Marcus, 1837).] Here we meet the representation for instance, that Lutheranism places the material principle foremost, the Reformed Church the formal; that the first has proceeded on the maxim of holding fast all that is not expressly condemned

Still all this, as compared with the wealth of the German literature, is but a small beginning. It would be easy to name more than a score of new works, of exegetical and dogmatic character in particular, which are full as worthy to be translated as those which have been mentioned, and some of them much more so. A special society has been formed in French Switzerland for transplanting the better theological literature of Germany into that country, which has already entered upon its work with good success. Much more might we look for some institution of the sort here, and that no such measure has been thought of only shows how little interest the Germans of this country take in the monuments which reflect the greatest honor on their own race. They are put to shame in this respect, even by the English themselves. The best literary institutions of the land are coming to understand that no modern education can be complete which does not include some acquaintance with German learning, and think it necessary accordingly to make some provision for the cultivation of it in their academical course. The most distinguished theologians in the country, such as Stuart, Hodge, Robinson, Stowe, etc., have bestowed their careful study on the theological literature of Germany, and acknowledge themselves under lasting obligations to its help. This study ought not indeed to be confined simply to the critical, isagogical, and antiquarian departments, which some appear to consider most valuable and safe; though in fact they have been occupied to a great extent by Rationalism. We need to have rather, in larger measure, the *spirit* and the *ideas* of the later German theology. We need to fortify ourselves in this way against errors, and tendencies to error, to which we are already exposed. Against the rationalism of the abstract understanding on the one hand, and a disposition to pantheistic sentimentalism and reverie on the other, we can have no better protection in the way of science than is here placed within our reach. In no other quarter have these false forms of thought been met and

---

by God's word, the last on the maxim of rejecting all for which no explicit authority is to be found in the bible; that the work of reformation with the first was carried on prevailingly in a doctrinal and theological way, while with the last it took also a practico-moral and political form; that the first was aristocratic and monarchial, the last democratic and republican; that the first showed itself exclusive and in the end hostile to the Reformed Church, while this last was always disposed to a union with Lutheranism, but perseveringly opposed to all peace with Rome; etc., etc. Even the examples on pp. 139, 148, and 160 are copied from Goebel.

All this is mentioned, not to depreciate at all the Genevan theologian, but only to show how ready the most distinguished French writers are to take lessons in the school of German learning, and to recommend their example to imitation in this country. Why should we undervalue in German, what we are ready to laud as exhibited to us at second-hand in French? What confidence is to be reposed in the judgment of those who undertake to proscribe the entire theological literature of Germany as worthless and full of peril only to the Church, without having read perhaps a volume of it themselves, while they suffer the same material to be smuggled in upon us in any quantity from a different quarter, as profitable and wholesome in the highest degree? The French theological literature, such as it is, owes nearly all its value to the use of German helps; and when all is done, it may be pronounced immeasurably poor and meager, as compared with the theological literature of Germany itself. [Schaff's critical comments about the popular Merle d'Aubigné won him few new American friends as responses in the *Christian Intelligencer* and the *Christian Evangelist* show. Review of "The Principle of Protestantism" in *Christian Intelligencer*; Cheever, "German Theology."]

vanquished in the same thorough style. Germany has produced the most pious as well as the most godless philosophers and theologians; those whose influence has been the most salutary, as well as those who seem to have been born only to work mischief and death. The greatest demerit of the land and its highest glory, are found here in close conjunction. So it was with Greece, where the *Sophists* appear in intimate connection with a SOCRATES and along with the followers of PLATO the followers of EPICURUS. One tendency is always naturally coupled with another, as its own opposite.

This then is one desideratum, in our circumstances. A fresh, vigorous theology, in which the most decided faith might appear in union with the most free and thorough scientific culture, could not fail to advance us to a new position, and to give us a triumphant advantage over infidelity and popery and semi-popery in all their forms.

This however of itself is not of course enough. We need also a change in our practical Church state, an antidote to the sect plague. What is first wanted in this direction is the conviction that the present distracted condition of Protestantism is contradictory to the idea of the Church, whose normal character necessarily includes catholicity and unity, as well as an earnest sacred grief on this account. Nor have we any right to console ourselves with the fancy of a vague spiritual unity, in the case. It belongs to the inward always, if it have life, to manifest itself in an outward way. The soul must form itself a body, as its appropriate organ. Visibility lies necessarily in the conception of the Church, which is the BODY OF CHRIST; the mark of unity consequently must also clothe itself in an outward form. The unity we are to seek must be no dead sameness indeed, but such as is full of life, one and endlessly manifold at the same time. Here again the case requires, not that we should go back to the old, but that we should go forward rather with all that has been won by Protestantism, in the way of developed subjectivity. Outward unity does not require *one* visible head, as the pope, who is called antichrist for this very pretension. This place belongs to Christ alone, and he needs no *vicarius*, since he is himself present in his own body. In the apostolic age, and long after, the unity of the Church was maintained without any such human chief bishop. Even at the end of the sixth century, GREGORY THE GREAT, it is known, wrote to the patriarch of Constantinople : "*Certe Petrus Apostolorum primus, membrum sanctae et universalis Ecclesiae, Paulus, Andreas, Ioannes*, quid aliud quam singularium sunt plebium capita, et tamen sub uno capite omnes membra?"[84] And in another letter :

> "*Ego autem fidenter dico, quia quisquis se universalem Sacerdotem vocat, vel vocari desiderat,* in elatione sue Antichristum praecurrit, *quia superbiendo se caeteris praeponit. Nec dispari superbia ad errorem ducitur, quia sicut perversus*

84. Lib. V, Epist. 18. [Trans. "Certainly Peter, the first of the apostles, himself a member of the holy and universal Church, Paul, Andrew, John—what were they but heads of particular communities? And yet all were members under one Head." *NPNF*, 2nd ser. 12:167.]

> *ille Deus videri vult super omnes homines; ita quisquis iste est, qui solus Sacerdos appellari appetit, super reliquos Sacerdotes se extollit.*"[85]

Neither is a single organization absolutely necessary, as the Puseyites dream. The unity must proceed from within, from the deepest ground of the religious life itself; and then it will provide for itself a suitable external form. What this will be, we are not prepared now of course to say. In any case however, a living outward intercommunication must come to hold among all Christian Churches, such as may furnish practical proof that they are not only one spirit, but one body also, that is the body of Jesus Christ.

What cheering indications now, the guaranty of a better future in this direction, can the time be said to bring to our view? There, to be sure, in England and America, is the mighty movement of Puseyism. With this however we can make no common cause; if for no other reason, yet simply as non-episcopal Protestants, whom it unchurches without ceremony altogether; on which account too, it can never find much favor on the continent in Europe. It has been already shown, in the way of objection to the system, that it has no proper sense of the world-historical importance of Protestantism in its origin and later development. It leads backwards rather than forwards. Still it must be counted on the other hand a salutary fermentation. It has served to bring up again, with powerful interest, the great questions of the Church, Catholicity and Unity. These questions belong not exclusively to the Episcopal Church, and there is no reason why they should be identified at all with the idea of Episcopacy. They challenge the attention of the entire Christian communion. We may make room for them, and yield ourselves to their power, without surrendering ourselves in so doing to the errors of the false tendency with which they stand connected in the Oxford Episcopal school. The force of them has already begun to be felt indeed, in some measure, in other denominations. The different sections of orthodox Protestantism have not by any means now the same quiet confidence in their own position, as the *ne plus ultra* of Church perfection, the unimprovable absolute of Christianity itself, which they had only ten or fifteen years ago. It is coming to be felt that the present posture of things cannot be rested in as permanent and ultimate, and along with this is waking the desire for something better. Single voices are heard here and there, from the bosom of the Evangelical Church, calling for a true union among all who belong to the household of faith, in spirit, soul, and body, and find a lively echo in many a breast. It is to me a source of great satisfaction and encouragement to find among these the man with whom I am called to labor as a colleague in the same institution; with whom altogether, notwithstanding the entirely independent and widely separate spheres of

85. Ad Mauricium Aug., Lib. VII, Ep. 33. [Trans. "Now I confidently say that whosoever calls himself, or desires to be called, Universal Priest, *is in his elation the precursor of the Antichrist*, because he proudly puts himself above all others. Nor is it by dissimilar pride that he is led into error; for as that perverse one wishes to appear as God above all men, so whosoever this one is who covets being called sole priest, he extolls himself above all other priests." *NPNF*, 2d ser., 12:226.]

our previous history—God be praised—I have been enabled, to my own no small surprise, so fully to sympathize, in the most weighty points, from the first moment of our acquaintance.[86]

True, appearances are not such at present as to encourage the idea that a general union will soon take place. The differences which prevail in doctrine, government and worship, and the abstract view too generally taken of the relation of Christianity to the world, stand hopelessly in the way. Rather, division threatens to go still farther; as the question of slavery, to say nothing of other difficulties, is fastening itself with resistless force upon the heart of the Church. Episcopal Methodism is already rent by it into two great sections, which are not likely soon to be reconciled. Other denominations, it is to be feared, will be gradually involved in similar division. At this very time, there are strong indications that the great Presbyterian body, of *both* schools, will very soon find it necessary to meet the question in its whole length and breadth; and already the most serious apprehensions are entertained of a new ecclesiastical rupture, on its account.[87]

In the Protestant Episcopal Church, on other grounds, as all know, there is still less show of peace. The mournful scandal of the ONDERDONK trial has brought the quarrel between the Puseyite and evangelical parties to its climax.[88] The Puseyites

86. [Nevin: A very long note occurs here in the German work, containing a special reference to the translator's sermon "On Catholic Unity," preached at the opening of the Convention of the Reformed Dutch and German Reformed Churches, Harrisburg, Aug. 8, 1844, with a series of extracts exhibiting its principal thoughts. For various reasons, it has been considered best to attach the whole sermon to the present publication, in the way of an appendix; to which of course it is enough at this place to refer. The original note closes with a notice also of the last chapter in particular of the second edition of the *Anxious Bench*, as unfolding the same general views.] ["On Catholic Unity" and *The Anxious Bench* will appear in Nevin, *"One Holy, Catholic, and Apostolic": John Nevin's Writings on Ecclesiology*, ed. Sam Hamstra, MTSS, vol. 5 (forthcoming).]

87. [The Methodist Episcopal Church, South, broke from the Methodist Episcopal Church in 1844. The New School Presbyterians divided over slavery in 1857 and the Old School in 1861, after the secession of Southern states had begun. The Southern Baptist Convention was formed in 1845. Goen, *Broken Churches*.]

88. [Benjamin Treadwell Onderdonk, the Episcopal bishop of New York, was tried by a panel of seventeen bishops in December 1844 for what a later generation would term sexual harassment. He was convicted in a divided vote. Due to the appeal of his supporters on the panel, he was not disposed, but suspended from exercising his ministry as bishop. Onderdonk had been elected bishop in 1830 and continued the work of his predecessor and mentor John Henry Hobart in championing the High Church movement and separating the Episcopal Church from the rest of Protestant evangelicalism. The emergence of the Oxford Movement, however, deepened the divide between Evangelical and High Church Episcopalians and Onderdonk lacked his mentor's tact. The controversy over his ordination of Arthur Carey in 1843, discussed earlier, and the forced resignation due to drunkenness of his brother, Henry Ustick Onderdonk, bishop of Pennsylvania, encouraged his critics to gather stories of his drunkenness and sexual harassment of women. While the trial was conducted under seal, a complete transcript was released soon after and a pamphlet war raged as Schaff wrote *Principle of Protestantism*. Appealing to irregularities in the testimony against him, and the way the women's stories failed to make sense within Victorian gender norms, Onderdonk's supporters continued to insist that the real issue was his churchmanship. Cohen, "Ministerial Misdeeds;" Mullin, *Episcopal Vision*, 160–166.]

are now in desperate plight, not only by reason of the moral wreck of their principal leader in the view of the public, but still more as they are drawn into collision with their own principles; since they declare the sentence of suspension which has taken place to be unjust, though passed by a decided majority of their own bishops, those anointed and inviolable bearers of the apostolical, succession, wronging thus in heart at least the duty of canonical obedience. The appeal of Dr. Seabury to the example of Fénelon (*si parva licet componere magnis*[89]), who himself, read in his Church the papal bull directed against his own person, is here of no avail.[90] For Fénelon submitted himself truly to the judgment of the Church; acknowledged the faults charged upon his work *Explication des Maximes des Saintes*; forbade the reading of it in his diocese; and burned all the copies of it he could reach, in a court belonging to his archiepiscopal palace, with his own hand.[91] This the Puseyites could not easily be brought to do in the case of their *Tracts for the Times*; and in the present instance they even proclaim the suspended Onderdonk openly to be their bishop still; so that even that outward subjection to the decision of the court of bishops, for which Dr. Seabury takes credit to himself in his noted sermon, amounts at last to nothing.[92] Whether they will now go over in mass to Rome, or form a Church of their own, remains to be seen. At all events the matter has gone so far that they must either bend or break.[93]

[4. Ultimate prospect.]

Still all these storms that gather in the horizon will but serve fully to purify the atmosphere. The disease must pass through its last crisis before it can be thoroughly cured.

89. [Trans. "if it be allowable to compare small things with great," Virgil.]

90. [Samuel Seabury, editor of the *The Churchman* and rector of Church of the Annunciation (Episcopal) in New York City was among Benjamin Onderdonk's champions. In his sermon preached after Onderdonk's conviction and first published in *The Churchman*, Seabury associated Onderdonk with the philosopher Socrates, English archbishop William Laud, and French archbishop François de Salignac de La Mothe Fénelon, each of whom he suggested had willingly submitted themselves to authorities without acknowledging the justice of their judgment. Seabury, *A Sermon by the Rev. Samuel Seabury, D.D., in Reference to the Trial of the Right Rev'd Benj. T. Onderdonk, D.D., Bishop of the Diocese of New-York* (New York: J. A. Sparks, 1845), 3.]

91. [First published in English with related documents on Quietism as *The Maxims of the Saints Explained, concerning the Interior Life* (London: Rhodes, 1698). In this 1697 text, Fénelon defended the idea of disinterested love championed by Madame Guyon.]

92. [In his sermon, Seabury emphasized that though he did not accept the truth of the guilty decision, he did accept Onderdonk's suspension. He equally insisted, however, that Onderdonk was still his bishop. Because there was no mechanism to reinstate him, Onderdonk remained suspended, but still bishop of New York, until his death in 1861. Widely supported by his diocese, he continued to draw his bishop's salary and live in the bishop's house, though he left it almost only to attend daily church services. Eventually an assistant bishop was elected to carry out Onderdonk's duties.]

93. [Individual American Anglo-Catholics became Roman Catholics, most notably North Carolina bishop Levi Stillman Ives in 1852. The acceptance of Anglo-Catholics within the Episcopal Church, however, led some evangelicals to follow evangelical bishop George David Cummins and found the Reformed Episcopal Church in 1873. Guelzo, *For the Union of Evangelical Christendom*.]

The growth of division will cause the longing after Christian union, to break forth at last with irrepressible force. The mighty advances of the Romish Church, stalking forward through the motley crowd of our sects, in proud confidence of victory, as a *single* man, though in very questionable alliance with the most rank political demagoguism, must in the end compel the Protestants to take another position, in order that they may save themselves. The conflict is waxing more earnest every day. Who would have thought twenty years ago, that popery was ever to acquire importance in the land of freedom?[94] Now according to the *Metropolitan Catholic Almanac* for the year 1845, it embraces in the United States: a population of 800,000 souls; 21 episcopal dioceses with one apostolical vicarship; 675 churches, 709 priests; 28 male, and 63 female seminaries; 94 orphan houses and other benevolent institutions; a multitude of convents and religious associations—as Jesuits, Redemptorists, Lazarists, Augustinians, Dominicans, Eudists, the Society of the Precious Blood, the Brethren of St. Joseph; also, Sisters of Charity, Carmelitesses, Nuns of the Visitation of Mary, Nuns of Loretto, Dominican Nuns, Ladies of the Good Shepherd, Sisters of Notre Dame, Sisters of Providence, Ursuline Nuns, Ladies of the Most Sacred Heart, etc. There appear among us besides *ten* weekly and *three* monthly Roman Catholic periodicals; to which must be added now the *Quarterly* of BROWNSON, a man of much reading and ready pen, whose accession to the Church has recently been hailed with no small triumph.[95] Romanism directs its eye mainly towards the West, well knowing that this

94. [Nevin: I remember very well that when the venerable DR. ALEXANDER, of Princeton, less than twenty years ago, solemnly warned the students under his care of the danger that was to be expected from this quarter, exhorting us to prepare for the conflict with Rome as the *great* controversy of the American Church, his words to most were very much like empty wind. And yet how prophetical they have proved to be already! What a change in fact have not the last five years only produced in the posture of Romanism in this country relatively to both Church and State? The numerical increase of the body is no proper measure of its actual gain. By far the largest amount of progress is in the form of preparation for action that is expected to tell with wide effect hereafter. It is actually startling, to find in what broad, comprehensive and far reaching style, the policy of the system is revealing itself on all sides, and with how much quiet, unaffected confidence, it is pursuing a course that looks confessedly to nothing less than the spiritual conquest of the whole land. Within a very short time, the Catholic press has gained immensely in point of respectability and power; and there is reason to believe that the literary weight of the system will be made to press upon us, in the course of the next ten years, in a way of which few have begun to dream. Most assuredly the American Church has need now to consider well the danger that is fast gathering upon her in this direction. But alas, how few seem to understand what the times require, or to be prepared for the emergency which is at hand. How few show themselves qualified to go to the *ground* of the controversy, and to deal with it in its principles. *Here* precisely is our greatest danger. For one who has only begun to comprehend something of the force of the *ideas* that are involved in the conflict, and who can feel at all the nature of the historical crisis to which we have come, it is truly alarming, to consider the style in which the championship of Protestantism among us is too generally conducted.] [Archibald Alexander (1772–1851) served as a professor at Princeton Seminary from 1812 to 1840.]

95. [Orestes Brownson, a noted essayist and New England Transcendentalist, became a Roman Catholic on October 20, 1844. The same year he withdrew from writing for the *Democratic Review* and founded *Brownson's Quarterly Review*.]

must hereafter give law to the whole land. "Give us the West," says one of its bishops, "and we will soon take care of the East."

For the final issue of the conflict we have no fear since the Lord of hosts reigns supreme. Let all human work fall to pieces, that the work of God may have the more free scope. In the end, all must advance the glory of his name, and the welfare of his children. We will not be dismayed then at the gathering conflict. We will carry on the sacred war in word and in life, keeping always in view the honor of God and the interest on the Church; forgetting not our own faults in our zeal against those of others; not with the rough weapons of the flesh in the way of wild fanaticism, but with the weapons of the Spirit: the sword of God's word, the breastplate of faith, and the helmet of hope [1 Thess 5:8]. Let it be a war of extermination against all error and division, but a conflict of prayer at the same time and love towards the souls of the blinded enemies of the Church, to win them if possible to eternal life. Then shall we be soldiers in the sense of Paul, worthy followers of this spiritual hero. Then shall we too at last be adorned with the crown of righteousness [2 Tim 4:8], which the glorified apostle has long since received from the judge, who holds life and death, heaven and hell, in his almighty hand.

As members of a particular division of the Church of Christ, we must be true to the patrimony of our fathers, conscientiously turn to profit the pound entrusted to our care [Matt 25:14–30], and advance with free, genuine historical progress as the wants of the time may require. To forsake the Church communion in which we have been born, naturally and spiritually, without urgent reason, is base perfidy. Let us labor then *within* our own denomination and *for* it, as knowing that God has given us here our own special commission to fulfill. We will manifest, in this very way, our Church feeling and regard for history. Only, let all be subordinated to the interest of the general kingdom of God. If we have any right idea of the Church, as the communion of the redeemed transcending all limits of time and space, we shall feel that we cannot extend our view too far. We may not exclude the Romanists themselves. Let them go on to treat us as lost heretics; we must still return good for evil. We believe confidently that even for this Church, which once thrust out our fathers with terrible ban from its bosom, the Lord has still great things in store. Why should we despair of another reformation, as impossible in the case of its vast and powerful communion? This is wished and hoped for, by many even of its own best members.[96] Protestantism

96. [Nevin: Who can say, what vast results may not yet proceed from the agitation, which is going forward in the German Roman Catholic Church at this very time, in connection with the case of priest Ronge, and the stirring example set by the congregation at *Schneidemühl*? [In October 1844, the Roman Catholic parish at Schneidemühl in East Prussia declared itself an independent German Catholic congregation and, under the direction of Johannes Ronge, published its own confession. Ronge protested against the authority of the Roman Catholic hierarchy, clerical celibacy, idolatry, and auricular confession, among other things. He was subsequently excommunicated. The "German Catholic Church" was organized the next March with delegates from fifteen congregations. Its expressed foundation was scripture alone, interpreted by reason. Its creed pointedly did not affirm the divinity of Christ and it rejected many traditional Catholic practices. "Ronge, Czerski and the

cannot be consummated without Catholicism; not in the way of falling back to the past, but as coming into reconciliation with it finally in a higher position, in which all past errors shall be left behind whether Protestant or Catholic, and the truth of both tendencies be actualized, as the power of one and the same life, in the full revelation of the kingdom of God. The consummation of both will be at the same time their union. It is written, John 10:16: "There shall be one fold and one Shepherd"— a word that can be accomplished in its full and absolute sense, only when all confessional antagonisms shall come to an end.

It is an interesting and beautiful thought (to be felt indeed only by those who have some sense for the *philosophy* of Church history), by which the three most conspicuous apostles—PETER, PAUL, and JOHN—are made to stand as the representatives in character of three great stages of development through which the Church is to be carried to its final consummation. We meet the idea even among some of the old theologians, particularly with the prophetic monk JOACHIM OF FIORE, in the twelfth century.[97] Among the moderns H. STEFFENS (in his *Four Norwegians*) and H. E. SCHMIEDER (in his *Introduction to the Holy Scriptures*) again bring it into view.[98]

German-Catholic Church, No. 1," *The Churchman* (New York, NY) 15, no. 23 (August 9, 1845): 92. An English translation of his writings was published in New York in 1845, Ronge, *John Ronge*.] All accounts concur in representing the excitement to be immense, and not likely soon to subside. The idea of a separation from the headship of Rome, with a general retention at the same time of the catholic system, is taking hold of many minds, in every direction, with extraordinary power. Steps indeed have begun to be taken, it would seem, towards the organization of churches on this plan in a number of the most prominent places: Berlin, Leipzig, Breslau, Dresden, Elberfeld, etc. If only the Catholic Church in Germany might be severed from Rome, what vast bearings the event must have, at the present crisis, on the history of Christianity!

Still, the whole movement as yet needs to be regarded and spoken of with caution. We know too little of its moral constitution, its secret principles and reigning spirit, to speak of it with much confidence. Let us hope that we shall soon be permitted to look upon it, through the medium of a proper critical review, on the part of the evangelical press in Germany itself. It is certainly very precipitate, to say the least, for our religious papers, on the authority of the notoriously rationalistic correspondence of the New York *Schnellpost*, to glorifiy JOHN RONGE at once as a second HUSS or LUTHER. His second letter furnishes painful evidence that he stands in the element of a widely different spirit. To say nothing of the air of self-reliance which runs through the whole article, what must we think of the Christianity of a man, who can say, "Humanity is the Church of God, and in it rules the Spirit; to this Church I am sworn"? Is not this the very cant of Rationalism itself? The whole movement however is deeply interesting, in this view at least, that it serves to show the force with which the spirit of the age, even in the Church of Rome itself, is struggling towards a new order of life. In such a case it is not strange that much should seem dark and chaotic. But the Spirit of God, we may trust, is moving on the face of the deep.] [Nevin's cautious optimism in this note about Ronge contrasts sharply with Schaff's discussion of him less than a year later in *What is Church History?* There, in light of Ronge's rationalism and the later history of his movement, Schaff is sharply critical of those who had any hope for his movement. See "What is Church History?," [p. 239] in this volume. By 1849, Nevin was also sharply critical of anti-Catholics who continued to celebrate Ronge. Nevin, "True and False Protestantism," 103.]

97. Compare on him, NEANDER's *Kirchengeschichte* [*Allgemeine Geschichte der christlichen Religion und Kirche* (Hamburg: Perthes, 1826–52)], Band V, Abth. 1, pp. 291 ff. [Joachim of Fiore (1130/35–1201/02) was well known for his influential philosophy of history which divided time into three successive ages of progress associated with the Father, the Son, and lastly the Spirit.]

98. [Henrich Steffens, *Die vier Norwger: ein Cyklus von Novellen*, 6 vols. (Breslau: J. Max, 1828);

Very recently however, it has been clothed with new poetically scientific interest by the greatest living philosopher; who in the evening of his days has again come forth, like the sun from behind the clouds, and is now pouring the last splendid rays of his genius from Berlin, over the philosophical horizon of Germany. Schelling closes his *Philosophy of Revelation,* promised in vain for twenty years past as the complement and crown of the negative system published in his youth, with a section on the great periods of the Church. So far as I can recollect from his lectures, this is the amount of his view.[99] The Lord chose three favorite disciples, who are to be regarded as types at the same time of as many stages of development for the Church. Peter, the apostle of the Father, the New Testament Moses, or the representative of the principle of authority and law, answers in his personality and form of doctrine to the first *stadium* [stage] of Church history, the period of Catholicism, flowing over in the end to popery itself. Paul, the apostle of the Son, the New Testament Elias, the representative of the principle of movement, and of the free justifying power of faith, is the type of Protestantism. Both stages, separately taken, are one-sided and incomplete. The principles of authority and freedom, law and gospel, hope and faith, must at last become united. The Roman Catholic Church, it is true, has like Peter denied her Lord by a threefold gradation in the way of apostacy; but she will one day yet go out and weep bitterly. Then will the Lord turn towards her with a look of compassion, and restore her again to confidence and trust. This will be, at the same time, the epoch of the final reconciliation of both communions. So united, they will form the ideal Church, whose type is exhibited to us in the disciple that lay on Jesus' bosom, the apostle of the Holy Ghost, the apostle of that love which shall never fail, the law of freedom made perfect and complete in the gospel. To him corresponds, under the old economy, John the Baptist, in whose person the rigor of the law and consolation of prophecy are united. As he immediately preceded the first appearance of Christ, like the dawn of morning, so also the revivification of the spirit of John the evangelist, in the Church, will open the way directly for his second coming, to establish the Church absolute and triumphant, in which law and freedom shall both be perfect in one, and the results of all previous development appear conserved as the constituent elements of a higher and more glorious state. To this refers the mystical sense of Christ's word, John 21:22, where he speaks enigmatically of John's tarrying till his second coming.

Such is an outline of this prophetical speculation of Schelling. We mean not of course, to endorse it as correct; though it is certainly ingenious and beautiful. But putting out of view all that may seem to be simply fancy, it still turns at least upon a great and most consoling truth as it regards the Church, to which, though in quite

Heinrich Eduard Schmieder, *Einleitung in die heilige Schrift* (Leipzig, 1836).]

99. [On these widely influential lectures see Penzel, "An Ecumenical Vision," and Penzel, *German Education*, 118–21.]

different form, the faith and hope of thousands upon thousands of Christians have been directed.[100]

May the Nineteenth Century, by a magnificent UNION, consummate the ever memorable Reformation of the sixteenth! May the New World, enwombing the life spirit of almost every nation of the Old, prove the birth soil of this new era for the Church! As the distractions of Protestantism have been most painfully experienced here, so here also may the glorious work of bringing all the scattered members of Christ's body into true catholic union be carried forward with the greatest zeal and soonest crowned with the great festival of reconciliation, transmitting its blessings, in grateful love, to the world we honor and love as our general fatherland.

100. The reader is referred to substantially the same thought, presented by the celebrated Church historian NEANDER, at the close of the third edition of his *History of the Planting [and Training] of the Christian Church*, [trans. J. E. Ryland (Philadelphia: J. M. Campbell, 1844)].

General Summary

The following THESES have been added by the author,[1] not for the purpose of presenting any new matter, but simply to furnish a clear synopsis of the leading thoughts exhibited in the treatise itself. Of course, to be fully understood, each proposition must be examined in the light of the connections in which it comes forward in the general work. If any should choose to disregard this admonition, and undertake to hold up single propositions to reproach, according to the sound simply which they may carry to the ear of popular prejudice, in their separate form, it will be quite easy to fix upon the author the charge of heresy, in the most opposite directions. This low polemic trick can be practiced here, without even the small amount of cleverness it calls for in ordinary cases. The author has himself furnished to its hand, in these Theses, all the opportunity it could wish, to do him wrong in this way. Can the trick itself however, in such circumstances, cease to be either dishonorable or immoral? —TRANSLATOR.

Theses for the Time

INTRODUCTION

1. Every period of the Church and of Theology has its particular problem to solve; and every doctrine, in a measure every book also of the bible, has its classic age, in which it first comes to be fully understood and appropriated by the consciousness of the Christian world.

2. The main question of *our* time is concerning the nature of the Church itself, in its relation to the world and to single Christians.

1. [The theses were part of the 1845 German edition. They were an addition to the main text, not to the English edition as Nevin's introduction might seem to imply.]

I. The Church in General

3. The Church is the body of Jesus Christ. This expresses her communion with her Head, and also the relation of her members to one another.

4. In the first respect, she is an institution founded by Christ, proceeding from his loins and animated by his Spirit, for the glory of God and the salvation of man through which alone, as its necessary organ, the revelation of God in Christ becomes effective in the history of the world. Hence out of the Church, as there is no Christianity, there can be no salvation.

5. In the second respect, she is, like every other body, a living unity of different members; a communion in faith and love, visible as well as invisible, external as well as internal, of the most manifold individualities, gifts and powers, pervaded with the same spirit and serving the same end.

6. The definition implies further that as the life of the parents flows forward in the child, so the Church also is the depository and continuation of the earthly human life of the Redeemer, in his threefold office of Prophet, Priest, and King.

7. Hence she possesses, like her Founder, a divine and human, an ideal and real, a heavenly and an earthly nature; only with this difference, that in her militant stage, freedom from sin and error cannot be predicated of her in the same sense as of Christ; that is, she possesses the principle of holiness and the full truth, mixed however still with sin and error.

8. To the Church belong, in the wider sense, all baptized persons, even though they may have fallen back to the world; in the narrower sense however, such only as believe in Jesus Christ.

9. The relation of the Church to the world, with its different spheres of science, art, government, and social life, is neither one of destruction on her part nor one of indifference; but the object of it is that she should transfuse the world with the purifying power of her own divine life, and thus bring it at last to its true and proper perfection.

10. The ultimate scope of history accordingly is this, that Christianity may become completely the same with nature, and the world be formally organized as the kingdom of Christ; which must involve the absolute identity of Church and State, Theology and Philosophy, Worship and Art, Religion and Morality; the state of the renovated earth, in which God will be All in all.

11. In relation to single Christians, the Church is the Mother from which they derive their religious life, and to which they owe therefore constant fidelity, gratitude and obedience; she is the power of the objective and general, to which the subjective and single should ever be subordinate.

12. Only in such regular and rational subordination can the individual Christian be truly free; and his personal piety can as little come to perfection apart from an inward and outward communion with the life of the Church, as a limb separated from the body, or a branch torn from the vine.

13. Christianity in itself is the *absolute* religion, and in this view unsusceptible of improvement.

14. We must not confound with this, however, the *apprehension* and *appropriation* of Christianity in the consciousness of mankind. This is a progressive process of development that will reach its close only with the second coming of the Lord.

15. All historical progress then, in the case of the Church, consists, not in going beyond Christianity itself, which could only be to fall back to Heathenism and Judaism, but in entering always more and more (materially as well as formally) into the life and doctrine of the Redeemer, and in throwing off by this means, always more and more, the elements of sin and error still remaining from the state of nature.

16. It is possible for the Church to be in possession of a truth, and to live upon it, before it has come to be discerned in her consciousness. So it was, for instance, with the doctrine of the Trinity before the time of Athanasius, with the doctrine of divine grace and human freedom before Augustine, and with the evangelical doctrine of justification during the Middle Ages. Thus the child eats and drinks long before it has the knowledge of food, and walks before it is aware of the fact, much less *how* it walks.

17. The idea, unfolded in comprehensive and profound style particularly by the later German Philosophy, that history involves a continual progress towards something better, by means of dialectic contrapositions (*Gegensätze*), is substantially true and correct.

18. It must not be forgotten however, in connection with this, that there is a corresponding movement also on the part of evil toward that which is worse. Light and darkness, the wheat and the tares, grow together till their development shall become complete.

19. We must distinguish in the Church accordingly between idea and manifestation. As to her idea, or as comprehended in Christ, she is already complete; in the way

of manifestation however, she passes, like every one of her members, outwardly and inwardly, through different stages of life, until the ideal enclosed in Christ shall be fully actualized in humanity, and his body appear thus in the ripeness of complete manhood.

20. Such a process of growth is attended necessarily with certain diseases and crises, as well theoretical—in the form of heresies; as practical—in the form of schisms.

21. These diseases are to be referred partly to the remaining force of sin and error in the regenerate themselves, and partly to the unavoidable connection of the Church with the still unchristian world, by means of which the corrupt elements of this last are always forcing their way into her communion.

22. They can never overthrow however the existence of the Church. The Church may fall down, sore wounded, divided and torn, without ceasing for this reason to be the body of Christ. Through her humiliation gleams evermore the unwasting glory of her divine nature.

23. In the wise providence of God, all heresies and schisms serve only to bring the Church to a more clear consciousness of her true vocation, a deeper apprehension of her faith, and a purer revelation of the power included in her life.

24. But the presence of disease in the body requires to the same extent a remedial or curative process, that is, a reformation.

25. Protestantism consequently, in the true sense, belongs indispensably to the life of the Church; being the reaction simply of her proper vitality, depressed but not destroyed, in opposition to the workings of disease in her system.

[II. The Reformation]

26. Protestantism runs through the entire history of the Church, and will not cease till she is purged completely from all ungodly elements. So, for instance, Paul protested against Jewish legalism and Pagan licentiousness as found insidiously at work in the first Christian communities; the Catholic Church of the first centuries against the heresies and schisms of Ebionitism, Gnosticism, Montanism, Arianism, Pelagianism, Donatism, etc.

27. The most grand and widely influential exhibition of Protestantism is presented to us, under the formal constitution of a special Church, in the Reformation of the

Sixteenth Century, as originated, and in its most deep, inward, and truly apostolic form, carried out and consummated by the German nation.

28. It is a jejune and narrow conception of this event to look upon it as a restoration simply of the original state of the Church, or a renewal of Augustinianism against the Pelagian system by which it had been supplanted.

29. Such a view proceeds on the fundamentally erroneous supposition that the religious life revealed in the person of Christ primarily, and by derivation from him in his apostles, has been fully actualized also from the beginning in the general mass of the Church.

30. Rather, the Reformation must be viewed as an actual advance of the religious life and consciousness of the Church, by means of a deeper apprehension of God's word, beyond all previous attainments of Christendom.

31. As little is the Reformation to be regarded as a revolutionary separation from the Catholic Church, holding connection at best perhaps with some fractionary sect of the Middle Ages, and only through this and the help of certain desperate historical leaps besides, reaching back to the age of the apostles.

32. This contracted view of Protestantism is not only unhistorical and unchurchly altogether, but conscious or unconscious treason at the same time to the Lord's promise that he would build his Church upon a rock, and that the gates of Hell should not prevail against it, as well as to his engagement: "Lo I am with you always even to the end of the world" [Matt 28:20]; and the apostolic word: "The Church is the pillar and ground of the truth" [I Tim 3:15].

33. Rather, the Reformation is the greatest act of the Catholic Church itself, the full ripe fruit of all its better tendencies, particularly of the deep spiritual law conflicts of the Middle Period, which were as a schoolmaster towards the Protestant doctrine of justification.

34. The separation was produced, not by the will of the Reformers, but by the-stiff-necked papacy which like Judaism at the time of Christ, identifying itself in a fleshly way with the idea of the absolute Church, refused to admit the onward movement.

35. Thus apprehended, Protestantism has as large an interest in the vast historical treasures of the previous period, as can be claimed rightfully by the Church of Rome. Hence the arguments drawn by Romanists from this quarter, and particularly from the Middle Ages, the proper cradle of the Reformation, have no application against our standpoint.

36. Equally false finally is the view, whether popular or philosophical, by which the Reformation is made to consist in the absolute emancipation of the Christian life subjectively considered from all Church authority, and the exaltation of private judgment to the papal throne.

37. This view confounds with the Reformation itself the foul excrescences that revealed themselves along with it in the beginning, and the one-sided character of its development since.

38. On the contrary, it is quite clear from history that the Reformers aimed only at such liberty of faith and conscience and such independence of private judgment, as should involve a humble subjection of the natural will, which they held to be incapable of all good, to God's grace, and of the human reason to God's word. Indeed their opposition to the Roman traditions was itself based on the conviction that they were the product of such reason sundered from the divine word.

39. The material, or life principle of Protestantism, is the doctrine of justification by grace alone, through the merits of Jesus Christ, by means of living faith; that is, the personal appropriation of Christ in the totality of the inner man.

40. This does not overthrow good works; rather they are rightly called for and made possible only in this way; with dependence however on faith, as being its necessary fruit, the subjective impression of the life of Christ, in opposition to Pelagianism, which places works parallel with faith, or above it even.

41. The formal or knowledge principle of Protestantism is the sufficiency and unerring certainty of the holy scriptures as the only norm of all-saving knowledge.

42. This does not overthrow the idea of Church tradition; but simply makes it dependent on the written word, as the stream is upon the fountain—the necessary, ever deepening onward flow of the sense of scripture itself, as it is carried forward in the consciousness of the Christian world; contrary to the Romish dogma, by which tradition, as the bearer of different contents altogether, is made co-ordinate with the bible or even exalted above it.

43. These two principles, rightly apprehended, are only different mutually supplementary sides of one and the same principle, and their living interpenetration forms the criterion of orthodox Protestantism.

44. Opposition to the Roman Catholic extreme, according to the general law of historical progress, led the Reformers to place the strongest emphasis on justification and faith, scripture and preaching; whence the possibility of a one-sided development, in

which holiness and love, tradition and sacrament, might not be allowed to come to their full rights.

45. Respect for the Reformation as a divine work in no way forbids the admission that it included some mixture of error and sin; as where God builds a Church, the Devil erects a chapel by its side.

46. In any view moreover the Reformation must be regarded as still incomplete. It needs yet its concluding act to unite what has fallen asunder, to bring the subjective to a reconciliation with the objective.

47. Puritanism may be considered a sort of second reformation, called forth by the reappearance of Romanizing elements in the Anglican Church, and as such forms the basis to a great extent of American Protestantism, particularly in New England.

48. Its highest recommendation, bearing clearly a divine signature, is presented in its deep practical earnestness as it regards religion, and its zeal for personal piety, by which it has been more successful perhaps than any other section of the Church, for a time, in the work of saving individual souls.

49. On the other hand, it falls far behind the German Reformation by its revolutionary, unhistorical, and consequently unchurchly character, and carries in itself no protection whatever against an indefinite subdivision of the Church into separate atomistic sects. For having no conception at all of a historical development of Christianity, and with its negative attitude of blind irrational zeal towards the past, it may be said to have armed its children with the same right, and the same tendency too, to treat its own authority with equal independence and contempt.

III. The Present State of the Church

50. Protestantism has formed the starting point and center of almost all important world movements in the history of the last three centuries and constitutes now also the main interest of the time.

51. The history of Protestantism in the spheres of religion, science, art, and government, especially since the commencement of the eighteenth century, may be regarded as the development of the principle of *subjectivity*, the consciousness of *freedom*.

52. In this development however, it has gradually become estranged to a great extent from its own original nature, and fallen over dialectically into its opposite, according to the general course of history.

53. Its grand maladies at this time are *Rationalism* and *Sectarism*.

54. *Rationalism* is one-sided *theoretic religious subjectivism*, and its fullest and most perfect exhibition has taken place accordingly in Germany, the land of theory and science, and in the bosom of the Lutheran Church.

55. *Sectarism* is one-sided *practical religious subjectivism*, and has found its classic ground within the territory of the Reformed Church, in the predominantly practical countries, England and America.

56. These two maladies of Protestantism stand in a relation to it similar to that of the papacy to Catholicism in the Middle Ages; that is, they have a conditional historical necessity, and an outward connection with the system to which they adhere, but contradict nevertheless and caricature its inmost nature.

57. The secular interests, science, art, government, and social life, have become since the Reformation always more and more dissociated from the Church, in whose service they stood though with unfree subjugation in the Middle Ages, and in this separate form are advanced to a high state of perfection.

58. This is a false position, since the idea of the kingdom of God requires that all divinely constituted forms and spheres of life should be brought to serve Him in the most intimate alliance with religion, that God may be All in all.

59. The orthodox Protestantism of our day, with all its different character in other respects, is distinguished in common with Rationalism and Sectarism, particularly in this country, by the quality of one-sided subjectivity; only with the advantage of course of a large amount of personal piety.

60. Its great defect is the want of an adequate conception of the nature of the Church and of its relation to the individual Christian on the one hand, and the general life of man on the other.

61. Hence proceeds, first, indifference towards sectarian, or at least denominational divisions, which are at war with the idea of the Church as the body of Christ.

62. Secondly, a want of respect for history, by which it is affected to fall back immediately and wholly upon the scriptures without regard to the development of their contents in the life of the Church as it has stood from the beginning.

63. Thirdly, an undervaluation of the sacraments as objective institutions of the Lord, independent of individual views and states.

64. Fourthly, a disproportionate esteem for the service of preaching, with a corresponding sacrifice in the case of the liturgy, the standing objective part of divine worship, in which the *whole congregation* is called to pour forth its religious life to God.

65. Fifthly, a circumscribed conception of the all-pervading leaven-like nature of the gospel, involving an abstract separation of religion from the divinely established order of the world in other spheres.

66. To this must be added in the case of a number of denominations the fancy of their own perfection, an idea that *their* particular traditional style of religion can never be improved into anything better; which is a rejection of the Protestant principle of mobility and progress, and a virtual relapse accordingly into the ground error of the Romish Church.

67. From all this it is clear that the standpoint, and with it the wants of our time, are wholly different from those of the sixteenth century.

68. Our most immediate and most threatening danger is not now from the Church of Rome, but from the in part heterodox and antichristian, in part orthodox and pious, but always one-sided and false subjectivism, by which the rights of the Church are wronged in our own midst; which however must itself be considered again as indirectly the most alarming aspect of the danger that does in fact threaten us on the side of Rome, since one extreme serves always to facilitate the triumph of another.

68. The redeeming tendency of the age therefore is not such as looks directly to the emancipation of the individual and subjective from the bonds of authority, as at the time of the Reformation, but it is that rather which regards the claims of the objective in the true idea of the Church.

70. Not until Protestantism shall have repented of its own faults, and healed its own wounds, may it expect to prevail finally over the Church of Rome.

71. As this duty has been thus far in a great measure neglected, it is to be taken as a divine judgment in the case, that Popery has been enabled to make such formidable advances latterly, especially in England and the United States.

72. *Puseyism* (with which of course we must not confound the spurious afterbirth of fantastic, hollow-hearted affectation, always to be expected in such a case) may be considered in its original intention and best tendency a well-meant, but insufficient and unsuccessful attempt, to correct the ultra-subjectivity of Protestantism.

73. In this view we have reason to rejoice in its appearance, as indicating on the part of the Protestant world a waking consciousness of the malady under which it labors in this direction, and serving also to promote right Church feeling.

74. By its reverence for Church antiquity it exerts a salutary influence against what may be viewed as the reigning error of our time, a wild revolutionary zeal for liberty coupled with a profane scorn of all that is holy in the experience of the past.

75. So also its stress laid upon forms exhibits a wholesome reaction against the irrational hyper-spiritualism, so common among even the best Protestants, which the doctrine of the resurrection alone, as taught in the bible, is enough to prove fallacious.

76. Church forms serve two general purposes: first, they are for the lower stages of religious development conductors over into the life of the spirit; secondly, they are for the Church at large the necessary utterance or corporealization of the spirit, in the view in which Oetinger's remark holds good, "Corporeity is the scope of God's way."[2]

77. All turns simply on this, that the form be answerable to the contents and be actuated by the spirit. A formless spiritualism is no whit better than a spiritless formalism. The only right condition is a sound spirit within a sound body.

78. The grand defect of Puseyism, on the other hand, is its unprotestant character, in not recognizing the importance of the Reformation and the idea of progress in the life of the Church since.

79. It is for this reason only half-historical and half-catholic; since its sympathy and respect for the past life of the Church stop short with the sixteenth century.

80. Its view of the Church altogether is outward and mechanical, excluding the conception of a living development through the successive periods of its history.

81. This character appears particularly in its theory of episcopal succession; which is only a new form of the old pharisaic Judaism, and moreover makes the apostolicity of the Church dependent on a historical inquiry (in the case of which besides no absolute certainty is possible), resting it thus on a wholly precarious human foundation.

82. Puseyism is to be viewed then as nothing more than a simple reaction, which has served to bring to light the evils of ultra pseudo-protestant individualism, but offers

2. [A frequently cited aphorism from Friedrich Chrisoph Oetinger, an eighteenth-century German Lutheran theologian and theosopher, expressing his criticism of the rationalist and idealistic tendencies of his day and his conviction that spiritual life must take physical expression.]

no remedy for it save the perilous alternative of falling back to a standpoint already surmounted in the way of religious progress.

83. The true standpoint, all necessary for the wants of the time, is that of *Protestant Catholicism*, or genuine historical progress.

84. This holds equally remote from unchurchly subjectivity and all Romanizing churchism, though it acknowledges and seeks to unite in itself the truth that lies at the ground of both these extremes.

85. Occupying this conservative historical standpoint, from which the moving of God's Spirit is discerned in all periods of the Church, we may not in the first place surrender anything essential of the positive acquisition secured by the Reformation, whether Lutheran or Reformed.

86. Neither may we again absolutely negate the later development of Protestantism, not even Rationalism and Sectarism themselves, but must appropriate to ourselves rather the element of truth they contain, rejecting only the vast alloy of error from which it is to be extracted.

87. Rationalism and Sectarism possess historical right, so far as the principle of subjectivity, individuality, singleness, and independence, can be said to be possessed of right; that is, so far as this comes not in contradiction to the principle of objectivity, generality, the Church, authority and law, so far then as it continues subordinate to these forces.

88. Rationalism was a necessary schoolmaster for the orthodox theology, destroying its groundless prejudices, and compelling it both to accept a more scientific form in general, and also in particular to allow the human, the earthly, the historical, in the theanthropic nature of Christ and the Church, to come more fully to its rights.

89. While however the earlier historico-critical Rationalism has promoted a right understanding of the natural and historical in Christianity, this understanding in its case remains still but *half* true, since it has no organ for IDEAS, the inward life of which history after all is but the body.

90. The later speculative Rationalism, or pantheistic mythologism, or the *Hegelingians*, as they have been deridingly styled (Dr. Strauss and his colleagues), which from the Ebionitic standpoint of the old system has swung over to the opposite extreme of docetic Gnostic idealism,[3] fails to apprehend the idea of Christianity in its full truth

3. [Ebionites were the ancient Jewish Christian community who regarded Jesus as the biological child of Mary and Joseph who received the Holy Spirit at his baptism, thus he was not divine in the

and vitality, and substitutes for it a phantom or mere shadow, since it has no organ for historical REALITY, the outward life without which after all the idea must perish.

91. As in the first centuries, the theology of the Catholic Church gradually developed itself through scientific struggles with the two ground heresies—Ebionism or christianizing Judaism, and Gnosticism or christianizing Heathenism—so now also we are to look for a higher Orthodoxy, overmastering inwardly both forms of Protestant Rationalism, which shall bring the real and the ideal into the most intimate union, and recognize in full as well the eternal spirit of Christianity as its historical body.

92. The germs of all this are at hand in the later movements and achievements of the believing German theology, and need only a further development to issue at last in a full dogmatical reformation.

93. Separation, where it is characterized by religious life, springs almost always from some real evil in the state of the Church, and hence Sectarism is to be regarded as a necessary disciplinarian and reformer of the Church in its practical life.

94. Almost every sect represents in strong relief some single particular aspect of piety, and contributes to the more full evolution of individual religious activity.

95. Since however the truths of the gospel form an inseparable unity, and the single member can become complete only along with the whole body of which it is a part, it follows that no sect can ever do justice fully even to the single interest to which it is one-sidedly devoted.

96. Sects then owe it to themselves, as soon as they have fulfilled their historical vocation, to fall back again to the general Church communion from which they have seceded, as in no other way can their spiritual acquisitions be either completed or secured, and they must themselves otherwise stiffen into monumental petrifactions, never to be revisited with the warm life pulse of the one universal Church.

97. It is a cheering sign of the time that in the most different Protestant lands, and particularly in the bosom of the Reformed Church, in which religious individualism both in the good and in the bad sense has been most fully developed, it is coming to be felt more and more that the existing divisions of the Church are wrong, and with this is waking more and more an earnest longing after a true union of all believers, in no communication whatever with the errors either of Oxford or Rome.

---

orthodox sense. Gnostics affirmed Jesus' divinity, but denied his physical humanity. They served for Baur and others as the dialectical extremes that shaped the development of early Christianity.]

98. Finally, also the liberation of the secular spheres of life from the Church since the Reformation, though not the ultimate normal order, forms—notwithstanding as compared with the previous vassalage of the world to a despotic hierarchy—an advance in the naturalization process of Christianity.

99. The luxuriant separate growth of these interests, as unfolded in the Protestant States, Sciences, Arts, and Social Culture, lays the Church under obligation to appropriate these advances to herself, and impress upon them a religious character.

100. The signs of the time then, and the teachings of history, point us not backward, but forward to a new era of the Church that may be expected to evolve itself gradually from the present process of fermentation, enriched with the entire positive gain of Protestantism.

101. As the movement of history in the Church is like that of the sun from East to West, it is possible that America, into whose broad majestic bosom the most various elements of character and education are poured from the Old World, may prove the theatre of this unitive reformation.

102. Thus far, if we put out of view the rise of a few insignificant sects and the separation of Church and State, which to be sure has very momentous bearings, American Church history has produced nothing original, no new *fact* in the history of the Church as a whole.

103. Nowhere else however is there at present the same favorable room for further development, since in no country of the Old World does the Church enjoy such entire freedom, or the same power to renovate itself from within according to its own pleasure.

104. The historical progress of the Church is always conditioned by the national elements, which form its physical basis.

105. The two leading nationalities, which are continually coming into contact in this country, and flowing into one another with reciprocal action, are the English and the German.

106. The further advancement of the American Church, consequently, must proceed mainly from a special combination of German depth and *Gemütlichkeit* ["generous hospitality"], with the force of character, and active practical talent, for which the English are distinguished.

107. It would be a rich offering then to the service of this approaching reformation, on the part of the German Churches in America, to transplant hither in proper measure the rich wealth of the better German theology, improving it into such form as our peculiar relations might require.

108. This their proper vocation however they have thus far almost entirely overlooked, seeking their salvation for the most part in a characterless surrendry of their own nationality.

109. In view of the particular constitution of a large part of the German emigration, this subjection to the power of a foreign life may be regarded indeed as salutary.

110. But the time has now come, when our Churches should again rise out of the ashes of the old German Adam, enriched and refined with the advantages of the English nationality.

111. What we most need now, is theoretically, a thorough, intellectual theology, scientifically free as well as decidedly believing, together with a genuine sense for history; and practically, a determination to hold fast the patrimony of our fathers, and to go forward joyfully at the same time in the way in which God's Spirit by providential signs may lead, with a proper humble subordination of all we do for our own denomination to the general interest of the One Universal Church.

112. The ultimate, sure scope of the Church, towards which the inmost wish and most earnest prayer of all her true friends continually tend, is that perfect and glorious unity the desire of which may be said to constitute the burden of our Lord's last, memorable, intercessory Prayer [John 17:21].

DOCUMENT 2

Review of *The Principle of Protestantism* by Charles Hodge (1845)

Editors' Introduction

The Reception of *The Principle of Protestantism*

Near the end of his life, Philip Schaff expressed no little amazement over the fact that *The Principle of Protestantism*, his "harmless book," was received with such opposition in the German Reformed Church.[1] Schaff's primary antagonist in his new denomination was Dr. Joseph Berg, pastor of First Reformed Church in Philadelphia and editor of the vehemently anti-Catholic newspaper *The Protestant Banner*. In contrast to the theory of historical development that Schaff advocated, Berg advanced a notion that the true fathers of the Reformed Church were the Waldensians, in whom coalesced a spirit of protest "against idolatry and the strong delusions of both pagan and papal Rome from the second to the twelfth century."[2] Key to Berg's understanding of "true" Protestant identity, then, was the belief that it had nothing to do with Roman Catholicism. Indeed, as a leader of the American Protestant Association, Berg had pledged himself "to an unremitting ideological war on popery" in print and in the councils of his own denomination.[3] In the spirit of this pledge, Berg brought charges of heresy against Schaff before the Philadelphia classis of the German Reformed Church, perceiving in the notion of "Protestant Catholicism" an endorsement of what Berg considered "the Great Apostasy."[4] After some time of tension, during which church leaders and seminary students joined together to support him, Schaff was vindicated by the synod of York in October 1845.

Sentiments similar to Berg's were noted by other Reformed Protestants, usually with less vehemence. Some of the earliest criticism of the *Principle of Protestantism* came from the Philadelphia Presbyterian editor of the *Christian Observer*, Amasa Converse. He objected to Schaff's views of the Reformation as an outgrowth of medieval

1. See David Schaff, *Life of Philip Schaff*, 114; and Schaff, "Farewell Address to the Eastern Synod of the Reformed Church in the United States" in *Philip Schaff: Historian and Ambassador*, 6.

2. Berg, "Opening Sermon," 1913.

3. Weigeley, Wainright, Wolf, et al, eds., *Philadelphia*, 356–57.

4. Shriver, *Philip Schaff*, 24–25.

Catholicism and what he saw as Schaff's exaltation of the church and depreciation of scripture, but these he regarded as "mistakes in *theory*, rather than errors in *doctrine*."[5]

George Cheever, the Andover-educated editor of the *New York Evangelist*, published a six-part review throughout the early fall refuting Schaff's "main propositions" which he regarded as "thoroughly false."[6] Like Converse, he insisted that the medieval church was nothing but a sinful corruption. The life of the church, Cheever insisted, was sustained not through any historical succession, but solely through God's "Word and Spirit."[7] Similarly, true theology was not rooted in any scientific or historical scholarship, but in "the simple humble study of God's Word in reliance on God's Spirit."[8] While Schaff appealed to John 17 to denounce "sectarism," Cheever defended "denominations" by invoking 1 Corinthians 12 and Ephesians 4. He dismissed Schaff's celebration of Germany as the "proper home" of Protestant theology extolling New England instead.[9] For a proper understanding of Christianity and history, Cheever referred Schaff to Jonathan Edwards's *A History of Redemption*. More than any other point, it was the relation of the Bible to the progress of the church stood between Cheever and Schaff. It was on this point that Schaff would respond to Cheever in *What is Church History*?[10]

In other quarters, *The Principle of Protestantism* was received with less hostility, often with a mixture of praise and expressions of cautious concern. The anonymous reviewer in the *Lutheran Observer* recommended the book's "enlarged spirit, fearless candor, and a devotion to Christianity which rises superior to all denominations."[11] A reviewer in the *Christian Intelligencer* of the Dutch Reformed Church welcomed Schaff as one for whom "feelings of the most affectionate regard" were maintained. He went on to critique Schaff's description of Puseyism, positing that Schaff inadvertently endorsed a "hierarchical system" in the effort to advance his theory of historical development.[12] Meanwhile, a reviewer in the *Catholic Telegraph* cautiously endorsed Schaff's willingness to engage with Roman Catholicism and its history but expressed suspicion over Schaff's suggestion that Protestantism and not contemporary Roman Catholicism represented the fruit of the "dark and middle ages."[13] The recent Catholic

5. Converse, "Excitement against Prof. Schaf's Work on Protestantism." Nevin's objection to the review and Converse's reply further reveal the depth of their differences. Nevin, "Schaf on Protestantism"; Converse, "Dr. Schaf's Work of Protestantism."

6. Cheever, "The Work of Dr. Schaf on Protestantism." Interestingly, the first note on Schaff's book in Cheever's paper was entirely positive. *New York Evangelist* 16 (July 10, 1845): 112.

7. Cheever, "Unity of the Protestant Church."

8. Cheever, "German Theology—Science apart from Life."

9. Ibid.

10. See p. 244 in this volume. For Cheever's reaction to the dismissal of Schaff's heresy charges see Cheever, "Strange Made Plain."

11. Review of *Das Princip des Protestantismus*, *Lutheran Observer*, 39.

12. Review of *Principle of Protestantism*, *Christian Intelligencer*, 14.

13. Review of *Principle of Protestantism*, *Catholic Telegraph*, 266.

convert Orestes Brownson was more direct. "We tell him, Hands off!," he exclaimed. The Middle Ages "are our property. We have borne the reproach, and will not be robbed of the glory."[14]

Schaff's Reception by Princeton's Hodge

Perhaps the most critically sustained and careful review was penned by Charles Hodge. Hodge was Professor of Oriental and Biblical Literature at Princeton Theological Seminary. He founded the publication *Biblical Repertory* in 1825 as a conduit for the translation and dissemination of European scholarship into the United States. His interest in European theological education was such that he undertook a sojourn to some of Europe's leading universities from 1826 to 1828. In Hodge's absence, his former student, John Nevin, taught his courses. Most of Hodge's extended sabbatical was spent in Germany where he was particularly influenced by Friedrich August Gottreu Tholuck at the University of Halle and Wilhelm Hengstenberg at Berlin. Both of these men would later be mentors to Philip Schaff. Hodge gained from his studies in Germany the sense of "a profound correlation between theology and biblical studies."[15] But although he developed an admiration for German scholarship, Hodge never fully embraced it. He was suspicious of the philosophical notions that grounded Hegel's theory of history and which were transported into church history by scholars such as Johann August Neander. For example, he also felt that scripture, not philosophy, should be the basis for theological inquiry.

Hodge's review of *The Principle of Protestantism* is important because it demonstrates how a leading American theologian, versed in Germanic modes of theological inquiry, received and wrestled with the work. Hodge admits from the outset that the book is difficult to comprehend. Indeed, he confesses that after reading the book twice in its entirety he was still left puzzling. Despite his familiarity with German scholarship, Hodge attributes his lingering befuddlement to the thoroughly German character of the work—especially the parts of the book written by his former student, John Nevin (namely the introduction and the concluding sermon "Catholic Unity"). Nevin and Hodge would clash subsequently and regularly over a variety of issues, in particular the Reformed doctrine of the Lord's Supper.[16] As for Schaff's portion of the book, he is more approving of it than Converse or Cheever. Hodge does not join them in denouncing Schaff's view of the development of Protestantism out of medieval Christianity. He also recommends the exposition on the twin principles of

14. Brownson, Review of *The Principle of Protestantism.*

15. Aubert, *German Roots of Nineteenth-Century American Theology*, 158. Aubert's book details the challenge to and influence upon Hodge's theological development that the mediating theology (*Vermittlungstheologie*) of the German universities posed.

16. See the MTSS volumes Nevin, *Mystical Presence* and Nevin and Hodge, *Coena Mystica*.

Protestantism (scripture alone and justification) as wholly orthodox and a welcome guide to New School Presbyterians, whom he believed had lost a proper sense of sin.

But Hodge joins others in criticizing aspects of the second part of the book. Hodge understood why, as a German, Schaff would see rationalism as a greater threat than Catholicism, but he disagreed. In general, and especially in America, he believed that a wrong religion was more threatening than irreligion. He also felt that Schaff insisted too much on the external unity of the church over its internal unity and thoroughly disagreed with his assessment of the depth of the divisions in American Protestantism. Yet, Hodge wrote much of this off to the young European's lack of familiarity with his new environment. Hodge thoroughly disagreed with those who accused Schaff or Nevin of Puseyism or heading toward Rome. The Mercersburg theologians' motto was "Forward," he explained, not back to Rome or even to the early church. While Hodge expressed caution with this faith in progress and deep reservations about trends in German theology, he strongly affirmed Schaff's piety, scholarship, and Protestant commitments and welcomed his new colleague to the New World. The animosity that would later develop between fundamentalist successors to Hodge and progressive successors to Schaff's Romanticism was wholly absent.

Review by Charles Hodge

***Principle of Protestantism as related to the present state of the Church.* By Philip Schaff, Ph. D. Professor of Church History and Biblical Literature in the Theological Seminary of the German Reformed Church. Translated from the German with an introduction. By John W. Nevin, D. D. Chambersburg: 1845. pp. 215.**[1]

The importance of the subject of which this book treats, the ability which it displays, and the attention which it has excited, all claim for it an elaborate review. Such a review would be a very difficult task; one which we should not be ambitious to assume, even if circumstances beyond our control had not shut us up to the necessity of confining ourselves to this short notice.

It is a book not easy to understand, especially that part of it, which has proceeded from the pen of Dr. Nevin. We have read the whole twice over, and yet we are very far from being satisfied that we adequately comprehend its principles. This obscurity is no doubt due, in part, to the nature of the subject. Every thing that involves the nature of the church, pertains to one of the most difficult departments of theology; one in which the indefiniteness of language almost unavoidably leads to more or less confusion. The obscurity, however, of which we complain, we are disposed to attribute in no small measure to the manner in which the subject is treated. The book is thoroughly German. The mode of thinking, and the forms of expression are so un-English, that it is not easy for an American to enter into the views of the authors. German writers have many characteristic excellencies; but they have also some characteristic faults. They are seldom very intelligible. Their preference for the reason over the understanding leads them to eschew *Begriffe*, definite conceptions, and to abound in ideas, whose import and limits are indeterminate. It is hard, therefore, in many cases, to tell precisely what they mean. This whole book is about the church, and yet we have tried in vain to find out what the authors mean by the church. Is it the body of professors? or the body of true believers? or the two in inseparable union as one body? These questions

1. [Originally published in in *Biblical Repertory and Princeton Review* 16 (October 1845): 625–36.]

we cannot answer; and therefore we cannot tell what interpretation is to be put upon their language. If a writer speaks of man in such a way that his readers are at a loss to determine whether what he says is to be referred to the soul or to the body, or to the whole as a unit, they must be at a loss whether to assent or dissent. This is precisely the state of mind in which the perusal of this book has left us. This remark is intended to apply in a measure to the whole work, but more particularly to the introduction and appendix, which are by far the most difficult to understand.[2]

The first point which Prof. Schaf endeavors to establish, is that the Reformation was neither a revolution nor a restoration. It was neither a violent disruption from all that preceded it, nor the return of the church to the state in which it had existed during any preceding century. As to both these points, we presume, he speaks the general sentiments of Protestants. The middle ages were no doubt pregnant with the Reformation; the church lived through all those ages, and Protestantism was the revival, through the word and Spirit of God, of a backslidden church, and not a new creation. It is also no doubt true, that as in the case of an individual believer, who is brought back from his declensions, and by the grace of God rendered more enlightened and stable than at any previous stage of his career, so the church of the Reformation was in a more advanced state than the church of the second or third centuries. No one would think of comparing the works of the Fathers with those of the Reformers as to enlightened, scriptural and comprehensive views of the gospel.

When again Prof. Schaf speaks of the distinguishing principles of Protestantism, he follows the common method of evangelical theologians. Those principles are the doctrine of justification by faith, and the supremacy of scripture as the rule of faith. The former is our continued protest against the error of a mediating church or priesthood. It is undoubtedly the vital principle of Protestantism that God is now accessible to all men by Jesus Christ; that all who hear the gospel may come to Christ, and through him to God, receiving, in virtue of union with Christ by faith, the imputation of his righteousness for justification, and the indwelling of his Spirit for sanctification. In this liberty of access lies the priesthood of all believers. And so long as this is asserted, do we protest against the great error of Rome, that men can only come to God through the church, or through the mediation of other men as priests, by whose ministrations alone the benefits of redemption can be applied to the soul. The reverse of this is true, and the reverse of this is Protestantism. We are in the church because we are in Christ, and not in Christ because we are in the church. The analysis and exposition which Prof. Schaf gives of this great doctrine of justification by faith alone, is thoroughly evangelical. We commend it to our new school brethren as a mirror in which they may see the true principle of the Reformation, and thence learn how far they have lapsed

2. [The introduction and appendix were composed by John Nevin, who is thus characterized as being more Germanic than his German colleague, Schaff. The appendix in question is Nevin's sermon, "On Catholic Unity" which will appear in *One, Holy, Catholic, and Apostolic: John Nevin's Writings on Ecclesiology*, ed. Sam Hamstra, Jr., MTSS, vol. 5 (forthcoming).]

towards Romanism in their denial or explaining away of the corruption of our nature by original sin, and in making justification mere pardon, to the exclusion of the imputation of the righteousness of Christ.[3] Our author, however, presents this doctrine too exclusively "in opposition to all Pelagian and Semi-Pelagian error." He does not present it sufficiently in its opposition to the doctrine of a mediating church, which was historically its most prominent aspect. When the sinner asked, "What must I do to be saved?" the answer which the Spirit of God, and their own dear-bought experience taught the Reformers to give, was: "Believe in the Lord Jesus Christ and thou shalt be saved. That alone can save you; and that can, and most certainly will."[4] And by faith they meant not mere assent, but, as Dr. Schaf says, a personal appropriation of the merits of Jesus Christ. That is all the sinner needs in order to secure his justification, and with that blessing, sanctification and eternal life are inseparably connected. The answer given by Rome and "ecclesiasticism" in general, to the momentous question, "What must I do to be saved?" is, "Come to me, I have the merits of Christ; I have the Spirit; I have the custody of the blessings of redemption. Your own act of faith will do you little good; you can only come to Christ by me; I give you his merits and grace in baptism; and if you lose them, I alone can restore them by the sacraments of penance." It was in opposition to all this, it was their protest against this, the very thing that made them Protestants,[5] that the Reformers said, "we are justified freely by faith alone. We need not your mediation, Christ is every where present. And we can and must, each one for himself, lay hold on him by faith, and we know that whosoever believes on him has eternal life, though he has never heard of the Church, or of a priest, or of the sacraments." It is this aspect of the doctrine of justification by faith alone, which Prof. Schaf has failed to render prominent; and it is the apparent denial of this view of the subject by Dr. Nevin, which form the stumbling block, presented in this book. It is this which gives his portion of the work, the Puseyite aspect which has created so much anxiety.[6] We say "apparent denial," because we are not satisfied that it is any thing more than apparent. For while he speaks somewhat too contemptuously of those who make the turning point between us and Rome the question, "whether salvation

3. [Charles Hodge was a leader of the Old School Presbyterians who maintained, in strict adherence to the Westminster Confession of Faith, that humanity exists in a state of sin and misery on account of Adam's fall. Pelagianism and semi-Pelagianism argue that human nature is basically good, to one degree or another. Hodge attributes this position to his New School Presbyterian opponents. The division of the Presbyterians into Old School and New School occurred at the Presbyterian general assembly in 1837.]

4. [See Acts 16:31 and 4:12.]

5. [In his discussion of the twin principles of Protestantism, Hodge incorporates the word "protest" to insist, contra Schaff, that protest against the Catholic Church is basic to the nature of Protestantism.]

6. [For Hodge, the Oxford Movement's emphases on the visible church, the priesthood, and the sacraments, all point to the church as an institution first of all. This creates anxiety for him and other like-minded Protestants inasmuch as these emphases seem to support Roman Catholicism (and lead toward it).]

be an individual concern or something that comes wholly by the church" (p. 12),[7] and says: "We are not Christians, each one by himself, but we become such through the church" (p. 200),[8] still he pronounces "ecclesiasticism, as held by Rome and also by Oxford," a terrible error; and declares it would be treason to the gospel to reject "the position that religion is an individual interest, a strictly personal concern, a question between a man singly and his maker. He that believeth shall be saved; he that believeth shall not be damned" (p. 12).[9] We can only repeat what we have already said, as to our inability fully to comprehend his meaning on this point; and comfort ourselves with the conviction that it is impossible to hold the doctrine of justification by faith alone, as it is stated in this book, and yet mean by saying, "we become Christians through the church," what Puseyites mean by such expressions.

In the exposition, given by Dr. Schaf, of the formal principle of Protestantism, viz., that the scriptures are the only infallible rule of faith and practice, we in general concur. As the doctrine of justification by faith is the protest of the Reformed against the Romish doctrine of a mediating church; so the assertion of the sole infallible authority of the written word of God, is their protest against the doctrine of an inspired church to whose teaching we obliged to bow. As the church, according to Rome, consists of all who profess the Christian religion and are subject to the Pope, the wisdom and teaching of that body, consisting in great measure of unsanctified men, is but another name for the wisdom and teaching of the world. But if by the church is meant the body of true believers, in whom Christ dwells by his Spirit, and whom he leads to knowledge of the truth, then indeed to differ from the church is a serious, and if on any essential doctrine, a fatal matter.[10] It is by losing sight too much of this distinction, that Prof. Schaf is led to attribute much more weight to the usages and opinions, i.e. to the traditions, of the visible church, than we think is due to them, consistently with Protestant principles. This is a subject, however, on which we cannot dwell. We only wish to express our dissent from the obvious or apparent meaning of some of his remarks on tradition; which though we think they admit of a good sense, yet more naturally express one with which we cannot concur. We are more sensible of the difference of views between our author and the mass of his American readers, as to this point, from the conclusions to which his principles lead him, than from the statement of those principles themselves. He condemns not only the more rigid Puritans, but most of the Reformed churches for repudiating the usages (ritual traditions) of the church, and commends the greater regard of the Lutherans for such traditions. In this respect he will find few American Protestants to agree with him.

7. [See p. 43 in this volume.]

8. [In Nevin's appendix, "Catholic Unity."]

9. [See p. 43 in this volume.]

10. [For Hodge's views on the right relation of the concepts of the invisible church and the visible church, see his *Discussions in Church Polity,* 55–67.]

The two great diseases of Protestantism our author represents to be Rationalism and Sectarism. He gives a historical sketch of the rise and progress of the former in Germany, and concludes with the expression of his conviction that "the most dangerous enemy with which we are threatened on theoretical ground, is not the catholicism of Rome, but the foe within our own borders; not the hierarchic papacy of the Vatican, but the worldly papacy of the subjective understanding; not the Concilium Tridentinum, but the theology of unbelief, as proclaimed by a Rhoer, a Wegscheider, a Strauss, a Feuerbach, and others of the same stamp."[11] This is a very natural view to be taken by a theologian born and educated in Germany, who has been accustomed to see comparatively little of the evils of Romanism, and before whose eyes the desolations wrought by Rationalism were constantly present. In itself considered, however, and in reference to the state of the church in America, we consider Romanism immeasurably more dangerous than infidelity. Not by any means, as some have said, a greater evil; but an evil more dangerous to Protestantism. This is only expressing our conviction that a false religion is more likely to spread than mere irreligion; and that the human mind has greater affinity for superstition, than for infidelity.

The section relating to "Sectarism" we consider as more marred by false principles and false views of facts and of their historical relations, than any other in the book. Here we think our author betrays erroneous principles as to the unity of the church, too much forgetting that it is a spiritual unity, arising from the union of believers with Christ and from the indwelling of his Spirit; and which manifests itself in unity of faith, of love and of communion. There is therefore more of real unity, more real brotherhood existing between the evangelical denominations of America, than is to be found in the church of Rome, the church of England, or in the Reformed or Lutheran church of Germany. The true unity of the church is therefore, in a measure, independent of external ecclesiastical union. It is marred by all diversity of faith, all want of love, and by all refusal of intercommunion and fraternal subjection and intercourse; and is destroyed by the entire absence of any of these bonds. It is not, however, necessarily interrupted by separate ecclesiastical organizations, or diversity as to modes of discipline and worship; uniformity and unity being very different things. We do not suppose that Dr. Schaf denies this, but he constantly speaks as though he regarded external union, that is, union secured and expressed by outward bonds as far more essential to unity of the church than appears to us consistent with its true nature.[12]

Again, his principles as to conformity and the preservation of outward union, seem to us erroneous. He says the Reformers had "they been permitted to preach the pure word of God with freedom, and to administer the sacraments according to

11. [See p. 124 in this volume.]

12. [Hodge defends American denominationalism here and maintains a position similar to the one Schaff will advocate ten years later in his book *America*. See Schaff, *Schaff's "America" and Related Writings*, ed. Stephen R. Graham, MTSS, vol. 11 (forthcoming).]

Christ's appointment, would have remained in their original communion."[13] He blames the Puritans for separating from the established church of England, and condemns the recent secession of the Free Church in Scotland. All this we think betrays very wrong notions as to the principles involved in such questions. Such separations are a duty, which we owe to God and to the real unity of the church, whenever unscriptural terms of communion are enjoined. If the Puritans, in order to their connexion with the church of England, were required to declare their "assent and consent" to all and every thing contained in the Book of Common Prayer, then those who could not assent to the baptismal or burial service, or to the semi-deification of Charles I, were bound in conscience to separate from that church, and to protest against the schismatical principle of making such matters terms of Christian communion.[14] The same remark may of course be applied to a multitude of other cases.

When our author says that sects have their origin in sinful ambition and pride, we think he is wrong as to the majority of the cases, as far as evangelical sects are concerned.—They have much more commonly had their origin in the imposition, by those in authority, of unscriptural terms of communion. In many cases no doubt they have arisen from narrow-mindedness, and scrupulosity, but even in such cases, there is something to respect in the assertion of the supremacy of conscience.[15] We miss in our author any definite conception of Sectarism, or what it is that constitutes a sect. Why are the Congregationalists, or Baptists any more a sect than the German Reformed, or the Episcopalians?

In the account given by Dr. Schaf of the Puritans, of Cromwell, of the relation of the church in this country with the English Independents, we think he shows that he is [away] from home. He is speaking of events, which as they did not occur in Germany, cannot be supposed to be so well understood by a scholar so thoroughly German. He betrays also the disadvantage under which he labours as a stranger, when he comes to speak of the state of things in his country. The paragraph on p. 116[16] in which he speaks of the multiplication of sects in America, is an extravagant exaggeration. It is easy to string together a number of names of religious parties, here and anywhere else, and not more here, than in England, or even Germany, but what do they amount to? The vast mass of our population belong either to the Romish, the Episcopal, the Baptist, Methodist, Congregational, or Presbyterian churches, including in the last

13. [See p. 139 in this volume.]

14. [The 1662 Book of Common Prayer required every January 30 to be observed as "the Martyrdom of the Blessed King Charles the First." The king was executed by the Puritan-led Parliament in 1649. Note again Hodge's use of the word "protest" to characterize the essence of Protestantism.]

15. [What Hodge esteemed as "the supremacy of conscience" Schaff and Nevin were more likely to repudiate as "private judgment." See particularly the scathing critique of American religious sects in Nevin's "The Sect System," *Mercersburg Review* 1 (1849): 482–507; 521–39 *One, Holy, Catholic, and Apostolic: John Nevin's Writings on Ecclesiology*, ed. Sam Hamstra, Jr., Mercersburg Theology Study Series, vol. 5 (Eugene, OR: Wipf and Stock, forthcoming).]

16. [See pp. 135–136 in this volume.]

named, the English, Dutch, and German Presbyterians.[17] Beyond these all other sects are made up of handfuls, and these are to be found wherever there is liberty enough for what actually exists to make itself known.

We are not to be considered as apologists for "Sectarism" because we object to the exaggerated statements of the nature and extent of the evil given by our author. We admit that it is a very serious evil, and one which the friends of the church, in the true sense of the term, should endeavor to correct. What then are the means by which these two diseases of Protestantism, viz., Rationalism and Sectarism, are to be cured? To the answer to this question Dr. Schaf addresses himself in the latter part of his book.

He begins by saying that Puseyism is a well meant, but mistaken effort to accomplish this cure. It is represented as a legitimate reaction from false or ultra-Protestantism; an attempt to cure Rationalism by subjecting the judgment of the individual to that of the church; and Sectarism, by merging all parties into the outward unity of established uniformity. There may be some truth in this genesis of Puseyism; but we are disposed to assign it a less honourable origin. We believe it had its birth in wrong views as to the nature of religion, and wrong principles as to the nature of the church. Prof. Schaf thinks its end legitimate, but its means mistaken. We think its end a mistaken one, and therefore its means mistaken. We think its end a mistaken one, and therefore its means illegitimate. Rationalism and Sectarism were not the real evils which it proposed to cure, but Protestantism itself, i.e. the gospel, salvation by grace, justification by faith, the worship of God in spirit and in truth, instead of outward forms or inward mysticism or superstitious reverence. The gospel is the great evil against which it is directed with consummate skill. We cannot therefore regard it as embodying any great truth. It is not the expression of the sense of need of Christian unity, in the proper meaning of the term, but rather of the desire to be religious and secure heaven by some means sanctioned by antiquity, but which does not include submission to the gospel.

What means then does our author propose for the cure of the diseases of Protestantism? "Historical Progress. Puseyism looks backwards; we look forwards. It looks towards Rome. . . We towards Jerusalem."[18] Here comes in again the idea of the gradual development of Christianity, with which the work commences. Not that Christianity admits of any improvement, but simply that it comes gradually to be better understood and more fully to pervade the church and the world. As the advanced Christian

17. [Due to similarities in theology and polity, Hodge regards the Dutch and German Reformed as "Presbyterians." The German Reformed Church in America operated as a classis of the Dutch Reformed Church for a time in the eighteenth century. In the introduction to his sermon "Catholic Unity," Nevin argued for the close affiliation of the two churches, a position also endorsed by the Dutch Reformed publication *The Christian Intelligencer*. Ironically, the catholic—and seemingly Catholic—pleas for unity had the effect of distancing the Dutch Reformed and the German Reformed from each other in response to the emerging Mercersburg position.]

18. [See p. 148 in this volume.]

believes just what he believed when a babe in Christ, but apprehends it more justly, and is more under its influence; so the church of the Reformation, was in advance of the church of the third century, and the consummated church will be in advance of the church of the Reformation. In all this there is much truth. In the manner in which it is presented, and in the exhibition of the means by which this development is to be carried on, there is a great deal that is due to the peculiar philosophical and historical training of the writer; much that we do not understand and much with which we cannot agree. And yet there is much that is healthful and encouraging. It is very plain from this brief analysis of the book before us, that the apprehension that Dr. Nevin and Prof. Schaf are tending toward Puseyism, if by Puseyism be meant prelacy and Rome and what is necessarily connected with them, is altogether unfounded. It would be suicidal in them, and entirely opposed to all their principles, to step out of the line "of historical development" to which they belong. They are in the Reformed church: that church is an immeasurable advance on the church of the middle ages, to go back to the ground which the Puseyites are endeavoring to regain, would, in their view, be for men to turn children. Their motto is Forwards. What is the future they have figured for themselves and for the church, we cannot distinctly discern.

We confess we have not much faith in the means of progress on which these gentlemen seem to place their main reliance. German philosophy and German theology appear to be the great sources of their hopes, as far as human agency is concerned. We once heard a distinguished German professor say, "England and America are the hands of the church, Germany is the head. She must do the thinking, they the work." A division of labour with which we ought to be content, especially if our working does not depend upon our understanding their thinking. Prof. Schaf's book is imbued with the same idea of the relative vocations of the several portions of the church. "Germany is the proper home not only of the Reformation, but of all the deeper spiritual movement which have been called forth by this, during the last three hundred years."[19] "It is the proper home of Protestant theology."[20] If we allude to German Rationalism, we are told "only an archangel can become a devil."[21] To Germany therefore we must look for the impulse and the light to impel and guide this onward movement of the church. We are very ready to admit the great superiority of Germany in all that can be attained by research and concentrated labour. We admit too that the German mind is in some of its attributes favourably distinguished from the English and American, but we think Dr. Schaf not only over estimates this superiority, but finds it, in some instances, in those very peculiarities where the advantage is on the other side. The Germans have never been celebrated for their ability to distinguish between the unknown and the unknowable, they cannot discern the limits of human knowledge; and by passing those limits they lose all the criteria of knowledge, and are unable to distinguish

19. [See p. 129 in this volume.]

20. [See p. 177 in this volume.]

21. [See p. [Ibid.] in this volume.]

between truth and the phantoms of their creative imaginations. To our apprehension the willingness of the English mind to rest content within the sphere which God has assigned it; to submit to the laws of its nature, and to confide in the principles of belief impressed upon our constitution, without attempting either to question the legitimacy of those laws, or the conclusions to which they lead, is worth more as a means of attaining truth, than all that mysterious "power of perceiving the supernatural, the infinite, the harmonious unity, the essence of things, the primal idea of the absolute,"[22] which is the peculiar excellence of our German brethren.

In order to decide what the church has to hope from German theology, in securing the anticipated progress in divine knowledge, it would seem natural to inquire what that theology, since its revival, has actually accomplished. A question we are not competent to answer. On the one hand, we are disposed to hope that it has not done much in unsettling old landmarks, when we find such thoroughly evangelical exhibitions of the doctrine of justification, as that given by Prof. Schaf, and when we see that the very best of the recent German theologians are precisely those who are most like the Reformers. On the other hand, we cannot repress our fears when we find that to those most imbued with this theology, every thing seems alike. Fichte, Schelling, Hegel, as philosophers; Daub, Schleiermacher, Marheinecke, as theologians, seem to be regarded as differing from each other, and differing from received standards, only as to their mode of presenting truth. When we express surprise, that men who seem to deny a personal God, to deny sin, to deny the continued personal existence of the soul after death, should be referred to as substantially sound, we are told we do not understand these writers, and therefore are not competent to form an opinion on the subject. The sufficiency of this answer we should feel bound to admit, were it not for two circumstances. First, we see the professed and thoroughly instructed disciples of these schools in Germany itself, asserting that these philosophers do in fact teach what their words seem to imply, viz., that there is no God, no sin, no conscious existence hereafter.—And secondly, when we hear some of the most highly educated and devout, among the Germans themselves, denouncing as an utter abomination those very systems and writers, who are so much lauded in this country. Here then are two classes of men, neither of which can summarily set down as destitute of the *Anschauungsvermögen*, the power of perceiving the absolute and infinite, who unite in condemning just what those among us most zealous for German philosophy and theology, unite in lauding. We confess that this, more than anything else, far more than any confidence in our own limited knowledge of these systems and writers, makes us fear their influence. We are afraid of their confounding all the landmarks of truth, of leading men to see no difference between holiness and beauty, sin and defect, fate and providence, a self-conscious universe and our Father who is in heaven.

While we say this from a deep conviction of its truth, we are not insensible either to the merits of this work or to the advantages which the author derives from his

22. Dr. Schaf's definition of reason, p. 102. [See p. 123, fn 4, in this volume.]

familiarity with the varied learning of his native country.—The evangelical character of the leading doctrines of his book, the seriousness and warmth of feeling which pervade it, and the high order of ability which it displays, give ground to hope that Dr. Schaf will prove a blessing to the church and country of his adoption.

DOCUMENT 3

What is Church History? A Vindication of the Idea of Historical Development

by Philip Schaff (1846)

Editors' Introduction

What is Church History? A Vindication of the Idea of Historical Development is Philip Schaff's most pointed statement about his philosophy of church history, and indeed his theology of the church. It is an expanded form of the introductory lectures to his church history course at Mercersburg. As David W. Lotz has noted, this essay accomplished two firsts. It is the first history of church historiography composed in the United States and "the first American exposition of the 'idea of *organic* development' in its import for church history."[1] Schaff later expanded parts of *What is Church History?* to form the "General Introduction to Church History" in his *History of the Apostolic Church* which was published in German in 1851 and in English in 1853.[2] Together with *The Principle of Protestantism*, and "German Theology and the Church Question," these works present Schaff's fundamental idea and philosophy of church history and thereby his philosophy of the church itself. Since it is commonly agreed that Schaff's philosophy of history changed little over his career, and since in later writings he did not write as systematically about it, *What is Church History?* is the best introduction to his view of organic, historical development and its place in the Mercersburg theology.[3]

By Schaff's own admission, the principle of organic development is treated more extensively in *What is Church History?* than in the "General Introduction."[4] The book is lively retaining many characteristics of the lecture hall, including its enumerated list of eleven characteristics of the organic development of the church and five concluding "practical" observations on the importance of a right view of church history. As with *The Principle of Protestantism*, John Nevin provided the oftentimes awkward translation; this must have annoyed Schaff who complained in this essay about the poor German style of historians Gottfried Arnold, Johann Mosheim, and August Neander. When Schaff published *History of the Apostolic Church* seven years later, a different

1. Lotz, "Philip Schaff and the Idea of Church History," 3.

2. Schaff, *History of the Apostolic Church*, 1–134.

3. Lotz, "Philip Schaff" provides an excellent introduction to Schaff's view of history. Pranger, *Philip Schaff*, 199–239 provides a detailed discussion of *What is Church History*? See also Penzel, "The Reformation Goes West."

4. Schaff, *History of the Apostolic Church*, 13.

translator was used with a notably different result.[5] Nonetheless, as Charles Hodge charitably noted in his review, the awkward English can encourage the reader to attend to Schaff's argument.[6]

Overview of the Book

What is Church History? opens with a brief preface in which Schaff emphasizes the importance of church history to readers who are accustomed to having little interest in it. Chastened by the experience of *Principle of Protestantism*, he also pleads for readers who will "take the trouble of *studying* a book *through*" before criticizing it.[7] The reception of the book suggested, however, that Americans' relative lack of interest in church history triumphed over their proclivity to casually criticize. With a few exceptions, it received a benign, but neglected reception.

In the Introduction, Schaff makes the basic point that the renewed interest in the church in the present day, the so called "church question," has led to a great interest in church history, and that American Protestantism with its sectarian nature naturally suffers from a lack of interest in this history. He then heads into Section I, a discussion of recent German church historiography. This is arranged primarily topically and exists chiefly to impress Americans with the sheer volume of recent writing and to urge them to take up and read. While this appears to be a portion of the book that Schaff added after the classroom lecture, it is important to remember the German-language environment of Mercersburg seminary where this book was birthed. Schaff gives little attention to whether works have been published in English or not, or more precisely he is interested in works *not* yet published in English. Little or no adjustments were made for this fact in the original translation.

In Schaff's early career in America, part of his mission was as an apostle of German learning and a nurturer of German-language intellectual culture in America. He would lecture in German, publish in German, especially through the *Kirchenfreund*, and celebrate German culture. He also is at pains to show that while some German philosophy is correctly denounced for its infidelity, there is also another part of German thought which is the answer to this. Germans, he insisted, are at all times given to ideas, and to systematic, or "scientific" statements of them. Given his dialectical vision of history and culture it is because of the power of German science that both the greatest infidelity and the greatest theology arises. One should not be expected to exist without the other. At the conclusion of the introduction, Schaff evokes the truly

5. For Nevin as translator of *What is Church History?* see David Schaff, *Life of Phillip Schaff*, 140. Edward D. Yeomans translated *History of the Apostolic Church*. Schaff, *History of the Apostolic Church*, iv-v.

6. Hodge, review of *What is Church History?*, 106.

7. See p. 236 in this volume.

scientific framework where the organic development of ideas is featured, not the passions of the human heart, nor the mere mechanical recitation of facts.

In Section II, which is the heart of Schaff's essay, he takes up the development of the idea of church history as a dialectical historical process involving a number of successive stages. He refers to these stages either as "stand-points" or, in Latin, as *stadia* (sing. *stadium*). Schaff begins this section with a discussion of the church. This he understands to be the body of Christ, his ongoing presence in the world through an organic unity of different individuals. He defends this proposition biblically, and insists that without this perspective histories of the church do not supply the deepest theological wants of Christians. In defining the church as an organic unity in Christ, Schaff appeals to humanity's organic unity, stemming from its head in Adam. The importance of this becomes more evident as he parses the meaning of history, which is likewise the history of humanity as a living organism. Thus the history of the church is not just a narrative about an institution, but the story of God's ongoing work of redemption, or more precisely sanctification. The history of the church is, for Schaff, God's story of the development of his kingdom.

The rest of Section II is divided into three unequal sections. The first discusses the orthodox historiography which was written from the perspective of faith, but which denied change and development except as departure from orthodoxy. The second discusses rationalistic historiography which recognized change, but lacked faith. Within this section, Schaff also discusses the transition out of this stage as figures such as Herder introduced the principle of organic development and historians such as Neander united this with faith. The third section, on modern historiography, does not discuss historians and their work, but instead lays out the characteristics of a faithful, organic, churchly vision of church history. Since Schaff regards Neander lacking in churchly feeling, he does not find this perspective perfectly displayed in any general account of church history.

In treating the orthodox historiography, Schaff considers first Roman Catholic and then Protestant viewpoints. With regard to Roman Catholics, he notes chiefly the various ways by which Roman Catholic historians have denied the change that he sees so evident in their tradition and the fact that they have simply seen other movements as schismatic or heretical, not a proper part of church history. Given the general protest against *Principle of Protestantism* for being too Catholic, this section is most interesting for the clear line Schaff reveals between his own developmental position and the static conception of the church in Catholic historiography. At the end of this section, Schaff devotes a long footnote to the newly published work of John Henry Newman, *An Essay on the Development of Christian Doctrine.* Here he argues that Newman's position is unlikely to be accepted by the Catholic Church, and also emphasizes the "broad differences" with his own position in that Newman sees development only in the Roman Catholic direction and generally seeks to minimize change over time.

With regard to the historiographic model of the older Protestant orthodoxy, Schaff faults it chiefly for failing to recognize change and for unhistorically seeking to show that minority medieval movements, such as the followers of Jan Hus and John Wickliffe, agreed with later Protestant orthodoxy. Toward the end of this section, he maintains that Protestants distort the early church in not seeing medieval Catholicism as the regular development of it.The key patristic ideas, he insists, all lead to medieval Catholicism. He also notes that even Protestants had to recognize some of the achievements of the medieval church in the place of piety and theology. As a transition out of the period of Protestant Orthodoxy, Schaff notes the "*supranaturalistic* style of Church History" which he associated with figures such as Johann von Mosheim. He terms this school "supranaturalistic" because it is willing to disassociate the unchanging truth from any historic institution, maintaining it as a supernatural idea. This leads to a more tolerant attitude toward sects and minority movements. Schaff sees this as a strength, but the abstraction introduced by this disassociation of the Christian ideal from historical reality leads this school to an "unchurchly" character that is only increased by the next stage in the development of unchurchly historiography.

Turning toward Schaff's discussion of the rationalistic method, readers should discern Schaff's discontent with the older scholastic Protestant theology. Its conception of unchanging doctrine forced historians, such as Johann Semler, toward a position of skepticism, if not toward the faith itself, at least toward the seemingly less-rational accomplishments of earlier time—such as creeds and confessions. This awareness of the changing nature of doctrine is one the most distinctively modernist aspects of Schaff's thought. He is critical of the very conception of early modern orthodoxy.

In the second half of Schaff's section on the "Rationalistic Method," he turns toward criticism of it and the growth of the stand-point of organic development. He credits Johann Herder with introducing the principle of organic historical development to German intellectual life. He then considers the contributions of Friedrich von Schelling, G. W. F. Hegel, F. C. Baur, David Strauss, Friederich Schleiermacher, and August Neander to a conception of the proper, organic view of church history. Schaff is not wholly content with the philosophies of history of any of these men. Certainly Baur and Strauss receive the most negative evaluation. In general, Schaff is very given to Hegel's conception of history, but finds that it does not give enough place to God, or to the individual. Here he shares Søren Kierkegaard's future critique of Hegel's "System." Neander fares the best because he gives a broader place to organic development and recognizes the qualities of individuals and their importance from a variety of Christian backgrounds. Schaff, however, faults him for insufficient attention to the church as an organism, Neander's view of Christianity tends to be too exclusively spiritual for Schaff.[8]

8. Schaff is much more detailed in his evaluation of all of these historians in his "General Introduction." This is particularly the case with Neander. He was willing to be more critical of him after

The section entitled "Modern Historiography" is the essay's most important. Here Schaff embraces the three-fold Hegelian concept expressed through the German verb *aufheben*, in which an earlier standpoint is at once abolished, conserved, and raised to a new standpoint. Accordingly each phase of church history, and each sect, is necessary and plays an important role in the advancement of the church. He articulates the characteristics of an organic development of church history in a numbered series of eleven points.

The most important claim here is that while the essence of the church, its germ or seed, is set for all time in the revelation of Jesus Christ, what the true church is at any point of time, and what it is at the completion of Christ's work of sanctification, is the result of a process of organic development. His view of this process is strongly Hegelian. It proceeds through dialectical opposites as one position emerges and then provokes an antithesis resulting in restoration, revolution, or reformation. Disease, distortion, error are a natural part of the development of the life of the church and these negative conditions are necessary for the progress of the church. These exist as part of the life of the church as surely as sin does, and they must be overcome as part of Christ's work of sanctification leading to the millennium. As history progresses, it is not that disease and error will fade away—on the contrary they will grow stronger—but so will the truth as the means to combat it. The truth, Schaff insists, is always to be found in the middle, in the mainstream. Schaff's vision of the church is a synthesis of the dialectical vision of history he learned from Baur, the mystical connection between the church and Christ he learned from Ludwig von Gerlach, and the emphasis on the contribution of the individual from his Pietist background and Neander's historiography.[9]

He closes this section with a triumphant passage. The eleventh point in a series of twelve affirms that the development of the Church is from "east to west;" thus Schaff assumes that the next great stage of the development for the church will take place in America, and then proceed to China, India, and the Holy Land to complete its course in time for the millennium. Schaff sees himself in a historical moment, the birth throes of a new creation in which rationalism is being corrected by a new church feeling and America is emerging as the place where all the divisions of Protestantism along with Catholicism are present so that synthesis can be achieved.

Schaff closes this essay with a discussion of five practical results of this proper understanding of church history. First, the knowledge that history is the working out of God's plan makes the subject interesting because it is inspiring and almost revelatory to see how God has worked in the past, it also provides both satisfaction and comfort that God is active in the world. It makes our own life appear significant, because it is part of God's plan. Lastly, it leads one above party spirit to universal sympathy and

---

Neander had died and Schaff had published the first portion of his own church history. Schaff, *History of the Apostolic Church*, 95–107.

9. Penzel, *German Education*, 109–16.

encourages movement toward Church unity as an organic process, not something to be created by one person.

Reception of the Book

As an elaboration of some themes first sounded in *Principle of Protestantism*, this book did not generate the same degree of controversy. The Classis of Philadelphia, smarting from the defeat of their heresy charges against *Principle of Protestantism*, did include it in a new set of heresy charges against Schaff, resulting in what he later termed his second trial for heresy. George Shriver has observed that this may be the only time in American religious history that "a strictly historiographical volume has been attacked for heresy."[10] But as we have seen, this book was far from strictly historiographical. The key charge against this volume was that he treated the Roman Catholic Church as part of the mainstream of Christian history. The complaints against *What is Church History?*, however, were not even considered by the 1846 synod meeting at Carlisle, Pennsylvania; instead attention focused on Schaff's view of the middle state, that is whether the unredeemed dead could still be saved. These charges were discussed without a formal trial and dismissed.[11]

In his review of *What is Church History?*, Charles Hodge took the opportunity to celebrate the substantial accomplishments of German historiography in the history of doctrine, even while attacking German philosophy. He also noted the similarity in perspective and substance between Schaff's book and Kliefoth's series of articles on the modern historiography of German Protestantism in the early 1845 issues of *Allgemeines Repertorium*.[12] Hodge seemed to some readers to have charged Schaff with plagiarism. That was not Hodge's intention and upon learning that Schaff had not read Kliefoth's *Dogmengeschichte* nor any but his first article in the *Repertorium*, he published a correction stating that he should have avoided "that ambiguity of language" which left "this unpleasant imputation on a writer."[13] In his review, Hodge dissented from Schaff's embrace of botanical images for the idea of historical development and engaged little with the ecclesiology that is at the heart of Schaff's essay. Instead he simply affirmed the work of historiography itself, commending the importance of historical research to the end that like Matthew's "scribe instructed unto the kingdom of heaven" they would "bringeth forth out of his treasure things new and old" [Matt 13:52][14]

10. Shriver, "Philip Schaff (1819–1893)," 331.

11. Ibid., 333–34.

12. Klieforth, "Die neuere Kirchengeschichtschreibung".

13. [Hodge], "Short Notices," 317; Hodge, review of *What is Church History?*, 103–4; Kliefoth, *Einleitung in Die Dogmengeschichte* (Introduction to the history of dogma).

14. Hodge, review of *What is Church History?*, 106–13.

Because of the general neglect of the book in the press, George D. Wolfe's review in the *Mercersburg Review* largely consisted of extracts as he sought to bring the book before a larger public.[15] As David Layman has noted, Nevin's embrace of Schaff's notion of development was at first enthusiastic, but by 1852 cautious. By 1870, he had abandoned it.[16] While Schaff did not treat it as extensively in his later writings, the developmental understanding of the church he defends here is the animating principle of his career, and arguably of the Mercersburg theology as it sought to lead the effort to reveal the unity of the church in evangelical catholicism.

15. Wolfe, review of *What is Church History?*, 122.

16. Layman, general introduction to Nevin, Schaff, and Gerhart, *Born of Water and the Spirit*, 23–24, 31.

Title Page of 1846

WHAT IS CHURCH HISTORY?

A

VINDICATION

OF THE IDEA OF

HISTORICAL DEVELOPMENT.

By
PHILIP SCHAF.

Translated from the German.

Philadelphia:
J. B. Lippincott and Co.,
1846.

Original Table of Contents
(from 1846 edition)

Preface

The essay which is here presented to the theological public has grown out of an introductory address delivered at the opening of my lectures on church history, last fall, in the seminary with which it is my privilege to be connected as an instructor. From various quarters, a wish has been repeatedly expressed, to have the discourse more extensively made known in a printed form. In complying with this request, it has seemed to me proper and necessary to enlarge it, and to throw it also in some measure into a new shape; so that the address has become a tract.

An exposition of the true nature of church history is undoubtedly needed among us at this time; and might be expected, if at all successful, to be attended with no small practical benefit. There is reason to apprehend, that very few of our theologians in this country have any thing like a thorough acquaintance with the history of the church, through all its periods. It is too common to rest satisfied with that part of it which each one may find to be of immediate practical concern in his own case. The late convert to Popery, Mr. Newman, who must be allowed at least to possess some amount of learning, openly acknowledges the great ignorance that prevails in England in relation to the church history in particular of the middle ages; "Our popular religion," he tells us,

> scarcely recognises the fact of the twelve long ages which lie between the councils of Nicaea and Trent, except as affording one or two passages to illustrate its wild interpretations of certain prophecies of St. Paul and St. John. It is melancholy to say it, but the chief, perhaps the only English writer, who has any claim to be considered an ecclesiastical historian is the infidel Gibbon.[1]

The same may be affirmed of course with equal or with still greater right, of our America. As a general thing, we are too much taken up with the present to trouble ourselves much about the past. Our religious relations and views are pervaded with the spirit of Puritanism, which is unhistorical in its very constitution, and with which, in fact, a

1. An Essay on the Development of Christian Doctrine, by John Henry Newman, New York, Appleton, Introd., p. 14. [John Henry Newman, *An Essay on the Development of Christian Doctrine*, 6th ed. (Notre Dame, IN: University of Notre Dame Press, 1989), 8. Newman, a leader of the Oxford Movement within the Church of England published this book shortly after he was received into the Roman Catholic Church in 1845. Schaff discusses him at length below.]

low esteem for history and tradition has itself stiffened long since into as tyrannical a tradition as is to be met with in any other quarter.

The dry, lifeless style too, in which the study of Church History is conducted in our theological seminaries, must necessarily tend to destroy all satisfaction or interest in its pursuit. MOSHEIM still holds his place as the infallible authority though German diligence and learning have long since left him far in the rear. History is still regarded and treated as a mere conglomeration of notices, more or less interesting, thrown together in a perfectly outward way. The body, the outward appearance simply, is considered to be enough. That which constitutes the main thing in history, the ideas which rule it and reveal themselves in the process, imparting to it its only true significance and importance, are too generally disregarded altogether. The conception of an organic development is wanting almost entirely; and yet without this it is not possible ever to come to any right understanding, especially of the history of the church.

This defect in our theology carries with it the most unhappy consequences for our church life, and works powerfully in favour of that ever extending curse of sectarianism under which it has come so deplorably to labour. How shall we labour with any effect to build up the Church, if we have no thorough knowledge of her history, or fail to apprehend it from the proper point of observation? History is, and must ever continue to be, next to God's word, the richest fountain of wisdom, and the surest guide to all successful practical activity. To reject her voice is to rob ourselves of our own right to exist, or, at least, to condemn our own life; since we owe to her, in fact, whether we choose to do so or not, all that we are and all that we can become.

Beyond all question the German theology stands here vastly in advance of the American; and it has seemed to be a matter of some account accordingly, to direct the attention of the inquiring and studious, as I have attempted to do in the first part of my essay, to the mighty achievements in Church History which have taken place latterly in this quarter, the more especially as they are as yet so little known, and the whole subject is so much exposed to all sorts of prejudice and misrepresentation. Even NEWMAN shows a wretched want of acquaintance with the better productions of modern German historical inquiry, when he allows himself as he does to involve the whole in a summary charge of unbelief.[2]

If I might only succeed in placing the historical theology of my native land in a more favourable light, and in recommending it to more earnest study, I should feel that an important purpose had been served by the present publication.

2. He goes on, namely, in the passage of which a part has already been quoted, to say: "German Protestantism on the other hand has been of a bolder character; it has calmly faced and carefully surveyed the Christianity of eighteen hundred years, and it frankly avows that it is a mere religion of man, and the accident of a period. It considers it a syncretism of various opinions springing up in time and place, and forming such combinations one with another as their respective characters admitted; it considers it as the religion of the childhood of the human mind, and curious to the philosopher as a phenomenon." [Newman, *Development of Christian Doctrine* (1846), 8. This passage does not appear the revised edition of 1878 used in recent reprints.]

I must add here one other remark. The essay is designed only for readers who have some theological culture and an inquiring spirit. This is implied in the very nature of the case; and I should not think it necessary to make the remark, were it not for the experience I have had in the case of my small work on the *Principle of Protestantism*. We live indeed in a glorious land of liberty and equality. But still this can by no means justify the presumption, with which it is often pretended in this country, in offhand newspaper articles, to pronounce judgment on scientific works, which the self-constituted critics show themselves, by their own enormous superficiality and poverty of mind, utterly disqualified for understanding. There are subjects in theology, which the unscientific divine even, has no right to meddle with in this way. Let all things be tried indeed, in order that we may hold fast that which is good; but let it not be, in such a case, at the bar of the common understanding, where empty self-conceit may feel itself authorized to pass off its smattering of knowledge for true learning, and affect to proscribe as heretical all that may not happen to fit the measure of its own contractedness, with an intolerance equal to any ever exhibited by popery in its darkest period. I ask for readers, at home in some measure in the subject, loving the truth and free from prejudice, who may be willing, to take the trouble of *studying* a book *through*, before they seat themselves on the critic's chair. This methinks is a demand which does no wrong to our republican constitution. The theme on which I have chosen to write is very difficult; and, in spite of all the pains I have taken to treat it in a clear as well as thorough way, it is quite likely that I shall again be subjected to frequent misunderstanding. Even the great Melancthon found occasion, from his own painful experience for the remark: *Nihil tam simpliciter, tam plane dictum est, unde acuti homines non possint, velut ex eadem cera, mille formas ducere.*[3] Still, however, truth cannot fail in the end to work itself into view from the midst of all perversions, whether well intentioned or malicious; and a storm of opposition even has this good effect among others, that the chaff at times, from which the present tract is by no means supposed to be free, is blown away by its means.

May the small publication contribute something at least, under the blessing of the Lord, towards the resolution of one of the most weighty theological questions; and serve especially to encourage and assist my pupils, to whom it is dedicated with heartfelt love, in the prosecution of their studies already commenced in the department of Church History!

The Author
Mercersburg, April, 1846

3. [Trans. "Nothing is so simply, so clearly said that clever men cannot make it mean a thousand different things." Melanchthon to Albert, archbishop of Mainz, September 1532.]

Introduction

The great central theme of the Present, around which all religious and theological movements revolves, is the *Church Question.* This is admitted by the most intelligent and learned men of the age, in the old world as well as in the new. No one can deny it without showing, either that he is destitute of the gift of historical observation or that he trembles for the existence of his own unchurchly position, and would fain quiet his well grounded fear by a self-illusion.[1]

In proportion, however, as the Church is thus brought into prominent and principal view, her *History* must also become for theologians an object of attention and inquiry. Church and History altogether, since the introduction of Christianity, are so closely united, that respect and love towards the first may be said to be essentially the same with a proper sense of what is comprised in the other. The Christian Church is itself the greatest fact in the history of the world, by which the ancient order of life both Jewish and Heathen has been overturned, and the way opened for a new course of existence altogether. It has formed, for eighteen hundred years past, the main stream of the world's history. Almost nothing has since occurred that can be counted great and important, which is not found to stand in nearer or more remote, friendly or hostile, connexion with the Church, and to acquire its true historical significance precisely from this relation. History, on the other hand, is the bearer of the Church;

1. [The "church question" refers to a variety of questions concerning the nature of the church and its relationship to the individual, society, and the state. During Schaff's two years in Berlin (1842–44) he was introduced to the "church question" as a central issue for German Protestantism. The reasons for this new attention to the church were several. Romantic thought directed new attention to the organic and collective nature of human existence. The end of the Napoleonic wars led to the political reorganization of several German states and with it their territorial churches. In Prussia to mark the tercentenary of Luther's Reformation, King Friedrich Wilhelm III had mandated the union of Lutheran and Reformed churches in his kingdom. His policy was imitated in many other states as well. At the same time, there was a resurgence of Lutheran confessionalism in opposition to both rationalism and this ecumenical union. Subsequent royal reforms of the church deepened the intensity of the question. The fact that a somewhat similar combination of forces motivated the Oxford Movement makes Schaff's sweeping statement about the "church question" more plausible even in American setting. Still the phrase was not a common one in American Protestantism. It is important to bear in mind, however, that his first audience were German Reformed seminarians in America. Penzel, *German Education*, 90–97.]

by whose means this last is made to possess a real existence, whereas, under any other form it could be nothing better than a baseless, fantastic abstraction, which for us who are ourselves the product of history, and draw from it all the vigour of our lives, would have no meaning or value whatever.

Whether we look then to the present or the past, we shall find always that true churchmen are ever characterized by their respect for history and a due regard to its authority; while the unchurchly sectarian and rationalist, in their contracted subjectivity, look down with contempt on all that has been wrought out by an earlier time, and make no conscience of profanely dashing it to pieces, as soon as it is found unsuitable to the purposes of their own small trade. The whole destructional process to which the Church has been subjected by Rationalism and Sectarianism, particularly since the beginning of the last century, the classical period of political and religious revolutions, is found joined with the overthrow of all previous History at the same time. So, on the other hand, the glorious work of building up the Church, to which the noblest and best powers of our own age are coming to be more and more devoted, stands strikingly associated with a disposition fondly to look after and collect the treasures of past centuries. Interest in the Church and a true reverential regard for History, every where and at all times go hand and hand together.

Hence it appears how important it is, in our time especially, to come to a right conception of Church History. It is proposed to contribute something if possible towards this object in the present essay, with a view of recommending the study in a thorough way. We will, in the *first* place, cast a glance over the latest achievements of German theology in this sphere. This will serve to confirm what has been already said of the close connexion of the church tendency with historical studies, and may perhaps help to open the eyes of some to the wealth and value of the literature of Germany. In the *next* place, we will endeavour to develop more particularly the modem conception of Church History, as it lies at the ground of the literature to be noticed in the first section. This is the most important part of our task, to which consequently the most room must be allowed. *Finally*, we propose to bring into view the practical bearings of the whole subject on church life and church action.

Section I

Survey of the More Important Recent Performances of German Theology in the Department of Church History

In all the deeper movements of the world of mind, Germany for three hundred years past has taken and led the way for other nations. She is the land that gave birth to those world-embracing ideas, which introduced the Protestant period of the Church, and have wrought such mighty changes in State, Science and Art, and the entire social life of the modern world. In the Reformation, she set in motion the whole course of Protestant history, as it has developed itself from that time to the present. But as Rome was twice the centre of the world's life, while the sword of the Capitol, transplanted with broken point to the dome of St. Peter, ruled western Christendom for a full thousand years; so Germany would appear to be called also to act the second time a world-historical part, in the fact that the spirit of the Reformation, resuscitated under a new form, is just at this time actively engaged on all sides with the work of a vast revolution in theology and the church; a revolution, whose power may be expected in the end to rule the life of the world, as before, for whole centuries to come.

No reference is had here to the so called "German Catholic movement" which the Protestant religious press of this country with a most marvellous want of critical discernment has already trumpeted as a second Reformation.[1] We will not deny that this movement is one of more than common interest, and that it may serve to open the way, in the character of a mere negative condition, to important results. But in itself considered, it is by no means promising. Thus far, in the form it carries at least as connected with the person of Ronge, it has shown itself to be idea-less, destructive

1. [Where, in *Principle of Protestantism*, Schaff had expressed hope for a reformation within the Catholic church, Nevin had inserted a note in 1845 expressing cautious optimism that the German Catholic movement led by Johannes Ronge would provide this reformation. See p. 188 in this volume. As noted there, the movement began at Schneidemühl in 1844 and the German Catholic Church was organized with fifteen congregations in March 1845. It grew quickly and by 1847 boasted 259 congregations. In 1850, most congregations merged with the *Lichtfreunde* ("Friends of the Light"), a similar, liberal rationalist movement emerging a few years earlier from Protestantism, to form the Religious Society of Free Congregations (*Religionsgesellschaft freier Gemeinden*). The society gradually declined throughout the nineteenth century.]

and rationalistic; to be regarded as a catholic counterpart to the noise of the Protestant "*Friends of Light*" as they call themselves, the last straggling remnant of the old Rationalism, instead of being associated in any way with the faith and power of the Reformation. Germany has minds of immeasurably greater depth than any that are connected with this new Catholic movement, although they make immeasurably less noise on the market place of public life. We have here in our eye rather the exploits, as they may be styled, of the later *Protestant Theology* of Germany. These must make their way in time over the whole cultivated world, and exert a mighty influence on the form and shape that shall be given hereafter to church relations.

Those who measure the importance of all things by their immediately apparent outward consequences, and in whose view nothing is counted eventful but what fills the general popular consciousness with its sound, will be ready, no doubt, to smile at this declaration. Such, however, would do well to consider how they are to get along with Christianity itself, which was present in history as the great regenerating principle of dying humanity, working silently but powerfully like leaven, long before the central power of the world as it then stood so much as thought of bestowing upon it the least notice. It has always been peculiar to truly world-historical principles, that they have in the first place dwelt retired in the secret chamber of earnest and profound thought, working from within from the hidden birth-place of spiritual life, and only after reaching a certain measure of ripeness in this way, have begun to exert a new organizing power on the theatre of the public world. So it must ever hold. Not outward power, not superficial talk, not the off-hand oracles of the common popular press, but *ideas* only (that is actual single emanations from the primal Truth, which is God himself) rule in the last instance the History of the World. Shame on the man who dare deny it, and still hold himself for a Christian, that is a believer in an all-comprehending providence. True, ideas may be obstructed and restrained in every sort of way by rude force. But it is equally certain that the truth at the last will rise again, purified and victorious through martyrdom itself, no more to die, but to see even her bitter foes prostrate at her feet.

From this point of view, our high expectations of the weighty results of German Evangelical Theology and German Philosophy ought not to be considered fanciful. No one who is thoroughly acquainted with the extended exegetical, critical and historical inquiries, as well as with the philosophical and dogmatic struggles of the last twenty or thirty years (reaching as they do, to the inmost ground of all things), can possibly yield to the discouraging thought, that such an extraordinary mass of acuteness, intellect and learning should have been all to no purpose; that the sore spiritual toil of the most gifted and most excellent men of the age should have been absolutely thrown away. It is true that the German theology, in the last century, became more estranged from its proper life-element of religion and the Church, than was the case in other lands. Whilst the Deism of England and the Naturalism of France failed to rise in general above the lowest and most shallow popular free-thinking, the unbelief of Germany formed itself into a scientific system, fortified with a fearful bulwark of learning and philosophy, which became thus immensely more difficult to overcome than in the other case. The German takes so deep an interest in science and religion as such, and is possessed at the same time of such inexhaustible energy and perseverance of mind, that this character proclaims itself even under a false, perverse tendency, and he cannot rest till he has pushed a principle out to its most extreme consequences. But for this very reason again he alone could produce a *scientific* remedy for the disease in question. A large shadow indicates always the presence of a large body. The process could not stop of course content with rationalism. For the Church of God must bid defiance even to the gates of hell. There arose accordingly with the beginning of the present century, and more particularly since the Jubilee of the Reformation, celebrated in the year 1817, in connexion with the false theology of Rationalism, in its different forms, still retaining some portion of its old life, a powerful reaction, which with the keen weapons of the latest scientific cultivation, and the force of a newly resuscitated religious feeling carried breach after breach into the system of unbelief and began once more to build up again the ancient faith with the most diligent zeal. This, however, is not a direct unconditioned return to the earlier stand-point of church theology, over against which rationalism must be allowed to have a certain kind of right; but a living reproduction rather and for this very reason at the same time an advance. The pure negation of a particular tendency, is never a true victory over it. Only such an opposition can be so considered, which recognises also and saves the element of truth in which the tendency has its life. Thus Christ abolished the law, not by destroying but fulfilling it. So in the case before us, Rationalism was not to be simply ignored, but in the hand of that Providence which allows nothing to take place in vain, must serve the purpose of bringing to a new form the old, which in its contracted sphere (that of the mere understanding), it had profanely demolished; by which means this might come to a more free activity and full development, and satisfy also what may be called the want that lies at the ground of all rationalism; this, namely, that religious truth shall not be confronted with the subjective spirit in the form of mere outward authority, but become fully reconciled to it in an inward way in the form of conviction and certainty.

Since the different branches of theology form an organic whole, through which streams always one and the same blood, this new spirit must of course make itself felt on all these branches. The Exegesis of the Old and New Testaments, with its various forms of preparatory discipline, Introduction, Archaeology, Hermeneutics and Criticism, has gone forward with huge strides, and seeks now in connexion with religious church interests to satisfy at the same time the requisitions of grammatical and historical knowledge, so one-sidedly regarded by Rationalism, and thus to place the practical object also on a more solid scientific basis. Systematic and Philosophical Theology, including Apologetik, Symbolik, Dogmatik and Ethics, has been raised mainly through the influence of the school of Schleiermacher and that of Schelling and Hegel, into a higher *stadium* ["stage"] of development, in which the speculative spirit struggles to grasp the contents of faith at every point as identical at the same time with the absolute reason. Of the practical disciplines, Homiletics, Liturgik and Church Polity, have been most particularly influenced by this new spirit.

The greatest activity, however, has been expended on Historical Theology, with which alone we are here immediately concerned. The ground of this has been already mentioned. Theology proceeds ever hand in hand with church life. In the classic period of the Greek Church, the great object was to fix in the way of creed the ground doctrines of Christianity, in opposition to the Judaizing and paganizing errors which might be said to reflect the outward persecutions of the church on the part of the State. Hence this period was mainly dogmatic, and the pride of the Greek Church was to be known as orthodox. In the age of the Reformation, the return of the religious spirit to the sacred scriptures, in the way of protest against the authority of tradition which had come to be a fetter upon all free thought, imposed on theologians the duty above all of cultivating biblical exegesis; which accordingly was prosecuted with wonderful interest and success, while historical and church theology fell into the shade. The theology of the Reformation was more exegetical than speculative. In *our* days, it is the growing significance of the Church, the interest which is coming to be taken more and more in the Body of Christ as a visible organization, which has called forth such a vast activity in Church History and its several connexions. True, there have been several separate causes which have been felt in the case; such as the jubilee of the Reformation, the "Union," the call for improvement in the psalmody and church service generally, Möhler's assault on Protestantism, the affair of Cologne, the Anglo-Germanic episcopate of Jerusalem, &.c.; but these all refer back continually to the deep and ultimate ground now mentioned, and are joined with it in the closest connexion.[2] The church-historical literature of Germany has produced, within the last thirty years, ten times as many volumes as the dogmatic. Winer, in the first supplement to his *Manual of Theological Literature*, which covers a period of only two years (1839–41) notices more than five hundred historical works.[3] If we subtract from this statement one-half, as being either insignificant or destitute of genuine historical

2. [Two of the events Schaff mentions here have been noted before, namely the three hundredth anniversary of the Reformation in 1817 and Friedrich Wilhelm III's formation of a union church in Prussia. The Roman Catholic theologian Johann Adam Möhler was most noted for emphasizing the church as a living body, rather than a static institution. Since this view was akin to that of Schaff and his mentors, the sharp line Möhler drew in *Symbolik* (1832), comparing Catholic and Protestant confessions, drew a vigorous response from Protestants. Similarly the decision of the Protestant rulers of Prussia to support the completion of the Catholic Cathedral in Cologne, and to create a joint Anglican-Prussian bishopric in Jerusalem generated considerable controversy. The bishopric was proposed in 1841 by Friedrich Wilhelm IV of Prussia. The compromises agreed upon to reconcile Anglican and Prussian church orders satisfied neither German Lutherans nor high-church Anglicans. Nevertheless, it functioned for several decades until a variety of disputes, including one over form of consecration of a new bishop, led the German emperor to abolish the agreement in 1886. Möhler, *Symbolism*; Jack, "No Heavenly Jerusalem."]

3. [Georg Benedikt Winer, *Handbuch Der Theologischen Literatur* (1842).]

character, there will still remain a very large number. Almost every theologian of any name has devoted a portion at least of his strength to some department of Church History. Besides this, however, it is found to receive the homage of all other departments, Exegesis, Introduction, Ethics, Practical Theology, in this respect at least; that for any work to be complete, it is felt necessary that it should, in the way of introduction, present a history of the subject with which it is employed, and have due regard moreover throughout to views different from its own. Let any one look into any of the later commentaries, by BLEEK, HARLESS, LÜCKE, THOLUCK, STEIGER, HENGSTENBERG, FRITZSCHE, RÜCKERT, or among dogmatic works into the systems of TWESTEN, NITZSCH, HASE, the monograph of JULIUS MÜLLER on Sin, &c., and he will soon learn how entirely the whole present theology is pervaded with historical material from beginning to end.[4]

It is now our business to take a general survey of the latest performances of German Theology in the sphere of Church History, and then to set forth their character. We must here distinguish between works that stretch themselves over the whole field, and monographs which devote themselves to particular persons, doctrines or events.

Prominent among the first class, laid out on a large plan, and not yet complete, are the works of NEANDER and GIESELER; both distinguished for their comprehensive and profound learning, but widely different in the spirit by which they are ruled.[5] Gieseler in his own theological views belongs rather to the rationalistic school. The main value of his work also consists not at all in the text; which is indeed concise and clear, but at the same time dry and without spirit. It lies in the full extracts from original sources that are presented in the way of notes. These are selections with great care, fine judgment, and impartial honesty; and make it possible for the reader who has no access to the sources, to construct a Church History for himself, at least in its leading features, as the truth may be felt to require. Neander on the other hand joins with the most thorough study of authorities, an uncommon religious amiability and goodness, and a peculiar method of grasping and setting forth his subject, that has won for him the honorable title "Father of Church History."[6] We will notice him more particularly hereafter.

4. [Schaff is referring to recent works by exegetes of a variety of persuasions and to theologians of the mediating school.]

5. [August Neander, *Allgemeine Geschichte der chirstlichen Religion und Kirche* (1825–52). The first portion appeared in English in 1831, with the English translation of the complete work published as *General History of the Christian Religion and Church*. Johann Karl Ludwig Giesler, *Lehrbuch der Kirchengeschichte* (1824–57). The first portion appeared in English in 1836, with the complete work published as *Text-Book of Church History*.]

6. An honor allowed him also by Merle D`Aubigne, in his *Disc. sur l'étude a'hist. du Christianisme et son utilite pour l'époque actuelle. Par. et Geneve, 1832. Dedication.* [Jean Henri Merle d'Aubigné, *Discours sur l'étude de l'histoire du Christianisme et son utilité pour l'époque Actuelle* (Paris: Risler, 1832), "dedication." An English translation of this work that includes the dedication to Neander lacks the honorary title. Merle d'Aubigné, *Discourse on the Study of the History of Christianism, and Its Usefulness at This Epoch: Delivered at Geneva, January 2, 1832* (1833).]

Of the other recent works covering the whole field of Church History, I will simply mention only the *Manual* of Engelhardt, in four volumes,[7] which may be recommended for its independent research; and the brief compend of Hase, already in its fourth edition;[8] the principal merits of which are lively representation, compact delineation and description, and a judicious regard to the history of Christian art—merits which only make it the more to be regretted, that the author, thus born to be a historian, should not be more deeply imbued with the element of positive faith and true spiritual earnestness.

We should have, however, a most inadequate conception of German diligence on this field, were we to judge of it solely from such general histories. A far greater activity is presented in the countless monographs, which accompany these works in a supplementary way, augment their material, and modify their method and plan. The general histories can notice particular personalities and tendencies, as they come forward, only as portions of a great whole; whereas the monographs give us a view of them from all sides, and introduce us into those retreats of private life, where the thoughts which have ruled the world were born and trained to maturity.

It would carry us much too far, to attempt here any thing like a full enumeration of the works that have appeared under this form recently in the different departments of Church History. The mere titles of books besides can be of no service. Here the word applies. *Come and see.* He who has come at all to know what these treasures are, must look down with pity on the noisy ignorance, which can allow itself—like the worthy editor of one of our most widely circulated religious journals lately—to deny to Germany a *living* theology; and what is still worse, is not ashamed to proclaim the poor, stale, reproductions of the worn out theology of New England, still appearing among us, as the culmination of modern science![9] A few hints on the direction which has been taken by this learned activity within the last twenty years, with some reference to its most prominent productions, will be sufficient for our present purpose.

The historical emulation of the German theologians has exhibited an admirable tact, in the choice of subjects. It has been directed mainly, for instance, to the creative epochs of the Church, and to those individuals in whom a whole age may be said to mirror itself, or rather to concentrate and corporealize its very life. Thus, accordingly, the Greek Church after the fifth century, when with its growing alienation from the

7. [Johann Georg Veit Engelhardt, *Handbuch der Kirchengeschichte* (Manual of church history, 1833).]

8. [Karl von Hase, *Kirchengeschichte* (1841).]

9. [Schaff is responding to the last of George Cheever's six critical editorials on *The Principle of Protestantism*, "German Theology—Science apart from Life," *New York Evangelist* 16 (October 16, 1845): 166. This editorial appeared about the time Schaff gave the lectures behind this book to his students at Mercersburg. The other editorials appeared in the *New York Evangelist* on August 28; September 4, 11, and 19; and October 9. In them, Cheever, a New Englander, indicted Schaff and Nevin for neglect of the primacy of the scriptures and the ongoing role of the Holy Spirit in interpreting them. He also asserted the worthiness of the Puritan tradition, particularly the works of Jonathan Edwards and the seventeenth-century English Puritan, John Howe.]

Western Church it began to retire always more and more from the theatre of world-history; and again the transition period in the Latin Church between Gregory the Great and Charlemagne; the dark tenth century on to the reformation by Hildebrand;[10] the scholastic period of the Protestant Church; and the time of dissolution embraced in the last century; have all been but little regarded in the way of historical research. Whereas, on the other hand, the age of the fathers, the brilliant period of the Romano-Germanic Catholicism, from the 12th to the 16th century, and the Reformation, have been illuminated, on all sides with the torch of investigation.

Almost all the more important Church fathers stand now embodied and living before our eyes. NEANDER here also takes the first rank by his monographs on Tertullian and Chrysostom.[11] With respect may be mentioned besides SEMISCH'S *Justin Martyr*,[12] the works of THOMASIUS and REDEPENNING on Origen,[13] MÖHLER'S *Athanasius the Great*,[14] ULLMANN'S *Gregory of Nyssa*,[15] KLOSE'S *Basil the Great*,[16] RETTBERG'S *Cyprian*,[17] and the still unfinished work of C. BINDERMANN on the most gifted and influential of all the fathers, Augustine.[18] Add the patristic biographies of BOHRINGER, also in progress.[19] The heretical tendencies of this period also have been handled with immense research, and an impartiality previously unknown; so that it is only now they are coming to be understood, in their true significance especially as concerned with the development of the orthodox theology. We barely specify here the works of NEANDER and BAUR on Gnosticism,[20] which the older historians were accustomed to regard generally as nothing better than the play of a brainless fancy. In the church polity of the first centuries, RICHARD ROTHE has furnished an admirable volume in his *Beginnings of the Christian Church* a work distinguished for the amazing

10. [Hildebrand, a monk of Cluny, led a major reform of the church both before and after he became Pope Gregory VII in 1073. He died in 1085.]

11. [Neander, *Antignostikus: Geist des Tertullianus und Einleitung in dessen Schriften* (Antignosticism: the spirit of Tertullian and an introduction to his writings, 1825); *Der heilige Johannes Chrysostomus* (1821).]

12. [Karl Gottlieb Semisch, *Justin der Märtyrer* (1840).]

13. [Gottfried Thomasius, *Origenes* (1837); Ernst Rudolf Redepenning, *Origenes* (1841).]

14. [Möhler, *Athanasius der Grosse* (1827).]

15. [Schaff identifies the wrong Cappadocian father. He means Carl Ullmann, *Gregorius von Nazianz* (Gregory Nazianzus, 1825).]

16. [Carl Rudolph Wilhelm Klose, *Ein Beitrag zur Kirchengeschichte: Basilius der Grosse* (A contribution to church history: Basil the great, 1835).]

17. [Friedrich Wilhelm Rettberg, *Thascius Cäcilius Cyprianus* (1831).]

18. [Carl Bindermann, *Der heilige Augustinus* (Saint Augustine), 3 vols. (1844–69).]

19. [Georg Friedrich Böhringer, *Die Kirche Christi und ihre Zeugen* (The church of Christ and its witnesses), 24 vols. (1842–58).]

20. [Neander, *Genetische Entwickelung der Vornehmsten Gnostischen Systeme* (Genetic development of the chief gnostic systems, 1818); Ferdinand Christian Baur, *Die Christliche Gnosis* (Christian gnosticism, 1835).]

subtlety of its combinations, often indeed carried too far and the learning which it brings to bear on the smallest particulars.[21]

Passing on to the bloom period of the Middle Ages, we find, first, the two most important of the popes honoured with special histories; Gregory VII by Voigt,[22] and particularly Innocent III by the late convert to the Roman Church, Hurter;[23] each monograph, written with devotion to its subject and the most comprehensive knowledge of facts, and made to include also the whole time to which it belongs. The theology of this period, under its twofold form of scholasticism and mysticism, related to each other like head and heart, could not of course escape the earnestness of German inquiry. F. R. Hasse's *Anselm of Canterbury* especially deserves notice; of which only the first part has yet made its appearance;[24] exhibiting, after a masterly introduction on the rise and progress of the monastic system, the rich life of the profound theologian and conscientious archbishop in the most attractive style, leaving far behind the previous works of Möhler and Frank.[25] On the schoolmen of the thirteenth century, those *Doctors irrefragabiles, seraphici et subtiles*,[26] who represent this tendency at its perfection, Alexander Hales, Thomas Aquinas, Bonaventura, and Duns Scotus, we have yet unfortunately no works answerable to the present state of science; but doubtless we shall not be left now to wait for them much longer. With fond and special partiality on the other hand, has the Mystic School of the middle ages been explored, the native growth of Germany, and the most active agent in preparing the way for the Reformation. Here above all are to be reckoned Neander's *Bernard of Clairvaux*,[27] Liebner's *Hugo St. Victor*,[28] Engelhardt's *Richard St. Victor and John Ruysbroek*,[29] C. Schmidt's *John Tauler*,[30] Martensen's *Master Eckart*.[31] Works on the principal forerunners of the Reformation, belonging to the fermentation period of the 15th century, are multiplying themselves yearly, Savonarola alone was a few years since made the subject of three different biographies at once, by Rudelbach, F. C. Meier,

21. [Richard Rothe, *Die Anfänge der Christlichen Kirche* (1837).]

22. [Johannes Voigt, *Hildebrand, Als Papst Gregorius der Siebente* (Hildebrand, as Pope Gregory VII, 1815).]

23. [Friedrich Emanuel von Hurter, *Geschichte Papst Innocenz des Dritten und seiner Zeitgenossen* (History of Pope Innocent III and his contemporaries), 4 vols. (1834–42).]

24. [Friedrich Rudolph Hasse, *Anselm von Canterbury* 2 vols. (1843–52).]

25. [Möhler's study of Anselm appeared in *Gesammelte Schriften und Aufsätze* (Collected writings and essays) (1839). It was published as a separate book in English, Möhler, *The Life of St. Anselm* (1842). Georg Friedrich Franck, *Anselm von Canterbury* (1842).]

26. [Schaff uses the traditional titles of these scholastic theologians. Alexander of Hales was styled *the irrefragable, or irrefutable, doctor, Bonaventure, the seraphic doctor, and Duns Scotus, the subtle doctor.]*

27. [Neander, *Der heilige Bernhard* (1813).]

28. [A. Liebner, *Hugo von St. Victor* (1832).]

29. [J. G. V. Engelhardt, *Richard von St. Victor und Johannes Ruysbroek* (1838).]

30. [Charles Schmidt, *Johannes Tauler von Strassburg* (1841).]

31. [H. Martensen, *Meister Eckart eine theologische Studie* (1842).]

and G. RAPP.[32] Of Erasmus we have a very clear portrait, by joining to his *Life* by AD. MÜLLER,[33] the admirable Review of ULLMANN in the *Studien and Kritiken* for 1829.[34] The last has exhibited besides, in clear order, all the different preparatory struggles which led the way to the great work of the 16th century, so far as Germany and the Netherlands are concerned, in his truly classic production, *The Reformers before the Reformation.*[35]

As for the glorious Reformation itself, the third centennial jubilee of 1817, formed naturally the most powerful inducement and stimulus to renewed inquiry into its history; calling forth as it did an affectionate yearning towards the pentecostal days of protestantism, and a desire for the restoration of the old faith; which CLAUS HARMS with his 95 memorable theses, dared at this time to drag from the rubbish in which it had become buried, in the face of all sorts of prevailing error and unbelief.[36] We have been furnished since that date accordingly with works of the highest value on the German and Swiss Reformation particularly by MARHEINECKE, RANKE more recently and HAGENBACH,[37] whose lectures are open to a wider public. Nor must we overlook AD. MENZEL's *History of the Germans*,[38] and the *Universal History* of LEO,[39] which notwithstanding their simply protestant stand-point, serve often to throw light also, on the opposite side of the great work and its consequences. FORSTEMANN, by the publication of his *Original Documents*,[40] HOTTINGER and VÖGELI by giving to the world H. BULLINGER's *History of the Reformation*,[41] BRETSCHNEIDER by his comprehensive *Corpus Reformatorum*,[42] have laid the student of history under special obliga-

32. [Hermann Rudelbach, *Heironymus Savonarola* (1835); Carolus Meier, *Girolamo Savonarola* (1844); Georg Rapp, *Die Erwecklichen Schriften des Martyrers Heironymus Savonarola* (The revivalist writings of the martyr Girolamo Savonarola) (1839).]

33. [Adolf Müller, *Leben des Erasmus von Rotterdam* (1828).]

34. [Carl Ullmann, review of *Leben des Erasmus von Rotterdam* by Adolf Müller, *Theologische Studien und Kritiken* (1829): 178–208.]

35. [Ullmann, *Reformatoren vor der Reformation* (1841). An English translation appeared in 1855.]

36. [Claus Harms (1778–1855), a German Lutheran pastor published Luther's *Ninety-Five Theses*, along with ninety-five theses of his own. Most of these were directed against rationalism. Harms, *Das sind die 95 Theses* (1817).]

37. [Philipp Marheinecke, *Geschichte der Deutschen Reformation* (1816). Unlike most of the works Schaff names, Leopold von Ranke, *Deutsche Geschichte im Zeitalter der Reformation* (1839) had been published in English in the United States at the time of Schaff's writing. Ranke, *History of the Reformation in Germany* (1844). K.R. Hagenbach, *Vorlesungen über Wesen und Geschichte der Reformation in Deutschland und der Schweiz* (1834).]

38. [Schaff intended to refer to Wolfgang Menzel the writer, not Adolf Menzel the painter. Menzel, *Geschichte der Deutschen*, 4th ed. (1843).]

39. [Heinrich Leo, *Lehrbuch der Universalgeschichte* (1835–44).]

40. [Karl Eduard Förstemann, *Neues Urkundenbuch zur Geschichte der evangelischen Kirchen-Reformation* (New documentary history of the Protestant church reformation) (1842).]

41. [Heinrich Bullinger, *Reformationsgeschichte*, ed. Johann Jakob Hottinger and H. H. Vögeli (1838–40).]

42. [The series *Corpus Reformatorum* included as vols. 1–28 Philip Melanchthon, *Phillipi*

tions. As a matter of course, the Reformers themselves have been subjected to the most full representation. So we have within the last few years, Henry's *Life of Calvin*,[43] Herzog's *Œcolampadius*,[44] Galle's *Characteristics of Melancthon*,[45] Baum's *Theodore Beza*,[46] all works, which as a rich collection of materials at least, though somewhat defective it may be in historical skill, must take an honourable rank in modern theological literature. It is to be lamented that, with all this activity the Reformation in France, the Netherlands, England, and Scotland, has been handled thus far in a most step-motherly way. It may be trusted however that Merle D'Aubigne, who belongs properly as a historian to the German school, will be able to fill up here many a chasm by his learned investigations, for which such special advantage is secured to him by the libraries of Geneva and Paris, and his personal acquaintance now, also, with England and Scotland.[47]

On the Protestantism of the 17th and 18th centuries, as before intimated, fewer works have appeared. Still we have some right excellent monographs on single prominent persons; as on Valentine Andreae and Spener by Hossbach,[48] on Paul Gerhardt, by Wildenhahn,[49] on A. H. Franke by Guericke,[50] on Zinzendorf by Varnhagen von Ense.[51] The English Revolution has been recently handled by Dahlmann,[52] though chiefly in a political point of view; the English deism thoroughly and completely by Lechler.[53] The present church state of England and Scotland, through the establishment of the Anglo-Prussian Episcopate, the Scotch Secession, and the mission of the Russian preachers in 1842, has been brought, by means of several valuable publications, much nearer to the Germans than before.[54] Among these may be mentioned in

Melanthonis Opera, ed. Karl Gottlieb Bretschneider (1834–60).]

43. [Paul Henry, *Das Leben Johann Calvins* (1835–44).]

44. [J. J. Herzog, *Das Leben Johannes Oekolampads* (1843).]

45. [Friedrich Galle, *Versuch einer Charakteristik Melanchthons* (Essay on Melanchton's characteristics, 1840).]

46. [G. Baum, *Theodor Beza* (1843).]

47. [Jean Henri Merle D'Aubigné published his first volume of Reformation history in French in 1835. Thirteen volumes appeared in two collections. English translations of his work were very popular.]

48. [Wilhelm Hossbach, *Johann Valentin Andreæ* (1819); *Philipp Jakob Spener* (1828).]

49. [August Wildenhahn, *Paul Gerhardt* (1845).]

50. [Heinrich Guericke, *August Herman Franke* (1827).]

51. [Karl August Varnhagen von Ense, *Leben des Grafen von Zinzendorf* (Life of Count von Zinzendorf, 1830).]

52. [F. C. Dahlmann, *Geschichte der englischen Revolution* (1844).]

53. [Gotthard Victor Lechler, *Geschichte des englishen Deismus* (1841).]

54. [The names "Gerlach, Sydow, Uhden" appear before "in 1842" in the original. This appears to be a printer's error representing perhaps a reference in Schaff's manuscript to Otto von Gerlach, et al. *Amtliche Berichte über die in neuerer Zeit in England erwachte Thätigkeit für die Vermehrung und Erweiterung der kirchlichen Anstalten* (Official reports on the recent revival of activity of England for the spread and expansion of church institutions, 1845) as well as the next three books mentioned.]

particular, *The State of the Anglican Church* by UHDEN; *Church Affairs in Great Britain* by SYDOW, the first volume of which contains a thorough view of the Secession in Scotland; and *The Church of Scotland* by SACK of Bonn. [55] For the post-reformation history of Romanism finally, a new sense also has been awakened, and a new field thrown open, especially by RANKE's *Popes of the 16th and 17th centuries*,[56] and H. REUCHLIN's *History of the Port Royal* and *Life of Pascal*.[57]

Along with historical persons and tendencies, the *doctrines* of the church are at this time also the object of special attention in the same way. Here again to works covering the whole field, such as those of MÜNSCHER, ENGELHARDT, BAUMGARTEN-CRUSIUS and HAGENBACH,[58] must be joined monographs that pursue a single dogma through the several stages of its development. In this line, the Hegelian school has undoubtedly done important service; proceeding as it does throughout, on the view that all spiritual life is a process, always carried forward with immanent necessity; the only basis on which there can be any true force in the idea of dogmatic history. BAUR of Tubingen has handled in this way the doctrine of the Atonement in one volume,[59] and the doctrine of the Trinity, together with that of the Incarnation, in three volumes of large size.[60] His splendid learning and boundless power of combination would be of more value for theology, if he were less enslaved to the Hegelian formalism; which finds no meaning in doctrines except in their scientific relations, and runs them out continually into more and more attenuated forms, till at last they are made to dissolve into sheer abstractions. Of a different character is DORNER's excellent *Christology*,[61] and the *History of the Doctrine of the Trinity* by G. A. MEIER,[62] which has only quite lately appeared. With the Hegelian theory of development, which needs essential

55. [Hermann F. Uhden, *Die Zustande der anglikanischen Kirche* (1843). Only one volume of Adolf Sydow's projected *Beiträge zur Charakteristik der kirchlichen Dinge in Grossbritannien* ever appeared. Sydow, *Die schottische Kirchenfrage* (1845). Karl Heinrich Sack, *Die Kirche von Schottland* (1844). Sack's book never appeared in English. The others did immediately. Uhden, *The Anglican Church in the Nineteenth Century* (1844); Sydow, *The Scottish Church Question* (1845).]

56. [Leopold von Ranke, *Die römischen Päpste* (1838–39) had also appeared in an American English edition as *The Ecclesiastical and Political History of the Popes of Rome during the 16th and 17th Centuries* (1841).]

57. [Reuchlin, *Geschichte von Port-Royal* (1839); *Pascal's Leben und der Geist seiner Schriften* (1840).]

58. [Wilhelm Münscher, *Lehrbuch der christlichen Dogmengeschichte* (1819) translated as *Elements of Dogmatic History* (1830); Engelhardt, *Dogmengeschichte* (1839); Ludwig Friedrich Otto Baumgarten-Crusius, *Lehrbuch der christlichen Dogmengeschichte* (1832); K R. Hagenbach, *Lehrbuch der Dogmengeschichte* (1840) translated as *Compendium of the History of Doctrines* (1846).]

59. [Ferdinand Christian Baur, *Die christliche Lehre von der Versöhnung* (The Christian doctrine of atonement, 1838).]

60. [Baur, *Die christliche Lehre von der Dreieinigkeit und Menschwerdung Gottes* (The Christian doctrine of the trinity and incarnation), 3 vols. (1841–43).]

61. [Isaac August Dorner, *Entwicklungsgeschichte der Lehre von der Person Christ* (History of the development of christology, 1839).]

62. [Georg August Meier, *Die Lehre von der Trinität in ihrer historischen Entwickelung* (1844).]

modification in various respects to satisfy the Christian consciousness, is found conjoined in these works a living sense of religion, and a true church spirit, which govern the scientific investigation at all points, and thus conduct it to much more satisfactory results, than any that are possible on mere Hegelian ground.

As before said, this survey is necessarily very incomplete. Several sections of historical theology, such as the history of missions, the history of worship, &c., I have left altogether untouched; nor has any notice been taken of the almost countless essays, many of them for the professional theologian invaluable, which have appeared simply in theological Journals, such as Ilgen's *Zeitschrift for Historical Theology*, and the *Studien und Kritiken* by Ullmann and Umbreit.[63] Enough has been said, however, to give some notion of the wonderful zeal, with which the German mind of the present day is exploring the gold and silver mines of the past. There are scribblers possibly in this country, where such a tendency prevails to look selfishly to the present, and to weigh all things by the standard of immediate utility, to whom all this may seem no better than labour thrown away, an occasion for ridicule rather than respect. We leave such to their humour; reminding them simply that the man who undertakes to work for the future without the knowledge of the past and constant regard to it, will build most certainly a castle in the air, which the lightest wind will be sufficient to blow down again—as many striking examples in our American Church life serve clearly to show.

When now we consider these performances only in an outward way, we must be struck immediately by the spirit of *catholicity* they display; which rising high above the interest of a mere party or confession, spreads itself out with almost equal love over all spheres of Church History, from the days of the apostles down to our own time, and recognises the traces of the divine Spirit, the footsteps of the Lord of the Church, in all climes and among all nations. History is no longer handled in that merely apologetic style, that requires it to lend itself as an instrument to the service of an established system, and to take always such cut and shape as this object may require. It presents itself to the inquiring mind as a region full of wealth and attraction that deserves to be explored for its own sake. It carries in itself such a weight of truth and experience, that it is only by means of it, in the first place, the subjective spirit can raise itself at all to an independent stand-point; and must have need, always afterwards also, to enlarge and correct its views from the lessons here exhibited, instead of making them bend to its own pleasure.

With this catholicity is joined of course an *impartiality* and *freedom from prejudice*, of which the merely apologetic style of history is not capable. This can see only light and truth on its own side; on the side of its opponent, darkness and falsehood. The truly catholic historian, on the other hand, has too exalted an idea of truth to think

63. [Christian Friedrich Illgen founded the *Zeitschrift für historische Theologie* in 1832. Carl Ullmann founded *Theologische Studien und Kritiken* in 1828. Frederich Wilhelm Umbreit joined him in editing it. It became a major organ of the mediating theology.]

of confining it to the narrow horizon of an individual or a party. He sees light and darkness every where distributed over the vast picture which he unrolls to our view, and measures every time and every character, not by a foreign standard, but by one that is drawn from its own nature and its own relations. Even heretical and schismatic tendencies are not set down by him as of purely arbitrary growth. He allows to them rather, so soon as they are found to have become, in fact, world-historical, by some determining influence on the course of the church, a certain sort of right, an element of truth and necessity, the traces of which are to be discerned in the development of the orthodox church itself. Aiming at truth only, he will not shrink from uttering censure, even where it falls upon himself and the stand-point of his own confession; and will be equally ready to speak well of an opposite interest, where the right may happen to be on its side. For this very reason, such impartiality is not to be confounded with mere indifferentism. This is absolutely unjustifiable, and disqualifies a man for writing history altogether. He that begins by holding all religions and confessions in like value, will soon end by holding them to be alike without any value. In opposition to such indifference, the true church historian must have a decided character and take a decided stand; but only for the truth, honouring this whenever and wherever it may come in his way.

A further peculiarity of the modern Church History discloses itself to us, on a close consideration of the foregoing literature, in the purely *scientific* spirit with which it is conducted. It is something more than an outward mechanical weaving together of facts and figures, without regard to the inward life, the proper world-pulse, so to speak, which alone gives meaning and worth to the whole. Happily, too, that poor pragmatism of the last century is surmounted, which had come in the end to make account only of subjective factors in history, the affections and passions, namely, of the human heart; and supposed itself to be on the inmost track of events, when it could refer them to motives and springs of this sort. Now, the historical material is taken as a fluid mass pervaded with spirit. Investigation is carried back to the most remote and scarcely perceptible beginnings of the object contemplated; which is then allowed to unfold itself from within according to the Law of its own nature and constitution, and to its proper maturity. The forms of the past are invoked from their graves, and made to walk and act before us in flesh and blood: events are reproduced, and all is brought in this way to put on the character of a true breathing life. And what is thus made to pass before our eyes is not the play of unmeaning blind forces. All is conducted by a higher spirit, which urges forward the wheel of history, turns even the passions and errors of men to its own service, and through all events bears the world on continually towards the glorious end established for it in the eternal counsel of God. Only in this way plainly can Church History come to its true interest and significance. Only in this way can it ever be rightly studied or fairly understood.

All this, and much that might be mentioned besides, in the character of the modern literature now under consideration, indicates that the whole theological stand-point of Church History has been changed. The science plainly has advanced to a new position. Into the nature of this, after the preliminary sketch just given, it is our business now more closely to inquire.

SECTION II
Development of the Idea of Church History

Christian Theology is the scientific knowledge of the Triune God, as he has revealed himself in Christ and still continues to manifest his presence in the church. This revelation is deposited for all times and for every people, pure and perfect, in the covenant records of our religion, the Old and New Testaments. Theology must begin then by being exegetical. *Exegesis,* or as it is sometimes styled *Biblical Literature*, may be called also *Fundamental Theology.* It has to do with the incipient form of Christianity, and comprehends the exposition of the sacred scriptures as a whole. Its way is prepared by the precursory studies, Biblical Hermeneutics, Criticism, Archaeology, and Introduction to the Old and New Testaments. It finds its natural conclusion in Biblical Theology, according to the technical sense of this term; that is, in the reduction of the collective results of exegesis to a connected, logically arranged system of Biblical history, doctrine and morality. This forms the natural starting point for the second great theological discipline. The revelation of the Triune God remains not bound in the mere letter of the Bible, but passes over continually more and more into the form of spirit and life, communicating itself like leaven to the mass of humanity, and gradually transforming it into its own image. This process from the close of the New Testament canon on to the present time, it is the business of *Historical Theology,* or *Church History,* faithfully to represent. It has respect throughout only to the past. Having reached the present, it makes room for *Systematic* or *Philosophical Theology;* to which must be reckoned particularly Dogmatik and Ethics, and as some will have it Apologetik also, and Polemik, and Statistik.[1] This unfolds for the understanding the present posture of the church, with her faith and life, and exhibits always her latest scientific self-consciousness, or in other words the religious spirit of the age. Here it is not enough to furnish an objective representation simply; as in the case of exegetical and historical theology; the subjective conviction, the entire religious faith and judgment of the theologian himself, and his church connexion, must come into

1. ["Statistik" refers to demographics and statistics that show the progress and state of church life. The collection of such data was part of governmental censuses in Germany and other lands in the nineteenth century.]

view. Systematic theology has no sooner come to exist, than it becomes itself again an object of historical theology; as the present is always falling over to the past. Out of the knowledge of the past and present, however, a church future also comes now into view. Hence a fourth discipline, in which theology as *Practical* has for its object the proper application of this knowledge to the further advancement of the church; so that what has been learned may be wrought again into new life. This is to be done, partly by the preaching of the gospel; partly by the religious instruction of the young; partly by the administration of the liturgical portions of divine worship, psalmody, prayer, confession and the sacraments; partly by the pastoral care strictly so called; and partly also by the conduct of ecclesiastical affairs on the part of those to whom this trust may belong. To these different methods of advancing and extending the life of the church, are found answering the particular branches of practical theology, Homiletik, Catechetik, Liturgik, Pastoral Care, and Church Government. Arrived at this point, the science has returned again to its beginning; since the main instrument of its practical activity in the church must be the same divine scriptures that form the object of exegetical inquiry at the start.

Thus have we assigned to Church History its proper organic place in the general system of theology. Admitting the superior importance of exegesis, it is found to be by far the most comprehensive of all theological studies. The birth-day of its subject, the Christian Church, on the first Pentecost (Acts ii. 1) forms its starting point; or if it be preferred, the incarnation itself so as to include the life of Jesus also in its range. The present, at any given time, constitutes its relative end. Its material, however, must go on to increase unceasingly, till all historical development shall come to a close with the end of the world or last judgment. Within these two poles, it comprehends all that can occur of any importance for the kingdom of God, whether of an internal or external character.

Before proceeding to a more particular exposition of the idea of Church History, it may be well to bestow a preliminary glance first upon the nature of the Church itself, and then upon history in general.

The Church, in its broad sense, and as manifested in the world, is composed of all who have been baptized into Christ, whether they be nominal Christians only or real. This, according to long traditional Protestant designation, is the *visible*, or, better, the *mixed* Church. In a narrower sense, however, and according to its inward and true character, the Church is the religious, spiritual and real communion of all true believers in Christ. This is the *invisible* or more correctly the *pure* Church; for it may also be seen and recognised in distinct expressions of life; only no one can know of particular individuals with absolute certainty, whether they are truly united to Christ or not. The visible Church is made up of different confessions, which in part hold a perfectly hostile relation to each other, as Catholics, Greeks, Protestants, &c. The invisible or true Church, on the other hand, is always one only; although her members are scattered in different sections of the visible Church. She is the truth, the pure substance, the quintessence as it were of all visible organizations. She exists thus, as long as she continues militant upon the earth, always within the visible Church;[2] is for this reason constantly associated with unworthy, openly unbelieving or hypocritical members; and cannot be delivered from this connexion before the end of the world. The two communions act together and influence each other continually; so that history must always keep both in view. Only an infallible man would be prepared to write the history of the pure Church; and even such a one must still have respect to the Church in a wider sense, to make his work a true and *faithful* life representation of its subject.

The true, pure, or invisible Church is made up of men and bears throughout a true human character. It is not, however, for this reason the product of men, but, as indicated even by its name,[3] stands before us as a purely supernatural organization. Viewed under this objective ideal aspect, it may be defined, according to its origin and end, as an institution established by God through Christ for the glory of his own name and the salvation of men. It is the bearer of all God's revelations, the channel of Christianity, the depository of all the life powers of the Redeemer, the habitation of the Holy Ghost. The apostle Paul styles it in several places the body of Jesus Christ, and calls believers the members of this body.[4] His meaning in this is, that Christ dwells in the Church as an organic unity of different personalities and powers, as the soul in the body; and that he acts through it as his organ, just as our soul by means of the body shows itself active and exerts an influence upon the world.

Paul's doctrine of the Church, in this view, rests on the supposition of the real presence of Christ with his people. This was promised to his disciples, and so to the Church which they represented, by the Lord himself. "Where two or three are gathered

2. Single instances of such as have died in faith before they could be baptized, and so received into the visible Church, as the thief upon the cross, are to be counted exceptions merely, that as such serve to establish the rule. The old Church maxim holds here: *Non defectus, sed contemptus sacramenti damnat.* [Trans. "Not the lack, but the contempt of the sacrament condemns."]

3. From κνριακον sc. δωμα or κνριακη sc. οικια. *Dominica*, as Basilica from βασιλενς, *Regia* from *rex*. In this etymology and that which follows, Schaff is showing that the German *Kirche*, the English "church," and related words in other languages, derive from titles for God. Specifically *Kirche* and "church," are from the Greek κνριακον, literally "Lord's," but Byzantine Greek used as a noun meaning "church building," as a shortened form of κυριακον δωμα ("the Lord's house"), or κυριακη, as a shortened form of κνριακη οικια ("the Lord's home"). He also mentions three words with similar origins that sometimes mean "church building," *dominica* from the Latin *dominius* ("Lord"), "basilica" from the Greek βασιλευς ("king") and *regia* from the Latin *rex* ("king").] The word has passed from the Greek, by means of the Gothic, into all the German dialects, the Swedish *Kyrka*, the Danish *Kyrke*, the English *Church*, &c. Others with less probability derive it from the old German *kisen* or *kieren*, in which case it would correspond with the Greek, εκκλησια, in the sense of the *called* or the *chosen* (of the Lord) *electa*. The name denotes sometimes the edifice, sometimes the assembled congregation, sometimes, as we take it here, the organic complex of all congregations. It involves always, however, a reference to the divine origin and divine intention of the Church. [Giesler, *Text-Book of Ecclesiastical History*, 1:1, provides a very similar, slightly more detailed, discussion and was probably Schaff's source. Etymologists continue to find the origin of the words for church in Germanic languages in the Greek for "lord" rather than for "called."]

4. Rom. xii. 5. 1. Cor. vi. 15; xii. 27. Ephes. iv. 12; v. 30. Coloss. i. 24.

together in my name, there am I in the midst of them" (Matt xvii. [xxviii] 20). "Lo, I am with you alway, even unto the end of the world" ([Matt] xxviii. 20). He says not simply, My Spirit, or My consolation, or My truth, is with you alway; but, *I*, that is, *my whole person, in which divinity and humanity are inseparably joined together.* We must admit then the presence of the Redeemer in the Church—invisible and supernatural of course, but none the less real and efficient on this account—in his whole undivided and indivisible glorified personality, with all the powers that belong to it, whether as human or divine.

But does not Christ then, since his ascension to heaven, sit at the right hand of God, from whence he shall come to judge the quick and the dead? Over against a rude contracted exegesis, which unhappily is too often to be met with still even on the part of educated theologians, especially on the sacramental question, it might be enough to answer simply, By all means! The right hand of God, however, is not bound to a particular place; and in any case is not to be taken literally, but denotes his Almighty power, as it upholds and fills the whole universe. When we pray to our Father in heaven, we do not hereby deny his presence upon the earth, nor conceive of him as in the strict sense seated upon a throne in some definite locality above us. This would be indeed a most crass and fleshly notion of God, the omnipresent absolute Spirit. At the same time, however, as it regards Christ, we have to make a distinction psychologically allowable between his individual and generic character; in order to harmonize different scriptural statements, and to solve especially the difficulties which connect themselves for the understanding with the doctrine of the Lord's Supper, the standing seal and pledge of the real presence of Christ in the Church. We say, then, Christ as that particular human individual who formerly moved through Palestine, a man among other men, is no longer upon the earth certainly, not even in his glorified form, and will only appear again when he shall return to judge the world. Of course, there is no room, according to our view, to think of any participation of his individual body, as such, in the eucharist, or of any corporeal reception whatever, whether in the way of transubstantiation or consubstantiation. But Christ is not merely a single man among other men; he bears at the same time a universal character; as the Saviour of the world, he is the representative of the whole race. Hence, the evangelist says, (John i. 14) not ὁ λογος ανθρωπος εγενετο ["the word became a man"], which would denote merely a human individual, but σαρξ εγενετο ["became flesh"]; to show that he assumed humanity, or the general human nature. The designation, υιος του ανθρωπου ["the Son of Man"], so frequently applied to himself by our Lord, involves probably the idea, that he was to be regarded as the ideal man, in whom the conception of the human race as a whole was fully actualized, and from whom as the source of a new creation all regenerated life among men was to spring. This undoubtedly is the doctrine of the Apostle Paul, when at different times (Rom. v. 12, ff.; l Cor. xv. 21, ff.; 45, ff.) he draws a parallel between Christ and the first man, and styles him the second Adam. Christ bears the same relation to regenerate humanity or the Church that is borne by

Adam to humanity in its natural, fallen and as such dying character. They have both a typical significance; each standing as a head to the whole race. Sin and death came into the world by Adam, righteousness and life by Jesus Christ. Ὁ πρωτος ανθρωπος εκ γης χοικος ὁ δευτερος ανθρωπος ὁ κυριος εξ ουρανου. Ὁιος ὁ χοικος, τοιουτοι και οι χοικοι και οιος ὁ επουρανιος τοιουτοι και οι επουρανιοι και καθως εφορεσαμεν την εικονα του χοικου φορεσομεν και την εικονα του επουρανιου (1 Cor. xv. 47–49.)[5]

We partake thus of the spiritual and corporeal nature of Adam, truly and properly, although his individual being, as a particular body and particular soul, passes not over into our persons. We are of his race, we have part in the general qualities of his being, as well as in his sinfulness and mortality. His individual person has been withdrawn from the world; but his generic existence is still present really and substantially, though not under a specific local form, perpetuates itself from generation to generation, and forms, so to speak, the root of the natural tree of humanity, from which the vital sap flows continually into all its particular branches. Only on the ground of such an organic conception of the relation of Adam to his posterity, can the church doctrine of Original Sin and its Imputation have any rational sense.[6] And so also it

5. [Trans. "The first man was from the earth, a man of dust; the second man is from heaven. As was the man of dust, so are those who are of the dust; and as is the man of heaven, so are those who are of heaven. Just as we have borne the image of the man of dust, we will also bear the image of the man of heaven." (NRSV)]

6. Dr. Nevin has done well to press this parallel of Paul, in his well known articles on *Pseudo-protestantism*, for his view of the Lord's Supper. [Nevin, "Pseudo-Protestantism," *Weekly Messenger of the German Reformed Church* n.s. 10, nos. 48–52 (1845).] There can be no doubt for one properly acquainted with the history of the Reformation, that Calvin, and the whole Reformed Church in its most important symbols, which were all formed under the influence of Calvin, much more than that of Zuingli, held a real participation in the eucharist by faith, not only of the merit, but of the flesh and blood, that is of the human nature of Christ. To the known passages from Calvin's *Institutes*, and his Controversy with Westphal, I will here add one less familiar, which is particularly clear. It is to be found in the *Confessio fidei de Eucharistia,* signed by Calvin, Farel, Viret, Bucer, and Capito, in the year 1537. It is there said: "*Vitam spiritualem, quam nobis Christus largitur* non *in eo duntaxat sitam. esse confitemur, quod Spiritu suo nos vivificat, sed quod Spiritus etiam eui virtute carnis suæ vivificæ nos facit participes, qua participatione in vitam æternam pascamur. Itaque cum de communione, quam cum Christo fideles habent, loquimur, non minus carni et sanguini ejus communicare ipsos intelligimus quam spiritui, ut ita totum Christum possideant.*" [Trans. "We confess that the spiritual life which Christ bestows upon us does not rest on the fact that he vivifies us with his Spirit, but that his Spirit makes us participants in the virtue of his vivifying body, but which participation we are fed on eternal life. Hence when we speak of the communion which we have with Christ, we understand the faithful to communicate not less in his body and blood than in his Spirit, so that thus they possess the whole Christ." Calvin, *Theological Treatises,* 168.] At the same time, the Reformed symbols decidedly reject the idea of a local presence of Christ's body, which in this form is in heaven only; and Calvin endeavours to solve the contradiction that seems to lie in the idea of communicating with an absent object by assuming that through the supernatural power of the Holy Ghost, in the case of believers, the soul is so raised by faith to heaven as to come within the life-giving influence of the Saviour's body.

This however is not properly to remove the difficulty, but only to transfer it to another place; yea it is made worse, since it is easier to conceive of the power of Christ's body extending itself by the Holy Ghost down to the earth; than that our souls should be in two places at the same time. Plainly, the Reformers were not willing on the one hand to let go the exegetical significance of the Lord's supper, and it must be allowed they preserved it in substance; while, on the other hand, they were anxious not

is only on the supposition of the indwelling of the incarnate Word in the Church, a like intimate, or rather far more intimate mystical life union of Christ with believers, that the cardinal doctrines of the Atonement, the Imputation of Christ's merits and Justification through faith, can be successfully maintained against Socinian and Rationalistic objections.[7] The Son of God became man, not for his own sake, but for ours; and for us he still continues man in eternity. His humanity then must avail to our advantage: only by means of it, can we be permanently united with the divine nature. Only through our participation in its imperishable vitality, is the power of sin and death within us gradually eradicated, and a new glorified body, which shall be like his own, prepared for our use. All other religions aim at the reconciliation of man with God. But they either fail to reach this object altogether, or at most it is secured imperfectly, as in the case of Judaism, in the way of prolepsis or shadowy anticipation of Christianity itself. The relation which holds in them between founder and follower is merely moral, such as we acknowledge towards the Reformers and Church Fathers. The specific character of Christianity, on the contrary, consists in this, that it is the full reconciliation and enduring life union of man with God, centring in the person of Jesus Christ, the life of Christ, which is neither simply divine nor simply human, but divine-human, flows over by the different means of grace to believers, so that, as far as their new nature reaches, they do not live themselves, but Christ lives in them, (comp. Gal. ii. 20). The Old Testament saints could not be said to be *in* Moses, or *in* Elias. Of believers under the new dispensation, however, Paul says, continually, they are *in* Christ, that is in living union with him.[8]

All this involves the uninterrupted presence of Christ, the God-man, in and among his people. His absence would rob us of the root of our religious existence from which all living sap is derived into the branches. The branch would be separated from the vine, and must of necessity wither (John xv. 6); the stream would be cut off from its fountain, and must accordingly fail. Only as the Church has part in the life of the God-man does she stand upon a rock against which the gates of hell shall not be able to

to wrong the Biblical declarations with regard to Christ's ascension, sitting at the right hand of God; and returning to judge the world, by assuming any such presence as might seem to overthrow these for the understanding. The scientific union of these two points they did not reach; and it is just here accordingly that the eucharistic doctrine of the Reformers needs to be carried forward to a more complete form. This seems to me to be secured by the distinction, which both scripture and philosophy sanction, between the individual body of Christ now enthroned in heaven, and the generic virtue of his human nature as actively present by the Holy Ghost in the entire church.

7. [Socinian refers to a Unitarian group emerging from sixteenth-century Poland and the theology of Lelio Francesco Maria Sozini (1525–62) and his nephew Fausto Paolo Sozzini (1539–1604). Socinians, like later English and American Unitarians, saw Christ's work of redemption as being accomplished through his example and teaching, rather than through the imputation upon others of the merits of his death. Like other rationalists, they found traditional doctrines of the atonement not in keeping with their understanding of the rational and moral nature of humans and God.]

8. [A fuller statement of this crucial Mercersburg theme regarding the relationship of Christianity to other world religions can be found in the opening of chapter four of Nevin's *The Mystical Presence*, published in the same year as this work. See Nevin, *The Mystical Presence*, MTSS, 1: 174–80.]

prevail (Matt. xvi. 18). "Because I live, ye shall live also. At that day, ye shall know that I am in my Father, and ye in me, and I in you" (John xiv. 19, 20). In the Church, Christ carries forward, so to speak, his divine human life, heals the sick, wakes the dead to a new existence, takes even young children into his arms by baptism, gives believers his atoning flesh and blood to partake of in the Lord's supper, speaks by his word and ministers comfort, peace and blessing to all that seek his grace, is crucified anew by the hostile world in the persecutions of his people, but still repeats also his glorious resurrection and ascension, and continues evermore to visit his little flock, assembled with one accord for prayer, with the fulness of light and life by his Holy Spirit.

A right conception of the Church is indispensable for a living apprehension and satisfactory exhibition of its history. This is itself indeed, in one respect, the product of a thorough insight into its actual development, the result of deep exegetical and historical study; but in another respect, it is the *spiritus rector*, the conducting genius of the Church historian. The relation here is that of reciprocal light and confirmation. Only the art which has wrought with master hand the wondrous dome of Church history, furnishes at the same time the key for understanding it. Without its guidance, we see indeed the solemn earnest halls, the lofty walls, and gigantic towers; but we cannot understand their deep symbolic meaning, the high and vast ideas that have taken body in their external forms. Hence it is that such works on Church History as those of ENGELHARDT and GIESELER, for instance, however distinguished and valuable for their thorough learning, still leave the deepest theological want unsatisfied, as having no true idea of the Church.[9] It is to be regretted that with NEANDER, also, this idea comes less clearly and distinctly into view than one could wish, especially now when the Church forms the life question of the time. GUERICKE, who borrows so slavishly and for a man of learning so very unbecomingly from NEANDER in other respects, shows himself independent of him here at least, that he is possessed of a strong church feeling, though under a very one-sided and exclusive form, since the idea of the true Church is for him identical with Lutheranism and the Form of Concord.[10]

Let us now come to some right understanding, before we go further, on the nature of *History*. The term denotes in its objective sense the general course of events; subjectively, the representation of these events. This definition, however, requires to be made more particular, so soon as History comes to be handled as a science. Only that can be called *historical* strictly speaking, which has exercised a determining influence upon the progress of humanity, and which has become incorporated with the image of its life at any given time. Thus, for example, the appearance of Luther at Worms is in an eminent sense historical, and in truth world-historical; while his domestic and

9. Comp. R. Hasse's Review of Engelhardt's *Manual of Church History* in the *Berl. Jahrb. für wissensch Kritik*, 1835, Bd. I. S. 543. [Hasse, review of *Handbuch der Kirchengeschichte* by J. G. V. Engelhardt and *Handburch der allgemeinen Kirchengeschichte* by H. E. Ferdinand Guerike, *Jahrbücher für wissenschaftliche Kritik* (April 1835): 534–49, 553–63. Johann Karl Ludwig Gieseler, *Lehrbuch der Kirchengeschichte*, 6 vols. (1824–57).]

10. [Heinrich Ernst Ferdinand Guericke, *Handbuch der allgemeinen Kirchengeschichte* (1833).]

private movements, though having the character of events, are only so far historical, as they may serve to illustrate and explain his importance for the Church, his character as a Reformer.

As every single individual has his history, so has humanity also as a whole. Its biography is Universal or World History. Revelation and enlightened reason teach us, to look upon the human race as a single family, which has sprung from one and the same common ancestor, and tends towards the same end, the exhibition of God's glory. Hence the history of the world must be conducted also as a living organism, in which the irresistible onward movement of humanity towards this end, the struggle of centuries to actualize in full the deep meaning of life, may be fairly represented. The histories of particular nations form the members of this organic body; through which, under all difference of character and calling and position and circumstances, one life blood still flows, and in which the idea of humanity, as formed from God and for God, dwells as a single soul. All nations however are not historical, any more than all individuals; but only such as have made themselves felt in a living way upon the actual development, inward and outward, of the world's life as a whole. The Hottentots, Caffrarians, Negroes and New Zealanders, for instance, have thus far played no part whatever in the grand drama of history.[11] Paganism in general, since the introduction of Christianity, is to be regarded as material merely, which must be Christianized in the first place, before it can fall into the stream of historical development; like the child, which has not yet come to years of responsibility, and can take no position of its own accordingly in human society.

As nations which have come to free action, and individuals that reciprocally complete one another, form thus the factors of world-history, so we are to recognize in different periods the several *stadia* ["stages"], inwardly connected and flowing necessarily one out of another, through which the idea of humanity must proceed, in order to come always to a more complete realization and exhibition of its own nature. Every period has a distinct character, which is impressed more or less on all its movements and tendencies. This is denominated the spirit of the age. It is nothing more than the world spirit, or the spirit of humanity itself, at a particular point of its age. For humanity, like the single man of which it is organically composed, passes through the stages of childhood, earlier and later youth, and manhood, onwards to old age. In a general way, we may style the history of the Oriental world, where the nations still stand wholly under the rod of absolute power, the childhood and boyhood of our race; Greece, the land of freedom, sprightliness and fancy, its youth; Rome, full of calculation and action, its manhood; and the period since Christianity, its old age, as surpassing in reason and wisdom all its previous life.[12]

11. [Hottentots and Caffrarians both refer to indigenous peoples of southern Africa. Similarly, by "New Zealanders," Schaff means Maori, the native people of those islands.]

12. [This view of civilizational evolution was a common place by Schaff's day and had its seminal expression by Johann Herder, whom Schaff discusses at length below.]

At the same time, every period and every people has also its several ages of life through which to pass; and then we must say again that Christianity, as such, includes a new course of development, peculiar to itself and essentially different from all that went before. Religion in this form is not to be viewed as an advance simply upon the Jewish system, exalting it to a higher state. It must be regarded rather as a new creation, by which a new principle, a divine life is communicated to humanity itself. Christianity forms the turning point of the world's history; and Christ, the true pole star of the whole, is the centre also around which all revolves; the key, as the great historian John von Müller towards the close of his life expressed himself, which alone can unlock the sense of all that has taken place before his advent or since. In Christ, the ideal of humanity has been actualized. All history before him must be viewed as a preparation for his presence; a preparation, which in Judaism carried a positive character, in the way of progressive revelations and condescensions on the part of God; while in Paganism it was more negative, a helpless struggle upwards on the part of man. All history since Christ, finds its central movement in the development of the divine principle of life, which he has introduced into human nature, and which is destined gradually to take all up into its own element, as revealed in his person. In this view it becomes *Church History*.

We are now to consider more closely the idea of Church History itself. In this, there are very different views. The principal of these, as measured by their historical significance, we proceed to examine. Church history itself, like every other theological discipline, has its own history; having reached the high position it now occupies only by degrees, and through a series of imperfect efforts, previously put forth for the purpose. We distinguish, in its course of development, three periods. The first two stand related to each other as extremes. By surmounting both, in the way of a true reconciliation, that higher view has come to prevail, which enters clearly into the ground of all the more important works of modern German science in this department.

The Orthodox Historiography

As the fact goes always before its representation, so it was necessary for the Church to act and form material before there could be any history of it in the subjective sense. The first and most incomplete form of ecclesiastical history was the simple record of the recollections which the Church had of its past doings and fortunes—brought together usually in a mere outward way, in their chronological order. Such chronicles and annals constitute down to the time of the reformation almost the only attempts that were made in the way of historical representation; of immense value, of course, as collections of material; but still no more than attempts at history, we may say, as consisting of such collections only. Church History as a science commences, where the Church comes to reflect upon herself; where the historian brings his own judgment into his work and represents his matter so as to put life into it spiritually from some particular point of view. The first stand-point which presents itself to us here, is that of the earlier *orthodoxy*, as well Roman Catholic as Protestant. We may style it the stand-point of *established orthodoxy* (*der fertigen orthodoxie*) and *exclusive ecclesiasticism.*[13] It consists in general, in this, that the Church, with her whole system of doctrine and life, is regarded as something complete from the start and is thus made to stand under some particular received visible form in abstract opposition to all diverging sects, as the absolute and only legitimate representative of the Christian faith. Outward changes in the fortunes of the Church by its growth in the way of missionary activity and aggression upon the world are of course admitted; but all idea of an inward development of the nature of the Church itself, is rejected. This general maxim, however, must assume practically, a different form in the Roman Catholic consciousness, from what is found to be in the Protestant.

The Roman Catholic Method of History

If any system may be said to have *become* what it is historically, this must be affirmed of the Roman Catholic, both as it regards its outward form and its inward constitution. What an immense distance between the Galilean fisherman, who as a common presbyter (1 Peter v. 1), not as a lord over the flock but as its example (verse 3), travels from place to place, in poor raiment, accompanied by his wife (1 Cor. ix. 5), to proclaim the simple word of the cross to the Jews and Gentiles: and a Gregory VII with his unyielding hierarchic pride, and his inexorable anathemas directed against all married priests as whoremongers and adulterers; or an Innocent III who arrayed in gorgeous pontifical attire, and bearing the triple crown upon his head, reverently encompassed with different patriarchs, seventy-one metropolitans and superior prelates, four hundred and twelve bishops, nine hundred abbots and priors, the lights of learning, and the ambassadors of almost all the princes of Europe, at the fourth Lateran Council, as the holy and infallible father of the whole family of Christian nations, orders with dictatorial spirit all the affairs of the Church, whether outward or inward, decrees a crusade against the Saracens, and treats the most powerful kings of the earth as mere vassals, who hold their crowns in fief from him as the vicegerent of Christ upon the earth! How much labour of the deepest thinkers, what changes, yea, contradictions in opinion, what devices and circuitous courses of religious thought, lie between the extremely simple and indefinite doctrinal views of the apostolical fathers and apologists of the second and third centuries and the wonderful scholastic system of the Middle Ages, carried out in the most insignificant subtleties in the way of question, distinction and division, or the symbolical settlement of its main results in the *Concilium*

13. I may remark here, that I place no particular weight either on this designation, or on the designations employed in the case of the other two stand-point, as there is no authority, so far as my knowledge extends, requiring their use. If any can be furnished more significant and comprehensive, they will be cheerfully adopted.

Tridentinum ["Council of Trent"]! Through what struggles of centuries, through what diseases, relapses and recoveries, was it not necessary for the monastic institution to pass, before it could work its way upwards from the renowned poverty of the hermit Anthony in the Lybian desert, to the mighty orders which embraced and ruled all Western Christendom, in the thirteenth century! What a chasm, what conflicts of the principle of image worship with the principle of image war, between the simple, almost puritanic worship of the time of the apostles, and the outwardly imposing, mysterious pomp of the mediæval religious service!

All this, for the unprejudiced view, is something more than merely outward change, in the case of which the interior state might be supposed to remain always the same. Notwithstanding this, however, the Roman Catholic historians down to the time of Stolberg, Ritter, and Döllinger maintain in substance the principle of stability;[14] with this difference only, that the more recent and liberal among them have been forced to yield more or less to the powerful pressure of Protestant criticism, at least in subordinate points, in the sphere particularly of the utterly untenable fables of the hierarchy. All that has come at any time to general authority in the papacy, having impressed upon it thus the seal of the infallible church, is referred to an immediately divine origin; found partly in the Bible, and partly in an oral tradition claiming to be derived from the apostles, on the maxim of Vincentius Lirinensis understood in an outward and literal way: *Teneamus, quod semper, quod ubique, quod ab omnibus creditum est.*[15] The Council of Trent expresses the fullest conviction, that all its decisions, doctrinal and moral, were drawn through the medium of an uninterrupted succession of bishops from the very time of the apostles.[16]

According to this assumption, for instance, the declaration of Christ to Peter, Matt. xvi. 18, and the delivery to him of the keys of the kingdom of heaven, contain in themselves the full idea of the papacy. When the Lord says, "He that eateth of this

14. [Friedrich Leopold Stolberg, *Geschichte der Religion Jesu Christi*, 15 vols. (1806–18); Joseph Ignatius Ritter, *Handbuch der Kirchengeschichte*, 3 vols. (1826–33); Johann Joseph Ignaz von Döllinger, *Geschichte der christlichen Kirche*. 2 vols. (1833–35), translated as *A History of the Church*, 4 vols. (1840–42).]

15. [Trans. "We hold that which was believed always, everywhere, by all." This dictum originates with Vincent of Lérins (d. c. 450).]

16. *Sacrosancta œcumenica et generalis Trid. Synodus, perspiciens, hanc veritatem et disciplinam contineri in libris scriptis et sine scripto traditionibus, quae ab ipsuis Christo ore ab Apostolis acceptæ, aut ab ipsis Apostolis Spiritu S. dictante quasi per manus traditiæ ad nos usque pervenerunt—traditiones ipsas—tanquam vel oretenus a Christo vel a Sp. S. dictatas et continua successione in Ecclesia cathoiica conservatas. pari pietatis affectu ac venerantia suscipit et veneratur.* Sess. iv. dec. 1. [Trans. "The holy ecumenical and general council of Trent clearly perceives that this truth and rule are contained in written books and in unwritten traditions which were received by the apostles from the mouth of Christ himself, or else have come down to us, handed on as it were from the apostles themselves at the inspiration of the Holy Spirit—These traditions—the council accepts and venerates with a life feeling reverence and piety as either directly spoken by Christ or dictated by the holy Spirit, which have been preserved in unbroken sequence in the catholic church." This translation of Schaff's abridgement of this passage is based on *DEC*, 2:663.] This principle is repeated often in the case of single doctrines, as S. xii. c. 4, xiii c. 8, xiv. c, 5, xxi. c. 9, &c.

bread shall live for ever," (John vi. 51–58); when Paul separates the cup from the bread by an "*or*," (1 Cor. xi. 27); when Luke mentions of the first Christians with approbation, that they continued steadfastly in "the breaking of bread," without any notice of the cup; this all is enough of itself to justify communion in one kind. In the imposition of hands by Paul and John, after previous baptism in the case of the Samaritan converts (Acts viii. 16–17), is found the actual sacrament of confirmation; in the remarkable passage (Eph. v. 25–32) the sacrament of marriage; in the casual direction of James to anoint a sick brother with oil (iv. 14), the sacrament of extreme unction; in the remark of our Lord on voluntary eunuchs (Matt. xix. 12) and Paul's wish that all might be like himself as regarded marriage (1 Cor. vii. 7) the celibacy of the clergy as a divine ordinance. When historical testimonies are wanting altogether, the strict Romanists find a convenient refuge in the willful assumption of a *disciplina arcani* ["discipline of the secret"]; according to which, certain apostolical doctrines and practices, which are first mentioned and ecclesistically established at a later period, are supposed for various reasons, the fear for example of profanation on the part of Jews and Pagans, or a tender regard to the weakness of catechumens, to have been originally kept secret. When, finally, clear testimonies speak directly against them; as, for instance, where pope Gelasius, of the fifth century, expressly affirms that the nature of the bread and wine remains in the eucharist,[17] or where pope Nicholas I, of the ninth century, in his second letter to the emperor Michael, teaches the true presence of Christ's body in this sacrament, *without* transmutation;[18] these zealous historians and dogmatists do violence both to the subject and themselves, by calling in question the genuineness of the documents thus brought into view.

If the Roman Catholic doctrine and discipline have been at all times the same, they must remain the same also for all time to come. Were the entire structure of the Church regarded only as the product of a necessary historical process, having a right humanly to be what it has been in its own time, it would not be so bad. But the *jus humanum* ["human law"] is made to pass here always for *divinum* ["divine"], the *jus historicum* ["historical law"] for a *jus absolutum* ["absolute law"]. What has once been acknowledged by the Church, is constituted a law obligatory for all time.

So far as the *sects* are concerned, the historical theory now before us reserves to the Catholic, that is to the Roman Church, the *exclusive* possession of God's truth and Spirit, as being invested in fact with the attribute of infallibility. All tendencies that set themselves in opposition to its authority, including of course the whole interest of Protestantism with all its mighty achievements, are regarded as heretical and schismatical, the working of Satanic wickedness against the divine will itself. As such, they

17. [Pope Gelasius I (d. 496) wrote in *Tract on the Two Natures in Christ* 14 "the substance of the bread and wine do not cease to be." Johnson, *Worship in the Early Church*, 3:154.]

18. [The statement of Pope Nicholas I (d. 867) on the eucharist was made in the context of his controversy with Byzantine emperor Michael III over who was rightfully the patriarch of Constantinople.]

exclude all hope of salvation. *Extra ecclesiam* Romanum, *nulla salus*.[19] They are not allowed even the merit of having assisted the orthodox Church, in coming to a clear consciousness of her own vocation, and in bringing her dogmas to proper perfection for the understanding. They are made to be the outward occasion only, by which the Church has been led to utter in the way of formal decree against the manifestation of heresy, what she had held materially in its full completeness from the beginning.[20]

19. [Trans. "Outside of the *Roman* church, there is no salvation."]

20. I may be permitted here, to say a word at least in the form of a note, on the late publication of John Henry Newman, An Essay on the Development of Christian Doctrine New York, Appleton & Co, *1846*. It forms his defence of the long expected and entirely natural transition he has made recently to the Roman Catholic Church. The very title seems to contradict what we have here given as the character of the Romanist view of history. He holds, in fact, a certain kind of development in the Church, and fancies that he has in this the later Catholic theologians, De *Maistre* and *Möhler* on his side. So far as this goes, it forms a concession in favour of Protestant science, and involves, to the same extent, a departure from the strict sense of Romanist principle. It is doubtful, accordingly, whether it will be sustained by theologians in this Church. Professor Butler, in a late article in the Irish Ecclesiastical Journal (N. Y. Churchman, Feb. 14th, 1846.) remarks on this point: "I must in the first place observe that it is much more than doubtful, how far Mr. Newman's doctrine is at all the received doctrine of the Roman Church, or would be regarded by its authorities as any other than *a most perilous innovation*. Convenient as it may now be to tolerate it (or any thing else from the same author) for temporary purposes, and to meet the present state of speculation, I shall be much surprised, if as the controversy proceeds, it be not in substance disavowed as a private and unauthorized hypothesis." [Later republished as William Archer Butler, *Letters on Romanism*, 3.] The reviewer then appeals to a judgment of the Sorbonne, and to various declarations of the Council of Trent, in which the principle of stability is asserted in the most unqualified terms.

Still, however, Mr. Newman's conception of development is not so perilous for Rome as the mere name might imply; and differs very materially from ours. For, in the first place, he allows this development to hold only in the Roman Catholic direction; so that Protestantism is regarded as a falling away from history, and of course an abiding progressive corruption. Then again, with his view of the infallibility of the Church, every Roman Catholic development is for him of force for all time; whilst *we* can see in the papacy for instance, only a temporary form of church government, necessary for the wants of a particular period. Finally, in the application of his principle to concrete points, he still approximates again to the Romanist stand point; since the slightest and most indistinct hints of Christian antiquity are taken as sufficient proofs by themselves for the existence at the time of doctrines and practices that belong to a much later period; thus at bottom referring all again to apostolical or with different expression, to divine authority. Romanism cannot give up the principle of stability, without unsettling its own foundations. The broad difference between our view of the development of the church, and that presented by Mr. Newman, will be made to appear more clearly as we proceed. Meanwhile, it were to be wished, that the book in question might be subjected to a separate review of a more earnest character than it is likely to receive among us at this time. Too many of our critics, in their immense Protestant self-complacency, to which all is clear and settled long ago as regards the whole subject, are utterly disqualified for every task of this kind.

[Newman's understanding of development held that later generations of theologians made explicit, given their own situations and philosophical vocabularies, what was implicit among the apostles. Thus, for example, the apostles did not teach the Immaculate Conception, but if it was explained to them would have agreed with it. In this way it guarded against the idea of continuing revelation. It also stipulated, as Schaff states, that once taught, each doctrine is permanently in force. For Newman, development was a key issue because, he reasoned, if some things that Anglicans and Catholics held in common were not explicitly taught in the scriptures, there was no necessary reason for him to reject other things that Catholics taught that were not explicit in the scriptures. (Ian Kerr, foreword in Newman, *Essay on the Development*, xvii–xxvii.) Within the Roman Catholic tradition, Newman

Historical Method of the Older Protestant Orthodoxy.

The Reformation had from its commencement properly a practical character, but was still sustained and carried throughout by the power of ideas. It included then necessarily a regeneration in full of theology, which is only the form in which the life of religion is brought to scientific consciousness. The science was emancipated from the chains of the scholastic philosophy, and referred to the formal principle of Protestantism, the holy scriptures as the living fountain and only rule of all saving divine knowledge. This brought into the foreground, the interpretation of the Bible; which now acquired, through Luther, Melancthon, Camerarius, Zuingli, Œcolampadius, and still more through Calvin and Beza, an impulse, a force and vigour, freshness and life, depth and fullness of spirit, which cast into the shade not only the sparse performances of the Middle Ages in this department, but even the whole Patristic period itself. On this biblical ground arose a renovated *Dogmatik*, whose most brilliant incomparable monuments are presented to us, in Melancthon's *Loci Theologici*, and the *Institutio Christianæ Religionis* of Calvin.[21] By reason of the organic connexion among all branches of theology, Church History was required also to undergo a change, as soon as the Protestant principle came to be applied to this department. This took place towards the end of the age of the Reformation itself, primarily in the *Magdeburg Centuries* and the *Catalogus Testium Veritatis* by Flacius.[22] In the period immediately following, the Lutheran Church was more occupied with dogmatic than with exegetical and historical studies; still a certain view of Church History lay at the ground of the school divinity of the age, which is extensively interwoven with all its representations of Christian doctrine. The Reformed theologians, on the other hand, besides giving their attention to the interpretation of the scriptures, employed themselves in a number of cases with particular portions of Church History, chiefly in a controversial way; and produced accordingly, in the course of the period here noticed, many works, which, for the learning of their details, and their critical acumen, carry with them in part at least a permanent value. The most celebrated names on this list are, among the French, Du Plessis Mornay, Pierre du Moulin, Jean Daille

is generally reckoned as being an early figure in affirming the development of doctrine, and thereby paving the way for later developments. His invocation of the Ultramontane Joseph de Maistre with Johann Möhler suggests his limited familiarity with the theology of both men. McCarren, "Development of Doctrine," 130. Since the era of the Second Vatican Council (1962–65), the principle of doctrinal development has been widely accepted in Roman Catholic theology, generally according to a reception model, where the unchanging content of the tradition of the church is continually re-received by the church, taking different forms in different cultural moments. This model and most contemporary models lack the progressive, eschatologically oriented focus of Schaff's view of development. It is at the same time, however, much more dynamic than Newman's. Thiel, "The Development of Doctrine," 260–62.]

21. [Melanchthon, *Melanchthon on Christian Doctrine*; Calvin, *Institutes*.]

22. [Matthias Flacius Illyricus, *Ecclesiastica historia*, 13 vols. (1560–74) was known since the eighteenth century as the *Magdeburg Centuries*. Catalogus Testium Veritatis (1556).]

(DALLŒUS), DAV. BLONDEL, SAUMAISSE (SALMASIUS), the two BASNAGES; among the English USHER, PEARSON, BEVERIDGE, BURNET, DODWELL, BINGHAM, BULL, CAVE, and GRABE. Of histories bearing a general character may be named particularly those by J. HOTTINGER, SPANHEIM, J. BASNAGE, JABLONSKY, TURRETIN, and VENEMA.

The emancipation, however, from the Roman stand-point was accomplished only by degrees. It was changed as to material, in the first place, but remained formally the same; so that it is to be comprehended still under the same general view. We shall now attempt to characterize somewhat more particularly, this orthodox protestant method of history.

In the first place, the conception of the Church became more broad and spiritual. It was no longer identified with the communion of Rome. Elements of evangelical truth and Christian life, were recognised in the sects also of the Middle Ages, which were the object of Rome's severe persecution. It was generally admitted indeed that the Lord had at all times reserved a people for himself, even under the dominion of the pope; but what might be called *Roman* properly in the Catholic Church, the papacy with its institutions, was regarded as an apostacy from the true church, towards which the posture of a simply negative criticism was accordingly maintained. After the Reformation it was no longer possible to look upon the Roman as the absolutely true church. It took the character of a heresy, a sort of hardened Judaism; whilst to Protestantism was now assigned the place, which had been previous claimed by Rome.

Notwithstanding this material change, however, the church continued to be for these historians also something complete in its nature from the beginning, not needing nor admitting any proper development. All activity in the sphere of doctrine, was apprehended only under the form either of a vindication or denial of the truth, as orthodoxy or heresy. The orthodox was the stable, always agreeing with itself; the heretical appeared as the subject of perpetual change; so that the history of doctrines resolved itself at last into a mere history of heresies. The apostolical fathers and early Christian apologists already exhibited the full system of truth in a pure form; the general councils established it symbolically in opposition to different heresies; the papacy overwhelmed it with unscriptural and superstitious traditions. Still it was always present beneath this rubbish, as gold covered with dross, and was brought more or less into view by the so called "witnesses of the truth," the WALDENSES, WICKLIFFE, HUSS, JOHN WESSEL, &C.;[23] till the Reformation finally raised it again to ecclesiastical authority. In this view, accordingly, the great religious movement of the 16th century itself forms no proper advance of church life and consciousness, but a simple process of purification, a return to the original truth of the scriptures and the stand-point of the first few centuries. The entire Protestant system was supposed to be found immediately and literally in the Bible, even in the Old Testament itself, and in the practice

23. [These movements and figures from the twelfth to the fifteenth centuries espoused some ideas and practices characteristic of later Protestantism. Judged to be heretics by the medieval church, many Protestants saw them as forerunners of the Reformation.]

and life of the first period of the Church; so that the whole intermediate history was made to sink in fact into the character of an unmeaning and useless episode. While the Reformers always laid great weight on the agreement of their views with JEROME, AUGUSTINE, CYPRIAN, ATHANASIUS, &C., their followers of the 17th century went still further. The English Episcopalians, in particular, made it their business, to establish a perfect identity between the primitive Church and their own. In this effort they showed themselves often more unhistorical, and less favourable to the idea of development, than even the Romanists themselves. So, for example, the learned DR. GEORGE BULL, in his celebrated *Defence of the Nicene Creed*, undertakes to show that the ante-Nicene fathers taught in full all that this creed contains, and that all differences which appear in the case are formal only, not affecting the substance at any point.[24] The distinguished Jesuit DIONYSIUS PETAVIUS was sufficiently free from prejudice not to deny absolutely the fact of some difference of doctrine in this period; and indeed went so far as to allow even that the Arian heresy itself had appeared among the earlier forms of thinking in the Church.[25] For this, however, BULL blames him strongly, and thinks that such a concession must overthrow the respect which is due to the fathers, and give the Church a right also to form new dogmas. As it regards government and worship, the more liberal among the earlier Protestant historians have indeed acknowledged changes, even within the true Church; but then they look upon these as the accidental rise and disappearance merely of indifferent ceremonies. At the same time, there have not been wanting those among the Reformed, to whom the Presbyterian system has seemed fully identical with the constitution of the Church as it stood in the days of the Apostles and the age of CLEMENS ROMANUS;[26] as indeed such are to be met with still. So Protestant Episcopalians have found their three *orders*[27] in the same way, directly

24. *Defensio Fidei Nicenæ, etc.*, ed, Grabe, London, 1703. Prooem. p. 5: *Scilicet hic operis et incœpti nostri scopus, hoc institutum est ut clare ostendamus, quod de Filii divinitate contra Arium aliosque hæreticos statuerunt Patres Nicæni, idem reipsa (quam aliis fortasse nonnumquam verbis alioque loquendi modo) docuisse Patres ac Doctores ecclesiæ probati ad unum omnes, qui ante tempora Synodi Nicænæ ab ipsa usque apostolorum opiate floruerunt.* [Trans. "As regards the chief point, of which I wish to persuade others,—I myself am quite convinced, and that on no hasty view, that, What the Nicene fathers laid down concerning the divinity of the Son, in opposition to Arius and other heretics, the same in effect (although sometimes, it may be, in other words, and in another mode of expression) was taught, without any single exception, by all the fathers and approved doctors of the Church, who flourished before the council of Nice, even from the very times of the Apostles." Bull, *Defensio Fidei Nicænæ* (1851), x-xi.]

25. *De Theol. Dogmatibus. De Trinity. I. 5, 7 and 8, 2.* [Dionysius Petavius, *Opus de theologicis dogmatibus* (Venice, 1757).] In this, however, other Catholic theologians decidedly differ from Petavius. Thus, according to [Heinrich] Klee, the approximation of the earlier apologists to Tritheism or Subordinationism is merely apparent, and to be accounted for satisfactorily, from the imperfection of human language, generally, and of the theological language of this period in particular (*Lehrb. der Dogmengeschischte*, Mainz[: Kirchheim, Schott & Thielmann], 1837, Th. i., S. 162). Passages that sound like subordination in Origen, he charges to the account of some unknown forger (S. 166, comp. S. 192).

26. [Clement of Rome, that is Pope Clement I (d. 99).]

27. [That is bishops, priests (or presbyters), and deacons, the three orders of clergy in the Anglican

in the New Testament; yea, Lutherans even failed not to appear in the 17th and 18th centuries, who believed, that they could very satisfactorily establish the Consistorial and Territorial order of their government churches from the Old Testament!

The view taken also of the relation between the reigning Church and dissenting bodies, remained formally the same that it had been before in the Roman Catholic conception of history; namely, that of exclusive ecclesiasticism. Tendencies and views which appeared in opposition to the established church doctrines, were not brought into any inward connexion with the historical life of the Church itself, but were set over against it abstractly, as purely negative phenomena. Here, however, this principle fell into a striking self-contradiction in its application. In the first period of the Church, it went hand in hand with the Romanist view; since Protestantism, in its orthodox character, acknowledged the authority of the œcumenical symbols. Of course it condemned and rejected the heresies of Ebionism, Gnosticism, Montanism, Subordinationism, Sabellianism, Arianism, Semi-arianism, Manicheism, Nestorianism, Eutychianism, Pelagianism and Semi-pelagianism, as decidedly as the Church of Rome, denying them in the same way all right to exist. On into the sixth century, we may say, the two systems moved thus together.

But the case changed in the Middle Ages; where the *Roman* became always more and more clearly the reigning Church, under the papacy, which stood in direct antagonism to the Reformation. Here the Protestant historians were constrained to take side rather with the non-catholic sects, the so called forerunners of the Reformation, and so to make these "*testes veritatis*" ["witnesses to the truth"] properly the Catholic Church itself in its true sense, in order to maintain some consistency with their previous rule of judgment. But this was attended with great difficulties.

For in the first place the Middle Ages are only the regular development of the Catholic Church of the first six centuries. All the germs even of the papacy itself may be shown to have existed thus early. Protestant orthodoxy, it is plain, apprehended the church fathers only on one side. Augustine, for example, has full as much objective, churchly, catholic feeling, as what may be called subjective and protestant in his character. Yea, he is the principal former of the Catholicism of the Middle Ages; his deep feeling lies at the ground of its mystic theology, as his dialectic understanding animates the scholastic. His spirit makes its process first through the whole period of the Catholic Church, till at length the Reformers rose to interpret its Protestant element, as comprehended in his doctrine of sin and grace. How can the great veneration of the Roman Church for this father be explained, except on the ground of an actual inward affinity with his spirit, in some view?

A second difficulty appears in the fact, that a large proportion of the sects which existed before the Reformation were further removed in a number of points from the Protestant orthodoxy, than the errors even of the Church of Rome itself. Zealous Reformed theologians spared no pains, indeed, to clear the anti-hierarchic bodies of

communion.]

the Middle Ages from all reproach of heresy. Anti-papistic and evangelical were taken to be almost interchangeable terms.

Thus, for instance, JAMES USHER and JOHN PAUL PERRIN would force the world to believe, at every cost, that the ALBIGENSES were entirely pure and sound in their faith, and that the accusation of Manicheism must be considered a groundless slander brought against them by the papists.[28] The Catholic historians, particularly Bossuet, defended, with much spirit and learning, the earlier opinion. A vigorous controversy was now waged on the subject; till the publication of the judicial *Records of the Inquisition of Toulouse* by PHILIP LIMBORCH, compelled the parties to relinquish a portion of their claims.[29] For these documents clearly distinguish the ALBIGENSES from the WALDENSES, and attribute to the first, the error of the Manichean dualism. Thus, the matter stood before the appearance of MOSHEIM.[30]

Finally, such Protestants as had carried their studies somewhat thoroughly into the Catholic theology of the Middle Ages, could not, with all their respect for the dissenting sects, shut their eyes to the fact that at least as much piety as they could exhibit and a great deal more learning had place also in the reigning Church. This was specially evident in the persons of such men as ANSELM OF CANTERBURY, BERNARD OF CLAIRVAUX, THOMAS AQUINAS, and THOMAS A KEMPIS. For these men a traditional reverence still continued to make itself felt in spite of their connexion with the papacy. Yea, with the Lutheran theologians of the 17th century, who notwithstanding the opposition of the Reformers formed themselves a new scholastic divinity, THOMAS AQUINAS came even to be honoured with the title of an *assertor veritatis evangelicæ* ["champion of gospel truth"]. It is now allowed, however, by all who understand the subject that this great divine has exerted, next to Augustine, more influence than any other on the formation of the Roman system, so far as its doctrinal side is concerned.

When we come down to the period after the Reformation, we find the state of things more favourable again to the application of the historical principle before us. There was now a predominant orthodox Protestant Church and over against it dissenting men and parties, as during the first centuries, in relation to the Catholic Church. Here then the Lutheran Church in particular conducted itself with great harshness towards all movement of the more free kind, even when connected with forms so worthy of respect as ARNDT, JACOB BÖHM, CALIXTUS, and afterwards SPENER and FRANKE; treating them as dangerous heretics, and rivalling Rome herself in

28. [The French Protestant Jean Paul Perrin's 1618 work on the subject remained popular and was published in an American edition in 1846. Perrin, *History of the Ancient Christians Inhabiting the Valleys of the Alps*.]

29. [Limborch, *Historia Inquisitionis, Cui subjungitur Liber sententiarum inquisitionis Tholosanae* (1692).]

30. See his judgment with regard to this controversy, in his *Versuch einer unparteiischen und gründlichen Ketzergeschichte. [Attempt at an impartial and thorough history of heresy] Helmstadt: Weygand, 1746]. Einleitung* [*introduction*], *s. 28 ff.*

exclusiveness.[31] But here also this rigoristic ecclesiastical standpoint could not long be maintained; especially after Pietism had grown into a powerful tendency, and the orthodox themselves were compelled to acknowledge its influence.

Thus, through the pressure of the difficulties and self-contradictions which have been mentioned, as well as by the continued process of development on the part of orthodox theology itself, there was gradually formed in the Lutheran Church, during the course of the 18th century, a sort of *mediating* view or *moderate* orthodoxy; which we may look upon as the transition to the second principal *stadium* in the progress of our science, though it still belongs in the main to the first. This is the *supranaturalistic* style of Church History. It belongs chiefly to the German Lutheran Church, and has produced the most important works that Protestant orthodoxy has to show in this sphere. Here are to be reckoned those eminent names of the last century, Weismann, J. G. Walch, C. W. F. Walch, Baumgarten, Cramer, Mosheim, Schröckh; historians, indeed, who for their intellectual ability, unwearied diligence and solid learning must always remain in honourable and grateful memory. Mosheim, take him altogether, is without question the greatest among them. He unites in himself the powers of historical inquiry and historical representation, in a high degree. Whilst others generally appear in the tedious, dry address, and antiquated tasteless style of the foregoing century, Mosheim's manner of writing, both in German and Latin, is pure, flowing, graphic and pleasant.[32] Along with this he has the advantage of general culture, a wide and full knowledge of men, and great power of description and illustration. In short, he has performed all that it was possible to perform in his time. Honour to his memory! Surely however he would himself be surprised, and as a historian especially must be filled even with displeasure, if he should now return again to the earth and find the English and Americans, after the lapse of a full century, not a step advanced beyond his position and contenting themselves, in their seminaries, to commit his text book to memory in a mere mechanical way, so far as practical purposes may require. He would bestow, beyond doubt, far greater praise on his German countrymen, who have placed his immortal labours at large interest, and would be able thus to show him his capital doubled and tripled in its amount.

It remains now to notice some of the characteristic features of this supranaturalistic method of history.

The term *supranaturalism* is employed, in the historical sense of the word, to designate the last representatives of the old protestant orthodoxy, as opposed to Pietism and still more to Rationalism, by which the theology of Germany was gradually

31. [These men were variously mystics, "ecumenists," and Pietists, underscoring Lutheran opposition to *all* movements toward greater freedom.]

32. Gustavus Schwab styles him in this respect "the father of modern pulpit eloquence, and as regards tact, force and taste, the first former of the German conversational language of the 18th century." (*German Prose from Mosheim to our Time.* Stuttgart, 1843.) [Schwab, *Die deutsche Prosa von Mosheim bis auf unsere Tage: eine Mustersammlung mit Rücksicht auf höhere Lehr-anstaltne* (Stuttgart: S. G. Liesching, 1843).]

overpowered during the last century. Against this powerful enemy, the established school divinity became always less and less able to maintain with decision its church character; and was brought thus into a sickly decline, in which the main truths of Christianity indeed were still retained, but at the same time the scientific principle of rationalism was admitted, and along with it a strong tendency to unchurchly subjectivity. Thus supranaturalism stood between two powers, in the case of which neology soon gained the ascendency. It was found insufficient to withstand permanently the stream of the age, lost continually more and more its church character, and capitulated finally with the foe with which it had undertaken to wage perpetual war. This whole process can be clearly traced, not only in the systematic divinity and exegesis of the period in question, but also in its style of Church History.

The supranaturalistic historians agree with their strict orthodox predecessors in this, that the conception of development is wanting to them altogether. They look upon the process of history simply as a course or series of favourable and unfavourable events; and the exhibition of it is considered to be, not a living reproduction or generic evolution, but a simple relation merely, of these events as they have occurred.[33] The Christian doctrines and precepts are viewed by them as a fixed unalterable system, standing over against the human mind in an outward way, as handed down in the Bible, under the same form always, from the beginning.

On the other hand a difference appears in this, that the old orthodox zeal against deviations in doctrine from the church theology, whether of the patristic or protestant period, is very considerably cooled; particularly after the pious Arnold, of whom we shall have more to say presently, allowed himself to treat them with such tender indulgence, while so many instances of wrong were shown to have had place on the part of the orthodox. The supranaturalists affected the credit of great liberality and impartiality; which must by all means be allowed to them also, in a certain sense. They no longer looked upon heresies as being the product exclusively of bad intention and rebellion directly against the divine authority; but rather as errors of thought or imagination, in many cases at least, that called for pity, various forms of enthusiasm, such, for instance, as Gnosticism, Montanism and Mysticism. Or they treated them as deviations merely from the church terminology, and so reduced not infrequently the most weighty doctrinal controversies to unmeaning logomachies. Or lastly they even justified the heretics in part, in opposition to the orthodox.[34] In this, however, they assailed their

33. Mosheim defines church history to be perspicua et sincera *narratio, &c.* [“*a clear and honest* narrative, etc.”], (*Inst. Hist. Eccl. Helmst.* 1755, *præparatio* § 1.) [Johann Mosheim, *Institvtionvm historiae ecclesiasticae antiqvae at recentiors libri qvatvor ex ipsis fontibva insigniter emendati* (Helmstedt: Weygand, 1755), *præparatio* § 1] and again a prudens et ingenua narratio [“*sensible and honest narrative*”]. (*Inst. Hist. Christ. Helmst.* 1739, *Sec.* 1, *Præp.* § 1.) [Mosheim, *Institutiones historiae christianae maiores. Saeculum primum*, Helmstedt, Weygand, 1739), section 1, *Præp.* § 1.] He divides it accordingly into *external* and *internal*, (p. 2 in both works), and the first again into a narratio fatorum *prosperorum* et *adversorum* [“*narrative of fate*, favorable *and* adverse”] (§ 3). Plainly a most mechanical and outward method, which shows at once an utter want of the conception of an organic development.

34. Mosheim expresses himself very mildly in relation to heretics in general; *Non exiguus hujus*

own assumption, that heresy must be regarded as sheer falsehood, which of course can never have *any* right in opposition to divine truth. To close the eyes then indulgently in favour of the falsehood could not fail to promote a spirit of indifference in relation to true and false, orthodoxy and heterodoxy, of very dangerous character. This did, in fact, towards the close of the century, become generally prevalent; so that it became an easy thing for Rationalism, with its growing strength, to overcome so poor an enemy, and even to bring it over to its own side. The last and most extensive work of Church History from this lenient and pliant school, namely, that of SCHRÖCKH with its continuation by TZSCHIRNER, reveals in its five and forty volumes, which appeared from 1768 to 1810, the gradual progress of the latitudinarianism here noticed, as it fell over always more and more towards the rationalistic camp.[35]

---

laboris (hist. *hæresium*) *fructus est, si sapienter et sine partium studio instituatur; verum arduus idem et molestus est. Nam factionum duces multis injuriis temere affecti sunt, et ipsa corum dogmata depravata. . . ; Quapropter qui ad hanc historiæ partem accedunt, invidiam omnem de vocabulo hæreticus detrahere secumque cogitate debent, generaliori tantum sensu adsumi pro homine, qui bellis et dissidiis inter Christianos sive sua sive aliena culpa, cecasionem præbait. Inst. Hist. Eccless.* Præp. §11, p. 5, [Trans. "This labor (*the history of heresies*), if wisely expended and *with impartiality*, will well repay the toil; but it is arduous and difficult. For the leaders of these parties *have been treated with much injustice, and their doctrines misrepresented*. . . . Those therefore, who approach this part of Church history *should exclude everything invidious* from the name *heretic*, and should consider it as used in its more general sense, to denote those who were the occasion, whether by their own or others' fault, of divisions and contests among Christians." Mosheim, *Mosheim's Institutes of Ecclesiastical History, Ancient and Modern*, 5th ed. (London, Tegg, 1867), introduction, paragraph 11, p. 2.] As a striking example of these concessions in favour of heretics, may be adduced the learned monograph of *Mosheim* on the Unitarian, *Michael Servetus,* whose burning was approved even by the gentle *Melancthon* himself. We may see, here, how far the supranaturalism of this period had deviated in its method of history, from the original strictness of Protestant orthodoxy. In the comparison which *Mosheim* draws between *Calvin* and Servetus, this last comes off nearly as well as the first. "I venture," says the writer, "to append to this sketch, a brief parallel of the unfortunate Spanish physician and his great antagonist *John Calvin*. In this, I mean not to put reproach on the last; nor honour on the first. One who is orthodox is not made a heretic, by being compared with a heretic; and a worthy man loses none of his merit, though it be shown that his opponent has not been wholly unlike himself. *Calvin* and *Servetus* were both extraordinary and remarkable men. The first was far more serviceable to the Church than the last; but both were actuated alike by the same fiery zeal in this direction. Both burned with an inextinguishable desire to purify the Lord's congregation, to overthrow the papacy, to destroy superstition, to restore banished truth, and to lift up prostrate piety, &c." He closes the representation thus: "*Calvin* and *Servetus,* with all their infirmities, were both sincerely pious. This is shown by their end. They both died as the righteous, whom no accusations of conscience trouble, *Servetus* acknowledged, before his execution, the wrong he had done to *Calvin,* and begged his forgiveness. Let us in charity believe that *Calvin* also repented, before his death, of the faults he had committed towards *Servetus.* Charity hopeth all things. Should it give offence to suppose that God has shown his grace to both souls, for the sake of that Jesus on whom they called in death? It is a supposition, at all events, that does no wrong to truth. It is an infirmity of charity, which charity will readily overlook." [*Mosheim, Versuch einer unpartheiischen und gründlichen*] *Ketzergeschichte, Helmst.* 1748, *Buch ii.* § 39, s. 254 *ff.*

35. [Johann Matthais Schröckh and Heinrich Gottlieb Tzschirner, *Christliche Kirchengeschichte*, 45 vols. (Leipzig, 1768–1812).]

II. The Rationalistic Historiography.

The second stand-point of ecclesiastical history may be styled, in opposition to that of the old orthodoxy, the stand-point of *fluctuating heterodoxy* and *unchurchly subjectivity.* This also, however, does not appear at once in its complete character, but has again its own historical process. In this we must distinguish two periods, the *Pietistic* and the proper *Rationalistic,* to which last the distinction just given, becomes first fully applicable. The two differ widely in their views; more we may say perhaps than even the Roman Catholic and Protestant Orthodoxy. The Pietistic school stands in close connection with inward subjective piety, as it came to a reaction in the 17th century against the dead orthodoxy of the Lutheran Church, though continuing to hold still, in the main, the same system of faith, and to reject also the idea of all doctrinal movement or progress. Rationalism, on the contrary, sets itself in hostile array against the substance of the orthodox theory, and against Christianity itself, reducing it to the character of a mutable and transient system. Both tendencies, however, the pietistic and the rationalistic, come together in the point of unchurchliness, and this sufficiently explains to us the transition of the first over into the last, as its proper and natural theoretic consequence.

The Pietistic Method of History, or that of sectarian religious Separation.

George Calixtus had already, in several historical publications, taken a more liberal course than was common among his orthodox contemporaries.[36] Instead of dividing light and shade regularly between a particular section of the visible church and all differing communions, he sought rather in love to find elements of truth and unity in all confessions. He was, however, cried down by the church zealots, and for a long time thrust out of sight entirely. Still he had not lived in vain. His irenical theology, directed towards practical and essential points, came forward again, with the close of the 17th century, and the beginning of the next, under a somewhat modified form. In opposition to the congealed church character and petrified orthodoxy of Lutheranism, stood forth from the bosom of practical religion the Pietism of Spener and Franke; as in England previously we find Puritanism rebelling against the lifeless forms which had come to prevail in the Episcopal Church. Pietism, of the same mind here with the United Brethren[37] and the Methodists, made very little account of doctrine, theology, theoretic Christianity. Its concern was all for practical religion, the exhibition of faith in action. This was, however, as one-sided as the opposite extreme of overvaluing theoretic orthodoxy. Pietism accordingly soon furnished historical proof, that a practical religion which rests on no solid knowledge of truth, and is indifferent towards the

36. [George Calixtus, was a Protestant professor a Helmstedt from 1614. His attempt to develop a theology uniting Lutherans, Reformed, and Roman Catholics was widely denounced as syncretism.]

37. [That is, the *Unitas Fratrum*, the Moravians.]

church, must lose all its energy, fall into false ways, and at last, contrary to its original design, make common cause even with unbelief. In the sphere of history, this form of thinking would of course try the worth of every person and church by the standard of subjective piety; and as this, in many cases at least, must appear to prevail among the oppressed sects rather than with the reigning church, a different view would naturally come to be taken of the relation of the church to the sects, from that which lies at the ground of the old orthodoxy.

This we find exemplified in the celebrated History of the pious and learned GOTTFRIED ARNOLD, who belongs properly to this pietistic school.[38] He had the enormous courage to reverse outright the orthodox principle of history, by which the Church is held to be always in the right against the sects, vindicating to these last all *religious life*, and so of course all true *historical legitimacy* at the same time. Some basis for this method had been furnished, it is true, by the orthodox Protestant mode of handling the Middle Ages, where the cause of the Waldenses, Wickliffites, Hussites, &c., was espoused against the ruling church. But the extension of the principle to the first six centuries also, and to the period subsequent to the Reformation, could not fail to revolutionize the form of Church History completely. As Pietism had been in every way mishandled, persecuted and slandered, by the church orthodoxy to which it stood opposed, it is easy to see how a mind like that of ARNOLD might come to the thought: the reigning church, in which so little living piety is to be found, and by which indeed it is treated with bitter hostility, cannot possibly be the bride of Christ. It is peculiar to this rather to appear without show, small, poor, gentle, and loving, and to be mocked and crucified always by the ruling powers of the world. So it was in the first three centuries; the period of persecution called forth the richest blossoms of piety. ARNOLD's view properly is this, that there was a perfectly pure church only in connection with the apostles, and that no particular church since can be said to be the only true one. Truth and error are according to him everywhere, though not in the same relative proportions. The most truth, it is to be assumed, is found where we have the largest amount of piety; and this, he believed, was to be placed to the credit of the sects.[39]

38. *Unpartheiische Kirchen und Ketzerhistorie, von Anfang des Neuen Testaments bis auf das Jahr Christi*, 1688, [Impartial history of the church and of heresy from the beginning of the New Testament to the year of our Lord 1688] in 4 Theilen, Zuerst erschienen zu Frankfurt a. M., [Thomas Fritsch,] 1699 and 1700. [Gottfried Arnold (1666–1714) was a Lutheran historian and theologian who was introduced to Pietism by Spener. A strong critic of orthodoxy in his publications of the late 1600s he gave great attention to the non-orthodox movements of the early church, insisting on studying them through their own writings rather than those of their critics. He also embraced Christian mysticism. After becoming a pastor and inspector at Werben in Prussia in 1704, he reconciled with Lutheran orthodoxy.]

39. Characteristic in this view is the following passage which I extract from the Preface, § 30 and 31. Its general style, slovenly and destitute of all taste, marks well the spirit of the age to which it belongs. [The difference between Arnold's German style and Schaff's is not represented in the translation.] "Many may perhaps bring forward again the common objection: our dear mother the Christian

As Arnold made religious life the measure of the true Church, and acknowledged this only as it appeared in the form of subjective piety, it was very easy to apply his principle to particular cases, especially when it came to controversies within the Lutheran Church itself, and thus to put to shame the one-sided exclusiveness of orthodoxy. To carry out his maxim, however, with full consistency, he was compelled to employ the greatest violence and perversion of facts, as have been proved against him with convincing force by his orthodox contemporaries Faustking, Cyprian, Corvinus, Löscher, Vejel, Wachter and others.[40] His depreciating judgments with regard to many of the greatest and most pious men of the Church, as well as his extravagant laudations of the sects and heretics, are often truly disgusting.

Then again Arnold fell into a palpable self-contradiction. He was himself orthodox as it regarded the essential doctrines of the gospel, and in opposition to the charges of heresy brought against him, expressly declared his faith to be that of the Lutheran Church.[41] It must be plain, however, to any attentive reader, even of Arnold's *Church History* itself, that the fundamental truths of the gospel, during the first six centuries, and in the period following the Reformation, were altogether more faithfully maintained by the reigning church, than by the sects; and that these last, with all their religious life and their zeal for some particular elements of the evangelical doctrine, were infected in part at least, with errors, which left even those of the Roman Church far in the rear. Let any one call to mind only the Ebionites, Gnostics,

Church ought not to be so *prostituted*, seeing she has had so much to suffer already before. To this I reply, that it is hard for the inexperienced to see which of those outward church societies is to be counted the true church, as everyone according to his own fancy and interest will have the religion to be meant hereby into which he has happened himself to be born. Besides, it is not a scriptural expression or opinion, that the church is a mother. The scriptures know only of one single mother of all saints, which is the Jerusalem above, Galat. iv, 26, Heb. xii. 22. They have never given those godless pretenders, and much less the apostate clergy, liberty to call her a mother, and in this way to intrench and secure themselves against all testimony, admonition, and improvement. The true, pure congregation of the Lord has been from the beginning of the gospel and the times of the apostles, a virgin and bride of Christ. But the false apostate church, according to the testimony of the first teachers and the report hereafter to follow in this history, has become a harlot; and by means of the miscellaneous and inconsiderate introduction of all hypocrites and wicked, under Constantine the Great, as also by the natural increase and propagation of false Christians, has given birth to millions of bastards, with whom no true members of Christ will have anything to do." [Arnold, *Unparteyische Kirchen- und Ketzer-Historie*, preface, sections 30–31.]

40. An ample collection of literature, for the learned professional historian, of great interest and value, in favour of this pietistic stand-point and against it, may be found in the third volume of the Schaffhausen edition of Arnold's History, 1742. [Arnold, *Unparteyische Kirchen- und Ketzer-Historien vom Anfang des Neuen Testaments biß auf das Jahr Christi 1688*, vol. 3 (Schaffhausen: Hurter, 1742).]

41. See particularly his declaration in the second edition of his work just noticed, Part iii. Sect. 2, p. 500, where among other things, he says: "I profess freely and without constraint, that I greatly and dearly prize Luther's doctrine and testimony, as well against the anti-christianity of the corrupt clergy, as in favour of the genuine way of the gospel. Yea, I find this old pure theology and religion to be best in practice for life, and in harmony with the true gospel, which he has again brought forth into view, out of the holy scriptures, and those witnesses of the truth and mystics, particularly Tauler and the German Theology, and asserted it against the schoolmen."

Manichæans, Socinians, Anabaptists, Quakers, &c. Altogether, moreover, the whole view of history exhibited by Arnold is adapted to make a most uncomfortable impression, and to serve powerfully the cause of skepticism; which calls in question, if not the existence, at least the success of any divine plan in history. We need not wonder then, that the founder of Pietism himself, the excellent and venerable Spener, was by no means satisfied with the work of his friend.[42]

The Rationalistic Method of History.

It is easy to see, that Arnold's view of history, as soon as it was admitted to be just, could not fail to shake the credit of the reigning Church in favour of the dissenting sects; nay, to bring its whole existence itself into question. Only the personal piety of Arnold kept him from surrendering himself to a perfectly destructive tendency. The time soon appeared, when not merely the life, but the faith and orthodoxy also of the predominant church were assailed, and the heresies of the sects taken under protection. As Pietism in general, by its comparatively anti-church character, prepared the way for Rationalism, so the work of Arnold served to make room for the stand-point of rationalistic history.

The principle of dissenting subjectivity had now put itself forward, and claimed to be regarded as the legitimate historical force. This required only the loss of that basis of religious feeling which Pietism still inherited from the church out of which it drew its fresh life in order to fall over necessarily to Rationalism. The work of ARNOLD, falling in as it did with the tendency of the age, found a favourable response in many quarters, during his own life-time; as for instance with the great jurist THOMASIUS, who, in a negative respect at least made common cause with the Pietists, in opposition to the reigning church.[43] As the term "orthodox" was brought into miscredit by the first, so also was the word "catholic" by this last, who applied it to every ecclesiastical regulation that did not happen to suit his taste. It became in Germany a proverb even to denote a desperate business, of any sort: "That is to become catholic." With this bug-bear many a wound has since been inflicted on the Lord's body.

The man however who first turned the principle of Arnold to full account, and who is to be considered the founder of the proper rationalistic view of history, was the

42. He mentions in relation to the work, that he had not read a page of it, as he was apprehensive from what he had learned of it by report, that he could not be satisfied with its contents; while at the same time he wished to avoid all occasion for coming out with a public declaration against one, whom he respected as an old friend. (*Letzte Bedenken. theol.* [*Letzte theologishe Bedencken* (Recent theological concerns; Halle: Waisenhaus, 1711)] Band iii, s. 582 f.).

43. See his judgment in Arnold's Church Hist. B. iii. Abth, 2. S. 6 [Arnold, *Unparteyische Kirchen- und Ketzer-Historien* (1742), vol. 3, sec. 2, p. 6.] where he says, among other things: "I hold this work of Mr. Arnold's to be the best, after the sacred scriptures, that is to be had in this line of writing, and hesitate not hereby to recommend it in the strongest terms to all my hearers, if they should have to stint themselves or beg money even to procure it."

celebrated Semler.[44] His early life was passed in pietistic connections; where however a sickly methodistical style of religion was cultivated. He retained also all his days a sort of loose connection with Pietism, in the way of what he called "private piety," as something wholly independent of all theological theories. This shows itself in various passages of his auto-biography, as, for example, in his account of the death of his daughter.[45] Hence it was that he was led earnestly to oppose the appointment of the infamous Bahrdt to a professorship in Halle, and to write against the *Wolfenbuttel Fragments*.[46] To Lessing, the publisher of them, who assured him that the work was given to the world only to promote inquiry, he replied forcibly: That is to set a town on fire in order to make trial of the engines. Still, however, his scientific tendency, and particularly his investigations in the form of historical criticism, ran, unconsciously to himself, directly into Rationalism.

With Arnold he had in common a strong prejudice against the ruling church, and in favour of all uncatholic dissenters. In his fruitful abstract of church history, he utters his regret, that "of the so called heretical writings of the first centuries, almost nothing remains"; and adds the remark "that from such fragments as have been saved, one may easily see that they would be probably *more worthy of being read than the wretched treatises of the catholics*." [47] For men like Tertullian, Bernard of Clairvaux, Thomas Aquinas, he had no taste whatever. Augustine's doctrine of sin and grace he hated from the bottom of his heart; while upon his dear, liberal-minded Pelagius he lost no opportunity of bestowing the warmest praise, and published his *Epistola ad Demetriadem* with full backing and defiance in the way of notes.[48]

To this was joined now, however, another most important element, which had no place with Arnold whatever; namely, the comprehension of the material of ecclesiastical history, and indeed of orthodoxy also itself, under the view of *mobility*, or strictly speaking, endless *mutability*; which we must take care not to confound with the conception of organic development. From his extensive historical studies he had received

44. Those who wish to know more of this man, who in spite of all his defects forms one of the most interesting and instructive characters in the history of theology, are referred to the spirited sketch of Tholuck in the 2d Part of his *Vermischte Schriften*, P, 39 ff. [August Tholuck, *Vermischte schriften grösstentheils apologetischen inhalts* (Various writings, mainly apologetic in content) (Hamburg: F. Perthes, 1839), 2:39 ff.]

45. Th. i., S. 248. [Johann Salomo Semler, *Lebensbeschreibung von ihm selbst abgefasst* (Autobiography; Halle, 1781–82), 1:248.]

46. [The *Wolfenbuttel Fragments* were Deistic writings by Hermann Samuel Reimarus that treated Jesus as a purely human figure and accused authors of the Bible of fraud. They were first published as fragments and anonymously by Gotthold Ephraim Lessing between 1774 and 1778. Reimarus, *Fragments*.]

47. Th. i., S. 40. [Semler, *Historiae ecclesiasticae selecta capita: cum epitome canonum excerptis dogmaticis et tabulis chronologicis* (Select chapters of the history of the church: with excerpts of dogmatic canons and chronological table; Halle, 1767), 1:40.]

48. [Pelagius, *Epistola ad Demetriadem cum aliis aliorum epistolis* (Letter to Demetrias, with other letters), ed. Johann Salomo Semler (Halle: Hemmerde, 1775).]

the indelible impression, that doctrines were always in a course of change, and that the church system as it stood in his own time was something which had existed constantly, under the same form, from the first. The whole history of doctrine appeared to him as a confused chaos of opinions, changing with every period, and hence of no account properly in a theoretic respect at all, but only so far as they might have a good effect morally for the time. His own restless spirit was reflected in this theory. Of an entirely sanguine nature, as he informs us himself,[49] he had a perfect literary voracity, and save in the field of polite learning for which his immeasurably prosaic spirit had no taste, wandered in his one hundred and seventy-one different writings, through all possible spheres of knowledge;[50] everywhere making new discoveries, and illuminating the darkest corners with the lightning flashes of his penetrating genius; but never finding rest or satisfaction, and never rising to a general view or true idea. He saw indeed in the whole history of the Church motion and flow, but no unity in this change, no helmsman on the storm-tost sea. He rose not to the conception of an organic process, a development including the regularity of law that unfolds always new treasures. History was for him a vast tumultuating waste, without guiding principle or certain aim; yea, in the case of the Church, a continually advancing disfiguration only of what might be regarded as the original biblical form of Christianity.

This view of Semler, according to which the church system itself was something that had grown up in the course of time, and this partly, at least, during the period which had been regarded previously as embracing the rise of popish corruption, served to inflict on the old orthodoxy and its theory of history a second stroke, that proved indeed to be deadly. For this whole school based itself on the assumption that whatever might have arisen in time could not be properly of divine or eternal right.

The tone which was thus struck by Semler found the most lively response, in a period, which through the influx of English deism and French materialism, and the prevalence of the philosophy of Wolff, leaned already with growing inclination to a shallow rationalistic *aufklärung* ["enlightenment"] in the sphere of religion. His followers soon cast off the last remains of his affectionate respect for Pietism. Now it first became an earnest matter, with Arnold's principle of partiality for dissent, Arius in opposition to Athanasius, Pelagius against Augustine, the Socinians against the Reformers, were made to have full right even doctrinally on their side. Their only fault was that they had not carried their opposition sufficiently far; and hence the eighteenth century could find no more important work, than to complete the business of destruction upon the Church and her history. The vast labour of centuries was looked upon as labour spent in vain; Rationalism would have history everywhere to be different from what it was in fact; and so, not being able to change it must needs come into

49. In his Account of his Life, Th. i., S. 70 [Semler, *Lebenschreibung*, 1:70.]

50. He even wrote a book on the Habits of Snails in Winter and showed a lively interest in the subject of making gold; in which however, as Tholuck supposes, not merely his scientific curiosity, but his devotion to the god Pluto also, may have been concerned.

a standing controversy with its contents, undertaking presumptuously to correct it after its own miserable subjective conceptions, and turning its greatest facts into insignificance. The acute dogmatical distinctions of the œcumenical councils were thrust aside as sophistical subtleties. The symbolical books of the Protestant Church were condemned as dishonorable shackles for the mind; the deep speculations of the most spiritual thinkers derided as empty dreams; the interior exercises of tender devotional souls, pitied as enthusiastic fancies; the vigorous manifestations of faith in opposition to unbelief, cried down as wild zealotism and intolerance; the greatest enterprises of the Church in other times or among other people branded as the product of dark religious fanaticism. All in one word that rose above the level of everyday life, was forced to become common.[51]

To give some account at the same time of all this past activity of the world, the *pragmatical* fashion was now carried to its perfection; represented under its most learned, skillful, and respectable character by MÜNSCHER and PLANCK. MOSHEIM, following French examples, had already indeed laid down the rule that Church History must be pragmatic; that is, must not simply relate events, but as he expresses it, "unfold also, under the guidance of psychology, the causes to which they are to be referred in the passions, tricks, and windings of the human heart." This pragmatism was not so dangerous with Mosheim and his school; since through the connection in which they still stood with the church orthodoxy, they had some regard to the authority of the scriptures and to Christian experience, as well as to psychology, and acknowledged, in conjunction with the subjective factors of history, the presence of objective forces also by which the course of events was held to be ruled always in the last instance. But now, in the hands of religious indifferentism and rationalism, the entire history of the Church was turned into a purely subjective play of human passions. The most important doctrines and events, all tried by the standard of the most miserable private judgment were deduced from idle speculation or the lowest motives of a selfish heart; the divinity of Christ, for instance, from the rhetorical fancy of Athanasius; the doctrine of free grace and original sin, from Augustine's stiff humor and fondness for writing; the papacy of the Middle Ages, from the imposition of the false Isodorian decretals and the ambition of "the rascal" Hildebrand;[52] the Reforma-

51. How shamefully Rationalism, which has been indeed scientifically conquered, but still retains its adherents among the half-learned, and appears lately resuscitated among the so called *Friends of Light* in Germany, can allow itself to deal with the most venerable names in Church History, may be seen, for instance, in the judgment of the general superintendent [Johann Friedrich] Röhr on Augustine; whom he styles, on account of his doctrine of sin and grace "a profaner of the gospel and a rake turned pious" (*Prediger-Bibliothek*, Heft. 1. s. 13). On the other hand he lauds *Pelagius* as "the venerable champion of reason against unreason who even in his own time had the satisfaction of seeing the wisest and best men take their stand on his side," (s. 15.).

52. [The Isidorian decretals (often spelled "Isodorian" in the nineteenth century) refers to a collection of canon law documents said to be composed by various early popes and compiled by an Isidore Mercrator, but likely forged in France c. 850. They deal with many issues, including papal supremacy. Many of them were drawn on in the canon law collections associated with the reform of Gregory VII

tion from the pecuniary embarrassment of Leo X; the Lutheran dogma of the Lord's Supper from the obstinacy and contentious spirit of Luther himself.[53]

Thus was God excluded from history altogether; which was at the same time, to thrust out its eyes and tear the living heart from its bosom. The life-course of the Redeemer's bride was caricatured into a "history of human folly." The theatre of the kingdom of God in the world was degraded into a wild arena of base, unholy passions. We might wonder, how with such a view, it was still possible to take any interest in the study of church history at all, were the maxim, *Similis simili gaudet* ["like takes pleasure in like"], not at hand to explain the seeming contradiction. The least that a still somewhat noble nature could do, in these circumstances, was to fall upon this fool-interlude in the drama of human life indignantly, with the scourge of sharp satire. This was done by HENKE, in his work, first published 1789, and in different editions since.[54] He wrote the History of the Church throughout, to adopt the mild judgment of HASE in the case, as "a representation of errors, in religion and judicial process against spiritual despotism in every shape."

It was in this period of cheerless destruction, that HAMANN, the Northern magus, in deep sorrow, uttered his complaint: "What a negative age we live in! What hosts of negative men! All plunder and rob, no one is willing to give. All are bent on destroying, nobody thinks to build. No earnestness, all frivolity; no dignity, all buffoonery; no object, all side references only!"[55] His friend and kinsman in spirit, HERDER longed also for deliverance from the self-styled philosophical century, that hated mortally, to use his own language, all that was either miraculous or mysterious; and from the depth of his warm heart, that burned with zeal for the beautiful and the noble, was heard, passionately to exclaim, "Would that I had been born in the Middle Ages!"[56]

This wish found a lively echo in many young hearts, whose time of appearing on the theatre of public life had not yet come. HERDER himself also contributed some

(Hildebrand).]

53. In the case of this last point, the American divine Joseph F. Berg goes still further, and refers Luther's doctrine of consubstantiation at once to the *devil.* See his *Lectures on Romanism*, [(Philadelphia: Weidner)] published 1840, p. 233; where he says—"On the whole, however, I am not disposed altogether to deny that the devil may have had some hand in originating Luther's notion of consubstantiation; it savours so much of transubstantiation, the *chef d'œuvre* of the evil one, that it would be hard to disprove the devil's agency in its invention!" And yet we have been told by the same theological authority in the *Protestant Banner*, deceased, that the eucharistic doctrine of Calvin and the Heidelberg Catechism is still more absurd than that of Luther; because forsooth the soul cannot literally eat flesh, as this doctrine is gravely charged with teaching! It must follow of course that the Reformed theory of the Lord's Supper, as it stood originally, is still more devilish even than the Lutheran. [The *Protestant Banner* was a biweekly published in Philadelphia by Berg from 1842 to 1844.]

54. [Heinrich Philipp Konrad Henke, *Geschichte der jüdischen und christlichen Religion für den ersten Unterricht* (History of the Jewish and Christian religion for the first lessons, 1789).]

55. [A characteristic saying of Johann George Hamann (1730–88). See Betz, *After Enlightenment*; Berlin, *Three Critics of Enlightenment*.]

56. [Jean Paul reported this famous exclamation of Herder many years after his death. Nevinson, *A Sketch of Herder and His Times*, 214.]

material at least towards the erection of the new dome that was to rise in the midst of these dreary ruins, by his philosophical and historical writings; which belong already, in their stand-point, to another time and tendency.

When necessity is greatest, help shows itself to be most near. Rationalism, with its full denial of the divinity of Christ, and its deistic degradation of God himself to the character of a private indifferent spectator merely of human events, from beyond the clouds, lost every deeper conception of man also, at the same time. For that which makes man to be man, and gives him his true worth, is the presence of God in him, in which he lives, moves, and has his being. It was quite in order therefore, that this spiritually bankrupt age, should be led first back again to the consciousness of the original, ideal dignity of the human nature itself, so as to see in this mirror with shame its own wretched visage, and thus come to repentance and a sound conversion. This took place chiefly by means of Herder; who without question is to be ranked among the richest, noblest, and most life-pregnant spirits, in the history of Literature. His nature was compounded of theological, philosophical, and poetical material, endowed with the most open sense for the beautiful and the grand in the most diversified forms, and adorned with the most comprehensive cultivation in a general way. He was the inspired and inspiring prophet of humanity in its purest sense. He came forward in the year 1774, with his small work (the sign of a new epoch) entitled, *A Philosophy of History for the Culture of Humanity*; which he extended ten years after, into his celebrated *Ideas for the History of Humanity*, so highly commended by the accomplished John von Müller.[57]

The first point in which Herder rose above the rationalistic historiography, and prepared the way for the modern, was in his apprehension of it as *living spirit*, a process of *organic development*. In this development, he saw a constant *progress towards the better*. This was a most fruitful thought that served to bring light and order into the chaotic confusion of the rationalistic history. It came to a reconciliation again between the subject and the objective constraint of the world. "Humanity," he tells us,[58] "always remains humanity; and still a plan of progress is visible—my great theme!" (S.76. [p. 76.]) He appeals, in favour of the theory of development, to the analogy of the single human life and of nature, where we meet it on all sides, and goes on to say:

> Clearly so also in human history! The Egyptian could not be without the Oriental; the Greek rested on him again as his basis; the Roman lifted himself into view on the back of the whole world. Actual *advance* and *constant development*, even though no individual gain should appear! All on a wide scale; the theatre of a ruling plan upon the earth, although the last purpose may be

57. [Johann Gottfried Herder, *Auch eine Philosophie der Geschichte* (1774); Herder, *Ideen zur Philosophie der Geschichte der Menschheit* (1784).]

58. In the first of the works just named. See *J. G. Herder's Sämmtliche Werke. zur Phil. and Gesch.* Th 3. S. 74. [Herder, *Auch eine Philosophie der Geschichte,* reprinted in *Johann Gottfried Von Herder's Sämmtliche Werke: Zur Philosophie Und Geschichte* (Stuttgart: Gotta, 1827–30), 3:74.]

> hidden from our sight; the theatre of divinity, though it should be only amid the ruins of life in its particular forms.

Hence he exhibits, for example, the old Oriental history as the childhood, the Grecian as the youth, and the Roman as the manhood of humanity. (S. 53, ff. [p. 53ff.])

Closely connected with this is the second point in which HERDER exerted a salutary influence. He created, namely, a *love* for history in *all* its stages; since no part can be torn from an organic whole without destroying its beauty. In the face of the ridiculous self-complacency of the eighteenth century, which claimed all illumination and wisdom to itself alone, he had the courage to show, that every people and every period, not excepting, even the so much decried Middle Ages, had possessed its peculiar glory and worth, and that his contemporaries, in their contempt for the past, only revealed their own poverty and disgrace. He will have nothing to do with that egotistical narrowness of mind that affects to bring everything to the measure of its own subjectivity. No single people, no single age, in his view, can represent the full ideal of humanity; it is distributed accordingly into a thousand forms, and "wanders a perfect Proteus through all climes and centuries."[59] With untiring affection, this gifted cosmopolite gathered, in his numerous works, the flowers of humanity of all zones, nations and times, and wove them into a wreath, whose fresh fragrance served wonderfully to quicken the genius, especially of the rising generation. Many of his words were like the morning breath that foretells a beautiful day. On all sides was awakened once more sympathy with humanity, and along with this a new enthusiasm in the study of its history. Still HERDER himself never came to a full, comprehending, general view of his subject. His reverence for humanity was of a somewhat unmeasured and indefinite character. JEAN PAUL says of him very aptly, in a letter to JACOBI: "It requires broad wings, to swim over so many remote fields. Herder is made up of half a dozen geniuses at once, *wanting only the binding force of a properly independent personal reflection*, without which neither poetry nor philosophy has ever become complete."

A number of other men now soon arose, who contributed in various ways to promote respect and affection for the past. Here especially is to be noticed the *Romantic School*, of the two SCHLEGELS, TIECK and NOVALIS; who chastised severely the shallow pretensions of the reigning, unhistorical Rationalism, and drew forth the rich religious poetry of the Middle Ages from its dark retreat. VON DER HAGEN, the two GRIMMS, LACHMANN, and others brought into view particularly the glories of German antiquity. The great antiquarians WOLF, NIEBUHR, CREUZER, produced a much more deep and living apprehension of Grecian and Roman history.

Of still more importance, however was the turn which took place at this time in philosophy; as it served to bring to clear consciousness, and systematic order, the ideas irregularly thrown out by Herder and his spiritual allies. SCHELLING overcame the stand-point of critical reflection as established by Kant, and the subjective

59. S. 76.

idealism of Fichte; planted himself on the ground of realism and the objective reason; and applied himself with fond partiality in his earlier years to the speculative study of nature, under the view of a self-unfolding organic process. His disciple and successor, Hegel, carried the principle of a dialectic development, with the most amazing energy of metaphysical thought, into every sphere of the philosophy of spirit. We wish not to endorse Hegel's theology of development without qualification; but whatever may be thought of it, one thing is certain. It has left an impression on German science that can never be effaced; and has contributed more than any other influence to diffuse a clear conception of the interior organism of history as a richer evolution continually of the idea of humanity, as well as a proper respect for its universal and objective authority, in opposition to the self-sufficient and arrogant individualism of the rationalistic school. The Hegelian method requires, moreover, that the historian should resign himself without prejudice to his subject, and thus suffer it to come to a living reproduction according to the law of its own nature. Hence it stands in direct contradiction to that subjective show of reason that is never satisfied with history as it stands, but must be always correcting it after the fashion of its own private fancies. According to the whole stand-point of this philosophy, history is a self-evolution of the absolute spirit, and hence supremely rational throughout. Such is the sense of that celebrated, though often misunderstood, dictum of Hegel: All that is rational is real, and all that is real (or absolutely existent, substantial) is rational.[60] Here, however, we come also on the fatal rock of this speculative method of history. While Rationalism had scarcely the most remote conception of a divine presence in history and resolved everything into free human activity, the philosophy before us falls over to the opposite extreme of pantheism and fatalism. The individual is regarded the blind organ of the world-spirit; evil is held to be a necessary medium for reaching the good; and thus the idea of guilt and moral accountability is necessarily lost. We may say indeed that the Hegelian *Method* rests on the supposition of the necessity of evil as the negative condition of moral progress. For sin in the sphere of morality is made to correspond exactly with contradiction in the sphere of logic; and this last, according to Hegel's dialectics, forms the impulsive force in the moving process of all thought. It results, moreover, from the pantheistic tendency just mentioned, that no sufficient account is made of the personal and individual. Such emphasis is laid upon the general, that life in the concrete dissolves into mere abstraction, the endlessly diversified fullness of history shrinks into a few logical forms, and living personalities are transformed into ideal shadows. All these defects are found united in the modern Tübingen school, with Dr. Bauer[61] and Dr. Strauss at its head. These, preceded[62] by Schwegler and Zeller, have handled particularly the history of primitive Christianity in the way of pretended dialectic construction, with a spirit altogether pantheistic and ruinous.

60. [The dictum is found in Hegel's preface to *Outlines of the Philosophy of the Right*, 14.]

61. Not to be confounded with the notorious Bruno Baur.

62. ["followed" is meant here.]

The Hegelian Philosophy then is in itself no safe conductor through the halls of Church History. Its logical forms of thinking are capable of being applied in the most opposite ways. Whilst it has led the way for many to a historical and churchly spirit, and proved an admirable help towards the overthrow of the common Rationalism and a thorough speculative understanding and defence of orthodoxy; it has served, on the other hand, when sundered from the real life revelation of Christianity, to produce itself a new form of Rationalism, very different from the first, more spiritual indeed, but for this reason also more dangerous, that from an opposite direction shows the most radical hostility to all concrete and individual historical life.

Of much more account than the philosophy of Schelling and Hegel for the formation of the modern German theology, has been the influence of SCHLEIERMACHER, the greatest theological genius, we may say, since the Reformation. The most various forms of cultivation belonging to his time were brought together, under an exceedingly original scientific combination, in his person; and there is not to be found now a single theologian of importance, in whom the influence of his great mind is not more or less to be traced. History, to be sure, was not his sphere and what has been published from him since his death, in this department, belongs to his weakest productions. Still, however, by his profound doctrinal and moral views, he has influenced *indirectly* the treatment of historical theology also, to a most important extent. The productive, strictly evangelical element in his system is found in this; that he placed the person of Christ as the Redeemer and the author of a new life in the centre of theology; put emphasis on the idea of *communion* in religion; and in this manner opened the way at least for a churchly tendency. He forms a supplementary counterpoise over against the Hegelian theory thus far, that he fastens his eye sharply in particular upon the original and specific in Christianity, and instead of starting from the idea, makes religious experience rather the fountain of dogmatic knowledge. On the whole, however, Schleiermacher's method is not so much historical as mathematical. The different constituents of an idea came into view with him, more as standing together in space than as growing forth one from another in time.

Out of his school has proceeded the most important church historian of our time, AUGUSTUS NEANDER; who however is to be considered some steps in advance of his position. He attaches himself, namely, still more closely than Schleiermacher, to the real and positive element of religion, and allows far more weight to the idea of organic development. In this respect he appears in a certain affinity with the Hegelian philosophy, although known as one of its bitter opponents. The greatest charm of his historical writing results precisely from this, that he causes religious characters to rise gradually, in the way of living reproduction, before the eyes of his readers; and all with such amiable pious artlessness of manner, that the picture becomes irresistibly at the same time a source of practical edification. His work, which is now brought down in *ten* parts to the time of Boniface VIII, deserves to be presented in full, under a worthy form, to the English and American public, and to take the place which has been heretofore allowed to Mosheim.[63] Possibly a judicious compilation or epitome as a manual for students of theology, might be better than a literal translation, which at all events, by reason of the easy carelessness of Neander's style, would be no easy task. This distinguished monument of sanctified learning is, without question, the most important product of the modern German theology in the sphere of church history, and must long maintain a high authority. At the same time, it is not to be denied that, in point of *church* character, it is no longer fully equal to the demands of the time. Neander stands still on Schleiermacher's ground in this respect, that the church spirit appears with him under an indefinite form, and in the general character too much of a mere feeling of communion. Hence his aversion to a pointedly distinct orthodoxy, and his partiality towards free dissenting tendencies. Since the Jubilee of the Reformation, however, in 1817, the evangelical theology of Germany has taken a strong and constantly growing church direction; and this, beyond all doubt, will give character more and more to the future. To be complete now, a Church History should unite in proper harmony a thorough use of original sources, clear apprehension, organic development, lively and interesting delineation, strong but liberal and universal church feeling, and fruitfulness in the way of practical edification. It may be long, perhaps, before we possess a work that shall satisfy equally all these requirements. Still however the elements which it calls for are all actually at hand in the different tendencies of the modern German theology. The material is prepared; the plan of the edifice too is ready in its main outline; only the master hand is waited for, that shall put the work together, and cause the parts to appear as a complete, magnificent and harmonious whole.

After this short review of the most conspicuous modern historical schools, let us endeavour now to bring into a single view the right conception of church history, as it may be gathered from all that has been said. The main point here is to set in proper light the idea of *organic development*; since this forms the key to the understanding of history, and the watchword of all the more important works, in this department, which we have already brought into view in the first part of this tract. True, this conception itself is differently held by different persons, and I also claim the right of deviating in several points from Hegel, Schleiermacher, Neander, &c., as has already been intimated in what goes before. But still there runs a common thread through the whole latter view of church history, which it is above all important to discern and understand. Such as are acquainted with the subject in any measure by correct personal reflection, will judge indulgently of the following attempt; since a philosophy of church history, and a complete theory of historical development from the theological stand-point, is something which is wanting to us as yet altogether. Any deficiency

63. [Only the first part of Neander, *Allgemeine Geschischte* (1825–52) had appeared in English by 1846 as *The History of the Christian Religion and Church during the Three First Centuries* (1831–41). The first complete edition began appearing in 1847 as *General History of the Christian Religion and Church*, 9 vols. (Edinburgh: T. & T. Clark, 1847–55).]

that may take place in my particular exposition of the idea of development, it must be remembered, can in no way impair the truth and value of the idea itself.

III. The Modern Historiography, or the Stand Point of Organic Development

The stand-point of the present historical theology of Germany is not something isolated, the sheer subjective product of some later theologians; but the necessary result of previous standpoints, resting itself in this way on the solid ground and bottom of history. The orthodox treatment of history, as well as the rationalistic, came to a dissolution by the irresistible process of their own development, under the one sided tendency which belonged to each. But this dissolution was only the necessary transition to a new life. Out of their ruins the elements of truth on both sides, divested of their perishable hull, rose and became united in a higher third, in which they now came to their true force. We allow both the former methods then up to a certain point, and incorporate them so far into our own view.

The *orthodox* theory of history we hold to be right in two essential points. First, in insisting upon something unchangeable and everlasting in history. But while the theory identifies this at once with the *church* doctrine, and affirms that *this* has been at all times the same, and has undergone neither decrease nor increase, but perversions only and obscurations; we, on the other hand, distinguish between truth as objectively present in Christ and in the scriptures, and truth as subjectively present in the consciousness of the church, and say: Christianity in itself and objectively considered is complete in Christ, in whom dwells the fulness of the Godhead bodily, and who is the same yesterday, today, and forever; as also in his word, which is exhibited in the holy scriptures of the New Testament, in a pure, original, perfect and absolutely normative form, for all times. Subjective Christianity, on the contrary, or the life of the God man in his Church, is a process, a development, which begins small, and grows always larger, till it comes at last to full manhood in Christ; that is, till the believing human world may have appropriated to itself, both outwardly and inwardly, the entire fulness of objective Christianity, or the life of Christ. In this view the word of God also was not at once understood by the church from the beginning, in all its depth and comprehension, but gradually always more and more with the advancing age of the church. We must say, accordingly, that the reformers, for instance, understood the word of God better than the church fathers and the schoolmen. Then we agree with the orthodox standpoint, in the second place, in believing the *church* to be the bearer of God's truth, and Christian life, the lawful and proper heir of all the promises of the gospel. But we do not, for this reason, agree with it in denying the sects all right to exist, and excluding them from all participation in the truth. On the contrary, we suppose them to play an indispensable part, in modifying and determining the development of the orthodox church itself.

Thus do we exhibit our position, also, with regard to the rationalistic theory of history. We consider it right in this respect generally, in the first place, that it apprehends the life and doctrine of the church as something moveable and flowing. But in determining more particularly the nature and character of this movement, we differ from it essentially. The rationalist sees in the movement only the lawless play of caprice, without any unity at the ground of the manifold, without any fixed and definite end, resolving all mainly into the course of mere human affections and passions. History is for him a continual ebb and flow, that still comes in the end always to the old thing; or, if he allows a progress, it is made to consist in a process of rarefaction, in the dissolution of previous church views, with nothing left at last but the miserable conceptions of an abstract religion of mere reason and nature. But we conceive of historical movement as an ever-increasing stream, whose course has been already prescribed in the plan of everlasting wisdom before the formation of the world, and that now rolls itself forward according to divine laws to empty itself finally in the ocean of eternity. We maintain, consequently, that the Spirit of Christ himself, uninterruptedly present in the church, is the chief factor in history, to whose power all human factors, which are also to be acknowledged in their place, must be regarded as subordinate; and that nothing which has once come to be of true historical weight can be absolutely negated or made to become null, but must ever incorporate itself as an abiding element into the subsequent part of the process. Those who have lived and died in the Lord, are followed by their works into the quiet abodes of everlasting blessedness (comp. Rev. xiv. 13). As it regards the relation, in which Rationalism places dissent to orthodoxy, the sects to the church, we agree with it thus far, that the sects are not to be counted as pure error; whilst we maintain, in direct opposition to it, that they are justifiable over against the church only so far as this may have come to labour under disease, and that after the restoration of the general body, *which always follows sooner or later*, they must be overwhelmed by the judgment of history. It is only the *church* which has the promise that the gates of hell shall not prevail against her.

We may characterize our standpoint, then, in few words, with regard to the first point here noticed, as that of *regular or organic development*, and with regard to the view taken of orthodoxy and dissent, as that of free, or *protestant, evangelically catholic, ecclesiasticism.*

It remains now to explain somewhat more particularly these terms of distinction, and to show their force. What then, in the first place, are we to understand by *organic or regular development*, in itself considered? And how, in the second place, is the general idea to be applied to the history of the Church?

Only that which is dead has the privilege of being *done.* All, on the other hand, that can lay claim to life is in its inmost nature a genesis, movement, process, development. So we find it even in nature; which is the presupposition, and, at the same time, the mirror, of spirit. The lowest kind of process, which indeed can be only improperly so termed, is the mechanical motion of the heavenly bodies, which revolve around their sun, obeying unconsciously the immanent law of their own constitution. This motion, however, always returning into itself, is not yet life, but at best an analogy only of life. The proper *genesis* first appears in the sphere of organic nature, in the life of the *plant.* The plant is possessed of a real life and is the subject thus of a development that begins with the seed, forms itself from this into root, stem, branch, leaf, and blossom, and becomes complete in its fruit. Here we have progress constantly from the lower to the higher; but still nothing is revealed that was not contained potentially at first in the germ. The last result accordingly of the vegetable development, the fruit, comprises in itself again new seed; so that the end returns always with new wealth to the beginning.

A still higher form of life is the animal; at the head of which (though of a specifically different order of existence) stands man, so far as his earthly nature is concerned. Man, to come to him at once, exists first as an embryo, still interwoven with the life of the mother, and as such is said to pass as it were cursorily, in his conformation, through all the lower stages of the animal life. After his birth, he makes the course of childhood, boyhood, youth, manhood, and old age. In all these stages he is *man* and preserves thus in his development the unity of his nature; but in all at the same time he is again different, inasmuch as his general nature takes continually a more definite form, and reveals itself in a higher and more perfect way. Still even the highest stage, the life of the old man, is but the full evolution of the life that was originally present in the child. This development we denominate regular and organic; since it follows with necessity an inward life force, proceeds with equal, steady, order, and continues always true to the original nature of the man, till in the end it has brought the whole fulness of it into view. The German language, which is uncommonly rich and philosophical, has an admirable word that expresses all that is comprised in this idea of organic development. It is the word, *aufheben,* which is so much used, and we may say so much *abused* also, in the Hegelian philosophy. It includes three meanings, namely, to *abolish* (*tollere*) to *preserve* (*conservare*) and to *raise* to a higher state (*elevare*). All these senses are wonderfully combined in the idea with which we are now concerned. We may say with the fullest truth, of man, that in every higher stage of his existence, his previous life is in this threefold view *aufgehoben*. The child is abolished in the young man, and yet is preserved at the same time, and raised unto a higher stage of life. The temporary outward form is abolished; the substance, the idea is preserved; not however by continuing to be what it was before, but by mounting upwards to a more exalted mode of out ward existence.

Parallel precisely with the bodily life of man in this view, is the life also of his spirit. For soul and body are by divine constitution most intimately bound together, and what God has thus joined, man has no right to put asunder. Both parts of his being develop themselves, hand in hand together. Man comes not into the world a scholar, an artist, or the possessor of a moral and religious character. He carries within him indeed the capacity for life in such form; but this only in the way of germ that must yet be developed by impulse from within and the influence of proper conditions without, as the plant grows through the action of air, sunshine and rain. Here, also, we have in full again, what we have just noticed in the case of his animal life. Spiritual growth or development is likewise a process of annihilation, preservation, and exaltation; in which it comes in the end to a complete explication only, of what was present by implication at the start. This must be affirmed even of the development of the life of religion itself. Its commencement is the new birth; its end, the resurrection of the body. This last is only the full consummation of the first, its proper ultimate consequence, by which the new spirit has added to it the new body also, as its needful organ and blessed habitation.

All this is so clear and so fully established by common experience that it is not likely to be called in question by any reflecting man. Is it not marvelous then, that the same simple, familiar truth, as soon as it comes to be applied to the history of the human *race,* should be so stoutly and stiffly denied, as we find it to be in fact by many?[64] What holds of the individual must hold also of humanity as a whole, since this is simply the organic totality of all single men. So precisely as the single Christian does not become complete at a stroke, but only by degrees, the Church as the complex of all Christians must admit and require too a gradual development. Christ himself, the head of the Church, submitted to the law of a genesis in time and grew from infancy up to manhood. This genesis was no apparition merely, no δοκησις[65] as many of the Gnostics supposed; but truth and reality. "Jesus *increased,*" it is written,

64. Dr. *Cheever,* the editor of the *New York Evangelist,* in his review of my work, the *Principle of Protestantism* ["Dr. Schaf's Work on Protestantism," *New York Evangelist*, 16, no. 36 (September 4, 1845), 142], roughly rejects the idea of a steadily advancing development of the Church, and affirms in opposition to it that Christendom moves always at like distance around the same centre, the Bible; so that the 19th century is just as near to this centre as the first! A fine compliment to humanity truly, on the part of this learned divine; by which it is thus sunk to such form of existence as belongs to a soulless and lifeless planet that likewise revolves, always at the same distance around its centre, the sun. As Dr. Cheever is no friend of German Theology, I will refer him to an English authority of some reputation, Bishop Butler, who in his *Analogy [of Religion],* Part II. Chap. iv., [192–93], towards the close, plainly sanctions the idea of a progressive development on the part of the human world, in the following words: "However, thus much is manifest, that the whole natural world and government of it, is a scheme or system; not a fixed, but a progressive one; a scheme, in which the operation of various means takes up a great length of time, before the ends they tend to can be attained. The change of seasons, the ripening of the fruits of the earth, the very history of a flower, is an instance of this. And so is human life. Thus vegetable bodies, and those of animals, though possibly formed at once, yet grow up by degrees to a mature state. And thus rational agents, who animate these latter bodies, are naturally directed to form each his own manners and character, by the gradual gaining of knowledge and experience, and by a long course of action. Our existence is not only successive, as it must be of necessity; but one state of our life and being is appointed by God, to be a preparation for another; and that to be the means of attaining to another succeeding one, infancy to childhood, childhood to youth, youth to mature age. . . . Thus, in the daily course of natural providence, God operates in the very same manner, as in the dispensation of Christianity, making one thing subservient to another, this somewhat farther; and so on, through a progressive series of means, which extend, both backward and forward, beyond our utmost view."

65. [Trans. "apparition." "Docetism," the term for the teaching that Jesus merely appeared to be human, is derived from δοκησις.]

"in wisdom and stature, and in favour with God and man" (Luke ii. 52.). "Though he were a Son, yet learned he obedience, by the things which he suffered" (Heb. v. 8). How then shall the Church, which repeats and continues the earthly human life of Christ, form an exception to this law of development. The Lord himself teaches the contrary, in the parables he employs to represent the nature of the kingdom of God; comparing it with the small mustard seed that gradually becomes a great tree (Matt. xiii. 31, 32); and with leaven that works and spreads till the whole lump is leavened (v. 33). Paul is full of the idea of a constantly advancing development on the part of the Church. He speaks of the whole building of the saints, as *growing* to a holy temple in the Lord (εν ω πασα η οιχοδομη συναρμολογουμενη αυξει εις ναον αγιον εν κυριω, Eph. ii. 21. Comp. 1 Peter ii. 5.)[66] He dwells on the *edifying* of the body of Christ, (εις οιχοδομην του σωματος του χριστου),[67] until we all come in the unity of faith and of the knowledge of the Son of God, unto a perfect man, unto the measure of the stature of the fulness of Christ (Eph. iv. 12, 13. Comp. v. 16; also, iii. 18, 19, and Col. ii. 19.).

We present now the particular characteristics of this development of the kingdom of God, as they disclose themselves in a thorough study of history.

1. The development of the church is partly *external* and partly *internal*. The first consists in the progressive diffusion of the gospel among those who are not Christians, by the activity of missions. This must go forward, as long as there may be a soul that has not yet heard of Christ crucified. It is not at all times equally active. It showed itself with the greatest power in the apostolic age, among the Jews, Greeks, and Romans; then on the threshold of the middle ages, when the Church received the Germanic nations as a new material into her bosom; and appears now again in the spirit of modern missions, which is turned with increasing earnestness towards Asia, Africa and Australia. In many periods, the Church has been so fully taken up with her internal concerns, in the way of establishing a principle or combating error, as to have no time left for missions. So in the heart of the middle ages and in the period of the reformation. Still action in this form can never fail wholly; since it belongs inseparably to the vocation of the militant church.

But the missionary work alone is by no means all that this vocation includes. As soon as Christianity has gained footing among a people, a more difficult *interior* mission begins; having for its object the transfusion of the manners and institutions of such a people with the Christian principle. This forms that *inward* development which we have here chiefly in view. It spreads itself over all portions of the natural life, as the outward missionary work does over all lands and people, agreeably to the claims of Christianity as the absolute world religion. Like leaven, the gospel must work itself into the universal mass of life, under all its established forms.

66. [Trans. "In him the whole structure is joined together and grows into a holy temple in the Lord" (NRSV).]

67. [Trans. "for building up of the body of Christ" (Eph 4:12b, NRSV).]

The Church finds at the start an existing *State,* in a certain stage of development; with which, as ruled by the principle of heathenism, she comes into violent collision, the source of bloody persecutions. Out of all these however she rises victorious, in the time of Constantine. Then, during the Middle Ages, she brings the state more and more into subjection, and occupies it with Christian laws and institutions. Under this discipline, the state gradually comes of age, and since the Reformation takes a more free posture towards the Church; either in the way of more or less direct control, as in Lutheran lands and in the English establishment; or in the way of peaceful indifference, as here in America. Since however the Church is itself social in its very nature, she must include a regimen also of some sort, a system of order and discipline, in her own organization. This *constitution* at first, while the nations still need education, appears under the episcopal or hierarchic form; but with the Reformation this has been exchanged, to a large extent at least, for the presbyterial in which the people are brought to take part in the government.

Again, the Church meets, among cultivated nations at least, the *Fine Arts.* With these she has nothing to do so far as they stand in the service of sin. But their proper human value she appropriates in the end to herself, and employs it, transfused with the religious principle for the purposes of worship; in which way, architecture, sculpture, painting, music, and poetry, find their proper place and lay their richest products on the altar of the Lord.

The Church requires, in the third place, a *Science*, in which she may come to clear self-consciousness, and have a full view of her relation to God, her peculiar life, her duties and privileges. This is *Theology;* that is, the scientific apprehension of religion. This again has its own development, of which no farther notice can be taken here. As science, she comes of course into contact with the secular or profane sciences, which serve her as a natural basis; in exegesis, for instance, with classic and oriental philology; as church history, with the history of the world; as apologetik, polemik, dogmatik and ethics, with philosophy; as homiletics, with rhetoric; &c. This relation too, like that to art, is partly hostile and in part friendly. Thus, for example, the Church in her theology separates what is heathenish from the philosophy of Plato and Aristotle; but appropriates their results in the way of pure thought, as well as their bold inquiring spirit and dialectic method. Plato, in the patristic age, and Aristotle, in the scholastic, have exerted an immense influence on the construction of theology; and so more recently, in England, Locke, and in Germany, the systems of Kant, Fichte, Schelling and Hegel, in their necessary consecution. The same thing might be shown also of other branches of secular science; but this would carry us here quite too far.

Finally, the Church transforms the *natural social life* of the nations; and causes her faith to show itself in a system of virtues and good works, which as Christian all rest on the principle of love to God. Hence we have a history of *Christian life,* understanding by this the manifestation of faith, or the morality of religion. This life is different according to the faith and doctrinal system lying at its ground. Thus the practical piety and morality of Roman Catholicism is characteristically legal, punctilious, unfree and anxious; but distinguished also for great sacrifices, the virtue of obedience, and full consecration to the Church. That of Protestantism is evangelically free, cheerful and joyous in the possession of justification by grace, and rests in the deep inward sense of union with God through Jesus Christ.

2. The development of the Church is *organic*. It is no mechanical accumulation of events, and no result simply of foreign influences. Certain outward conditions are indeed required for it, as the plant needs air, moisture, and light, in order to grow. But still the impelling force in the process is the inmost life of the church herself. Christianity is a new creation that unfolds itself continually more and more from within, and extends itself by the necessity of its own nature. It takes up, it is true, foreign material also in the process; but changes it at once into its own spirit and assimilates it to its own nature, as the body converts the food required for its growth into flesh and blood, marrow and bone. The church accordingly, in this development, remains true always to her own nature and reveals only what it contained in embryo from the start. Through all changes—first Greek, then Roman Catholic, then German evangelical—she never ceases still to be the church. So the oak also changes, but never becomes an apple tree. The expression *organic* implies farther that the stages of development, like the links of a chain, or better, like the members of a living body, are indissolubly bound together. Just because the church does unfold itself from within, as now affirmed, obeying its own life-law throughout, the process itself must form a whole, in which the several parts mutually complete each other. It is only the entire history of the church, from her commencement in the congregation at Jerusalem to her consummation in the general judgment, which can fully represent her conception. Here, however, will be found no trait superfluous, no trait wanting, and every part in its proper place, as is required by the nature of a beautiful and complete organism.

3. The development in question includes the threefold form of action, which has been already described as expressed by the German word *aufheben*. Each new stage negates the preceding one, by raising its inmost being to a more adequate form of existence. Annihilation is thus required. The seed must die to make way for the plant. The bud is burst by the flower. The child must put off childhood in becoming a youth. But it is only the outward, the transient, that is thus annihilated. The substance abides. So Judaism is taken up (*aufgehoben*) by Christianity; that is, it exists no longer as the legal and particularistic institute it was before; but all the truths of the Old Testament, at the same time, are preserved in the gospel, by being fulfilled. The Grecian and Roman nationalities came to an end, in their pagan form, as soon as they became Christian; but under a higher character they still continue to exist and have done specific service for the church. The Greek Church, by means of Grecian culture, was the organ for producing speculative doctrine and forms of worship. The Roman Church, true to the spirit of ancient Rome under Christian form, brought forward ecclesiastical government and law and the idea of a catholicity that should embrace and pervade all lands

and nations as well as all departments of life. She has not forgotten, of a truth, the line of Virgil: "*Tu regere imperio populos, Romane, memento!*"[68] The Middle Ages have been *taken up* by Protestantism; that is, the period exists here no longer as that theocratic universal monarchy, which had its centre in Rome and the pope for its head; but its deepest meaning has been fulfilled in the reformation, and its intellectual and spiritual acquirements have descended to the evangelical church, as its heir, to be improved still farther under a new character. Rationalism, as a system of unbelief, is scientifically and morally annihilated by the reviving evangelical theology of Germany; but its grammatico-historical interpretation of the scriptures and its whole effort to reach a critical scientific apprehension of Christianity and the church on their natural, human side, have been preserved by being raised into higher connexions and brought under the power of a living faith. Only in this form, indeed, could the previous effort at all reach its own proper end. How the orthodox and rationalistic methods of history, have been made to pass away in the modern, we have shown already at some length.

4. The development of the Church is carried forward, by means of *dialectic opposites* and *extremes*. This is a very weighty point which is indispensable to a right understanding of Church History. Here the history of mankind shows itself different from the history of the divine Redeemer. His life unfolded itself quietly, like a clear stream flowing with smooth regularity in a straight course. It was a line that led, without the least deviation, to God. He suffered indeed and died; but this came not properly from the constitution of his own nature morally considered; it grew out of his voluntary assumption of the place of men, in order to redeem them from the power of sin. His own life, as such, remained always calm and serenely clear, in uninterrupted communion with his heavenly Father. This was because he knew no sin, neither was guile found in his mouth. If Adam had not fallen, his life would have unfolded itself in his posterity in the same way, without being required either to pass through death, that sharpest and hardest of all contradictions. He fell, however, and the human nature along with him, including of course the whole race; as partaking of the same life. Hence, in history, all errors, contradictions, conflicts and sufferings, with death at their head. Christ has appeared indeed as the second Adam, and introduced into humanity a new principle of life that must in the end triumph over all contradiction, all sin and all evil. But this principle can realize itself only in a gradual way. The Church on earth consists not of perfect saints, but of dying sinners, comprehended in a process of sanctification, which will end only with the outward resurrection. Freedom from sin and error may be predicated of Christ and the Church triumphant, but not of the Church militant. So long accordingly as the elements of a still unrenewed

68. [Trans. "Roman, be sure to rule the world." The context of this line relates to Schaff's positive view of Rome's role and to his understanding of national gifts and mission. "Others, I doubt not, shall with softer mould beat out the breathing bronze, coax from the marble features to the life, plead cases with greater eloquence and with pointer trace the heaven's motions and predict the rising of the stars; you, Roman, be sure to rule the world (be these your arts), to crown peace with justice, to spare the vanquished and to crush the proud." Virgil, *Aeneid* VI. 843–56.]

life continue to work in her constitution, her development must necessarily involve hard struggles and conflicts. The stream of church history flows with abrupt turns, in a zigzag course. At one time, it winds, soft and clear, through flowery meadows and smiling fields; but again it rushes headlong, wild, foaming, over towering precipices, bearing giant oaks and huge rocks irresistibly in its way, and forming the while also cataracts to be gazed upon with admiration and terror. Here it meets no resistance; but now, a mountain comes in its way, which it must go around or break through. Such is the complex variety, the terrific, though deeply interesting romance, the tragic scenery, which sin has introduced into the drama of the world's history.

This view may be established first in a general way by referring to the most comprehensive leading periods of history. With the reformation of the 16th century, the main stream of the Church took a direction wholly opposite to that which it had before. Thus far, the history of Christianity had been a development of the principle of objectivity, authority, obedience, Jewish Christian legalism. This was carried so far, that the power of the church became at last an insupportable bondage. Then the spirit of personal freedom, trained by such discipline to ripe self-possession, rose in revolt, and struck into quite another way. With this begins the evolution of the principle of subjectivity, the Gentile Christian element, evangelical liberty and independence. At the first, this movement carries along with it still the force of the old church life, as derived from the Middle Ages; but in proportion as it recedes from where it started, it is found to lose more and more its objective church character. Evangelical freedom has degenerated into fleshly self-will and licentiousness. The original common life of Protestantism has run out into a multitude of separate interests. The authority of God's word and of history is made to bend to private will and private judgment; which of course are different in different cases, and only affect subordination to the Bible, while in fact by their contempt for history they set themselves above it. Thus, for the papacy of the one bishop of Rome, is substituted the papacy of endless sect systems and sect heads. No wonder, then, that the historical stream should even now be turning from this pseudo-protestant extreme, towards a higher form of true church life in the opposite direction.

Not only on this large scale however is the law in question illustrated; it repeats itself also, in each single period, within more narrow compass. Everywhere one extreme calls forth another. Take, for instance, the image controversy in the Greek Church. The superstitious veneration for images, which had there become prevalent excited the emperor, LEO III, to put them away altogether, and the council of Constantinople, in the year 754, confirmed his judgment. This ultra-spiritualism, however, again produced a reaction the other way; which found a powerful patron in the empress IRENE, and was ecclesiastically sanctioned also, at least in part, by the second council of Nice,[69] A. D. 787. So we see the scholastic and mystic systems of the 12th century again in the persons of ABELARD and BERNARD OF CLAIRVAUX, violently opposing each other;

69. [That is, Nicaea.]

although they could as little bear to be divorced as light and heat, or head and heart. The formality of the English Episcopal Church causes Puritanism to appear; and when this swings over to the opposite extreme, a reaction follows in the restoration of the Stuarts. The orthodoxy of the school Lutheranism, which exalted knowledge at the expense of action, gives rise to *Pietism*; which now undervalues orthodoxy again in favour of practical religion. To refer finally to a quite recent case, Puseyism owes its rise mainly to its arch-enemy, the ultra-protestantism of the day.

We might illustrate the same truth also, from the lives of single Christians; in the case of whom, the strongest characters precisely, and those which have exerted the widest influence, are found to have been formed through a process of sharp extremes, while the essential identity of their nature has still been preserved in the midst of all. We will simply refer, in the way of example, to Paul, Augustine, and Luther.

5. The truth, in this whole case, lies not in the extremes, but in the *middle,* or the *deep* rather, in which they may be said to meet! The very nature of an extreme is that it pushes one side of a truth into prominence at the cost of another; wronging thus the interest itself which it seeks to uphold, since the organic nature of truth makes it impossible for any part of it to be fairly represented without due regard at the same time to other parts. Let this be illustrated again, by actual historical examples. The orthodox christology holds in the midst, between the one-sided theories of Nestorianism and Eutychianism. The first has right, so far as it insists upon the distinction of the divine and human natures in Christ, and opposes all pantheistic confusion of the one with the other. But with this, it overlooks the personal unity that binds them together; and hence its distinction of the divine and human, becomes abstract and only half true. Eutychianism presses the unity of both at the expense of their difference, and runs out accordingly into a monophysitic mingling of the two into a single nature. The church christology, as it was established by the councils of Ephesus and Chalcedon, unites the truth of both sides, in each case sundered from its accompanying error, into a complete general view, in which the unity as well as the distinction of the divine and human in the Redeemer's person are allowed to come to their right. In the image controversy already mentioned, the extremes of iconoclasm and iconolatry are alike one-sided and half-true. The right stand-point, that for instance maintained by Gregory I and by the French Church of the Carlovingian period in the so called *libris Carolinis*, distinguishes wisely between the image and its object, between the use of images and their abuse. It vindicates all worship to God and Christ alone; but allows religious images, at the same time, as representations of Christian art, and helps to devotion in the way of calling into lively recollection the saints and their virtues, and exciting pious imitation.[70] In like manner, Luther and his Church held themselves

70. Libri Carol. III. c. 16: *Nam dum nos nihil in imaginibus spernamus præter adorationem, quippe qui in basilicis sanctorum imagines non ad adorandum, sed ad memoriam rerum gestarum et venustatem parietum habere permittimus, etc.* [Trans. "We do not despise the images, but the worship of them. For the images of saints which are in the church, we do not permit for the purpose of adoration, but to remind us of their achievements, and to beautify the walls." The *Libris Carolinis*, also known as

equally aloof, from Romanist image worship and Carlostadt's[71] image demolition. Again, scholasticism and mysticism are both equally right and wrong; only as completed by each other, do they become fully true. The best theology is that in which the clearest understanding and deepest feeling appear harmoniously interfused. In the apostle Paul, Augustine, Anselm of Canterbury, Hugo of St. Victor, Bonaventura, Luther, Melancthon, John Gerhard, J. A. Bengel, Schleiermacher, and others, we find in fact both tendencies, though in very different ways, more or less united. In the controversy between Lutheran orthodoxy and Pietism, the venerable J. A. Bengel asserted the right medium; insisting on the union of practical piety with a firm adhesion to the established church doctrines, and opposing thus, with like decision, dead school divinity and mere religious subjectivism, that must ever become rationalistic in the end. Finally, we may say also, that the grand leading phases of church historical development, Catholicism and Protestantism, do not, separately taken, exhibit the *full* compass of Christian truth; and we look forward accordingly, with earnest longing, to a higher *stadium* of development, when error shall be effectually surmounted on both sides, and the divine element comprehended in each, appear happily preserved and perfected, in a higher form of church life, that shall be neither the one nor the other; a consummation, already anticipated and prefigured, we may say, in some single characters, that for instance of Augustine, and more especially in the circle of the apostles. The realization of this evangelical Catholicity or churchly Protestantism forms more and more clearly the great problem of the present age.

This right middle, of which the old word holds good, *Medium tenuere beati,*[72] is removed heavenwide from a characterless halting between two opinions, or from that loose eclecticism, which throws heterogeneous elements together, and then dignifies the undigested mish-mash with the name of a system. Such a middle must be pronounced rather something worse than the extremes it seeks to avoid; since it lacks courage and energy to attach itself decidedly either to the one or the other.

6. Every stage of development has its own corresponding *disease.* That the process should pass through diseases might be presumed even from the analogy of our natural existence; it results with necessity from the elements of sin and error that still cleave to the Church in her militant state, as well as from her connexion with the unregenerate world whose influence she is made continually to feel. These diseases form the Antichristian power in the Church, which also has a development of its own. Along with the wheat grow the tares till the last judgment, when both shall be separated, the first gathered into the heavenly granary, the other consigned to hell-fire. As

Opus Caroli regis contra synodum (The work of King Charles against the council), were composed at the command of Charlemagne around 790 to refute the supposed conclusion of the Second Council of Nicaea (787) on the role of images in worship. While it is a major statement of the early medieval Western theology of images, it is responding to a very problematic translation of the council's Greek decrees.]

71. [That is, Andreas von Carlstadt.]

72. [Trans. "Happy are they who have kept a middle course."]

every stage in the life of the individual has its *peculiar* derangements and dangers, so also has each life-period of the Church; and the more advanced any stage of development may be, the more dangerous will be also the disease to which it is exposed. The secularized tyrannical papacy is a diseased excrescence or swelled tumour of Catholicism. Rationalistic and sectaristic pseudo-protestantism is a distortion of the original spirit of the Reformation. Both diseases form a revelation of the mystery of iniquity, an apostacy, it may be said, a manifestation of the man of sin, who exalteth himself in the temple of God and exhibits himself as God. The last is the case particularly with the logical pantheism of the latest German philosophy and anti-theology, which claims to be the most perfect birth of the Reformation itself. While the pope acknowledges the existence of a personal God, and the fundamental doctrines of the gospel in general, and professes to derive his power by apostolical succession from Christ; this false protestantism of the school of Hegel and Strauss sets aside the divine personality altogether and raises the idea of humanity to the throne of the world; so that all theology or christology are made to lose themselves in mere anthropology. The opposers of Puseyism in our own country, at the present time, are but too often chargeable with the great fault of forgetting, over the mote in a brother's eye, the beam that is in their own, unwittingly helping in this way the enemy they oppose. We ought to acknowledge and love Christ always, wherever and in whatever form he may appear. So also, we ought to contend against Antichrist in all places; and he is to be found assuredly in all Christian confessions. Where God builds a temple, the devil is sure to have a chapel alongside.

7. These diseases however attending the development of the church prove in the hand of an all-wise God, who in the end rules all for his own glory, the *negative conditions* precisely of her *progress*. Want and help are closely joined together. With the consciousness of disease awakes also the desire for improvement. The physician is called, and offered remedies are thankfully received. When the church is thus brought to thorough repentance for her sin, and the proper means of cure are employed, her original life returns again more fresh and vigorous than ever before; as the natural body, after having surmounted the diseases of early life, goes on to unfold itself subsequently with increased strength. The storm makes way for a purer atmosphere and more genial sun. So it was in the 16th century. The Reformation was conditioned historically throughout by the shocking abuses of the papacy; and the fire was immediately kindled, we know, by the shameless traffic in indulgences as carried on by Tetzel. In our own time, pseudo-protestantism tends to awaken a strong church feeling, and so to break the way for a new tendency. The horrid strumpet government of Rome, when the highest ecclesiastical dignity had become the play-ball of avarice and lust, called forth the Hildebrandic reaction, which rescued the church from her slavery, and carried the idea of the papacy to its world-historical completion. The degeneracy of the works in the 9th and 10th centuries, when the ancient discipline had yielded to all sorts of libertinism, and the abbeys were occupied almost entirely by avaricious

laymen, served powerfully to assist the reformation which issued from the convent of Clugny;[73] a reformation, that fell back once more to the strictness of the Benedictine rule, and carried the monastic institute forward to its highest and last stage of development, as presented in the mighty orders of the 11th and 12th centuries. Thus does God, in his infinite wisdom, bring good out of all evil and turn the purposes and plans of his foes to the benefit of his children.

8. The starting points of new stages of development, or the epochs that unfold themselves into periods, carry, according to the want of the time, the character prevailingly, either of *restoration* or *revolution,* or *reformation;* of which three forms of change, the last must be considered the highest and most influential. By *restoration,* we understand the simple re-establishment of a state which has existed before without any advance. It takes place commonly after a violent revolution. History revenges the wrongs she has been made to suffer, by falling back once more to the earlier position from which she had been forcibly expelled. Here belongs, in the political sphere, the restoration of the Bourbons, after the fall of Napoleon; in the religious, the restoration of the Stuart family and the English Episcopal Church, after the Puritan revolution. Puseyism and old Lutheranism in our day are to be placed essentially in the same catalogue. Such a tendency however can maintain itself ordinarily only for a short time and calls forth new reactions. Thus the last hour of the Bourbons struck already in the year 1830; and the Romanizing Stuarts were required soon to yield to a new Protestant succession. Puseyism, as such, will hardly be able to endure long. Its more consistent leaders, completing their own principle, will pass over to Rome, as a number of the English clergy, with Newman at their head, have quite recently done already; others will fall back to the ordinary high church stand-point.

Revolution is the unsparing violent overthrow of what is at hand. It bears accordingly a character that is prevailingly negative and destructive. It becomes historically legitimate only where a diseased political or ecclesiastical condition has grown so inveterate, as to defy all help in the way of ordinary quiet and regular improvement. In such circumstances, revolution is like a terrible thunder storm that purifies the air. As examples from political history, we may mention the French Revolution of the preceding century and the emancipation of the United States from the dominion of Great Britain. The last, however, has a much more regular, worthy, and historical character than the other, and approaches rather the conception of a reformation; while the first produced the most horrible fruits of political fanaticism, and was followed thus with no stability in its results. From church history, we notice the course pursued by Carlostadt and the Anabaptists at the time of the reformation, and the Puritanism of England in the century following; which overturned the entire constitution and worship of the English church, and thrust the spiritual and civil authorities quite aside. At the same time, Puritanism carries with it a grand character, and has left deep traces of its power; inasmuch as it held fast all the fundamental truths of the gospel, and

73. [Cluny, the Benedictine foundation established in France in 910.]

proceeded from a fiery zeal, though not according to full knowledge, for the honour of God and his word, partaking in this way of the nature of a reformation. In the history of German theology we have an example of unbelieving revolution in Rationalism. To the same category belongs the movement of Ronge, now making so much noise, the moral value of which has been so blindly exaggerated by our protestant press.

Revolution is in its own nature something unnatural, which, especially when it springs from unbelief, cannot last long. The less it may have been the result of historical necessity; the less care it may have shown to distinguish between the good and the bad in the previous order of things; the more it has cast away truth along with error; it must ever come the more rapidly to nothing, and fall the more certainly into the same contempt with posterity which it has itself exercised towards previous time. Where it is possible to reform in a legal and regular way, revolution must be abhorred as godless.

In the midst, between restoration and revolution, stands *reformation;* the improvement and productive advancement of what is at hand; or such an overthrow of the old, as is its fulfilment, by raising its truth to a higher position. A reformation includes in itself both restorational and revolutionary elements, and the organic union of these, through the force of a positive life principle, is that precisely which constitutes its peculiarity. It strikes root backwards always, in the first place, in an earlier flourishing state of the church, above all the age of the apostles, so as to reproduce its life. Thus the Reformers of the 16th century betook themselves to the sacred scriptures and the church fathers, particularly Augustine, and re-asserted the primitive doctrines and practices that had been gradually thrust aside by popery; as, for instance, the universal priesthood, the use of the cup for the laity, the right of the people to choose their preacher, to read the Bible in their own tongue, &c. On the other side, they rejected all ordinances and institutions of the Roman church which were opposed to the scriptures; such as the papacy, the Pelagian merit of good works, indulgences, monkery, the doctrine of transubstantiation, purgatory, &c. In the Reformed church of Switzerland, France, and Scotland, this revolutionary element showed itself more powerful than in the Lutheran and Anglican, and remodelled accordingly the whole life of Roman Catholicism, in a more radical way, after the supposed pattern of the scriptures. John Knox in particular was already a puritan in principle. But notwithstanding this, the Reformed church grew with historical necessity out of Catholicism, and served to fulfil the deep longing of the Middle Ages after evangelical freedom. Reformatory also, though in a different direction, must be considered the activity of Gregory the Great, and Hildebrand, in the sphere of church government; that of Benedict, Odo, Francis of Assisi, in the history of monasticism; that of Augustine, Anselm, Schleiermacher, in theology; and that of Spener, Franke, Zinzendorf, Wesley, in the sphere of practical piety.

To the age in which a reformatory movement has place, it appears always to be revolutionary, and is denounced as schism or heresy. Public opinion is against it;

though it meets directly, on the other hand, the deepest wants of time, and is sure accordingly to triumph in the end. So was it indeed even with the Lord himself and his apostles, who were persecuted by public opinion even to death. When Luther came forward, he had the highest spiritual and civil powers against him. That his work prevailed notwithstanding, shows its uncompromisable necessity. The violent opposition of the orthodox against Spener is known; still Pietism carried the day, since it had its ground in the wants of the Lutheran church at the time. The necessity of a reformation of the Protestant church is making itself more and more felt in our own time. Our circumstances are defective enough to call for an improvement, both in head and branch; but not so desperate, on the other hand, that they need to be assailed in a violent, radical way. Rather the defects, are of a negative sort; so that restorational action should prevail, in the case, over the revolutionary. What is first of all needed, is a more thorough apprehension of the original stand-point of the reformation of the 16th century, from which a large part of the Protestant church has notoriously fallen away; then a living regress also to the earlier history of the church, and especially to her covenant archives, the sacred scriptures. Only from this objective positive ground, is it possible to combat successfully the reigning evils, so as to advance to a new and higher position.

9. Reformatory movements are characterized by having at their head *great religious personalities,* which have become filled and ruled, in mind and heart, by the power of a deep religious idea. History proceeds aristocratically. Talk as we may of the sovereignty and self-government of the people, the first impulse of great events springs almost always from prominent individuals, in whom the spirit of the age as it were becomes flesh, and whom the mass of other men follow by a sort of spiritual instinct. These master spirits, if they are truly to carry the church forward, must be animated with deep moral earnestness, must have gone through much spiritual conflict in their own souls, and wrestled with all their might to secure salvation in the church they are called to reform. Only one who has learned, by thorough study and practical experiment, to understand a system, and judge correctly of its advantages as well as its faults, is prepared to overcome it and carry it beyond itself. Think only of the apostle Paul. He had been honestly zealous for the law of his fathers, and had fully mastered the rabbinical theology of his day. For this very reason, he was the most powerful and successful opponent of pharisaic Judaism. Augustine wrestled as a Manichean, to solve the deep mystery of evil, and to find peace for his own anxious soul; and it was this precisely that qualified him to overcome scientifically the errors of that heretical system. Luther did not set out against the Roman Catholic church with ridicule and abuse; but as one of the most conscientious among monks, he laboured to secure the sanctification of his nature in her bosom, bore willingly and humbly her legal burdens, and even after he came to a better knowledge of the truth, felt it a heavy task still to renounce in full his connexion with the pope. It is just this that authenticates his call to be a reformer. ULLMANN, in his interesting "Thoughts of the German

Catholic movement," doubts with full right RONGE's capacity to be a reformer, on the ground of his being so easily done with the Roman Catholic system, clearly without having himself gone through its system of moral discipline. "Whoever," says Ullmann beautifully,

> may be called by a truly divine mission, to make a passage in history, and to assist in the production of something new, it is necessary that he should himself in the first place have had an inward religious history, have passed through a momentous, rich, peculiar, life-process, in the way as it were of pattern for others. This has appeared to us to be essentially wanting, in this German Catholic movement. Men, such as we are accustomed to find at the head of church creations; men, full of deep, holy, earnestness; full of experimental, living, rock-firm faith; devoted in humility and self-forgetfulness to the will and purpose of God; standing at the head of their age, not simply in their Christian life, but in all its more important and influential forms of culture; who have wrestled with themselves in the sweat of their brow, and then after coming to solid divine rest in their own spirits, are found standing forth in sharp opposition to the errors of their time; carried by the true, deeper spirit of the age, but yet in conflict with the false, as it moves on the mere surface of life:—*such* men, like many of the great teachers of Christian antiquity and the middle ages, like our German and Swiss reformers, like some of the later founders too of smaller Christian societies, have not here presented themselves to our view. [74]

10. The main stream of development, though full of turns, moves always *forwards*. We say purposely the *main stream;* which was formed first by the Greek-Roman universal church; then by the Romano-Germanic Catholicism; and since the Reformation appears in evangelical Protestantism. Along with this there are side-currents that may dry away entirely. Thus we find sects which having fulfilled their historical call, without uniting themselves afterwards with the general life of the church, are as it were turned into stone; the *Dunkards,* for instance, whose religion now consists in their long beards and their opposition to all culture and civilization. Large churches also, that once formed the main stream of history, may sunder themselves from the historical movement, and then stagnate and waste away in dead formalism. This is the case with the Greek church since its separation from the West, and with those sections of the Roman Church since the Reformation that stand in no connexion whatever with Protestantism.

With this restriction now we affirm an uninterrupted progress in the history of the church. As soon as we are set free from the cheerless view, that takes history to be the product of mere human activity, without the living intervention of the almighty love and wisdom of God himself, we must necessarily come to this idea of a

74. [Ullmann, "Zwei Bedenken über die deutsch-catholiche Bewegung,"] *Studien und Kritiken.* Jahrgang, 1845. Heft. 4. S. 1013.

progressive movement. The idea of a divine providence and government of the world if only we be in earnest with it, requires a steady advance towards the latter. God has proposed for his kingdom upon the earth a definite end. If so, however, all history must look and move this way. It would imply, either that God is not almighty, or that he deals not seriously with men, to suppose that the church is not always in fact coming ever to this end, or that it is never to be reached. The revelation of God under the Old Testament exhibits to our view an analogous progress; commencing with the faint germ-like promise of the serpent bruiser, immediately after the fail; advancing to more distinct announcements of the blessing for all nations, that should spring from Abraham's seed, in the patriarchal period; then to the more magnificent representation of the Messianic salvation, by the greater and smaller prophets; till all becomes complete at last in the palpable testimony of the Baptist, pointing to the Lamb of God that taketh away the sins of the world. Not only in knowledge, but in the religious life also we can trace, on the part of ancient Israel, such a progressive development. First, the child-like piety of the patriarchs; then the manly, earnest discipline of the law; afterwards, the almost evangelical joy of Isaiah in the consciousness of an approaching deliverance from the curse; finally, the sum and culmination of all preceding revelations, the union of the severity of the law and the consolation of prophecy in the person of John the Baptist with whom the Old Testament comes to an end. The history of God's ancient people, however, is a type of the Christian church. Hence, this too, is carried through a similar, though far richer development, always advancing towards the point, when she shall be ripe to receive the Lord at his second coming in glory. The history of the individual believer, finally, goes to confirm this view. He advances, in fact, not simply in his bodily life, but in that of the spirit also; his history is a *growth* in grace, from repentance to faith, from one measure of knowledge and holiness to another, till he is brought to see God face to face and is made free from all sin and death.

It is true now indeed, that the Rationalists also talk much of an ever-advancing "*aufklärung*" [enlightenment] of humanity, in their sense. But they mean by this, an advance *beyond* Christ and the Bible. Every such conception we decidedly reject; and affirm, rather, that this would be no advance, but a relapse only to Paganism and Judaism. According to our view, on the contrary, Christ is the alpha and omega, the beginning and the end, and all true progress, as we have before remarked, consists simply, in a more full appropriation continually of his divine human life, and a deeper understanding of his word, which is the absolute truth and eternal life itself.

It would be a misunderstanding again, if this theory were supposed to imply that the *personalities* of a later stage of development must be greater than those of an earlier stage. Rather the case may be precisely opposite. We allow, for instance, without hesitation, that our present Protestantism has no such profound, spiritually productive spirits, no such grand self-renouncing characters, to show, as the Middle Ages or the period of the Reformation. It is just at the head of an epoch, that we meet with personal forms transcending all that belong to its subsequent course; which is employed simply with the application of the new life principle to particular instances and relations, in the way of detail, and of course does not require the same spiritual power. We maintain only, that the *stand-point*, the *principle*, of a later time, surpasses that of an earlier period; or that a new element at least is made to come forward in it, which had not previously been apprehended with clear consciousness, but at most was present only in an implicit way. We may apply here the word of our Lord in relation to John the Baptist: "Among them that are born of women, there hath not arisen one that is greater; and yet the least in the kingdom of God is greater than he" [Luke 7:28]. This does not mean plainly, that the *person* even of the smallest Christian was to be counted superior to that of John; for this would not suit the first part of the declaration. It is the *stand-point* of one dispensation that is compared with that of the other; in such way as to affirm the endless superiority of the second over the first.

Particular periods, however, may be held up to our view, that seem wholly at variance with our affirmation; periods in which religious life has almost entirely failed, and dark superstition, or daring unbelief, or both perhaps together, have reigned supreme in the Church. Such was the tenth century, emphatically designated dark; also the fifteenth, when papal corruption was at its height; and then, again, the eighteenth, in which rationalism and religious indifference took possession of almost every Protestant land. But here we refer to our previous exposition, in which we have shown that the development before us is carried forward through diseases, that cause the vital energy to give way at times for a season; only, however, that, it may afterwards, as soon as the disease has been overcome, display itself again more actively than before. Just before creative epochs in particular, there is usually a falling away, in which old truths, forms and usages, are torn down, to make room for a new structure. These are transition periods accordingly, which are also necessary in order to progress. Compared merely with the previous state, they form a deterioration; but still they are nearer the redemption of a new epoch, and in this respect higher, as viewed in connexion with the subsequent course of history.[75]

75. Comp. the excellent remarks of *Dr. Nevin*, in his Introduction to the *Principle of Protestantism*, p. 21, sq. [p. 51 in this volume.]: "Assuredly those who hold the idea of historical progress with any proper knowledge do not conceive of it as a continuous movement, under the same form, in the same direction. They mean by it only a movement, whose general, ultimate tendency is forwards and not backwards; and which, though it may seem at times to be differently turned, is still found in the end steadily recovering and pursuing its original course; as a stream of water, carried aside, or pressed back upon itself, by some obstruction, does but force for itself a more circuitous way, or only gather strength to burst or overflow the barrier, that so it may roll onward as before. Truth can be said to advance, only as error is surmounted and thrown into its rear. But this requires that the error should always in the first place, make itself known and felt. A position in which the elements of a still latent error are included, is of course less advanced than a position, which has been gained by overcoming the same error after it has come to light; and as this can be reached only through the manifestation of the error, we may say that the intermediate stage itself in which such in an manifestation takes place, though it may seem to be a falling away as compared with the period before, is nevertheless also an onward movement in fact."

Finally, we may be referred to our Lord's prediction concerning the moral state of the world at his second coming (Matt. xxiv. 37–39), and to other similar passages, that foretell an increase of *corruption*, as militating against our view. But we have already shown that along with the kingdom of Christ, that of Antichrist also is steadily advancing to its completion, in the opposite way. The tares grow towards full ripeness, as well as the wheat in the midst of which they stand; but only to be cast in the end into the fire and burned, while the last is gathered into the store-house of eternal life. The more advanced the state of the Church may be, the more dangerous will be found the power of the world with which she is called to contend. Partly, because the world itself appropriates what Christianity has won in the way of culture, in order to employ it by abuse against the Church; and partly, because the prince of darkness may be expected of course to increase the vigour of his assaults, in proportion to the vigour with which he is withstood. Thus, for example, the popish errors and abuses were a worse enemy to the cause of Christ than pagan Rome with all its persecutions; and Protestant infidelity, as it has been systematically perfected, especially in connexion with the German theology, is more dangerous again, and more profoundly and directly opposed to the truth, than all the superstition of the Roman Catholic church at the time of the Reformation.

11. The last feature of the development of the Church which we shall mention, is found in its *geographical* course. This proceeds in general, like that of the sun, from *east to west*. The cradle of Christianity, as also of history and cultivation generally, is the orient; and in particular that remarkable land, which by its central relation to three quarters of the globe, has been found so peculiarly fitted to be the birth-place of a universal religion. But even in the time of the apostles, the gospel passed over from Palestine to Asia Minor, Greece and Italy. In the centuries next following, the Greek Church held the rudder of Church History. She fulfilled especially, by means of her philosophic culture, the momentous task of unfolding the objective, fundamental doctrines, of the trinity, the divine incarnation, and the two natures in the God-man. During this period, the rise of the Latin Church took place, from the time of Tertullian, in Africa. In Augustine, who may be regarded as the reproduction of Tertullian's spirit under a higher and more perfect form, the philosophical acumen and theological depth of the Grecian mind were united with the practical tendency of the West. He brought out in the controversy with Pelagius, the subjective anthropological dogmas of human freedom and the work of grace. His boundless spiritual wealth, and noble greatness of heart, fell as an inheritance to the Latin Church. This now fixed its centre for centuries, in the world metropolis; whose bishop gradually raised himself from the rank of co-ordinate patriarchs to that of universal Christian pope; while the Greek Church in time, separated from the West, lost all its historical significance and weight. Meanwhile, from Rome as a centre, the Germanic nations of the north of Europe and the Anglo-Saxons of the British Islands were Christianized, the arts and sciences advanced, the idea formed of catholicity that should embrace all lands and

pervade all relations, and the unity and independence of the Church triumphantly defended against the particular, secular interests of single States. Towards the close of the Middle Ages, the spiritual strength of the Church appears already in the progress of transplantation from its old seat. France and the university of Paris became the central ground of theology. The celebrated chancellor of this university, John Gerson, it is well known, Nicholas of Clamenge and Peter d'Alliaco, exerted the most important influence, with their liberal principles, on the great reformatory councils of the fifteenth century. With the Reformation of the century following, Germany became the birth-place of a new epoch in Church history, and Wittemberg is made to take the place of Paris. The power of the papacy, in the feudal system of former times, is broken in its principle, and its historical importance henceforward, which is by no means lost, comes to rest mainly upon its antagonism to the new creation, by which it has been thrown into the shade. Protestantism shakes the whole vast structure of the Roman Church, and in particular gains possession of that wonderful island also, that is to succeed Rome, and the Romano-Germanic empire, in the supremacy of the world. Whilst Protestant theology still finds its congenial home in Germany, the heart of Europe, England on the other hand represents the political world-force of the evangelical Church, by a dominion on which the sun never sets.

From England and Scotland mainly, the northern half of the new world has been settled. The United States of America are essentially a Protestant land; as in language and manners, so also in religion and church life, the daughter of Great Britain. They are in an eminent sense the land of the future. It is pleasing, and natural at the same time, to look upon this free and friendly asylum for all pilgrims from Europe, now growing old and weary of life, as the main theatre of world and church history in time to come. From this country again perhaps, when its civilization shall reach to Oregon, may proceed principally the evangelization of China and India, still bearing the gospel westward in its sun-like course; till finally it shall return, with the millennium and the coming of the Lord in his glory, to the point from which it started on its circuit round the globe. At present, we lie in the birth throes of a new creation. All still rolls in wild confusion. But the time is not far, when the divine word shall sound, *Let there be light!* and a beautiful world shall rise from the midst of the struggling chaos. As the church of the Future is called to take up into herself the truth of all previous development, and to be thus the proper sum of all Church History, it is quite in order that all the divisions of Protestantism should be represented in our land, and Catholicism too as a sort of counterpoise to any extreme on the opposite side. This imparts to our religious condition an aspect of disorder, and constitutes our free land an arena of violent ecclesiastical conflict, on which the European is inclined to look down with a compassionate smile. But such wild fermentation always characterizes the transition periods, that go before a reformation; and the more manifold and mighty the conflicting elements may be, the more rich must the result prove to which they ultimately give birth. May our American church soon come to the consciousness of this her great calling; subordinate her sectarian activities to the general interest that lies far beyond that of any single existing denomination; assume in this struggle towards a better future, the genuine historical stand-point; and never forget, at the same time, what she owes to the old world, not excepting the still so much misunderstood and reviled German theology, from whose ideas in the end whole protestantism lives and thrives, nor how much she ought still to learn from the history of her fathers.

Section III
Practical Importance of a Right View of Church History

Such in general are the laws and conditions that rule the development of the kingdom of God in the world. The correctness of our view can be fully established only by an actual representation of Church History itself; a work that is worthy to engross a whole life. It devolves upon us now, to present some practical observations that flow from the whole subject. Truth, so far as it has life, is never simple theoretic, but includes always a bearing also on practice. Our beloved America has especially the great merit of at once turning all thoughts into flesh and blood, life and deed. The practical consequences of any theory form the best test of its truth, according to the old maxim, "By their fruits ye shall know them" [Matt 7:16a]. The foregoing view of history, it is believed, has no reason to shrink from the test; as we shall now attempt to show.

The study of history in general has its use at large in this, that it promotes a proper understanding of the present, and serves thus to secure efficiency and success to the labours which have respect to the future. Only such points, however, as follow with necessity from the peculiar theory of Church History, which has now been exhibited, will here he brought into notice.

1. This view first inspires us with a genuine *living interest in the study of Church History.* It is regarded as the evolution of God's plan of redemption, proceeding according to rational and necessary laws. All that it includes is bound together in a living way. Nothing comes too soon, and nothing too late. Every period possesses its own peculiar greatness, its imperishable worth, and is entitled to our attention and admiration. Every great and truly considerable manifestation has indeed a mortal body, but reveals also an undying soul, and positively or negatively, with will or without it, must ever issue in the glory of God and the salvation of the Church. Such a spectacle, whether in a scientific or religious point of view, cannot fail to be in a high degree attractive. We may well say indeed, that history must become in this way a study of the first interest, a fountain of the richest spiritual enjoyment and instruction. The mighty dead, who have died in the Lord, rise from their dust, and move before us, clothed in flesh and blood, as though they belonged to our own time. Like the different tones of a glorious anthem, they hymn the praise of their Redeemer, in whose blood they have

washed their garments white. Every one has a word to say to us, in the way of consolation, exhortation, animation. Every one becomes to us a lively monument of God's mercy and truth. We feel ourselves happy and at home, in their society. The wonderful riddle of the communion of the saints, comprehending heaven and earth, eternity and time, is solved; and we fall down in adoration before him, who has caused his grace to abound, under such manifold forms, in all Christian lands, and nations, and times.

How all is changed when history is viewed as a mere outward conglomeration of facts, numbers and names, that are held together by no living principle, and etherialized by no everlasting thought. In such an atomistic heap no interest can be taken, unless by one who uses mechanically his memory only, without thought. What attraction can be found, for instance, in the study of the middle ages, where one has his head crammed full beforehand with the prejudice, that darkness and corruption only, hatred to the truth and hostility to all true religion, ruled throughout this whole period the Catholic Church? It were much better, certainly, in such a case, to be employed with other things entirely, that might he expected to refresh and edify the spirit; and it is not strange accordingly, that so few of our Protestant theologians, in consequence of such prejudice, which has wrought itself into the character of a stiff tradition, should be found to possess even a tolerable acquaintance with the school divinity, mysticism, and other forms of spiritual grandeur, belonging to the mediaeval church.

2. A second practical fruit of the theory is found in the *satisfaction* and *comfort*, which the idea of an ever advancing development of the Church imparts to the mind, in looking at the past and present. The rationalistic imagination, that history at last is but a tangled web of human passions, a fruitless contest for words and systems, is well suited to lead an earnest spirit to despair. And certainly the view of many who count themselves orthodox, is not much better; according to which, during certain centuries at least, God has as it were withdrawn himself from the stage, and abandoned humanity wholly to itself; so that whole vast periods, in particular the middle ages, are to be set down as times of pure deterioration, spiritually void and waste, a moral blank at best, or horrible yawning chasm; by which the present, instead of being joined with the past, is only sundered from it, and that must be overleaped entirely, in order that all things may go forward again as by a fresh, original, start. Appalling imagination, if it only were fairly and solemnly laid to heart! It turns, not only the fallen world as such, but the new creation in Christ also, who is the principle of all order and life, into a formless chaos! The doctrine of an all-comprehending divine Providence, in which we live and move and have our being, affirmed by the Bible and all Christian experience, it completely overturns.

According to our view, on the other hand, Church History presents on every one of its pages, an impressive confirmation of the truth of our Lord's precious promise: "Lo, I am with you alway, even to the end of the world!" [Matt 28:20] and constitutes thus one of the most powerful arguments for the divine origin of Christianity. On one who is able thus to discern the footsteps of the Lord in the Church as a power that has bid defiance to the gates of hell in all ages, no impression will be made against the gospel by any objections, however plausible they may appear. The overwhelming might of history, has already long since demolished them in the way of fact. Such a one can look also with confidence and comfort, towards the present and future. Confused as may be the first, and dark as may be the second, the past still gives him the assurance that the omnipotent head of Zion will unravel the confusion and cause the darkness to become light, and to bring his most frantic enemies to bow at his feet.

The man, who in the midst of such a heaving, tumultuating time as our own, for instance, is found resting on his own mere private judgment, or that of his party, has under him the most unstable ground, and cannot come to any true and solid quiet in his own spirit at the last. Our nature involves in itself a demand for communion with the general and universal that must sooner or later, in every such case, make itself painfully felt. The subjectivity, that affects to carry itself high towards objective history, closes its ear against the voice of centuries, and retires self-sufficient into its own poor and narrow life, is deserving of contempt, or at least compassion. We will bear in mind, that Christianity, in its very nature, seeks communion. We will cherish sympathy then with the whole family of Christian nations, and feel our own heart's blood in the veins of every century. We will make the gain of history, true mistress of experience, to become our own. Thus have we a solid rock, on which to rest secure. And when we know not, as we gaze into the future, what is to be done, in order to help the hurt of Israel and loose the bands of Zion, we are still not disconcerted. A thousand examples teach us, that it is not we that make history, but history that makes us. There moves in the whole onward course of time a spirit of infinite wisdom and love, in whose hand we are simple instruments. The general reigns over the single. This objective force of history will, at the proper season, bring the right remedy; and it belongs to us only to follow freely the working of the divine Spirit, and obediently to execute his commands. When Luther posted his 95 theses on the castle-church at Wittemberg, he had no presentiment what consequences this seemly unimportant event would draw in its train. Most innocently, we may say, did he become a reformer. The force or history bore him forward from one act to another and before he himself dreamed of it, the church had taken another form. Only such a creation on the part of the individual, as is at the same time a creation wrought by history through him, can have any permanent stability. A purely subjective fabrication, however skilfully and vigorously framed, goes quickly as it comes. The presumptuous spirits that bark against her, history hurls unmercifully to the ground, and proceeds in triumph over the golgotha of their impotent deeds. Luther's work still stands; because it was called forth by the necessity of history. The artificial effort of Julian, the apostate, to restore Judaism to life, went to ruin with its author, with the tragic cry: *Galilaeus vicisti*![1] The English *Book of Common Prayer*, which gathered into itself, with reverential affection,

1. [Trans. "You have conquered, Galilean!" A statement acknowledging Christian supremacy commonly, but falsely, attributed to the Roman emperor Julian the Apostate (c. 332–63) as his last words.]

the liturgical creations of the ancient church, continues to this day a rich source of edification and the pride of the Episcopal Church; while the numerous liturgies and hymn-books of Rationalism and unhistorical Protestantism generally, have been able to maintain themselves only for a short time. The German Churches in this country, might have spared themselves the trouble of manufacturing so many new liturgies and hymn-books, had they but respected more the treasures of the primitive Church and the Reformation.—This leads us to another point, which we will notice separately.

3. It is only the conservative historical standpoint that can authorize any right *satisfaction in our own work.* Unbelieving Rationalism and believing Puritanism alike, with their revolutionary attitude towards history, have properly no right whatever to expect that they shall be regarded and loved by those who come after them. He that despises his spiritual ancestry should reckon upon no grateful posterity. If the work of whole *centuries* has been vain, so that there is nothing better than to extirpate it root and branch, how should *we* then be able to bring any thing permanent to pass? Are we formed of higher material than our predecessors? Are we not men, even as they were? It is a ridiculous, if not wicked, presumption, for any one to exalt his own individuality, as such, over the authority of all history.

The man, on the other hand, who knows how to join the royal rights of freedom, as they are included in the very idea of personality wherever found, with due reverence for authority, may calculate that to him also the tribute of free respect and love will be paid in time to come. He that holds the works of the past in honour, and attaches himself with self-renouncing love to existing relations, holding fast in them what is of divine right, and correcting their defects with wise forbearance, has ground to hope that his own work too, appointed of God, will leave behind it some benefit for following generations. Robespierre and Danton are branded names.[2] Voltaire, Bahrdt and Bruno Bauer, are mentioned with horror. Thomas Münzer has become as a spectral dream. Even men like Carlstadt and Cromwell, though of a much higher nature, on account of their wild, stormful behaviour towards the work of their fathers, enjoy but a very qualified respect in a small circle. But the men of reverence, that holy power which exalts the man while it causes him to bow—an Augustine, Anselm, Thomas a Kempis, Luther, Melancthon, Calvin, Leighton, Spener, Zinzendorf, J. A. Bengel—rise from their centuries like light-towers for all times, and will continue to live in blessed remembrance with the Church for ever.

4. The modern German view of history lends to overthrow all *narrow party spirit* and *intolerant party zeal.* What rashness it is, to bind the Spirit of God to a fixed form and party! Only too often, however, do we find this done. Especially also in the war against the Church of Rome. How many forget, over the dross of this system, the

2 [Maximilien de Robespierre (1758–94) and Georges Danton (1759–94) were leaders of the French Revolution. Robespierre was a leader of the Reign of Terror in which Danton was executed for his growing moderation. Robespierre himself was executed at the end of the Reign. As recent political revolutionaries, Schaff lists them first in this litany of radicals.]

gold of catholicity still contained in it, which is much older than popery. We must maintain for this Church a historical respect, and may not consent for any price, that on account of its great and terrible errors, the evangelical truths also which are among them, and which we too hold, should be assailed with profane hand. Under the influence of such blind zeal, that casts away the wheat with the chaff, the mind shrinks within itself more and more, and loses all capacity for development. With the mind, at the same time, the heart and character are also contracted. Love and humanity die, and dark intolerance, a fanatical persecuting temper, takes full possession of the soul.

With *our* principle of history, on the contrary, we remain open continually to humiliation, encouragement, instruction, enlargement of every sort. We gather with fond affection the flowers of the Christian life, out of all times and generations, and adorn with them our own altars. *Nihil humani, et multo magis nihil Christiani, a me alienum puto*, is our watchword;[3] sympathy with all that is great, and noble, and beautiful, though under a rough shell, our high and cherished enjoyment. We seek to stand in living communion with the saints of all centuries, of whatever tongue or confession, and however much the form of their piety also may differ from ours. In a common garden we find various flowers, and it is the intermingling of all sorts of hues and odours, precisely that serves most to regale the senses. And shall the Church, the garden of the Lord, be characterized by tedious, monotonous uniformity?

We are ready thus to turn to account, in our own Church activity, all the treasures that history brings within our reach; even though derived in part from the so called dark ages themselves. Let us leave to the papists the spirit of uncharitable intolerance; we will count it our honour to admit instruction, though with self-denial, even from them. Let us leave to the Seceders and *Alt-lutheraner*[4] the fancy, that they alone are the elect, possessed of the pure and perfect doctrine of Christ. We envy them not their principle of stagnation and their self-sufficiency. With the apostle Paul, we hold that we have not yet attained the whole of Christianity, nor become perfect; and forgetting what lies behind, we reach joyfully after that which is before, towards the prize of the high calling of God in Christ Jesus.[5]

5. Closely connected with what has just been said is the last and most important point to be presented. I mean, the bearing of this view of Church History on the great work of *Christian Union*. The Church of Christ, and in particular the Protestant Church in our own country, is at present so deplorably divided, the professors of the same faith are so filled with envy and jealousy, and so sadly estranged from one another by bitter, uncharitable, sectarian feuds, that even those who have the least church feeling

3. [Trans. "I consider nothing human, and even more nothing Christian, alien to me." Here Schaff adapts the famous aphorism of Terence (d. 159 BCE), the Roman playwright. He would later use a slightly different form of this aphorism as the motto of his *History of the Christian Church* and the American Society of Church History.]

4. [Trans. "Old Lutherans." The confessional Lutherans of Schaff's day who refused to unite in the Church of the Prussian Union.]

5. Cf. Philippians 3:12–14.

begin at last to see the evil; and, God be praised, thousands are brought to sigh after a permanent deliverance from such vast curse. While Rome triumphs maliciously over our divisions, and some are urged, in despair of the future, and dazzled with the show of unity exhibited by this corrupt Church, to forsake the ranks of Protestantism and throw themselves into her bosom; we have various plans proposed among ourselves for a union of our scattered strength; and in August of the present year a grand universal Protestant council is to be held in London with reference to this very object, in prosecution of steps already taken by the convention of last year at Liverpool.[6] We will not suffer ourselves to be deceived, however, with this fair talk of union. We acknowledge with joy indeed the right feeling that lies at the ground of these movements. They show a painful sense of the wrong state of the Church at the present time, and a desire for something better. They are a practical testimony furnished by the conscience of the Church against the great evil of sects, which some are so ready to extenuate and excuse theoretically. But, notwithstanding all this, we must enter our decided dissent from the general movement. Many appear to wish a union of Protestants only in order to a more successful conflict with the power of Rome. This is to sink the interest to a mere instrument, in the service too of a party motive. But it should be remembered, that church unity is not a means simply for something else, but an end in itself; which requires to be sought accordingly for its own sake. We should long for it, and struggle to reach it, as the object for which our Lord himself so solemnly prayed, when about to leave the world [John 17:21]. We should seek to realize it, because it is involved in the very conception of the Church as the one body of Christ, as the organic communion of saints, that it should be united. So far as it is divided, it falls short of its own idea in its actual form among men.

And then, it is besides an altogether too contracted conception of union, to confine it exclusively to the Protestant world; as though *all* Christianity belonged to this, and the elements of a perfect church organization were *all* at hand in it, *as it now stands*. It is surely an intolerant and narrow imagination, to regard the whole Roman and Greek communions, so far exceeding us as they do in numbers, as out of the Church entirely, and only worthy of course to be blotted out of history altogether as a gigantic spiritual zero. Thus to excommunicate the greatest part of Christendom at a single stroke, is to imitate the bigotry of Rome herself, and cast a reproach upon the whole Protestant profession. We mean not assuredly to plead the cause of Rome, as such; and think of no union with the false power that involves a return to her bosom, constituted as the Church is at the present time; with the whole strength and beauty of her original catholic life infolded in the deadly coils of the papacy, and wickedly refusing to acknowledge God's truth as saved by the Reformation. We go not *back* to

6. [An international, Protestant association, the Evangelical Alliance was formed in London in 1846. A preparatory meeting took place in Liverpool in 1845. Because of disputes over slavery, its development in America was delayed. Schaff played a major role in the alliance later in his career. Pranger, *Philip Schaff*, 242–45, 248–57; Jordan, *The Evangelical Alliance for the United States of America*; Randall, *One Body in Christ*.]

that hard, iron captivity, which has been left full three hundred years behind in the onward march of the true Israel of God. But we have no right to say, that *all* truth and life have departed from this Church. It will yet be brought to occupy new and higher ground; or rather the truth and life which it includes be carried forwards and upwards as a constituent element at least, not simply to the present posture of protestantism (which no sound mind can hold to be itself complete), but to that last best state of Christianity, in which full justice shall be done to the truth on all sides and the Church shall appear one and universal in fact as she is now one and universal in idea. We dream of no other union. But for this we long and pray, even as we long and pray for the coming of the millennium itself; and shall be hindered from doing so by no fanatical intolerance, either on the one side or on the other.

Another defect too generally characteristic of our efforts for union is doctrinal indifferentism and an undervaluation of history. The differences that exist among religious parties are viewed as of small account; and so to make room for union, peculiarities of doctrine are to be surrendered, for which our fathers contended and made the greatest sacrifices, as for points of vital solemnity. Whole centuries of separation are to be sunk into nothing, only to come together again at the common point of departure. The process must be from the definite to the indefinite, from the concrete and particular backwards to abstract generalities. Thus, for instance, the Apostles' Creed, or some loose compilation made up of the most formal propositions (anti-papistical in particular) from the different protestant symbols, are to represent these symbols themselves! With such a so called "United Apostolical Protestant Confession," we have been lately favoured in fact, from a worthy and zealous leader in the cause of Christian union.[7] But what a full mistake it is to project a symbol before the *body* is formed that

7. [Samuel S. Schmucker,] "Overture for Christian Union, submitted for the consideration of the evangelical denominations in the United States" [(1845)]; subscribed by quite a number of distinguished names. [This overture was initially published as a large four-page folder. Drafted by Schmucker it was signed by forty Protestant leaders. It was essentially a summary of the plan of federal union first proposed in Schmucker, *Fraternal Appeal to the American Churches, with a Plan for Catholic Union on Apostolic Principles* in 1838. Schmucker's proposed confession was also first published in *Fraternal Appeal*. The *Overture* was later included in Schmucker, *Church of the Redeemer*, 242–63, and in the 1965 edition of *Fraternal Appeal*, 199–212. When the Evangelical Alliance was organized in London in 1846, Schmucker agreed to substitute a much briefer theological statement for the Confession.]

[Formed in Lutheran pietism, Schmucker (1799–1873) graduated from Princeton Theological Seminary and throughout his career sought to bring Lutherans into the mainstream of American Protestantism with its emphasis on revivalism and social reform. He founded Gettysburg Theological Seminary in 1826. He became a champion of Christian unity because of his concern for missionary work and his millennialism, but more confessionally-oriented Lutherans saw him as betraying everything distinctive to the tradition. Schaff did indeed count Schmucker, a Lutheran leader and president of the Gettysburg Theological Seminary a worthy leader and maintained a cordial friendship with him throughout his life. Schmucker, however, was much more in tune with American evangelical life than Schaff in terms of his anti-Catholicism and lack of a sense of organic development. Beginning with *Fraternal Appeal*, his ecumenical proposals focused on the federation, rather than the union of churches, an approach which Schaff also later championed. Wentz, *Pioneer in Christian Unity*, 269–96; Wentz, "Samuel Simon Schmucker and Philip Schaff."]

shall take it for its confession! It is as though one should think to speak before he has a mouth, or to walk before he has feet. What is a symbol; in its only true and proper sense? A formal representation on the part of the church, of a *common living faith already at hand.*[8] It supposes the presence of a certain form of life, in its very nature, of which it is simply the expression and transcript. The Apostles' Creed appeared long after the time of the apostles; the Augsburg Confession full thirteen years after the commencement of the Lutheran Reformation; the Heidelberg Catechism and other protestant symbols still much later. But where now is the United Protestant church, in which Lutherans, German Reformed, Presbyterians, Congregationalists, Episcopalians, Methodists, Baptists, &c., join hands fraternally in *twelve* articles of faith? It has not yet come to light; and it will not be called into being, I am afraid, by this "United, Apostolic, Protestant Confession." A church is not to be fabricated in the study, by simply extracting, and putting together in an outward way, some propositions of apparently like sound, out of different symbolical books.[9] It comes not by the pious wish and operation of a human individual as such. God alone can produce a union, by the objective course of history itself; which does indeed concentrate, and as it were corporealize itself, in single towering personalities; but in doing so, forms these also as organs for its service, and thrusts them forward in it as by a divine force, instead of

8. We would respectfully submit to our honoured friend Dr, S. *Schmucker,* the author of this symbol, the following words of one of the most eminent German theologians, for consideration: "True confessions again, such as are grounded in a specific, living, deep-rooted conviction, are not accustomed to make their appearance as this one (the symbol formed by the adherents of Ronge at the council of Leipzig) has done. They start not, in their original form at least, from the joint action of many, met to discuss, and to consult and vote, and concerned to produce by suppression and concession, something that may satisfy all. Rather, in the quiet, holy depths of a soul that has passed through great trials and conflicts, a mind possessed of the power of faith and pervaded with the noblest cultivation of the time, there springs up a new, fuller, purer apprehension of Christianity; along with this faith is kindled a fire that with contagious force lays hold also of other spirits; in common, inspiring and inspired, they break a new path of religious knowledge, a new highway of salvation; and then they give to that with which all are filled, a clear utterance also in the way of confession, to lay the ground thus of an enduring communion. Always, however, where things have their natural course, what thus becomes the word of confession for many will be found to have been in the first place the original, full life of some prominent, spiritually mighty individual man, from whom, as a germ, the whole communion grows. But for this very reason, a new faith, a new confession, is not made, it rises, it becomes, it grows. It is not the man who has the faith, but the faith has the man and seeks to express itself through him. And hence it follows again; first, that a system of faith, a confession, is not so quickly and easily brought to pass, but involves earnest and great spiritual toil; and secondly, that where the work proceeds properly, the contents of the system will be such as are acknowledged to be, not something made by the man himself, ordered and settled according to his pleasure; but something divinely true, a higher power, before which he bows and prostrates himself in his inmost soul." ULLMANN. ["Zwei Bedenken über die deutsch-catholiche Bewegung" (Two concerns about the German-Catholic movement),] *Studien und Kritiken*, 1845. Heft. 4, S. 1011 ff.

9. [This exactly describes Schmucker's approach. His "United Apostolic Protestant Confession" consisted of the Apostles' Creed and "The United Protestant Confession" composed of twelve articles carefully footnoted to indicate their source in existing Episcopal, Presbyterian, Congregationalist, Baptist, Methodist, Lutheran, and Moravian confessions.]

allowing itself to be fashioned according to their pleasure, or even to be anticipated by them in any way.

And what a wretched union must not that be counted in the end, which might thus be constructed, in any case, only on the ruins of history! Have the dogmatic struggles of our ancestors then been all in vain? Has the peculiar development of the different branches of Protestantism gone forward thus far, without meaning or fruit? After the toil of so many hundred years, must we go back again to the most indefinite beginnings, the A B C we may say, of our church life? Is it not in fact an enormous presumption, when we look at it properly, to suppose that a few men of the 19th century, in such an outward mechanical way, should succeed in bringing something permanently stable to pass, where the whole Christian past is practically charged with having laboured to no purpose?

No; if a union is to come, as we pray and hope in reliance upon Christ's promise, it will not present itself destructively towards history, but take up rather the whole contents of it into its own life. Every single denomination, every Christian people, every Christian century, has something to contribute to this great result. The end then plainly requires, as the means by which it may be best reached, that the different branches of the church should be brought, by a thorough study of her history, to know and respect and love one another more; and thus come more and more clearly to the consciousness, that no one of them is perfect, but that they are mutually necessary one to the other, and should severally leave their faults behind, and unite their advantages and virtues into a harmonious whole. The exposition which we have now attempted to give of the nature of Church History is sufficient to show its importance as it regards this object. In the light in which it has been presented, it is precisely adapted to awaken and promote such a genuine catholic spirit of union as the ease requires; and thus we come to the result that a thorough knowledge of the historical development of the body of Christ, in all its parts, is an indispensable condition to the farther advancement of the church, and to a permanent union of its different branches. The cultivation of Church History, and that of the church itself, go hand in hand together. Here lies the strongest challenge to an unremitting prosecution of the study, for all who are called to take part in the solution of the great church questions of the present time, and who are concerned to build, not upon the sand, but upon an immoveable rock.

FINIS.

DOCUMENT 4

"German Theology and the Church Question" (1853) by Philip Schaff

Editors' Introduction

"German Theology and the Church Question" is a direct defense of the key controversial claim of *The Principle of Protestantism*, namely, that the Roman Catholic Church was the legitimate predecessor of Protestantism as the true Church of Christ in the middle ages. Indeed Schaff here maintains that the Roman Catholic Church remains an important and legitimate part of the Church. In this respect, Schaff sought to contribute to "the Church Question," the key animating question of his early career, namely what was the nature of the true Church: was it Catholic, Protestant, or Confessional Lutheran? Specifically, the essay can be read as in part a defense of his colleague John Nevin, who was under increased attack by his critics in the early 1850s for the positions he took in his articles in the *Mercersburg Review* on "Cyprian" and "Early Christianity."

The essay was initially published in German in September 1852, immediately after the conclusion of a series of five essays on contemporary German university theologians that appeared in *Kirchenfreund*, a German language literary magazine published by Schaff.[1] It was translated and published in the *Mercersburg Review* where it appeared in the January 1853 issue. The translator is unknown. It could be Nevin or Schaff himself.[2]

Der Deutsche Kirchenfreund: Organ fur die gemeinsamen Interessen der amerikanisch-deutschen Kirchen. (The German Church-friend: Organ for the common interests of American-German churches) was founded by Schaff in 1848 and edited by him for six years, after which time his lifelong friend, William Julius Mann (1819–92), became editor. The magazine addressed an inter-denominational audience of mainline German-American Protestants, including members of Reformed, Lutheran, United, and Moravian churches. It aimed to occupy a middle ground between the weekly religious press and academic journals. It sought both to elevate the quality of religious

1. Schaff, "Die deutsche Theologie und die Kirchenfrage." Schaff, "Gallerie der bedeutendsten jezt lebenden Universitätetheologen Deutschlands."

2. Schaff indicates in *History of the Apostolic Church* published later the same year that he was capable of producing an English translation, but in that work he employed the assistance of Edward D. Yeomans. Yeomans provided a notably fluid translation in that book and thus is probably not the translator of this article.

discourse among German Americans and to help sustain a German-language culture in America. The latter project was one that Schaff would later have less enthusiasm for as the Americanization of immigrant communities proceeded rapidly.[3]

In this essay, Schaff confronts the sharp anti-Catholicism of this period in American Protestantism and its intersection with German theology. These are precisely the issues which animated his heresy trial seven years earlier. He defends the conclusion of recent German church historians that the Roman Catholic Church was in the medieval period *the* church, "the bearer of true Christianity." Furthermore, the church fathers were the progenitors of this medieval Catholicism and had much more in common with Catholicism than they did with Protestantism.

Like much of his writing on this topic, Schaff situated this essay in the intersection between German and British-American culture. What was for German researchers a more abstract and theoretical matter, was quickly put on practical grounds by British and American church leaders. His key argument was that German church historians had shown that the medieval Roman Catholic Church was the organic development of the Christianity of the church fathers of the second to sixth centuries. Furthermore they had shown that there was much to be esteemed in the medieval church. Given the scriptural promise of Christ to be with the church always, the medieval Catholic church, he concluded, must be seen as the true church of Christ of which the modern Catholic church was still a part. Accordingly the best defense of Protestantism was not to attack the medieval church, but to celebrate its accomplishments and to show that Protestantism is the organic outgrowth of it.

Similarly, Schaff concluded that Protestants must maintain that they are rooted in the apostolic church. Yet the apostolic church had three types of doctrine: Jewish or Petrine Christianity with its emphasis on law, Gentile or Pauline Christianity with its emphasis on freedom, and the higher harmony of Johannine Christianity with its emphasis on the living communion of the faithful with one another and with Christ. Historically Catholicism had sustained the Petrine and Protestantism the Pauline; if Protestantism recovered the full theology of Paul, however, including his theology of the church as expressed in Ephesians, then, Schaff insisted, the way will be prepared for the reconciliation of Catholicism and Protestantism through mutual repentance in which Catholicism will necessarily need to confess and amend its faults.

The essay begins by discussing the conclusions of modern church history about the middle ages and then about the early church. Then it turns to the relevance of this research for the church question. Schaff rejects a simple biblicism that assumes that present-day interpreters are more reliable than earlier generations and insists that the scriptural promises of Christ to be with the Church always are clearer than any identification of the Roman church with the antichrist. Then evoking the current debate and sectarian spirit among Anglo-American Protestants, he presents his argument that the best defense of Protestantism is one premised on organic development that

3. Pranger, *Philip Schaff*, 84–87; David Schaff, *Life of Philip Schaff*, 160–62.

celebrates the accomplishments of the medieval church, sees Protestantism as built upon these, and looks to the future combination of the present strengths of both Catholicism and Protestantism.

German Theology and the Church Question[1]
(Translated from "Schaf's Kirchenfreund," for September 1852.)

[The Catholic Church in Recent German Protestant Church Historiography]

If we compare the present theological literature of English and American Protestantism with that of the modern Evangelical school of Germany, we meet with a remarkable difference in their conception of *Catholicism*. Of this we have already had occasion to speak, more fully, in our review of Dr. Ullmann's *Reformers before the Reformation*, which rests throughout on the assumption that Protestantism can be properly understood and defended only as the legitimate and necessary product of mediæval Catholicism, and not as an abrupt unhistorical revolution.[2] To unchurch the Catholic Church, to cut her off entirely from the kingdom of God, and to identify her with the kingdom of Antichrist, as was almost unanimously done by the General Assembly of the Old School Presbyterian Church, during its sessions at Cincinnati, 1845 (and which that Church, notwithstanding the well-founded protest of her able and learned Professors at Princeton, has not yet rescinded) would, upon German ground, be absolutely impossible.[3] The Evangelical Theology of Germany is indeed also thor-

1. [Originally published in *Mercersburg Quarterly Review* 5 (January 1853): 124–44.] This essay is the conclusion of a series of articles on the most distinguished contemporary University-theologians of Germany, which appeared in the May, July, August and September numbers of the *Kirchenfreund* for 1852. [The five-part series, "Gallerie der bedeutendsten jetzt lebenden Universitätetheologen Deutschlands," actually began in April. This essay, "Die deutsche Theologie und die Kirchenfrage," appears immediately after the last of the series under a separate heading.]

2. [Schaff, "Gallerie der bedeutendsten jetzt lebenden Universitätetheologen Deutschlands (Schluss)," *Der deutsche Kirchenfreund*, 5 (August 1852), 290–93. Carl Ullmann, *Reformatoren vor der Reformation* (Hamburg: Perthes, 1841).]

3. [In responding to a question from the Presbytery of Ohio, "Is Baptism in the Church of Rome valid?" this assembly concluded that such baptisms were not valid. The committee appointed to express the mind of the assembly on this matter stated that valid baptisms could only be performed by "a duly ordained minister of the true Church of God visible." Roman Catholic priests, the committee concluded, "are not ministers of Christ, for they are commissioned as agents of the papal hierarchy, which is not a church of Christ, but the Man of Sin, apostate from the truth, the enemy of righteousness

oughly Protestant in principle and spirit, and rests upon that freedom of thought, and impartiality of investigation, which we properly owe to the Reformation. But this very freedom and impartiality of research has also led her to conceive and judge of the Catholic Church in a manner totally different from the old Protestant polemics of the sixteenth and seventeenth centuries. This, however, does by no means necessarily involve an approach towards Rome, but indicates rather a new and advanced position of Protestantism itself, which we understand to be the progressive principle of modern church history, whilst Romanizing tendencies are retrograde movements and deadly hostile to a proper conception of progressive development, which underlies all living German theology of the present day, especially its best works on church history.

[The Middle Ages]

First of all, the modern investigation of ecclesiastical and profane historians have entirely overthrown the earlier views concerning the *Middle Ages*. It may now be received as an established fact, admitted by all learned judges, that the Roman Catholic Church as such, during that age, was, by no means, the great Apostacy or kingdom of Antichrist, but the bearer of true Christianity, with its sacred canon and saving ordinances, the mother of the Romanic and Germanic nations, and of the whole modern European civilization, and not withstanding her adherent corruption, carried within herself a vast amount of elevated piety and heroic virtue. The Papacy itself is regarded now, by the most distinguished modern church historians, and even by profane historians, such as John von Müller, Leo, Ranke, and Macaulay, as an institution absolutely indispensable for that time, and upon the whole highly beneficial, for the education of the Germanic nations, for the preservation of the unity and security of the freedom and independence of the Church over against the encroachments of the secular power.

---

and of God." Here they invoked the Westminster Confession of Faith 25.6 which identifies the papacy with the "man of sin" mentioned in 2 Thess 2:3. The committee also invoked the declaration of the 1835 General Assembly that the Church of Rome was an apostate body. Presbyterian Church in the U. S. A. (Old School), General Assembly, *Minutes* 11 (1845): 14–15, 34–37.

Charles Hodge of Princeton Theological Seminary was not present at the assembly, but vigorously dissented and tried unsuccessfully to get his fellow Presbyterians to change their minds. He argued that the assembly was wrong because it departed from the precedent of the reformers, including Luther and Calvin, because Roman Catholics held the major truths of the Christian religion and maintained the proper matter and form of baptism, and because the Roman Catholic Church was indeed part of the visible church even though it was apostate. The Westminster Confession's statement about the "man of sin" referred to the papal hierarchy, he insisted, not to the Roman Catholic Church, its members as a whole, or its priests. Gutjahr, *Charles Hodge*, 235–39; Hoffecker, *Charles Hodge*, 248–51. This debate is an excellent example of the church question being taken up by a denomination in the mainstream of American Protestantism.

As merely the resolution of one particular General Assembly, the decision did not formally enter into the standards of the denomination or its successors. In 2011 the Presbyterian Church (USA) formalized its recognition of Catholic baptism when it, the U. S. Conference of Catholic Bishops, and other American Reformed churches, including the United Church of Christ, celebrated the approval of "The Common Agreement on the Mutual Recognition of Baptism."]

As the law of Moses was a schoolmaster to Christ,[4] so the new Christian legalism of medieval Catholicism prepared the way for Evangelical Protestantism. "Whatever opinion we may hold," says the Protestant historian Ranke,

> concerning the Popes of former times, they had ever important interests in view—the fostering of an oppressed religion, the contention with Heathenism, the spread of Christianity throughout the Northern nations, and the establishment of an independent hierarchical power; it belongs to the dignity of human nature to will and to accomplish something great: these movements the Popes kept alive, and gave them a higher direction.[5]

To what extent similar conceptions have gradually taken root, of late, in English Protestant literature, notwithstanding the opposition of religious prejudices, the highly gifted Macaulay bears testimony, who leaves it undecided whether England is not more indebted for her greatness to Catholicism than to Protestantism, and thus frankly speaks concerning the Papacy of the Middle Ages:

> Even the spiritual supremacy arrogated by the Pope was, in the dark ages, productive of far more good than evil. Its effect was to unite the nations of Western Europe in one great commonwealth. What the Olympian chariot course, and the Pythian oracle were to all the Greek cities, from Trebizond to Marseilles, Rome and her bishop were to all the Christians of the Latin communion, from Calabria to the Hebrides. Thus grew up sentiments of enlarged benevolence. Races separated from each other by seas and mountains acknowledged a fraternal tie, and a common code of public law. Even in war, the cruelty of the conqueror was not seldom mitigated by a recollection that he and his vanquished enemies were all members of one great federation.[6]

The proper *coryphei* ["party leaders"] of the Papacy, such as Nicholas, Hildebrand, and Innocent III,[7] heretofore regarded as scarcely anything better than incarnate devils, are now looked upon as heroes and benefactors of humanity. Even Neander, who is well known to have naturally a great antipathy to every thing priestly and hierarchical, and who zealously endeavors to place the opposers of the ruling Church in the most advantageous light possible, candidly expresses his profound admiration for

4. [Cf. Gal 2:24.]

5. Roman Popes in the Sixteenth and Seventeenth Centuries, 1 part, p. 44 second edition. [This is Schaff's own translation from the German edition. Leopold von Ranke, *Die römischen Päpste: ihre Kirche und ihr Staat im sechzehnten und siebzehnten Jahrhundert*, 2nd ed. (Berlin: Duncker und Humblot, 1838–39), 1:44.]

6. History of England, ch. 1. [Thomas Babington Macaulay, *The History of England from the Accession of James the Second* (London: Longman, Brown, Green, and Longmans, 1849). Pagination for edition used by Schaff unknown. Macaulay, *Macaulay's History of England from the Accession of James II* (London: Dent, 1906), 9.]

7. [Nicholas I (c. 800–67, pope from 858), Gregory VII (c.1025–85, pope from 1073), Innocent III (1160/61–1216, pope from 1198). Each notably advanced the authority of the Roman pontiff.]

the moral character and great merits of these popes. In the same manner has the judgment concerning the other prominent phenomena of the Middle Ages—the crusades, the monastic orders and their founders, religious art, scholasticism and mysticism—assumed a more favorable form, in proportion as they are brought from the dust of the past to light, and understood in their organic connection with the nature and wants of that period. It is impossible, e. g., to read with attention, Neander's *Bernard*, or Hasse's *Anselm*, without being filled with profound admiration for the spirit, virtue and piety of these men, although they move throughout in the spirit and mould of the Catholic Church, and belong, as is well known, to her most distinguished teachers and saints.[8]

But this altered conception of the Middle Ages involves an enormous concession to Catholicism, and a fatal blow against a bigoted ultra-Protestantism. A Church, which throughout this whole transition period, from ancient to modern times, sent out such a host of self-denying missionaries to heathen nations, who carried the Gospel to the Germans, Scandinavians, Anglo-Saxons, Picts and Scots, and Sclavonians[9]—a Church, which had power to excite all Europe to a heroic conflict against the false prophet for the recovery of the holy sepulchre of the Redeemer[10]—a Church, which contended vigorously and successfully against the despotism of worldly potentates, slavery, barbarity, and a thousand other evils of society, which gave wholesome laws to the states, raised the female sex to its present dignity, which interested herself in behalf of the poor and suffering of all classes, which established asylums for misery, and institutions of benevolence in all places, which erected unto the Lord numberless churches, chapels, and those Gothic cathedrals, which even yet command the admiration of the world, which gave the first impulse to a general education of the people, which founded and sheltered almost all those European universities, which even to this day exert an immeasurable influence—a Church which has produced within her bosom such an incalculable number of profound minds, elevated characters and devoted saints—such a Church cannot possibly, in the nature of the case, be the Antichrist and synagogue of Satan, notwithstanding the many anti-Christian elements which she may have included within her bosom, and of which no age and no denomination is entirely free. That extreme representation, which the majority of our popular religious papers continue to repeat from week to week, cannot for one moment maintain itself against the results of later Protestant historical research, and must therefore in due time disappear from the consciousness of all educated and unprejudiced minds.

8. [August Neander, *Der heilige Bernhard und sein Zeitalter* (Saint Bernard and his age, 1813); Friedrich Rudolph Hasse, *Anselm von Canterbury* (1843–52).]

9. [Sclavonians is a nineteenth-century term for the medieval Slavs of central Europe.]

10. [Schaff is referring to the Crusades. By "false prophet" he means Muhammad, the prophet of Islam.]

[The Early Church]

Moreover, not only the Middle Ages, but also the *first six centuries* of the Christian Church, have been thoroughly re-examined, and documents have been brought to light, which for the most part were unknown even by name at the time of the Reformation, when historical study and the publication of ancient works had scarcely begun. Even Luther once calls Tertullian, who lived as late as the end of the second and beginning of the third centuries, "the *oldest* teacher which we have since the time of the Apostles," (*Works*, ed. Walch XX, 1063),[11] so that for him the line of the Apostolical Fathers and the numerous Apologists of the second century did not exist, with the exception of uncertain fragments which he could not but know from the legends of the martyr Ignatius, Polycarp and Clemens,[12] "for whom," as he once remarks, "a bad boy forged books." The Reformers were best acquainted with Augustine, and their reverence and love for this profoundly pious, as well as spirited and highly gifted father, was of immeasurable importance for their theological and moral training and position, as otherwise the Reformation would most probably have assumed a far more radical character. Through the indefatigable diligence and zealous inquiry of modern times, and through the impulse, which more especially Neander has given to historical Monography, we have at present, in the German language, thorough and complete works on Leo, Augustine, Chrysostom, Gregory of Nazianzen, Basil, Athanasius, Origen, Cyprian, Tertullian, Irenæus, Justin Martyr, and even back to the immediate successors of the Apostles; so that the Nicene and Ante-Nicene Christianity, with the corresponding heresies of Arianism, Gnosticism and Ebionism, &c., are as clearly presented to our view, or at least as accessible as the Christianity of the seventeenth century. If we now read impartially those valuable monographies, or similar and more comprehensive works, such as Rothe's *Anfänge der christlichen Kirche*, Dorner's *Geschichte der Christologie*, Möhler's *Patrologie*, &c.,[13] and if we, in connection with these, candidly study only some of the more important productions of patristic theology, such as Chrysostom, *On the Priesthood*, Augustine's *Confessions*, Cyprian, *On the Unity of the Church*, Tertullian, *On the Prescription of Heretics*, Irenæus, *Against the Gnostics*, and the *Epistles* of Ignatius, we must inevitably receive the impression that the Church of antiquity was in its predominant spirit and tendency, far more Catholic than Protestant, and that the Middle Ages are only a natural continuation of

11. [Martin Luther, *D. Martin Luthers . . . sämtliche Schriften*, ed. Johann Georg Walch, vol. 20 (Halle im Magdeburgischen: Johann Justinus Gebauer, 1740), 1063. The phrase appears in Luther's 1527 treatise *That These Words of Christ, 'This is My Body,' etc. Still Stand Firm against Fanatics*, *LW* 37:108.]

12. [Pope Clement I (d. 99).]

13. [Richard Rothe, *Die Anfänge der christlichen Kirche* (The beginnings of the Christian church, 1837); Isaac August Dorner, *Entwicklungsgeschichte der Lehre von der Person Christi* (History of the development of christology, 1839); Johann Adam Möhler, *Patrologie, oder christliche Literärgeschichte* (Patristics, or Christian literary history, 1840).]

the Nicene Christianity. Could Ambrosius,[14] Athanasius, Cyprian, Irenæus, Ignatius, Clemens and Polycarp suddenly arise from their graves, and be transferred to Puritan New England, they would scarcely there recognize the Christianity of those venerable Martyrs and Confessors, for which they lived and suffered; but, on the contrary, would much sooner discover, not only amongst the Universalists and Unitarians, but amongst the Baptists and Puritans themselves, distinct traces of a congeniality of spirit with the heretics and schismatics of their own days. We state this, however, without any disrespect whatever, but simply as the impression received from an impartial comparison of historical facts. The most striking difference between the Primitive Church and Protestantism, lies in the doctrine of the Rule of Faith,[15] of the Relation of the Scriptures to Tradition, of the Church, her Unity, her Catholicity, her Exclusiveness, and of the Sacraments. Even of the material principle of Protestantism, the doctrine of Justification by Faith *alone*, in LUTHER's sense, the Fathers know nothing, not even Augustine;[16] and instead of making this the article of the standing and falling Church, they assign rather to the Christology, to the mystery of the Incarnation and to the Holy Trinity, the central position in the Christian system, and the confession or denial of Christ's real humanity, is with them, according to 1 John 4, the sure criterion of orthodoxy or heterodoxy.[17] In all these points of doctrine, as well as in the hierar-

14. [Ambrose of Milan (339–97).]

15. [The rule of faith is the standard by which Christian teaching and practice are to be judged. It and synonymous terms were also used by Irenaeus of Lyon and others in the second century to designate short statements, such as a baptismal creed, that distinguished their teachings from heretics. Mercersburg theologians, such as J. A. H. Bomberger, objected to the claim of some Protestants that the Bible alone was the rule of faith, or that individual Christians had the autonomy to discern the rule of faith. Instead Bomberger insisted that "the only true rule of faith" was "the combined testimony of the Word and the Church, past, present, and to come, to all fundamental doctrines, and essential ordinances." Bomberger, "The Rule of Faith—Concluded," 371.]

16. Neander, for instance, clearly shows, that Augustine's conception of justification is not a forensic outward imputation (however important this may be), but a really making just, and hence substantially the same with sanctification. This by no means interferes necessarily with the doctrine of free grace, of which the same father is well known to have been one of the most zealous defenders. We may indeed say, that the substance of the Protestant doctrine of justification by faith properly understood is salvation by free grace, and in this general form it underlies no doubt the piety of all ages and of all true Christians.

17. We cannot refrain from citing here a remarkable confession of Dr. W. J. Tiersch, in his valuable work on the New Testament Canon (1845, p. 280), [Heinrich Wilhelm Josias Thiersch, *Versuch zur Herstellung des historischen Standpuncts für die Kritik der neutestamentlichen Schriften: eine Streitschrift gegen die Kritiker unserer Tage* (Essay to establish the historical foundation for criticism of the New Testament: a polemic against the critics of our day) (Erlangen: Heyder, 1845), 280] as it serves to illustrate, in a most impartial manner, the impression of this contrast between Patristic and Protestant Theology, even in its most churchly and orthodox form:—"What a strange impression do the Church Fathers, for the most part, make upon him who, filled with a strictly Protestant consciousness, betakes himself for the first time to their study. Thus it happened with the author of these discussions. Nourished by the best devotional works of the older Protestant writers, and educated theologically in the Dogmatics and Exegesis of the sixteenth and seventeenth centuries, he turned to the Church Fathers. He remembers well how strange it appeared to him from the beginning, in not being able to find here anything of those truths which formed the well-springs of his entire religious life; nothing of that (Protestant) way, which

chical constitution, the sacrificial worship, and the ascetic conception of Christian virtue and piety, we clearly discover, in the Church Fathers, from Gregory and Leo up to Cyprian, Irenæeus and Ignatius, at least the germs of that system, which afterwards completed itself in the Roman Catholic Church.[18] This is continually becoming acknowledged the more in proportion as researches are extended in this sphere, and their results produced in a popular form. Without this resemblance, it would be absolutely impossible to account for the fact, that the Roman Catholic Church has canonized the most distinguished and pious of the fathers and cherishes their memory with filial veneration and gratitude to this day. It is only through want of knowledge, or a singular delusion, that any section of Protestantism could ever imagine itself to be a simple restoration of the Nicene or ante-Nicene age.

---

the sinner must tread in order to obtain peace, and become assured of divine grace; nothing of the merit of Christ as the only ground of pardon (?), nothing of an unceasing repentance, and continually fresh drawings from the fountain of free grace, and nothing of that lofty assurance of a justified Christian. Instead of this, he found that all stress was laid upon the Incarnation of the Divine Logos, upon a correct knowledge of this sublime object of worship, upon the objective mystery of the Trinity and Incarnation, upon the connection of creation, redemption and the future restoration of the creature in the glorification even of the human corporeality, upon the freedom of man, and upon the reality of the divine workings of grace in the Sacraments. Yet it was not too much for him to live himself into this whole method of thought, and, without giving up anything that is true and inalienable in the Protestant, especially the Lutheran Protestant consciousness, to conquer its onesidedness by means of a living appropriation of the theology of the Fathers. He soon learned that the Christian Church, over against the errors of the present, the Pantheism and Fatalism, the Spiritualism, sad misapprehension of the significance of corporeality, stood in need of a decided re-assumption of the truths preserved in the Patristic Theology, and of an assimilation of her entire existence to the peculiar character of the ancient Church, at least internally, since the Reformation of external circumstances lies not within the reach of human power. The Primitive Christian Church appeared to him more and more in her full splendor and exalted beauty, of which only fragmentary lineaments are to be recognized in the churches, confessions and sects of the present. But the knowledge of this truly Apostolic-Catholic Church, which is neither identical with the Greek nor the Roman Church—but which differs still *far more* from Protestantism—this it is which gradually emancipated him from all polemical and denominational fanaticism, and afforded him the happiness of a disposition as decided and uncompromising against that which is unchristian and antichristian, as irenical and liberal towards that which is true and Christian in the manifold confessions of the present."—Those who wish to convince themselves that the views of the Fathers from Ignatius down to Augustine on the nature of the *Church*, which in some respects is the most important and comprehensive point of difference between Romanism and Protestantism, are essentially Catholic, and that the article of the creed, *Credo unam sanctam apostolicam ecclesiam* [Trans. "I believe in one holy apostolic church"], with them, did not refer to an invisible abstraction, but to a visible historical reality, are respectfully referred to the third book in Dr. Rothe's masterly work on the early Church [Richard Rothe, *Die Anfänge Der Christlichen Kirche* (1837)]. The articles of Dr. Nevin on Early Christianity, and on Cyprian too, [John W. Nevin, "Early Christianity," *Mercersburg Review* 3 (1851): 461–90, 513–62; 4 (1852), 1–54; Nevin, "Cyprian," *Mercersburg Review* 4 (1852), 259–77, 335–87, 417–52, 513–63] with which the readers of the *Mercersburg Review* are familiar, are quite to the point, and bring out a great many facts in clear and strong light which are worthy of the most serious attention, and cannot be put aside by mere categorical protests or ungentlemanly insinuations.

18. [Schaff lists these fathers in reverse historical order, from Pope Gregory I (c.540–604), often counted as the last western "father," to Pope Leo I (c.400–61), Cyprian of Carthage (c. 200–58), Irenaeus of Lyon (d. c. 202), Ignatius of Antioch (d. between 98 and 117). Thus he argues that Christianity began to develop in a Roman Catholic direction from at least the end of the first century.]

[Implications for the Church Question]

If however we concede this much, from a mere historical standpoint, it is easy to see what an enormous influence such an admission must have upon the final solution of *the Church Question*. For whoever despises the judgment of History, robs himself at the same time of all foundation and basis. If the fifteen centuries prior to the Reformation are deserving of no confidence, neither are the last three centuries entitled to any respect. "If any one neglect to hear the voice of the Church," saith our Lord, "let him be unto thee as a heathen man and a publican." (Matt 18:17). In proportion as we undermine and reject the testimony of Church History, in theological and religious questions, do we also open the door to skepticism and nihilism. Herein precisely lies the great ecclesiastical and religious importance of modern church-historical research, even if this should not yet be duly acknowledged by many German theologians. The time will and must come, when the practical conclusions will be drawn from the theory.

[The Bible and the Church]

But some will at once ask, "Of what concern is the testimony of history to me, if I have the *Word of God* in my favor, which is, after all, the only certain Rule of Faith and Life; whilst the greatest schoolmen and Church Fathers, according to their own confession, were themselves sinful men, and liable to err?" Very true! But who has made you an infallible *interpreter* of this Word? Has not this Word already existed in the Church before the sixteenth century, and as such been highly honored, read, transcribed, translated and commented upon? Whence then have you the canon, save directly from the faithful collection and transmission of the Catholic Church? Who furnishes you the proof of the genuineness and integrity of the apostolical writings, except the testimonies of the ancient ecclesiastical authors? If already the immediate disciples of the Apostles, if Ignatius, Clemens and Polycarp, if the fathers and martyrs of the second and third centuries, have radically misunderstood the New Testament, what guaranty have we then that *you*, in the nineteenth century, understand it properly throughout, wherever you may differ from them? Are you then made of better stuff than the Confessors and Martyrs of the blooming period of the Church? Have you done and suffered more for Christ? You say: The clear letter of Paul and John condemns the Catholic Church as Antichrist, as the Man of Sin, the Beast from the abyss, as the Babylon destined to be destroyed.[19] But whence do you know that this interpretation is correct? Since you totally reject the infallibility of the Pope, and perhaps also of the Church in general, you will certainly not be so inconsistent, and ridiculously presumptuous, as to claim it for yourself or any other Protestant inter-

19. [For identification of the Roman Catholic Church with the "anti-christ," the beast from the abyss, and Babylon some Protestants pointed to various chapters in Revelation especially 13, 18, and 19. For the "man of sin," 2 Thess 2:3–4, for Babylon, Rev 17–18.]

preter? Moreover, such an application of the passages in question was wholly unheard of until within the later period of the Middle Ages, when it was invented by certain fanatical sects, to suit their polemical ends. The Church Fathers, without exception, even Irenæus, who through Polycarp stood in close relation to the Apostle John himself, have referred them to Gnosticism and to the World-Empire of *heathen* Rome. At all events, the Reformers could not have used consistently the Revelation of John for any polemical purpose, since Luther and Zwingli denied its Apostolical origin, and Calvin, with all his masterly skill as a commentator, wisely suffered it to remain unexplained. Later Protestant interpreters, such as Hammond and Grotius, and all modern expounders of Scripture (quite lately the orthodox Hengstenberg, in his commentary on the Apocalypse, and even the Puritan Stuart)[20] have, almost without exception, rejected the Anti-Roman interpretation, as entirely untenable, and again returned to the explanation of the Church Fathers.[21]

However this may be, there are, at all events, many more *clear* and *distinct* passages in Scripture, which, according to the unanimous explanation of Catholic and Protestant commentators, promise to the Church of Christ an *indestructible continuation and an uninterrupted presence of her divine Head, even to the end of the world.* Of this there cannot be the least doubt, and therefore must we above all, build our theory of Church History upon *such* declarations, and not upon a very doubtful interpretation of the darkest passages in the most mysterious book of the Bible—which, not without reason, stands last in our canon. But if it should appear as the result of the modern thorough and impartial investigations of the greatest Protestant Historians, that the Christian Church, before the Reformation, even back to the days of the Apostolic Fathers, was not in her predominant spirit and character Protestant, but essentially Catholic, in most of those points where the two systems are at war with each other, and that the protesting sects, from the Ebionites and Gnostics, down to the Cathari and Albigenses[22] present a confused mixture of contradictory opinions, and

20. [Ernst Wilhelm Hengstenberg, *Die Offenbarung des heiligen Johannes* (The Revelation of Saint John, 1849); Moses Stuart, *A Commentary on the Apocalypse* (1845).]

21. We must remark, however, that the *exclusive* reference of the 18th and 17th chapters of the Apocalypse does not seem to do justice to the inspired vision of John, which seems to include several successive world-powers opposed to the kingdom of Christ. Still less can we adopt Hengstenberg's view of the Millenium. [All of these seventeenth- and nineteenth-century interpreters espoused a preterist interpretation of most events in Revelation, in which the events revealed to John had been fulfilled in the history of the early church and the downfall of the Roman Empire. Thus they rejected the anti-Roman Catholic interpretation of many early Protestants by embracing the anti-Roman Empire interpretation of the church fathers. About Rev 17 and 18, Hengstenberg wrote, "the overthrow of heathen Rome, which is simply and in some sharp features announced in ch. xvii, is vividly portrayed in ch. xviii." *The Revelation of St. John*, 2:227. In this note, Schaff is questioning this interpretation and dissenting from Hengstenberg's identification of the millennium as beginning with the inauguration of the Western Christian empire with the crowning of Charlemagne at Christmas in 800 and thus lasting until about 1800. Hengstenberg, *Revelation*, 2:334–37.]

22. [Ebionites and Gnostics were ancient alternative Christian movements dating from the second century. In the twelfth and thirteenth centuries Cathars and Albigensians also claimed to practice a more

as such cannot possibly constitute the uninterrupted continuation of the Life of Christ and evangelical truth: it necessarily follows that such a defense of Protestantism, which rests upon an entire rejection of Catholicism—as a system of falsehood—be it Baptistic, Puritanic, Presbyterian or Anglican—stands in direct contradiction to the testimony of history and those unequivocal sayings of Christ and his Apostles, and must therefore be abandoned.

[Challenges for Protestantism's Current Relationship to Catholicism]

This is the deciding point to which the controversy between Protestantism and Catholicism, which has lately arisen with renewed zeal and energy in Germany, England and the United States, is forced; and should some German theologians, who have aided in bringing about this issue, in their predominantly theoretical tendency and scientific self-complacency, concern themselves little about the practical consequences, there are many divines in practical England and America, who will draw the final conclusions. Examples might readily be pointed out, which in reality confirm this. It is a remarkable and interesting fact that German evangelical theology becomes far more practical and serious in its consequences upon English ground, than in Germany itself. For the Englishman seldom contents himself with naked theories and speculations, but endeavors directly to bring them into practical life, to organize them externally and realize them in some concrete form. This can easily be seen in Methodism, compared with the congenial, but unorganized Pietism. Puseyism exhibits the same tendency, though in an opposite direction; for in it, the idea of the Church has long since emerged from the sphere of theological research, and has become a solemn practical life-question, which has already driven a considerable number of the Clergy and Laity from the Protestant into the Roman camp. Neither would it greatly surprise us should we live to see also in America a larger secession of educated men towards Rome, arising partly at least from an earnest but one-sided study of Church history. For here such a step could be more easily accounted for than in Germany, as a necessary reaction against extreme forms of anti-catholic theology. To do this, we need only consider that the Protestant press of America, with few honorable exceptions, from the city papers, with their ten and twenty thousand subscribers, down to the most obscure country sheets, rests upon this totally anti-scriptural and anti-historical theory; that it contends against the Roman Church with weapons of the blindest fanaticism, and that it suffers itself to make use of such rude and uncharitable misrepresentations, which we should be obliged to stigmatize directly as barefaced lies, could they not be accounted for, on the ground of ignorance and prejudice, and did not the otherwise religious character of these Intelligencers and non-Intelligencers,[23] compel us to

perfect form of Christianity and were deemed heretical by Catholic theologians. Together these two sets of groups frame the major pre-Reformation history of alternative Christian sectarian movements.]

23. [Schaff is parodying the common title of many nineteenth-century newspapers, *Intelligencer*,

adopt the latter expedient. He who has ever thoroughly and impartially studied the history of the Church before the Reformation and the classical productions of Roman Divines, such as Bellarmine, Bossuet, Möhler, Wiseman, Balmes, and Newman, must possess a more than ordinary amount of patience and stoical tranquility of mind, if he can behold those caricatures which are circulated from week to week without being filled with indignation against the conscious or unconscious calumniators, and with an increasing sympathy, for the slandered party. Add to this, the growing confusion in Protestantism, which notwithstanding its great advantages in many other respects is, precisely in this country, more than in any other, split into numberless denominations and sects, without any human prospect for a consolidation or union, and presents a confused mixture of private opinions and subjective, ever changing notions, which threaten finally to wash away all the solid ground of real supernatural faith and fixed doctrine from under our feet, unless important conservative powers should stay the wild stream. The most trifling cause is considered sufficient to mangle the Body of Christ, and to transgress the Apostle's command: "Forbearing one another in love; endeavoring to keep the unity of the spirit in the bond of peace."[24] And along with this, there is such an abuse made of the Word of God, that it must furnish proof texts for the wildest dreams, as if it were a nose of wax and a book of all sorts of contradictions. If then we have any idea of the Church, its inherent unity and catholicity, of law and authority, and regard Christianity as a supernatural power, to which we must humbly submit, instead of fashioning it according to a rationalistic common sense, and the conceptions of modern times, until it is finally sunk to the sphere of Nature, and becomes the product of our reason and imagination; we must have an unusually strong confidence in History, and continually look to the past, and with hope to the future, so as not to become disheartened sometimes by the present Babel of Protestant sects. Without such a confidence in God—who, as a Portuguese proverb says, writes also on a crooked line, and can call a beautiful creation out of chaos; without the virtue of patient expectation and hope, there is a strong inducement for serious minds, which have become fully conscious of the weight and difficulties of this subject, to cast themselves into the arms of Roman uniformity, if only for the purpose of escaping this eternal fluctuation, and experimenting to acquire a firm foundation and basis, and to enjoy as they hope at least, the feeling of comfortable rest and security.

If therefore Protestantism is to be defended, without surrendering the thoroughly scriptural idea of an indestructible Church, and an uninterrupted indwelling presence of Christ, and without doing violence to the clear testimony of History, prior to the Reformation, it can only be done by conceding, at the same time, a relative title to Catholicism, and allowing it to have been the chief, if not the only bearer of Christianity, down to the sixteenth century, and that it even yet constitutes a vital member of the Body of Christ. Dr. Rothe says in his learned and not sufficiently appreciated work,

perhaps particularly the Dutch Reformed newspaper published in New York, *The Christian Intelligencer*.]

24. [Eph 4:2b-3.]

entitled *Die Anfänge der christlichen Kirche* (Preface, p. ix.): "There can be no more powerful apology for Protestantism, than the acknowledgment, yea even the positive affirmation of the fact, that in the *past*, Catholicism, according to its substance, has had full historical reality and necessity, deep inward truth, and high moral excellence and power."[25] So we say also: The noblest and most efficient way of defending Protestantism, is not to run down and abuse, but rather to glorify and defend Catholicism, as the bearer of mediæval Christianity, and as a necessary preparation for Protestantism itself, without which the latter could as little have made its appearance, as Christianity without Judaism, or as liberty without the school of authority and obedience. In the same way we may say that the honor of the New Testament is not diminished, but increased rather and properly guarded, by giving the Old Testament all due credit and importance as a preparatory dispensation of the gospel.

But even this alone is not sufficient. For a Church, which, in spite of the tremendous shock experienced in the sixteenth century, depriving her of the most vigorous nations, has yet power to revive herself, and replace, at least to a great extent, the lost territory by means of important conquests in the heathen world; which has since been able to reproduce in the sphere of theology, a Bellarmine, a Baronio, a Pétau, a Bossuet, a Möhler, in the sphere of missions and Christian Life, a Xavier, a Borromeo, a Filippo of Neri, a Vincens of Paula, a Pascal, a Fenelon, a Sailer; which in later times has attracted talented men so differently constituted, such as Haller, Stolberg, Novalis, Schlegel, Hurter, Florencourt, Newman, Manning, Wilberforce and Brownson; which subsequent to the Revolutionary storm of 1848, has elevated herself with renewed energy, extended her arms towards the North and West, into the very heart of Protestant civilization, and the bulwark of Protestant power, and wherever she goes, throws the Government, Clergy and Laity into a feverish agitation, and sets a thousand tongues and pens in motion against her:[26]— such a Church cannot have her significance in the past *alone*, but must possess even yet an important life-power, a relative necessity for the present, and a significant mission for the future. This is, of course, at once to

25. [Rothe, *Die Anfänge der christlichen Kirche* (The origins of the Christian church), ix. No English translation of the book has been published.]

26. There is only too much truth in the following remarks of the distinguished Anglican convert, Dr. Newman, in the preface to his lectures to Anglicans: "there is an instinctive feeling of curiosity, interest, anxiety, and awe, mingled together in various proportions, according to the tempers and opinions of individuals, when the Catholic Church makes her appearance in any neighborhood, rich or poor, in the person of her missionary or her religious communities. Do what they will, denounce her as they may, her enemies cannot quench this emotion in the breasts of others, or in their own. It is their involuntary homage to the Notes of the Church; it is their spontaneous recognition of her royal descent and her imperial claim; it is a specific feeling, which no other religion tends to excite. Judaism, Mahometanism [i.e., Islam], Anglicanism, Methodism, old religions and young, romantic and common-place, have not the spell. The presence of the Church creates a discomposure and restlessness, or a thrill of exultation, wherever she comes. Meetings are held, denunciations launched, calumnies spread abroad, and hearts beat secretly the while." [John Henry Newman, *Lectures on Certain Difficulties Felt by Anglicans in Submitting to the Catholic Church* (London: Burns & Lambert, 1850), v-vi. The "Notes of the Church" are that it is one, holy, catholic, and apostolic.]

confess that Protestantism does not describe the entire circumference of the Church, even since the time of the Reformation—although it is evidently the chief bearer of modern civilization—but that it is in its own nature, onesided, that it suffers from imperfections, as well as its adversary, although of an opposite character, that it, on this account, again stands in need of a Reformation, that it has in Catholicism its necessary complement, and that it can never complete itself without it. The signs of the times also, point clearly enough to this issue. Protestantism is just at this time undergoing a thorough examination and sifting in Germany, England and North America, and it is to be hoped that the sermon of repentance, which is thus delivered unto it, may not be overheard, but that it may reap similar benefits from the progress of its old hereditary enemy, whilst the Roman Church has evidently gained to a great extent, in activity and zeal, by means of the reacting and arousing influence of Protestantism. For wherever they have come into contact, it can easily be seen, that Romanism is in a far more living and hopeful condition, than where it sways the sceptre of undisturbed dominion, e.g., in the spiritually dead Mexico, Brazil, Portugal and Croatia.

This liberal position towards Rome is, at all events, more generous, far more consistent with the spirit of Christian charity, and much better calculated to gain over the adversary, than that harsh and repulsive fanaticism, which hesitates not even to make common cause with Rationalists, Pantheists, Atheists, Socialists and impure Revolutionary spirits of every possible character, over against Catholicism, as is too frequently the case with many of our religious sheets. Only think of the many Protestant patrons, such miserable apostates and unprincipled slanderers as Maria Monk, Ronge, Leahy (who lately turned out a murderer), Achilli, etc., have found in our midst! "What communion hath Christ with Belial, or light with darkness?"[27] But the

27. [2 Cor 6:15. Maria Monk, Johannes Ronge, Giancinto Achilli, and Edward Leahy were each converts from Roman Catholicism who achieved notoriety for their criticisms of Catholicism before being discredited for their personal lives or intellectual positions. Each is discussed in the glossary of names. Edward Leahy is the least well known, but the most closely connected to Mercersburg. An Irish immigrant to the United States, he claimed to have been a monk at La Trappe Abbey in France. He was converted to Protestantism by Joseph Berg and sent to Marshall College in Mercersburg in 1844, the same year Schaff arrived. Leahy was scandalized to be taught that the Roman Catholic Church was part of the visible church. Berg, the prominent Philadelphia German Reformed minister, became Schaff's leading opponent, criticizing *Principle of Protestantism* on precisely this point. Though the *Weekly Messenger* claimed Leahy had never been a regular student at Mercersburg, he promoted himself as "late of Marshall College" as he traveled the United States giving salacious anti-Catholic lectures. Even though his monastic background was quickly discovered to be false, he enjoyed a national reputation for several years and was supported by some anti-Catholic Protestant clergy. His lectures caused significant riots in various cities including Milwaukee, Wisconsin, in 1851. Mercersburg theologians regularly complained about the support of anti-Catholic Protestant clergy of this disreputable character. Nevin, "True and False Protestantism," 103; Bomberger, "Dr. Nevin and his Antagonists," 91.

In 1852, Leahy was convicted of murdering a man, whom Leahy accused of seducing his wife in the courthouse of Padreville, Wisconsin. He was sentenced to life in prison. (Wisconsin did not have capital punishment.) In 1856 he was reconciled to the Catholic Church, and upon being pardoned and released in 1860, announced that he would begin lecturing against Protestantism. The dates of his birth and death are unknown. De Courcy, *The Catholic Church*, 249–50, provides a brief biography. Billington, *The Protestant Crusade*, 319 n.72, lists newspaper articles documenting his career. On his

main point here is, that this mild and moderate polemic is more in keeping with *truth*, the Word of God, and the testimony of History, than the other, which rests purely on historical suppositions, caricatures and perversions.

[Historical Development is the Proper Foundation for Theology and the Church]

But now it may be asked, How can one remain a Protestant any longer, with a good conscience, if he makes such significant concessions to the Catholic Church, regarding her as the only true Church down to the Reformation, and attributing to her even to this day such an important position and mission? Is not that which was once the true Church, always the true Church? How can Christianity be first Catholic, then Protestant, without contradicting itself? Of course, from the standpoint of a mechanical conception of Christianity and History, this difficulty is not easily solved. Just as soon as we conceive of ecclesiastical Christianity as a system, pre-concluded from the start, and completed in its outward form, for all time, so soon must we consistently become either Roman Catholic or Ultra-Protestant. There is no middle ground. But far otherwise is it from the standpoint of *historical development*, which underlies all the more important German historical works of modern times, although the thing itself is as old as history, and has a firm foundation in the Bible. The only merit which German theology can claim in this respect is that it has brought out the idea in a scientific form and applied it to the treatment of history. This conception, it seems to us, affords the only tenable foundation upon which to justify the Reformation and Protestantism, without doing violence to preceding history, and destroying the nature of an uninterrupted Church. Hence its vast practical importance for the solution of the Church question. We speak here, of course, only of the *theological* and *scientific* defense of Protestantism. For the plain practical Christian is not and ought not to be troubled with these historical difficulties; he bases his faith in Protestantism very properly on the Word of God, as he understands it, on his own religious experience, and on the practical fruits of the system which he finds to compare very favorably on the whole with those of the opposite system. But the theologian must battle with the solemn problem of the Church question, as it stares him in the face from the pages of history. To him, it cannot possibly be indifferent what Christianity has been in the different ages of the world, and what relation his own view of it sustains to the great and good men of bygone days who have suffered all for Christ.

Development is properly identical with history itself; for history is life, and all life involves growth, evolution and progress. Our bodily existence, all our mental faculties, the Christian life, and the sanctification of every individual, constitute such a process

---

brief stay at Mercersburg see Good, *History of the Reformed Church in the U.S.*, 221; "The Rev. Mr. Leahey," 134. On later events in Wisconsin see Buck, *Milwaukee under the Charter*, 334–40; "Another Development," 4258; "Ex-Monk Leahy Revived," 2.]

of development from the lower to the higher. Why should not the same law hold, when applied to the whole, the communion which is made up of individuals? Any reasonable person will allow a progress in trade, business, in politics, arts, science and civilization; why not also in the Church? Why should she alone, which is a communion of individual believers, and something historical, yea the greatest fact and phenomenon of history, be made an exception to the laws of all organic life and development? The New Testament itself distinctly applies this law to the Church. For Christ compares his kingdom to a mustard seed which growth into a mighty tree, and to a leaven which gradually leaveneth the whole lump, and the Apostles, especially St. Paul, speak continually of the growth of the body of Christ as well as of individual believers.

Even Roman Catholic Divines, such as Möhler and Newman, must resort to the idea of development in some form—whether this naturally follows from the Roman standpoint of stability or not, is another question[28]—in order to understand and explain the history of their own Church. Much less can a Protestant historian advance a single step, and justify the Reformation, without the torchlight of this idea. It is now determined, as before remarked, that Protestantism in those doctrines differing from Catholicism, is not the Christianity of the Schoolmen and Mystics, not the Christianity of the Church Fathers of the Nicene age, not the Christianity of the Apologists, of the Apostolic Fathers, of the Martyrs and Confessors of the second and third centuries, but that all these are substantially more closely related to the Catholic standpoint, although this itself had only gradually developed and perfected itself. This is placed beyond doubt already, by the character of the Greek Church, which remains stationary at the point of the Ancient Church, and is evidently far more Catholic than Protestant. The doctrine of the Trinity, of the Divinity of Christ, of the Relation of the two Natures in Christ, of the Atonement, in short all the articles of the Apostolic and Nicene creeds, are here not brought into view; for these are not specifically and exclusively Protestant, but in their origin and substance Catholic, and manifestly inherited from an earlier Catholicism, fully as much so as the canon of Scripture and the doctrine of Inspiration. They constitute the primitive foundation common to all orthodox Churches, in opposition to all heretical sects. If then the Reformation is not

28. Brownson, in several articles of his *Review*, violently opposes Newman's theory of development as subversive to Catholicism and Christianity, and predicts that a new and dangerous heresy will spring out of this view of the Anglican converts, unless it be speedily condemned by the authorities of the Roman Church. [Brownson, review of *An Essay on the Development of Christian Doctrine* by John Henry Newman, *Brownson's Quarterly Review*, 3, no. 3 (July 1846): 342–68.] We believe that Brownson is very unjust to Newman, personally and perhaps unconsciously influenced by jealousy against his most distinguished fellow-convert; at the same time, however, we agree with him, that the idea of development is not congenial to the genuine spirit of Romanism, but essentially of Protestant growth. [Patrick Carey suggests that Brownson did have some jealousy of Newman because he and other former Anglo-Catholics had not needed to sacrifice as much of their prior intellectual perspectives upon conversion to Roman Catholicism as Brownson did. As a Protestant, Brownson had espoused the idea of development through his own doctrine of communion and initially gave this up upon his conversion in 1844. Carey, *Orestes A. Brownson*, 171–76.]

a work of Satan, but a divine fact, which we for good reasons believe, it must be viewed and defended as a new phase in the progressive development of Protestantism, as an advance on the earlier periods of the history of the Church.

This is then the last but safe anchor for a Protestant divine of the German historical school. To this position has, for example, Dr. NEVIN been forced, who is thoroughly acquainted with all the forms of English[29] and German Protestantism. The Puritan, Presbyterian and Anglican historical hypotheses, have proved wholly untenable to him, and in his late articles on "Early Christianity" and "Cyprian," in the *Mercersburg Review*, he has produced arguments against them, which none of his many dissatisfied opponents have attempted to refute, and which indeed, in a historical view, so far as the main facts are concerned, can scarcely ever be refuted.[30] Consequently there remains for him nothing except the German theory of Development, which, in the mean time, is held in reproach by almost all English theologians. As long as he adheres to this theory, an exodus to Rome will be impossible, as it would be it retrogression, and consequently a nullification of the fundamental law of historical development.[31] For this, in the nature of the case, implies progress, an advance from the lower to the higher, and this must hold good when applied to the Church, although in the individual parts of all the divisions of the Church, retrogressive movements and temporary stagnation may occur.

29. [Here and elsewhere, Schaff employs the vernacular of German Americans: by English, Schaff means "English-speaking."]

30. It is a fact by no means creditable to our American theology, that the many and earnest writings of this distinguished divine on the Church question, in its various aspects, have been met almost on every side with misrepresentation, slander and abuse, instead of earnest, solid argument. The only respectable articles, which have thus far appeared against Dr. Nevin, are Dr. Hodge's review of the *Mystical Presence* [Charles Hodge, "Doctrine of the Reformed Church on the Lord's Supper," review of *The Mystical Presence: A Vindication of the Reformed or Calvinistic Doctrine of the Holy Eucharist* by John W. Nevin, *The Biblical Repertory and Princeton Review* 20 (1848): 227–78. For this complete review and Nevin's detailed reply see *Coena Mystica: Debating Reformed Eucahristic Theology*, ed. Linden J. DeBie, MTSS, vol. 2.] and two articles of Dr. Proudfit in the *Princeton Review* [John Williams Proudfit, "The Apostles' Creed," *Biblical Repertory and Princeton Review* 24 (1852): 602–77; Proudfit, "The Heidelberg Catechism and Dr. Nevin," *Biblical Repertory and Princeton Review* 24 (1852): 91–134] and even the latter ones are by no means free from misrepresentation, and escape the real points at issue. We hope for the honor of Puritanism, Presbyterianism and Anglicanism, that they will be able and willing to defend themselves is a truly scholarly and gentlemanly way against the powerful attacks made upon them from that quarter, which, however, in our estimation, could only be done by assuming a much more historical and at the same time far less bigoted and exclusive position than they have occupied heretofore. Unhistorical and unchurchly Protestantism, we apprehend, cannot stand ultimately against the powerful strides of Romanism, which has now fairly entered into the very heart of Anglo-American Protestantism, with renewed energy and the boldest hopes of final success.

31. [On Nevin's consideration of entering the Roman Catholic Church see Wentz, *John Williamson Nevin*, 26–30, Hart, *John Williamson Nevin*, 153–68, Nichols, *Romanticism in American Theology*, 192–217.]

[Necessary Proofs for the Authenticity of Protestantism in the Developmental Theory]

For the purpose, however, of justifying Protestantism satisfactorily, on the ground of the development theory, two important points must be settled. First, it must be proved that it was not a *radical* rupture with the religious life of the early, i.e., the Catholic Church, but that it has, *in common with her a primitive Christian and a primitive Church basis*, which we, in our opposition, should never lose sight of. For, in the course of her development, the Church must yet continually remain identical in her nature, and dare not advance beyond herself, without falling into heresy, and thus make the promise of Christ to her of none effect. Thus man from childhood to old age still remains man, and each successive step is but a higher evolution of the idea contained already in the infant. Hence it is of immense importance that the Reformers without exception retained the Catholic Canon of Scripture, the ancient ecumenical symbols, and especially the Apostles' Creed, and incorporated them in their own confessions, and that they stood in direct opposition to the ultra Protestant sects of their times. Certain portions of modern Protestantism manifest, indeed, a fearful tendency in their bitter hostility against Rome, to separate themselves from this fundamental basis, and in like proportion sink into the character of heresies and sects. But the main branches of Protestantism will, by no means, surrender this Apostolic symbol, which connects them with the Ancient Church, and never cease to claim an interest in the Christianity before the Reformation, especially in the Patristic literature. Indeed there are evidently manifold strivings to recover numerous treasures, which have been cast overboard, and particularly to reconstruct, enlarge and conform their worship to the Church principle.

Then again it must be proved that Protestantism has its foundation substantially in *Apostolical* Christianity. For the New Testament, the Word of Christ and his inspired organs, is, after all, the final resort in all religious questions, and whatever has no connecting point with it cannot be sustained in the end. The germs of all legitimate stages of progress must already appear in the Apostolic Church, whilst a development beyond Christ himself and his Apostles, in the sense of Rationalists and Free-thinkers of all classes, must naturally assume the character of a degeneration, and a relapse into Heathenism or Judaism. With *such* development we, of course, have not the least sympathy whatever, but abhor it as essentially antichristian. But the Reformers, we all know, without exception placed themselves on the Bible as the only infallible rule of Christian faith and practice. Now it would indeed be an inextricable historical riddle, if the close association which Protestantism has from the start formed with the Bible, and if the seal with which it continually devotes itself to its translation, interpretation and promulgation throughout the world, should rest finally upon a mere delusion. It is, indeed, manifestly impossible for the Bible to contain *all* that the various denominations and sects imagine to find in it—but which, in truth, they force into it, by means of their private interpretation—or it would contradict itself, and cease to be the truth any longer. It cannot possibly contain at once the contrary doctrines of Episcopalianism, Lutheranism, Calvinism, Zuinglianism, Presbyterianism, Congregationalism, Methodism, the Baptists and Quakers (if by special indulgence, we should still number the last two with orthodox Protestantism); it cannot, at the same time teach and condemn the doctrine of Predestination, or both affirm and deny the real presence of Christ in the Eucharist; it cannot at one time declare Baptismal Regeneration, and yet degrade the Sacrament to the level of an empty sign; it cannot enjoin the baptism of Infants, and yet reject it as unchristian; it cannot establish three orders in the Ministry, and then again, but one, or teach no peculiar spiritual office at all, but only a universal Priesthood, and favor whatever other points of difference there may be in Doctrine, Constitution and Cultus, partly essential, partly non-essential, concerning which Protestants have quarreled already for three hundred years, with equally zealous appeal to the Bible, without advancing a single step towards each other. Still justice requires us to allow that they agree, we will not say in all—as this would evidently be saying too much—but in most of the fundamental articles of the Gospel; for if it were otherwise, we would, according to the incontrovertible maxim, "out of the Church, no salvation," be compelled to deny the possibility of salvation in one or the other of these communions, to which extent, even the extreme Puseyites, and Old-Lutherans will not venture.

Some such relation then must evidently exist between the Bible and orthodox Protestantism in order to explain intelligently their close connection for three hundred years. In this dilemma, German Theology again comes to our relief and transfers us, to what appears to us, the only correct point of view.

[Conclusion: The Three Apostolic Stages in the Development of the Church]

Modern exegetical investigations, in which sphere, as is well known, it has displayed an extraordinary activity, place it beyond all doubt for us at least, that we must distinguish three stages of development and types of doctrine in the apostolic Church, which of course, in no way, contradict or exclude each other, as the school of Dr. Baur in Tubingen, after the precedence of the ancient Gnostics, maintains, but mutually complete each other, to wit:—*Jewish Christianity*, represented by the Apostles, Peter and James, *Gentile Christianity*, represented by the Gentile Apostle Paul and his colaborers, and *the higher union of both* by John, the beloved disciple, who, surviving all his colleagues, exhibits the third and last period and completion of the Apostolic Church, and looks forward, at the same time, as the Prophet of the new covenant, through the most distant future, to the new heavens and the new earth, wherein dwelleth righteousness and peace for evermore.[32] If this view be correct—and we find

32. [Schaff presumes the traditional teaching that John son of Zebedee was the author of the three letters of John, the Revelation to John, and was the beloved disciple who authored of the Gospel of John.]

it more and more confirmed the longer we study the New Testament in its proper connection—we have a polar star to guide us through the entire labyrinth of Church History, in her manifold phases and stages of development. According to this view then, the history of the Catholic Church, which stays herself on Peter as her rock,[33] and derives her doctrine on justification, faith and good works chiefly from the first two Gospels and from the Epistle of James, corresponds to Apostolic Jewish Christianity, and with it lays stress principally on authority, law and the closest possible connection with the theocracy of the Old Testament. Protestantism, which originally proceeded from a renewed study of the Epistles of Paul, is a onesided enforcing of the paulino-Gentile Christianity with its spirit of evangelical freedom and independence, over against the Jewish Christian excesses. In its relation to Catholicism it has thus far imitated St. Paul far more in his temporary inimical collision with Peter at Antioch (Gal. 2:11, 19), than in his subsequent friendly co-operation with him, and has frequently given occasion to his antagonist to repeat the warning of Peter against the abuse of the writings of Paul "in which there are some things hard to be understood" (2 Peter 3:16). Then again Protestantism has unfolded thus far almost exclusively the anthropological and soteriological doctrines of Paul, his Epistles to the Galatians and Romans whilst the later Epistles of the same Apostle, especially his profound doctrine of the Church, as the one, undivided body of Christ, the fulness of him that filleth all in all, have evidently not yet received their full share of attention.[34] As soon as this shall be done, there will be at the same time a certain approximation to the Catholic, church-principle, and the way become prepared for the third and last Period of the Christian Church, in which the great truths of Catholicism and evangelical Protestantism, with the exclusion of their mutual errors, may become united in a higher union and harmony, through the renewal and complete appropriation of the spirit of John, especially of his doctrine of the person of Christ, and the living communion of the faithful with Him and with each other. But this union must be preceded by a universal repentance, and we may here appropriate to ourselves the significant words of the great and generous Catholic Divine, Möhler (*Symbolik*, Page 353, sq. 6 Ed.) who, after frankly acknowledging the unwarrantable lack of principle in so many priests, bishops and Popes, "whom hell has swallowed up," as the cause of corruption in his Church and of the Reformation in the sixteenth century, adds—

33. We may admit with Count Zinzendorf, and Dr. Stahl, in his late address to the German Church Diet in Bremen, that "the Pope is not the Antichrist, but the legitimate chief of the Roman Church," as Peter was the head of Jewish Christianity, without surrendering thereby the true interests of Protestantism. For the Roman Church is not the Catholic Church, but only it part of it. The Greek Church in her best days never disputed the authority and even primacy of the Bishop of Rome for the Latin Church, but refused to submit to it in the absolute and universal sense. [Friedrich Julius Stahl (1802–61), was a professor at Berlin, and held senior positions in the state government of the Prussian church.]

34. [Schaff is particularly referring to Colossians and Ephesians.]

> This is the point (the consciousness of guilt) at which Catholics and Protestants will in great multitudes one day meet and give each other the hand of friendship. Both conscious of guilt, must exclaim, We *all* have erred—it is the Church only—as an institution of Christ—which cannot err; we *all* have sinned—the Church alone is spotless on earth. This open confession of mutual guilt will be followed by the festival of reconciliation.[35]

[Epilogue]

Herewith we bring the series of essays on German Theology to a close. We have rendered it high praise, and joined bright hopes with it. But we would not be so misunderstood, as though we were blind to its manifold wants and imperfections; we have rather distinctly stated the contrary, and intimated that its principle practical task has by no means yet been accomplished. We know also full well that salvation comes not from theology, science or learning, under any form, as many German closet-scholars imagine, but from *life*, from those *divine-human powers*, those aged, yet ever youthful *supernatural facts*, which alone have founded and which alone can renew and complete the Church. But if the evangelical theology of Germany, in connection with the other instruments of the age, should, in the hands of a merciful God, serve the purpose of preparing the way, from the Protestant side, through the inward, quiet, yet deeply working "power of thought," for such a reconciliation between Catholicism and Protestantism, and aid in bringing to an end the great schism of the sixteenth century by a greater and more difficult act of reunion: it would truly deserve the praise and gratitude of all true friends of the kingdom of God, which is a kingdom of love, harmony and peace. For what can be more grand and glorious than to heal the bleeding wounds of the body of Christ, and to labor for the realization of the last prayer of our Eternal High Priest: "Neither pray I for these alone, but for them also which shall believe on me through their word; that they all may be one; as thou, Father, art in me, and I in thee, that they also may be one in us: that the world may believe that thou hast sent me !"[36]

Mercersburg
December 6th, 1852.[37]

35. [This is Schaff's own translation of Johann Adam Möhler, *Symbolik, oder Darstellung der dogmatischen Gegensätze der Katholiken Und Protestanten nach ihren öffentlichen Bekenntnisschriften* (On the creeds, or exposition of the doctrinal differences between Catholics and Protestants as evidenced by their creeds and confessions), 6th ed. (Mainz: F. Kupferberg, 1843), 353. The passage appears in a very similar translation without the interjection "as an institution of Christ" or the italics in Möhler, *Symbolism*, 276.]

36. [John 17:20–21.]

37. [This appears to be the date the English translation of this article was completed.]

Glossary of Names

Achilli, Giacinto (c. 1803–c. 1860), Italian Dominican discharged from the Roman Catholic priesthood for sexual misconduct. He became an advocate of evangelical Protestantism and was supported by the Evangelical Alliance in England. Strong allegations of sexual misconduct continued throughout his career. After John Henry Newman gave voice to these in an 1850 speech, Achilli had Newman tried for libel. Newman was convicted but sentenced only with a modest fine. Achilli's reputation suffered, all but ending his public ministry.

Ammon, Christoph Friedrich von (1766–1850), rationalist, professor, preacher, and principal of the theological school at Erlangen. His most important theological work was *Die Fortbildung des Christenthums zur Weltreligion* (The development of Christianity into a world religion), 4 vols. (1833–40).

Anselm of Canterbury (1033–1109), pioneering scholastic theologian. He became a monk in 1060 at the abbey in Bec, in Normandy, where he served as prior beginning in 1063. His duties took him to England often but his appointment as archbishop of Canterbury did not materialize until 1093. He is best known for his reflections on theological metaphysics, the *Monologion* and *Proslogion*, and his theory of the atonement in *Cur Deus homo?* In the latter, Anselm argued that God's honor suffered injury on account of human sin and therefore required "satisfaction" for the sake of justice—either by punishing human beings or through the death of the God-man whose sacrifice compensates for the injury to God's honor.

Aquinas, Thomas (c.1225–74), Dominican scholar, theologian, and prolific writer. His *Summa theologica* and other writings were decreed by Pope Leo XIII (1879) to be the basis of all Church teaching.

Arminius (c. 18/17 BCE–21 CE), leader of the Germanic Cherusci tribe that defeated the legion in the Battle of the Teutoburg Forest (9 CE). Arminius's victory had a far-reaching effect on the subsequent history of both the ancient Germanic peoples and on the Roman Empire. The Romans made no further attempts to conquer and permanently hold German lands to the east of the Rhine River.

Arndt, Johann (1555–1621), German mystic who advocated moral purification as a means of bringing the soul into communion with God. He is revered as the precursor of Pietism.

Athanasius (293–373), bishop of Alexandria, theologian, and church father. He defended the doctrine of the Trinity against Arianism.

Augustine of Hippo (354–430), bishop of Hippo, and one of the most prolific writers among the church fathers. Among his key writings are *The City of God* and *The Confessions*. His wide-ranging doctrinal concerns included "just war" theory, the Trinity, the concept of "original sin," and the nature of the church as "catholic."

Bahrdt, Karl Friedrich (1741–92), German theologian, writer, and innkeeper. He produced a rationalist version of the New Testament in modern German, which led to his expulsion from an academic post in Giessen in 1775 and to a devastating critique by Goethe. In 1779 he settled at Halle where through the offices of a liberal Prussian minister, he was permitted to lecture on subjects other than theology. In 1789, however, after he parodied an edict of the Prussian minister of religion, he was sentenced to a year in prison. Considered one of the most disreputable characters in German scholarship, he died shortly after his release.

Balmes, Jaime (1810–48), Spanish Roman Catholic priest known for his writings defending Catholicism, particularly his *Protestantism and Catholicity Compared in their Effects on the Civilization of Europe*, originally published in Spanish in 1842–44.

Baronio, more commonly Caesar Baronius (1538–1607), Italian cardinal. He was the leading Roman Catholic church historian of the sixteenth century.

Basnage, Jacques (1653–1723), cousin of Samuel Basnage, French Reformed pastor in France and the Netherlands. He authored many polemical-historical works.

Basnage, Samuel (1638–1721), cousin of Jacques Basnage, a French Protestant who settled in the Netherlands, author of *Annales politico-ecclesiastici* (Political-ecclesiastical Annals).

Bauer, Bruno (1809–82), biblical critic and writer, who lost his academic post at Bonn in 1842 after the publication of a series of books questioning the origin and veracity of biblical texts. He argued that Christianity was essentially Greek Stoicism that had undergone a Jewish metamorphosis.

Baumgarten, Siegmund Jacob (1706–57), theologian and church historian at Halle. Among his works was *Geschichte der Religionsparteien* (History of religious parties) (Halle, 1760). He represents a transition from the Pietism of Spener and Francke to modern rationalism. His disciple, Johann Semler continued this transition.

Baur, Ferdinand Christian (1792–1860), German Protestant theologian, biblical scholar, and historian of Christianity. He was influenced by Hegel's understanding of historical development and saw emergent Christianity as shaped by the dialectic between Jewish and Gentile Christianity. He founded the Tübingen school of Biblical criticism and argued that Galatians, I & II Corinthians, and Romans were the only genuinely Pauline epistles. Among his works are *The Church History of the First Three Centuries.*

Bellarmine, Robert (Roberto Francesco Romolo Bellarmino) (1542–1621), Italian Jesuit theologian known for his defense of Roman Catholic doctrine against Protestants. Becoming a professor at Louvain in 1570, he came into contact with Protestant thought and gained a reputation for learning and eloquence. In 1576 he moved to Rome where he joined the faculty of the newly formed *Collegium Romanum.* His major work, which presented careful, reasoned arguments for Roman Catholic teaching, was *Disputationes de controversis Christianae fidei adversus hujus temporis haereticus* (Lectures concerning the controversies of the Christian faith against the heretics of this time, 1586–83). He was named a cardinal in 1599.

Bengel, Johann Albrecht (1687–1752), German Lutheran professor at the cloister school at Denkendorf and biblical scholar. His *Apparatus criticus* (1734) is regarded as the starting point for modern text criticism. Concerning textual variants in New Testament manuscripts, he originated the principle "the more difficult reading is to be preferred" as the one more likely to be original. On a more popular level, his brief commentary on the complete New Testament, *Gnomon of the New Testament*, exercised great influence. His Pietism, based in the dogmatic understanding of salvation typical of Württemberg, was opposed to the more flexible, ecumenical, and tolerant piety advanced by the Moravians and Zinzendorf.

Bernard of Clairvaux (1090–1153), prominent preacher, writer, abbot, and monastic reformer. He emphasized the importance of the *lectio divina*, or divine reading as a religious practice. His conception of justification influenced both Luther and Calvin.

Beveridge, William (1637–1708), Anglican bishop of Asaph and noted scholar of Greek canons.

Beza, Theodore (1519–1605), French Protestant scholar and theologian, follower of John Calvin and his immediate successor at Geneva. He exerted great influence on the development of Reformed theology, particularly on the doctrines of ecclesiology and predestination.

Bingham, Joseph (1688–1723), Anglican author of *Origines Ecclesiasticae; or the Antiquities of the Christian Church,* a systematically arranged compendium of the rites, hierarchy, organization, discipline, and calendar of the early church.

Bleek, Friedrich (1793–1859), Protestant theologian and exegete who was professor at Bonn from 1829. He was known for his clarity and thoroughness. A critic of Baur and the Tübingen school, he defended the integrity and authenticity of the Gospel of John. He was also a frequent contributor to *Studien und Kritiken*.

Blondel, David (1590–1655), one of the leading defenders of Protestantism against Catholicism among French Reformed clergy. He is particularly noted for his work on pseudepigrapha.

Boehm, Jacob, (Jacob Böhm, Jakob Boehme) (1575–1624), shoemaker and famous German Lutheran mystic whose writings influenced a variety of pacifist and mystical societies including the Society of Friends and the Ephrata Cloisters. He was opposed in his own day, but highly esteemed by Hegel and other German Romantics.

Borromeo, Charles (1538–84), archbishop of Milan, one of the leading reformers of sixteenth-century Catholicism particularly in the areas of education and pastoral administration.

Boos, Martin (1762–1825), Roman Catholic priest and ascetic who, in response to his own ascetic practices, came to develop a doctrine of salvation by faith that resembled the Lutheran view. Despite the popularity of his preaching, he was driven from Bohemia and Austria by church authorities.

Bossuet, Jacques-Bénigne (1627–1704), French Catholic preacher, bishop, and theologian. He was a major leader of Catholicism in France and widely acclaimed as a preacher. His *Discourse on Universal History*, first published in 1681 emphasized God's overruling of history. He supported the revocation of the Edict of Nantes, which had granted to substantial rites to French Protestants.

Bretschneider, Karl Gottlieb (1776–1848), German theologian, writer, and controversialist. In his *Handbuch der Dogmatik der evangelisch-lutherischen Kirche* (Dogmatics handbook of the Evangelical Lutheran Church, 1814), he originated the notion of the two principles of Protestantism.

Brownson, Orestes (1803–76), American journalist and essayist. At one time a Universalist and then a Unitarian minister, he was a leading New England Transcendentalist who converted to Roman Catholicism in October 1844. The same year he founded *Brownson's Quarterly Review*, which he published until 1865, and again from 1872 until his death. He and the Mercersburg theologians, especially John Williamson Nevin, engaged one another several times in print. Carey, *Orestes A. Brownson*.

Bull, George (1652–1710), Anglican high-church theologian and bishop of St. David's. He is best known for his *Defensio Fides Nicaenae* (1685) which, largely against Petavius, maintained that that the teaching of the pre-Nicene fathers agreed with the orthodoxy of the fourth century.

Burnet, Gilbert (1643–1715), Anglican bishop of Salisbury, born in Scotland and a latitudinarian in theology. He unsuccessfully sought to incorporate Nonconformists in to the Church of England. His historical works include *History of the Reformation of the Church of England*.

Bush, George (1796–1859), professor of Hebrew and Oriental Literature at New York University. He studied at Dartmouth College and at Princeton Seminary, serving as a tutor at the latter in John Nevin's first year, 1823–24. Ordained into the Presbyterian ministry, he served as a missionary in Indiana before joining the faculty of New York University in 1831. In his book *Anastasis: or the Doctrine of the Resurrection of the Body, Rationally and Scripturally Considered* (1845), he advanced an argument against bodily resurrection and for the "progressive development of Scriptural truth." In 1845 he affiliated with the Church of the New Jerusalem, the denomination based on the teachings of the scientist and mystic, Emanuel Swedenborg.

Butler, William Archer (1814?–48), Anglican professor of moral philosophy at Dublin and author of nine "Letters on Development," a response to John Henry Newman initially published in the *Irish Ecclesiastical Journal* from December 1845 to November 1846.

Calovius, Abraham (1616–86), Lutheran dogmatician at Wittenberg who opposed Calvinism and the "syncretism" of his opponent Georg Calixtus. He is best known for his massive twelve-volume dogmatics, *Systema locorum theologicorum* (1655–77), which represented a high point of Lutheran scholasticism.

Calixtus, Georg (1586–1656), Protestant professor of theology at Helmstedt from 1614. He had high regard for Philip Melanchthon. He endeavored to build a theological system that would reconcile Lutherans, Reformed, and Roman Catholics. The term "syncretism" first came into prominence to condemn his position.

Calvin, John (1509–64), French theologian and a principal figure in the development of the system of Christian theology later called Reformed or Calvinism. Originally trained as a lawyer, he broke from the Roman Catholic Church around 1530 and, from 1541 onward, was preacher, theologian, and reformer in Geneva. His system of theology is recorded in *The Institutes of the Christian Religion*, the fifth and final edition of which appeared in Latin in 1559.

Carlstadt, Andreas Rudolf Bodenstein von (c. 1480–1541), early supporter of Martin Luther who departed from him for more radical reforms including iconoclasm.

Camerarius, Joachim (1500–74), humanist scholar and Lutheran theologian. A friend and student of Philip Melanchthon, he was assigned to reorganize the University of Leipzig in 1541.

Caraffa, Giovani Pietro (1476–1559), Italian Catholic bishop, reformer, founder of Theatine order, and from 1555 Pope Paul IV. As bishop of Chieti (Theate) from 1504 to 1524 he was involved with the reform of his diocese and the church and participated in the Oratory of Divine Love in Rome. He resigned his see to found the Theatine Order with Thomas de Vio Cajetan. Building on the practices and spirituality of the Oratory of Divine Love, the order focused on reforming the church from abuses and deepening the spirituality of priests. As pope, he advanced two activities: the inquisition and the prosperity of the Jesuits.

Carlyle, Thomas (1795–1881), Scottish philosopher, essayist, and translator of Goethe's *Wilhelm Meister's Apprentice* (1824). Through his translations and writings he helped introduce German Romanticism to the English-speaking world. His *Sator Resartus* (1833–34) strongly reflects Romantic ideals.

Cave, William (1637–1713), Anglican patristic author. His major works include *Apostolici* (1677) on the chief Christian figures of the first three centuries and *Ecclesiastici* (1683) which focuses on the fourth century.

Charles I (1600–49), son of King James I and king of England and Scotland from 1625 to 1649. His marriage to Henrietta Maria of France, among other factors, put him at odds with Parliament. After his forces were defeated by the Parliamentary armies in the English Civil War, he was executed for high treason in 1649.

Cheever, George Barrell (1807–90), graduate of Andover Seminary who pastored Congregationalist and Presbyterian churches. Throughout his youth he was attracted to Unitarianism but by the early 1830s he became vigorous proponent of orthodoxy. From 1844 to 1846 he was principal editor of the *New York Evangelist*, a significant voice of New School Presbyterianism. In 1846 he founded the Church of the Puritans, a Congregational church, in New York City. A consistent opponent of slavery, in the late 1850s, he became an abolitionist. Between August and October 1845 he authored six editorials against *The Principle of Protestantism.*

Chemnitz, Martin (1522–86), referred to as "the second Martin" in Lutheran tradition; theologian, controversialist, and author of *Examination of the Council of Trent* (1565–73).

Coleridge, Samuel Taylor (1772–1834), English poet, philosopher and critic, he composed "The Rime of the Ancient Mariner" and "Kubla Khan" among other poems. He was a key figure in the English Romantic movement. During a trip to Germany with poet William Wordsworth, he undertook a study of Kant's philosophy and subsequently helped introduce German Idealist philosophy to the English-speaking world. Particularly important in this regard was his *Aids to Reflection* (1825).

Contarini, Gasparo (1483–1542), Italian diplomat and cardinal, who advocated dialogue with Protestants after the start of the Reformation. A member the Oratory of Divine Love, he was a major leader of the reform group within Rome. He chaired the commission that produced the 1537 report *Consilium de emendanda ecclesia* calling for the reform of church. Contarini was persuaded of the doctrine of justification by faith in 1511, but did not draw Luther's conclusions from it. In 1541 he served as papal legate at the Colloquy of Regensburg which sought reconciliation between Lutherans and Catholics. The colloquy agreed to Contarini's proposed article on justification, but it was rejected by both Luther and the pope. He defended it in his *Epistola de justificatione*. Gleason, *Gasparo Contarini*.

Corvinus, Johann Friedrich (active 1701), conservative Lutheran minister from Hornburg in Halberstadt who was one of Gottfried Arnold's chief opponents.

Cousin, Victor (1792–1867), leading French philosopher of the 1830s and 40s. He had traveled in Germany (1817–18) where he met and was influenced by Hegel and Schelling. Teaching at the École *Normale*, he espoused an eclectic philosophy.

Cramer, Johann Andreas (1723–88), German Protestant theologian and hymn writer. He held several ecclesiastical and academic positions including at ones in the university of Copenhagen and Kiel. While he may have exercised his greatest influence through his sermons, hymns, and catechism, his historical work included translations of the sermons and minor writings of John Chrysostom.

Creuzer, Georg Friedrich (1771–1858), German classical scholar, professor of philology and ancient history at University of Heidelberg. His first and most famous work was *Symbolism and Mythology of the Ancients, Especially the Greeks*, which argued that the mythology of Homer and Hesiod came from an eastern source.

Cyprian, Ernst Salomon (1673–1745), one of the few learned defenders of Lutheran orthodoxy in the mid-eighteenth century. He was an opponent of Gottfried Arnold. He also opposed Friedrich Wilhelm I's efforts to unify Lutherans and the Reformed.

d'Ailly, Pierre also rendered Peter d'Alliaco (1350 or 1352–1420), chancellor of the University of Paris, preacher, bishop of Cambrai, and later cardinal. He advocated a general council as the means to restore unity to the divided church during the great papal schism (1378–1429), and attended the councils of Pisa (1409) and Constance (1414–18).

Daillé, Jean (1564–1670), French Reformed minister, his writings against Roman Catholics included *A Treatise Concerning the Right use of the Fathers*.

Daub, Karl (1765–1836), German Protestant theologian who served as professor at Heidelberg from 1795. In his effort to reconcile philosophy and theology, his thought went through three distinct phases. The first was influenced by Kant, the second by Schelling, and the last by Hegel.

De Maistre, Joseph (1752–1821), one of the most important French Ultramontane theologians. His most famous work *Du pape* (On the pope) (1819) argued that the basis of society rested in authority, with spiritual authority vested in the pope and temporal authority in kings.

Dodwell, Henry (1641–1711), Anglican patristic scholar and editor of the works of John Pearson. He was among the foremost apologists of the nonjuroring bishops who refused to swear allegiance to William of Orange when he claimed the British throne in the place of the still-living James II in 1688.

Döllinger, Johann Joseph Ignaz von (1799–1890), Bavarian priest and historian. Schaff refers to him chiefly as the author of *A History of the Church*, published in German, 1833–38. Subsequent to his mention in these writings, he became a leader of the Old Catholic movement which broke with the Roman Catholic Church over papal authority.

Dorner, Isaak August (1809–84), one of the foremost German theologians of the nineteenth century. A leader among the mediating theologians, he appropriated elements of Hegel and Schleiermacher and emphasized the divine-human personality of Christ as the highest revelation of God, ideal of humanity, and savior from sin and death. His *Entwicklungsgeschichte der Lehre von der Person Christi* (History of the development of the teaching on the person of Christ, 1839) was written in direct opposition to David Friedrich Strauss's *Leben Jesu* and traces the Christ of the Gospels throughout church history, representing Christ as the greatest fact in Christian thought and experience.

Du Moulin, Pierre (1568–1658), French Reformed minister and theologian who wrote many books in disputes with Roman Catholics.

Du Plessis Mornay, Philippe (Philippe de Mornay, seigneur du Plessis-Marly) (1549–1623), one of the most outspoken publicists of the Protestant cause during the French Wars of Religion. He was possibly the author of the defense of popular resistance, *Vindiciae contra tyrannos, or, Concerning the Legitimate Power of a Prince over the People, and of the People over a Prince* (Latin original, 1579) now attributed to Hubert Languet. His major historical work was on the papacy and published in English as *The Mysterie of Inquitie* (1612).

Edelmann, Johann Christian (1698–1767), German rationalist who denied the validity of the Bible as a source of religious knowledge and sought to base religion on nature and human thought.

Engelhardt, Johann Georg Veit (1791–1855), German Protestant theologian and historian who was professor at Erlangen. He was noted for his work on patristics and on mystics. He authored studies of Plotinus, pseudo-Dionysius, and Richard of St. Victor, but did not complete a planned history of mystical theology.

Erasmus (Desiderius Erasmus Roterdamus) (1466–1536), Dutch humanist, satirist, and theologian. Among his many scholarly works, he prepared important Latin and Greek editions of the New Testament. These works figured significantly in Reformation-era debates about the content of Scripture.

Ernesti, Johann August (1707–81), professor of theology at Leipzig, who defended orthodox Protestant teaching while advancing the historical study of the New Testament. His *Principles of Biblical Interpretation*, first published in Latin in 1761, argued against mystical interpretation and unhistorical rationalists that the work of an interpreter was the establishment of the grammatical or literal sense.

Eschenmeyer, Adam Karl August von (1768–1852), German philosopher and physician, who in many respects closely echoed the philosophy of Schelling. He differed from him in affirming that in order to understand the absolute one must supplement philosophy by non-philosophy, a mystical illumination.

Ewald, Georg Heinrich August (1803–75), German philologist and biblical scholar. His most important work was on the Hebrew language and scriptures, particularly his *Grammar of the Hebrew Language of the Old Testament* (1836, first German edition 1827).

Fritzsche, Karl Friedrich August (1801–46), German New Testament exegete who was rationalistic in his theology. He was professor of theology at Rostock from 1826 and then at Giessen from 1841. He focused on the linguistic element of exegesis and was a leading textual critic. He made many contributions to later editions of Winer's *Treatise on the grammar of New Testament Greek.*

Eusebius (c.260–c.240), Roman historian, theologian, and bishop who wrote, among many books, *The Ecclesiastical History*, the oldest surviving history of the Christian church.

Faustking (Feustking), Johann Heinrich (1672–1713), German Lutheran theologian. Educated at Wittenberg, he held a number of ecclesiastical and academic appointments. He was an opponent of Pietism and published *Gynaeceum haeretico fanaticum* (1704) against Gottfried Arnold.

Fénelon, François de Salignac de La Mothe (1651–1751), French Roman Catholic archbishop, educator, and spiritual writer who defended the Quietist spiritual writer Madame Guyon. His spiritual writings had significant influence on Protestants.

Feuerbach, Ludwig Andreas (1804–72), German philosopher and anthropologist who advocated liberalism and atheism. He is best known for his *The Essence of Christianity* (German, 1841) and the idea that religion is an outward projection of an inner human nature.

Fichte, Johann Gottlieb (1762–1814), German philosopher and student of Immanuel Kant. His conception of religion originally centered on ethics, but changed after he moved to Berlin in 1799 to affirm that faith surpasses moral reason. In this fashion he helped facilitate the transition from Enlightenment rationalism to Hegel's idealism. While professor of philosophy at the University of Jena (1793–99), he published *Kritik der praktischen Vernunft* (Critique of practical reason) (1788), which sought to demonstrate that moral reason was the ground of all knowledge and of human nature. After moving to the University of Berlin he became friends with leaders of Romanticism including Schlegel and Schleiermacher. His *Die Anweisung zum seligen Leben, oder auch die Religionslehre* (The way towards the blessed life) (1806) discussed the relationship between finite self-consciousness and God, affirming that God is over and above the distinction between subject and object and human knowledge, but a reflection of his infinite existence.

Ficino, Marsiglio (Marsilio Ficino, Marsilius Ficinus) (1433–99), Italian scholar and Platonic philosopher. His Latin translations of Greek writers advanced Platonic studies in Italy and influenced the development of European philosophy.

Filippo of Neri (Philip Romolo Neri) (1515–95), Italian Roman Catholic mystic and leading reformer of sixteenth-century Catholicism. He founded the Congregation of the Oratory, which John Henry Newman would later join.

Flacius Illyricus, Matthias (1520–75), Lutheran theologian and historian, who opposed Melanchthon as one of the leaders of the so-called "Gnesio-Lutheran" party. An influential church historian, he published *Catalogus Testium Veritatis* (Catalog of the witnesses of the truth) in 1556, and in 1574 completed the *Ecclesiastical historia* (known since the eighteenth-century as the *Magdeburg Centuries*).

Flaminio, Marcantonio (1498–1550), Italian poet engaged in efforts to reform the Catholic church from within, principally with respect to the doctrine of justification by faith. His Neapolitan associates were pursued by the inquisition at the instigation of Pope Paul IV.

Florencourt, Franz Chassot von (1803–86), German writer and journalist who converted to Roman Catholicism in 1851.

Franke, August Hermann, also spelled Francke (1663–1727), German Pietist and educational leader who became professor of theology at Halle.

Fritzsche, Karl Friedrich August (1801–46), German New Testament exegete who was rationalistic in his theology. He was professor of theology at Rostock from 1826 and then at Giessen from 1841. He focused on the linguistic element of exegesis and was a leading textual critic. He made many contributions to later editions of Winer's *A Grammar of the Idiom of the New Testament*.

Fox, George (1624–91), founder of the Society of Friends (Quakers). Exercising a ministry in marketplaces and fields, he was often arrested for unauthorized worship and refusing to take an oath. He organized meetings in Barbados, the American colonies, and Holland, among other places. He taught a highly spiritualized form of Christianity in which the Inner Light was supreme and outward forms including water baptism and the Lord's supper were to be abandoned.

Gerhard, Johann (1582–1637), Lutheran scholastic theologian and theology professor at the University of Jena. His *Loci Theologica*, nine volumes (1610–25), stands in the Lutheran dogmatic tradition of Melanchthon.

Gerlach, Otto von (1801–49), German theologian, mission worker, and court preacher in Berlin.

Gerson, John von (Jean de) (1363–1429), chancellor of the University of Paris and prominent figure in the ecclesiastical disputes of his age. He authored many mystical and spiritual works, championed the supremacy of councils over the pope, and referred to the contemporary church as "not apostolic but apostate."

Giesler, Johann Karl Ludwig (1792–1854), noted church historian, educated at Halle. He was professor of theology at Bonn (1819) and Göttingen (1831), where he lectured in church history. His popular *Text-Book of Church History* began to be published in English in 1836.

Giberto, (Giovanni Matteo Giberti) (1495–1543), Roman Catholic reformer, member of the Oratory of Divine Love, and bishop of Verona from 1524. He sought to raise the educational and moral standards of the Catholic clergy and helped author *Concilium de emendanda ecclesia* (1537), a report on the reform of the Roman church commissioned by Pope Paul III.

Goch, John (Johann) von (c. 1410–c. 1475), founder of the priory of Thabor and its governor. Often referred to as a reformer before the Reformation, he opposed monasticism, minimized the traditions of the church, and acknowledged the authorities of the Bible and the church fathers.

Goerres (Görres), Johann Josef von (1776–1848), German Roman Catholic professor at Münich and proponent of moderate Catholicism.

Goeschel (Göschel), Karl Friedrich (1784–1861), German jurist and philosopher, whose primary intellectual endeavor was to reconcile Christianity and modern culture as represented by Hegel and Goethe. He was a leader of the right-wing Hegelian party.

Gossner, Johannes Evangelista (1773–1858), Roman Catholic parish priest in Munich who subsequently converted to Protestantism. He served as pastor in Berlin and established a missionary society that sent missionaries to East India.

Grabe, Johannes Ernst (1666–1711), Anglican priest of German birth and education, he immigrated to England because he questioned the apostolic validity of Lutheran orders. He published many works of patristic and biblical scholarship.

Grapheus, Cornelius (1482–1558), Flemish humanist and town clerk at Antwerp. As publisher of two works by Johann von Goch, Grapheus included prefaces critical of clerical practices. A forced recantation was extracted from him by the Inquisition.

Grimm, Jacob Ludwig Carl (1785–1863), German philologist and pioneer in the study of folklore. He worked closely with his brother Wilhelm. Among many other works, they are best known for *Grimm's Fairy Tales* (1812–22), a collection of traditional stories collected mainly from oral sources.

Grimm, Wilhelm Carl (1786–1859), German philologist and pioneer in the study of folklore. He was the brother of Jacob Grimm.

Groot, Gerhart (1340–84), Dutch religious reformer, preacher, educator. He founded the Roman Catholic pietist religious community called the Brethren of the

Common Life (*Fratres communis vitae*). The community was open to both laymen and clergy and required no vows. It founded many schools.

Grotius, Hugo (Huigh de Groot) (1583–1645), Dutch theologian and statesman. Noted for his irenic tendency in doctrinal matters. As a scholar, he was the first to apply the historical-philological method to the explanation of Scripture and determined, for example, that Solomon had not authored Ecclesiastes. He is also renowned for his work on jurisprudence, politics, and the theory of natural law.

Guericke, Heinrich Ernest Ferdinand (1803–78), professor at Halle. He authored a respected biography of August Franke (1833). His *Handbuch der allgemeinen Kirchengeschichte* was published in English as *A Manual of Church History* in 1857.

Hagen, Friedrich Heinrich von der (1780–1856), German philologist who reawakened interest in Old German poetry.

Haller, Albrecht von (1708–77), Swiss scientist and poet, who defended the reasonableness of Christianity.

Hamann, Johann Georg (1730–99), leading counter-Enlightenment German religious thinker and critic of rationalism. A friend but sharp critic of Immanuel Kant, he regarded himself as the rejuvenator of Lutheranism.

Hammond, Henry (1605–60), chaplain to British king Charles I who advanced a preterist interpretation of the Revelation to John. He argued that the events it prophesied were fulfilled mainly during the early church and that the millennium lasted from the conversion of Constantine to the rise of the Ottoman Turks. He thus refuted the historicist interpretation that animated many radical Protestants, including the opponents of his king. See Johnston, *Revelation Restored*, 61–62.

Harless, Gottlieb Christoph Adolf von (1806–79), New Testament exegete, theologian, and German Lutheran leader. After an early orientation toward the philosophy of Hegel and Schelling, he was converted to Lutheran orthodoxy and its doctrine of justification by Tholuck. He served at the University of Erlangen (1833–45) and Leipzig (1845–50). He first attracted scholarly attention with his commentary on Ephesians (1834). As president of the supreme consistory in Bavaria, he advanced the interests of the orthodox, or high Lutheran, school by opposing the organic union of Lutheran and Reformed communions. His chief work is *Christliche Etik* (1842; translated as *System of Christian Ethics*, 1868).

Hase, Karl August von (1800–90), Lutheran theologian and church historian at Jena from 1830. Influenced by Schelling and Hegel, he wrote widely on many subjects, and is most important to Schaff for his compilation of sixteenth-century Lutheran confessions, the *Libri Symbolici* (1827).

Hasse, Friedrich Rudolf (1808–62), German theologian, professor of church history at Bonn, and author of an important work on Anselm's life and theological system.

Haug, Lodewijk Frederik Christiaan (1773–1834), German-born historian and professor at military schools in the Netherlands. He authored a general world history published in 1820 that highlighted the role of Christianity.

Hegel, Georg Wilhelm Friedrich (1770–1831), German philosopher who served as professor at Berlin beginning in 1818. His philosophy is a dialectical system of logic proceeding from thesis to antithesis to synthesis or from positive through negative to the absolute. After his death, his adherents spilt into three distinct groups representing supernaturalism on the right wing, naturalism on the left, and a mediating tendency (to which Schaff shared an affinity) in the center.

Hengstenberg, Ernst Wilhelm (1802–69), German Lutheran biblical scholar and professor of Old Testament at Berlin. He exercised enormous influence as editor of the *Evangelische Kirchenzeitung*. Against rationalism, he favored the primacy of Scripture and the authority of the Protestant confessions. He was a leader among the orthodox Protestants at Berlin in opposition to Schleiermacher, among others. While he is best remembered as a champion of Lutheran orthodoxy, when Schaff knew him in Berlin (1842–44), Hengstenberg still supported the Prussian union of Reformed and Lutheran churches. Only after the economic and political crises of 1846 and 1848 did he and his circle turn against this union. For Hengstenberg's influence on Schaff see Penzel, *German Education*, 102–6, 116, 122–23.

Henke, Heinrich Philipp Konrad (1752–1809), professor of theology at Helmstadt. Unorthodox in this theology, he nevertheless had a great reverence for the person of Jesus. He regarded the church as having abandoned the original simplicity of Christ's teaching at a very early date, this shaped his general negative view of Christian history in his general history of the church which first began to appear in 1789.

Herder, Johann Gottfried (1744–1803), from 1776 the general superintendent and court preacher at Weimar. A significant figure in many aspects of German intellectual life, his most important contribution was to the philosophy of history. He discerned in the development of different nations an ascending process toward a fuller manifestation of humanity.

Hermes, Georg (1775–1831), German Catholic theologian, who taught that "a man can believe only that which he has recognized as true from evidence furnished by his reason," thereby calling into question hierarchical authority. He was professor of theology at Bonn starting in 1819.

Hilary of Poitiers (c. 320–67), after marriage and converting to Christianity, he was made bishop of Poitiers some time before 355. His commentary on Matthew's gospel is of particular interest because it is the first Latin commentary of a complete biblical text. In his *Expositions of the Psalms* (c. 360) he lists only the Hebrew Scriptures as comprising the Old Testament, but includes in this the Letter of Jeremiah and notes that some add Tobit and Judith.

Hirscher, John Baptist (1788–1865), Roman Catholic professor of moral and pastoral theology at the University of Freiburg 1834–63. His best known work *Die christliche Moral als Lehre von der Verwirklichung des göttlichen Reiches in der Menschheit* (Christian morality as the doctrine of the realization of the divine kingdom in humanity) went through five editions from 1835 to 1851.

Hitzig, Ferdinand (1807–75), German scholar of the Hebrew Bible. He was professor at Zürich from 1833 until 1861 when he became professor of theology at Heidelberg. He authored influential commentaries on prophets, psalms, and other portions of the canon.

Hodge, Charles (1797–1878), Presbyterian theologian at Princeton Theological Seminary. While pursuing a leave of absence from Princeton between 1826 and 1828, he studied in Europe and became familiar with the work of the mediating theologians at Halle (Müller and Tholuck) and Berlin (Neander and especially Hengstenberg). John Nevin substituted for Hodge during the latter's absence from the seminary, and was later to clash with him over the doctrine of the Eucharist and other issues.

Hoffmann, Wilhelm (1806–73), influential church official who was appointed court preacher at Berlin in 1853 by Friedrich Wilhelm IV (king of Prussia, 1840–61).

Hohenstaufen Dynasty, German family that ruled the Holy Roman Empire from 1138 to 1252. As emperors, Frederick I (1155–90) and Frederick II (1220–50) were particular active in struggles against the papacy. Frederick II was called by Nietzsche "the first European." He ruled a vast territory from his base in Sicily.

Hottinger, Johann Jakob (1652–1735), professor in Zürich and historian of Christianity in Switzerland. He was the son of the biblical scholar Johann Heinrich Hottinger. His *Life and Times of Ulric Zwingli* was translated into English.

Hugo (Hugh) of St. Victor (1097–1141), one of the most influential theologians of the 12th century. His theological system, as presented in the *Sacramenta* (On the mysteries of the Christian faith, c. 1140), was foundational for the development of Christian dogma while his mystical system provided the basis for the French mystical school including, among others, Bernard of Clairvaux.

Hurter, Friedrich Emanuel von (1787–1865), Swiss Protestant pastor who was converted to Roman Catholicism in 1844 through his historical studies, particularly his history of Pope Innocent III.

Huss (Hus), Jan (c. 1369–1415), Czech priest and reformer. Influenced by the writings of Wycliffe, Hus advocated clerical reform in the church. His ideas were well-received and spread throughout Bohemia. Eventually he was condemned as a heretic at the Council of Constance where he was burned at the stake and his ashes were tossed into the Rhine River.

Hutten, Ulrich von (1488–1523), German knight who tried to establish a standing army of knights and soldiers for the protection of the empire and to counterbalance papal force. His efforts to resist extradition to Rome caused him to seek refuge in various cities until he came at last to Zurich where he received protection and care from Zwingli.

Hutter, Leonhard (1563–1616), professor of theology at Wittenberg, orthodox Lutheran, and fierce advocate for the Formula of Concord. He opposed efforts to harmonize Lutheran and Reformed doctrine.

Ignatius of Antioch (c. 50–c. 98–115), bishop of Antioch and martyr. He wrote a series of letters that are key to an understanding of early church history as they describe the work of bishops, presbyters, and deacons and discuss the Eucharist and the "catholic" nature of the church.

Innocent III, Pope (Lotario dei Conti di Degni) (1160–1261), among the most powerful of popes, he exercised authority over secular princes, initiated crusades (including the 4th Crusade which captured Constantinople and led to the schism between Eastern and Western Christianity), and inaugurated reforms within the church, notably with the Fourth Lateran Council.

Jablonsky, Daniel Ernst (Jablonski) (1660–1741) Moravian bishop and historian. He consecrated Count Zinzendorf bishop and thus provided the continuity between the historic Moravian church and the Herrnhuter. He promoted the union of Protestants and, unsuccessfully, the introduction of the episcopate into the Prussian Lutheran church.

Jansen, Cornelius Otto (1585–1638), theologian and Roman Catholic bishop who championed the teachings of Augustine of Hippo on grace and the effects of original sin against the emphasis on free will and human ability by the counter-reformation church, particularly the Jesuit order. His followers, known as Jansenists, were the subject of considerable controversy in sixteenth and seventeenth-century France. Pope Innocent X condemned several teachings associated with Jansen in 1653.

Jerome (c. 347–420), Latin historian, and scholar best known for his translation of the Bible into Latin. The "Vulgate" served as the commonly used biblical text for centuries and was adopted as the official version of the Bible in the Roman Catholic Church in response to the Reformation.

Kant, Immanuel (1724–1804), German philosopher, professor at Königsberg, and arguably the central figure in modern philosophy. The fundamental idea underlying his system is "human autonomy," that is to say: human understanding is the source of the laws that structure experience and the moral laws.

Kempis, Thomas à (1380–1471), German priest, copyist, and author of *The Imitation of Christ*, one of the most popular Christian devotional books. He was educated at Deventer at the school of the Brethren of the Common Life before becoming an Augustinian Canon.

Kepler, Johannes (1571–1630), German mathematican, astronomer, and astrologer. He is best known for his laws of planetary motion. They provided a foundation for Isaac Newton's theory of universal gravitation. He had financial difficulties periodically throughout his life, especially just before his death. Schaff employs a common heroic image of him resolutely pursuing his research into scientific truth despite personal suffering.

Klee, Heinrich (1800–40), German orthodox Roman Catholic theologian and biblical scholar who opposed liberal and Rationalist trends in Catholic thought.

Knox, John (c.1513–72), Scottish Reformed church leader. He was the leading figure of the Scottish Reformation and author of many of the Church of Scotland's foundational documents.

Koellner (Köllner), Wilhelm Heinrich Dorotheus Eduard (1806–94), Lutheran theologian and church historian who studied at Göttingen before joining the faculty at Giessen. His research focused on creeds and confessions.

Lachmann, Karl (1793–1851), German philologist in Berlin. He was a leader in the study of Old and Middle High German, and a pioneer in text criticism.

Laud, William (1573–1645), Anglican churchman and scholar. As archbishop of Canterbury during the reign of Charles I he sought to restore some pre-Reformation liturgical practices and enforce liturgical conformity. Perceived by Puritans as a danger, he was indicted by Parliament and executed after a long and dubious trial.

Lange, Johann Peter (1802–84), German evangelical theologian and exegete. When David Strauss was prevented in becoming professor at Zürich, Lange took his place and authored a multi-volume refutation of Strauss's *Life of Jesus*. He later succeeded Dorner as professor of dogmatic theology at Bonn.

Leighton, Robert (1611–84), Anglican archbishop of Glasgow, who sought reconciliation between Presbyterians and Episcopalians in Scotland. He was also known for his devotional life and writings influenced by his readings of Thomas à Kempis and Bernard of Clairvaux.

Leo, Heinrich (1799–1878), conservative Prussian historian and leading opponent of Leopold von Ranke. His most ambitious work was his *Lehrbuch der Universalgeschichte* (Textbook of universal history).

Leo X (Giovanni de Medici) (1475–1521), served as pope from 1513. He was responsible for granting indulgences to those who contributed funds toward the reconstruction of Saint Peter's Basilica—a practice defended by Tetzel and condemned by Luther.

Lessing, Gotthold Ephraim (1729–81), son of a Lutheran pastor and one of the principal figures of the German Enlightenment.

Limborch, Philipp (Phillippus) van (1633–1712), Dutch Remonstrant theologian. He was professor of theology at the Remonstrant seminary in Amsterdam from 1667 and became the leading Remonstrant, or Arminian, theologian of the seventeenth century. His chief theological work was his 1686 systematic theology published in English as *A Compleat System, or Body of Divinity* (1702). His transcription of the records of the inquisition in Toulouse continues to be of importance to historians.

Lindanus, William Damasus (1528–88), Roman Catholic bishop and inquisitor of the Low Countries. With the help of Philip II, he founded the royal college at Louvain for the education of young clerics. In addition to numerous texts composed in Latin, he wrote works in Dutch for the instruction of his co-religionists in order to keep them from Protestantism.

Lippomano, Luigi (1500–59), Italian bishop present at the Council of Trent from 1551 to 1552 when various decrees on reform were published.

Lirinensis, Vincentius see Vincentius Lirinensis

Locke, John (1632–1704), philosopher and one of the most influential Enlightenment thinkers. He argued that knowledge is gained only through experiences determined by individual consciousness. In his famous "Letters Concerning Toleration" (1689–92), Locke presented the case for religious toleration.

Loescher (Löscher), Valentin Ernst (1673–1749), German Lutheran professor, pastor of the Kreuskirche in Dresden. He opposed Pietism and defended Lutheran orthodoxy.

Lücke, Gottfried Christian Friedrich (1791–1855), German Lutheran theologian and friend of Schleiermacher who supported the Prussian union. He is best known for his works on the Gospel of John and Revelation.

Ludvigh, Samuel (1801–69), freethinker, writer, and newspaper publisher. Son of a bookseller, he immigrated to the United States from the Austrian empire in 1837, becoming editor of the *Alte und neue Welt* (Old and New World), in Philadelphia. In 1843 he moved to New York City, founding *Die Fackel. Literaturblatt zur Förderung geistiger Freiheit* (The torch: literary journal for the promotion of intellectual freedom), which he published until his death. He traveled widely lecturing in German-American communities and publishing many books.

Luther, Martin (1483–1546), Augustinian monk whose debates in Wittenberg with papal representative John Tetzel over the selling of indulgences inaugurated the Protestant Reformation. He was excommunicated by Pope Leo X in 1521. In 1534 he published a complete translation of the Bible into German. He was the progenitor of the evangelical or Lutheran branch of Protestantism.

Macaulay, Thomas Babington (1800–59), English politician and historian best known for his *History of England*. He is regarded as one of the founders of the Whig interpretation of history. That is, a view of the past which sees it leading steadily toward greater liberty and enlightenment culminating in modern liberal democracies.

Mani (c.216–74), Persian prophet and founder of Manichaeism, a sharply dualistic religion influenced by Hinduism, Buddhism, and Zoroastrianism, and developed primarily in the context of gnostic Christianity. After finding favor in the court of Persian emperor Shapur I, Mani eventually died in prison shortly after the ascension of Bahram I, who favored Zoroastrianism.

Manning, Henry Edward (1808–92), Anglican clergyman who converted to Roman Catholicism in 1851. He became archbishop of Westminster in 1865, and a cardinal in 1875. Unlike his fellow convert John Henry Newman, he became a strong supporter of the doctrine of papal infallibility.

Marheinecke, Phillip Konrad (1780–1846), professor of theology at Berlin and an ardent Hegelian. He led the battle against Pietist theologians and those who followed Schleiermacher, identifying himself as a theologian of the "idea."

Martensen, Hans Lassen (1808–84), Danish theologian and bishop, influenced significantly by Hegel and Schleiermacher. He pointed to Scripture as the critical and organic norm for dogmatics. A mediating theologian, his views on the relationship between faith and reason were challenged by Søren Kierkegaard.

Maurice, John Frederick Denison (1805–72), Anglican pastor, theologian, and professor at Cambridge. His philosophically oriented *The Kingdom of Christ, or Hints to a Quaker concerning the Principle, Constitution, and Ordinances of the Catholic Church* (1838) ignited a controversy about his orthodoxy which endured until his dismissal from Cambridge in 1853. In addition to his voluminous writings, he was a social reformer and in this capacity he helped found Queens College in London for governesses as well as the Working Men's College and the Working Women's College.

Melanchthon, Philipp (1497–1560), worked closely with Luther at Wittenberg and with the publication of his *Loci communes* (1521) became the first systematic theologian of the Protestant Reformation. He represented the Protestant position at the Diet of Augsburg and was chiefly responsible for preparing the Augsburg Confession (1531).

Merle D'Aubigné, Jean Henri (1794–1872), Swiss Protestant, who served churches in Hamburg, Brussels, and Geneva. He studied in Berlin and was a friend of Neander. The first volume of his history of the Reformation appeared in 1835, the thirteenth and last in 1878. English translations of his histories were very popular.

Moehler (Möhler), Johann Adam (1796–1838), Roman Catholic historian and theologian who wrote in opposition to the use of Latin in the mass and the practice of withholding the cup from the laity. Professor of church history at Tübingen from 1837, he was one of the leading representatives of the Tübingen school of Roman Catholic theology. He emphasized the nature of the church as a living community, rather than as an institution. His comparative study of Catholic and Protestant confessions, *Symbolik* (English *Symbolism*), sought to clarify similarities and differences between the two communions, but precipitated considerable controversy with German Protestants.

Monk, Maria (1816–49), Canadian who claimed to have been sexually exploited as a Roman Catholic nun in Montreal. Her story was published serially in the *American Protestant Vindicator* in 1835 and in book form as the *Awful Disclosures of Maria Monk* (1836). It was sensationally popular and fueled anti-Catholicism. Despite the fact that the story was soon shown to be a fraud, the book remained popular and influential among anti-Catholics.

Morus, Samuel Friedrich Nathanael (1736–92), student and successor of Johann August Ernesti at Leipzig. He developed his mentor's focus on the grammatical historical study of the New Testament.

Moser, Friedrich Karl von (1723–98), German writer, lawyer, and diplomat. His varied accomplishments included the establishment of the first German ecumenical faculty at the University of Giessen and the publication of *Actenmäßige Geschichte der Waldenser* (1798) (A documentary history of the Waldensians).

Mosheim, Johann Lorenz von (1694–1755), historian and professor of theology at Helmstedt and then Göttingen. Because he introduced objectivity to the study of church history with his *Institutiones historiae ecclesiasticae* (1726), he was sometimes regarded as the first modern church historian. He lacked, however, the sense of piety and historical development that Schaff found vital.

Mueller (Müller), Johannes (John) von (1752–1809), Swiss historian whose *Geschichten der Schweizer* (Histories of the Swiss), 5 vols. (1780–1808), was much admired by the Romantics.

Mueller (Müller), Julius (1801–78), German Lutheran mediating theologian best known for his work on *The Christian Doctrine of Sin* (German, 1839–44, English translation 1852–53). Nevin's examination of this work, "*Cur Deus Homo?*" *Mercersburg Review*, vol. 3 (1851) is in *The Incarnate Word*, ed. Evans, MTSS, vol. 4, 113–35.

Muehl (Mühl), Edward (1800–54), with his brother-in-law Carl Procopius Strehly the publisher of the *Licht-Freund* in Hermann, Missouri. Mühl and Strehly were freethinkers who emphasized the supremacy of reason. Most controversially, the *Licht-Freund* advocated the abolition of slavery. The paper discontinued upon his death.

Münscher, Wilhelm (1766–1814), moderate rationalist theologian at the University of Marburg. His chief contributions were to the history of doctrine.

Münzer (Müntzer), Thomas (1490–1525), radical Protestant Reformer who participated in the Peasants' War (1524–25). He was executed at its end.

Neander, Johann August Wilhelm (1789–1850), named David Mendel until his conversion to Christianity in 1806, Neander served as professor of church history at Berlin beginning in 1813. He conceived of church history as a life force and not merely a dogma. This perception animated his major work, *Allgemeine Geschichte der chritlichen Religion und Kirche*, 6 vols. (1825–52) translated in various editions including *General History of the Christian Religion and Church*, 5 vols. (1872).

Newman, John Henry (1801–90), priest of the Church of England who led the Catholic revival within it, known as the Oxford Movement. Newman edited the *Tracts for the Times* and authored many of them including *Tract 90* which sought to show that the Articles of Religion, the key confessional document of the Church of England, could be subscribed to by people who affirmed the Catholic faith as taught by the ancient church fathers and the Council of Trent. Newman was received into the Roman Catholic Church on October 9, 1845, and subsequently became a Catholic priest and cardinal. The fact that his catholicity led him into the Catholic church supported the charge of Schaff's Protestant critics that evangelical catholicism was merely a halfway house on the path toward the abandonment of Protestantism and the acceptance of Roman Catholicism.

Nicolas of Clamenge, (Nicholas of Clémanges) (c. 1363–1437), French theological author and colleague of d'Ailly and Gerson. He wrote numerous treatises critiquing the errors and corruptions he saw in the church of his time. As secretary to Pope Benedict XIII, he worked to bring about the Council of Constance (1414–18).

Nicolai, Friedrich (1733–1811), German writer and bookseller. He was a significant leader of the Enlightenment in Germany and editor of the journal *Allgemeine deutsche Bibliotek* (German general library).

Niebuhr, Barthold Georg (1776–1831), Danish-born German historian. His *History of Rome*, 3 vols. (1811–32), was of great influence both in the study of its subject and in historical method. He was a pioneer in source criticism.

Nitzsch, Karl Immanuel (1787–1864), a prominent representative of the mediating theology and author of *System of Christian Doctrine* (1829, English translation, 1849).

Novalis, pseudonym of Georg Philipp Friedrich Freiherr von Hardenberg (1772–1801), poet, writer, and key figure in the Romantic movement. In his literary works he sought to connect science and poetry. His essay *Christendom or Europe* (1799) called for a universal Christian church to restore Europe whose medieval unity has been destroyed by the Reformation and Enlightenment.

Œcolampadius, Johannes (1482–1531), humanist scholar who became the Protestant reformer at Basel. He sided with Zwingli in his debates with Luther on the eucharist and introduced lay elders into the government of the church.

Oetinger, Friedrich Christoph (1702–82), German theologian and pastor, whose sermons and other writings exerted a significant influence in the circles of Pietism and among scholars such as Schelling and Rothe.

Origen (c.182–c.251), distinguished father of the early church. His theological writings included biblical exegesis, speculative theology, hermeneutics, and preaching.

Papias, bishop of Hierapolis, died as martyr circa 150. In *Against Heresies* (V, xxxiii, 4), Irenaeus quotes Papias's "Exposition of the Words of Jesus" and identifies Papias (incorrectly) as an associate of the disciple John.

Pascal, Blaise (1623–62), French Roman Catholic mathematician, religious philosopher, and mystic. He was known for his emphasis on spiritual experience and defense of the rigorous spiritual life of the Jansenists against the Jesuits.

Paul, Jean, pseudonym of Johann Paul Friedrich Richter (1763–1825), German novelist and humorist whose works were popular in the early nineteenth century and formed a bridge to early Romanticism.

Paulus, Heinrich Eberhard Gottlob (1761–1851), Protestant theologian and professor at Heidelberg. He proposed natural explanations for the biblical miracles stories. He also argued for the conversion of Jews and their assimilation into German culture.

Pearson, John (1613–86), Anglican bishop of Chester, most influential as a systematic theologian, among his historical works was a defense of the authenticity of the letters of Ignatius of Antioch against Jean Daillé.

Pelagius (c. 354–after 418), monk, probably of British origin, who entered into controversy with Augustine over the doctrine of grace and the freedom of the will. Pelagius insisted that such teachings undermined the moral law. He taught that the human nature was basically good and responsible for choosing the good. He was excommunicated in 417.

Petavius, Dionysius (Denis Pétau) (1583–1682), French Jesuit professor of theology at Paris. He opposed scholasticism and conceded the imperfection of the theology of some early church fathers in light of later standards. George Bull's *Defensio Fidei Nicaenae* was written primarily to refute these claims. Petavius's work influenced John Newman's idea of doctrinal development.

Petrarch (Francesco Petrarca) (1304–74), Florentine poet and scholar, called the "father of humanism," his rediscovery of Cicero's letters is often pointed to as the start of the 14th-century Renaissance.

Planck, Gottlieb Jakob (1751–1833), German Lutheran, church historian, and professor of church history at Göttingen. His most important work was the *Geschichte der Entstehung, der Veränderung, und der Bilding unseres protestantischen Lehrbegriffs von Anfang der Reformation bis zur Einführung der Koncordienformel* (History of the origin, change, and development of our Protestant doctrine from the Reformation to the Formula of Concord,

1781–1800). It was the earliest attempt at a non-partisan account of the Reformation and the rise of Lutheranism.

Plutarch, Lucius Mestrius (46–120), Greek historian, magistrate, essayist, priest at Delphi, and biographer, he is known for his works *Moralia* and *Parallel Lives*. The latter work consist of biographies of famous Greek and Roman historical figures arranged in pairs to emphasize similarities between the pairs and the virtues and vices of each character.

Pole, Reginald (1500–58), English cardinal and the last Roman Catholic archbishop of Canterbury. Pole withheld his support for Henry VIII's divorce from Catherine of Aragon leading to his departure from England in 1536. He returned as archbishop in 1554 after the ascension of Mary I to the throne.

Polycarp (c. 70–155), bishop of Smyrna and martyr. According to a letter written by Ignatius, Polycarp was an acquaintance of the disciple John and others who had been associated with Jesus. He is best known for the anonymous account of his death at the hands of Roman authorities, *The Martyrdom of Polycarp*.

Pusey, Edward Bouverie (1800–82), Regius Professor of Hebrew and canon of Christ Church at Oxford beginning in 1829, and leader in the Oxford Movement. In 1835, he joined forces with this Catholic revival within the Church of England with the publication of his treatise on baptism, "Scriptural Views on Holy Baptism" (*Tracts for the Times*, nos. 67–68, 1835). By 1838, some were referring to the movement as Puseyism. The popularity of this name increased in 1843, after he was suspended from preaching in the university for two years for preaching a sermon that advanced a doctrine of "real presence" akin to medieval Catholicism..

Quenstedt, Johannes Andreas (1617–88), professor of theology at Wittenberg, an orthodox Lutheran noted for his piety and irenic spirit.

Ranke, Leopold von (1795–1886), the leading German historian of the nineteenth century. Influenced by the philosophy of Friedrich Schelling, he sought to discern God's action in history. He was appointed associate professor at the University of Berlin in 1825 and professor in 1834. His seminars helped establish the modern discipline of history. Among his early works, well-known to Schaff, was his *The Ecclesiastical and Political History of the Popes of Rome during the 16th and 17th Centuries*, a masterpiece of narrative history that rose above confessional perspectives to present the papacy not only as an ecclesiastical institution, but as a worldly power.

Reuchlin, Johannes (1455–1522), German humanist, scholar of Greek and Hebrew. He studied the kabbalah and published several volumes on Hebrew grammar. He recommended his great nephew, Melanchthon, to be professor of Greek at Wittenberg.

Ritter, Joseph Ignatius (1787–1857), German Catholic priest and professor at Bonn who authored *Handbuch der Kirchengeschichte* (1826–33).

Robinson, Edward (1794–1863), American biblical scholar. He founded the journal *Biblical Repository* in 1831. His academic career included tenures at Andover Theological Seminary (1821–26, 1830–33) and Union Theological Seminary (1837–63). He met his wife during his first sojourn in Germany (1826–30) to which he made four additional extended visits later in life.

Roehr (Röhr), Johann Friedrich (1777–1848), German Lutheran rationalist and chief pastor at Weimar. He was a defender of popular rationalism, maintaining that the final end of religion was moral behavior and categorically denying the divinity of Christ.

Ronge, Johannes (1813–87), founder of the German Catholic movement. Ordained a Roman Catholic priest in 1841, his liberal views immediately brought him into conflict with the hierarchy. When the archbishop of Tier displayed the Holy Coat of Christ in 1844, Ronge attacked the pilgrimage as a money-raising fraud. Immediately he was widely hailed by English-speaking Protestants as the leader of a new German Reformation, even a new Luther. The following year he organized the German Catholic movement with a creed that denied the divinity of Christ. Also in 1845 a volume of his writings was published in English as *John Ronge, the Holy Coat of Treves, and the New German-Catholic Church.* Despite his liberal views, anti-Catholic Protestants still viewed him positively, rejoicing in his criticism of Catholicism, and hoping that his movement would become more orthodox. It did not and Schaff and Nevin frequently faulted their anti-Catholic critics for their positive view of the rationalist Ronge. After supporting the revolutionaries in 1848, Ronge lived in exile in England, where he and his wife founded kindergartens. In 1861 he returned to Germany and sought to revive his waning movement. In his later years he also spoke out against anti-semitism.

Rosenblut (Rosenplüt), Hans (c.1400–70), master gunner in the city of Nurenberg who was also reputed to have written a series of *Fastnachtspiele* (Carnival plays), satires concerning the misgovernment of the empire and the misdeeds of the princes.

Rothe, Richard (1799–1867), German theologian, professor, and church official. He was a leader of the conservative branch of the Hegelian school devoted to the Christian faith and in opposition to rationalism and agnosticism.

Rückert, Leopold Immanuel (1797–1871), German Lutheran who advanced a rationalistic theology and authored commentaries on Romans, Galatians, Ephesians, and Corinthians.

Sachs, Hans (1494–1576), German Lutheran poet and polemicist. He used his poetic skills to present Lutheran doctrine in verse and in contrast to Roman Catholic doctrine, notably in *Der gut und der bös Hirt* (The good and the bad shepherd, 1531).

Sadolet (Sadleto), Jacopo (1477–1547), Italian Roman Catholic bishop who sought reconciliation with Protestants through peaceful persuasion. He wrote a famous letter in 1539 to the citizens of Geneva asking them to return to the Catholic Church. John Calvin, from Strasbourg, responded to the letter. He was a member of the Oratory of Divine Love.

Sailer, Johann Michael von (1751–1832), Jesuit and Roman Catholic bishop of Regensburg known for his promotion of spirituality. His aim was the internal reform of Roman Catholicism and the restoration of confidence in the Church.

Sartorius, Ernst Wilhelm Christian (1797–1859), German Lutheran theologian who taught at Marburg and Dorpat. After the publication of *The Person and Work of Christ* (German, 1831; English translation, 1838), he became court chaplain at Königsberg and general superintendent of the province of Prussia. In these capacities he defended "true" Lutheranism and opposed rationalism.

Saumaise, Claude de (Claudius Salmasius) (1588–1653), author of many works of historical and classical scholarship, he also published a defense of the monarchy of the British king Charles I.

Savonarola, Girolamo (1452–98), Italian Dominican priest, reformer, and prophet. He announced that Florence would be the New Jerusalem and resisted papal efforts to include Florence in the Holy League against the French. He continued to defy the pope, was excommunicated, and under torture confessed to having concocted the visions and prophecies that had made him popular. He was hanged and his body burned in Florence's main square.

Schelling, Friedrich Wilhelm Joseph von (1773–1854), German idealist philosopher. He held academic appointments at Jena, Würzburg, Erlangen, Munich, and from 1841 at Berlin. Influenced by Fichte, Kant, and Spinoza, his *Vom Ich als Prinzip der Philosophie* (On the ego as principle of philosophy, 1795) acknowledged one reality, the infinite Absolute. His friendship with Hegel ended when Hegel sharply criticized Schelling's system in *The Phenomenology of Mind* (1807). His later philosophy was strongly influenced by Neo-platonist and theosophist speculation especially that of Jakob Boehme. In 1809, he began to seek to reconcile Christianity with his philosophy in *Philosophical Investigations into the Essence of Human Freedom,* an effort he continued in his later Berlin lectures. There he distinguished three periods of church history that became fundamental to Schaff's own perspective, the Petrine, or Catholic, the Pauline, or Protestant, and the Johannine or church of the future.

Schlegel, August Wilhelm von (1767–1845), German poet, translator, and key figure in the Romantic movement along with his younger brother Karl, Novalis, and Ludwig Tieck. His translation of Shakespeare's works had a profound effect on German literature and also influenced Felix Mendelssohn (to whom he was related through his brother's marriage) to compose his overture to *A Midsummer Night's Dream.* In his later years he undertook the study of

Sanskrit and published translations of the *Bhagavad Gita* (1823) and the *Ramayana* (1829).

Schlegel, Karl Wilhelm Friedrich von (1772–1829), German poet, philosopher, Indologist, and key pioneer of the Romantic movement along with his older brother August, Novalis, and Ludwig Tieck. The son of a Lutheran pastor, he was for a time an atheist but converted to Roman Catholicism in 1806. That same year he published Über *die Sprache und Weisheit der Indier* (On the language and wisdom of India).

Schleiermacher, Friedrich Daniel Ernst (1768–1834), Protestant theologian, pastor, professor and first dean of the theology faculty at Berlin beginning in 1810. He emphasized the role of feeling and the importance of ethics in religion. His early book, *On Religion: Speeches to Its Cultured Despisers* (1799), betrays the influence of the Romantic movement in its call for a more open culture based on fantasy and feeling. Schleiermacher viewed his *The Christian Faith (*1822) as an early testament to the recent union of Lutheran and Reformed churches in Germany. He defines piety as the feeling of absolute dependence upon God; the articles of Christian belief as propagated by the church, therefore, function as testimonies to personal faith, not tests of common conviction.

Schott, Heinrich August (1780–1835), German Lutheran preacher and professor at Wittenberg and Jena.

Schröckh, Johann Matthais (1733–1808), German Lutheran historian at Wittenberg. His most important work was the forty-five volume *Christliche Kirchengeschichte*.

Schubert, Gotthilf Heinrich von (1780–1860), German physician and naturalist who aimed to create a religiously-grounded interpretation of nature that found evidence for God in nature and in the human soul, utilizing the philosophy of Herder and Schelling.

Schwegler, Friedrich Carl Albert (1819–57), church historian of the Tübingen School. He held that early Christianity was pure Ebionism, a Jewish Christianity that saw Jesus as Messiah, but in no sense divine.

Seabury, Samuel (1801–72), American Episcopal priest, grandson of Bishop Samuel Seabury of Connecticut (1729–96), and champion of high church interests. As editor of *The Churchman* (1833–49) he was one of the period's leading journalistic voices. He also served as rector of Church of the Annunciation in New York City (1838–68) and in various positions at General Theological Seminary.

Semler, Johann Salomo (1725–91), German church historian, professor of theology at Halle, and critic of prevailing notions of "revelation" as applied to Scripture. He is sometimes referred to as "the father of German rationalism."

Servetus, Michael (1511–53), Spanish physician and anti-trinitarian opponent of Calvin who was ordered by the Geneva council to be burned at the stake.

Sickingen, Franz von (1481–1523), was a knight of the German Empire who pledged his service to Luther. Martin Bucer served as his chaplain in 1522, the same year he waged battle, ultimately unsuccessfully, against the archbishop of Treves (Tier).

Simon, Richard (1638–1712), French Roman Catholic biblical scholar. He was the first to write a history of the Bible as a work of literature. His critical histories of both the Old and New Testaments were attacked during his lifetime for favoring critical discussion about matters such as the nature of the Septuagint or the Vulgate over more traditional and dogmatic concerns.

Soto, Peter à (1500–63), Spanish Dominican and professor of theology in Oxford during the reign of Mary I. After his departure from England, he participated in the later sessions of the Council of Trent.

Spanheim, Friedrich (1632–1701), Calvinist theologian and church historian. He was professor at Leiden from 1670. His father Friedrich Spanheim (1600–49) was also professor of theology at Leiden from 1642.

Spener, Philip Jakob (1635–1705), German Protestant theologian, preacher, and founder of the Pietist movement. His theology emphasized personal devotion. The University of Halle was founded under his influence in 1649.

Staupitz, John von (d. 1524), Augustinian vicar-general, first dean of the theological faculty at Wittenberg. He encouraged Martin Luther to study for the theology doctorate and supported Luther's early activities but remained loyal to the Roman Catholic Church and, consequently, was critical of the Protestant movement.

Steffens, Henrik (1773–1845), Norwegian-born philosopher, scientist, and poet. In his childhood, his family moved to Copenhagen where he received part of his education. After studying with Schelling at the University of Jena, he spent most of his career in Germany. He was professor at Halle and Breslau before coming to Berlin in 1832. At Berlin he was a close associate of Schleiermacher and Schelling. His own writings combined scientific knowledge with the speculation of Schelling.

Steiger, Wilhelm (1809–36), a Swiss theologian who wrote against rationalism. He authored commentaries on I Peter (1832) and Colossians (1835).

Strehly, Carl Procopius, a native of Prague, with his brother-in-law Edward Muehl, he published the *Licht-Freund*, in Hermann, Missouri.

Stolberg, Friedrich Leopold (1750–1819), German count who converted to Roman Catholicism in 1800, He authored the fifteen-volume *Geschichte der Religion Jesu Christi*.

Strauss, David Friedrich (1808–74), German radical theologian and student of Ferdinand Christian Baur and Hegel. His *The Life of Jesus* (1835–36) applied various Hegelian concepts to a reading of the gospel narratives and rejected the historicity of all supernatural elements. The book led to his dismissal from his position at Tübingen. It is considered a turning point in modern theology as it inaugurates what subsequently was called, by Albert Schweitzer, "the quest for the historical Jesus."

Stowe, Calvin Ellis (1802–86), American Congregationalist biblical scholar. Educated at Bowdoin College and Andover Theological Seminary, he was professor of biblical literature at Lane Theological Seminary in Cincinnati, Ohio, from 1833 to 1850, where his wife, Harriet Beecher Stowe wrote her famous anti-slavery novel, *Uncle Tom's Cabin*. Later he taught at Bowdoin (1850–52) and Andover (1852–64). An 1837 tour of Europe to investigate elementary education brought him into contact with German theological education.

Stuart, Moses (1780–1852), American pastor and professor of sacred literature at Andover Theological Seminary. He was called "the father of American Biblical literature" for his early efforts to publish a Hebrew grammar and his introduction to American students of German biblical scholarship.

Suso, Henry (Heinrich Amandus) (1300–66), Dominican and German mystic whose "Book of Eternal Wisdom" was among the favorite books of meditation during the Middle Ages.

Tauler, Johann (1300–61), Dominican mystic from Strasbourg. His practical sermons, addressing moral and spiritual concerns, were published widely and praised by, among others, Luther.

Terence (Publius Terentius Afer) (c. 195/185–159 BCE), Roman playwright who was brought to Rome as a slave but was freed eventually. He wrote six plays at Rome then disappeared from the city. His plays survived along with his famous expression "*Homo sum, humani nihil a me alienum puto*": "I am a human being, I consider nothing that is human alien to me."

Tholuck, Friedrich August Gottreau (1799–1877), German mediating theologian and professor at Halle from 1826. He was known for his personal attention to students, and exercised a profound influence on Schaff during Schaff's six months at Halle in 1839. Charles Hodge also studied under Tholuck and translated an essay by him in 1828 for inclusion in the *Princeton Review*. A leader of the "neo-Pietist" school, he was primarily a biblical scholar and widely respected in America as an exegete.

Thomasius, Christian (1655–1728), Lutheran jurist and natural law theorist, who helped found the University of Halle and served as professor of jurisprudence. He counted himself an ally of the Pietists in his opposition to theological systems, emphasis on practical piety, and liberality on the creeds. He lacked the Pietists' emphasis on sin and grace.

Tetzel, Johann (c. 1450–1519), was made commissioner of indulgences for all of Germany in 1517 by Pope Leo X. He defended the doctrine of indulgences against Luther for which he was awarded the degree doctor of theology from the University of Frankfurt-on-the-Oder in 1518.

Tieck, Ludwig (1773–1853), German writer, translator, critic, and key figure, alongside Novalis and the two Schlegels, in founding the Romantic movement. A writer of novels, poetry, and criticism, he also edited August Schlegel's translation of Shakespeare.

Turretin, Jean Alphonse (1671–1737), son of François Turrentin, and professor of church history at Geneva. He departed from his father's strict Calvinism and sought the reunion of all Christians. He contributed to the abolition in 1725 of the Helvetic Confession in Geneva.

Twesten, August Detlev Christian (1789–1876), German mediating theologian. He succeeded his teacher, Schleiermacher, at Berlin where Twesten occupied a middle position between the Hegelianism of Marheineke and the confessional orthodoxy of Hengstenberg.

Tzschirner, Heinrich Gottlieb (1778–1828), German Lutheran professor at Leipzig who completed Schröckh's history of the Reformation and authored various works defending Protestantism against Roman Catholics, on liturgy, and on marriage.

Ullmann, Karl (or Carl) (1796–1865), German church historian and mediating theologian. To promote the mediating theology he founded the journal *Theologische Studien und Kritiken* in 1828, with the help of F. W. C. Umbreit. He also wrote *Reformers before the Reformation*, first published in German in 1841. Nevin considered him "one of the finest living writers of Germany." He was professor of church history, dogmatics, and symbolics, at Halle and Heidelberg. Between 1853 and 1861 he also officiated as prelate (spiritual leader) of the United Evangelical Protestant Church of Baden.

Umbreit, Friedrich Wilhelm Carl (1795–1860), professor of theology at Göttingen who with Carl Ullmann served as editor of *Theologische Studien und Kritiken*. His own scholarship was chiefly on the Old Testament.

Usher (Ussher), James (1581–1656), Anglican archbishop of Armagh, best known today for his calculation of the date of creation from biblical genealogies, he wrote many other histories from a Protestant perspective.

Veith, Johann Emanuel (1787–1876), Jewish convert to Roman Catholicism and a noted Redemptorist preacher in Bohemia.

Vejel (Veiel), Elias (1635–1706), German Lutheran theologian, a native of Ulm. He spent most of his career there as pastor and teacher. He declined an offer to succeed Calovius at Wittenberg in order to remain at Ulm. A friend of Spener, he was nonetheless a critic of Gottfried Arnold.

Venema, Hermannus (1697–1787), Dutch Reformed clergyman most significant for his work on the Hebrew scriptures.

Vincens of Paula (Vincent de Paul, 1581–1660), French Roman Catholic priest, known for his work with the poor and sick.

Vincentius Lirinensis (Vincent of Lérins), (d. c. 450), presbyter of Lérins. Under the pseudonym "Peregrinus" ("pilgrim"), he wrote the *Commonitorium* to establish the principles whereby orthodoxy might be distinguished from heresy with reference to both scripture and the tradition of the church. In the sentence for which he is best known, he declares truly Catholic only "that which is believed always, everywhere, and by all."

Voltaire, pseudonym of François-Marie Arouet (1694–1778), gifted French writer, a deist in religion. He was a critic of the Catholic church and a champion of religious freedom. In Schaff's time he was seen as partially responsible for the French Revolution and its atrocities.

Walch, Christian Wilhelm Franz (1726–84), son of Johann Georg Walch, professor at Jena and then Göttingen. He published many works on church history.

Walch, Johann Georg (1693–1775) Lutheran professor at Jena and historian of the Reformation. Well known as the editor of the works of Martin Luther. He published other collections of Reformation documents and histories of the Reformation, including *Historische und theologische Einleitung in die Religionsstreitigkeiten der evagnelishe-lutherischen Kirche* (Historical and theological introduction to the religious controversies of the Evangelical-Lutheran Church, 1733–36).

Wegscheider, Julius (1771–1849), German Protestant professor at Halle and a leading dogmatic theological rationalist. He was aligned with Wilhelm Gesenius in disputes against supernaturalism and maintained that supernatural revelation was impossible.

Weismann, Christian Eberhard (1677–1747), Lutheran professor at Tübingen, author of a history of emergent Christianity, *Introductio in memorabilia ecclesiastica historiae sacrae Novi Testamenti.*

Wesel, John von (de Wesalia), (c. 1400–82), professor of theology at Erfurt, preacher at the Worms and the cathedral at Mainz. Often referred to as a reformer before the Reformation, his attacks on the sacraments, teaching, and tendencies of the church and his later association with a member of the Hussites attracted the attention of the inquisitors. He recanted, his writings were burned, and he was sequestered in the Augustinian monastery in Mainz where he subsequently died.

Wessel, John (Wessel Harmensz Gansfort) (1419–89), Dutch theologian and member of the Brethren of the Common Life. Often referred to as a reformer before the Reformation, he was critical of the papacy, church traditions, and the role of human will as it related to the doctrine of justification. Though commonly known as John Wessel, the "John" appears to have come solely through confusion with John von Wesel.

Wickliffe (Wyclif, Wycliffe), John (c. 1320–84), English theologian and professor at Oxford who completed by 1382 a translation of the Bible from the Vulgate text into English. Wycliffe, often referred to as the first church reformer, was an ardent opponent of papal authority and even taught that the pope was the Antichrist. His followers, called Lollards, believed in a lay priesthood and sought the basis for their religious ideas in Scripture.

Wieland, Christoph Martin (1733–1813), German poet and man of letters, his work spanned the trends of his age from the rationalism to pre-Romanticism. Between 1762 and 1766 he published the first German translations of twenty-two of Shakespeare's plays. His allegorical verse epic *Oberon* (1780) foreshadowed many aspects of Romanticism.

Wilberforce, Henry William (1807–73), the youngest son of the British anti-slavery leader William Wilberforce and an Anglican clergyman. He entered the Roman Catholic Church in 1850.

Winer, Johann Georg Benedikt (1789–1858), German philologist and professor at Erlangen from 1823 and then Leipzig from 1832. His *Grammatik des Neutestamenlichen Sprachidioms* was first published in 1822. An English translation appeared as *A Greek Grammar of the New Testament* in 1825. Through subsequent editions and various English titles it remained the standard work for nearly three-quarters of a century.

Wiseman, Nicholas Patrick Stephen (1802–65), English Roman Catholic leader. He became the first archbishop of Westminster when the Roman Catholic episcopacy was restored to England for the first time since the Reformation in 1850.

Wolf, Friedrich August (1759–1824), German classical scholar considered the founder of modern philology.

Wolff, Christian (1679–1754), German enlightenment philosopher. He taught at Halle, repaired to Marburg after his teachings fell into disfavor with the king, then returned to Halle in triumph in 1740 at the instigation of the new king, Frederick the Great. Wolff argued that human reason alone was able to determine and respond to moral truth.

Xavier, Francis (1506–1552), Spanish Roman Catholic, one of the first seven members of the Society of Jesus. He was a pioneering missionary to India, the Malay Archipelago, and Japan.

Zeller, Eduard, (1814–1908), Tübingen historian and philosopher whose published works were largely on Greek philosophy.

Zinzendorf, Nikolaus Ludwig Graf von (1700–60), aristocrat, Pietist, and student of Francke. He helped found the Moravian Brethren by creating the colony of Herrnhut on his estate. Attacked at times by orthodox Lutherans and other Pietists, his "religion of the heart" had considerable influence on English evangelicals such as John Wesley and on nineteenth-century theology through Friedrich Schleiermacher.

Bibliography

Works Included in this Volume

Hodge, Charles. Review of *The Principle of Protestantism* by Philip Schaf. *Biblical Repertory and Princeton Review* 16 (October 1845): 625–36.

Schaff, Philip. "German Theology and the Church Question." *Mercersburg Quarterly Review* 5 (January 1853): 124–44

———. *The Principle of Protestantism as Related to the Present State of the Church.* Translated with an introduction by John W. Nevin. Chambersburg, PA: Publication Office of the German Reformed Church, 1845.

———. *What Is Church History?: A Vindication of the Idea of Historical Development.* Philadelphia: J. B. Lippincott, 1846.

Works Cited by the Editors

(Works which were also cited in the original can be found in the next section of the bibliography.)

Albanese, Catherine L. *A Republic of Mind and Spirit: A Cultural History of American Metaphysical Religion.* New Haven, CT: Yale University Press, 2007.

"Another Development." *German Reformed Messenger.* February 20, 1856, 4258.

Anselm of Canterbury. *The Major Works.* Edited by Brian Davies and G. R Evans. New York: Oxford University Press, 1998.

Appel, Theodore. "The Life of Dr. Philip Schaff." *The Reformed Church Review*, 4th ser., 3, no.1 (1899): 90–110.

Atwood, Craig D. *Community of the Cross: Moravian Piety in Colonial Bethlehem.* University Park: Pennsylvania State University Press, 2004.

———. *Theology of the Czech Brethren from Hus to Comenius.* University Park: Pennsylvania State University Press, 2009.

Aubert, Annette G. *The German Roots of Nineteenth-Century American Theology.* New York: Oxford University Press, 2013.

Augustine. *Homilies on the Gospel of John 1–40.* Edited by Allan D. Fitzgerald. Translated by Edmund Hill. Part 3, vol. 12 of *The Works of Saint Augustine: A Translation for the 21st Century.* Hyde Park, NY: New City, 1990–2014.

Bacon, Francis. *Two Bookes of the Proficience and Advancement of Learning, Divine and Human.* London, 1605.

Bains, David R., and Theodore Louis Trost. "Philip Schaff: The Flow of Church History and the Development of Protestantism." *Theology Today* 71 (January 2015): 416–28.

Balmes, Jaime Luciano. *Protestantism and Catholicity Compared in Their Effects on the Civilization of Europe*. Translated by C. J. Hanford and Robert Kershaw. Baltimore: J. Murphy, 1851.

Basnage, Samuel. *Annales politico-ecclesiastici*. 3 vols. Rotterdam, 1706.

Baumgarten, Siegmund Jacob. *Geschichte der Religionsparteien*. Halle, 1760.

Baur, Ferdinand Christian. *The Church History of the First Three Centuries*. Translated by Allan Menzies. 3rd ed. 2 vols. London: Williams and Norgate, 1878.

Bek, William Godfrey. *The German Settlement Society of Philadelphia: And its Colony, Hermann, Missouri*. Hermann, MO: Americana Germanica, 1907.

Bellarmine, Robert. *Disputationes de Controversis Christianae Fidei adversus hujus temporis Haereticus*. Ingolstadt, 1586–83.

———. *Opera Omnia*. 12 vols. Paris: Vines, 1874.

Bengel, Johann Albrecht. *Gnomon of the New Testament*. Edited by Andrew R. Fausset. Edinburgh: T. & T. Clark, 1858.

Berg, Joseph F. *The Old Paths; or, a Sketch of the Order and Discipline of the Reformed Church before the Reformation as Maintained by the Waldenses Prior to that Epoch, and by the Church of the Palatinate, in the Sixteenth Century*. Philadelphia: J. B. Lippincott, 1845.

———. "Opening Sermon." *Weekly Messenger* 9 (November 6, 1844): 1913.

Berlin, Isaiah. *Three Critics of the Enlightenment: Vico, Hamann, Herder*. Edited by Henry Hardy. Princeton, NJ: Princeton University Press, 2000.

Betz, John R. *After Enlightenment: The Post-Secular Vision of J. G. Hamann*. Malden, MA: Wiley-Blackwell, 2008.

Billington, Ray Allen. *The Protestant Crusade*. New York: Macmillan, 1938.

Black, Christopher F. *Italian Confraternities in the Sixteenth Century*. Cambridge: Cambridge University Press, 1989.

Bingham, Joseph. *Origines ecclesiasticae or, the antiquities of the Christian Church*. 10 vols. London, 1711–22.

Bomberger, J. A. H. "Dr. Nevin and his Antagonists." *Mercersburg Review* 5 (1853): 89–124.

———. "The Rule of Faith." *Mercersburg Review* 1 (1849): 44–68.

———. "The Rule of Faith—Concluded." *Mercersburg Review* 1 (1849): 347–69.

Bossuet, Jacques-Bénigne. *Discourse on Universal History*. Translated by Elborg Forster. Edited by Orest Ranum. Chicago: University of Chicago Press, 1976.

Bowden, Henry Warner, ed. *A Century of Church History: The Legacy of Philip Schaff*. Carbondale: Southern Illinois University Press, 1988.

Broadie, Alexander. *The Scottish Enlightenment*. Edinburgh: Birlinn, 2001.

Brown, Stewart J. and Michael Fry, ed. *Scotland in the Age of the Disruption*. Edinburgh: Edinburgh University Press, 1993.

Brownson, Orestes Augustus. Review of *The Principle of Protestantism* by Philip Schaf. *Brownson's Quarterly Review* 2, no. 4 (October 1, 1845): 546.

Buck, James S. *Milwaukee under the Charter, from 1847 to 1853 Inclusive*. Vol. 3 of *Pioneer History of Milwaukee*. Milwaukee: Milwaukee News, 1884.

Bull, George. *Defensio Fidei Nicænæ: A Defence of the Nicene Creed, out of the Extant Writings of the Catholick Doctors, Who Flourished During the Three First Centuries of the Christian Church*. Oxford: John Henry Parker, 1851.

Burnet, Gilbert. *The History of the Reformation of the Church of England*, 1679–1714. New edition edited by Nicholas Pocock. 7 vols. Oxford: Clarendon, 1865.

Butler, Joseph. *The Analogy of Religion*. London: J. F. Dove, 1828.

Butler, William Archer. *Letters on Romanism: In Reply to Mr. Newman's Essay on Development*. Edited by Thomas Woodward. 2d ed. rev. by Charles Hardwick. Cambridge: Macmillan, 1858.

Calovius, Abraham. *Systema Locorum Theologicorum*. Wittenberg: Schrödter, 1655–77.

Calvin, John. *Institutes of the Christian Religion*. Translated by Ford Lewis Battles. Edited by John T. McNeill. Philadelphia: Westminster, 1960.

———. *Theological Treatises*. Translated by J. K. S. Reid. Philadelphia: Westminster, 1954.

Casey, Michael W. and Douglas A. Foster, eds. *The Stone-Campbell Movement: An International Religious Tradition*. Knoxville: University of Tennessee Press, 2002.

Carey, Patrick W. *Orestes A. Brownson: American Religious Weathervane*. Grand Rapids, MI: Eerdmans, 2004.

The Catechism of the Council of Trent. Translated by Theodore Alois Buckley. London: Routledge, 1852.

Cave, William. *Apostolici*, London: Richard Chiswel, 1677.

———. *Ecclesiastici*, London: Richard Chiswel, 1683.

Cheever, George. "The Church of Christ in the Middle and the Modern Ages." *New York Evangelist* 16, no. 41 (October 9, 1845): 162.

———. "Position of Protestantism." *New York Evangelist* 16, no. 35 (August 28, 1845): 138.

———. "The Strange Made Plain." *New York Evangelist* 16, no. 51 (December 18, 1845): 202.

———. "Unity of the Protestant Church." *New York Evangelist* 16, no. 38 (September 18 1845): 151.

———. "The Work of Dr. Schaf on Protestantism." *New York Evangelist* 16, no. 37 (September, 11, 1845): 146.

Chemnitz, Martin. *Examination of the Council of Trent*. Translated by Fred Kramer. 4 vols. Saint Louis: Concordia, 1971.

Cohen, Patricia Cline. "Ministerial Misdeeds: The Onderdonk Trial and Sexual Harrassment in the 1840s." In *A Mighty Baptism: Race, Gender, and the Creation of American Protestantism*, edited by Susan Juster and Lisa MacFarlane, 81–106. Ithaca, NY: Cornell University Press, 1996.

Conser, Walter H. *Church and Confession: Conservative Theologians in Germany, England, and America, 1815–1866*. Macon, GA: Mercer University Press, 1984.

Converse, Amasa. "Dr. Schaf's Work of Protestantism." *Christian Observer* 24, no. 30 (July 25, 1845): 118.

———. "Excitement against Prof. Schaf's Work on Protestantism." *Christian Observer* 24 (July 11, 1845): 110.

Courcy de Laroche-Héron, Henri de. *The Catholic Church in the United States: Pages of its History*. Translated by John Gilmary Shea. 2nd ed. New York: Edward Dunigan and Brother, 1857.

Cross, F. L., and Elizabeth A. Livingstone, eds. *The Oxford Dictionary of the Christian Church*. 3rd ed. New York: Oxford University Press, 1997.

Daillé, Jean. *A Treatise concerning the right use of the Fathers, in the decision of the controversies that are this day in religion*. London, 1675.

De Maistre, Joseph Marie. *Du Pape*. Lyon: J .B. Pélaguad, 1854.

DeBie, Linden J. "Biographical Essay: Parallel Lives, Antagonistic Aims." In John Williamson Nevin and Charles Hodge, *Coena Mystica: Debating Reformed Eucharistic Theology*, edited by Linden J. DeBie, Mercersburg Theological Study Series, vol. 2., xiii-xxxvii. Eugene, OR: Wipf & Stock, 2013.

———. *Speculative Theology and Common-Sense Religion: Mercersburg and the Conservative Roots of American Religion*. Eugene, OR: Pickwick, 2008.

Deming, James C. "Philip Schaff, Europe, and American Exceptionalism." *Journal of Presbyterian History* 84, no. 1 (Spring-Summer 2006): 46-51.

Detzler, Wayne A. "Protest and Schism in 19th-Century German Catholicism: The Ronge-Czerski Movement, 1844-45." In *Schism, Heresy and Religious Protest*, edited by Derek Baker, 341-49. Cambridge: Cambridge University Press, 1972.

"Dr. Schaff's Sermon at Elberfeld." *Weekly Messenger* 9 (September 4, 1844): 1866–70.

Edwards, Jonathan. *A History of the Work of Redemption*. Edited by John Frederick Wilson. Vol. 9 of *The Works of Jonathan Edwards*. New Haven, CT: Yale University Press, 1989.

Erasmus, Desiderius. *The Praise of Folly*. Translated by Clarence H. Miller. New Haven, CT: Yale University Press, 1979.

Erb, Peter C. *Schwenkfelders in America: Papers presented at the Colloquium on Schwenckfeld and the Schwenkfelders, Pennsburg, Pa., September 17–22, 1984*. Pennburg, PA: Schwenkfelder Library, 1987.

Eusebius. *The History of the Church from Christ to Constantine*. Translated by G. A. Williamson. New York: Penguin, 1989.

Ewald, Georg Heinrich August von. *A Grammar of the Hebrew Language of the Old Testament*. Translated by John Nicholson. London: Whittaker, 1836.

"Ex-Monk Leahy Revived." *German Reformed Messenger*. August 8, 1860, 2.

Feuerbach, Ludwig A. *The Essence of Christianity*. Translated by George Elliot. New York: Harper, 1957.

Feustking, Johann Heinrich. *Gynaeceum haeretico fanaticum, oder, Historie und Beschreibung der falschen Prophetinnen, Quäckerinnen, Schwärmerinnen, und andern sectirischen und begeisterten Weibes-Personen durch welche die Kirche Gottes verunruhiget worden: sambt einem Vorbericht und Anhang entgegen gesetztet denen Adeptis Godofredi Arnoldi*. Frankfurt: Gottfried Zimmermanns Buchladen, 1704.

Fichte, Johann Gottlieb. *Characteristics of the Present Age; the Way Towards the Blessed Life: Or, the Doctrine of Religion*. Translated by William Smith. Washington, DC: University Publications of America, 1977.

Franchot, Jenny. *Roads to Rome: The Antebellum Protestant Encounter with Catholicism*. Berkeley: University of California Press, 1994.

Gäbler, Ulrich. "Philipp Schaff in Chur, 1819–1834: Herkunft, Jugendjahre und geistiges Unfeld des späteren Amerikanischen Theologen." *Zwingliana* 18, nos. 1 & 2 (1989): 143–65.

Garraty, John A., and Carnes Mark C., eds. *American National Biography*. 24 vols. New York: Oxford University Press, 1999.

Gigot, Ernest. *General Introduction to the Holy Scriptures*. New York: Benziger, 1904.

Gleason, Elisabeth G. *Gasparo Contarini: Venice, Rome, and Reform*. Berkeley: University of California Press, 1993.

Goen, C. C. *Broken Churches, Broken Nation: Denominational Schisms and the Coming of the Civil War*. Macon, GA: Mercer University Press, 1985.

Good, James I. *History of the Reformed Church in the U.S. in the Nineteenth Century*. New York: Board of Publication of the Reformed Church in America, 1911.

Graham, Stephen R. *Cosmos in the Chaos: Philip Schaff's Interpretation of Nineteenth-Century American Religion*. Grand Rapids, MI: Eerdmans, 1995.

Guelzo, Allen C. *For the Union of Evangelical Christendom: The Irony of the Reformed Episcopalians*. University Park: Pennsylvania State University Press, 1994.

Gutjahr, Paul C. *Charles Hodge: Guardian of American Orthodoxy*. New York: Oxford University Press, 2011.

Hamburger, Jeffrey F. *St. John the Divine: The Deified Evangelist in Medieval Art and Theology*. Berkeley: University of California Press, 2002.

Hamm, Thomas D. *The Quakers in America*. New York: Columbia University Press, 2003.

Harless, Gottlieb Christoph Adolf von. *System of Christian Ethics*. Edinburgh: T. & T. Clark, 1868.

Hart, D. G. *John Williamson Nevin: High-Church Calvinist*. Phillipsburg, NJ: P & R Publishing, 2005.

Hatch, Nathan O. *The Democratization of American Christianity*. New Haven, CT: Yale University Press, 1989.

Hegel, Georg Wilhelm Friedrich. *Outlines of the Philosophy of Right*. Translated by T. M. Knox. Edited by Stephen Houlgate. New York: Oxford University Press, 2008.

———. *The Phenomenology of Mind*. Translated by J. B. Baillie. New York: Harper & Row, 1967.

———. *G. W. F. Hegel: Theologian of the Spirit*. Edited by Peter C. Hodgson. Minneapolis: Fortress, 1997.

Hempton, David. *Methodism: Empire of the Spirit*. New Haven, CT: Yale University Press, 2005.

Hengstenberg, Ernst Wilhelm. *The Revelation of St John: Expounded for Those Who Search the Scriptures*. 2 vols. Translated by Patrick Fairburn. Edinburgh: T. & T. Clark, 1851.

Hirscher, Johann Baptist. *Die Christliche Moral als Lehre von der Verwirklichung des göttlichen Reiches in der Menschheit*. 2nd ed. Tübingen, 1836.

Hodge, A. A. *The Life of Charles Hodge*. New York: T. Nelson and Sons, 1881.

Hodge, Charles. *Discussions in Church Polity: From the Contributions to the "Princeton Review."* New York: Charles Scribner's Sons, 1878.

———. Review of *What is Church History?: A Vindication of the Idea of Historical Development* by Philip Schaf. *The Biblical Repertory and Princeton Review* 16 (January 1847): 91–113.

Hoffecker, W. Andrew. *Charles Hodge: The Pride of Princeton*. Phillipsburg, NJ: P & R Publishing, 2011.

Holifield, E. Brooks. *Theology in America: Christian Thought from the Age of the Puritans to the Civil War*. New Haven, CT: Yale University Press, 2003.

Hottinger, Johann Jakob. *The Life and Times of Ulric Zwingli*. Translated by Thomas Conrad Porter. Harrisburg, PA: T. F. Scheffer, 1856.

Howard, Thomas A. *God and the Atlantic: America, Europe, and the Religious Divide*. New York: Oxford University Press, 2011.

———. "Philip Schaff: Religion, Politics, and the Transatlantic World." *Journal of Church and State* 49, no. 2 (spring 2007): 191–210.

———. *Protestant Theology and the Making of the Modern German University*. New York: Oxford University Press, 2006.

Hutchison, William R. *The Modernist Impulse in American Protestantism*. Cambridge, MA: Harvard University Press, 1982.

Irwin, Karla. "Chaos in the Streets: The Philadelphia Riots of 1844," Falvey Memorial Library, Villanova University, http://exhibits.library.villanova.edu/chaos-in-the-streets-the-philadelphia-riots-of-1844.

Jack, Sybil M. "No Heavenly Jerusalem: The Anglican Bishopric, 1841–83." *Journal of Religious History* 19, no. 2 (1995): 181–203.

Jackson, Samuel Macauley, and Lefferts Augustine Loetscher, eds. *The New Schaff-Herzog Encyclopedia of Religious Knowledge*. 13 vols. Grand Rapids, MI: Baker, 1949.

Jerome. *St. Jerome's Commentaries on Galatians, Titus, and Philemon*. Translated by Thomas P. Scheck. Notre Dame, IN: University of Notre Dame Press, 2010.

Johnson, Lawrence J., ed. *Worship in the Early Church: An Anthology of Historical Sources*. 4 vols. Collegeville, MN: Liturgical, 2009.

Johnston, Warren. *Revelation Restored: The Apocalypse in Later Seventeenth-Century England*. Woodbridge, Suffolk: Boydell, 2011.

Jordan, Philip D. "Cooperation without Incorporation: America and the Presbyterian Alliance, 1870-1880." *Journal of Presbyterian History* 55, no.1 (1977): 13–35.

———. *The Evangelical Alliance for the United States of America, 1847–1900: Ecumenism, Identity, and the Religion of the Republic*. New York: Mellen, 1982.

Jorgenson, Kenneth J. "The Oratories of Divine Love and the Theatines: Confraternal Piety and the Making of a Religious Community." Ph.D. diss., Columbia University, 1989.

Ker, Ian. *John Henry Newman: A Biography*. Oxford: Oxford University Press, 1998.

Kliefoth, Theodor. "Die neuere Kirchengeschichtschreibung in der deutsch-evangelischen Kirche." *Allgemeine Repertorium für die theologishe Litteratur und kirchliche Stastisik* (1845).

———. *Einleitung in Die Dogmengeschichte*. Parchim: Hinstorff, 1839.

Kolb, Roberrt and Timothy J. Wengert, ed. *The Book of Concord: The Confessions of the Evangelical Lutheran Church*. Philadelphia: Fortress, 2000.

"Krummacher's Address." *Weekly Messenger* 9 (August 28, 1844): 1866.

Languet, Hubert. *Vindiciae contra tyrannos, or, Concerning the Legitimate Power of a Prince over the People, and of the People over a Prince*. Edited and translated by George Garnett. New York: Cambridge University Press, 1994.

Layman, David R. General introduction to *Born of Water and the Spirit: Essays on the Sacraments and Christian Formation* by John Williamson Nevin, Philip Schaff, and Emanuel V. Gerhart, edited by David R. Layman, Mercersburg Theology Study Series, vol. 6., 1–33.

Leo, Heinrich. *Lehrbuch der Universalgeschichte: zum gebrauche in höheren Unterrichtsanstalten*. 6 vols. Halle: Eduard Anton, 1835–44.

Limbroch, Philippus van. *A Compleat System, or Body of Divinity, Both Speculative and Practical, Founded on Scripture and Reason*. 2 vols. Translated by William Jones. London: John Taylor, 1702.

Littlejohn, W. Bradford. *The Mercersburg Theology and the Quest for Reformed Catholicity*. Eugene, OR: Pickwick, 2009.

Lotz, David W. "Philip Schaff and the Idea of Church History." In *A Century of Church History: The Legacy of Philip Schaff*, edited by Henry Warner Bowden, 1–31. Carbondale: Southern Illinois University Press, 1988.

Luther, Martin. *Luther's Works*. Minneapolis: Fortress, 1955–.

———. *The Theologia Germanica of Martin* Luther. Translated by Bengt Hoffman. New York: Paulist, 1980.

Macaulay, Thomas Babington. *Macaulay's History of England from the Accession of James II*. London: Dent, 1906.

Mann, Wilhelm J. *Erinnerungsblätter*. Reading, PA: Pilgersbuchhandlung, 1894.

Maxwell, Jack Martin. *Worship and Reformed Theology: The Liturgical Lessons of Mercersburg*. Pittsburgh: Pickwick, 1976.

McCarren, Gerald H. "Development of Doctrine." In *The Cambridge Companion to John Henry Newman*, ed. Ian T. Ker and Terrence Merrigan. New York: Cambridge University Press, 2009.

Mechthild of Magdeburg. *The Flowing Light of the Godhead*. Translated by Frank J. Tobin. New York: Paulist, 1998.

Melanchthon, Philipp. *The Chief Theological Topics: Loci praecipui theologici 1559*. Translated by J. A. O. Preus. St. Louis: Concordia, 2011.

———. *Loci Communes 1543*. Translated by J. A. O. Preus. St. Louis: Concordia, 1992.

———. *Melanchthon on Christian Doctrine: Loci communes, 1555*. Translated and edited by Clyde Leonard Manschreck. New York: Oxford University Press, 1965.

Merle d'Aubigné, J. H. *History of the Reformation in Europe in the Time of Calvin*. New York: R. Carter, 1863.

———. *History of the Reformation of the Sixteenth Century*. Rev. ed. Translated by Henry White. 5 vols. New York: American Tract Society, 1849–53.

Meyer, John Charles. "Philip Schaff's Concept of Organic Historiography as Related to the Development of Doctrine a Catholic Appraisal." Ph. D. diss., Catholic University, 1968.

Miller, Perry. Editor's introduction in Philip Schaff, *America: A Sketch of its Political, Social, and Religious Character*, edited by Perry Miller. Cambridge, MA: Harvard University Press, 1961.

Missouri: A Guide to the 'Show Me' State. American Guide Series. New York: Duell, Sloan, and Pierce, 1941.

Möhler, Johann Adam. *Symbolism: Exposition of the Doctrinal Differences between Catholics and Protestants as Evidenced by Their Symbolical Writing*. Translated by James Burton Robertson. New York: Crossroad, 1997.

Monk, Maria and Rebecca Reid. *Veil of Fear: Nineteenth-Century Convent Tales by Rebecca Reed and Maria Monk*. Edited by Nancy Lusignan Schultz. West Lafayette, IN: Purdue University Press, 1999.

Mornay, Philippe de, seigneur du Plessis-Marly. *The Mysterie of Iniquitie; That Is to Say, the Historie of the Papacie*. Translated by Samson Lennard. London: Adam Islip, 1612.

Moser, Friedrich Carl Freiherr von. *Actenmassige Geschichte der Waldenser*. Zürich: Orell, Gessner, Fussli, 1798.

Mosheim, Johann. *Mosheim's Institutes of Ecclesiastical History, Ancient and Modern*. 5th ed. Translated by J. Murdock. London: Tegg, 1867.

Müller, Johannes von. *Die Geschichten der Schweizer*. Bern, 1780.

Mullin, Robert Bruce. *Episcopal Vision / American Reality: High Church Theology and Social Thought in Evangelical America*. New Haven, CT: Yale University Press, 1986.

Münscher, Wilhelm. *Lehrbuch der christlichen Kirchengeschichte*. Marburg, 1804.

Neander, August. *General History of the Christian Religion and Church*. Translated by Joseph Torrey. 9 vols. Edinburgh: T & T Clark, 1847–55.

Nellen, H. J. M. "De zinspreuk 'In necessariis unitas, in non necessariis libertas, in utrisque caritas.'" *Nederlands archief voor kerkgeschidenis* 79 (1999): 99-106.

Nevin, John Williamson. "The Mercersburg Theology" in *The Anxious Bench, Antichirst, and the Sermon on Catholic Unity*, edited by Augustine Thompson, v–vii. Eugene, OR: Wipf & Stock, 1999.

———. *My Life: The Earlier Years*. Lancaster, PA: The Historical Society of the Evangelical and Reformed Church, 1964.

———. *The Mystical Presence and the Doctrine of the Reformed Church on the Lord's Supper*. Edited by Linden DeBie. Mercersburg Theological Study Series, vol. 1. Eugene, OR: Wipf and Stock, 2012.

———. "Schaf on Protestantism." *Christian Observer* 24 (July 25, 1845): 118.

———. "True and False Protestantism." Review of *The Principle of Protestantism* by Philip Schaff. *Mercersburg Review* 1 (1849): 83–104.

Nevin, John Williamson, and Charles Hodge. *Coena Mystica: Debating Reformed Eucharistic Theology*. Edited by Linden DeBie. Mercersburg Theological Study Series, vol. 2. Eugene, OR: Wipf & Stock, 2013.

Nevin, John Williamson, Philip Schaff, and Daniel Gans. *The Incarnate Word: Selected Writings on Christology*. Edited by William B. Evans. Mercersburg Theology Study Series, vol. 4. Eugene, OR: Wipf & Stock, 2014.

Nevinson, Henry Woodd. *A Sketch of Herder and His Times*. London: Chapman and Hall, 1884.

Newman, John Henry. *An Essay on the Development of Christian Doctrine*. 6th ed. Notre Dame, IN: University of Notre Dame Press, 1989.

Nichols, James Hastings, ed. *The Mercersburg Theology*. New York: Oxford University Press, 1966.

———. *Romanticism in American Theology: Nevin and Schaff at Mercersburg*. Chicago: University of Chicago Press, 1961.

Noll, Mark A. *America's God: From Jonathan Edwards to Abraham Lincoln*. New York: Oxford University Press, 2002.

———. *Princeton and the Republic, 1768-1822: The Search for a Christian Enlightenment in the Era of Samuel Stanhope Smith*. Princeton: Princeton University Press, 1989.

Novalis. *Philosophical Writings*. Edited and translated by Margaret Mahony Stoljar. Albany: State University of New York Press, 1997.

Payne, John. "Philip Schaff: Christian Scholar and Prophet of Ecumenism." *Prism* 9. no. 2 (1994): 28-42.

Pelikan, Jaroslav, and Valerie R. Hotchkiss, eds. *Creeds & Confessions of Faith in the Christian Tradition*. 4 vols. New Haven, CT: Yale University Press, 2003.

Penzel, Klaus. "Church History and the Ecumenical Quest: A Study of the German Background and Thought of Philip Schaff." Ph. D. diss., Union Theological Seminary, 1962.

———. Editorial introduction to Philip Schaff, *Philip Schaff: Historian and Ambassador of the Universal Church: Selected Writings*, edited by Klaus Penzel, xv–lxviii. Macon, GA: Mercer University Press, 1991.

———. "An Ecumenical Vision of Church History: F. W. J. Schelling." *Perkins School of Theology Journal* 17 (Winter–Spring 1964): 3–19.

———. *The German Education of Christian Scholar Philip Schaff: The Formative Years, 1819–1844*. Lewiston, NY: Mellen, 2004.

———. "The Reformation Goes West: The Notion of Historical Development in the Thought of Philip Schaff." *Journal of Religion* 62 (July 1982): 225.

———. "Toward a New Reformation." In Philip Schaff, *Philip Schaff: Historian and Ambassador of the Universal Church: Selected Writings*, edited by Klaus Penzel, 75–80. Macon, GA: Mercer University Press, 1991.

Peters, Edward, ed. *Heresy and Authority in Medieval Europe: Documents in Translation*. Philadelphia: University of Pennsylvania Press, 1980.

Planck, Gottlieb Jakob. *Geschichte der Entstehung, der Veränderungen und der Bildung unseres protestantischen Lehrbegriffs von Anfang der Reformation bis zur Einführung der Konkordienformel*. 6 vols. Leipzig, 1781–1800.

Pranger, Gary K. *Philip Schaff (1819–1893): Portrait of an Immigrant Theologian*. New York: Peter Lang, 1997.

Presbyterian Church in the U. S. A. (Old School). General Assembly. *Minutes of the General Assembly of the Presbyterian Church in the United States of America*. Vol. 11. Philadelphia: Stated Clerk of the Assembly, 1845.

Randall, Ian M. *One Body in Christ: The History and Significance of the Evangelical Alliance*. Carlisle, Cumbria: Paternoster, 2001.

Reid, Thomas. *An Inquiry into the Human Mind, On the Principles of Common Sense*. 1785. Reprint, Bristol: Thoemmes, 1990.

Rauch, Frederick A. *Psychology: Or, a View of the Human Soul, Including Anthropology*. Introduction by Eric T. Carlson. Delmar, NY: Scholars' Facsimiles & Reprints, 1975.

"The Rev. Mr. Leahey, formerly monk of La Trappe." *Weekly Messenger*. Reprinted in *Catholic Telegraph*, April 23, 1846, 134.

Review of *Das Princip des Protestantismus* by Philip Schaf. *Lutheran Observer* 12 (April 11, 1845): 39.

Review of *The Principle of Protestantism* by Philip Schaf. *Christian Intelligencer* 16 (August 7, 1845): 14.

Review of *The Principle of Protestantism* by Philip Schaf. *New York Evangelist* 16 (July 10, 1845): 112.

Rex, Richard. *The Lollards*. New York: Palgrave, 2002.

Richey, Russell E. "Denominations and Denominationalism: An American Morphology." In *Reimagining Denominationalism: Interpretive Essays*, edited by Robert Bruce Mullin and Russell E. Richey, 74–98. New York: Oxford University Press, 1994.

Richards, George "The Life and Work of Philip Schaff." *Bulletin of the Theological Seminary of the Evangelical and Reformed Church* 15, no. 4 (October 1944): 155–72.

"Ronge, Czerski and the German-Catholic Church, No. 1," *The Churchman* 15, no. 23 (August 9, 1845): 92.

Ronge, Johannes. *John Ronge, the Holy Coat of Treves, and the New German-Catholic Church*. New York: Harper & Brothers, 1845.

Roxburgh, Kenneth B. E. *Thomas Gillespie and the Origins of the Relief Church in 18th Century Scotland*. New York: Peter Lang, 1999.

Ryan, Emmett Ryan. *Imaginary Friends: Representing Quakers in American Culture, 1650–1950*. Madison: University of Wisconsin Press, 2009.

Sachs, Hans. *Werke in Zwei Bänden*. 2nd ed. Edited by Karl Martin Schiller. 2 vols. Berlin: Aufbau-Verlag, 1966.

Sartorius, Ernst Stearns Oakman S. *The Person and Work of Christ*. Translated by Oakman S. Stearns. Boston: Gould, Kendall & Lincoln, 1848.

Schaff, David S. *The Life of Philip Schaff, in Part Autobiographical.* New York: Scribner's, 1897.

Schaff, Philip, *America: A Sketch of its Political, Social, and Religious Character.* Edited by Perry Miller. Cambridge, MA: Harvard University Press, 1961.

———. *A Catechism for Sunday Schools and Families: In Fifty Two Lessons.* Philadelphia: Lindsay and Blakiston, 1862.

———, ed. *The Creeds of Christendom.* 3 vols. 4th ed. New York: Harper Brothers, 1919.

———. *Das Princip des Protestantismus.* Chambersburg, PA: Hochdeutsch Reformirten Kirche, 1845.

———, ed. *Deutsches Gesangbuch: Eine Auswahl Geistlicher Leider aus allen Zeiten Der Christlichen Kirche.*. Philadelphia: Lindsay und Klakiston: Berlin, 1859.

———. "Die deutsche Theologie und die Kirchenfrage." *Der Deutsche Kirchenfreund* 5 (September 1852): 338–53.

———. "Gallerie der bedeutendsten jetzt lebenden Universitätetheologen Deutschlands." *Der Deutsche Kirchenfreund* 5 (April 1852): 129–140.

———. "Gallerie der bedeutendsten jetzt lebenden Universitätetheologen Deutschlands (Fortsetzung)." *Der Deutsche Kirchenfreund.* 5 (May 1852): 161–179.

———. "Gallerie der bedeutendsten jetzt lebenden Universitätetheologen Deutschlands (Fortsetzung)." *Der Deutsche Kirchenfreund* 5 (July 1852): 241–55.

———. "Gallerie der bedeutendsten jetzt lebenden Universitätetheologen Deutschlands (Fortsetzung)." *Der Deutsche Kirchenfreund* 5 (August 1852): 289–306.

———. "Gallerie der bedeutendsten jetzt lebenden Universitätetheologen Deutschlands (Schluss)." *Der Deutsche Kirchenfreund* 5 (September 1852): 321–38.

———. *Germany: Its Universities, Theology, and Religion.* Philadelphia: Lindsay and Blakiston, 1857.

———. *History of the Apostolic Church: With a General Introduction to Church History.* Translated by Edward D. Yeomans. New York: Scribner, 1853.

———. *History of the Christian Church.* 8 vols. New York: Scribner's, 1891.

———, ed. *Nicene and Post-Nicene Fathers of the Christian Church.* Reprinted. Grand Rapids MI: Eerdmans, 1956.

———. *Reformed and Catholic: Selected Historical and Theological Writings of Philip Schaff.* Edited by Charles Yrigoyen and George M. Bricker. Pittsburgh: Pickwick, 1979.

———. "The Reunion of Christendom" in *Philip Schaff: Historian and Ambassador of the Universal Church,* edited by Klaus Penzel, 302-40. Macon, GA: Mercer University Press, 1992.

Schelling, Friedrich. *Philosophie der Offenbarung (1841/42).* Edited by Manfred Frank. Frankfurt: Suhrkampf Verlag, 1977.

———. *Vom ich als Prinzip der Philosophie.* Leipzig: Meiner, 1911.

Schleiermacher, Friederich. *The Christian Faith.* Edited by H. R. Mackintosh and James S. Stewart. Edinburgh: T & T Clark, 1999.

Schmucker, Samuel Simon. *The Church of the Redeemer.* Baltimore: T. N. Kurtz, 1867.

———. *Fraternal Appeal to the American Churches; with a Plan for Catholic Union on Apostolic Principles.* 1838. Edited by Frederick K. Wentz. Philadelphia: Fortress, 1965.

Shea, William M. *The Lion and the Lamb: Evangelicals and Catholics in America.* New York: Oxford University Press, 2004.

Shriver, George H. "Philip Schaff (1819–1893)." In *Dictionary of Heresy Trials in American Christianity,* by George H. Shriver, 327–36. Westport, CT: Greenwood, 1997.

———. *Philip Schaff: Christian Scholar and Ecumenical Prophet:* Macon, GA: Mercer University Press, 1987.

———. "Phillip Schaff: Heresy at Mercersburg." In *American Religious Heretics; Formal and Informal Trials*, edited by George H. Shriver, 18-55. Nashville: Abingdon, 1966.

Smylie, James H. *A Brief History of the Presbyterians.* Louisville, KY: Geneva, 1996.

Splitter, Wolfgang. "The Fact and the Fiction of Cotton Mather's Correspondence with August Herman Francke." *The New England Quarterly*, 83, no. 1 (March 2010): 102–22.

Stewart, Dugald. *Elements of the Philosophy of the Human Mind.* Brattleborough: William Fessenden, 1813.

Tanner, Norman P., ed. *Decrees of the Ecumenical Councils.* 2 vols. Washington, DC: Georgetown University Press, 1990.

Tappert, Theodore G., ed. *The Book of Concord: The Confessions of the Evangelical Lutheran Church.* Philadelphia: Fortress, 1959.

Theil, John E. "The Development of Doctrine." In *The Blackwell Companion to Catholicism*, edited by James J. Buckley, Frederick Christian Bauerschmidt, and Trent Pomplun, 237–67. Malden, MA: Blackwell, 2007.

Tomaschewsky, Michaela. "Dress Rehearsal for 1848: Johannes Ronge and the German Catholic Movement." In *Consortium on Revolutionary Europe, 1750–1850*, edited by Ronald Caldwell, Donald D. Horward, John W. Rooney, Jr. and John K. Severn, 116–22. Tallahassee, FL: Institute on Napoleon and the French Revolution, 1994.

Thompson, Bard and George Bricker. Editors' preface in Philip Schaff. *The Principle of Protestantism*, edited by Bard Thompson and George H. Bricker, 7–17. Philadelphia, PA: United Church Press, 1964. Reprint Eugene, OR: Wipf & Stock, 2004.

Trost, Theodore L., Jr., "Philip Schaff's Concept of the Church with Special Reference to his Role in the Mercersburg Movement, 1844-1864." Ph. D. diss., Edinburgh University, 1958.

Trost, Theodore Louis. "The Ecumenical Trajectory of the Mercersburg Movement." *The New Mercersburg Review* 53 (Fall 2015): 1-25.

———. "Exposing, Experiencing, and Explaining America: Philip Schaff's Progress from *The Principle of Protestantism* to *America*." *The New Mercersburg Review* 23 (Spring 1998): 3–24.

Turner, Frank M. *John Henry Newman: The Challenge to Evangelical Religion.* New Haven, CT: Yale University Press, 2002.

Presbyterian Church (USA), Christian Reformed Church in North America, Reformed Church in America, United States Council of Catholic Bishops, and United Church of Christ. "Common Agreement on Mutual Recognition of Baptism." September 29, 2011. http://www.usccb.org/beliefs-and-teachings/ecumenical-and-interreligious/ecumenical/reformed/baptism.cfm

Van Engen, John. *Sisters and Brothers of the Common Life: The Devotio Moderna and the World of the Later Middle Ages.* Philadelphia: University of Pennsylvania Press, 2008.

Virgil. *Aeneid.* Translated by H. Rushton Fairclough and G. P. Goold. Loeb Classical Library, vol. 63. Rev. ed. Cambridge, MA: Harvard University Press, 1999.

Walch, Johann Georg. *Historische und theologische Einleitung in die Religionsstreitigkeiten der evagnelishe-lutherischen Kirche.* 5 vols. Jena, 1733–36.

Weismann, Christian Eberhard. *Introductio in memorabilia ecclesiastica historiae sacrae Novi Testamenti.* 2 vols. Stuttgart, 1718–19.

Wentz, Abdel Ross. *Pioneer in Christian Unity: Samuel Simon Schmucker.* Philadelphia: Fortress, 1967.

Wentz, Frederick K. "Samuel Simon Schmucker and Philip Schaff: Nineteenth-Century Ecumenical Pioneers." *Currents in Theology and Mission* 15, no. 6 (1988): 574–88.

Wentz, Richard E. *John Williamson Nevin: American Theologian.* New York: Oxford University Press, 1997.

White, James F. *The Cambridge Movement: The Ecclesiologists and the Gothic Revival.* Cambridge: Cambridge University Press, 1962.

Whitley, Lawrence A. B. *A Great Grievance: Ecclesiastical Lay Patronage in Scotland until 1750.* Eugene, OR: Wipf & Stock, 2013.

Wieland, Christoph Martin. *Oberon: A Poetical Romance in Twelve Books.* Translated by John Quincy Adams. New York: F. S. Crofts, 1940.

Wigger, John H. *Taking Heaven by Storm: Methodism and the Rise of Popular Christianity in America.* New York: Oxford University Press, 1998.

Winer, Georg Benedikt. *A Treatise on the Grammar of New Testament Greek: Regarded as a Sure Basis for New Testament Exegesis.* 3rd ed. Translated by William Fiddian Moulton. Edinburgh: T. & T. Clark, 1882.

Winer, George Benedikt. *Grammatik des Neutestamenlichen Sprachidioms.* Leipzig: Vogel, 1822. English translation by Moses Stuart and Edward Robinson as *A Greek Grammar of the New Testament* (Andover, MA: Flagg & Gould, 1825).

Wolfe, George D. Review of *What is Church History? A Vindication of the Idea of Historical Development* by Philip Schaf. *Mercersburg Review* 2 (March 1847): 117–141.

Yates, Nigel. *Buildings, Faith, and Worship: The Liturgical Arrangement of Anglican Churches 1600–1900.* Oxford: Clarendon, 1991.

WORKS CITED IN THE ORIGINAL

(In most cases we have provided the edition known to Schaff. If the work was translated into English at a later time, information on the translation appears in the second half of the entry.)

Ammon, Christoph Friedrich von. *Die Fortbildung des Christenthums zur Weltreligion.* 4 vols. Leipzig: Vogel, 1833–40.

Arnold, Gottfried. *Unparteyische Kirchen- und Ketzer-Historie von Anfang des Neuen Testaments biss auff das Jahr christi 1688.* 4 vols. Frankfurt: Thomas Fritsch, 1699–1700.

Arnold, Gottfried. *Unparteyische Kirchen- und Ketzer-Historien vom Anfang des Neuen Testaments biß auf das Jahr christi 1688.* 3 vols. Schaffhausen: Hurter, 1742.

Bacon, Francis. *Two Bookes of the Proficience and Advancement of Learning, Divine and Human.* London, 1605.

Baum, G. *Theodor Beza: nach handschriftlichen Quellen dargestellt.* 2 vols. Leipzig: Weidmann'sche Buchhandlung, 1843.

Baumgarten-Crusius, Ludwig Friedrich Otto. *Lehrbuch der christlichen Dogmengeschichte.* Jena: Cröker, 1832.

Baur, Ferdinand Christian. *Der Gegensatz des Katholicismus und Protestantismus.* Tubingen: L. F. Fues, 1834.

———. *Die christliche Gnosis oder die christliche Religions-Philosophie in ihrer geschichtlichen Entwicklung.* Tübingen: Osiander, 1835.

———. *Die christliche Lehre von der Dreieinigkeit und Menschwerdung Gottes in ihrer geschichtlichen Entwicklung.* 3 vols. Tübingen: C. F. Osiander, 1841–43.

———. *Die christliche Lehre von der Versöhnung in ihrer geschichtlichen Entwicklung von der ältesten Zeit bis auf die neueste.* Tübingen: C. F. Osiander, 1838.

Berg, Joseph F. *Lectures on Romanism.* Philadelphia: Weidner, 1840.

Bindemann, Carl. *Der heilige Augustinus.* 3 vols. Berlin: H. Schultze, 1844–69.

Bretschneider, Karl Gottlieb. *Handbuch der Dogmatik der evangelish-lutherischen Kirche.* 2 vols. Leipzig: Barth, 1814.

Böhringer, Georg Friedrich. *Die Kirche christi und ihre Zeugen; oder, Die Kirchengeschichte in Biographien.* 24 vols. Zürich: Meyer & Zeller, 1842.

Bull, George. *Defensio fidei Nicænæ.* Edited by Johannes Ernestus Grabe. London: Richard Smith, 1703.

Bullinger, Heinrich. *Reformationsgeschichte.* Edited by Johann Jakob Hottinger and H. H. Vögeli. 3 vols. Frauenfeld: Beyel, 1838–40.

Bush, George. *Anastasis: or the Doctrine of the Resurrection of the Body, Rationally and Scripturally Considered.* New York: Wiley and Putnam, 1845.

Butler, Joseph. *The Analogy of Religion, Natural and Revealed, to the Constitution and Course of Nature.* London, 1736.

Calvin, Jean. *Ioannis Calvini opera quae supersunt omnia.* Corpus Reformatorum, vols. 29–87. Braunschweig: Schwetschke, 1863–1900.

Carlyle, Thomas. *On Heroes, Hero-Worship & the Heroic in History.* New York: Appleton, 1841.

Cheever, George. "Dr. Schaf's Work on Protestantism." *New York Evangelist* 16, no. 36 (September 4, 1845), 142.

———. "German Theology—Science apart from Life," *New York Evangelist* 16, no. 42 (October 16, 1845): 166.

Conversations-Lexicon der neuesten Zeit und Literatur. 4 vols. Leipzig: Brockhaus, 1832–34.

Dahlmann, F. C. *Geschichte der englischen Revolution.* Leipzig: Weidmann, 1844. English translation by H. Evans Lloyd as *The History of the English Revolution* (London: Longman, Brown, Green, and Longmans, 1844).

Döllinger, Johann Joseph Ignaz von. *Geschichte der christlichen Kirche.* 2 vols. Landshut : G.J. Manz, 1833–35. English translation by Edward Cox as *A History of the Church*, 4 vols. (London: C. Dolman, 1840–42).

Dorner, Isaac August. *Entwicklungsgeschichte der Lehre von der Person Christi: von den ältesten Zeiten bis auf die neueste.* Stuttgart: S. G. Liesching, 1839.

Engelhardt, Johann Georg Veit. *Dogmengeschichte.* 2 vols. Neustadt: J. C. Engelhardt, 1839.

———. *Handbuch der Kirchengeschichte.* 4 vols. Erlangen: Palm and Enke, 1833.

———. *Richard von St. Victor und Johannes Ruysbroek: zur Geschichte der mystischen Theologie.* Erlangen: Palm, 1838.

Ess, Leander. *Auszüge über das nothwendige und nützliche Bibellesen aus den heiligen Kirchenvätern und andern katholischen Schriftstellern zur Aufmunterung der Katholiken.* 2nd ed. Sulzbach: J.C. Seidel, 1816.

Fénelon, François de Salignac de La Mothe. *The Maxims of the Saints Explained, concerning the Interior Life.* London: Rhodes, 1698.

Flacius Illyricus, Matthias. *Catalogus testium veritatis.* Basel, 1556.

———. *Ecclesiastica historia.* 13 vols. Basel, 1560–74.

Förstemann, Karl Eduard. *Neues Urkundenbuch zur Geschichte der evangelischen Kirchen-Reformation*. Hamburg: Perthes, 1842.

Franck, Georg Friedrich. *Anselm von Canterbury*. Tübingen: C. F. Osiander, 1842.

Galle, Friedrich. *Versuch einer Charakteristik Melanchthons als Theologen und einer Entwickelung seines Lehrbegriffs*. Halle: Johann Friedrich Lippert, 1840.

Gerhard, Johann. *Loci Theologica*. 9 vols. Jena, 1610–25.

Gerlach, Otto von, H. F. Uhden, Albrecht von Sydow, and Friedrich August Stüler. *Amtliche Berichte über die in neuerer Zeit in England erwachte Thätigkeit für die Vermehrung und Erweiterung der kirchlichen Anstalten*. Potsdam: Stuhr, 1845.

Gieseler, Johann Karl Ludwig. *Lehrbuch der Kirchengeschichte*. 6 vols. Bonn: Adolph Marcus, 1824–57. An English translation by Francis Cunningham of the early volumes appeared as *Text-Book of Ecclesiastical History*, 3 vols (Philadelphia: Carey, Lea, and Blanchard, 1836). English translation of the complete work by Samuel Davidson, John W. Hull, and Mary A. Robinson, edited by Henry B. Smith as *A Text-Book of Church History*, 5 vols. (New York: Harper, 1857).

Goebel, Max. *Die religiöse Eigenthümlichkeit der lutherischen und der reformirten Kirche*. Bonn: Adolph Marcus, 1837.

Guericke, Heinrich Ernst Ferdinand. *August Herman Franke: Eine Denkschrift zur Secularfeyer seines Todes*. Halle, 1827. English translation by Samuel Jackson as *The Life of Augustus Herman Franke, Professor of Divinity, and founder of the Orphan-House in Halle*. (London: Seeley & Burnside, 1837).

———. *Handbuch der allgemeinen Kirchengeschichte*. Halle: In der Gebauerschen Buchhandlung, 1833. English translation by William G. T. Sheed as *A Manual of Church History*, 2 vols. (Andover, MA: W. F. Draper, 1857).

Hagenbach, K. R. *Lehrbuch der Dogmengeschichte*. 2 vols. Leipzig: Weidmann, 1840. English translation by Carl W. Buch as *Compendium of the History of Doctrines* (Edinburgh: T. & T. Clark, 1846).

———. *Vorlesungen über Wesen und Geschichte der Reformation in Deutschland und der Schweiz: mit später Beziehung auf die richtungen unserer Zeit*. 6 vols. Leipzig: Weidmann'sche Buchhandlung, 1834. English translation by Evelina Moore as *History of the Reformation in Germany and Switzerland Chiefly*, 2 vols. (Edinburgh: T. & T. Clark, 1878).

Harms, Claus. *Das sind die 95 Theses oder Streitsätze Dr. Luthers*. Kiel, 1817.

Hase, Karl von. *Kirchengeschichte*. 4th ed. Leipzig: Breitkopf and Härtel, 1841.

———, ed. *Libri symbolici Ecclesiae evangelicae, sive, Concordia*. 2nd. ed. Leipzig, 1837.

———. Review of *Handbuch der Kirchengeschichte* by J. G. V. Engelhardt and *Handburch der allgemeinen Kirchengeschichte* by H. E. Ferdinand Guerike. *Jahrbücher für wissenschaftliche Kritik* (April 1835): 534–49, 553–63.

Hasse, Friedrich Rudolph. *Anselm von Canterbury*. 2 vols. Leipzig: W. Engelmann, 1843-52. Partial English translation by William Turner as *The Life of Anselm, Archbishop of Canterbury: Translated and Abridged from the German of F.R. Hasse* (London: F. & J. Rivington, 1850).

Hegel, G. W. F. *Vorlesungen über die Philosophie der Geschichte*. Edited by Eduard Gans. In *Georg Wilhelm Friedrich Hegel's Werke*. Vol. 9. Berlin: Duncker und Humblot, 1837.

Hengstenberg, Ernst Wilhelm. *Die Offenbarung des heiligen Johannes: für solche die in der Schrift forschen*. Berlin: Ludwig Oehmigke, 1849. English translation by Patrick Fairburn as *The Revelation of St John: Expounded for Those Who Search the Scriptures*, 2 vols. (Edinburgh: T. & T. Clark, 1851).

Henke, Heinrich Philipp Konrad. *Allgemeine Geschichte der christlichen Kirche nach der Zeitfolge*. 9 vols. Brunswick: Verlag der Schulbuchhandlung, 1804–23.

Henry, Paul. *Das Leben Johann Calvins des grossen Reformators*. 3 vols. Hamburg: F. Perthes, 1835–44.

Herder, Johann Gottfried. *Auch eine Philosophie der Geschichte*, 1774.

———. *Ideen zur Philosophie der Geschichte der Menschheit*. 4 vols. Riga and Leipzig: Johann Friedrich Hartknoch, 1784. English translation by T. Churchill as *Outlines of a Philosophy of the History of Man* (1800, repr. New York, Bergman, 1966).

———. *Johann Gottfried von Herder's sämmtliche Werke: Zur Philosophie und Geschichte*. 22 vols. Stuttgart: J. G. Cotta, 1827–30.

Herzog, J. J. *Das Leben Johannes Oekolampads und die Reformation der Kirche zu Basel*. 2 vols. Basel: Schweighauser, 1843.

Hodge, Charles. "Doctrine of the Reformed Church on the Lord's Supper." Review of *The Mystical Presence: A Vindication of the Reformed or Calvinistic Doctrine of the Holy Eucharist* by John W. Nevin. *The Biblical Repertory and Princeton Review* 20 (1848): 227–78. A modern critical edition is included in John Williamson Nevin and Charles Hodge, *Coena Mystica*.

Hossbach, Wilhelm. *Johann Valentin Andreæ und sein Zeitalter dargestellt*. Berlin: G. Reimer, 1819.

———. *Philipp Jakob Spener und seine Zeit: eine kirchenhistorische Darstellung*. 2 vols. Berlin: F. Dümmler, 1828.

Hurter, Friedrich Emanuel von. *Geschichte Papst Innocenz des Dritten und seiner Zeitgenossen*. 4 vols. Hamburg: Friedrich Perthes, 1834–42.

Klee, Heinrich. *Lehrbuch Der Dogmengeschichte*. 2 vols. Mainz: Kirchheim, Schott & Thielmann, 1837–38.

Klose, Carl Rudolph Wilhelm. *Ein Beitrag zur Kirchengeschichte: Basilius der Grosse nach seinem Leben und seiner Lehre dargestellt*. Stralsund: Löffler, 1835.

Koellner, Eduard. *Symbolik der heiligen apostolischen katholischen römischen Kirche*. Hamburg, 1844.

Lang, J. P. *Vermischte Schriften*. Vol. 4. Göttingen: Rheinischen Schulbuchhandlung, 1841.

Lechler, Gotthard Victor. *Geschichte des englischen Deismus*. Stuttgart: J. G. Cotta, 1841.

Leo, Heinrich. *Lehrbuch der Universalgeschichte: zum Gebrauche in höheren Unterrichtsanstalten*. 6 vols. Halle: Eduard Anton, 1835–44.

Liebner, A. *Hugo von St. Victor und die theologischen Richtungen seiner Zeit*. Leipzig: A. Lehnhold, 1832.

Limbroch, Philipp van. *Historia Inquisitionis, Cui subjungitur Liber sententiarum inquisitionis Tholosanae ab a. Chr. 1307 ad annum 1323*. Amsterdam, 1692.

Luther, Martin *D. Martin Luthers sowol in geutscher als lateinischer Sprache verfertigte und aus der letztern in die erstere übersetzte sämtliche Schriften*. Edited by Johann Georg Walch. 24 vols. Halle im Magdeburgischen: Johann Justinus Gebauer, 1740.

Macaulay, Thomas Babington. *The History of England from the Accession of James the Second*. London: Longman, Brown, Green, and Longmans, 1849.

Marheinecke, Philipp. *Geschichte der deutschen Reformation*. 2 vols. Berlin: Nicolais, 1816.

Martensen, H. *Meister Eckart eine theologische Studie*. Hamburg: F. Perthes, 1842.

Maurice, Frederick Denison. *The Kingdom of Christ, or Hints to a Quaker concerning the Principle, Constitution, and Ordinances of the Catholic Church*. 2 vols. 1838. Reprint, Cambridge: Lutterworth, 2002.

Meier, Carolus. *Girolamo Savonarola: aus Grossen Theils handschriftlichen Quellen*, Berlin: G. Reimer, 1836.

Meier, Georg August. *Die Lehre von der Trinität in ihrer historischen Entwickelung*. 2 vols. Hamburg: F. und A. Perthes, 1844.

Melanchthon, Philipp. *Loci communes theologici*. Basel: Ioannem Oporinum, 1562.

Melanchthon, Philipp. *Philippi Melanthonis Opera quae supersunt omnia*. Edited by Karl Gottlieb Bretschneider. Corpus Reformatorum, vol. 1–28. Halle: Schwetschke, 1834–60.

Menzel, Wolfgang. *Wolfgang Menzel's Geschichte der Deutschen: bis auf die neuesten Tage*. 4th ed. 2 vols. Stuttgart: J. G. Cotta, 1843.

Merle d'Aubigné, Jean Henri. *Discours sur l'étude de l'histoire du Christianisme et son utilité pour l'époque actuelle*. Paris: Risler, 1832. English translation by Thomas Smith Grimké as *Discourse on the Study of the History of Christianism, and Its Usefulness at This Epoch: Delivered at Geneva, January 2, 1832* (Charleston, SC: Observer Office, 1833).

———. *History of the Reformation of the Sixteenth Century*. Translated by Henry White. 4 vols. New York: American Tract Society, 1835–45.

———. "Lutheranism and the Reform: Their Diversity Essential to their Unity." *The Biblical Repository and Classical Review*, 3rd ser., 1, no. 1 (January 1845): 130–168

Möhler, Johann Adam. *Athanasius der Grosse und die Kirche seiner Zeit, besonders im Kampfe mit dem Arianismus*. Mainz: Kupferberg, 1827.

———. *Die Einheit in der Kirche; oder, Das Princip des Katholicismus, dargestellt im Geiste der Kirchenväter der drei ersten Jahrhunderte*. Tübingen: Heinrich Laupp, 1825. English translation by Peter C. Erb as *Unity in the Church or the Principle of Catholicism: Presented in the Spirit of the Church Fathers of the First Three Centuries* (Washington, DC: Catholic University of America Press, 1996).

———. *Gesammelte Schriften und Aufsatze*. Edited by Johann Joseph Ignaz von Döllinger. 2 vols. Regensburg: G.J. Manz, 1839. English translation of the biography of Anselm included here by Henry Rymer as *The Life of St. Anselm, Archbishop of Canterbury: A Contribution to a Knowledge of the Moral, Ecclesiastical, and Literary Life of the Eleventh & Twelfth Centuries* (London: Jones, 1842).

———. *Patrologie, oder christliche Literärgeschichte*. Regensburg: Manz, 1840.

———. *Symbolik, oder Darstellung der dogmatischen Gegensätze der Katholiken und Protestanten nach ihren öffentlichen Bekenntnisschriften*. 1st ed. Mainz: F. Kupferberg, 1832.

———. *Symbolik, oder Darstellung der dogmatischen Gegensätze der Katholiken und Protestanten nach ihren öffentlichen Bekenntnisschriften*. 5th ed. Mainz: F. Kupferberg, 1838. English translation by James Burton Robertson as *Symbolism: Exposition of the Doctrinal Differences between Catholics and Protestants as Evidenced by Their Symbolical Writings* (1843; repr., New York: Crossroad, 1997).

Mosheim, Johann Lorenz. *Institutiones historiae christianae maiores. Saeculum primum*. Helmstedt: C. F. Weygand, 1739.

———. *Institvtionvm historiae ecclesiasticae antiqvae at recentiors libri qvatvor ex ipsis fontibva insigniter emendati*. Helmstedt: Christianvm Fridericvm Weygand, 1755. English translation by J. Murdock as *Mosheim's Institutes of Ecclesiastical History, Ancient and Modern* 5th ed. (London, Tegg, 1867).

———. *Versuch einer unpartheiischen und gründlichen Ketzergeschichte*. Helmstadt: Christian Friederich Weygand, 1746.

Müller, Adolf. *Leben des Erasmus von Rotterdam: Mit einleitenden Betrachtungen über die analoge Entwicklung der Menschheit und des einzelnen Menschen.* Hamburg: F. Perthes, 1828.

Müller, Julius. *Die christliche Lehre von der Sünde.* 2 vols. Breslau: Josef Max und Komp, 1839-44. English translation by William Pulsford as *The Christian Doctrine of Sin* (Edinburgh: T. & T. Clark, 1852–53).

Münscher, Wilhelm. *Lehrbuch der christlichen Dogmengeschichte.* 2nd ed. Marburg: J. C. Krieger, 1819. English translation by James Murdock as *Elements of Dogmatic History* (New Haven, CT: A. H. Maltby, 1830).

Neander, August. *Allgemeine Geschischte der chirstilischen Religion und Kirche* 6 vols. Hamburg, 1825–52. An English translation of the first volume by Henry John Rose was published as *The History of the Christian Religion and Church during the Three First Centuries*, 2 vols. (London, 1831–41). English translation of the complete work by Joseph Torrey as *General History of the Christian Religion and Church; from the German of Dr. Augustus Neander*, 11th American ed. 5 vols. (Boston: Crocker and Brewster, 1872).

———. *Antignostikus: Geist des Tertullianus und Einleitung in dessen Schriften.* Berlin: F. Dümmler, 1825.

———. *Der heilige Bernhard und sein Zeitalter.* Berlin: Realschulbuchhandlung, 1813. English translation by Matilda Wrench as *The Life and Times of St. Bernard* (London: Rivington, 1843).

———. *Der heilige Johannes Chrysostomus und die Kirche, besonders des Orients, in dessen Zeitalter.* Berlin: F. Dümmler, 1821. English translation by John Charles Stapleton as *The Life of St. Chrysostom* (London: R. B. Seeley and W. Burnside, 1845).

———. *Genetische Entwickelung der vornehmsten gnostischen Systeme.* Berlin: Ferdinand Dümmler, 1818.

———. *History of the Planting and Training of the Christian Church by the Apostles.* Translated by J. E. Ryland. Philadelphia: J.M. Campbell, 1844.

Nevin, John Williamson. "Cyprian: First Article." *Mercersburg Review* 4 (1852): 259–77.

———. "Cyprian: Fourth Article." *Mercersburg Review* 4 (1852): 513–63.

———. "Cyprian: Second Article." *Mercersburg Review* 4 (1852): 335–87.

———. "Cyprian: Third Article." *Mercersburg Review* 4 (1852): 417–52.

———. "Early Christianity: First Article." *Mercersburg Review* 3 (1851): 461–90.

———. "Early Christianity: Second Article." *Mercersburg Review* 3 (1851): 513–62.

———. "Early Christianity: Third Article." *Mercersburg Review* 4 (1852): 1–54.

———. "Pseudo-Protestantism." *Weekly Messenger of the German Reformed Church* n.s. 10, nos. 48–52 (1845).

Newman, John Henry. *An Essay on the Development of Christian Doctrine.* New York: Appleton, 1845.

———. *Lectures on Certain Difficulties Felt by Anglicans in Submitting to the Catholic Church.* London: Burns & Lambert, 1850.

———, ed. *Lives of the English Saints.* 14 vols. London: James Toovey, 1844–45.

Niemeyer, H.A. *Collectio confessionum in ecclesiis reformatis publicatarum.* Leipzig: Klinkhardt, 1840.

Nitzsch, Carl Immanuel. *System der christlichen Lehre.* 4th ed. Bonn: Marcus, 1839. English translation by Robert Montgomery and John Hennen as *System of Christian Doctrine* (Edinburgh: T. & T. Clark, 1849).

Pelagius. *Epistola ad Demetriadem cum aliis aliorum epistolis*. Edited by Johann Salomo Semler. Halle: C .H. Hemmerde, 1775.

Perrin, John Paul. *History of the Ancient Christians Inhabiting the Valleys of the Alps: I. The Waldenses. II. The Albigenses. III. The Vaudois*. Philadelphia: Griffith and Simon, 1847.

Petavius, Dionysius. *Opus De Theologicis Dogmatibus*. Venice, 1757.

Pigghe, Albrecht. *Heirarchiae ecclesiasticae absertio*. Cologne: Neuss, 1544.

Proudfit, John Williams. "The Apostles' Creed." *The Biblical Repertory and Princeton Review* 24 (1852): 602–77.

———. "The Heidelberg Catechism and Dr. Nevin." Review of *The Commentary of Dr. Zacharias Ursinus on the Heidelberg Catechism* translated by G. W. Williard with an introduction by John W. Nevin. *The Biblical Repertory and Princeton Review* 24 (1852): 91–134.

Quenstedt, Johann Andreas. *Theologia didactico-polemica, sive, System theologicum : in duas sectiones, didacticam et polemicam, divisum . . . in quatuor partes distributum*. Leipzig: Thomam Fritsch, 1702.

Ranke, Leopold von. *Deutsche Geschichte im Zeitalter der Reformation*. Berlin: Duneker und Humblot, 1839. English translation by Sarah Austin as *History of the Reformation in Germany* (Philadelphia: Lea and Blachard, 1844; repr. New York: Unger, 1966).

———. *Die römischen Päpste: ihre Kirche und ihr Staat im sechzehnten und siebzehnten Jahrhundert*. 2nd ed. 3 vols, Berlin: Duncker und Humblot, 1838–39. English translation by Sarah Austin as *The Ecclesiastical and Political History of the Popes of Rome during the 16th and 17th Centuries*, 2 vols. (Philadelphia: Lea and Blanchard, 1841).

Rapp, Georg. *Die erwecklichen Schriften des Märtyrers Hieronymus Savonarola zur belebung christlichen und kirchlichen Sinnes*. Stuttgart: Liesching, 1839.

Redepenning, Ernst Rudolf. *Origenes: eine Darstellung seines Lebens und seiner Lehre*. 2 vols. Bonn: E. Weber, 1841.

Reimarus, Hermann Samuel. *Fragments*. Edited by Charles H. Talbert. Translated by Ralph S. Fraser. Philadelphia: Fortress, 1970.

Rettberg, Friedrich Wilhelm. *Thascius Cäcilius Cyprianus, Bischof von Carthago*. Göttingen: Vandenhoeck und Ruprecht, 1831.

Reuchlin, Hermann. *Geschichte von Port-Royal: der Kampf des reformirten und des jesuitischen Katholicismus unter Louis XIII und XIV*. 2 vols. Hamburg: Perthes, 1839.

———. *Pascal's Leben und der Geist seiner Schriften: zum Theil nach neu aufgefundenen Handschriften mit Untersuchungen ueber die Moral der Jesuiten*. Stuttgart: Tübingen, 1840.

Ritter, Joseph Ignatius. *Handbuch der Kirchengeschichte*. 3 vols. Bonn: A. Marcus, 1826–33.

Rothe, Richard. *Die Anfänge der christlichen Kirche und ihrer Verfassung: Ein geschichtlicher Versuch*. Wittenberg: Zimmermann, 1837.

Rudelbach, A. G. *Hieronymus Savonarola und seine Zeit. Aus den quellen dargestellt*. Hamburg: F. Perthes, 1835.

Rupp, I. Daniel. *An Original History of the Religious Denominations at Present Existing in the United States*. Philadelphia: J. Y. Humphreys, 1844.

Sack, Karl Heinrich. *Die Kirche von Schottland: Beitræge zu deren Geschichte und Beschreibung*. Heidelberg: Karl Winter, 1844.

Schmucker, Samuel S. *Overture for Christian Union, Submitted for the Consideration of the Evangelical Denominations in the United States*. 1845.

Sarpi, Paolo. *The History of the Council of Trent.* Translated by Nathanael Brent. London, 1676.

Schaff, Philip. "Ein Wort über die theologische Kritik: I Wahre und falsche Kritik." *Literarische Zeitung* 20, no. 40 (May 20, 1843): 969–75.

———. "Ein Wort über die theologische Kritik: II Der Selbstvernichtungsprocess der neueren Evangelienkritik," *Literarische Zeitung* 20, no. 61 (August 2, 1843): 633–37.

———. "Katholizismus und Romanismus." *Literarische Zeitung* 20, no. 87 (October 31, 1843): 1385–90, no. 100 (December 16, 1843): 1597–603.

———. "Ordination of Professor Schaf." *Weekly Messenger* 9 (September 4, 1844): 1869–70.

———. Ordination sermon. *Palmblätter* 1 (May/June, 1844) 49.

Schelling, Friedrich Wilhelm Joseph von. *Philosophical Investigations into the Essence of Human Freedom.* Translated by Jeff Love and Johannes Schmidt. Albany: State University of New York Press, 2006.

———. *Vorlesungen über die Methode des academischen Studium.* Tübingen: T.G. Cotta, 1803. English translation by E. S. Morgan as *On University Studies*, edited by Norbert Guterman (Athens: Ohio University Press, 1966).

Schleiermacher, Friederich. *On Religion: Speeches to Its Cultured Despisers.* Translated by Richard Crouter. Cambridge: Cambridge University Press, 1988.

Schmidt, Charles. *Johannes Tauler von Strassburg: Beitrag zur Geschichte der Mystik und des religiösen Lebens im vierzehnten Jahrhundert.* Hamburg: F. Perthes, 1841.

Schröckh, Johann Matthais and Heinrich Gottlieb Tzschirner. *Christliche Kirchengeschichte.* 45 vols. Leipzig, 1768–1812.

Schwab, Gustav Benjamin *Die deutsche Prosa von Mosheim bis auf unsere Tage: eine Mustersammlung mit Rücksicht auf höhere Lehr-anstaltne.* Stuttgart: S. G. Liesching, 1843.

Seabury, Samuel. *A Sermon by the Rev. Samuel Seabury, D.D., in Reference to the Trial of the Right Rev'd Benj. T. Onderdonk, D.D., Bishop of the Diocese of New-York.* New York: J. A. Sparks, 1845.

Semisch, Karl Gottlieb. *Justin der Märtyrer: eine kirchen- Und dogmengeschichtliche Monographie.* 2 vols. Breslau: August Schulz, 1840. English translation by J. E. Ryland as *Justin Martyr: His Life, Writings, and Opinions*, 2 vols. (Edinburgh: T. Clark, 1843).

Semler, Johann Salomo. *Historiae ecclesiasticae selecta capita: cum epitome canonum excerptis dogmaticis et tabulis chronologicis.* 3 vols. Halle, 1767.

———. *Lebensbeschreibung von ihm selbst abgefasst.* 2 vols. Halle, 1781–82.

Smith, Hugh and Henry Anton. *The True Issue for the True Churchman: Statement of Facts in Relation to the Recent Ordination in St. Stephen's Church.* New York: Harper and Brothers, 1843.

Spener, Philipp Jacob. *Letzte theologische Bedencken.* Halle: Waisenhaus, 1711.

Stolberg, Friedrich Leopold. *Geschichte der Religion Jesu Christi.* 15 vols. Hamburg, 1806–18.

Stowe, Calvin E. "Teutonic Metaphysics or Modern Transcendentalism." *Biblical Repository and Classical Review*, 3rd ser. 1, no.1 (January 1845): 64–97.

Strauss. David Friedrich. *The Life of Jesus, Critical Examined.* Edited by Peter C. Hodgson. Translated by George Eliot. Philadelphia: Fortress, 1973.

Stuart, Moses. *A Commentary on the Apocalypse.* Andover, MA: Allen, Morrill, and Wardwell, 1845.

Steffens, Henrich. *Die vier Norwger: ein Cyklus von Novellen.* 6 vols. Breslau: J. Max und Komp., 1828.

Schmieder, Heinrich Eduard. *Einleitung in die heilige Schrift.* Leipzig, 1836.

Sydow, Adolf. *Die schottische Kirchenfrage mit den darauf bezüglichen Documenten: ein kirchliches Rechtsgutachten.* Vol. 1 of *Beiträge zur Charakteristik der kirchlichen Dinge in Grossbritannien.* Potsdam: Stuhr, 1845. Also published in English as Adolphus Sydow, *The Scottish Church Question* (London: James Nisbet, 1845).

Thiersch, Heinrich Wilhelm Josias. *Versuch zur Herstellung des historischen Standpuncts für die Kritik der neutestamentlichen Schriften: eine Streitschrift gegen die Kritiker unserer Tage.* Erlangen: Heyder, 1845.

Tholuck, August. *Vermischte schriften grösstentheils apologetischen inhalts.* 2 vols. Hamburg: F. Perthes, 1839.

Tholuck, August. *Die Glaubwürdigkeit der evangelischen Geschichte: zugleich eine Kritik des* Lebens Jesu *von Strauss: für theologische und nicht theologische Leser.* Hamburg: F. Perthes, 1837. Partial English translation by J. R. Beard as *The credibility of the evangelical history illustrated,* in *Voices of the Church, in Reply to Dr. D.F. Strauss . . . Comprising Essays in Defence of Christianity* (London: Simpkin, Marshall, 1845), 117–60.

Thomasius, Gottfried. *Origenes: ein Beytrag zur Dogmengeschichte des dritten Jahrhunderts.* Nürnberg: L. Schrag, 1837.

Twesten, August Detlev Christian. *Vorlesungen über die Dogmatik der Evangelisch-Lutherischen Kirche: nach dem Compendium des herrn dr. W. M. L. de Wette.* 2 vols. (Hamburg: F. Perth, 1837–38).

Uhden, Hermann F. *Die Zusthnde der angliecanischen Kirche mit besonderer Berucksiehtigung der Verfassung und des Cultus dargestellt.* Leipzig, 1843. English translation by W. C. C. Humphreys as *The Anglican Church in the Nineteenth Century: Indicating Her Relative Position to Dissent in Every Form; and Presenting a Clear and Unprejudiced View of Puseyism and Orthodoxy* (London: Hatchard, 1844).

Ullmann, Carl. *Gregorius von Nazianz, der Theologe. ein Beitrag zur kirchen- und dogmengeschichte des vierten Jahrhunderts.* Darmstadt: Carl Wilhelm Leske, 1825. English translation by G.V. Cox as *Gregory of Nazianzum. Ho Theologos 'the Divine'. A Contribution to the Ecclesiastical History of the Fourth Century* (London: J. W. Parker, 1851).

———. *Reformatoren vor der Reformation: Vornehmlich in Deutschland und den Niederlanden.* 2 vols. Hamburg: Perthes, 1841. English translation by Robert Menies as *Reformers before the Reformation: Principally in Germany and the Netherlands.* 2 vols. (Edinburgh: T. & T. Clark, 1855).

———. Review of *Leben des Erasmus von Rotterdam* by Adolf Müller. *Theologische Studien und Kritiken* (1829): 178–208.

———. "Zwei Bedenten über die deutch-catholiche Bewegung." *Studien und Kritiken* (1845), 985–1026.

Varnhagen von Ense, Karl August. *Leben des Grafen von Zinzendorf.* Vol. 5, *Biographische Denkmale.* Berlin: G. Reimer, 1830.

Voigt, Johannes. *Hildebrand, als Papst Gregorius der siebente und sein Zeitalter.* Weimar: Landes Industrie Comptoirs, 1815.

Wildenhahn, August. *Paul Gerhardt: kirchengeschichtliches Lebensbild aus der Zeit des grossen Churfürsten.* 2 vols. Leipzig: Gebhardt und Reisland, 1845.

Winer, George Benedikt. *Grammatik des neutestamentlichen Sprachidioms als sichere Grundlage der neutestamentlichen Exegese.* 3rd ed. Leipzig: F. C. W. Vogel, 1830.

———. *Handbuch der theologischen Literatur, hauptsächlich der protestantischen. Erstes Ergänzungsheft zur dritten Auflage.* Leipzig: C. H. Reclam, 1842.

Index of Subjects, Authors, and Names

[Bold type indicates the glossary entry for the subject.]

Index of Biblical Citations

www.ingramcontent.com/pod-product-compliance
Lightning Source LLC
LaVergne TN
LVHW061218100826
845148LV00004B/790
* 9 7 8 1 6 2 5 6 4 5 2 3 4 *